MANAGING IN THE MODULAR AGE

To the memory of Herbert A. Simon

*"How complex or simple a structure is depends critically upon
the way in which we describe it."*

Simon, 1962

MANAGING IN THE MODULAR AGE

ARCHITECTURES, NETWORKS, AND ORGANIZATIONS

EDITED BY

RAGHU GARUD
New York University

ARUN KUMARASWAMY
Rutgers University

RICHARD N. LANGLOIS
University of Connecticut

Blackwell
Publishing

350 Main Street, Malden, MA 02148-5018, USA
108 Cowley Road, Oxford OX4 1JF, UK
550 Swanston Street, Carlton South, Melbourne, Victoria 3053, Australia
Kurfürstendamm 57, 10707 Berlin, Germany

First published 2003 by Blackwell Publishers Ltd

Library of Congress Cataloging-in-Publication Data

Managing in the modular age: architectures, networks, and organizations
/edited by Raghu Garud, Arun Kumaraswamy, Richard N. Langlois.
    p.   cm.
  Some article originally published 1962–2000.
  Includes bibliographical references and index.
    ISBN 0–631–23315–6 (hbk: alk. paper)—ISBN 0–631–23316–4 (pbk:
  alk. paper)
    1. Organization. 2. Management. 3. Modularity (Psychology)
  I. Garud, Raghu. II. Kumaraswamy, Arun. III. Langlois, Richard N.
    HD31 .M294178 2003
    658—dc21

                                                            2002004409

A catalogue record for this title is available from the British Library.

Set in 10/12 Galliard
by Graphicraft
Printed and bound in the United Kingdom
by MPG Books Ltd, Bodmin, Cornwall

For further information on
Blackwell Publishing, visit our website:
http://www.blackwellpublishing.com

CONTENTS

ACKNOWLEDGEMENTS

The editor and publishers wish to thank the following for permission to use copyright material:

American Philosophical Society for Herbert A. Simon, "The architecture of complexity," *Proceedings of the American Philosophical Society*, 106 (1962) pp. 467–82;

Copyright Clearance Center, Inc. on behalf of the journal for M. A. Schilling, "Toward a general systems theory and its application to interfirm product modularity," *Academy of Management Review*, 25:2 (2000) pp. 312–34;

Elsevier Science for M. L. Tushman and J. P. Murmann, "Dominant designs, technological cycles and organizational outcomes" in B. Staw and L. L. Cummings, eds. *Research in Organizational Behavior*, vol. 20 (1998) pp. 232–66; Nicholas Economids, "The economics of networks," *International Journal of Industrial Organization*, 14:6 (1996) pp. 673–99; Richard N. Langlois and Paul L. Robertson, "Networks and innovation in a modular system: Lessons from the microcomputer and stereo component industries," *Research Policy*, 21 (1992) pp. 297–313; and K. Ulrich, "The role of product architecture in the manufacturing firm," *Research Policy*, 24 (1995) pp. 419–40;

Harvard Business Review for C. Y. Baldwin and K. B. Clark, "Managing in an age of modularity," *Harvard Business Review*, Sept/Oct (1997) pp. 84–93. Copyright © 1997 by the President and Fellows of Harvard College;

The Regents of the University of California for Carl Shapiro and Hal R. Varian, "The art of standards wars," *California Management Review*, 41:2 (1999) pp. 8–32. Copyright © 1999 by the Regents of the University of California;

John Wiley & Sons, Ltd. for Raghu Garud and Arun Kumaraswamy, "Technological and organizational designs to achieve economies of substitution," *Strategic Management Journal*, 16 (1995) pp. 93–109; Ron Sanchez and Joseph T. Mahoney, "Modularity, flexibility, and knowledge management in product and organizational design," *Strategic Management Journal*, 17 (1996) pp. 63–76; and James Wade, "Dynamic of organizational communities and technological bandwagons: An empirical investigation of community evolution in the microprocessor market," *Strategic Management Journal*, 16 (1995) pp. 111–13.

Every effort has been made to trace copyright holders and to obtain their permission for the use of copyright material. The authors and publishers will gladly receive any information enabling them to rectify any error or omission in subsequent editions.

MANAGING IN THE MODULAR AGE: ARCHITECTURES, NETWORKS, AND ORGANIZATIONS

Raghu Garud, Arun Kumaraswamy and Richard N. Langlois

The world is full of complex systems. Nature provides an abundance of complex organisms and ecosystems, and humans have constructed complex mechanical, intellectual, organizational and social systems. But what exactly does it mean for a system to be complex? For Herbert Simon (in this volume), a complex system is "one made up of a large number of parts that have many interactions . . . [i]n such systems the whole is more than the sum of the parts in the weak but important pragmatic sense that, given the properties of the parts and the laws of their interaction, it is not a trivial matter to infer the properties of the whole." Complexity is thus a matter both of the sheer number of distinct parts the system comprises and of the nature of interactions among those parts.

Decomposability Principle

One way to manage complexity is to reduce the number of distinct elements in the system by grouping elements into – and therefore hiding the elements within – a smaller number of subsystems. This is the basic idea of *decomposability* that Simon offers both as a prescription for human designers and as a description of the systems we find ready-made in nature. To establish the importance of decomposability, Simon offered the parable of the watchmakers. Tempus and Hora both made watches from myriad parts, and both were interrupted frequently in their work. Tempus organized his work in a manner that if he had "one [watch] partly assembled and had to put it down – to answer the phone, say – it immediately fell to pieces and had to be reassembled from the elements" (Simon, in this volume). Consequently, every time Tempus was interrupted and forced to set aside his work, the entire unfinished assembly fell to pieces. In contrast, Hora first built stable subassemblies that he could then put together in a hierarchic fashion into larger stable subassemblies. Thus, when Hora was interrupted, only the last unfinished subassembly fell apart, preserving most of his earlier work.

It is easy to appreciate the complexity that Tempus confronted due to the way he organized his work. Unlike Hora, who organized his work such that there was a one-to-one mapping between functions and subassemblies, there was no such one-to-one mapping for Tempus. For Tempus, the functioning of each part was dependent upon the functioning of other parts. The parts interacted with one another in non-linear ways, making it difficult to complete a watch – even without interruptions. Of course, interruptions made matters worse by compelling Tempus to retrace his steps (at least cognitively) to determine the point he had reached before the interruption. In the end, it was the "perpetual incompleteness" of the watchmaking process that doomed Tempus.

Stated differently, the architecture that Tempus was working with did not possess a high degree of modularity. In contrast, Hora's architecture was modular – the successful operation of any given subassembly was not dependent upon the performance of another. That is, there was a clear one-to-one mapping between functions and subassemblies (Ulrich, in this volume). Consequently, Hora's approach preserved the subassemblies that he had finished between interruptions.

In an evolutionary selection environment, such stability is rewarded with survival (Simon, in this volume; Loasby, 1976). And there are other benefits as well (see for example, Garud and Kumaraswamy, 1993; Langlois and Robertson, Sanchez and Mahoney, Baldwin and Clark, and Schilling, all in this volume). For example, modularity facilitates the retention and reuse of system parts and enhances the speed, scope and reach of innovation.

In organizational and social systems – and perhaps in mechanical ones as well – it is possible to think of interdependency and interaction among the parts as a matter of information transmission or *communication*. Consider, with Eric von Hippel (1990), the problem of organizing product innovation. Here, the issue is how to decompose the organization of a research and development project by partitioning tasks among development teams. As von Hippel pointed out, in order to solve this decomposition problem, one has to focus on the interdependencies among the various tasks the project comprises.[1] If the project is organized in a non-decomposable manner, then interdependency will be high, meaning that each development team will need constantly to receive and use information about what all the other development teams are doing.

For example, the development of the OS/360 operating system for the original IBM 360 line of computers was evidently organized in a relatively non-decomposable way. The manager of the project, Frederick Brooks, insisted on a conscious attention to interdependencies and a high level of communication among all participants. This included the creation and maintenance of a formal project workbook that documented every aspect of the system so that, in principle at least, every worker could determine how changes elsewhere would affect his or her part of the project. Brooks decided "that *each* programmer should see *all* the material, that is, should have a copy of the workbook in his own office" (Brooks, 1975: 76). But, there was one small problem. Within six months

> The workbook was about five feet thick! If we had stacked up the 100 copies serving programmers in our offices in Manhattan's Time-Life Building, they would have towered above the building itself. Furthermore, the daily change distributions averaged two inches, some 150 pages to be interfiled in the whole. Maintenance of the workbook began to take a significant time from each workday (Brooks, 1975: 77).

The team soon switched to microfiche. And, clearly, with modern technology, the workbook could reside online and be updated rapidly. But the point remains that a non-decomposable system incurs high communication cost. Indeed, it is for this insight that Brooks is well known: in the design of complex systems, the costs of communication among workers will eventually outweigh the benefits of the division of labor as more and more workers are added to a project (Brooks, 1975: 18–19).

At one point, Brooks briefly considered a "radical" alternative proposed by D. L. Parnas, whose "thesis is that the programmer is most effective if shielded from, rather than exposed to the details of construction of system parts other than his own" (Brooks, 1975: 78). This radical alternative is in fact the strategy of seeking decomposability in the design of the development project and of the underlying software. Parnas (1972) is the inventor of the notion of *information hiding*, a key concept in the modern object-oriented approach to computer programming. Programmers had long understood the importance of modularity, that is, of breaking programs into manageable pieces. But not all modular systems are automatically decomposable, since we can break the systems into modules whose internal workings remain highly interdependent on one another. Parnas argued that, especially in large projects, programmers should abandon modularization based on simple flow charts and pay attention instead to minimizing interdependencies. If knowledge is hidden or *encapsulated* within a module, that knowledge cannot affect, and therefore need not be communicated to, other modules of a system. Under this scheme, every module "is characterized by its knowledge of a design decision which it hides from all others. Its interface or definition was chosen to reveal as little as possible about its inner workings" (Parnas, 1972: 1056).

Modular Systems and Standards

Baldwin and Clark (in this volume and 2000) have drawn on similar ideas from computer science to formulate some general principles of modular systems design. The decomposition of a system into modules, they argue, should involve the partitioning of information into *visible design rules* and *hidden design parameters*. The visible design rules (or *visible information*) consist of three parts:

- An *architecture* specifies what modules will be part of the system and what their functions will be.

- *Interfaces* describe in detail how the modules will interact, including how they fit together and communicate.
- And *standards* test a module's conformity to design rules and measure the module's performance relative to other modules.

These visible pieces of information need to be widely shared and communicated. (In contrast, the hidden design parameters are encapsulated within the modules, and they need not be communicated beyond the boundaries of the module.) As Baldwin and Clark pointed out, the literature on modular systems tends to collapse the three kinds of visible information together, calling them all either "the architecture," "the interfaces," or "the standards."

Clearly, there is much to be gained by pursuing each of these design rules in greater depth. In economics, it has been the word "standards" that has caught on, and indeed the economics of standards and standard setting has grown to considerable prominence in the last few years. Economides (in this volume) provides a thorough survey. At the center of this literature is a series of influential models of "network effects" (see Katz and Shapiro, 1985; Farrell and Saloner, 1986). Network effects occur when the value to an individual of adopting a standard depends on the number of others who have already adopted it or who can be expected eventually to adopt it.

There are basically two types of networks. In *physical connection networks*, users are literally connected to one another. For example, the value to a person of being connected to a telephone system (in the late nineteenth century, let us say) depends on how many friends and business associates are connected to the system (rather than to a rival system, perhaps).[2] Standards also play a role in the second type, *virtual networks*, sometimes also called hardware-software networks. Here there is no literal connection; instead, users are connected by their adherence to the same set of standards. For example, the value to a person of a piece of hardware (a personal computer in the late twentieth century, let us say) depends on the availability of complementary hardware and software, which in turn typically depends on the number of others who have chosen or will choose the standard of compatibility embodied in the hardware (rather than a rival standard).

These networks effects generate positive feedback. As a result, a single standard is likely to win out and become dominant under most circumstances (Shapiro and Varian, in this volume). A firm whose technology defines the industry-wide standard is the winner who "takes most." It is to realize such a competitive advantage that firms attempt to sponsor their proprietary technologies as standards (Garud and Kumaraswamy, 1993). In this regard, issues such as first and second movement, alliances, dynamic appropriability and managing expectations all take on great strategic significance.

Yet, the sponsorship of standards is not straightforward. Standardization is always contested and fragility is inherent in the apparent stability of standards (Garud, Jain, and Kumaraswamy, 2002; Wade, 1996). Many are required to subscribe to a new standard before a winner can take most. To the extent that the new standard is an architectural innovation, it may attract sufficient organizational support to challenge an existing dominant standard (Wade, in this volume). Still, stitching together a coalition to support a standard is a difficult socio-political process (Tushman and

Murmann, in this volume). As many begin subscribing to a standard, competitive pressures to innovate increases, thereby increasing the likelihood that the standard itself may fragment. In an environment where advantages are transient, it is not clear that the first mover, even with a significant market lead, always wins.

PATH DEPENDENCE AND CREATION

Underlying these political and strategic dynamics are path dependencies that standards generate. Paul David (1985) set the tone here with his now legendary account of how the QWERTY keyboard came to be the dominant layout of typewriter keys. Other favorite examples have included computers, telecommunications systems, and various kinds of home entertainment systems such as stereos (Langlois and Robertson, in this volume), VCRs (Cusumano, Mylonadis, and Rosenbloom, 1992), or high-definition television (Farrell and Shapiro, 1992). In most of these cases, the issue is one of the compatibility of physical components or electronic signals.

Besides technical standards, behavioral standards are another important class of standards that generates path dependencies. In the QWERTY case, human touch-typing skills were part of the technological system QWERTY standardized. Indeed, David (1987) distinguishes between *standards of technical design* and *standards of behavioral performance*. The two are closely related, of course: standards are at base a kind of social institution; and social institutions are recurrent patterns of behavior that help to coordinate human activity (Langlois, 1986; North 1990).

Much of the allure of Paul David's keyboard story comes from the contention that QWERTY is not the best of all possible configurations and that "lock-in" has prevented change to a better keyboard.[3] This same logic is true of social institutions more generally. The convention that we all drive on the same side of the road is a standard that brings order out of disorder and increases the efficiency of driving; but to change such a convention can be difficult, as places such as Sweden and Okinawa discovered when they switched sides of the road.

These behavioral or technical standards are anchors to the past, encapsulating learning and network effects that make it all the more difficult for a new technology to emerge. In this regard, a key issue is to understand how firms might break away from standards even while building upon them. The essential tension between flexibility and commitment is perhaps the most intriguing aspect of standard setting that underlies path creation (Garud and Karnoe, 2001; Langlois and Savage, 2001). To use the language of Garud and Jain (1996), standards can be at once *enabling* and *constraining*. When there are no standards, there is complete flexibility, but very little enablement, as "customers and vendors might be prone to wait for the emergence of a dominant design before they are induced to make significant investments" (Garud and Jain, 1996: 393). But when standards are too tight, they can suffocate progress, leading to a "stuck" technology with little innovation of any kind. Only when the institutional environment (the standards) "just embeds" the technological matrix do those standards most fully enable, and not constrain, technological development. In such a "just-embedded" world, technology and standards co-evolve, "each of these reciprocally and continually shaping the other" (Garud and Jain, 1996: 393).

ECONOMICS OF STANDARDS

Charles Kindleberger (1983) pointed out that standards serve to create economies of scale and to lower transactions costs. Economies of scale arise from the increase in the extent of the market that results from reduced variety. For example, in the 1910s, the Society of Automotive Engineers set standards for automobile parts that winnowed the kinds of steel tubing in use from 1,600 to 210 and the types of lock-washers from 800 to 16 (Epstein, 1928: 41–3). Independent parts suppliers could then take advantage of longer production runs to reduce costs, which especially helped the smaller car companies who did not have high internal demands for parts.

Standards help reduce transactions costs by acting as mechanisms for coordination and by helping align expectations. In the classic case, for example, the convention that we all drive on the same side of the road is a standard that reduces the "transaction" costs of ascertaining the intentions of each oncoming driver, not to mention the resource costs of failed coordination. As David (1987) points out, behavioral standards of this kind can be thought of as ensuring "interface compatibility" much as do standards of technical design, since such standards help to coordinate the way individuals "connect together."

Standards can also reduce transactions costs (and agency costs) by facilitating measurement and by reducing monitoring costs. A single standard of weights and measures, for example, makes easier the comparison of goods in exchange and increases the cost of cheating. More generally, normative standards can reduce costs of monitoring by providing a benchmark against which quality or performance can be judged. In a sense, standards are always normative in that they take the form: "do it this way." This is true whether the standard is an injunction to drive on the right or a technical specification constraining design choices.[4]

Conformance to a standard also generates economies of scope and substitution (Garud and Kumaraswamy, in this volume). For instance, economies of scope are realized to the extent that a common technological platform is used for a variety of product classes.[5] Economies of substitution can be realized to the extent that subsystems at lower levels of the system hierarchy are mixed and matched to generate different combinations.[6] Degrees of freedom available at the platform level determine the range of possibilities that are available at a lower level of system hierarchy.

ORGANIZATIONAL ISSUES

These economies are manifest and realized in the ways we organize. For instance, with the advent of the Internet, there has been a disaggregation of the traditional value chain into value nets. A reduction in transactions costs made possible by standards makes it possible for firms in the value net to specialize just in the development of some components of the larger technological system and to build upon external economies, that is upon the strength of others (Langlois and Robertson, in this volume). Such specialization enables each firm in the value net to derive economies of scale from the aggregation of demand. To the extent that firms in the value net adopt the same technological platform across their different product classes, they derive economies of scope. They also derive economies of substitution when they mix and match standardized components available within the value net to offer different new products and services (Garud and Kotha, 1994).

Indeed, standards, as coordination mechanisms, make it possible for firms in a value net to operate in a distributed and parallel manner. There are critical differences in the functioning of such value nets when compared to traditional mass production chains. Value nets are hetrarchical whereas traditional mass production chains are hierarchical. Coordination of value nets is not in the form of boss-subordinate relationships, but rather in the form of peer-to-peer relationships. Such coordination is accomplished by a "shared" rather than a "clean" division of labor (Imai, Nonaka and Takeuchi, 1985), a second difference between value nets and mass production chains. In other words, each "module" in the value net has specialized capabilities, and, yet, has other in-built capabilities.

Such a redundancy in functions within each "module" ensures that the net possesses emergent properties. The interlaced structure also reduces network vulnerability to which a sequentially interdependent system is susceptible when any module fails (Morgan, 1986; Garud and Kotha, 1994). Indeed, these interlaced structures enable modules to combine and split apart to generate new functionality (Fleming and Sorenson, 2001). Moreover, such an interlaced structure is critical for dealing with changes in standards even as they are applied.

As may be apparent, the design of such an ultra-modular system violates the near decomposability principle suggested by Simon. However, the reason that such a structure possesses evolutionary capabilities is that the whole, to some extent, is contained in the parts. Consequently, intermediate states provide the architectural genetic codes for larger structures to emerge. Such is the design of the human brain and of the Internet. These designs are very different from the non-decomposable design adopted by Tempus. They are also different from the one adopted by Hora, whose watches were subassemblies of stable parts clumped and nested together in a hierarchical fashion.

RESEARCH DIRECTIONS

As we can see from these discussions, modularity is a rich entry point to a broader set of issues cutting across technological, organizational and strategic domains. For instance, we cannot talk about the benefits of modularity without acknowledging the socio-political processes involved in the shaping of industry-wide standards. Or, we cannot talk about co-evolutionary dynamics associated with the disaggregation of technical and organizational forms without reflecting upon the transaction costs and translations costs involved.

There is exciting research being and to be conducted in this regard. For instance, an important line of inquiry is to understand the underpinnings, scope and limits of modularity. Gaining such an understanding accords greater explanatory power to a concept that is increasingly being used by many with respect to both products and services markets. For instance, it would be useful to understand different types of modularity and the costs and benefits associated with each. An understanding of different types of modularity may result in directing our attention to other less studied system attributes such as integrity and upgradability and the tradeoffs that we may have to make among them.

Another fruitful avenue for exploration is the relationship between standards (including architectures and interfaces) and modularity. After all, standards provide the "vanishing hand" which enables the decentralized design and production of modular systems (Langlois, 2001; see also Garud and Kumaraswamy, in this volume). But, how do these standards emerge? Once they emerge, how extensible are these standards? To the extent that standards themselves continue to change (Jain, 2001), is it possible to modularize components of a technological system into neatly decomposable elements? We know that standards enable and constrain at the same time and that these properties generate path dependencies. In this regard, how should standards be articulated to allow for the emergence of new paths?

These issues hint at the many organizational and strategic issues associated with modularity and standards. For instance, we know that standards require collective action and that the outcomes of these collective initiatives often provide private benefits. In this regard, how are property rights and appropriability issues to be sorted out within the collective? Given the winner-takes-all dynamics and lock-in associated with standards, what economic and legal frameworks would be most appropriate for network industries? From the perspective of a firm sponsoring an open standard, how much of its own technology should it place in the public or collective domain to mobilize support? Under what conditions would a sponsor be able to mobilize sufficient organizational support to displace a dominant design? If modularity allows firms to be a part of a value net, what are the governance processes most appropriate for harnessing distributed and parallel development? What are the new transaction modes involved and how do these transactions evolve over time?

A relatively understudied issue is the role of organizational arrangements to benefit from modularity. For instance, many have noted the importance of building technological platforms as the base on which modular forms might emerge (Kogut and Kulatilaka, 1994). How do organizations justify the investments of building a platform that will be used in the future? (see Baldwin and Clark, 2000). What incentives are required to develop and use platforms and modules across generations? What capabilities and organizational infrastructure should a firm possess to gain the options value inherent in technological platforms? How does a shift in industry-wide standard change the options value inherent in platforms and modules? And coming full circle once again to the relationship between modularity and standards, what actions should a firm undertake to shape emerging standards so as to gain the economies associated with the investments it has made in a technological trajectory?

CONCLUSIONS

There is no doubt that we are living in a modular age. Even as we embrace modularity and its virtues, we are also gaining an understanding of systems such as the brain that depart from "near decomposability." We are also beginning to appreciate broader issues related to the harnessing and exploitation of modularity. And, as we have suggested in our indicative list of research questions, these issues are not "nearly decomposable" in the Simon sense.

This is the larger message that this edited volume attempts to communicate. It includes seminal articles that address modularity issues from different disciplinary perspectives and from different levels of analysis. As readers navigate through this mosaic of ideas, it is our hope that they will encounter beneficial spillovers and rich connections among the different domains and, in the process, formulate new research questions and hypotheses.

We have designed this volume to be modular, but with overlaps to highlight key interdependencies among the concepts of modularity, networks and architectures. We have also included commentaries by the authors that "upgrade" the insights present in their original articles. It is our hope that readers will find sufficient integrity in the set of articles and commentaries we have included in this volume.

NOTES

1   von Hippel defines "the interdependence between any two innovation project tasks with respect to problem-solving as the probability that efforts to perform one of the tasks to specification will require related problem-solving in the other. The higher this probability in a given instance, the greater the problem-solving interdependence" (von Hippel 1990: 409).

2   If you visit the Mark Twain House in Hartford, Connecticut, you will discover that Samuel Clemens was among the first users of a telephone in the city. Although he couldn't call many people, he could communicate with his editors. It is a comment on Twain's ambiguous attitude toward technology, however, that he kept the phone in a closet in the foyer.

3   Liebowitz and Margolis (1990, 1995) have, however, challenged David's specific contention about QWERTY and have engendered debate about the extent to which lock-in situations can be considered to be sub-optimal.

4   A useful distinction is whether a standard is self-enforcing or it requires some other enforcement mechanism. For example, the standards of cleanliness and efficiency that McDonald's sets for its franchise holders require monitoring by company inspectors. In contrast, network effects can instill self-regulative characteristics to compatibility standards once they have become widely accepted.

5   In language now popular in economics, a common technological platform of this type would be called a general-purpose technology (GPT). Such technologies are an important engine of economic growth (Bresnahan and Trajtenberg, 1995).

6   On the hierarchy of designs in technological systems, see Clark (1985).

REFERENCES

Baldwin, C. Y. and Clark, K. B. (2000). *Design Rules, Volume 1, The Power of Modularity*, Cambridge, MA: MIT Press.

Bresnahan, T. F. and Trajtenberg, M. (1995). "General Purpose Technologies: 'Engines of Growth'?" *Journal of Econometrics*, 65 (January): 83–108.

Brooks, Jr., F. P. (1975). *The Mythical Man-Month: Essays on Software Engineering*, Reading, MA: Addison-Wesley.

Clark, K. B. (1985). "The interaction of design hierarchies and market concepts in technological evolution," *Research Policy*, 14: 235–51.

Cusumano, M., Mylonadis, Y., and Rosenbloom, R. (1992). "Strategic Maneuvering and Mass-Market Dynamics: The Triumph of VHS Over Beta," *Business History Review*, 66 (Spring): 51–94.

David, P. A. (1985). "Clio and the Economics of QWERTY," *Economic History*, 75: 227–332.

David, P. A. (1987). "Some new standards for the economics of standardization in the information age". In P. Dasgupta and P. Stoneman (eds.), *Economic Policy and Technological Performance*, Cambridge, UK: Cambridge University Press, 206–39.

Epstein, R. C. (1928), *The Automobile Industry: Its Economic and Commercial Development*, Chicago, IL: A. W. Shaw.

Farrell, J. and Saloner, G. (1986). "Installed base and compatibility: Innovation, product preannouncements and predation," *American Economic Review*, 76: 940–55.

Farrell, J. and Shapiro, C. (1992). "Standard Setting in High Definition Television," *Brookings Papers on Economic Activity: Microeconomics*, 1–93.

Fleming, L. and Sorenson, O. (2001). "The dangers of modularity," *Harvard Business Review*, September: 20–1.

Garud, R. and Jain, S. (1996). "The embeddedness of technological systems," in J. Baum and J. Dutton (eds.), *Advances in Strategic Management*, 13, Greenwich, CT: JAI Press, 389–408.

Garud, R., Jain, S., and Kumaraswamy, A. (2002). "Institutional entrepreneurship in the sponsorship of common technological standards: The case of Sun Microsystems and Java," *Academy of Management Journal*, Special Forum on Institutional Theory and Institutional Change, 45(1): 196–214.

Garud, R. and Karnoe, P. (2001). "Path creation as a process of mindful deviation," in R. Garud and P. Karnoe (eds.), *Path dependence and creation*, Mahwah, NJ: Lawrence Earlbaum Associates, 1–38.

Garud, R. and Kotha, S. (1994). "Using the brain as a metaphor to model flexible production systems," *Academy of Management Review*, 19: 671–98.

Garud, R. and Kumaraswamy, A. (1993). "Changing competitive dynamics in network industries: An exploration of Sun Microsystems' open systems strategy," *Strategic Management Journal*, 14: 351–69.

Imai, K., Nonaka, I., and Takeuchi, H. (1985). "Managing the New Product Development Process: How Japanese Companies Learn and Unlearn," in K. B. Clark, R. Hayes, and C. Lorenz (eds.), *The Uneasy Alliance: Managing the Productivity Technology Dilemma*, Cambridge, MA: Harvard Business School.

Jain, S. (2001). "A process framework of collective standards emergence," Unpublished doctoral dissertation, New York, NY: New York University.

Katz, M. L. and Shapiro, C. (1985). "Network externalities, competition, and compatibility," *American Economic Review*, 75: 424–40.

Kindleberger, C. P. (1983). "Standards as Public, Collective and Private Goods," *Kyklos*, 36(3): 377–96.

Kogut, B. and Kulatilaka, N. (1994). "Options thinking and platform investments: Investing in opportunity," *California Management Review*, 36(2): 52–71.

Langlois, R. N. (1986). "Rationality, Institutions, and Explanation," in R. N. Langlois (ed.), *Economics as a Process: Essays in the New Institutional Economics*, New York: Cambridge University Press, 225–55.

Langlois, R. N. (2001). "The Vanishing Hand: The Changing Dynamics of Industrial capitalism," working paper, Center for Institutions, Organizations and Markets, Storrs, CT: University of Connecticut.

Langlois, R. N. and Savage, D. A. (2001). "Standards, Modularity and Innovation: The Case of Medical Practice," in R. Garud and P. Karnoe (eds.), *Path dependence and creation*, Mahwah, NJ: Lawrence Earlbaum Associates, 149–68.

Liebowitz, S. J. and Margolis, S. E. (1990). "The fable of the keys," *Journal of Law and Economics*, 22: 1–26.

Liebowitz, S. J. and Margolis, S. E. (1995). "Path dependence, lock-in, and history," *Journal of Law, Economics and Organization*, 11, 205–26.

Loasby, B. J. (1976). *Choice, Complexity and Ignorance*, Cambridge, UK: Cambridge University Press.

Morgan, G. (1986). *Images of Organization*, Beverly Hills, CA: Sage Publications.

North, D. C. (1990). *Institutional, Institutional Change and Economic Performance*, Cambridge, UK: Cambridge University Press.

Parnas, D. L. (1972). "On the Criteria To Be Used in Decomposing Systems Into Modules," *Communications of the ACM*, 15: 1053–8.

von Hippel, E. (1990). "Task Partitioning: An Innovation Process Variable," *Research Policy*, 19: 407–18.

Wade, J. (1996). "A Community-Level Analysis of Sources and Rates of Technological Variation in the Microprocessor Market," *Academy of Management Journal*, 39: 1218–44.

PART ONE

OVERVIEW

CHAPTER ONE

THE ARCHITECTURE OF COMPLEXITY

Herbert A. Simon

A number of proposals have been advanced in recent years for the development of "general systems theory" that, abstracting from properties peculiar to physical, biological, or social systems, would be applicable to all of them.[1] We might well feel that, while the goal is laudable, systems of such diverse kinds could hardly be expected to have any nontrivial properties in common. Metaphor and analogy can be helpful, or they can be misleading. All depends on whether the similarities the metaphor captures are significant or superficial.

It may not be entirely vain, however, to search for common properties among diverse kinds of complex systems. The ideas that go by the name of cybernetics constitute, if not a theory, at least a point of view that has been proving fruitful over a wide range of applications.[2] It has been useful to look at the behavior of adaptive systems in terms of the concepts of feedback and homeostasis, and to analyze adaptiveness in terms of the theory of selective information.[3] The ideas of feedback and information provide a frame of reference for viewing a wide range of situations, just as do the ideas of evolution, of relativism, of axiomatic method, and of operationalism.

In this essay I should like to report on some things we have been learning about particular kinds of complex systems encountered in the behavioral sciences. The developments I shall discuss arose in the context of specific phenomena, but the theoretical formulations themselves make little reference to details of structure. Instead they refer primarily to the complexity of the systems under view without specifying the exact content of that complexity. Because of their abstractness, the theories may have relevance – application would be too strong a term – to other kinds of complex systems observed in the social, biological, and physical sciences.

In recounting these developments, I shall avoid technical detail, which can generally be found elsewhere. I shall describe each theory in the particular context in which it arose. Then I shall cite some examples of complex systems, from areas of science other than the initial application, to which the theoretical framework appears relevant. In doing so, I shall make reference to areas of knowledge where I am not expert – perhaps not even literate. The reader will have little difficulty, I am sure, in distinguishing instances based on idle fancy or sheer ignorance from instances that cast some light on the ways in which complexity exhibits itself wherever it is found in nature.

I shall not undertake a formal definition of "complex systems."[4] Roughly, by a complex system I mean one made up of a large number of parts that interact in a nonsimple way. In such systems the whole is more than the sum of the parts, not in an ultimate, metaphysical sense but in the important pragmatic sense that, given the properties of the parts and the laws of their interaction, it is not a trivial matter to infer the properties of the whole. In the face of complexity an in-principle reductionist may be at the same time a pragmatic holist.[5]

The four sections that follow discuss four aspects of complexity. The first offers some comments on the frequency with which complexity takes the form of hierarchy – the complex system being composed of subsystems that in turn have their own subsystems, and so on. The second section theorizes about the relation between the structure of a complex system and the time required for it to emerge through evolutionary processes; specifically it argues that hierarchic systems will evolve far more quickly than nonhierarchic systems of comparable size. The third section explores the dynamic properties of hierarchically organized systems and shows how they can be decomposed into subsystems in order to analyze their behavior. The fourth section examines the relation between complex systems and their descriptions.

Thus my central theme is that complexity frequently takes the form of hierarchy and that hierarchic systems have some common properties independent of their specific content. Hierarchy, I shall argue, is one of the central structural schemes that the architect of complexity uses.

HIERARCHIC SYSTEMS

By a *hierarchic system*, or hierarchy, I mean a system that is composed of interrelated subsystems, each of the latter being in turn hierarchic in structure until we reach some lowest level of elementary subsystem. In most systems in nature it is somewhat arbitrary as to where we leave off the partitioning and what subsystems we take as elementary. Physics makes much use of the concept of "elementary particle," although particles have a disconcerting tendency not to remain elementary very long. Only a couple of generations ago the atoms themselves were elementary particles; today to the nuclear physicist they are complex systems. For certain purposes of astronomy whole stars, or even galaxies, can be regarded as elementary subsystems. In one kind of biological research a cell may be treated as an elementary subsystem; in another, a protein molecule; in still another, an amino acid residue.

Just why a scientist has a right to treat as elementary a subsystem that is in fact exceedingly complex is one of the questions we shall take up. For the moment we shall accept the fact that scientists do this all the time and that, if they are careful scientists, they usually get away with it.

Etymologically the word "hierarchy" has had a narrower meaning than I am giving it here. The term has generally been used to refer to a complex system in which each of the subsystems is subordinated by an authority relation to the system it belongs to. More exactly, in a hierarchic formal organization each system consists of a "boss" and a set of subordinate subsystems. Each of the subsystems has a "boss" who is the immediate subordinate of the boss of the system. We shall want to consider systems in which the relations among subsystems are more complex than in the formal organizational hierarchy just described. We shall want to include systems in which there is no relation of subordination among subsystems. (In fact even in human organizations the formal hierarchy exists only on paper; the real flesh-and-blood organization has many interpart relations other than the lines of formal authority.) For lack of a better term I shall use "hierarchy" in the broader sense introduced in the previous paragraphs to refer to all complex systems analyzable into successive sets of subsystems and speak of "formal hierarchy" when I want to refer to the more specialized concept.[6]

Social systems

I have already given an example of one kind of hierarchy that is frequently encountered in the social sciences – a formal organization. Business firms, governments, and universities all have a clearly visible parts-within-parts structure. But formal organizations are not the only, or even the most common, kind of social hierarchy. Almost all societies have elementary units called families, which may be grouped into villages or tribes, and these into larger groupings, and so on. If we make a chart of social interactions, of who talks to whom, the clusters of dense interaction in the chart will identify a rather well-defined hierarchic structure. The groupings in this structure may be defined operationally by some measure of frequency of interaction in this sociometric matrix.

Biological and physical systems

The hierarchical structure of biological systems is a familiar fact. Taking the cell as the building block, we find cells organized into tissues, tissues into organs, organs into systems. Within the cell are well-defined subsystems – for example, nucleus, cell membrane, microsomes, and mitochondria.

The hierarchic structure of many physical systems is equally clear-cut. I have already mentioned the two main series. At the microscopic level we have elementary particles, atoms, molecules, and macromolecules. At the macroscopic level we have satellite systems, planetary systems, galaxies. Matter is distributed throughout space in a strikingly nonuniform fashion. The most nearly random distributions we find, gases, are not random distributions of elementary particles but random distributions of complex systems, that is, molecules.

A considerable range of structural types is subsumed under the term "hierarchy" as I have defined it. By this definition a diamond is hierarchic, for it is a crystal structure of carbon atoms that can be further decomposed into protons, neutrons, and electrons. However, it is a very "flat" hierarchy, in which the number of first-order subsystems belonging to the crystal can be indefinitely large. A volume of molecular gas is a flat hierarchy in the same sense. In ordinary usage we tend to reserve the word "hierarchy" for a system that is divided into a *small or moderate number* of subsystems, each of which may be further subdivided. Hence we do not ordinarily think of or refer to a diamond or a gas as a hierarchic structure. Similarly a linear polymer is simply a chain, which may be very long, of identical subparts, the monomers. At the molecular level it is a very flat hierarchy.

In discussing formal organizations, the number of subordinates who report directly to a single boss is called his *span of control*. I shall speak analogously of the *span* of a system, by which I shall mean the number of subsystems into which it is partitioned. Thus a hierarchic system is flat at a given level if it has a wide span at that level. A diamond has a wide span at the crystal level but not at the next level down, the atomic level.

In most of our theory construction in the following sections we shall focus our attention on hierarchies of moderate span, but from time to time I shall comment on the extent to which the theories might or might not be expected to apply to very flat hierarchies.

There is one important difference between the physical and biological hierarchies, on the one hand, and social hierarchies, on the other. Most physical and biological hierarchies are described in spatial terms. We detect the organelles in a cell in the way we detect the raisins in a cake – they are "visibly" differentiated substructures localized spatially in the larger structure. On the other hand, we propose to identify social hierarchies not by observing who lives close to whom but by observing who interacts with whom. These two points of view can be reconciled by defining hierarchy in terms of intensity of interaction, but observing that in most biological and physical systems relatively intense interaction implies relative spatial propinquity. One of the interesting characteristics of nerve cells and telephone wires is that they permit very specific strong interactions at great distances. To the extent that interactions are channeled through specialized communications and transportation systems, spatial propinquity becomes less determinative of structure.

Symbolic systems

One very important class of systems has been omitted from my examples thus far: systems of human symbolic production. A book is a hierarchy in the sense in which I am using that term. It is generally divided into chapters, the chapters into sections, the sections into paragraphs, the paragraphs into sentences, the sentences into clauses and phrases, the clauses and phrases into words. We may take the words as our elementary units, or further subdivide them, as the linguist often does, into smaller units. If the book is narrative in character, it may divide into "episodes" instead of sections, but divisions there will be.

The hierarchic structure of music, based on such units as movements, parts, themes, phrases, is well known. The hierarchic structure of products of the pictorial arts is more difficult to characterize, but I shall have something to say about it later.

THE EVOLUTION OF COMPLEX SYSTEMS

Let me introduce the topic of evolution with a parable. There once were two watchmakers, named Hora and Tempus, who manufactured very fine watches. Both of them were highly regarded, and the phones in their workshops rang frequently – new customers were constantly calling them. However, Hora prospered, while Tempus became poorer and poorer and finally lost his shop. What was the reason?

The watches the men made consisted of about 1,000 parts each. Tempus had so constructed his that if he had one partly assembled and had to put it down – to answer the phone, say – it immediately fell to pieces and had to be reassembled from the elements. The better the customers liked his watches, the more they phoned him and the more difficult it became for him to find enough uninterrupted time to finish a watch.

The watches that Hora made were no less complex than those of Tempus. But he had designed them so that he could put together subassemblies of about ten elements each. Ten of these subassemblies, again, could be put together into a larger subassembly; and a system of ten of the latter subassemblies constituted the whole watch. Hence, when Hora had to put down a partly assembled watch to answer the phone, he lost only a small part of his work, and he assembled his watches in only a fraction of the man-hours it took Tempus.

It is rather easy to make a quantitative analysis of the relative difficulty of the tasks of Tempus and Hora: suppose the probability that an interruption will occur, while a part is being added to an incomplete assembly, is p. Then the probability that Tempus can complete a watch he has started without interruption is $(1 - p)^{1000}$ – a very small number unless p is 0.001 or less. Each interruption will cost on the average the time to assemple $1/p$ parts (the expected number assembled before interruption). On the other hand, Hora has to complete 111 subassemblies of ten parts each. The probability that he will not be interrupted while completing any one of these is $(1 - p)^{10}$, and each interruption will cost only about the time required to assemble five parts.[7]

Now if p is about 0.01 – that is, there is one chance in a hundred that either watchmaker will be interrupted while adding any one part to an assembly – then a straightforward calculation shows that it will take Tempus on the average about 4,000 times as long to assemble a watch as Hora.

We arrive at the estimate as follows:

1 Hora must make 111 times as many complete assemblies per watch as Tempus; but
2 Tempus will lose on the average 20 times as much work for each interrupted assembly as Hora (100 parts, on the average, as against 5); and
3 Tempus will complete an assembly only 44 times per million attempts (0.99^{1000} = 44×10^{-6}), while Hora will complete nine out of ten ($0.99^{10} = 9 \times 10^{-1}$). Hence Tempus will have to make 20,000 as many attempts per completed assembly as Hora. $(9 \times 10^{-1})/(44 \times 10^{-6}) = 2 \times 10^4$. Multiplying these three ratios, we get

$$1/111 \times 100/5 \times 0.99^{10}/0.99^{1000} = 1/111 \times 20 \times 20{,}000 \sim 4{,}000.$$

Biological evolution

What lessons can we draw from our parable for biological evolution? Let us interpret a partially completed subassembly of k elementary parts as the coexistence of k parts in a small volume – ignoring their relative orientations. The model assumes that parts are entering the volume at a constant rate but that there is a constant probability, p, that the part will be dispersed before another is added, unless the assembly reaches a stable state. These assumptions are not particularly realistic. They undoubtedly underestimate the decrease in probability of achieving the assembly with increase in the size of the assembly. Hence the assumptions understate – probably by a large factor – the relative advantage of a hierarchic structure.

Although we cannot therefore take the numerical estimate seriously, the lesson for biological evolution is quite clear and direct. The time required for the evolution of a complex form from simple elements depends critically on the numbers and distribution of potential intermediate stable forms. In particular, if there exists a hierarchy of potential stable "subassemblies," with about the same span, s, at each level of the hierarchy, then the time required for a subassembly can be expected to be about the same at each level – that is, proportional to $1/(1 - p)^s$. The time required for the assembly of a system of n elements will be proportional to $\log_s n$, that is, to the number of levels in the system. On would say – with more illustrative than literal intent – that the time required for the evolution of multicelled organisms from single-celled organisms might be of the same order of magnitude as the time required for the evolution of single-celled organisms from macromolecules. The same argument could be applied to the evolution of proteins from amino acids, of molecules from atoms, of atoms from elementary particles.

A whole host of objections to this oversimplified scheme will occur, I am sure, to every working biologist, chemist, and physicist. Before turning to matters I know more about, I shall mention three of these problems, leaving the rest to the attention of the specialists.

First, in spite of the overtones of the watchmaker parable, the theory assumes no teleological mechanism. The complex forms can arise from the simple ones by purely random processes. (I shall propose another model in a moment that shows this clearly.) Direction is provided to the scheme by the stability of the complex forms, once these come into existence. But this is nothing more than survival of the fittest – that is, of the stable.

Second, not all large systems appear hierarchical. For example, most polymers – such as nylon – are simply linear chains of large numbers of identical components, the monomers. However, for present purposes we can simply regard such a structure as a hierarchy with a span of one – the limiting case; for a chain of any length represents a state of relative equilibrium.[8]

Third, the evolution of complex systems from simple elements implies nothing, one way or the other, about the change in entropy of the entire system. If the process absorbs free energy, the complex system will have a smaller entropy than the elements; if it releases free energy, the opposite will be true. The former alternative is the one that holds for most biological systems, and the net inflow of free energy has to be supplied from the sun or some other source if the second law of thermodynamics is not to be violated. For the evolutionary process we are describing, the equilibria of the intermediate states need have only local and not global stability, and they may be stable only in the steady state – that is, as long as there is an external source of free energy that may be drawn upon.[9]

Because organisms are not energetically closed systems, there is no way to deduce the direction, much less the rate, of evolution from classical thermodynamic considerations. All estimates indicate that the amount of entropy, measured in physical units, involved in the formation of a one-celled biological organism is trivially small – about -10^{-11} cal/degree.[10] The "improbability" of evolution has nothing to do with this quantity of entropy, which is produced by every bacterial cell every generation. The irrelevance of quantity of information, in this sense, to speed of evolution can also be seen from the fact that exactly as much information is required to "copy" a cell through the reproductive process as to produce the first cell through evolution.

The fact of the existence of stable intermediate forms exercises a powerful effect on the evolution of complex forms that may be likened to the dramatic effect of catalysts upon reaction rates and steady-state distribution of reaction products in open systems.[11] In neither case does the entropy change provide us with a guide to system behavior.

Problem solving as natural selection

Let us turn now to some phenomena that have no obvious connection with biological evolution: human problem-solving processes. Consider, for example, the task of discovering the proof for a difficult theorem. The process can be – and often has been – described as a search through a maze. Starting with the axioms and previously proved theorems, various transformations allowed by the rules of the mathematical systems are attempted, to obtain new expressions. These are modified in turn until, with persistence and good fortune, a sequence or path of transformations is discovered that leads to the goal.

The process ordinarily involves much trial and error. Various paths are tried; some are abandoned, others are pushed further. Before a solution is found, many paths of the maze may be explored. The more difficult and novel the problem, the greater is likely to be the amount of trial and error required to find a solution. At the same time the trial and error is not completely random or blind; it is in fact rather highly selective. The new expressions that are obtained by transforming given ones are examined to see whether they represent progress toward the goal. Indications of progress spur further search in the same direction; lack of progress signals the abandonment of a line of search. Problem solving requires *selective* trial and error.[12]

A little reflection reveals that cues signaling progress play the same role in the problem-solving process that stable intermediate forms play in the biological evolutionary process. In fact we can take over the watchmaker parable and apply it also to problem solving. In problem solving, a partial result that represents recognizable progress toward the goal plays the role of stable subassembly.

Suppose that the task is to open a safe whose lock has 10 dials, each with 100 possible settings, numbered from 0 to 99. How long will it take to open the safe by a blind trial-and-error search for the correct setting? Since there are 100^{10} possible settings, we may expect to examine about one half of these, on the average, before finding the correct one – that is, 50 billion billion settings. Suppose, however, that the safe is defective, so that a click can be heard when any one dial is turned to the correct setting. Now each dial can be adjusted independently and does not need to be touched again while the others are being set. The total number of settings that have to be tried is only 10×50, or 500. The task of opening the safe has been altered, by the cues the clicks provide, from a practically impossible one to a trivial one.[13]

A considerable amount has been learned in the past 30 years about the nature of the mazes that represent common human problem-solving tasks – proving theorems, solving puzzles, playing chess, making investments, balancing assembly lines, to mention a few. All that we have learned about these mazes points to the same conclusion: that human problem solving, from the most blundering to the most insightful, involves nothing more than varying mixtures of trial and error and selectivity. The selectivity derives from various rules of thumb, or heuristics, that suggest which paths should be tried first and which leads are promising. We do not need to postulate processes more sophisticated than those involved in organic evolution to explain how enormous problem mazes are cut down to quite reasonable size.[14]

The sources of selectivity

When we examine the sources from which the problem-solving system, or the evolving system, as the case may be, derives its selectivity, we discover that selectivity can always be equated with some kind of feedback of information from the environment.

Let us consider the case of problem solving first. There are two basic kinds of selectivity. One we have already noted: various paths are tried out, the consequences of following them are noted, and this information is used to guide further search. In the same way in organic evolution various complexes come into being, at least evanescently, and those that are stable provide new building blocks for further construction. It is this information about stable configurations, and not free energy or negentropy from the sun, that guides the process of evolution and provides the selectivity that is essential to account for its rapidity.

The second source of selectivity in problem solving is previous experience. We see this particularly clearly when the problem to be solved is similar to one that has been solved before. Then, by simply trying again the paths that led to the earlier solution, or their analogues, trial-and-error search is greatly reduced or altogether eliminated.

What corresponds to this latter kind of information in organic evolution? The closest analogue is reproduction. Once we reach the level of self-reproducing systems, a complex system, when it has once been achieved, can be multiplied indefinitely. Reproduction in fact allows the inheritance of acquired characteristics, but at the level of genetic material, of course; that is, only characteristics acquired by the genes can be inherited. We shall return to the topic of reproduction in the final section of this essay.

On empires and empire building

We have not exhausted the categories of complex systems to which the watchmaker argument can reasonably be applied. Philip assembled his Macedonian empire and gave it to his son, to be later combined with the Persian subassembly and others into Alexander's greater system. On Alexander's death his empire did not crumble to dust but fragmented into some of the major subsystems that had composed it.

The watchmaker argument implies that if one would be Alexander, one should be born into a world where large stable political systems already exist. Where this condition was not fulfilled, as on the Scythian and Indian frontiers, Alexander found empire building a slippery business. So too, T. E. Lawrence's organizing of the Arabian revolt against the Turks was limited by the character of his largest stable building blocks, the separate, suspicious desert tribes.

The profession of history places a greater value upon the validated particular fact than upon tendentious generalization. I shall not elaborate upon my fancy therefore but shall leave it to historians to decide whether anything can be learned for the interpretation of history from an abstract theory of hierarchic complex systems.

Conclusion: the evolutionary explanation of hierarchy

We have shown thus far that complex systems will evolve from simple systems much more rapidly if there are stable intermediate forms than if there are not. The resulting complex forms in the former case will be hierarchic. We have only to turn the argument around to explain the observed predominance of hierarchies among the complex systems nature presents to us. Among possible complex forms, hierarchies are the ones that have the time to evolve. The hypothesis that complexity will be hierarchic makes no distinction among very flat hierarchies, like crystals and tissues and polymers, and the intermediate forms. Indeed in the complex systems we encounter in nature examples of both forms are prominent. A more complete theory than the one we have developed here would presumably have something to say about the determinants of width of span in these systems.

NEARLY DECOMPOSABLE SYSTEMS

In hierarchic systems we can distinguish between the interactions *among* subsystems, on the one hand, and the interactions *within* subsystems – that is, among he parts of those subsystems – on the other. The interactions at the different levels may be, and often will be, of different orders of magnitude. In a formal organization there will generally be more interaction, on the average, between two employees who are members of the same department than between two employees from different departments. In organic substances intermolecular forces will generally be weaker than molecular forces, and molecular forces weaker than nuclear forces.

In a rare gas the intermolecular forces will be negligible compared to those binding the molecules – we can treat the individual particles for many purposes as if they were independent of each other. We can describe such a system as *decomposable* into the subsystems comprised of the individual particles. As the gas becomes denser, molecular interactions become more significant. But over some ranges we can treat the decomposable case as a limit and as a first approximation. We can use a theory of perfect gases, for example, to describe approximately the behavior of actual gases if they are not too dense. As a second approximation we may move to a theory of *nearly decomposable* systems, in which the interactions among the subsystems are weak but not negligible.

At least some kinds of hierarchic systems can be approximated successfully as nearly decomposable systems. The main theoretical findings from the approach can be summed up in two propositions:

1   in a nearly decomposable system the short-run behavior of each of the component subsystems is approximately independent of the short-run behavior of the other components;
2   in the long run the behavior of any one of the components depends in only an aggregate way on the behavior of the other components.

Let me provide a very concrete simple example of a nearly decomposable system.[15] Consider a building whose outside walls provide perfect thermal insulation from the environment. We shall take these walls as the boundary of our system. The building is divided into a large number of rooms, the walls between them being good, but not perfect, insulators. The walls between rooms are the boundaries of our major subsystems. Each room is divided by partitions into a number of cubicles, but the partitions are poor insulators. A thermometer hangs in each cubicle. Suppose that at the time of our first observation of the system there is a wide variation in temperature from cubicle to cubicle and from room to room – the various cubicles within the building are in a state of thermal disequilibrium. When we take new temperature readings several hours later, what shall we find? There will be very little variation in temperature among the cubicles within each single room, but there may still be large temperature variations *among* rooms. When we take readings again several days later, we find an almost uniform temperature throughout the building; the temperature differences among rooms have virtually disappeared.

We can describe the process of equilibration formally by setting up the usual equations of heat flow. The equations can be represented by the matrix of their coefficients, r_{ij}, where r_{ij} is the rate at which heat flows from the ith cubicle to the jth cubicle per degree difference in their temperatures. If cubicles i and j do not have a common wall, r_{ij} will be zero. If cubicles i and j have a common wall and are in the same room, r_{ij} will be large. If cubicles i and j are separated by the wall of a room, r_{ij} will be nonzero but small. Hence, by grouping together all the cubicles that are in the same room, we can arrange the matrix of coefficients so that all its large elements lie inside a string of square submatrices along the main diagonal. All the elements outside these diagonal squares will be either zero or small (see figure 1.1). We may take some small number, ε, as the upper bound of the extradiagonal elements. We shall call a matrix having these properties a *nearly decomposable matrix*.

	A1	A2	A3	B1	B2	C1	C2	C3
A1	—	100	—	2	—	—	—	—
A2	100	—	100	1	1	—	—	—
A3	—	100	—	—	2	—	—	—
B1	2	1	—	—	100	2	1	—
B2	—	1	2	100	—	—	1	2
C1	—	—	—	2	—	—	100	—
C2	—	—	—	1	1	100	—	100
C3	—	—	—	—	2	—	100	—

Figure 1.1 A hypothetical nearly decomposable system.
In terms of the heat-exchange example of the text, A1, A2, and A3 may be interpreted as cubicles in one room, B1 and B2 as cubicles in a second room, and C1, C2, and C3 as cubicles in a third. The matrix entries then are the heat diffusion coefficients between cubicles:

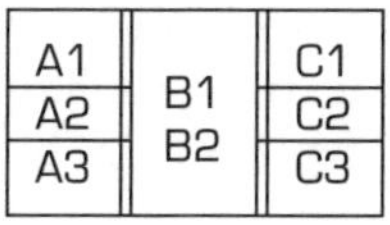

A1	B1	C1
A2	B2	C2
A3		C3

Now it has been proved that a dynamic system that can be described by a nearly decomposable matrix has the properties, stated earlier, of a nearly decomposable system. In our simple example of heat flow this means that in the short run each room will reach an equilibrium temperature (an average of the initial temperatures of its offices) nearly independently of the others and that each room will remain approximately in a state of equilibrium over the longer period during which an overall temperature equilibrium is being established throughout the building. After the intra-room short-run equilibria have been reached, a single thermometer in each room will be adequate to describe the dynamic behavior of the entire system – separate thermometers in each cubicle will be superfluous.

Near decomposability of social systems

As a glance at figure 1.1 shows, near decomposability is a rather strong property for a matrix to possess, and the matrices that have this property will describe very special dynamic systems – vanishingly few systems out of all those that are thinkable. How few they will be depends of course on how good an approximation we insist upon. If we demand that epsilon be very small, correspondingly few dynamic systems will fit the definition. But we have already seen that in the natural world nearly decomposable systems are far from rare. On the contrary, systems in which each variable is linked with almost equal strength with almost all other parts of the system are far rarer and less typical.

In economic dynamics the main variables are the prices and quantities of commodities. It is empirically true that the price of any given commodity and the rate at which it is exchanged depend to a significant extent only on the prices and quantities of a few other commodities, together with a few other aggregate magnitudes, like the average price level or some over-all measure of economic activity. The large linkage coefficients are associated in general with the main flows of raw materials and semifinished products within and between industries. An input-output matrix of the economy, giving the magnitudes of these flows, reveals the nearly decomposable structure of the system – with one qualification. There is a consumption subsystem of the economy that is linked strongly to variables in most of the other subsystems. Hence we have to modify our notions of decomposability slightly to accommodate the special role of the consumption subsystem in our analysis of the dynamic behavior of the economy.

In the dynamics of social systems, where members of a system communicate with and influence other members, near decomposability is generally very prominent. This is most obvious in formal organizations, where the formal authority relation connects each member of the organization with one immediate superior and with a small number of subordinates. Of course many communications in organizations follow other channels than the lines of formal authority. But most of these channels lead from any particular individual to a very limited number of his superiors, subordinates, and associates. Hence departmental boundaries play very much the same role as the walls in our heat example.

Physicochemical systems

In the complex systems familar in biological chemistry, a similar structure is clearly visible. Take the atomic nuclei in such a system as the elementary parts of the system, and construct a matrix of bond strengths between elements. There will be matrix elements of quite different orders of magnitude. The largest will generally correspond to the covalent bonds, the next to the ionic bonds, the third group to hydrogen bonds, still smaller linkages to van der Waals forces.[16] If we select an epsilon just a little smaller than the magnitude of a covalent bond, the system will decompose into subsystems – the constituent molecules. The smaller linkages will correspond to the intermolecular bonds.

It is well known that high-energy, high-frequency vibrations are associated with the smaller physical subsystems and low-frequency vibrations with the larger systems into which the subsystems are assembled. For example, the radiation frequencies associated with molecular vibrations are much lower than those associated with the vibrations of the planetary electrons of the atoms; the latter in turn are lower than those associated with nuclear processes.[17] Molecular systems are nearly decomposable systems, with the short-run dynamics relating to the internal structures of the subsystems and the long-run dynamics to the interactions of these subsystems.

A number of the important approximations employed in physics depend for their validity on the near decomposability of the systems studied. The theory of the thermodynamics of irreversible processes, for example, requires the assumption of macroscopic disequilibrium but microsopic equilibrium, exactly the situation described in our heat-exchange example.[18] Similarly computations in quantum mechanics are often handled by treating weak interactions as producing perturbations on a system of strong interactions.

Some observations on hierarchic span

To understand why the span of hierarchies is sometimes very broad – as in crystals – and sometimes narrow, we need to examine more detail of the interactions. In general the critical consideration is the extent to which interaction between two (or a few) subsystems excludes interaction of these subsystems with the others. Let us examine first some physical examples.

Consider a gas of identical molecules, each of which can form covalent bonds in certain ways with others. Let us suppose that we can associate with each atom a specific number of bonds that it is capable of maintaining simultaneously. (This number is obviously related to the number we usually call its valence.) Now suppose that two atoms join and that we can also associate with the combination a specific number of external bonds it is capable of maintaining. If this number is the same as the number associated with the individual atoms, the bonding process can go on indefinitely – the atoms can form crystals or polymers of indefinite extent. If the number of bonds of which the composite is capable is less than the number associated with each of the parts, then the process of agglomeration must come to a halt.

We need only mention some elementary examples. Ordinary gases show no tendency to agglomerate, because the multiple bonding of atoms "uses up" their capacity to interact. While each oxygen atom has a valence of two, the O_2 molecules have a zero valence. Contrariwise, indefinite chains of single-bonded carbon atoms can be built up, because a chain of any number of such atoms, each with two side groups, has a valence of exactly two.

Now what happens if we have a system of elements that possess both strong and weak interaction capacities and whose strong bonds are exhaustible through combination? Subsystems will form, until all the capacity for strong interaction is utilized in their construction. Then these subsystems will be linked by the weaker second-order bonds into larger systems. For example, a water molecule has essentially a valence of zero – all the potential covalent bonds are fully occupied by the interaction of hydrogen and oxygen molecules. But the geometry of the molecule creates an electric dipole that permits weak interaction between the water and salts dissolved in it – whence such phenomena as its electrolytic conductivity.[19]

Similarly it has been observed that, although electrical forces are much stronger than gravitational forces, the latter are far more important than the former for systems on an astronomical scale. The explanation of course is that the electrical forces, being bipolar, are all "used up" in the linkages of the smaller subsystems and that significant net balances of positive or negative charges are not generally found in regions of macroscopic size.

In social as in physical systems there are generally limits on the simultaneous interaction of large numbers of subsystems. In the social case these limits are related to the fact that a human being is more nearly a serial than a parallel information-processing system. He can carry on only one conversation at a time, and although this does not limit the size of the audience to which a mass communication can be addressed, it does limit the number of people simultaneously involved in most other forms of social interaction. Apart from requirements of direct interactions, most roles impose tasks and responsibilities that are time consuming. One cannot, for example, enact the role of "friend" with large numbers of other people.

It is probably true that in social as in physical systems the higher-frequency dynamics are associated with the subsystems and the lower-frequency dynamics with the larger systems. It is generally believed, for example, that the relevant planning horizon of executives is longer, the higher their location in the organizational hierarchy. It is probably also true that both the average duration of an interaction between executives and the average interval between interactions are greater at higher than lower levels.

Summary: near decomposability

We have seen that hierarchies have the property of near decomposability. Intra-component linkages are generally stronger than intercomponent linkages. This fact has the effect of separating the high-frequency dynamics of a hierarchy – involving the internal structure of the components – from the low-frequency dynamics – involving interaction among components. We shall turn next to some important consequences of this separation for the description and comprehension of complex systems.

THE DESCRIPTION OF COMPLEXITY

If you ask a person to draw a complex object – such as a human face – he will almost always proceed in a hierarchic fashion.[20] First he will outline the face. Then he will add or insert features: eyes, nose, mouth, ears, hair. If asked to elaborate, he will begin to develop details for each of the features – pupils, eyelids, lashes for the eyes, and so on – until he reaches the limits of his anatomical knowledge. His information about the object is arranged hierarchically in memory, like a topical outline.

When information is put in outline form, it is easy to include information about the relations among the major parts and information about the internal relations of parts in each of the suboutlines. Detailed information about the relations of subparts belonging to different parts has no place in the outline and is likely to be lost. The loss of such information and the preservation mainly of information about hierarchic order is a salient characteristic that distinguishes the drawings of a child or someone untrained in representation from the drawing of a trained artist. (I am speaking of an artist who is striving for representation.)

Near decomposability and comprehensibility

From our discussion of the dynamic properties of nearly decomposable systems, we have seen that comparatively little information is lost by representing them as hierarchies. Subparts belonging to different parts only interact in an aggregative fashion – the detail of their interaction can be ignored. In studying the interaction of two large molecules, generally we do not need to consider in detail the interactions of nuclei of the atoms belonging to the one molecule with the nuclei of the atoms belonging to the other. In studying the interaction of two nations, we do not need to study in detail the interactions of each citizen of the first with each citizen of the second.

The fact then that many complex systems have a nearly decomposable, hierarchic structure is a major facilitating factor enabling us to understand, describe, and even "see" such systems and their parts. Or perhaps the proposition should be put the other way round. If there are important systems in the world that are complex without being hierarchic, they may to a considerable extent escape our observation and understanding. Analysis of their behavior would involve such detailed knowledge and calculation of the interactions of their elementary parts that it would be beyond our capacities of memory or computation.[21]

I shall not try to settle which is chicken and which is egg: whether we are able to understand the world because it is hierarchic or whether it appears hierarchic because those aspects of it which are not elude our understanding and observation. I have already given some reasons for supposing that the former is at least half the truth – that evolving complexity would tend to be hierarchic – but it may not be the whole truth.

Simple descriptions of complex systems

One might suppose that the description of a complex system would itself be a complex structure of symbols – and indeed it may be just that. But there is no conservation law that requires that the description be as cumbersome as the object described. A trivial example will show how a system can be described economically. Suppose the system is a two-dimensional array like this:

$$
\begin{array}{cccccccc}
A & B & M & N & R & S & H & I \\
C & D & O & P & T & U & J & K \\
M & N & A & B & H & I & R & S \\
O & P & C & D & J & K & T & U \\
R & S & H & I & A & B & M & N \\
T & U & J & K & C & D & O & P \\
H & I & R & S & M & N & A & B \\
J & K & T & U & O & P & C & D
\end{array}
$$

Let us call the array $\begin{vmatrix} AB \\ CD \end{vmatrix}$ a, the array $\begin{vmatrix} MN \\ OP \end{vmatrix}$ m, the array $\begin{vmatrix} RS \\ TU \end{vmatrix}$ r, and the array $\begin{vmatrix} HI \\ JK \end{vmatrix}$ h. Let us call the array $\begin{vmatrix} am \\ ma \end{vmatrix}$ w, and the array $\begin{vmatrix} rh \\ hr \end{vmatrix}$ x. Then the entire array is simply $\begin{vmatrix} wx \\ xw \end{vmatrix}$. While the original structure consisited of 64 symbols, it requires only 35 to write down its description:

$$S = \frac{wx}{xw}$$

$$w = \frac{am}{ma} \qquad x = \frac{rh}{hr}$$

$$a = \frac{AB}{CD} \qquad m = \frac{MN}{OP} \qquad r = \frac{RS}{TU} \qquad h = \frac{HI}{JK}$$

We achieve the abbreviation by making use of the redundancy in the original structure. Since the pattern $\begin{vmatrix} AB \\ CD \end{vmatrix}$, for example, occurs four times in the total pattern, it is economical to represent it by the single symbol, a.

If a complex structure is completely unredundant – if no aspect of its structure can be inferred from any other – then it is its own simplest description. We can exhibit it, but we cannot describe it by a simpler structure. The hierarchic structures we have been discussing have a high degree of redundancy, hence can often be described in economical terms. The redundancy takes a number of forms, of which I shall mention three:

1 Hierarchic systems are usually composed of only a few different kinds of subsystems in various combinations and arrangements. A familiar example is the proteins, their multitudinous variety arising from arrangements of only 20 different amino acids. Similarly the 90-odd elements provide all the kinds of building blocks needed for an infinite variety of molecules. Hence we can construct our description from a restricted alphabet of elementary terms corresponding to the basic set of elementary subsystems from which the complex system is generated.

2 Hierarchic systems are, as we have seen, often nearly decomposable. Hence only aggregative properties of their parts enter into the description of the interactions of those parts. A generalization of the notion of near decomposability might be called the "empty world hypothesis" – most things are only weakly connected with most other things; for a tolerable description of reality only a tiny fraction of all possible interactions needs to be taken into account. By adopting a descriptive language that allows the absence of something to go unmentioned, a nearly empty world can be described quite concisely. Mother Hubbard did not have to check off the list of possible contents to say that her cupboard was bare.

3 By appropriate "recoding," the redundancy that is present but unobvious in the structure of a complex system can often be made patent. The commonest recoding of descriptions of dynamic systems consists in replacing a description of the time path with a description of a differential law that generates that path. The simplicity resides in a constant relation between the state of the system at any given time and the state of the system a short time later. Thus the structure of the sequence 1 3 5 7 9 11 ... is most simply expressed by observing that each member is obtained by adding 2 to the previous one. But this is the sequence that Galileo found to describe the velocity at the end of successive time intervals of a ball rolling down an inclined plane.

It is a familar proposition that the task of science is to make use of the world's redundancy to describe that world simply. I shall not pursue the general methodological point here, but I shall instead take a closer look at two main types of description that seem to be available to us in seeking an understanding of complex systems. I shall call these *state description* and *process description*, respectively.

State descriptions and process descriptions

"A circle is the locus of all points equidistant from a given point." "To construct a circle, rotate a compass with one arm fixed until the other arm has returned to its starting point." It is implicit in Euclid that if you carry out the process specified in the second sentence, you will produce an object that satisfies the definition of the first. The first sentence is a state description of a circle; the second, a process description.

These two modes of apprehending structures are the warp and weft of our experience. Pictures, blueprints, most diagrams, and chemical structural formulas are state descriptions. Recipes, differential equations, and equations for chemical reactions are process descriptions. The former characterize the world as sensed; they provide the criteria for identifying objects, often by modeling the objects themselves. The latter characterize the world as acted upon; they provide the means for producing or generating objects having the desired characteristics.

The distinction between the world as sensed an the world as acted upon defines the basic condition for the survival of adaptive organisms. The organism must develop correlations between goals in the sensed world and actions in the world of process. When they are made conscious and verbalized, these correlations correspond to what we usually call means-ends analysis. Given a desired state of affairs and an existing state of affairs, the task of an adaptive organism is to find the difference between these two states and then to find the correlating process that will erase the difference.[22]

Thus problem solving requires continual translation between the state and process descriptions of the same complex reality. Plato, in the *Meno*, argued that all learning is remembering. He could not otherwise explain how we can discover or recognize the answer to a problem unless we already know the answer.[23] Our dual relation to the world is the source and solution of the paradox. We pose a problem by giving the state description of the solution. The task is to discover a sequence of processes that will produce the goal state from an initial state. Translation from the process description to the state description enables us to recognize when we have succeeded. The solution is genuinely new to us – and we do not need Plato's theory of remembering to explain how we recognize it.

There is now a growing body of evidence that the activity called human problem solving is basically a form of means-ends analysis that aims at discovering a process description of the path that leads to a desired goal. The general paradigm is: given a blueprint, to find the corresponding recipe. Much of the activity of science is an application of that paradigm: given the description of some natural phenomena, to find the differential equations for processes that will produce the phenomena.

The description of complexity in self-reproducing systems

The problem of finding relatively simple descriptions for complex systems is of interest not only for an understanding of human knowledge of the world but also for an explanation of how a complex system can reproduce itself. In my discussion of the evolution of complex systems, I touched only briefly on the role of self-reproduction.

Atoms of high atomic weight and complex inorganic molecules are witnesses to the fact that the evolution of complexity does not imply self-reproduction. If evolution of complexity from simplicity is sufficiently probable, it will occur repeatedly; the statistical equilibrium of the system will find a large fraction of the elementary particles participating in complex systems.

If, however, the existence of a particular complex form increased the probability of the creation of another form just like it, the equilibrium between complexes and components could be greatly altered in favor of the former. If we have a description of an object that is sufficiently clear and complete, we can reproduce the object from the description. Whatever the exact mechanism of reproduction, the description provides us with the necessary information.

Now we have seen that the descriptions of complex systems can take many forms. In particular we can have state descriptions, or we can have process descriptions – blueprints or recipes. Reproductive processes could be built around either of these sources of information. Perhaps the simplest possibility is for the complex system to serve as a description of itself – a template on which a copy can be formed. One of the most plausible current theories, for example, of the reproduction of deoxyribonucleic acid (DNA) proposes that a DNA molecule, in the form of a double helix of matching parts (each essentially a "negative" of the other), unwinds to allow each half of the helix to serve as a template on which a new matching half can form.

On the other hand, our current knowledge of how DNA controls the metabolism of the organism suggests that reproduction by template is only one of the processes involved. According to the prevailing theory, DNA serves as a template both for itself and for the related substance ribonucleic acid (RNA). RNA in turn serves as a template for protein. But proteins – according to current knowledge – guide the organism's metabolism not by the template method but by serving as catalysts to govern reaction rates in the cell. While RNA is a blueprint for protein, protein is a recipe for metabolism.[24]

Ontogeny recapitulates phylogeny

The DNA in the chromosomes of an organism contains some, and perhaps most, of the information that is needed to determine its development and activity. We have seen that, if current theories are even approximately correct, the information is recorded not as a state description of the organism but as a series of "instructions" for the construction and maintenance of the organism from nutrient materials. I have already used the metaphor of a recipe; I could equally well compare it with a computer program, which is also a sequence of instructions governing the construction of symbolic structures. Let me spin out some of the consequences of the latter comparison.

If genetic material is a program – viewed in its relation to the organism – it is a program with special and peculiar properties. First, it is a self-reproducing program; we have already considered its possible copying mechanism. Second, it is a program that has developed by Darwinian evolution. On the basis of our watchmaker's argument, we may assert that many of its ancestors were also viable programs – programs for the subassemblies.

Are there any other conjectures we can make about the structure of this program? There is a well-known generalization in biology that is verbally so neat that we would be reluctant to give it up even if the facts did not support it: ontogeny recapitulates phylogeny. The individual organism in its development goes through stages that resemble some of its ancestral forms. The fact that the human embryo develops gill bars and then modifies them for other purposes is a familiar particular belonging to the generalization. Biologists today like to emphasize the qualifications of the principle – that ontogeny recapitulates only the grossest aspects of phylogeny, and these only crudely. These qualifications should not make us lose sight of the fact that the generalization does hold in rough approximation – it does summarize a very significant set of facts about the organism's development. How can we interpret these facts?

One way to solve a complex problem is to reduce it to a problem previously solved – to show what steps lead from the earlier solution to a solution of the new problem. If around the turn of the century we wanted to instruct a workman to make an automobile, perhaps the simplest way would have been to tell him how to modify a wagon by removing the singletree and adding a motor and transmission. Similarly a genetic program could be altered in the course of evolution by adding new processes that would modify a simpler form into a more complex one – to construct a gastrula, take a blastula and alter it!

The genetic description of a single cell may therefore take a quite different form from the genetic description that assembles cells into a multicelled organism. Multiplication by cell division would require as a minimum a state description (the DNA, say), and a simple "interpretive process" – to use the term from computer language – that copies this description as a part of the larger copying process of cell division. But such a mechanism clearly would not suffice for the differentiation of cells in development. It appears more natural to conceptualize that mechanism as based on a process description and a somewhat more complex interpretive process that produces the adult organism in a sequence of stages, each new stage in development representing the effect of an operator upon the previous one.

It is harder to conceptualize the interrelation of these two descriptions. Interrelated they must be, for enough has been learned of gene-enzyme mechanisms to show that these play a major role in development as in cell metabolism. The single clue we obtain from our earlier discussion is that the description may itself be hierarchical, or nearly decomposable, in structure, the lower levels governing the fast, "high-frequency" dynamics of the individual cell and the higher-level interactions governing the slow, "low-frequency" dynamics of the developing multicellular organism.

There are only bits of evidence, apart from the facts of recapitulation, that the genetic program is organized in this way, but such evidence as exists is compatible with this notion.[25] To the extent that we can differentiate the genetic information that governs cell metabolism from the genetic information that governs the development of differentiated cells in the multicellular organization, we simplify enormously – as we have already seen – our task of theoretical description. But I have perhaps pressed this speculation far enough.

The generalization that we might expect ontogeny partially to recapitulate phylogeny in evolving systems whose decriptions are stored in a process language has applications outside the realm of biology. It can be applied as readily, for example, to the transmission of knowledge in the educational process. In most subjects, particularly in the rapidly advancing sciences, the progress from elementary to advanced courses is to a considerable extent a progress through the conceptual history of the science itself. Fortunately the recapitulation is seldom literal – any more than it is in the biological case. We do not teach the phlogiston theory in chemistry in order later to correct it. (I am not sure I could not cite examples in other subjects where we do exactly that.) But curriculum revisions that rid us of the accumulations of the past are infrequent and painful. Nor are they always desirable – partial recapitulation may, in many instances, provide the most expeditious route to advanced knowledge.

Summary: the description of complexity

How complex or simple a structure is depends critically upon the way in which we describe it. Most of the complex structures found in the world are enormously redundant, and we can use this redundancy to simplify their description. But to use it, to achieve the simplification, we must find the right representation.

The notion of substituting a process description for a state description of nature has played a central role in the development of modern science. Dynamic laws, expressed in the form of systems of differential or difference equations, have in a large number of cases provided the clue for the simple description of the complex. In the preceding paragraphs I have tried to show that this characteristic of scientific inquiry is not accidental or superficial. The correlation between state description and process description is basic to the functioning of any adaptive organism, to its capacity for acting purposefully upon its environment. Our present-day understanding of genetic mechanisms suggests that even in describing itself the multicellular organism finds a process description – a genetically encoded program – to be the parsimonious and useful representation.

CONCLUSION

Our speculations have carried us over a rather alarming array of topics, but that is the price we must pay if we wish to seek properties common to many sorts of complex systems. My thesis has been that one path to the construction of a nontrivial theory of complex systems is by way of a theory of hierarchy. Empirically a large proportion of the complex systems we observe in nature exhibit hierarchic structure. On theoretical grounds we could expect complex systems to be hierarchies in a world in which complexity had to evolve from simplicity. In their dynamics hierarchies have a property, near decomposability, that greatly simplifies their behavior. Near decomposability also simplifies the description of a complex system and makes it easier to understand how the information needed for the development or reproduction of the system can be stored in reasonable compass.

In science and engineering the study of "systems" is an increasingly popular activity. Its popularity is more a response to a pressing need for synthesizing and analyzing complexity than it is to any large development of a body of knowledge and technique for dealing with complexity. If this popularity is to be more than a fad, necessity will have to mother invention and provide substance to go with the name. The explorations reviewed here represent one particular direction of search for such substance.

NOTES

1   See especially the yearbooks of the Society for General Systems Research. Prominent among the exponents of general systems theory are L. von Bertalanffy, K. Boulding, R. W. Gerard, and J. G. Miller. For a more skeptical view – perhaps too skeptical in the light of the present discussion – see H. A. Simon and A. Newell, "Models: Their Uses and Limitations," in L. D. White (ed.), *The State of the Social Sciences* (Chicago: University of Chicago Press, 1956), pp. 66–83.

2   N. Wiener, *Cybernetics* (New York: Wiley, 1948). For an imaginative forerunner, see A. J. Lotka, *Elements of Mathematical Biology* (New York: Dover Publications, 1951), first published in 1924 as *Elements of Physical Biology*.

3   C. Shannon and W. Weaver, *The Mathematical Theory of Communication* (Urbana: University of Illinois Press, 1949); W. R. Ashby, *Design for a Brain* (New York: Wiley, 1952).

4   W. Weaver, in "Science and Complexity," *American Scientist, 36* (1948): 536, has distinguished two kinds of complexity, disorganized and organized. We shall be concerned primarily with organized complexity.

5   See also John R. Platt, "Properties of Large Molecules that Go beyond the Properties of Their Chemical Sub-groups," *Journal of Theoretical Biology, 1* (1961): 342–58. Since the reductionism-holism issue is a major *cause de guerre* between scientists and humanists, perhaps we might even hope that peace could be negotiated between the two cultures along the lines of the compromise just suggested. As I go along, I shall have a little to say about complexity in the arts as well as in the natural sciences. I must emphasize the pragmatism of my holism to distinguish it sharply from the position taken by W. M. Elsasser in *The Physical Foundation of Biology* (New York: Pergamon Press, 1958).

6   The mathematical term "partitioning" will not do for what I call here a hierarchy; for the set of subsystems and the successive subsets in each of these define the partitioning, independent of any systems of relations among the subsets. By "hierarchy" I mean the partitioning in conjunction with the relations that hold among its parts.

7   The speculations on speed of evolution were first suggested by H. Jacobson's application of information theory to estimating the time required for biological evolution. See his paper "Information, Reproduction, and the Origin of Life," in *American Scientist, 43* (January 1955): 119–27. From thermodynamic considerations it is possible to estimate

the amount of increase in entropy that occurs when a complex system decomposes into its elements. (See for example, R. B. Setlow and E. C. Pollard, *Molecular Biophysics* (Reading, Mass.: Addison-Wesley, 1962), pp. 63–5, and references cited there.) But entropy is the logarithm of a probability; hence information, the negative of entropy, can be interpreted as the logarithm of the reciprocal of the probability – the "improbability," so to speak. The essential idea in Jacobson's model is that the expected time required for the system to reach a particular state is inversely proportional to the probability of the state – hence it increases exponentially with the amount of information (negentropy) of the state.

Following this line of argument, but not introducing the notion of levels and stable subassemblies, Jacobson arrived at estimates of the time required for evolution so large as to make the event rather improbable. Our analysis, carried through in the same way, but with attention to the stable intermediate forms, produces very much smaller estimates.

8 There is a well-developed theory of polymer size, based on models of random assembly. See, for example, P. J. Flory, *Principles of Polymer Chemistry* (Ithaca: Cornell University Press, 1953), chapter 8. Since *all* subassemblies in the polymerization theory are stable, limitation of molecular growth depends on "poisoning" of terminal groups by impurities or formation of cycles rather than upon disruption of partially formed chains.

9 This point has been made many times before, but it cannot be emphasized too strongly. For further discussion, see Setlow and Pollard, *Molecular Biophysics*, pp. 49–64; E. Schrödinger, *What Is Life?* (Cambridge: Cambridge University Press, 1945); and H. Linschitz, "The Information Content of a Bacterial Cell," in H. Quastler (ed.), *Information Theory in Biology* (Urbana: University of Illinois Press, 1953), pp. 251–62.

10 See Linschitz, "The Information Content." This quantity, 10^{-11} cal/degree, corresponds to about 10^{13} bits of information.

11 See H. Kacser, "Some Physico-chemical Aspects of Biological Organization," appendix, pp. 191–249, in C. H. Waddington, *The Strategy of the Genes* (London: George Allen and Unwin, 1957).

12 See A. Newell, J. C. Shaw, and H. A. Simon, "Empirical Explorations of the Logic Theory Machine," *Proceedings of the 1957 Western Joint Computer Conference*, February 1957 (New York: Institute of Radio Engineers); "Chess-Playing Programs and the Problem of Complexity," *IBM Journal of Research and Development*, 2 (October 1958): 320–35; and for a similar view of problem solving, W. R. Ashby, "Design for an Intelligence Amplifier," pp. 215–33 in C. E. Shannon and J. McCarthy, *Automata Studies* (Princeton: Princeton University Press, 1956).

13 The clicking safe example was supplied by D. P. Simon. Ashby, "Design for an Intelligence Amplifier," p. 230, has called the selectivity involved in situations of this kind "selection by components." The even greater reduction in time produced by hierarchization in the clicking safe example, as compared with the watchmaker's metaphor, is due to the fact that a random *search* for the correct combination is involved in the former case, while in the latter the parts come together in the right order. It is not clear which of these metaphors provides the better model for biological evolution, but we may be sure that the watchmaker's metaphor gives an exceedingly conservative estimate of the savings due to hierarchization. The safe may give an excessively high estimate because it assumes all possible arrangements of the elements to be equally probable.

14 A. Newell and H. A. Simon, "Computer Simulation of Human Thinking," *Science*, 134 (December 22, 1961): 2011–2017.

15 This discussion of near decomposability is based upon H. A. Simon and A. Ando, "Aggregation of Variables in Dynamic Systems," *Econometrica*, 29 (April 1961): 111–38. The example is drawn from the same source, pp. 117–18. The theory has been

further developed and applied to a variety of economic and political phenomena by Ando and F. M. Fisher. See F. M. Fisher, "On the Cost of Approximate Specification in Simultaneous Equation Estimation," *Econometrica*, 29 (April 1961): 139–70, and F. M. Fisher and A. Ando, "Two Theorems on *Ceteris Paribus* in the Analysis of Dynamic Systems," *American Political Science Review*, 61 (March 1962): 103–13.

16 For a survey of the several classes of molecular and intermolecular forces, and their dissociation energies, see Setlow and Pollard, *Molecular Biophysics*, chapter 6. The energies of typical covalent bonds are of the order of 80–100 k cal/mole, of the hydrogen bonds, 10 k cal/mole. Ionic bonds generally lie between these two levels; the bonds due to van der Waals forces are lower in energy.

17 Typical wave numbers for vibrations associated with various systems (the wave number is the reciprocal of wave length, hence proportional to frequency):

$$
\begin{aligned}
&\text{Steel wire under tension} - 10^{-10} \text{ to } 10^{-9} \text{ cm}^{-1} \\
&\text{Molecular rotations} - 10^{0} \text{ to } 10^{2} \text{ cm}^{-1} \\
&\text{Molecular vibrations} - 10^{2} \text{ to } 10^{3} \text{ cm}^{-1} \\
&\text{Planetary electrons} - 10^{4} \text{ to } 10^{5} \text{ cm}^{-1} \\
&\text{Nuclear rotations} - 10^{9} \text{ to } 10^{10} \text{ cm}^{-1} \\
&\text{Nuclear surface vibrations} - 10^{11} \text{ to } 10^{12} \text{ cm}^{-1}
\end{aligned}
$$

18 S. R. de Groot, *Thermodynamics of Irreversible Processes* (New York: Interscience Publishers, 1951), pp. 11–12.

19 See, for example, L. Pauling, *General Chemistry* (San Francisco: W. H. Freeman, 2nd ed., 1953), chapter 15.

20 George A. Miller has collected protocols from subjects who were given the task of drawing faces and finds that they behave in the manner described here (private communication). See also E. H. Gombrich, *Art and Illusion* (New York: Pantheon Books, 1960), pp. 291–6.

21 I believe the fallacy in the central thesis of W. M. Elsasser's *The Physical Foundation of Biology*, mentioned earlier, lies in his ignoring the simplification in description of complex systems that derives from their hierarchic structure. Thus (p. 155):

> If we now apply similar arguments to the coupling of enzymatic reactions with the substratum of protein molecules, we see that over a sufficient period of time, the information corresponding to the structural details of these molecules will be communicated to the dynamics of the cell, to higher levels of organization as it were, and may influence such dynamics. While this reasoning is only qualitative, it lends credence to the assumption that in the living organism, unlike the inorganic crystal, the effects of microscopic structure cannot be simply averaged out; as time goes on this influence will pervade the behavior of the cell "at all levels."

But from our discussion of near decomposability it would appear that those aspects of microstructure that control the slow developmental aspects of organismic dynamics can be separated out from the aspects that control the more rapid cellular metabolic processes. For this reason we should not despair of unraveling the web of causes. See also J. R. Platt's review of Elsasser's book in *Perspectives in Biology and Medicine*, 2 (1959): 243–45.

22 See H. A. Simon and A. Newell, "Simulation of Human Thinking," in M. Greenberger (ed.), *Management and the Computer of the Future* (New York: Wiley, 1962), pp. 95–114, esp. pp. 110 ff.

23   *The Works of Plato*, B. Jowett, translator (New York: Dial Press, 1936), vol. 3, pp. 26–35.

24   C. B. Anfinsen, *The Molecular Basis of Evolution* (New York: Wiley, 1959), chapters 3 and 10, will quality this sketchy, oversimplified account. For an imaginative discussion of some mechanisms of process description that could govern molecular structure, see H. H. Pattee, "On the Origin of Macromolecular Sequences," *Biophysical Journal, 1* (1961): 683–710.

25   There is considerable evidence that successive genes along a chromosome often determine enzymes controlling successive stages of protein syntheses. For a review of some of this evidence, see P. E. Hartman, "Transduction: A Comparative Review," in W. D. McElroy and B. Glass (eds.), *The Chemical Basis of Heredity* (Baltimore: Johns Hopkins Press, 1957), pp. 442–54. Evidence for differential activity of genes in different tissues and at different stages of development is discussed by J. G. Gall, "Chromosomal Differentiation," in W. D. McElroy and B. Glass (eds.), *The Chemical Basis of Development* (Baltimore: Johns Hopkins Press, 1958), pp. 103–35. Finally, a model very like that proposed here has been independently, and far more fully, outlined by J. R. Platt, "A 'Book Model' of Genetic Information Transfer in Cells and Tissues," in M. Kasha and B. Pullman (eds.), *Horizons in Biochemistry* (New York: Academic Press, 1962), pp. 167–87. Of course this kind of mechanism is not the only one in which development could be controlled by a process description. Induction, in the form envisaged in Spemann's organizer theory, is based on a process description in which metabolites in already formed tissue control the next stages of development.

COMMENTARY
Mie Augier and Herbert A. Simon

The architecture of complexity: background and central idea

Complexity has recently become a fashionable topic; it shows up most evidently in biological and human systems (such as organizations and markets). Most complex systems – be they natural, human or artificial – are hierarchical in structure. This does not refer to their internal relations of power or authority but to the fact that they are divided into parts, and the parts into parts, and so on, like an elaborate collection of Chinese boxes. So molecules are divided into atoms, and these into elementary particles; multi-celled organisms are divided into organs and tissues, and these into cells; and so on. The components at each lever are not independent of each other, but there is much denser and more rapid interaction within the components at any level than between components at that level. Such systems are said to be nearly decomposable. To discuss and explore this idea was one of the central themes in *The Architecture of Complexity* (Simon, 1962).

The core ideas in *The Architecture of Complexity* were initiated during Simon's work with Albert Ando on near decomposability (Simon and Ando, 1961) which in turn was stimulated by Richard Goodwin's paper in *Econometrica* in 1947. At that time, Simon was playing with a mental image of the matrix of coefficients of the dynamic system and he recognized that the rows and columns of the matrix could be arranged in a number of diagonal blocks with large coefficients in them and small coefficients outside the diagonal blocks. So the matrix was "nearly block diagonal."

This got Simon thinking about the metaphor of a building divided into rooms, each room divided into cubicles.

When Simon later was invited to join the American Philosophical Association, he chose this subject as a topic for his introductory talk (later published as Simon, 1962). The intent was to provide a topic that was of interest to the general academia – it applied to economics, to biology, to the hierarchy of the sciences, and so on. The editor of the journal had originally suggested that the word "social science" be in the title, but Simon insisted that his ideas applied to structured systems in general.

The paper was intended to use Simon's newly acquired metaphor to contribute to our understanding of a central and fundamental property of multi-celled organisms. This fundamental property is the fact that such organisms consist of a hierarchy of components, such that at any level of the hierarchy, the rates of interaction within components at the level are much higher than the rates of interaction between different components. These systems are *nearly decomposable*. To characterize, consider the following metaphor: imagine a large building, with very many rooms with thick walls, each room divided into smaller cubicles with thinner walls. Then, some external disruption occurs, causing the temperature in each cubic centimeter of air to be different from each adjoining cubic centimeter; each cubicle exhibiting a sizeable temperature difference from each adjoining cubicle; each room from each adjoining room, and the whole set of rooms from the outdoors. We hold the outdoor temperature constant and shut off the heating and air conditioning, close all doors and see what happens.

Rapidly, the temperatures of all the air particles in any single cubicle will become essentially equal. By the end of an hour, the temperature of all the cubicles in a given room will be the same. By the end of eight hours, the temperatures of all the rooms will be about the same. And by the end of a day, all the rooms will be at the same temperature as the outside air. Never mind that the exact times of equilibration of the place would depend on the Newton coefficients of heat transmission through the walls and ceilings; the sequence is clear.

Such a system is the archetype of a nearly decomposable system. It can be thought of as a boxes-within-boxes hierarchy with an arbitrary number of levels. Its special characteristic is that equilibrating interactions within boxes at any level take place much more rapidly than do interactions between boxes at that same level, and similarly all the way to the top of the hierarchy.

Organizations and markets

A central task of the social and the behavioral sciences (important for both theory and practice) is to build a theory of how markets and organizations (such as business firms) behave and how they come into being, how they grow, and eventually disappear. Markets have played a key role in human economic affairs since classical Greek times, and even much earlier. The growth and power of Athens, for example, was highly dependent on its colonies, as distant as the Black Sea and the Western Mediterranean, with which it exchanged its products for agricultural commodities and minerals. What has always been thought remarkable about markets (by von

Hayek, to mention a well-known example), is their low degree of explicit organization: the independence of their participants in going their several ways, yet bringing
about, through their activities, an orderly pattern of (usually) equilibrated transactions. This property of markets has been widely proclaimed in economics as making
them indispensable to efficient economic organization. Many questions can be raised
about this description of market systems and may also remind us that effective
markets are only part of what makes effective social and economic organization and
that human organizations are sometimes very effective means.

In the days of Adam Smith, markets had little competition as economic organizers.
The corporation, in its modern form and functions, was nearly unknown, and non-
market competition, at least in Western Europe largely took the form of the putting-
out system, itself an extension of market mechanisms. Why did this system which
had prevailed for several thousand years as the main organizer of economic activity
find itself rapidly inhabited by large corporate organizations within which the vast
bulk of the gainfully active population now carry on their work? Contemporary
American or Western economies are not "market economies" – they are "organization
and market economies" and could not do what they are currently doing without
both components, in particular the organizational one (Simon, 1991).

Given the important role of markets and organizations in economies, a high
priority needs to be given, in research on complex systems, to deepening our understanding of the real natures of these kinds of structures. Many topics will appear
on this agenda. We will have to learn why exchanges in markets frequently call for
information about many things besides prices. We will have to take account of
motives besides self-interest, especially organizational identification, that play a central role in the decisions of members of organizations. We will have to reassess the
circumstances under which markets exhibit greater effectiveness than organizations,
and the circumstances under which they are less effective. In particular, we will have
to understand how bounded rationality – limits on knowledge and computation by
humans and computers – affects these relative advantages and disadvantages. In sum,
the theory of markets and organizations, and their mutual relations, deserves a high
place on the agenda of the study of complex systems.

Coordination and organizations as complex systems

Organizations often come into being because of the need for some activities to
be coordinated more closely than can readily be done through market exchange.
The basic idea of coordination is simple: the effectiveness of one activity depends on
what other and related activities are being performed and how. To take an obvious
example, it is desirable that all drivers on the streets use the same conventions about
direction of movement in left and right lanes.

When there is a limited number of products and these are highly standardized,
enforcement of the necessary coordination conventions may not require organization, but simply wide communication of what the conventions are. As variety and
the rate of innovation of products increases – and technological advance has been a
powerful force for such increases – coordination by convention is no longer adequate.

Even with an understanding of such principles as interchangable parts, centralization of decision may be required to set the standards of interchangeability.

The problem of coordination is seen most simply if we imagine the process of designing a system, say a piece of machinery, that has two components. If the design that is most efficient for each component is independent of the design that is adopted for the other component, independent designers can produce each component, which can then be assembled into the finished machine. If, however, the effectiveness of each component depends on the design of the other, we cannot depend on a pure market to bring about the desired coordination. In this case we could do better with an organization that would coordinate the design of the two components.

Of course, coordination is not without its costs, among them the costs of communication and the costs of providing motivation for organization members to work toward the organizational goal. The choice between organization and markets depends on a comparison of these costs with the quality of the product that is likely to result under either arrangement. We shall return to the motivational issues later, and for now focus on the problem of coordination.

To minimize the costs of coordination, organizers try to divide up their activities in such a way that there is as much independence as feasible for each of the component divisions and departments. As long as the appropriate motivation can be provided for those who staff the components, the effort of coordination will decline with the degree of mutual independence. Thus, a central principal of organizational design is to divide the work among components in such a way as to minimize needs for coordination. City governments have their police departments, fire departments, and public works departments with only a minimum of coordination and cooperation among them. As the need for coordination diminishes, so the choice between organizations and markets approaches a toss-up. Automobiles may be sold by their manufacturers, or by semi-independent dealers who contract with the manufacturers. The modern economy has many cross-breeds between market connected agents and near organizations. Sole suppliers of parts are an example of hybridization, and large divisionalized conglomerates constitute another.

Organizations are prime examples of nearly-decomposable systems and organizations are the most powerful tools that human beings have found to cope with their bounded rationality by combining their thinking powers. The near decomposability of organizational structures is a means of securing the benefits of coordination while holding down its costs by an appropriate division of labor among subunits (Simon, 2000). Moreover, complex systems, such as organizations, must be created so as to meet the needs of coordination and the prospects for the emergence of an effective complex system are much greater if it has a nearly decomposable structure than if the interconnections are less departmentalized (Simon, 1996, chapters 7 and 8). Let us see why.

Suppose that we have a system of two components, and that the efficiency of the whole is some function of the efficiencies of the components and their interactions. Suppose, further, that this system is evolving through a process either of natural selection or design, where designs are evaluated as wholes with respect to their "fitness." Changes in the components may be thought of as mutations. The effect of a mutation in a component upon the fitness of the system will depend on the total fitness function. For example, improvement of one component, in terms of its own performance, may cause the other component to perform more poorly. Under these circumstances, it will be very hard for the evolving system to find its way through the space of possible designs. It is highly likely to get stuck at some local maximum in this space, where further improvements in one component are countered by deterioration of the other.

Suppose, by contrast, that the effectiveness of each component is nearly independent of the design of the other component. Then, improvements in either or both will improve the functioning of the whole system. The system (and this is true of any system evolving by mutation and natural selection) is still likely to be stalled at a local maximum, but will almost always reach much higher equilibria than the system without near-independence of its parts.

This is not just a matter of speculation. Very impressive simulations, using genetic algorithms, have shown that when nearly decomposable systems are put into competition with systems of comparable complexity that lack near decomposability, and when both sets of systems have comparable mutation rates, the nearly decomposable systems very soon greatly outnumber the others and take over the ecosystem. Hence, one reason we see in the world only complex systems that are nearly decomposable is because such systems are the ones that survive the fitness competition (Frenken, Marengo, and Valente, 1999).

There has been a classical debate, since mid-century, in economics, initiated by Alchian (1950) and Friedman (1953) about whether competition will guaranty the survival of the fittest. In terms of what we now know about fitness landscapes and the presences of numerous local optima that bare the path to the global optima, we know that market competition will not maximize fitness, or even assure its rapid growth, unless the competitors are nearly decomposable so that improvement is not blocked by the need for coordinating design over many components. Market competition is not an adequate substitute for effective design (near decomposability) of complex organizations. And if there is a strong need for coordination of economic activities, in the senses described above, there is a strong need for organizations other than markets.

Connecting to issues of organizational identification

Let us discuss the relative advantages of markets and organizations with respect to the motivations of the participants. One argument that has been made strongly for the advantages of markets is that their effectiveness depends solely on the self-interest of the economic actors. This even can be, and has been, bolstered by the argument that self-interest is the only motive that can survive the forces of natural selection. Simon (1990) has argued that the latter argument is incorrect. In a world of bounded rationality, individuals who are endowed with docility (that is, who are receptive to social influences), have a substantial fitness advantage over those not so endowed, and can (and often will) absorb a large measure of altruism from their social environments while still retaining a net fitness advantage.

Furthermore, the altruism is likely to take the form of loyalty to social groups (such as a family, an organization, or a nation), and identification, both motivational and cognitive, with the objectives of these groups. Organizational identification, thus, provides a strong psychological mechanism for a major part of the motivation, a mechanism that is consistent with what we know about both evolution and bounded rationality.

A look at history will perhaps add further strength to this argument. Not only must we explain the rapid gain of organizations over markets in the two centuries since Adam Smith. We must also explain why large organizations, especially military organizations and organizations for managing irrigated agricultural areas, flourished at a very early stage in human history, before written language appeared to record their exploits. Military organizations and irrigation projects represent two very old technologies that benefit greatly from a relatively high level of coordination of effort, and that can only with difficulty be conceived of as being replaced by markets. To be sure, "identification" with these organizations was heavily reinforced by the sheer autocratic power exercised over their members, but one has only to read Xenophon's story, in the *Anabsis*, of the march of the Four Hundred to the sea, or the tales of tribal warfare in the Old Testament, to recognize that group loyalty and identification were already powerful forces in those early times.

Conclusions

Complexity and hiearachical systems are central to modern thinking in economics, biology, and so on. In recent years, the idea of hierarchy and how one uses it to accomplish goals and the opportunity it gives for systems to evolve and become more effective have been taken up by people in many domains, either from an evolutionary standpoint or from an organizational efficiency standpoint. Starting with Nelson and Winter (1982), these ideas got some hold in economics, but the biologists saw the implications earlier.

At the same time, increasing focus on complexity has increased the need to think about the architecture of these systems. Everybody is much more aware now of the structure of complex systems than when *The Architecture of Complexity* was first written. Near decomposability has been a subject of much discussion and research, and that research has added to our understanding of the relations between organizations and markets.

The idea of near decomposability provides some guidelines for designing an organization and information systems for it. It can also add to our understanding of the existence of economic organizations in two ways. First, great increases in effectiveness are obtainable by introducing mechanisms of coordination between interrelated activities. But only after organizing these activities in nearly decomposable form so as to reduce the need for and costs of coordination as far as is possible without losing the advantages it affords, and only with the help of organizational identification to complement and supplement self-interest as a motivating force. Second, in the Darwinian competition among systems for survival and growth, near decomposability provides a major advantage for the systems possessing it, with the consequence that many, possibly all of the world's complex systems, including economic and other human organizations, come to possess this property.

But our purpose here has not been to provide a finished story of the understanding of modern business organizations and how they have emerged. It was rather to reaffirm the centrality of near decomposability in the light of the presence of large economic organizations and the need to deepen our understanding of their structure and workings in order to better understand the system of organizations and markets in which we live, and to enlarge our ability to redesign and manage that system so that we may use it more effectively to meet our human needs.

NOTE

This commentary was drafted by Mie Augier and Herbert A. Simon in December, 2000, after the invitation to participate in this volume. Due to Herbert Simon's unexpected death, the manuscript was edited and the references added by Mie Augier. This editing process could not have been completed without the helpful comments and encouragement from Raghu Garud, Richard Langlois, James G. March, and Kathie Simon.

REFERENCES

Alchian, A. (1950). "Uncertainty, Evolution and Economic Theory," *Journal of Political Economy*, 58: 211–22.

Frenken, K., L. Marengo and M. Valente (1999). "Interdependencies, near-decomposability and adaptation," Working Paper 1999–03, CEEL, Department of Economics: University of Trento.

Friedman, M. (1953). "The Methodology of Positive Economics," *Essays in Positive Economics*, Chicago: University of Chicago Press.

Goodwin, R. (1947). "Dynamic Coupling with especial reference to Markets having Production Lags," *Econometrica*, 15: 181–204.

Nelson, R. and S. G. Winter (1982). *An Evolutionary Theory of Economic Change*, Cambridge: Harvard University Press.

Simon, H. A. (1962). "The Architecture of Complexity," *Proceedings of the American Philosophical Society*, 106: 467–82.

Simon, H. A. (1990). "A Mechanism for Social Selection and Successful Altruism," *Science*, 250: 1665–8.

Simon, H. A. (1991). "Organizations and Markets," *Journal of Economic Perspectives*, 5: 25–44.

Simon, H. A. (1996). *The Sciences of the Artificial*, Cambridge: MIT Press.

Simon, H. A. (2000). "Public Administration in Today's World of Organizations and Markets," *Political Science and Politics*, 33(4): 749–56.

Simon, H. A. and A. Ando (1961). "Aggregation of variables in dynamic Systems," *Econometrica*, 29: 111–38.

CHAPTER TWO

TECHNOLOGICAL AND ORGANIZATIONAL DESIGNS FOR REALIZING ECONOMIES OF SUBSTITUTION

RAGHU GARUD AND ARUN KUMARASWAMY

The Schumpeterian era during which "gales of creative destruction" brought about revolutionary changes over long periods of time (Schumpeter, 1942) is past. In recent times, we have entered a neo-Schumpeterian era where technological change appears to be ceaseless. To survive in this new era, firms have to innovate continually (Klein, 1977). Continual innovation, however, imposes limits on a firm's ability to realize scale economies. Moreover, rapid change dampens the diffusion of new technologies as customers postpone purchases due to fear of obsolescence (Rosenberg, 1982). Slower diffusion of technological changes creates problems for firms attempting to recoup investments made in technologies that change continually.

There is another facet to this new era that renders contemporary environments different from those prevalent during Schumpeter's time. Specifically, many of these technologies are "systemic" in nature (Winter, 1987); i.e., they are embodied in multicomponent products that connect to each other. The development and production of such technological systems require significant investments on several complementary technologies (Hakansson, 1989; Powell and Brantley, 1992; Quinn, 1992; Teece, 1987). It is difficult for any one firm to invest in all complementary technologies because, after a point, bottlenecks arise in the form of overxtended scientists, engineers, and manufacturing personnel (Penrose, 1959; Teece, 1980). Such congestion imposes limits on the firm's ability to realize scope economies.

How may firms deal with these challenges? We propose that firms take advantage of a different source of economies – economies of substitution – instead of relying exclusively on economies of scale and scope. We use the term "substitution" to suggest that technological progress may be achieved by substituting certain components of a technological system while reusing others. The potential for such economies increases if technological systems are modularly upgradable. By designing

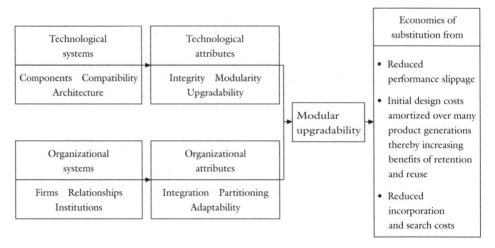

Figure 2.1 Technological and organizational designs for economies of substitution.

modularly upgradable systems, firms can reduce product development time, leverage their past investments, and provide customers with continuity.

Additionally, we suggest that firms reorganize their internal and external relationships to reduce the costs of component reuse, while enhancing associated benefits. The network mode of governance, with its emphasis on knowledge sharing, adaptability, and continual innovation, appears to be best suited for this task (Powell, 1990). Indeed, networks form the basis for a variety of arrangements ranging from giant Japanese "keiretsus" to small Italian firms linked by cooperative associations (see Best, 1990; Kenney and Florida, 1993; Nelson and Wright, 1992; Piore and Sabel, 1984; Porter, 1990; Quinn, 1992). Increasingly, these network forms are challenging traditional "Fordist" organizations based on Taylor's scientific management principles.

Figure 2.1 summarizes our core thesis and depicts the organization of this paper. First, we discuss how technological systems are built of components that interact with one another under an overall system architecture. We identify three system-level attributes: integrity, modularity, and upgradability. All three attributes must be considered while designing technological systems for economies of substitution. We substantiate why technological systems must be modularly upgradable to yield economies of substitution. Then, we explore organizational issues that arise in realizing these economies of substitution. We emphasize the similarity between the design of technological systems and organizational systems for realizing substitution economies. Just as technological systems are composed of components interacting with one another within an overall architecture, these organizational systems are composed of individual firms interacting with each other within an overall institutional framework. We explore how modularly upgradable organizational systems may be created, and how modular upgradability gives rise to both cooperative and competitive dynamics. Finally, we discuss the implications of our thesis for firms operating in the neo-Schumpeterian era.

Technological Systems for Economies of Substitution

A technological system comprises a set of components that, together, provide utility to customers. System performance is dependent not only on the performance of individual components, but also on the extent to which they are compatible with one another (Gabel, 1987; Henderson and Clark, 1990; Tushman and Rosenkopf, 1992). Compatibility is a relational attribute that defines rules of fit and interaction between components across boundaries called interfaces. The overall set of rules that defines acceptable fit and interactions constitutes a system's architecture.

The degree of compatibility among components defines three important attributes of technological systems: integrity, modularity, and upgradability. *Integrity* represents "the consistency between a product's function and its structure: the parts fit smoothly, components match and work well together, the layout maximizes available space" (Clark and Fujimoto, 1990: 108). Although individual system components may have been designed to yield high performance, a lack of compatibility among them results in suboptimal system performance. In other words, incompatibility between components comprises the integrity of a technological system.

Firms may ensure system integrity by custom-designing components and assembling them through an iterative process of rework to obtain requisite fit and interaction, as in craft production (Cox, 1986; Womack, Jones, and Roos, 1990). Firms may also ensure system integrity by designing and producing components to standard dimensional and interface specifications. Conformance to standard specifications enables the production of identical (and therefore interchangeable) components in large numbers, as in mass production (Marshall, 1961).

Production of components conforming to standard interface specifications also leads to modularity. *Modularity* allows components to be produced separately and used interchangeably in different configurations without compromising system integrity (Demsetz, 1993; Flamm, 1988; Garud and Kotha, 1994).[1] The degree of modularity of a technological system varies, depending on whether interfaces are standardized within only a single firm or throughout an industry. In the former case, components my be used interchangeably only within a firm's own product lines. In the latter case, components manufactured by different firms may be mixed and matched. This ability to mix and match allows firms to offer a variety of system configurations, and to economize on product development investments (Baldwin and Clark, 1994; Pine, 1993; Sanchez, 1995). At the same time, it offers customers the flexibility to buy components from different firms and create technological systems that are most appropriate for their requirements (Matutes and Regibeau, 1988).

In rapidly changing environments, a third system-level attribute – *upgradability*, or the ease with which system performance can be enhanced over time – also becomes important. If a system is not upgradable, performance improvements may involve its complete redesign. Such a process entails the destruction of existing knowledge and competence. Given the rapidity of technological change, the repetitive destruction and creation of knowledge and competencies for each new generation may increase firms' R&D investments to levels that cannot be recouped within ensuing short product life cycles. At the same time, customers will be wary of adopting new technologies that become obsolete rapidly, thereby decreasing the rate at which these technologies diffuse (Rosenberg, 1982).

To be upgradable, a technological system must possess degrees of freedom that enable improvements in existing capabilities and the addition of new capabilities.[2] To understand how degrees of freedom may be created, we have to appreciate the hierarchical organization of components within a technological system (Clark, 1985; Hughes, 1987; Simon, 1962). Component choices at any given level of the hierarchy outline operational boundaries for lower-order components. For instance, the performance capability of a computer is dependent on the speed of its microprocessor. Over time, technological advances in microprocessor design have led to significant increases in the speed of the entire computer. These innovations in microprocessor design represent a movement "up the system hierarchy" and, typically, represent revolutionary changes where system foundations are built afresh (Clark, 1985): movement up the system hierarchy makes it more difficult to maintain compatibility between product generations because core components are replaced.

Firms, however, may design higher-order components with performance capabilities that are not fully exploited at early design stages. These unutilized degrees of freedom in higher-order components can be exploited progressively through innovations in lower-order components. Clark (1985) labels such innovations as a movement "down the system hierarchy." Specifically, movement down the hierarchy represents incremental change where core components are preserved even as innovations occur in lower-order components. In this case, it is easier to maintain compatibility between product generations because innovations occur only in lower-order components.

In sum, firms may impart upgradability to technological systems by designing unutilized degrees of freedom into higher-order components. These unutilized degrees of freedom enable designers to enhance system performance by substituting only those lower-order components whose potentials have been exhausted. However, the benefits of upgradability and associated retention of components must be weighed against the costs of component reuse. We now explore these benefits and costs in greater detail, and suggest how to design technological systems that yield economies of substitution.

Economies of substitution

Economies of substitution exist when the cost of designing a higher-performance system through the partial retention of existing components is lower than the cost of designing the system afresh (Garud and Kumaraswamy, 1993). Component retention yields several benefits. The most obvious benefit is the reutilization of the existing base of knowledge associated with the retained components. Other benefits include savings in testing and production costs. Savings in testing costs arise when test programs developed for retained components are reused. This benefit is especially valuable in cases where test program development takes as much time as the actual design of the system itself. For instance, Texas Instruments (TI) cites such savings in testing costs as one of the main benefits that it expects to receive from its new PRISM methodology. TI's PRISM methodology allows circuit modules to be combined in different configurations to create new chips (*Texas Instruments*, September 1992). Additionally, the reuse of circuit modules enables TI to standardize chip fabrication processes, thereby yielding significant savings in production costs. In general, savings in production costs accrue from the reutilization of capital equipment and production routines associated with reused components.

Yet, these benefits have to be balanced against performance slippage and several costs incurred in reusing components. *Performance slippage* may occur when designers try to incorporate newly developed components into a technological system. This is because newly developed components may not fit or interact well with existing components, thereby compromising system integrity.

Designers can minimize performance slippage by using gateway technologies, such as adapters and converters, that enable the coexistence of incompatible components within a technological system (David and Bunn, 1990). Gateway technologies, however, imply higher costs because they involve the development and usage of additional components. Moreover, gateway technologies seldom restore system integrity completely. Therefore, they may not provide the best way for firms to realize economies of substitution.[3]

A better way for firms to realize economies of substitution is by designing modularity into technological systems. Modularity minimizes performance slippage arising from incompatibility between the newly designed and reused components. Additionally, modularity makes it easier for designers to integrate newly developed components into the existing system; that is, modularity reduces *incorporation costs* for both designers and customers. Incorporation costs in a modular system are limited to eliminating incompatibilities that were not anticipated while designing standard interfaces.

Therefore, modularity and upgradability are both important system attributes for realizing economies of substitution. Modularity increases the ease with which system designers can substitute certain system components while retaining all others. Upgradability provides designers with the opportunity to work on an already-established technological platform thereby preserving their core knowledge base (Wheelwright and Clark, 1992). In this manner, modular upgradability simplifies the task of coping with very short life cycles.

Besides enabling the preservation of knowledge over successive generations, modular upgradability creates new knowledge that enhances, rather than destroys, existing knowledge. This competency-enhancing knowledge (Tushman and Anderson, 1986) is derived from experience as designers gain a deeper appreciation of (1) which aspects of the platform will lead to future improvements, (2) which aspects of the platform will lead to dead ends, and (3) how new lower-order components fit in with the base platform.

Modular upgradability leads to economies of substitution in another way. Modular upgradability allows firms to listen to customer feedback and modify their systems accordingly by substituting some components while retaining the others. Rosenberg (1982) points out that such learning by using is essential for the evolution of complex multicomponent systems whose optimization only occurs through large-scale customer trials. In so far as the system design incorporates modular upgradability, designers will find it easy and economical to carry out modifications. Wheelwright and Clark (1992) call this process "rapid prototyping."

Increasingly, firms competing in neo-Schumpeterian environments are designing modularly upgradable systems to enable component reuse. In computer hardware, for instance, Sun Microsystems had created the modularly upgradable Sparcstation 10 family of computer workstations (see Garud and Kumaraswamy, 1993, for more details). In computer software development, object-oriented programming (OOP), a technique that allows reuse of program modules and easy upgradability, has gained in popularity and usage by firms. By using OOP techniques, Brooklyn Union Gas Company created 20 percent more functionality (over the previous nonobject-oriented system) with 40 percent fewer lines of code; Shearson Lehman, Inc. reduced development costs by 30 percent through reuse of objects (*Business Week*, 30 September 1991); and the US Marine Corps reduced prototype time from the normal 6 to 8 weeks to just 2 weeks. In general, OOP users report two- to five-fold increases in programmer productivity (*Financial Executive*, July/August 1991).[4]

Firms in the automobile industry, too, have designed models that allow for the sharing and reuse of key components. For instance, Honda developed a single basic 1994 Accord model and customized it later for different markets. Honda held its total development costs down by reusing components from other models. All versions of the 1994 Accord had at least 50 percent common components (*Business Week*, 21 December 1992). Additionally, Honda reduced retooling and procurement costs by (1) reusing components, (2) designing new components so that these could be manufactured using existing equipment in its Japanese and US plants, and (3) delegating design of certain components entirely to its suppliers (*Wall Street Journal*, 1 September 1993).

However, modularly upgradable technological designs alone are inadequate for firms to realize economies of substitution. This is because several costs are implicit in the design of modularly upgradable systems: initial design costs, testing costs, and search costs. *Initial design costs* refer to the additional costs that designers incur in creating components for reuse over and above those incurred in designing components for one-time use. These additional costs are incurred up-front to impart additional degrees of freedom to a system, such as standardized interfaces or the design of higher-order components with unutilized capabilities. For instance, analysts of OOP estimate that initial design costs of reusable objects may be as high as three to ten times the costs incurred in building an object for one-time use (Balda and Gustafson, 1990; Kain, 1994).

Baldwin and Clark (1994) highlight that *testing costs* constitute a high proportion of product innovation costs. They suggest that the ability to perform tests at the component level (rather than at the system level) is essential for reducing testing costs. Although testing at the commandant level and the reuse of testing programs reduce costs, overall testing costs increase cumulatively with the number of modular components to be tested. Additionally, as Baldwin and Clark point out, designers of different components must strike prior agreements on the interface specifications and the encompassing system architecture to develop testing programs. This increases initial design costs.

Finally, designers incur *search costs* to locate reusable components. Typically, search costs increase with the proliferation of modular, reusable components. For instance, in OOP, Banker et al. (1993) found that reuse percentage decreased with an increase in the number of reuse candidates. They cite the case of Carter Hawley Hale Information Services where reuse dropped by more than 15 percent when the number of reusable objects in the firm's repository grew by four times. In these cases, even libraries that allowed searches by key words did not promote reuse.

To realize economies of substitution, then, initial design costs and testing costs need to be amortized over a number of reuses, and search costs need to be minimized. These demands raise issues concerning the design of appropriate organizational systems. For instance, consider a firm that does not consciously encourage component reuse. In such a firm, the extra costs associated with the creation of modularly upgradable components may not be amortized fully. Consequently, the firm will not realize economies of substitution. Or consider a firm that does not institute effective mechanisms to search for reusable components. In such a firm, high search costs may prevent reuse altogether; or even if reuse occurs, costs may outweigh benefits. Again, the firm will not realize economies of substitution.

ORGANIZATIONAL SYSTEMS FOR ECONOMIES OF SUBSTITUTION

Technological systems consist of components that together provide utility to users. Similarly, firms that manufacture the components of a technological system together comprise an organizational system for that technology. Relationships between these firms are analogous to interactions between components of the technological system. The mosaic of rules, procedures, and norms that comprise the institutional environment of this organizational system parallels the architecture of a technological system.

A key challenge in realizing economies of substitution is the design of organizational systems that enhance component retention or reuse while reducing associated costs. We suggest that this challenge be met by designing organizational systems to be "modularly upgradable." A modularly upgradable organizational system allows constituent members to work independently and in unison, even as they evolve over time.[5]

Intrafirm issues

Realization of economies of substitution requires knowledge sharing and the reuse of components. Traditional hierarchical and SBU structures, however, inhibit realization of these economies. Specifically, these traditional structures result in "knowledge hoarding" by independently functioning units. To encourage "knowledge sharing," Prahalad and Hamel (1990) propose that firms organize themselves around core competencies. Garud and Nayyar (1994) recommend that firms enhance knowledge sharing and reuse by cataloguing, updating, and distributing lists of available "shelved projects" (see also Kogut and Zander, 1992). Kotha (1995) reports how the National Bicycle Company rotates personnel between its plants, thereby creating a mechanism for the sharing of tacit knowledge (see also Nonaka, 1994). Indeed, Hill, Hitt, and Hoskisson (1992) report that related-diversified firms that install mechanisms to promote cooperation and knowledge sharing between constituent units tend to perform well.

Cusumano (1991) illustrates how a knowledge-sharing organization might look in his description of Toshiba's software production facilities. Toshiba has instituted elaborate procedures to evaluate, catalogue, store, and disseminate reusable software throughout the company, thereby reducing search costs. Toshiba has also created special "committees," "departments," and "centers" to ensure that designers create reusable software and reduce incorporation costs by conforming to company-wide standards. Additionally, committees help overcome the short-term concerns that may arise with knowledge sharing and reuse.

There are yet other challenges involved in designing reusable components, and in reusing components designed by others. As Mary Wells, erstwhile training program manager to Tektronix Inc., asserted: "There will always be tension between those pushing for a library and reuse, and those trying to get a job done. People focusing on reuse want to make (objects) as general as possible, while the application developers want things as specific as possible" (*Datamation*, 15 November 1989: 90). In a similar vein, Graham (1994) states: "We are used to rewarding analysts and programmers according to the amount of code they produce rather than the amount of other people's code they reuse. . . . Furthermore, project managers are paid to make projects come in on time and not to write code for the benefit of subsequent projects" (also see Banker et al., 1993; Cusumano, 1991). Therefore, firms need to realign their incentives to encourage reuse.

Cusumano (1991) describes Toshiba's integrated set of incentives and controls associated with knowledge sharing and reuse. At the beginning of each project, managers at Toshiba agree to productivity targets that can be met only if a certain percentage of software specifications, designs, or code is reused. Design review meetings held at the end of each phase in the development cycle monitor progress against reuse targets. Moreover, when building new software, management requires project members to register a certain number of components in data bases for reuse in later projects. Personnel receive awards for registering particularly valuable or frequently reused modules, and their formal evaluations from superiors report on whether they have met their reuse targets. An overall committee, meanwhile, monitors reuse levels at Toshiba as well as deviations from targets both at the project and individual levels, and provides regular reports to managers.

Although reuse and knowledge sharing lead to economies of substitution, they have the potential to trap firms within the confines of old knowledge. To overcome this eventuality, Garud and Nayyar (1994) suggest that firms must continually create new knowledge through a combination of the old. (See also Jelinek and Schoonhoven, 1990.) Moreover, Hamel and Prahalad (1994) note that firms must upgrade their core competencies over time, partially by continually retraining employees. Lei, Hitt, and Bettis (1995) provide a more complete thesis on how firms can update core competencies through a meta-learning process that consists of information transfer, continuous improvement based on experimentation, and the development of firm-specific skills based on dynamic routines.

These arguments, and the Toshiba example in particular, establish a firm's capabilities to reorganize its structure, routines, and incentives to encourage reuse and realize economies of substitution. However, there are limits to the number of activities any one firm can perform within the purview of its administrative structure. To appreciate these limits, we have to compare the costs of internalizing activities within the firm with the costs of sharing some of these activities with other firms.

Internalizing activities within a firm involves two costs: managerial and production costs. *Managerial costs* increase with the number of components produced in-house (lateral integration) and with the number of stages required to produce a given component (vertical integration). First, as the extent of vertical and lateral integration increases, managerial costs of coordinating different activities increases disproportionately (Demsetz, 1993; Piore, 1992). These coordination costs will increase further if congestion occurs in the deployment of scarce resources among competing activities (Teece, 1980). Second, cognitive complexity faced by managers also increases. This is particularly true in neo-Schumpeterian environments where each change brings with it disproportionate cognitive demands. As cognitive complexity increases, at some point, it becomes more costly for a firm to undertake any more activities in-house than it is to delegate them to other firms.

Additionally, in-house *production costs* will increase if the demand experienced by a firm is low or uncertain. In such circumstances, the firm cannot justify production facilities that operate at a minimum efficient scale for each component.[6] However, a specialized firm that consolidates demand for a particular component can justify building a minimum efficient scale plant, thereby realizing scale economies.[7]

Thus, in neo-Schumpeterian environments, increases in managerial and production costs are key forces for the disaggregation of activities. To understand fully why disaggregation is occurring, however, we must trade off the benefits of depending upon external component manufacturers with increases in transactions costs (Langlois and Robertson, 1992). Transactions costs arise from asset specificity under uncertainty, and from the potential for opportunistic behavior under conditions of information asymmetry and bounded rationality (williamson, 1985). However, the advent of information technologies (such as electronic data interchange) allows firms to coordinate activities more closely (Manzi, 1994), thereby reducing information asymmetry and opportunism. Furthermore, a steady movement in many systemic industries toward industry-wide standards has reduced asset specificity and small numbers bargaining. Consequently, transactions costs are progressively decreasing (Malone, Yates, and Benjamin, 1987; Quinn, 1992). With decreases in transactions costs and increases in managerial and production costs, firms are focusing on a set of conceptually related activities and outsourcing the rest (Demsetz, 1993; Langlois, 1992; Piore, 1992; Piore and Sabel, 1984; Richardson, 1972).[8]

Interfirm issues

As firms manufacture only some components and outsource others, they implicitly "partition" the technological system.[9] Partitioning a technological system can create an organizational system whose organizational modules (firms) can engage and disengage in response to market and technological changes (also see Miles and Snow, 1986; Sanchez and Mahoney, 1994). However, to accomplish such "flexible specialization" (Piore and Sable, 1984), it is important that these organizational modules coordinate among themselves to design and produce compatible components. Otherwise, performance slippage and the costs associated with integrating the various components into a technological system will become prohibitively high.

A key question is whether such integration should be left to markets, or whether some other governance mode is required. If we were dealing with a static technological system, perhaps markets could serve as a forum for integration. However, when technological systems are changing rapidly, the cost of creating and maintaining interface standards within a market mode of governance will be prohibitively high. Standardization requires much closer coordination among firms than markets can offer.

Coordination between vertically interdependent firms requires an approach to contracting that emphasizes long-term relationships based on trust and reputation (Macneil, 1980; Powell, 1990).[10] Analogous to the notion of unutilized degrees of freedom in technological systems, relationships between firms are defined broadly, allowing enough latitude for evolution over time. Once relationships are established, continual interactions (including the exchange of strategic information, personnel and knowledge) among collaborating firms create an environment that engenders trust and mutual accommodation. That is, the relationships between firms become "upgradable." Indeed, as Morgan (1986) points out, the broadest agreement would be one in which only those eventualities that definitely must be avoided (noxiants) are specified.

The classical approach to contingent claims contracting reduces such upgradability. This is because contingent claims contracts create a rigid framework for relationships by attempting to prespecify performance under all likely contingencies (Macneil, 1980). However, when technology is evolving rapidly and it is difficult to foresee the future, the very notion of a contingent claims contract becomes questionable.[11]

Furthermore, a zero-sum mentality which prescribes that firms should view buyer–supplier relationships as a source of competition also inhibits upgradability (Garud, 1994). For instance, Porter (1980) has suggested that firms should develop "bargaining advantage" over suppliers to "squeeze out the best deal." Such a zero-sum mentality engenders distrust (Kelley and Stahelski, 1970; Weick, 1979) and leads to conflict in a self-fulfilling way. Eventually, such a mentality destroys the coordination required to realize economies of substitution.

There are indications that some firms in the USA are increasing their emphasis on upgradable relational contracts. For instance, vertically related firms are focusing on the practical aspects of building relationships and trust among themselves. In particular, some firms are reducing the number of suppliers and focusing their energies on building long-term relationships with this core group.[12] Such long-term relationships seek to ensure that ". . . [e]ach player's destiny will be joined with that of the other. And mutual dependence will characterize the relationships" (Davidow and Malone, 1993: 142).

The advent of new information-mediated technologies (Zuboff, 1984) makes coordination between firms all the more possible (Fombrun and Astley, 1982). If we view firms as modules of knowledge, mechanisms such as electronic data interchange (Malone et al., 1987) enable connections between these modules and promote interfirm coordination. These information technologies reduce transactions costs, thereby improving the management of disaggregated systems (Quinn, 1992).

A neo-Schumpeterian industrial landscape requires cooperation between horizontally interdependent firms as well. As technologies change, firms may find that they do not have all the required competencies to create a viable technological system. These competencies may be resident in their rivals. Given the difficult task of creating new competencies rapidly as and when they are required, firms may be compelled to forge hybrid arrangements with rivals.[13] Taligent is one such hybrid arrangement. IBM and Apple, two direct competitors, created the Taligent collaborative venture and gave it wide latitude to create a common object-oriented operating system.

Another form of cooperation between horizontally interdependent firms is knowledge sharing without the formation of a formal alliance such as a joint venture (Langlois and Robertson, 1992). Knowledge sharing between rivals is desirable to the extent that it increases the density of firms manufacturing technological systems that conform to a common standard. As the density of firms manufacturing systems to a common standard increases, so do the benefits to customers who get a wider choice of complementary products from which to create their preferred system configurations (see Wade, 1994). The larger customer base, in turn, provides incentives to manufactures of complementary components to invest in innovation.

In their study of the music and computer industries, for instance, Langlois and Robertson (1992) note that a firm can earn higher profits by sharing knowledge with rivals than by attempting to appropriate all the benefits itself. They add that "when a component maker is unable to offer customers enough variety to justify the purchase of associated components in a modular system, the most successful firms will be those that abandon a proprietary strategy in favor of membership in a network of competitors employing a common standard of compatibility" (Langlois and Robertson, 1992: 301).

Eventually, distinctions between horizontal and vertical interdependence become blurred. As vertically interdependent firms learn from one another, they may become horizontally interdependent over time (Hamel, Doz, and Prahalad, 1989). For instance, Donnelley Corporation, a supplier of glass for making mirrors, became a rival to its own buyers when it built a plant to supply Honda with exterior mirrors (*Fortune*, 21 February 1994). As winners and losers arise in a technological race, firms that were horizontally interdependent may become vertically interdependent over time. For instance, Next Corporation, an erstwhile rival to workstation manufacturers like Hewlett-Packard and Sun Microsystems, exited the workstation hardware market and currently supplies its object-oriented tools and operating system software to these companies. Moreover, two firms that are vertically interdependent in one organizational system may become horizontally interdependent in another organizational system. In the telecommunications industry, for instance, AT&T supplies wireless communications equipment to the Baby Bells. However, with its recent acquisition of McCaw, AT&T will compete with the Baby Bells in the cellular services market.

In summary, the partitioning of the technological system among specialized manufacturers confers modularity on the organizational system. The coordination of specialized firms manufacturing components of the partitioned technological system occurs under a governance mode that is neither a hierarchy nor a market (Best, 1990; Powell, 1990; Richardson, 1972). This governance mode is characterized by a "lattice type" network of relationships (Powell and Brantley, 1992) wherein the distinction between horizontal and vertical relationships becomes blurred. This network structure must be generally, rather than specifically, defined to allow enough latitude for interfirm relationships within the organizational systems to evolve with time. The result is a modularly upgradable organizational system.

Piore and Sabel (1984) note that the partitioning of tasks in the production process need not map neatly on to customers' preferred system configurations. In this regard, intermediary firms, commonly known as value-added resellers or system integrators, play an important role. Such firms perform two functions. First, they provide customized solutions to meet specific customer needs. In doing so, they reduce the cognitive complexity customers confront in mixing and matching the components manufactured by different firms. Second, when performance slippage occurs due to incompatibilities created by technological change, these firms ensure that the integrity of the technological system is maintained. To this extent, the role of system integrators in an organizational system is analogous to the role of gateway technologies in a technological system.[14]

Whereas system integrators reduce cognitive complexity, their presence increases transactions costs. These costs can be minimized to the extent that members of an organizational system subscribe to a common set of standards. According to Astley and Brahm (1989: 258), for "the functional integration of modules as part of a coherent system, an overarching 'framework' of planning and coordination would be necessary" (see also Toffler, 1985). Indeed, we are now witnessing a growing movement toward "open standards" in the institutional environment of standards. Open standards act as mechanisms for coordinating the emerging network mode by reducing transaction costs. We now direct our attention to the institutional aspects of open standards creation.

Institutional issues

Langlois and Robertson (1992) distinguish between two types of networks: "centralized" and "decentralized." They suggest that a centralized network is one in which network members are tied to a "lead" firm, as in the Japanese automobile industry. A decentralized network is one in which no one firm exercises exclusive control over common standards; moreover, any firm that tries to dictate standards in a decentralized network risks being isolated if network members and customers do not follow its lead.

Increasingly, we are witnessing the growth of such decentralized networks in rapidly changing systemic environments, because of network externalities (Rotemberg and Saloner, 1991). Network externalities arise when the benefits a user derives from a product increase from current levels as others use compatible products (e.g., Farrell and Saloner, 1986; Katz and Shapiro, 1985).[15] In the presence of network externalities, the larger the network, the greater is its attraction. In such a situation, firms are finding it in their best interests to adhere to industry-wide standards and promote compatibility, thereby increasing network benefits.[16] Even the largest of firms have been forced to participate in the joint setting of industry-wide standards. For instance, in the computer industry, dominant computer manufacturers (e.g., IBM in the USA and NEC in Japan) were reluctant to adopt open standards, fearing loss of market control. However, over time, customers have compelled even these firms to offer systems based on open standards.[17]

Although the impetus for open standards stems from market demands for compatibility, the actual process of standard-setting is political – one that unfolds in the institutional environment of standards-setting bodies. The political process manifests itself in the form of broad agreements on system architecture, rather than in the form of precise definitions of standards. Indeed, only such broad agreements provide organizational and technological systems with the degrees of freedom required for future evolution. Recognizing the importance of this upgradability, Graham (1994) suggests that open standards must be specified at a high level of abstraction to allow greater degrees of freedom. At the same time, if standards are specified to loosely, they may result in the creation of incompatible components.

Working with open standards leads to decentralized innovation wherein individual firms can autonomously create differentiated components. At an extreme, a proliferation of components occurs, thereby increasing the costs involved in identifying and selecting appropriate components (both for system manufacturers and users). Under these circumstances, specialized information brokers arise to reduce these search costs. For instance, in the case of OOP, the Object Management Group has created an information brokerage that provides information as well as a market for component software. Participating firms list their products with the brokerage, along with descriptive information and product specifications (Object Management Group, 25 July 1994: 1).

Thus, open standards reduce asset specificity and information asymmetry between interdependent firms manufacturing complementary components of a larger system. Moreover, with open standards, the negative consequences of opportunistic behavior are mitigated because no one firm can change industry-wide standards on its own. No firm is held hostage by others because open standards create second sources for the supply of components. Therefore, as more firms embrace open standards, transaction costs decline. In turn, a reduction in transactions costs makes it possible for firms to form dynamic networks (Miles and Snow, 1986). In these dynamic networks, coordination occurs through institutional mechanisms that comprise both the standard-setting bodies and the open standards they foster. While modularity in the organizational system makes it highly adaptive to external contingencies, the overarching institutional umbrella of standards maintains overall consistency of action.

In sum, just as relational contracting imparts hierarchy-like characteristics to the network organizational system, the institutional environment of open standards imparts market-like characteristics to it. Reliance on open standards allows firms to "trade" knowledge encapsulated in reusable components. Just as markets comprise regulatory bodies and institutional arrangements to guarantee efficiency, the organizational system comprises autonomous bodies to maintain and guarantee conformance to open standards. In markets, changes in customer demand result in resource reallocation between competing activities. In organizational systems too, customers play an important role in providing incentives for firms to conform to a common set of standards. Specifically, customers are the arbiters of whether or not a technological system has greater network benefits, and firms that offer "incompatible" systems pay a price. At the same time, institutionalized standards endow memory on the organizational system – a feature missing in traditional atomistic markets. Thus, open standards create a unique institutional environment that coordinates activities of the organizational system.

Cooperative and Competitive Dynamics in a Modularly Upgradable World

We have introduced three levels of analysis – intrafirm, interfirm, and institutional – to explain how organizational systems may be designed to realize economies of substitution. A fundamental attribute of these emerging organizational systems is the presence of both cooperation and competition at each of the three levels. Within the firm, for instance, competition for a limited pool of resources between individuals creates incentives for increasing current performance even at the expense of future performance. Contributions to current performance provide instant recognition and rewards, whereas contributions to future performance (through the design of reusable components) may yield little recognition or rewards. Moreover, creators of reusable components may have to face an additional burden when problems arise with their reusable components. Consequently, there will be a tendency to avoid or postpone the creation of reusable components. In addition, there may be a reluctance to reuse components designed by others (even if created). Clearly, cooperation is required to create and reuse such components. Firms need to balance the tension between cooperation and competition by instituting appropriate systems, structures, and incentives to encourage the creation of reusable components.

This tension between cooperation and competition is manifest at the interfirm level as well. Firms confronting a rapidly changing technological system will have to rely on others for complementary components even as they focus on the creation of core components. Indeed, firms will have to share knowledge with one another to ensure that the components they manufacture are compatible. Knowledge sharing, in turn, increases competitive pressures on firms.[18] In such a situation, firms have to innovate continually, destroying some core competencies and enhancing others to suit current requirements (see Lei et al., 1995, for a detailed discussion of how core competencies can be changed over time).

As Powell and Brantley (1992) and Mowery and Rosenberg (1989) suggest, these efforts to extend and adapt core competencies essentially serve as a "ticket of admission" into the wider organizational network to which they belong. Indeed, from this perspective, the main question is not whether to "make or buy." Rather, it is "What competencies are complementary to our own?" so that access to these may be secured through appropriate realignment of relationships within organizational networks

(Quinn, 1992; see also Black and Boal, 1994). Depending on how firms answer this question, they may terminate some relationships and forge new ones to create a dynamic learning environment that enables them to adapt to the demands of an evolving technological system.

The tension between cooperation and competition pervades the institutional level as well. Because of network benefits, firms will try to create or join as large a network as possible. As we saw earlier, this implies the creation of, or conformance to, open standards. To this extent, cooperation is required. However, confronting the prospect of subscribing to common standards, firms would want to be proactive in shaping these standards to suit their competencies better. Specifically, each firm would want its own component specifications built directly into emerging standards. To this extent, firms compete to define standards that favor their own conceptualization of the technological system.

Thus, firms operating in a neo-Schumpeterian world of rapidly changing systemic technologies have to focus their attention on some core components while depending upon others for complementary ones. To ensure compatibility between these components, firms have to share their knowledge with others and subscribe to open standards. Such cooperation leads to competition as firms differentiate their activities through innovation and attempt to shape their institutional environment of standards. In this way, the tension between cooperation and competition is manifest between levels of the organizational systems.

Conclusion

Kenney and Florida (1993) state that the "challenge facing American industry is similar to that faced by Britain at the turn of the century – the need to restructure according to the organizational principles of a new production paradigm in the face of social inertia resulting from the legacy of a past industrial order." These authors caution that American industry may lose its global leadership role if contemporary industrial challenges are not articulated in appropriate technological and organizational terms.

This paper is an attempt to pose these challenges in appropriate technological and organizational terms. Specifically, firms are operating in a neo-Schumpeterian environment where systemic technologies are changing rapidly. In such an environment, firms have to design technological systems to yield economies of substitution, and at the same time, design organizational systems to exploit these economies.

Implicit in the design of technological and organizational systems for economies of substitution is an ability to manage what were once considered to be mutually exclusive concepts – incremental vs. radical technological change, markets vs. hierarchies, cooperation vs. competition, and craft vs. mass production. Already, we can see a trend toward the coexistence of these mutually exclusive concepts as evidenced by the prevalence of terms such as "modular upgradability" (*New York Times*, June 25 1991), "networks" (Powell, 1990), "co-opetition" (Mr. Sam Albert in *Fortune*, 14 December 1995) and "mass customization" (Pine, 1993). Clearly, we need new theoretical frames to understand the basis for these concepts.

Our paper provides a basis for understanding how these new terms are the order of the new industrial landscape. For instance, consider the dichotomy between radical and incremental technological change. As our paper suggests, technological change need not be radical breakthroughs that destroy previous knowledge.[19] Innovating from scratch each time is difficult, if not impossible, given the systemic nature of technologies and the rapidity of change. At the same time, reliance on incremental change may stifle technological progress and lead to stagnation. Instead, firms may create higher-performing systems by reusing some components and substituting others, thereby building on existing knowledge and reaping economies of substitution. Thus, the technological change process need not be either incremental or radical, but can incorporate aspects of both.

Similarly, consider the traditional dichotomy between markets and hierarchies. As our paper suggests, the network mode of governance integrates both the decentralization of market governance and the coordination of hierarchical governance. Moreover, we argue that the network mode requires reconceptualization of current practices at the intrafirm, interfirm, and institutional levels. For instance, at the intrafirm level, we need to design systems, incentives, and structures that promote knowledge sharing rather than knowledge hoarding. At the interfirm level, we need to conceptualize alliances and relationships in fluid terms calling into attention relational aspects of contracting. At the institutional level, we need to explore the sociopolitical processes involved in the creation and evolution of self-regulatory mechanisms such as open standards. Emphasizing the unique status of networks, Powell (1990: 299) declared that they are "neither fish nor fowl, nor some mongrel hybrid, but a distinctly different form." Indeed, Powell argues that network governance is the most appropriate mode for organizing complex and idiosyncratic exchanges (such as knowledge) under dynamic conditions.

Next, consider the dichotomy between cooperation and competition. As our paper suggests, firms need to cooperate and compete with one another simultaneously. Firms need to cooperate with suppliers and even rivals to secure complementary resources, skills, or components. At the same time, they may have to compete with their collaborators in the product markets. For instance, standards creation requires cooperation among firms; at the same time, these firms compete with one another to ensure that their own technical specifications are included in the evolving standards.

Together, the technological and organizational designs that we have described in this paper address another dichotomy – the trade off between craft and mass production. Specifically, modular upgradability makes it possible for customers to mix and match components to create customized solutions to their technological needs. At the same time, modular upgradability allows firms to realize scale and scope economies. For instance, firms realize scale economies when they partition the system and specialize in mass producing specific components (an aspect that Baldwin and Clark, 1994, term as modularity-in-production). Firms realize scope economies by reusing components across different product lines (Goldhar and Jelinek, 1983). Thus, modular upgradability leads to mass customization (Pine, 1993).

Although our paper provides a framework with which to view these emerging phenomena, it is but a first step. As is the case with most new frameworks, ours raises as many questions for future research as it attempts to answer. For instance, what are the limits to economies of substitution? Clearly, after a point, modularity results in too many options, thereby increasing cognitive complexity and search costs for designers, manufacturers, and customers. Upgradability too has its limits; the degrees of freedom built into a system will be exhausted eventually. How can firms anticipate these limits and plan ahead to sustain continual innovation?

Consider another issue. How can firms create organizational systems that balance conflicting demands created by the coexistence of cooperation and competition? We offered one description of a network form that is illustrative of industries characterized by network externalities and built around technological systems. Others have reported network forms in industries ranging from biotechnology to textiles (Best, 1990; Kenney and Florida, 1993; Nelson and Wright, 1992; Piore and Sabel, 1984; Porter, 1990; Powell, 1990; Quinn, 1992). What are the idiosyncratic features of these network forms? These are but illustrative questions that we as researchers and practitioners need to address. Indeed, our ability to raise the appropriate questions and address them is critical for the continued success of American firms in the emerging industrial order.

ACKNOWLEDGMENTS

We thank several colleagues for their comments at various stages of this paper's development. These include participants at the Strategic Management Society Conference held at Chicago, 1993; anonymous reviewers for the *Strategic Management Journal*; editors of the special issue, Richard Bettis and Michael Hitt; participants of a conference on "Technological Transformation and the New Competitive Landscape" held at the University of North Carolina, Chapel Hill, 1994; Warren Boeker, Deborah Dougherty, Roger Dunbar, Rebecca Henderson, Sanjay Jain, and Praveen Nayyar. We also thank Ian Graham for graciously sharing with us chapters of his yet-to-be published book on object-oriented programming and Chris Stone of the Object Management Group.

NOTES

Key words: technological innovation; networks; reuse; modularity; upgradability; standards.

1   Baldwin and Clark (1994) make a useful distinction among *modularity-in-design*, *modularity-in-production*, and *modularity-in-use*. In this paper, we make a general argument that encompasses all three types of modularity. Specifically, modularity-in-design creates a potential for the reuse of components and knowledge, modularity-in-production arises from the partitioning of production tasks, and modularity-in-use provides customers the benefits of speed and scope flexibility.

2   The design of cochlear implants provides an illustration of all three system-level attributes. Cochlear implants are biomedical devices that provide the profoundly deaf with a sensation of sound. For illustrative purposes, consider two parts of the implant: the electrode that is implanted within the cochlea, and the processor that is worn outside the body. Here, system integrity represents how well the processor works with the electrodes to create a sensation of sound. Modularity refers to the decoupling of the electrode from the processor. Recipients may disconnect the processor when desired, even though they

are compelled to wear the electrode in the cochlea. Moreover, modularity provides the recipient with the flexibility to use different types of processors. The type of electrode implanted (single-channel or multichannel), however, limits the benefits that a recipient may derive from processor improvements. It is here that the notion of upgradability is best illustrated. A multichannel electrode possesses greater technological degrees of freedom. Therefore, it allows recipients to benefit from the development of new processing schemes that utilize more than one channel in the implanted electrode. In contrast, a single-channel electrode has fewer degrees of freedom, thereby limiting its upgradability (see Garud and Rappa, 1994, for more details). Moreover, in attempting to migrate from a single-channel device to a multichannel device, designers have not been able to retain either the electrode or the processing scheme associated with the single-channel device. This is because it is difficult to create a multichannel device by replacing only one or the other subsystem of the single-channel device. Both subsystems need to be replaced, thereby entailing a complete redesign of the device.

3   However, for systems that were originally designed for obsolescence, gateway technologies remain the only way to retain or reuse existing components. See Toffler (1971) for reasons why systems were designed for obsolescence in earlier periods.

4   Several researchers have studied and catalogued the actual costs and benefits of employing OOP techniques. Based on these studies, several simulation models that perform cost–benefit analysis for OOP and predict productivity increases and returns on investment have been generated (e.g., Banker, Kaufman, and Zweig, 1993; Gaffney and Durek, 1989; Graham, 1994, 1995; Henderson-Sellers, 1993; Pfleeger, 1991). As data on the costs and benefits of employing OOP have accumulated, these simulations are yielding more accurate estimations of productivity and return on investment.

5   Following Weick (1976) and Granovetter (1985), we must design various elements of an organizational system such that they are coupled neither too tightly nor too loosely. Very tight coupling between elements will constrain the evolution of the system. Very loose coupling, on the other hand, will undermine the coordination required for system elements to function in an integrated manner.

6   A firm could establish minimum efficient scale plants and sell excess production to other system manufacturers. But, as the number of system components manufactured in-house increases, the firm will encounter greater cognitive complexity and higher coordination costs in dealing with multiple activities in several different markets.

7   Even with the usage of flexible manufacturing technologies, eventually cognitive complexity will set in as the variety of product configurations increases.

8   For several illustrations, see a recent *Fortune* (14 December 1994) article which provides the benefits of outsourcing and examples of firms that benefited from outsourcing.

9   von Hippel (1994) offers the notion of sticky data to explain why such a task partitioning is important. Data are sticky when there are costs associated with replicating and diffusing location-specific information. Consequently, if different components of a technological system require conceptually different kinds of knowledge, it makes sense to partition the system into modules that different members can manufacture in a distributed manner.

10   Relational contracting is an important characteristic of the Japanese Keiretsu system (Abegglen and Stalk, 1985; Aoki, 1990; Piore and Sable, 1984; Womack et al., 1990). Keiretsus are characterized by a governance mode that possesses features of both markets and vertically integrated hierarchies while being neither. Reflecting on the benefits of such a "quasi-integrated" system, Aoki (1990: 3) states: "A key to an understanding of Japan's industrial performance can be found in the ability of firms in certain industries to

coordinate their operating activities flexibly and quickly in response to changing market conditions and to changes in other factors in the industrial environment, as well as to emergent technical and technological exigencies."

11 This line of reasoning has led many researchers to suggest that these types of transactions be internalized within firms. However, as we have noted earlier, there are limits to the different kinds and number of activities that can be internalized.

12 A recent *Fortune* (21 February 1994) article describes these emerging practices in the USA. For instance, AMP, a manufacturer of electronic connectors, supplied Silicon Graphics, a workstations manufacturer, with an order over the weekend to replace defective connectors (supplied by a competitor) on the basis of just a phone call. Similarly, Donnelley Corporation built a new plant to manufacture exterior mirrors for Honda based on a verbal agreement to initiate a new partnership. From Honda's point of view too, this agreement involved a lot of trust because Donnelley neither had prior experience in making exterior mirrors nor did it have the requisite production facilities.

13 In dynamic environments, in-house development of components as and when they are required is prohibitively expensive because of time compression diseconomies (Dierickx and Cool, 1989). Time compression diseconomies arise when an attempt is made to reduce the time taken to accomplish a set of activities by allocating additional resources. The diseconomies result because the resources additionally required are disproportionately more than the benefits that accrue from time compression.

14 For instance, in OOP, several firms, including Visual Edge Software Ltd., Iona Technologies Inc., and Digital Equipment Corporation, have created products to bridge various systems based on incompatible object models from Object Management Group (OMG) and Microsoft Corporation (*Computerworld*, 3 October 1994, p. 8). Recently, however, Microsoft and OMG have agreed to make their object models compatible with each other (*Computerworld*, 5 September 1994, p. 1).

15 The importance of compatibility in OOP is captured by Graham (1994: 5), who states: "Object technology can only succeed against the inertia of existing practice if users can achieve the confidence in moving to it that they require from a move to open systems. If object-oriented applications are all mutually incompatible, if object-oriented databases cannot interwork with each other and with relational databases and if there are no standard notations and terms for object-oriented analysis there is little hope of this (success)."

16 See Arthur (1988), David (1993), and Garud and Kumaraswamy (1993) for a deeper appreciation of why the presence of network externalities is leading to the creation of open standards in contemporary environments.

17 For instance, the Network Applications Consortium, a group of 25 large users with annual revenues of almost $200 billion, hopes to use its buying capacity to exert pressure on hardware and software vendors to conform to standards, so that applications, operating systems, and network services from various vendors can work smoothly together (*Computerworld*, 12 September 1994).

18 For instance, Motorola, Apple, and IBM have had to share technical knowledge with one another in order to create the Power PC microprocessor; this effort eventually will increase competitive pressures on each firm to innovate (*Fortune*, 14 December 1994).

19 We are not alone in suggesting this. Usher (1954) offers the thesis of cumulative synthesis where invention occurs through accumulation of incremental progress in seemingly unconnected areas until such time the stage is set for an act of insight (the actual invention) to take place. Similarly, Dougherty (1992) suggests that product innovations do not occur in a vacuum, but typically build upon available knowledge.

REFERENCES

Abegglen, J. and G. Stalk, Jr. (1985). *Kaisha: The Japanese Corporation*. Basic Books, New York.

Aoki, M. (1990). "Toward an economic model of the Japanese firm," *Journal of Economic Literature*, 28, pp. 1–27.

Arthur, W. B. (1988). "Self-reinforcing mechanisms in economics." In P. Anderson, K. Arrow and D. Pines (eds.), *The Economy as an Evolving Complex System*. Addison-Wesley, Reading, MA, pp. 9–31.

Astley, W. G. and R. Brahm (1989). "Organizational designs for post-industrial strategies: The role of interorganizational collaboration." In C. Snow (ed.), *Strategy, Organization Design, and Human Resources Management*. JAI Press, Greenwich, CT, pp. 233–70.

Balda, D. and D. Gustafson (1990). "Cost estimation models for the reuse and prototype software development life-cycles," *ACM SIGSOFT Software Engineering Notes*, 15(3), pp. 42–50.

Baldwin, C. and K. Clark (July 1994). "Modularity-in-design: An analysis based on the theory of real options." Working paper, Harvard Business School, Boston, MA.

Banker, R., R. Kaufman and D. Zweig (1993). "Repository evaluation of software re-use," *IEEE Transactions on Software Engineering*, 19(4), pp. 379–89.

Best, M. (1990). *The New Competition: Institutions of Industrial Restructuring*. Harvard University Press, Cambridge, MA.

Black, J. A. and K. B. Boal (1994). "Strategic resources: Traits, configurations and paths to sustainable competitive advantage," *Strategic Management Journal*, Summer Special Issue, 15, pp. 131–148.

Business Week (30 September 1991). "Software made simple," pp. 92–7.

Business Week (21 December 1992). "How Honda hammered out its new Accord," p. 86.

Clark, K. (1985). "The interaction of design hierarchies and market concepts in technological evolution," *Research Policy*, 14, pp. 235–51.

Clark, K. and T. Fujimoto (1990). "The power of product integrity," *Harvard Business Review*, 68(6), pp. 107–18.

Computerworld (5 September 1994). "Object standard accelerates: Microsoft blesses emerging standard," p. 1.

Computerworld (12 September 1994). "Group brings order to interoperability," p. 4.

Computerworld (3 October 1994). "Object standard conflict rises . . . as compatibility issue gets an 'Edge'", p. 8.

Cox, B. (1986). *Object Oriented Programming: An Evolutionary Approach*. Addison-Wesley, Reading, MA.

Cusumano, M. (1991). *Japan's Software Factories: A Challenge to US Management*. Oxford University Press, New York.

Datamation (15 November 1989). "Cultural barriers slow reusability," pp. 87–92.

David, P. (1993). "Path-dependence and predictability in dynamic systems with local network externalities: A paradigm for historical economics." In F. Dominique and C. Freeman (eds.), *Technology and the Wealth of Nations: The Dynamics of Constructed Advantage*. Pinter, New York, pp. 209–31.

David, P. and J. A. Bunn (1990). "Gateway technologies and network industries." In A. Heertje and M. Perlman (eds.) *Evolving Technology and Market Structure*. University of Michigan Press, Ann Arbor, MI, pp. 121–56.

Davidow, W. and M. Malone (1993). *The Virtual Corporation*. HarperCollins, New York.

Demsetz, H. (1993). "The theory of the firm revisited." In O. E. Williamson and S. G. Winter (eds.), *The Nature of the Firm: Origins, Evolution, and Development*. Oxford University Press, New York, pp. 159–78.

Dierickx, I. and K. Cool (1989). "Asset stock accumulation and sustainability of competitive advantage," *Management Science*, 35, pp. 1504–11.

Dougherty, D. (1992). "A practice-centered model of organizational renewal through product innovation," *Strategic Management Journal*, Summer Special Issue, 13, pp. 77–92.

Farrell, J. and G. Saloner (1986). "Installed base and compatibility: Innovation, product preannouncements and predation," *American Economic Review*, 76, pp. 940–55.

Financial Executive (July/August 1991). "Major technology trends for the 1990s," pp. 11–15.

Flamm, K. (1998). *Creating the Computer: Government, Industry and High Technology*. Brookings Institution, Washington, DC.

Fombrun, C. and W. Astley (1982). "The telecommunications community: An institutional overview," *Journal of Communications*, 32, pp. 56–68.

Fortune (21 February 1994). "The new golden rule of business," pp. 60–4.

Fortune (14 December 1995). "Outsourcing," Special Advertising Section.

Gabel, H. L. (1987). "Open standards in the European computer industry: The case of X/OPEN." In H. L. Gabel (ed.), *Product Standardization and Competitive Strategy*. Elsevier Science, New York, pp. 91–123.

Gaffney, Jr., J. and T. Durek (1989). "Software reuse – key to enhanced productivity: Some quantitative models," *Information and Software Technology*, 31(5), pp. 258–67.

Garud, R. (1994). "Cooperative and competitive behaviors during the process of creative destruction," *Research Policy*, 23(4), pp. 385–94.

Garud, R. and S. Kotha (1994). "Using the brain as a metaphor to model flexible production systems," *Academy of Management Review*, 19, pp. 671–89.

Garud, R. and A. Kumaraswamy (1993). "Changing competitive dynamics in network industries: An exploration of Sun Microsystems' open systems strategy," *Strategic Management Journal*, 14(5), pp. 351–69.

Garud, R. and P. Nayyar (1994). "Transformative capacity: Continual structuring by intertemporal technology transfer," *Strategic Management Journal*, 15(5), pp. 365–85.

Garud, R. and M. Rappa (1994). "A socio-cognitive model of technology evolution: The case of cochlear implants," *Organization Science*, 5(3), pp. 344–62.

Goldhar, J. and M. Jelinek (1983). "Plan for economies of scope," *Harvard Business Review*, 61(6), pp. 141–8.

Graham, I. (1994). *Object Oriented Methods* (2nd ed.) Addison-Wesley, Workingham, UK.

Graham, I. (1995). *Migrating to Object Technology*. Addison-Wesley, Workingham, UK.

Granovetter, M. (1985). "Economic action and social structures: The problems of embeddedness," *American Journal of Sociology*, 91, pp. 481–510.

Hakansson, H. (1989). *Corporate Technological Behavior: Cooperation and Networks*. Routledge, New York.

Hamel, G. and C. K. Prahalad (1994). *Competing for the Future*. Harvard Business School Press, Boston, MA.

Hamel, G., Y. Doz and C. K. Prahalad (1989). "Collaborate with your competitors – and win," *Harvard Business Review*, 67(1), pp. 133–9.

Henderson, R. and K. Clark (1990). "Architectural innovation: The reconfiguration of existing product technologies and the failure of established firms," *Administrative Science Quarterly*, 35, pp. 9–30.

Henderson-Sellers, B. (1993). "The economics of reusing library classes," *Journal of Object-Oriented Programming*, 6(4), pp. 43–50.

Hill, C., M. Hitt and R. Hoskisson (1992). "Cooperative versus competitive structures in related and unrelated diversified firms," *Organization Science*, 3, pp. 501–21.

Hughes, T. (1987). "The evolution of large technological systems." In W. E. Bijker, T. P. Hughes and T. J. Pinch (eds.), *The Social Construction of Technological Systems.* MIT Press, Cambridge, MA, pp. 51–82.

Jelinek, M. and C. B. Schoonhoven (1990). *The Innovation Marathon: Lessons from High Technology Firms.* Basil Blackwell, Cambridge, MA.

Kain, J. B. (June 1994). "Measuring the ROI of reuse," *Object Magazine*, pp. 49–54.

Katz, M. and C. Shapiro (1985). "Network exeternalities, competition, and compatibility," *American Economic Review*, 75, pp. 424–40.

Kelley, H. and A. Stahelski (1970). "Inference of intentions from moves in prisoners-dilemma games," *Journal of Experimental Social Psychology* 6, pp. 401–19.

Kenney, M. and R. Florida (1993). *Beyond Mass Production: The Japanese System and Its Transfer to the U.S.* Oxford University Press, New York.

Klein, B. (1997). *Dynamic Economics.* Harvard University Press, Cambridge, MA.

Kogut, B. and U. Zander (1992). "Knowledge of the firm, combinative capabilities, and the replication of technology," *Organization Science*, 3, pp. 383–97.

Kotha, S. (1995). "Mass customization: Implementing the emerging paradigm for competitive advantage," *Strategic Management Journal*, Summer Special Issue, 16, pp. 21–42.

Langlois, R. (1992). "External economies and economic progress: The case of the micro-computer industry," *Business History Review*, 66, pp. 1–50.

Langlois, R. and P. Robertson (1992). "Networks and innovation in a modular system: Lessons from the microcomputer and stereo component industries," *Research Policy*, 21, pp. 297–313.

Lei, D., M. Hitt and R. Bettis (1996). "Dynamic core competence through meta-learning and strategic context," *Journal of Management*, 22(4), 546–69.

Macneil, I. (1980). *The New Social Contract: An Inquiry into Modern Contractual Relations.* Yale University Press, New Haven, CT.

Malone, T., J. Yates and R. Benjamin (1987). "Electronic markets and electronic hierarchies," *Communications of the ACM*, 30(6), pp. 484–97.

Manzi, J. (6 February 1994). "Computer keiretsu: Japanese idea, U.S. style," *New York Times*, Money Section, p. 15.

Marshall, A. (1961). *Principles of Economics.* Macmillan, London.

Matutes, C. and P. Regibeau (1988). "'Mix and match': Product compatibility without network externalities," *Rand Journal of Economics*, 19, pp. 221–34.

Miles, R. and C. Snow (1986). "Organizations: New concepts for new forms," *California Management Review*, 27(3), p. 62–73.

Morgan, G. (1986). *Images of Organization.* Sage, Beverly Hills, CA.

Mowery, D. and N. Rosenberg (1986). *Technology and the Pursuit of Economic Growth.* Cambridge University Press, New York.

Nelson, R. and G. Wright (1992). "The rise and fall of American technological leadership: The postwar era in historical perspective," *Journal of Economic Literature*, 30, pp. 1931–64.

New York Times (25 June 1991). "Tandon's modular upgradability" p. C9.

Nonaka, I. (1994). "A dynamic theory of organizational knowledge creation," *Organization Science*, 5, pp. 14–37.

Object Management Group (25 July 1994). "Objects get on-line with the Information Brokerage," Press information bulletin.

Penrose, E. (1959). *The Theory of the Growth of the Firm.* Basil Blackwell, Oxford.

Pfleeger, S. (1991). "Model of software effort and productivity," *Information and Software Technology*, 33(3), pp. 224–31.

Pine II, B. J. (1993). *Mass Customization.* Harvard Business School Press, Boston, MA.

Piore, M. (1992). "Fragments of a cognitve theory of technological change and organizational structure." In N. Nohria and R. G. Eccles (eds.), *Networks and Organizations: Structure, Form and Action*. Harvard Business School Press, Boston, MA, pp. 430–44.

Piore, M. and C. Sabel (1984). *The Second Industrial Divide*. Basic Books, New York.

Porter, M. (1980). *Competitive Strategy*. Free Press, New York.

Porter, M. (1990). *The Competitive Advantage of Nations*. Free Press, New York.

Powell, W. (1990). "Neither market not hierarchy: Network forms of organization." In B. Staw and L. Cummings, (eds.), *Research in Organizational Behavior*, 12. JAI Press, Greenwich, CT, pp. 295–336.

Powell, W. and P. Brantley (1992). "Competitive cooperation in biotechnology: Learning through networks." In N. Nohria and R. G. Eccles (eds.), *Networks and Organizations: Structure, Form and Action*. Harvard Business School Press, Boston, MA, pp. 366–94.

Prahalad, C. K. and G. Hamel (1990). "The core competence of the corporation," *Harvard Business Review*, 68(3), pp. 79–91.

Quinn, J. (1992). "The intelligent enterprise: A new paradigm," *Academy of Management Executive*, 6(4), pp. 48–63.

Richardson, G. (1972). "The organization of industry," *Economic Journal*, 82, pp. 883–96.

Rosenberg, N. (1982). *Inside the Black Box: Technology and Economics*. Cambridge University Press, Cambridge, UK.

Rotemberg, J. and G. Saloner (1991). "Interfirm competition and collaboration." In M. Morton (ed.), *The Corporation of the 1990s: Information Technology and Organizational Transformation*. Oxford University Press, New York, pp. 95–121.

Sanchez, R. (1995). "Strategic flexibility in product competition: An options perspective on resourcebased competition," *Strategic Management Journal*, Summer Special Issue, 16, pp. 135–59.

Sanchez, R. and J. Mahoney (1994). "The modularity principle in product and organization design: Achieving flexibility in the fusion of intended and emergent strategies in hypercompetitive product markets." Office of Research working paper #94-0139, University of Illinois at Urbana-Champaign.

Schumpeter, J. (1942). *Capitalism, Socialism and Democracy*. Harper and Brothers, New York.

Simon, H. (1962). "The architecture of complexity," *Proceedings of the American Philosophical Society*, 106, pp. 467–82.

Teece, D. (1980). "Economies of the scope and the scope of the enterprise," *Journal of Economic Behavior and Organization*, 1, pp. 223–47.

Teece, D. J. (1987). "Profiting from technological innovation: Implications for integration, collaboration, licensing and public policy." In D. J. Teece (ed.)., *The Competitive Challenge: Strategies for Industrial Innovation and Renewal*. Ballinger, Cambridge, MA, pp. 185–219.

Texas Instruments (September 1992). News Release #SC-92075, SC-92076.

Toffler, A. (1971). *Future Shock*, Bantam Books, New York.

Toffler, A. (1985). *The Adaptive Corporation*. McGraw-Hill, New York.

Tushman, M. and P. Anderson (1986). "Technological discontinuities an organizational environments," *Administrative Science Quarterly*, 31, pp. 439–65.

Tushman, M. and L. Rosenkopf (1992). "Organizational determinants of technological change: Toward a sociology of technological evolution." In B. Staw and L. Cummings, (eds.), *Research in Organizational Behavior*, Vol. 14. JAI Press, Greenwich, CT, pp. 311–47.

Usher, A. (1954). *A History of Mechanical Inventions*, Harvard University Press, Cambridge, MA.

von Hippel, E. (1994). "'Sticky information' and the locus of problem solving: Implications for innovation," *Management Science*, 40, pp. 429–39.

Wade, J. (1994). "Dynamics of organizational communities and technological bandwagons: An empirical investigation of community evolution in the microprocessor market," working paper, University of Illinois, Urbana-Champaign.

Wall Street Journal (1 September 1993). "Redesign of Honda's management faces first test with unveiling of new Accord," p. B1.

Weick, K. (1976). "Educational organizations as loosely coupled systems," *Administrative Science Quarterly*, 21, pp. 1–19.

Weick, K. (1979). *The Social Psychology of Organizing*. Random House, New York.

Wheelwright, S. and K. Clark (1992). *Revolutionizing Product Development: Quantum Leaps in Speed, Efficiency, and Quality*. Free Press. New York.

Williamson, O. (1985). *The Economic Institutions of Capitalism*. Free Press, New York.

Winter, S. (1987). "Knowledge and competence as strategic assets." In D. J. Teece (ed.), *The Competitive Challenge: Strategies for Industrial Innovation and Renewal*. Ballinger, Cambridge, MA, pp. 159–84.

Womack, J., D. Jones and D. Roos (1990). *The Machine that Changed the World*. Rawson Associates, New York.

Zuboff, S. (1984). *In the Age of the Smart Machine: The Future of Work and Power*. Basic Books, New York.

COMMENTARY
Raghu Garud and Arun Kumaraswamy

Many scholars focus on modularity as a way to deal with the complexities of contemporary economic life. Modularity refers to an ability to "decompose" technological and organizational systems such that the internal functioning of one subsystem does not significantly affect the functioning of the others in the short term (see Baldwin and Clark, 1997; Simon, 1962; Garud and Kumaraswamy, 1995; Langlois and Robertson, 1992; Sanchez and Mahoney, 1996; Schilling, 2000; Ulrich, 1995). Such ability facilitates the retention and reuse of system components (Garud and Kumaraswamy, 1996; Baldwin and Clark, 1997) and enhances the speed and scope of innovation (Garud and Kotha, 1994). Furthermore, it provides firms with an opportunity to harness external economies – economies deriving from the efforts of other firms comprising the knowledge ecosystem (Langlois and Robertson, 1992). Especially in network industries built around complex and systemic products, an ability to harness external economies is critical as no one firm can possess all the competencies required to produce the goods and services valued by customers (Hughes, 1983).

Notwithstanding the many benefits that it provides, we must remember that modularity is only one of the three attributes that define a system. The other two attributes are integrity and upgradability. Integrity is a measure of how well the overall performance of a technological system is optimized at any given time by appropriately matching the form, function and interactions of individual components (see Clark and Fujimoto, 1990; Ulrich, 1995). Upgradability, an attribute that is increasingly important in today's dynamic environments, is a measure of how easily the system can evolve over time to offer higher performance, new functions and uses.

On each of these three attributes, a system may lie at any point along a continuum stretching from a very high level to a very low level (or lack thereof) of that attribute.

For instance, on the modularity attribute, a system may lie anywhere along a continuum ranging from very high modularity to very low modularity. In other words, a system may be designed to possess a specific level of each of these attributes depending on designers' objectives, decisions and implementations.

Therefore, it is important for us to consider all three system attributes to understand how technological systems evolve and why certain technological systems prevail over others. Additionally, consideration of all the three attributes directs our attention to tradeoffs that influence system performance and costs. These tradeoffs formed the basis of our notion of economies of substitution. *Economies of substitution arise when the cost of designing a higher performance system through the partial retention of existing components is lower than the cost of designing the system afresh.*

These economies are shaped as much by technical issues as they are by organizational and strategic ones. For instance, these economies are shaped by organizational incentives to design system platforms and reuse system components in the future. They are also shaped by strategic considerations of the value of conforming to emerging industry-wide standards. We had covered these issues in greater detail in our original article. Here, we provide a brief summary and an extension to our argument.

Three attributes of technological systems

We routinely confront technological and organizational systems that are complex and subject to non-linear dynamics. One way to deal with the complexity is to disaggregate the system into constituent components such that intra-component dynamics are greater than inter-component dynamics. This generates a system that possesses a high level of modularity. Such decomposability is possible to the extent that each system component performs one function and is not dependent upon some other component to perform that function. Each component interfaces with the other through standardized interfaces. These interfaces are part of a larger architecture that governs the form and function of components and the interactions among them. Under such conditions, systems can be designed to have different kinds of modularity such as slot, bus and sectional modularity (Pine, 1993; Ulrich, 1995).

Simon pointed out that such a "strong" form of modularity, that is, perfect decomposability, may be impossible to achieve.[1] Instead, he suggested that most systems are only "nearly" decomposable, a state in which interactions among system components are weak but not non-existent. This is especially true of technological systems within which components are arranged within a hierarchy (Clark, 1985; Hughes, 1987) and interact with one another directly across interfaces or through the system hierarchy according to rules prescribed by the system's architecture. We label such near decomposability as the "semi-strong" form of modularity.

In practice, however, we find that several systems are not even as nearly decomposable as Simon suggested, but still possess modularity. The human brain, for instance, is an example of a system with such "weak form" of modularity. The brain is organized into several "modules" that are specialized and yet generalized (see Garud and Kotha, 1994). In other words, each module of the brain is primarily responsible for a specific function, but it also shares peripheral responsibility for several other functions with other modules.[2] As we will explain later in this document, such a weak form of modularity may occur for strategic, transitional, or practical reasons.

Whether or not a system is modular does not address the question of how well it performs as a system. System components may be put together in different configurations, with each configuration yielding a different level of overall system performance. Indeed, as Henderson and Clark (1990) pointed out, components can be put together in different configurations to yield what they label as "architectural" innovations. This issue of overall system performance is addressed by a second system attribute, its integrity.

It is also important for us to recognize that upgradability, the third system attribute, cannot be subsumed completely under modularity. Modularity, even the semi-strong form (near decomposability), offers only one type of upgradability – the ability to add new components or modify existing ones within the confines of the system's current architecture. However, modularity may not facilitate another type of upgradability – an evolution of the very system architecture over time to hitherto-unanticipated or emerging functionality and use.

In sum, we must pay attention not only to modularity but also to the integrity and upgradability of a system. Indeed, there are inherent tradeoffs among these system attributes that complicate the task of designing complex and networked systems. These tradeoffs are manifest as fundamental choices in whether to build upon an already established platform or to design the entire system afresh.

Tradeoffs among system attributes

Before offering details, it is useful for us to gain an intuitive appreciation of the tradeoffs among the three system attributes. Consider Java, Sun Microsystem's revolutionary "write-once, run-anywhere" software technology. Sun designed Java to be modular using object oriented programming (OOP) principles so that software developers could write their programs just once and run them easily on different platforms without appreciable loss of speed or functionality. However, Microsoft was able to modify Java to run faster on its Windows operating system and, in doing so, offer better performance and functionality to Windows users than Sun could with its modular, standard Java version. In other words, Microsoft's version of Java was much less modular than Sun's standard version, but had much higher integrity when used with the Windows operating system.

Meanwhile, Sun's other partners were finding it difficult to conform to the Sun-specified Java standard while at the same time innovating to add new functionality and features to Java. Indeed, depositions in the Sun-Microsoft "Java poisoning" court case revealed that several firms such as IBM, Novell and Spyglass too had innovated on Java and, in the process, developed versions that did not pass Sun's stringent Java compatibility tests (see Garud, Jain, and Kumaraswamy, 2002). In sum, Sun's efforts to maintain Java's modularity (platform independence) compromised the ease and speed with which the technology could be upgraded.

As this brief example suggests, integrity and upgradability cannot be subsumed under modularity. Indeed, there are tradeoffs among these three system attributes. The design of technological systems requires a consideration of the tradeoffs among these system attributes. In the remainder of the commentary, we discuss these tradeoffs and their implications in greater detail.

Modularity versus integrity

One tradeoff between modularity and integrity stems from the fact that subsystems are, at best, "nearly" decomposable. In other words, despite our best attempts, we may not be able to control or eliminate all incidental interactions among system components (see Ulrich and Eppinger, 2000). As a consequence, the complexity of the system (in terms of nonlinear interactions) actually may increase with excessive modularization, thereby reducing overall system performance.

Second, as we modularize, the number of interfaces among components increases. To the extent that there are performance losses across interfaces (analogous to friction in the case of physical systems), overall system performance will suffer. Such performance losses may occur even across standardized interfaces, because robust interface standards typically allow a range of inputs/outputs rather than a single optimized input/output.

Finally, designers may opt to deliberately bring together two or more components together, that is de-modularize, to minimize redundancies or gain from the synergistic interactions among the components (Schilling, 2000). For instance, Ulrich (1995) provides an example of how, in high-performance motorcycles, the transmission and engine casing assemblies are integrated to also serve the function of the load-bearing frame to reduce total system mass.[3]

Modularity versus upgradability

The general consensus is that modularity automatically ensures upgradability because standardized interfaces allow components to be mixed and matched, added or replaced with higher-performing versions without affecting other system components. Such ability, however, represents just one kind of upgradability, which we term as "add" and "replace" designs (Garud and Kumaraswamy, 1996). Such designs are possible to the extent that the pre-specified system architecture and interfaces possess unexploited degrees of freedom.

But, even with such designs, tradeoffs arise between modularity and upgradability. First, excessive modularization may make it difficult to reuse components because the search costs associated with reuse increases disproportionately with the number of alternatives and the total number of reusable components.[4] Moreover, excessive modularization may reduce the actual degrees of freedom available for a system's evolution by triggering complex non-linear interactions among components.

Additionally, pre-specification of the system architecture may not allow the system to evolve to a new architecture First, adherence to anticipatory standards can result in path dependencies that can be strategically costly in the future. Second, a limit is reached eventually when the entire architecture has to be abandoned for a new one. Moreover, designing modules to reduce interactions may prevent the emergence of new functionality through the combination and remodularization of two or more modules over time (Fleming and Sorenson, 2001).

To avoid such a possibility, technological systems need to be designed to evolve to new architectures even as they are being used – a transmutation akin to rebuilding a ship plank by plank even as it is sailing. We label such designs as "transmutational" designs (Garud and Kumaraswamy, 1996). As might be apparent in this metaphor, the planks (or modules) may have redundancy of functions thereby creating overlaps with one another (Garud and Kotha, 1994). Such "shared division of labor" (Imai, Nonaka, and Takeuchi, 1985) facilitates the spontaneous cross connections between modules that are specialized yet generalized to generate new functionality.

Indeed, the melding of exploration and exploitation that is implicit here characterizes many contemporary systems such as the Internet, web browsers, PDAs and cell phones that are continually morphing their designs as different elements converge (Garud, Jain, and Phelps, 1998). Such morphing requires an ability to change the very standards and architecture as new technologies with completely new functionality emerge through cumulative synthesis (Usher, 1954; Garud, Kumaraswamy, and Prabhu, 1995). As a system transitions to a new architecture, the coupling between once de-coupled components may increase, thereby compromising modularity.

Integrity versus upgradability

The tradeoff between integrity and upgradability is best characterized by Schumpeter's (1975) observation that any system designed to be efficient at a given time is likely to be inefficient over time. Although articulated at the macro level of the economy, this observation is applicable at the more micro level of technological and organizational systems as well. Specifically, a system designed to exploit all degrees of freedom at a given time may become trapped in a local maximum because it offers no freedom for evolution over time.

For "add" and "replace" designs, this tradeoff is manifest in a decision to build in degrees of freedom up front that will only be used later. For instance, the more interfaces are designed to enable upgradability in the future, the less the system is fully optimized for performance in the present. For transmutational designs, tradeoffs between integrity and upgradability arise because of performance losses during transitions. As we have all experienced, migration to a new architecture typically involves at least a temporary loss of performance.[5]

Economies of substitution

From these tradeoffs, it is apparent that at any stage of a technology's development, choices present themselves as to the extent to which existing system components can be reused for developing the next generation of products with improved functionality. It is to capture these tradeoffs that we had offered the notion of economies of substitution. Beginning afresh is preferable when performance slippages and costs of adding or modifying existing components are too high. In situations where benefits outweigh the costs, added system functionality and higher overall performance can be achieved by building on the existing platform.

This choice is informed by organizational issues that critically shape the economies arising through substitution. After all, organizations represent the supply side of the process wherein knowledge for producing technological systems is embedded, whereas technological systems represent the demand side wherein knowledge produced through organizational processes is embodied. Indeed, organizational systems that produce knowledge and the technological systems that embody the knowledge co-evolve.

Therefore, when the partitioning of organizational systems does not map onto the partitioning of technological systems, significant "translation costs" may arise. These costs increase to the extent that an attempt is made to use components from one system interchangeably with those of an alternative system. This is because the architectures of the two systems may be so different that mixing and matching of components among them may require translators or gateways.

These translation costs are particularly high during early stages of industry emergence when many alternative technological systems vie for dominance (Tushman and Anderson, 1986). During such eras of ferment, incentives to reuse or build afresh are informed by several factors, some within firms and some outside. For instance, within firms, one factor is the extent to which a firm invests in creating a technological platform for retention and reuse. A factor outside the firm pertains to the economics associated with following one technological trajectory over the other at any given time, given the path dependencies that emerge (Dosi, 1982).

As may be apparent from these discussions, standards represent the larger architecture within which technological and organizational systems are embedded. The specific nature of embedding can have a profound impact on the dynamics of change within technological fields (Garud and Jain, 1996). Systems that are "over-embedded" become prisoners of the standards that enable their use, as is the case with the QWERTY keyboard. Systems that are "under-embedded" may be unable to generate the momentum required to gain widespread acceptance, as was the case with IBM's OS/2 operating system. Only systems that are "just" embedded in the standards that govern their functioning may be able to preserve dynamic capabilities required to continually move to new functionality, as may be the case with Linux or Sun Microsystems's Java technology. Key, then, is the design of appropriate institutional mechanisms – for instance, licensing regimes – for developing and then governing dynamically evolving standards.

A strategic issue that cuts across technological and organizational domains also comes into play. Firms may want to sponsor a modular design despite loss of system integrity as this enables distributed and decentralized innovation. Or, firms may decide to de-modularize or create integral designs for control and strategic reasons. Indeed, making a distinction between modularity and integrity allows us to see interesting dynamics between modular systems with low integrity and high-integrity systems with low modularity (for instance, between PCs and Macs).

Another strategic issue pertains to the sponsorship of standards. Considerable network benefits accrue to firms that subscribe to the same architecture or standard (David and Greenstein, 1990; Katz and Shapiro, 1985). However, the very act of cooperation among firms in the institutional domain to create a common standard also sets the stage for future competition among them in the product-market domain. Realizing this, rivals that cooperate to set the standard also try to interpret and implement the standard to their advantage in the product markets. In other words, a standard is as much an agreement to conform to a common architecture as an implied intention to depart from it. Accordingly, the emergence of a common standard is always contested and marked with battles for control over its future (Wade, 1996; Garud, Jain, and Kumaraswamy, 2002).

Implications

Economies of substitution and the tradeoffs that drive these economies offer several important implications for practitioners operating in network industries. A fundamental choice is whether or not to invest in technology platforms and interfaces for the future – in other words, in the creation of easily upgradable systems. Creating platforms and interfaces for the future require investments in the present that may yield returns only in the future. Traditional NPV-based approaches to capital budgeting result in overly conservative evaluation processes that reject such upfront investments. Instead, a real options approach is required to recognize and evaluate the benefits of such investments (Baldwin and Clark, 1997).

Not only do these investment opportunities in technological platforms require a different evaluation approach, but they also require a corresponding organizational capability to maintain real options and strike at the right time (Garud, Kumaraswamy, and Nayyar, 1998; Garud and Nayyar, 1994; Kumaraswamy, 1996). In this regard, an important capability is for the organization to enable exploration and exploitation activities simultaneously, not sequentially or one at the expense of the other. As a result, the system's design itself becomes endogenous and as the system slowly evolves, technological change becomes metamorphic instead of being disruptive.

Another implication pertains to the boundary of the firm. Traditional theories suggest that the boundaries of firms are informed by transactions costs and economies of scale (Langlois and Robertson, 1992). In this regard, conformity to common standards can reduce transactions costs by reducing asset specificity, information asymmetry and the problems of hold up that are possible with stand-alone systems. Furthermore, common standards enable the partitioning of the organizational system to more easily map on to the partitioning of the technological system that it designs and produces.

A final implication is for the strategy that a focal firm may use to sponsor its own technologies as common standards. Sponsorship may require the opening up of a firm's proprietary technology to makers of complementary products and rivals alike. A firm that chooses to do this confronts several challenges (Garud and Kumaraswamy, 1993). First, it needs to manage cooperation and competition with mutualistically interdependent firms. Second, it has to continue to innovate to stay ahead of its "partners." Third, it has to make sure that the standard does not fragment due to the setting in of diminishing returns for adopters of the technology. Such fragmentation may take place as firms strategically enter to fill in niches that have been left unattended by industry giants as they exploit economies of scale (Wade, 1995).

Managing these tensions effectively may be very difficult, as Sun Microsystems's experiences with sponsoring its Java technology illustrates (Garud, Jain, and Kumaraswamy, 2002). It is, therefore, not surprising that we are recently witnessing interesting battles between open and proprietary approaches to standards setting and governance – for instance, Microsoft's Windows versus Linux. Indeed, the specific governance approach may be conditional upon the stage of industry emergence (Langlois and Robertson, 1992; Tushman and Murmann, 1998) and the specific characteristics of the industry (Rotemberg and Saloner, 1991).

Conclusions

In our original article, we had suggested that it is important to identify economies associated with the technologies of the twenty-first century. In this regard, we had suggested the concept of "economies of substitution" to summarize the tradeoffs between three important system attributes – modularity, integrity and upgradability. Just as economies of scale and scope have been important in understanding the dominant organizational forms of the twentieth century, economies of substitution is important for understanding the emerging forms of the twenty-first century.

NOTES

1 Bounds to human rationality may render it impossible to design ex-ante system architectures that decompose a complex system perfectly to remove interactions among system components. Furthermore, designers or managers may be guided by considerations other than perfect decomposability in designing technological and organizational systems.
2 This is one reason humans are able to partially regain skills/functions even if parts of the brain are damaged.
3 In such cases where designers resort to function-sharing or geometric nesting, cost and ease of manufacturing may be as important a concern as improvement in system performance (Ulrich and Eppinger, 2000).
4 High search costs is one reason why object oriented programming techniques have not contributed to programmer productivity through reuse as much as expected.
5 For instance, Mac users who upgraded to Apple's new OS-X operating system found it difficult to utilize all the software applications they have grown accustomed to over time. Also, the early versions of OS-X did not provide all the functionality of the previous generation operating system version it replaced. The same was true of Microsoft's migration to Windows NT and Windows 2000 from Windows 9x.

REFERENCES

Baldwin, C. Y. and Clark, K. B. (1997). "Managing in an age of modularity," *Harvard Business Review*, September–October: 84–93.

Clark, K. B. (1985). "The interaction of design hierarchies and market concepts in techno-logical evolution," *Research Policy*, 14: 235–51.

Clark, K. B. and Fujimoto, T. (1990). "The power of product integrity," *Harvard Business Review*, November–December: 107–18.

David, P. and Greenstein, S. (1990). "The economics of compatability standards: An intro-duction to recent research," *Economics of Innovation and New Technology*, 1: 3–41.

Dosi, G. (1982). "Technological paradigms and technological trajectories," *Research Policy*, 11: 147–62.

Fleming, L. and Sorenson, O. (2001). "The dangers of modularity", *Harvard Business Review*, September: 20–1.

Garud, R. and Jain, S. (1996). "The embeddedness of technological systems," in J. Baum and J. Dutton (eds.), *Advances in Strategic Management*, 13, Greenwich, CT: JAI Press, 389–408.

Garud, R., Jain, S., and Kumaraswamy, A. (2002). "Institutional entrepreneurship in the sponsorship of common technological standards: The case of Sun Microsystems and Java," *Academy of Management Journal*, Special Forum on Institutional Theory and Institutional Change, 45(1).

Garud, R., Jain, S., and Phelps, C. (1998). "Technological linkages and transience in network fields: New competitive realities," in J. Baum (ed.), *Advances in Strategic Management*, 14, Greenwich, CT: JAI Press, 205–37.

Garud, R. and Kotha, S. (1994). "Using the brain as a metaphor to model flexible production systems," *Academy of Management Review*, 19: 671–98.

Garud, R. and Kumaraswamy, A. (1993). "Changing competitive dynamics in network indus-tries: An exploration of Sun Microsystems' open systems strategy," *Strategic Management Journal*, 14: 351–69.

Garud, R. and Kumaraswamy, A. (1995). "Technological and organizational designs to achieve economies of substitution," *Strategic Management Journal*, 16: 93–110.

Garud, R. and Kumaraswamy, A. (1996). "Technological designs for retention and reuse," *International Journal of Technology Management*, (Special Issue on Unlearning and Learn-ing for Technological Innovation), 11: 883–91.

Garud, R., Kumaraswamy, A., and Nayyar, P. R. (1998). "Real options or fool's gold? Perspective makes the difference," *Academy of Management Review*, 23: 212–17.

Garud, R., Kumaraswamy, A., and Prabhu, A. (1995). "Networking for Success in Cyberspace," *IEEE Proceedings of the International Conference on Multimedia Computing and Systems*, 335–40.

Garud, R. and Nayyar, P. R. (1994). "Transformative capacity: Continual structuring by inter-temporal technology transfer," *Strategic Management Journal*, 15: 365–85.

Henderson, R. M. and Clark, K. B. (1990). "Architectural innovation: The reconfiguration of existing product technologies and the failure of established firms," *Administrative Science Quarterly*, 35: 9–30.

Hughes, T. (1983). *Networks of Power*, Baltimore, MD: The Johns Hopkins University Press.

Hughes, T. (1987). "The evolution of large technological systems," in W. E. Bijker, T. P. Hughes and T. J. Pinch (eds.), *The Social Construction of Technological Systems*, Cambridge, MA: MIT Press, 51–82.

Imai, K., Nonaka, I., and Takeuchi, H. (1985). "Managing the New Product Development Process: How Japanese Companies Learn and Unlearn," in K. B. Clark, R. Hayes and C. Lorenz (eds.), *The Uneasy Alliance: Managing the Productivity Technology Dilemma*, Cambridge, MA: Harvard Business School.

Katz, M. L. and Shapiro, C. (1985). "Network externalities, competition, and compatibility," *American Economic Review*, 75: 424–40.

Kumaraswamy, A. (1996). "A real options perspective of firms' R&D investments," Unpublished doctoral dissertation, New York, NY: New York University.

Langlois, R. N. and Robertson, P. L. (1992). "Networks and innovation in a modular system: Lessons from the microcomputer and stereo component industries," *Research Policy*, 21: 297–313.

Pine II, B. J. (1993). *Mass Customization*, Boston, MA: Harvard Business School Press.

Rotemberg, J. J. and Saloner, G. (1991). "Interfirm competition and collaboration," in M. S. Morton (ed.), *The Corporation of the 1990s: Information Technology and Organizational Transformation*, New York, NY: Oxford University Press.

Sanchez, R. and Mahoney, J. T. (1996). "Modularity, flexibility and knowledge management in product and organizational design," *Strategic Management Journal*, 17: 63–76.

Schilling, M. A. (2000). "Towards a general modular systems theory and its application to interfirm product modularity," *Academy of Management Review*, 25: 312–34.

Schumpeter, J. A. (1975). *Capitalism, Socialism and Democracy*, Reading, MA: Addison-Wesley.

Simon, H. A. (1962). "The Architecture of Complexity," Proceedings of the American Philosophical Society 106: 467–82, reprinted in idem, *The Sciences of the Artificial*, 4th edn. Cambridge, MA: MIT Press, 1998: 183–216.

Tushman, M. L. and Anderson, P. (1986). "Technological discontinuities and organizational environments," *Administrative Science Quarterly*, 31: 439–65.

Tushman, M. L. and Murmann, J. P. (1998). "Dominant designs, technological cycles and organizational outcomes," in B. Staw and L. L. Cummings (eds.), *Research in Organizational Behavior*, Greenwich, CT: JAI Press, 20: 231–66.

Ulrich, K. T. (1995). "The role of product architecture in the manufacturing firm," *Research Policy*, 24: 419–40.

Ulrich, K. and Eppinger, S. D. (2000). *Product Design and Development.*, New York, NY: Irwin McGraw-Hill.

Usher, A. (1954). *A History of Mechanical Inventions*, Cambridge, MA: Harvard University Press.

Wade, J. (1995). "Dynamics of organizational communities and technological bandwagons: An empirical investigation of community evolution in the microprocessor market," *Strategic Management Journal*, 16: 111–33.

Wade, J. (1996). "A Community-Level Analysis of Sources and Rates of Technological Variation in the Microprocessor Market," *Academy of Management Journal*, 39: 1218–44.

CHAPTER THREE

NETWORKS AND INNOVATION IN A MODULAR SYSTEM: LESSONS FROM THE MICROCOMPUTER AND STEREO COMPONENT INDUSTRIES

RICHARD N. LANGLOIS AND PAUL L. ROBERTSON

INTRODUCTION

The degree of vertical integration in an industry depends on both supply and demand conditions. In this paper, we explore the relationship between supply and demand conditions in shaping the nature of an industry and the scope of activities of specific firms.

The effects of such supply factors as the division of labor, economies of scale, and the presence or absence of external economies have been thoroughly explored over a period of more than 200 years. Demand factors have received less attention. In particular, the tendency of economists to assume product homogeneity has obscured the fact that the structure of an "industry" and the characteristics of the firms it comprises can vary greatly depending on how consumers define its "product." Over time, the nature of what consumers believe is the essence of a given product often changes. Consumers may add certain attributes[1] and drop others, or they may combine the product with another product that had been generally regarded as distinct. Alternatively, a product that consumers had treated as an entity may be divided into a group of subproducts that consumers can arrange into various combinations according to their personal preferences.

We call this kind of network of subproducts a *modular system*. The nature of an industry and the extent of vertical integration therefore depend not only on what patterns of production minimize production and transaction costs, but also on which attributes consumers may wish. As a result of "bundling," "unbundling," and "rebundling" various attributes, the definition of a product and the structure of the industry that manufactures it may change dramatically.

Recently, formal price theory has turned its attention to some of the demand-side aspects of modular systems. But this literature does not simultaneously address the supply-side issues of technology, innovation, and firm boundaries.[2] Our objective in this paper is to look at both sides of the market. On the demand side, we look at how autonomous changes in consumer tastes and the reaction of consumers to changes introduced by suppliers help to shape the definition of a product. On the supply side, we consider the importance of technical and organizational factors in influencing the production cost, and therefore the price to consumers, of employing various degrees of vertical integration. We also recognize the vital role of suppliers as innovators who can bring new components and new arrangements of existing components to the notice of consumers.

This first section of the paper outlines the theoretical underpinnings of the relationship between vertical integration and desired product attributes. The next two sections examine these concepts through case studies of the stereo component and microcomputer industries.

Attributes and product differentiation

For most kinds of products – toasters or automobiles, say – manufacturers offer preset packages. We can choose from a multiplicity of packages, but we can't choose the engine from one kind of car, the hood ornament from another, and the front suspension from a third. Not only are there transaction costs of such picking and choosing (Cheung [2, pp. 6–7]), there are also economies of scale in assembling the parts into a finished package. Indeed, it is these economies of scale more than transaction costs that explain the tendency of assemblers to offer preset packages. If there were only transaction costs of discovering which parts are available and what their prices are, we would expect to see not preset packages but a proliferation of middlemen who specialize in packaging components tailored to buyers' specific tastes. For most appliance-like products, however, the economies of scale of assembly lead to integration of the packaging and assembly functions.

One way to think about this is in terms of the modern theory of product differentiation.[3] Instead of seeing a product as an ultimate entity, view it instead as an input (or set of inputs) to the production of utility through the consumer's "consumption technology" (Lancaster [10]). In technical terms, the consumer chooses among available bundles (or combinations of bundles) to reach the highest indifference surface possible. Each bundle represents a location (technically speaking: a vector) in "product space," and each consumer has a preferred place in that space – a bundle with his or her favorite combination of attributes. If there are scale economies, some producers can gain advantage by choosing the locations in this space where they think the density of demand will be highest. An example of this is Ford's Model T. The undifferentiated, no-frills product may not have suited everyone's (or, indeed, anyone's) tastes exactly. But the progressive reductions in price that long production runs made possible brought the Model T within the budget constraints of a growing number of people who were willing to accept a relatively narrow provision of attributes rather than do without.[4]

In the extreme case of no economies of scale, the entire space can be filled with products, and each consumer can have a product tailored exactly to his or her requirements. The type of product we have called a modular system approximates this extreme: both the transaction costs of knowing the available parts and the scale economies of assembling the package are low for a wide segment of the user population. By picking and choosing among an array of compatible components, the consumer can move freely around a large area of the product space.

In the case of sound reproduction, for example, the list of attributes can be extensive and the tradeoffs among them complex. The product technology the consumer chooses is a function of the attributes sought. As the range of the voice is limited, high fidelity can be achieved more easily for voice than for music: in contrast to lovers of piano sonatas, consumers who confine their listening to news broadcasts can get by easily with small radios and have no practical use for a sophisticated combination of components. When immediacy is needed, a radio or telephone will provide better service than a phonograph. The ability to store sound, on the other hand, can be accomplished using a record, tape, or compact disk, but not directly by a telephone or radio. When reciprocal communication is wanted, a telephone suits the purpose while a radio receiver does not.

When the bundle of overlapping attributes for different consumption technologies is small or they conflict in some way, consumers will use different appliances or systems. Although there are considerable technical similarities between the telephone and radio voice transmission, the differences have been more significant, ensuring that two distinct networks and sets of reception appliances have remained in use. Where attributes do not conflict, however, the presence of a high degree of technological convergence will open the way for the development of multipurpose appliances or modular systems, as in the case of a stereo set featuring several sound media that share amplification and reproduction equipment. Again, compatibility is crucial. Producers may have an incentive to create proprietary products in an attempt to capture sales of most or all potential subcomponents. But, as we suggest below, such a strategy often backfires, and the high demand that unbundling allows can often force a compatible modularity on the industry.

Thus innovation can affect consumption technology in two major ways. First, new products can satisfy a desire for attributes that has not yet been satisfied or, perhaps, even noticed. Second, through technological convergence, new ways of packaging or bundling consumption technology, and therefore providing attributes, become feasible.

For example, there may be five components involved in the production of a particular good, the famous widget (figure 3.1a). Through a form of technological convergence,[5] two new components developed in other industries may turn out to be desirable adjuncts to the original good (figure 3.1b). The question is, will these new components be supplied by outside firms, perhaps their original manufactures, or will they be internalized through vertical integration by the widget makers? The answer, as usual, will depend on the extent of economies of scale and the transaction costs involved. If the minimum efficient scale (MES) of production of the new components exceeds the needs of any individual widget maker, then the component

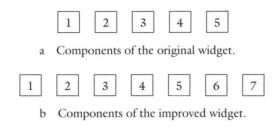

a   Components of the original widget.

b   Components of the improved widget.

Figure 3.1   Producing the improved widget.

Firm 1   Firm 2   Firm 3

Figure 3.2   Firms involved in the production of improved widget.

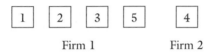

Firm 1   Firm 2

Figure 3.3   Production of widgets with changing component 4.

manufacturers are likely to remain independent as long as the transaction costs of dealing with outside suppliers are smaller than the additional production costs the widget firms would incur by production at less than MES.[6] (Williamson [30, chapter 4]).

Suppose, however, that the new components are not necessary – that they may, in fact, be superfluous or even repugnant to many widget users. In this case, the decision to purchase them could be delegated to the users rather than to the widget manufacturers. Users would buy the same type of widgets that they had traditionally purchased and then, if they wished, buy one or both of the additional components, perhaps from a different shop. The production of new widgets would then come to resemble figure 3.2. Alternatively, the rate of technological change of the various components that make up the widget may vary. Component 4, for example, might enter a new phase of rapid development while the remaining inputs do not vary. Furthermore, customers might have reason to believe that this component would continue to improve dramatically for some years. They would then wish to purchase a widget that embodies the traditional components 1, 2, 3, and 5, but that offers the opportunity to upgrade component 4 as improved variations come on the market.

Again, whether component 4 would be manufactured by the widget maker or by someone else would depend on the relationship between production costs and transaction costs. If the widget firm decides that internalization is impractical, the situation in figure 3.3 would arise. Customers would purchase component 4 separately and the remainder as a package. This assumes, of course, that the new variant is compatible with the other components. The established widget firms will have an interest in trying to avoid compatibility so that they can continue to sell the existing models that embody all five components. But the developers of the new variant of component 4 will want to achieve compatibility to allow consumers to adopt their product without fuss. In fact, if possible, the component developers will want to achieve compatibility with the products of all widget manufacturers.

In the situations portrayed in figures 3.2 and 3.3, customers are no longer purchasing an appliance as they were in figure 3.1. Instead, they have moved to a modular system in which they can take advantage of interchangeable components rather than having to accept an entire package that is pre-chosen by the manufacturer.

Networks

The vertical specialization that modular systems encourage leads also to the establishment of networks of producers. Two basic types of networks among firms are possible. The first (figure 3.4) is a centralized one in which suppliers are tied to a "lead" firm, as in the Japanese automobile industry. *Decentralized networks*, however, of the type illustrated in figure 3.5, are of more interest to the argument developed here (Best [1]).

W_1, W_2, and W_3 are the users of modular systems, which they assemble according to their individual requirements. A_1, A_2, A_3, C_1, C_2, and C_3 are the manufacturers of A and C, two of the components of systems of type W, and B_1, B_2, and B_3 are makers of subassemblies used in component C. Makers of components A and C must, therefore, ensure compatibility with each other's products and with other potential components if their output is to be suitable for modular systems of type W. But subassembly B needs to be compatible only with component C and not directly with other components.

Taken together, all of the component manufacturers (A, C) and the ultimate users (W) make up a decentralized network. In contrast to centralized networks, in which

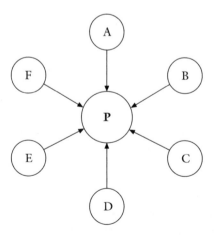

Figure 3.4   A centralized network.

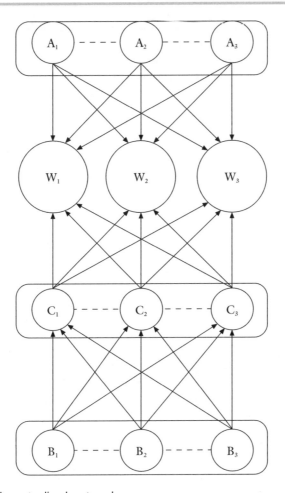

Figure 3.5 A decentralized network.

the standards of compatibility are laid down by the lead manufacturers and may differ from one lead firm to another, in decentralized networks the standards are determined jointly by components producers and user/assemblers through market processes or negotiation. No single member of the network has control, and any firm that tries to dictate standards in a decentralized network risks being isolated if users and other producers do not follow. Even component variations that are demonstrably superior in a technical sense may be disregarded if users and other manufacturers are "locked in" to existing standards because the costs of change would be greater than the benefits permitted by the new variation (David and Bunn [3]).

A second type of network is important here. Even when there is no patent or other protection, horizontal networking of firms – for example, among A_1, A_2, and A_3 or C_1, C_2, and C_3 – can allow an innovator to earn higher profits than if it attempted to appropriate all of the benefits itself. As we suggest in the case studies, when a component maker (especially of software) is unable by itself to offer customers enough variety to justify the purchase of the associated components in a modular system, the most successful firms will be those that abandon a proprietary strategy in favor of membership in a *network of competitors* employing a common standard of compatibility.

Autonomous versus systemic innovation

The benefits of modularity appear on the producer's side as well as on the consumer's side. A modular system is open to innovation of certain kinds in a way that a closed system – an appliance – is not. Thus a decentralized network based on modularity can have advantages in innovation to the extent that it involves the trying out of many alternate approaches simultaneously, leading to rapid trial-and-error learning. This kind of innovation is especially important when technology is changing rapidly and there is a high degree of both technological and market uncertainty (Nelson and Winter [18]). In a decentralized network, there are many more entry points for new firms, and thus for new ideas, than in a vertically integrated industry producing functionally similar appliances. To this extent, then, a modular system may progress faster technologically, especially during periods of uncertainty and fluidity.

Another reason that innovation may be spurred on by modularity lies in the division of labor. A network with a standard of compatibility promotes autonomous innovation,[7] that is, innovation requiring little coordination among stages. By allowing specialist producers (and sometimes specialist users) to concentrate their attention on particular components, a modular system thus enlists the division of labor in the service of innovation. We would expect innovation to proceed in the manner Rosenberg [24, p. 125] and Hughes [8] suggest: with bottleneck components – those standing most in the way of increased consumer satisfaction – as the focal points for change.

Systemic innovation would be more difficult in a modular system, and even undesirable to the extent that it destroyed compatibility across components. We would expect, however, to see systemic innovation *within* the externally compatible components. The internal "stages of production" within a modem or a tape deck can vary greatly from manufacturer to manufacturer so long as the component continues to connect easily to the network.[8] The components may, in other words, be appliances. To the extent that the coordination this internal systemic innovation requires is costly across markets, we would expect to see greater vertical integration by makers of components than by purveyors of the larger systems.

THE DEVELOPMENT OF HIGH-FIDELITY AND STEREO SYSTEMS

The evolution of modular high-fidelity and stereo component systems in the post-World War II period resulted from two separate but related developments.[9] The first, the spread of an underground movement for greater fidelity in reproduction, involved better recording techniques and superior reproduction equipment. The second was the introduction of 33- and 45-rpm records and the associated use of vinyl, which greatly enhanced the usefulness of recordings, particularly for lovers of classical music. Thus the connection between changes in hardware (the components) and software (records and later tapes and compact disks) was established from the beginning.

Early developments

Before the 1930s, the phonograph[10] was an appliance. Records were still recorded and played back acoustically, using mechanical vibrations to cut grooves into wax originals and to transmit sound from records to listeners via a horn. Although various instruments operate over a range of approximately 20 Hz to 20,000 Hz, from the lowest note on the organ to the highest overtones of the oboe, acoustic records generally reproduced a range of 350 to 3,000 Hz [6, September 1939, pp. 74–5, 92; 20, p. 237; 9, p. 29].

The origins of modularity in subsequent decades can be traced to the development of the Brunswick Panatrope. Although there had been earlier radio-phonograph combinations, they were essentially two appliances encased in a common cabinet, since radio signals could not be reproduced acoustically [20, pp. 268–9]. The Panatrope, which had a vacuum-tube amplifier and a speaker, therefore permitted technological convergence, since both radio signals and signals transmitted from the phonograph pickup were now reproduced identically. This soon led to a degree of modularity, as record players could be played through a radio's amplifier.

However, significant improvements in fidelity did not occur before the end of World War II. As late as 1945, most records cut off at 8,000 Hz because of distortion in the higher ranges. This limited span was further truncated by contemporary phonographs, which seldom reproduced sounds above 4,000 Hz. American record and phonograph manufacturers of the interwar period resisted attempts to improve the range of their products on the grounds that their customers preferred a diluted sound. One survey, conducted by the Columbia Broadcasting System, indicated that, by a margin of more than two to one, listeners liked standard broadcasts of up to 5,000 Hz better than wide-range programs that went up to 10,000. If, as it appeared, the most discerning of listeners were content with a cut-off of 5,000 Hz, there seemed to be no reason to improve recordings or equipment [6, October 1946, p. 161; 20, pp. 346–7].

The move toward systems in the post-war period

Even before the war, there was a move for greater fidelity among some enthusiasts. The most famous of these was Avery Fisher, who in 1937 began to produce high-quality radio sets. The high-fidelity movement gained impetus during World War II when US servicemen stationed in Europe became aware of the extent to which America lagged in both record and phonograph technology. In addition, many servicemen were trained in radio or electronic technologies that were transferable to high-fidelity uses, and some brought back equipment with them [4, pp. 76–7; 20, pp. 333, 347–8; 17, pp. 62–4]. When their suggestions for improvement were rebuffed by the established firms, a number of them set up as components manufacturers.

While a few manufacturers like Fisher, Capehart, and Scott did produce high-quality phonographs and combinations in the immediate postwar years [6, October 1946, pp. 190, 193, 195], there was a movement from integrated appliances to components that resulted from both supply and demand conditions. Many of the new firms were run by specialists who could not afford to manufacture across a broad scale even if they had had the expertise. On the demand side, interest in modularity was fueled by rapid but uneven rates of improvement across components that encouraged buyers to maintain the flexibility to update. The individualistic and subjective nature of "fidelity" also encouraged a proliferation of components as buyers sought to build systems to suit their idiosyncratic preferences.[11]

Components in the sense of add-on equipment had been available for many years. In 1933, for example, RCA began to offer the Duo Jr. record player that could be played through a radio. Available for $9.95, it was part of a successful attempt to revive the sale of records during the Depression. In general, the "war of the speeds" between Columbia and RCA, who introduced 33- and 45-rpm records, respectively,[12] opened the field to component makers by disturbing consumer perceptions of the existing paradigm. This was soon reinforced in the early 1950s by even more options, such as tape recorders [20, p. 350]. Listeners who took fidelity seriously now had a wide choice of equipment.

The importance of compatibility

Compatibility among the range of options was developed through the market as component manufacturers were forced to cooperate, at least up to a point, in order to be able to sell their products at all. Many promoters of high-quality components could not interest established producers and were forced to enter manufacturing themselves and to market directly to the public. Separate stores for high-fidelity and later stereo equipment developed in which customers could hear various combinations before deciding [20, pp. 351–2]. Only components that were compatible could be demonstrated. Similarly, the growth of the kit industry relied on interchangeability. Moreover, as many of the best components were developed in Britain or on the Continent, international standards became common.[13]

The origins of 33-rpm records

The first mass-produced disks with a reasonable range of fidelity, Decca's Full Frequency Range Recordings (FFRR), appeared originally on the 78-rpm format. The introduction of long-playing 33-rpm records and 45-rpm singles, however, provided a major impetus behind the development of high-fidelity reproduction. As the maximum playing time per side for a 12-inch 78 was barely five minutes, longer classical works required several disks and were frequently disrupted, sometimes in mid-movement. In addition, the quality of sound available on 78s produced from a shellac mixture was poor. In 1932, therefore, RCA introduced 33-rpm records made of vinyl, which reduced surface noise. The RCA records featured grooves that were only a little narrower than standard 78 grooves, however, which limited 33-rpm playing times to only around twice that of 12-inch 78s. More importantly, the wide grooves required wide styli and heavy pickups, which cut through the soft vinyl after the records had been played a few times. RCA did not address these hardware problems. Because of the scarcity of suitable turntables and the fragility of the records, RCA terminated the experiment the following year [28, p. 57; 20, pp. 339–40].

Networks in hardware and software

Following World War II, Columbia decided to reintroduce 33-rpm vinyl records. In order to increase playing time and (literally) reduce the wear and tear on vinyl, Columbia engineers concentrated on 1-mil microgrooves that could be used with a lighter stylus and pickup. Narrower grooves provided only part of the solution, however, as long as they were spaced as far apart as 78-rpm grooves of shellac-based records. As late as 1946, Columbia could provide only 11 to 12 minutes per side. To determine the desired length, Wallerstein surveyed the classical repertoire and found out that, with 17 minutes per side, 90 percent of classical pieces would fit on a single two-sided disk. By approximately doubling the number of grooves to between 190 and 225 per inch, Columbia engineers were soon able to exceed the 17-minute standard, and the firm decided to market 33-rpm long-playing records from the fall of 1948 [28, pp. 57–8; 20, p. 340].

Columbia recognized, of course, that simply offering the records would not be sufficient. Easy availability of 33-rpm record players would also be required. As Columbia, in contrast to RCA, did not itself manufacture electrical equipment, the success of the LP (a Columbia trademark) depended on convincing one or more outside firms to manufacture players. Recalling RCA's success with the Duo Jr. record player in 1933, Columbia approached several existing manufacturers to develop an inexpensive 33-rpm player. The company picked Philco as the initial supplier, with Columbia providing much of the basic technology. Wallerstein's recognition of the importance of networks was shown by his initial disappointment that only a single player manufacturer was chosen. "I was a little unhappy about this, because I felt that all of the manufacturers should be making a player of some sort – the more players that go on the market, the more records could be sold" [28, p. 58].

The price of the Philco "attachments" was soon reduced from $29.95 to $9.95, the cost at which Philco supplied them to Columbia. Columbia was able to leave the attachment business within a year as other manufacturers followed Philco's lead [28, p. 61].

Columbia also realized the importance of networks of competitors. Recognizing that it would prosper if other recording companies adopted the 33-rpm microgroove standard, it offered to license the process, a proposition that was quickly taken up by other, smaller, companies. Buyers of classical records responded to the convenience of the LP, the alleged unbreakability of vinyl disks (which RCA had begun to market as 78s in 1946), and the sharp reduction in price. Moderate-length classical works such as Beethoven's Fifth Symphony, which had previously required four 78-rpm records selling for $2 each, now appeared on a single LP at a fraction of the cost [28, pp. 58, 60; 20, pp. 339–430; 6, September 1939, p. 100]. Given the high price-elasticity of records, the lower price of LPs permitted an important broadening of the repertoire, which reinforced the density of the network and further encouraged consumers to switch to the new standard.

Thus, although there were no basic patents covering the LP process, Columbia was able to appropriate a large share of the profits by positioning itself as the leading firm in the network of competitors. Other firms that joined the network also prospered, but those that initially held out lost heavily and were eventually forced to conform. RCA, for example, lost $4.5 million on records between June 1948 and January 1950, when it began to issue its own LPs. Its classical sales were decimated, and a number of its most important artists, including Pinza, Rubinstein, and Heifetz, either deserted or threatened to do so. Over the same period. Columbia cleared $3 million [28, pp. 60–1].

RCA's response

RCA's first approach to the threat of the LP was to try to block the network by establishing its own incompatible system. Columbia had considered issuing six- or seven-inch 33-rpm records for the large singles market, but abandoned the idea. This left an opening for RCA, which introduced 45-rpm singles and produced its own record players and phonographs. In order to forestall competition, RCA chose to use a larger spindle that could not accommodate 33 (or 78) records [28, pp. 60–1; 20, pp. 340–2]. Although other companies followed RCA with large-hole 45s, however, the incompatibility turned out to be in one direction only, since 45-rpm records could easily be fitted in the center with a metal or plastic disk that permitted use with a standard spindle.[14] Moreover, the 45-rpm microgrooves could be played with a stylus designed for 33-rpm records. In the end, RCA was unable to develop a proprietary hardware system fed by its own software variation. Even though the seven-inch 45-rpm format became the standard for singles, 12-inch 33-rpm LPs captured the market for longer works and collections. RCA eventually joined independent manufacturers in producing phonographs and turntables that operated at all of the major speeds (including 78-rpm) and provided two styli (one for 78 rpm and one for 33- and 45-rpm microgrooves).

The importance of networks to the adoption of the LP and FM

The rapid spread of 33- and 45-rpm record formats contrasts sharply with the long delays required for FM receivers to become a vital part of high-fidelity systems. The use of frequency, rather than amplitude, modulation of radio signals and of very-high-frequency (VHF) waves for transmission permits reductions in atmospheric and man-made interference; relative immunity from other stations operating on the same frequency; and better fidelity of reproduction, especially in regard to dynamic volume range and frequency response. Despite these advantages, FM transmission spread slowly following its introduction in the United States in 1940. The number of FM stations actually fell significantly in the early 1950s, and as late as 1975 the FM share of the total radio listening audience was only 30 percent, as opposed to 75 percent in 1988 [9; 25].

The principal reason that purchasers of high-fidelity components were converted to LP turntables so quickly but resisted the charms of FM tuners for almost two decades was that LPs offered such important advantages when compared to 78-rpm records that a software network was created almost immediately, which consumers were then able to take advantage of through a series of individual purchases of relatively inexpensive record players and phonographs. The great majority of radio listeners, however, could see no immediate technical advantage in investing in FM equipment because popular music, in contrast to classical, had a limited dynamic range during the early decades of FM broadcasting. Moreover, radio listeners had less control because they were dependent on a network with two stages: the records and the stations that transmitted them. When the dynamic range of popular music broadened in the late 1950s and then stereo multiplex became available, the interests of popular- and classical-music listeners merged. Only at this point did the market become dense enough to justify greater investment by broadcasters in FM programming. The interests of FM consumers and producers therefore both evolved, but each faced its own bottlenecks that had to be overcome before further progress was possible.

From modular systems to appliances?

More recent developments, including cassette recorders and CD players, have streng-thened the old principle of attaching new options to existing systems. After more than four decades of development, however, it is possible that high sophistication is no longer of much value to the consumer. According to one estimate, 80 percent of listeners are "rather deaf" at ranges above 10,000 Hz. Casual empiricism also suggests that many listeners prefer extra volume to better tone when playing music.

In contrast to microcomputers, stereo equipment serves only one basic use: the reproduction of sound. New components represent variations on a theme rather than departures into new realms. Except for the most golden of ears or snobs, the point has probably been reached at which packaged systems[15] by such firms as Pioneer and Sony meet all reasonable technical specifications. At this mature stage of the product life cycle, the transaction costs of choice for most consumers may outweigh the benefits arising from picking and choosing. Preset packages cover almost the entire product space, not because consumers demand an undifferentiated no-frills product analogous to the Model T, but because with maturity a standardized product has become so well developed that it now meets the needs of almost all users. It remains to be seen whether a new era of modularity will emerge when, as is often predicted, stereo systems become more integrated into video and computer networks.

THE MICROCOMPUTER INDUSTRY

Early developments

The first microcomputer is generally acknowledged to have been the MITS/Altair, which graced the cover of *Popular Electronics* magazine in January 1975.[16] Essentially a microprocessor in a box, the machine was built around the Intel 8080 chip. Its only input/output devices were lights and toggle switches on the front panel, and it came with a mere 256 bytes of memory. But the Altair was, at least potentially, a genuine computer. Its potential came largely from a crucial design decision: the machine incorporated a number of open "slots" that allowed for additional memory and other devices to be added later. These slots were hooked into the microprocessor by a network of wires called a "bus," which came to be known as the S-100 bus because of its 100-line structure.

Add-ons – especially memory boards – were definitely the first bottleneck of the Altair system. Very quickly, third-party suppliers sprang up, many of them literally garage-shop operations. Using a microcomputer, especially a primitive early model, required some less-tangible complementary activities as well; software and know-how. Both of these gaps were filled exclusively by third parties, the latter by grass-roots organizations called user groups. In effect, the machine was captured by the hobbyist community and became a truly open modular system. Like most manufacturers, the Altair's designers wanted to keep the system as proprietary as possible. But when they tried to tie the sale of some desirable software to the purchase of inferior MITS memory boards, the main result was the dawn of software piracy. Moreover, the first clone of the Altair – the IMSAI 8080 – appeared within a matter of months.

The early success of MITS, IMSAI, and others anchored the popularity of the 8080/S-100 standard, especially among hobbyists, who were still the primary buying group. Lee Felsenstein, the influential leader of the Homebrew Computer Club in Northern California, argued that the standard had reached "critical mass," and, sounding like a present-day theorist of network externalities, forecast the demise of competing chips and buses [16, p. 123]. The main reason was the impressive library of software that S-100 users had built up.

The Apple II

The predicted dominance of the S-100 (and the CP/M operating system it used) never materialized. In 1977, three new machines entered the market, each with its own proprietary operating system, and two using an incompatible non-Intel microprocessor. The Apple II, the Commodore PET, and the Radio Shack TRS-80 Model I quickly outstripped the S-100 machines in sales and, by targeting users beyond the hobbyist community, moved the industry into a new era of growth.

The most important of the three machines was the Apple II. Apple Computer had been started a year earlier by Stephen Wozniak and Steven Jobs, two college drop-outs and tinkerers. The hobbyist Wozniak insisted that the Apple be an expandable system with slots and that technical details be freely available to users and third-party suppliers. Jobs saw the Apple as a single-purpose product, and he objected to the slots as unnecessary. Fortunately for Apple, Wozniak won the argument, and the Apple II contained eight expansion slots. Unlike the hobbyist S-100 machines, however, it was compact, attractive, and professional, housed with its keyboard in a smart plastic case.

With early revenues coming almost entirely from sales of the Apple II, the company took in three quarters of a million dollars by the end of fiscal 1977; $8 million in 1978; $48 million in 1979; $117 million in 1980 (when the firm went public); $335 million in 1981; $583 million in 1982; and $983 million in 1983. With the development of word processors like WordStar, database managers like dBase II, and spreadsheets like VisiCalc, the machine became a tool of writers, professionals, and small businesses. And, because of its slots, it could accommodate new add-ons – and therefore adapt to new uses – as they emerged.

Modularity again: the IBM PC

By mid 1981, the uses of the microcomputer were becoming clearer than they had been only few years earlier, even if the full extent of the product space lay largely unmapped. A microcomputer was a system comprising a number of more-or-less standard elements: a microprocessor unit with 64K bytes of RAM memory: a key-board, usually built into the system unit; one or two disk drives; a monitor; and a printer. The machine ran operating-system software and applications programs like word processors, spreadsheets, and database managers. CP/M, once the presumptive standard, was embattled, but no one operating system reigned supreme.

One response to this emerging paradigm was the bundled transportable computer – like the Osborne and later the Kaypro – that packaged together most of the basic hardware and software into an inexpensive package. These machines achieved a modicum of success. But the signal event of 1981 was not the advent of the cheap bundled portable. On 12 August 1981, IBM introduced the computer that would become the paradigm for most of the 1980s. Like the Osborne and Kaypro, it was not technologically sophisticated, and it incorporated most of the basic features users expected. But, unlike the bundled portables, the IBM PC was a system, not an appliance: it was an incomplete package, an open box ready for expansion, reconfiguration, and continual upgrading.

In order to introduce quickly a PC bearing its own nameplate, IBM embarked on an uncharacteristic strategy. Rather than building the machine inhouse, as was typical for IBM's large computers, the company produced the PC almost entirely by assembling parts bought on the market. Moreover, to save time, the design team followed the open architecture of the S-100 machines and initially resisted the temptation to produce its own add-ons.

The emergence of a network of competitors

Because the machine used the Intel 8088 instead of the 8080, the PC needed a new operating system. IBM wanted its system to become dominant in the industry. But, despite a long attachment to the proprietary strategy in mainframes, the company contracted out the design of the software, and, in a bold move, allowed Microsoft, the contractor, to license MS-DOS (as the operating system was called) to other manufacturers. One result was a legion of clones that offered IBM compatibility, generally at a price lower than IBM charged. But the other result was that MS-DOS – and the IBM PC's bus structure – did indeed become the new industry standard. Makers of IBM-incompatible machines went out of business, converted to the new standard (like Tandy and Kaypro), or retreated to niche markets (like Commodore and Apple, even if the latter's niche is quite roomy).

IBM did have one trick up its sleeve to try to ward off cloners, but it turned out not to be a very powerful trick. The operating system that Microsoft designed for the IBM PC – called PC-DOS in its proprietary version – differs slightly in its memory architecture from the generic MS-DOS IBM allowed Microsoft to license to others. IBM chose to write some of the BIOS (or basic input-output system, a part of DOS) into a chip and to leave some of it in software. They then published the design of the chip in a technical report, which, under copyright laws, copyrighted part of the PC-DOS BIOS. IBM sued Corona, Eagle, and a Taiwanese firm for infringing the BIOS copyright in their earliest models. These companies, and all later cloners, responded, however, with an end run. They contracted with outfits like Phoenix and AMI to create a BIOS that does what the IBM BIOS does, but does it in a different way. This removed the principal proprietary hurdle to copying the original PC.

What is especially interesting is the diversity of sources of these compatible machines. Many come from American manufacturers like Compaq and Tandy, who sell under their own brand names. Another group would be foreign manufacturers selling under their own brand names. The largest sellers are Epson and NEC of Japan and Hyundai of Korea. But there is also a large OEM (original-equipment manufacturer) market, in which firms – typically Taiwanese or Korean, but sometimes American or European – manufacture PCs for resale under another brand name. Perhaps the most interesting phenomenon is the no-name clone – the PC assembled from an international cornucopia of standard parts and sold, typically, through mail orders. Most manufacturers, even the large branded ones, are really assemblers, and they draw heavily on the wealth of available vendors. But the parts are also available directly, and it is in fact quite easy to put together one's own PC from parts ordered from the back of a computer magazine. By one 1986 estimate, the stage of final assembly added only $10 to the cost of the finished machine – two hours work for one person earning about $5 per hour. As the final product could be assembled this way for far less than the going price of name brands – especially IBM – a wealth of backroom operations sprang up. The parts list is truly international. Most boards come from Taiwan, stuffed with chips made in the US (especially microprocessors and ROM BIOS) or Japan (especially memory chips). Hard-disk drives come from the United States, but floppy drives come increasingly from Japan.

A power supply might come from Taiwan or Hong Kong. The monitor might be Japanese, Taiwanese, or Korean. Keyboards might come from the US, Taiwan, Japan, or even Thailand.

The importance of the network

It is tempting to interpret the success of the original IBM PC as merely the result of the power of IBM's name. While the name was no doubt of some help, especially in forcing MS-DOS as a standard operating system, there are enough counter examples to suggest that it was the machine itself – and IBM's approach to developing it – that must take the credit. Almost all other large firms, many with nearly IBM's prestige, failed miserably in the PC business. The company that Apple and the other early computer makers feared most was not IBM but Texas Instruments, a power in integrated circuits and systems (notably electronic calculators). But TI flopped by entering at the low end, seeing the PC as akin to a calculator rather than as a multipurpose professional machine. When TI did enter the business market in the wake of the IBM PC, its TI Professional also failed because the company refused to make the machine fully IBM compatible. Xerox entered the market with a CP/M machine that – in 1981 was too little too late. Hewlett-Packard was also slow out of the blocks.

Consider, in particular, the case of Digital Equipment Corporation [22]. DEC is the second-largest computer maker in the world, and the largest maker of mini-computers. In 1980, the company decided to enter the personal computer business. The Professional series was to be the company's principal entry into the fray. It would have a proprietary operating system based on that of the PDP-11 minicom-puter; bit-mapped graphics; and multitasking capabilities. But, despite winning design awards, the computer was a commercial flop. All told, the company lost about $900 million on its development of desktop machines. DEC's principal mistake was its unwillingness to take advantage of external economies. The strategy of propriet-ary systems and inhouse development had worked in minicomputers: put together a machine that would solve a particular problem for a particular application. The PC is not, however, a machine for a particular application; it is a machine adaptable to many applications – including some its users had not imagined when they bought their machines. Moreover, DEC underrated the value of software. And, unlike IBM, DEC chose to ignore existing third-party capabilities. Except for the hard disk and the line cord, DEC designed and built every piece of the Professional.

The importance of modularity

Why were the most successful machines – the Apple II and the IBM PC – also the most modular? Microcomputer software is a popular example of the importance of network externalities. The value of owning a computer that runs a particular kind of software (IBM-compatible software under MS-DOS, for example) is dependent on the number of other people who own similar machines, since the amount of software available is proportional to the total installed base of computers that can use that kind of software. But although this is certainly part of the story, its impact is less than might have been expected because the development of software networks has turned out to be a cheaper and more flexible process than was originally envisaged. By the summer of 1980, Microsoft had in place a system of software development in which code was first written in "neutral" language on a DEC minicomputer and then run through a translator program that would automatically convert the neutral software into the form needed by a specific machine. This made it possible to write machine-independent software. Now, smaller companies without this facility would still be tempted to write software specifically for one machine first, and the system with the largest installed base would offer the greatest temptation. But there are profits to be made writing or adapting software for even idiosyncratic machines, and a cottage industry like software development is particularly likely to seize such opportunities.

The explanation for modularity in microcomputers – modularity in hardware as well as software – is broader than, albeit related to, the phenomenon of network externalities. As we argued above, the benefits of modularity can appear on both the demand side and the supply side.

Demand-side benefits

In microcomputers, the economies of scale of assembling a finished machine are relatively slight. The machines are user-friendly in comparison with their larger cousins, and ample information is available through books, magazines, and user groups. There is also a lively middleman trade in the industry, revolving around so-called value-added resellers, who package hardware and software systems to the tastes of particular non-expert buyers. At the same time, the uses of the microcomputer are multifold, changing, and, at least in the early days, were highly uncertain. A modular system can blanket the product space with little loss in production or transaction costs.

Moreover, the microcomputer benefited from a kind of technological convergence, in that it turned out to be a technology capable of taking over tasks that had previously required numerous distinct – and more expensive – pieces of physical and human capital. By the early 1980s, a microcomputer costing $3,500 could do the work of a $10,000 stand-alone word processor, while at the same time keeping track of the books like a $100,000 minicomputer and amusing the kids with space aliens like a 25-cents-a-game arcade machine.

Supply-side benefits

On the producer side, again, a decentralized and fragmented system can have advantages in innovation to the extent that it involves the trying out of many alternate approaches simultaneously, leading to rapid trial-and-error learning. This kind of innovation is especially important when technology is changing rapidly and there is a high degree of both technological and market uncertainty. That the micro-computer industry partook of external economies of learning and innovation is in many ways a familiar story that need not be retold. Popular accounts of Silicon Valley sound very much like Marshall's localized industry in which the "mysteries of the trade become no mysteries; but are as it were in the air, and children learn many of them unconsciously" [14, IV.x.3, p. 225]. Compare, for example, Moritz's dis-cussion of the effect of Silicon Valley culture on one particular child: Wozniak, "In Sunnyvale in the mid-sixties, electronics was like hay fever: It was in the air and the allergic caught it. In the Wozniak household the older son had a weak immune system" [16, p. 29]. One could easily multiply citations. This learning effect went beyond the background culture, however. It included the proclivity of engineers to hop jobs and start spinoffs, creating a pollination effect and tendency to biological differentiation that Marshall would have appreciated.

Also, as we suggested earlier, innovation in a modular system typically proceeds in autonomous fashion, taking advantage of the division of labor. So long as it main-tains its ability to connect to a standard bus, an add-on board can gain in capabilities over a range without any other parts of the system changing. Graphics boards can become more powerful, modems faster, software more user-friendly, and pointing devices more clever. The prime focal points of this innovation are often technolog-ical "bottlenecks," in this case bottlenecks to the usefulness of the microcomputer in meeting the many needs to which it has been put. The lack of reliable memory boards was a bottleneck to the usefulness of the early Altair. The 40-column display and the inability to run CP/M software were bottlenecks of the Apple II. The IBM PC's 8088 microprocessor could address only a limited amount of internal memory. All of these – and many more – were the targets of innovation by third-party suppliers, from Cromemco and Processor Technology to Microsoft and Intel. Sometimes a bottleneck is not strictly technological, as when IBM's copyrighted ROM BIOS became the focus of inventing-around by firms like Phoenix and AMI. Although "innovations" of this sort may not directly yield improvements in per-formance, they do help to keep the system open. In a wider sense, we can also include as bottleneck-breakers those innovations that extended the system's abilities in new directions – modems, machinery-controller boards, facsimile boards, graphics scanners, etc. The microcomputer as a modular system has also partaken of certain types of integrative innovations, that is, innovations that allow a single device to perform functions that had previously required several devices. A good example of this would be the chip set designed by Chips and Technologies to integrate into a few ICs 63 of the 94 circuits on the original IBM AT, thus greatly facilitating the making of clones.

Other types of networks and systems

So far the discussion has been couched in terms of user/assemblers. But the analysis also applies to intermediate products where consumers are often even more sophis-ticated and well-informed about product attributes than typical final consumers.

The early history of the automobile industry provides an instructive example of the purposes and limitations of decentralized networks.[17] Recognition of the value of networks and external economies resulted in an important agreement in 1910: sponsored by the Society of Automotive Engineers, it led to the establishment of a set of standards for component parts. In the early period of the industry, most independent suppliers built to specifications laid down by the assembler. As a result, there were more than 1,600 types of steel tubing used and 800 standards of lock washer, with a similar proliferation of varieties of other components (Epstein [5, pp. 41–3]). Early attempts to set common standards had been unsuccessful, but the panic of 1910 brought a crisis among assemblers. The failure of suppliers in the panic emphasized the vulnerability of small assemblers who were not readily able to switch to other firms because of peculiarities in specifications. Led at first by Howard E. Coffin of the Hudson Motor Car Company, over the next decade the SAE set detailed standards for numerous parts, in the process creating interchangeability across firms. After standardization, for example, the number of types of steel tubing had been reduced to 210 and the number of lock washers to 16. Throughout the initial period of standardization, until the early 1920s, most interest was shown by the smaller firms, who had the most to gain. The larger firms such as Ford, Studebaker, Dodge, Willys-Overland, and General Motors tended to ignore the SAE and relied instead on internally established standards (Thompson [27, pp. 1–11]).

Similar behavior has been common in other industries. Beginning in 1924, for example, radio manufacturers established a variety of standards committees to allow greater interchangeability and embed themselves in a decentralized network (Graham [7, p. 40.]). A more recent case is the ongoing debate among semiconductor fabricators and equipment manufacturers over the Modular Equipment Standards Architecture (MESA) [31, p. 26]. Here a consortium of equipment makers is pushing for an open control and interface protocol that will allow semiconductor fabricators to mix and match equipment from many different suppliers on a single assembly line. This movement stands in opposition to Applied Materials, Inc., the largest maker of "monolithic," or non-distributed, fabrication systems, which is trying to use its large installed base to leverage a more open version of its Precision 5,000 system as the industry standard.

CONCLUSIONS

There are a number of striking similarities between the cases of high-fidelity and stereo systems and microcomputers. These similarities in turn illustrate a number of theoretical points.

In both cases, first of all, the industry adopted a modular structure with a common standard of compatibility rather than a structure of competing prepackaged entities. In both cases, large firms tried the appliance approach in an effort to appropriate the rents of innovation. But these attempts ultimately failed, and companies who relied heavily on an external network of competitors and suppliers were clearly more successful. Columbia encouraged the production of 33-rpm records and players, and

IBM allowed Microsoft to license MS-DOS widely. These firms became significant players in networks that were not under their control, thereby garnering larger payoffs than if they had attempted to market a proprietary product. Teece [26] has suggested some ways in which the desire to appropriate the rents of innovation can lead to vertical integration. These cases suggest the opposite possibility, in which the same desire can lead to vertical (and horizontal) *disintegration.*

In both cases, aficionados and enthusiasts, with more sophisticated tastes and a higher willingness to pay, played an important role in edging the systems onto a modular path. These hobbyists and audiophiles tested the limits of the systems and helped identify the bottlenecks that became foci of innovation. In many cases, these individuals set up in business to supply (and typically improve) the bottleneck components.

In both cases, one driving issue was the compatibility of hardware and software. Cast in these terms, the story revolves around the much-discussed phenomenon of network externalities leading to technological "lock in" (David and Bunn [3]). What has not been stressed in the literature, however, is the modular nature of these systems. Quite apart from any network externalities, the modularity of stereo and microcomputer systems allowed producers to participate in a system that was better able to blanket the product space – and thereby generate greater consumer demand – that a system of competing prepackaged entities.

There is perhaps a message in this for the debate over competitiveness and industrial policy; namely, that the definition of the "product" matters. As we argued above, vertical integration may have its benefits (or at least relatively few disbenefits) for the production of components fitting into the system. This is because subassemblies need to be compatible only with a particular brand of component, as in figure 5, and a vertically integrated firm may have some advantages in coordinating systemic innovation of the internal subcomponents of the module. But large size and vertical integration are of little benefit in coordinating across the compatibility boundaries of the larger system. Especially in the early stages of development, experimentation is a much more important concern than coordination. And rapid trial-and-error learning is one forte of a decentralized network.

There is evidence that stereo systems, and even microcomputers to some extent, have matured to an extent that they are becoming more like appliances. Because of technological progress and learning about demand, a standard system can now meet the needs of a large fraction of users without modification. But it is dangerous to extrapolate trends too far. For example, the home-entertainment industry may be entering a new phase of change, as convergence with computer and video technology opens up new possibilities for the consumer. The home-entertainment system today no longer produces merely sound but also video, with the monitor and videocassette recorder tied into the system and capable of high-fidelity stereo sound. Technological convergence with the microcomputer is already occurring in the case of the compact-disk player, which uses basically the same technology in its guises as audio source and data source. Many audio and video products now include microprocessors, and can be programmed in limited ways. If the predictions of the popular press hold true, further convergence will take place with the advent of computer-interactive audio and video and high-definition television.

Indeed, one might speculate in general that modular systems are likely to take on greater importance in the future. This is so for two reasons. First of all, the predicted advent of flexible manufacturing would reduce the cost advantages of large production runs. This would in turn reduce the advantages of integrating the functions of assembly and packaging. Second, a continued increase in consumer incomes would mean more sophisticated tastes and a greater relative demand for the finely tuned products a modular system permits.

NOTES

1   In the sense of Lancaster [10]. We discuss this approach in greater detail below.
2   The work most relevant to our concerns is that of Matutes and Regibeau [15], who cast the problem of "mix and match" in the form of a game. In this model, two firms who produce a two-component system must each decide whether to make parts compatible or incompatible with those of the competitor. Apart from being rather stylized, however, this model does not look at the issue of vertical integration, assuming instead that both firms produce both components. The model also does not examine the effect of the compatibility decision on innovation or production costs.
3   For a straightforward introduction, see Waterson [29, chapter 6].
4   Although price factors can be important, we must be careful not to place too much emphasis on them. Poor or unsophisticated consumers will be much more susceptible to low-cost products (have lower budget constraints); but, as incomes and sophistication increase, a higher proportion of buyers will seek a better selection of attributes. A sufficient number of people were able to afford better bundles of attributes that, even at the peak of its popularity, the Model T did not force Cadillac, Lincoln, or Packard from the market. And, as incomes rose generally in the 1920s, the Model T itself succumbed as a higher proportion of consumers had the means to purchase superior selections of non-price features (Langlois and Robertson [13]).
5   On which see Rosenberg [24, chapter 1].
6   Neoclassical economics has taught us to think of MES as a matter of technology independent of the firm using the technology. In fact, of course, production cost is an extremely firm-specific matter. As Nelson and Winter [19, chapters 4 and 5] suggest, production is a matter of the skills a firm possesses; and such skills are often inarticulate and learned gradually over time. The firm's cost of internalizing a given activity will depend on how appropriate to the task the firm's skills are, which often means how similar the activity is to the activities the firm already engages in (Richardson [21]). One force for vertical specialization, then, is the dissimilarity among stages of production. The skills necessary to make turntables may be significantly dissimilar from those needed to make amplifiers, the skills applicable to making disk drives may be significantly dissimilar from those needed to fabricate semiconductor memories. One might indeed go so far as to wonder whether such dissimilarity does not increase with the complexity and technical sophistication of the final product.
7   The notions of autonomous and systemic innovation are borrowed from Teece [26].
8   For example, the relationship between the manufacturers of subassembly B and those of component C in figure 3.5.
9   For a fuller discussion of the early development of modular stereo sets, see Robertson and Langlois [23].
10   A phonograph included all the equipment necessary for reproduction. With the advent of electric models in the late 1920s, this meant a speaker and an amplifier as well as the

turntable. A record player was only a turntable and had to be plugged into a radio. Finally, a "combination" included both a radio and a phonograph in single unit.

11 For the famous case of one such listener, the possessor of "a 'golden ear' of the richest sheen," see [6, October 1946, p. 161].

12 Columbia's offered a 33-rpm attachment in 1948, and RCA placed its 45-rpm rapid-drop changer on the market in the following year.

13 Garrard, for instance, used different-sized flywheels for the American and European markets to allow for local differences in the number of cycles per second in electricity transmission. Otherwise, the same record changers were compatible with other components everywhere.

14 In the terminology of David and Bunn [3], the RCA system was susceptible to a unidirectional "gateway technology."

15 Although these systems are sold as entities, most are in fact composed of separate components manufactured by a single firm. When they do not include the full range of options such as CD players, they usually offer provisions for plug-in sets for buyers who wish to diversify later.

16 For a much longer and better-documented history of the microcomputer, see [12], on which this section draws. A condensed version of this case study also appears in [11].

17 Although they were not final consumers, the smaller automobile assemblers were in a position analogous to W_1, W_2, and W_3 in figure 3.5 in that, for many components, they could not individually use the total output of a supplier operating at MES. As a result, the smaller assemblers tended to purchase components from outside firms that, to achieve efficiency, also needed to supply competing assemblers. This, of course, increased the commercial attractiveness of compatibility of components across assemblers and was also consistent with the delegation of a degree of component design to the suppliers.

The larger automobile assemblers, however, were more frequently able to absorb the entire production of their suppliers and were, therefore, in a position similar to that of P in figure 3.4. Alternatively, they were well placed to integrate vertically if their sources of supply were inadequate or under threat. Thus the large assemblers were less interested in compatibility.

REFERENCES

[1] M. Best, *The New Competition: Institutions and Industrial Restructuring* (Harvard University Press, Cambridge, 1990).

[2] S. N. S. Cheung, The Contractual Nature of the Firm. *Journal of Law and Economics* 26 (1983) 1–22.

[3] P. David and J. A. Bunn, Gateway Technologies and Network Industries, in: A. Heertje and M. Perlman (eds.). *Evolving Technology and Market Structure* (University of Michigan Press, Ann Arbor, 1990).

[4] N. Eisenberg, High Fidelity Pathfinders: The Men Who Made an Industry, *High Fidelity Magazine* (April 1976).

[5] R. C. Epstein, *The Automobile Industry: Its Economic and Commercial Development* (A. W. Shaw, Chicago, 1928).

[6] *Fortune* various issues.

[7] M. B. W. Graham, *The Business of Research: RCA and the VideoDisc* (Cambridge University Press, New York, 1986).

[8] T. P. Hughes, *Networks of Power: Electrification in Western Society, 1880–1930* (The Johns Hopkins University Press, Baltimore, 1983).

[9] A. F. Inglis, *Behind the Tube: A History of Broadcasting Technology and Business* (Focal Press, Boston, 1990).

[10] K. Lancaster, *Consumer Demand: A New Approach* (Columbia University Press, New York, 1971).

[11] R. N. Langlois, Creating External Capabilities: Innovation and Vertical Disintegration in the Microcomputer Industry, *Business and Economic History*, Second Series, 19 (1990) 93–102.

[12] R. N. Langlois, External Economies and Economic Progress: The Case of the Microcomputer Industry, Working Paper 91–1502. Department of Economics, the University of Connecticut, January 1991.

[13] R. N. Langlois and P. L. Robertson, Explaining Vertical Integration: Lessons from the American Automobile Industry, *Journal of Economic History* 49 (1989) 361–75.

[14] A. Marshall, *Principles of Economics*, 8th edition (Macmillan, London, 1920).

[15] C. Matutes and P. Regibeau, "Mix and Match": Product Compatibility without Network Externalities, *RAND Journal of Economics* 19 (1988) 221–34.

[16] M. Moritz, *The Little Kingdom: The Private Story of Apple Computer* (William Morrow, New York, 1984).

[17] J. Mullin, Creating the Craft of Tape Recording, *High Fidelity Magazine* (April 1976).

[18] R. R. Nelson and S. G. Winter, In Search of More Useful Theory of Innovation, *Research Policy* 5 (1977) 36–76.

[19] R. R. Nelson and S. G. Winter, *An Evolutionary Theory of Economic Change* (Harvard University Press. Cambridge, 1982).

[20] O. Read and W. L. Welch, *From Tin Foil to Stereo: Evolution of the Phonograph* (Howard W. Sams and Bobbs-Merrill, Indianapolis, 1976).

[21] G. B. Richardson, The Organisation of Industry, *Economic Journal* 82 (1972) 883–96.

[22] G. Rifkin and G. Harrar, *The Ultimate Entrepreneur: The Story of Ken Olsen and Digital Equipment Corporation* (Contemporary Books, Chicago, 1988).

[23] P. I. Robertson and R. N. Langlois, Modularity. Innovation, and the Firm: the Case of Audio Components, in: M. Perlman (ed.). *Entrepreneurship, Technological Innovation, and Economic Growth: International Perspectives* (University of Michigan Press, Ann Arbor, 1992).

[24] N. Rosenberg, *Perspectives on Technology* (Cambridge University Press, New York, 1976).

[25] C. H. Sterling, WTMJ-FM: A Case Study in the Development of Broadcasting, *Journal of Broadcasting* 12(4): 341–52, reprinted in: L. W. Lichty and M. C. Topping (eds.). American Broadcasting: A Source Book on the History of Radio and Television (Hastings House, New York, 1968).

[26] D. J. Teece, Profiting from Technological Innovation: Implications for Integration, Collaboration, Licensing, and Public Policy, *Research Policy* 15 (1986) 285–305.

[27] G. V. Thompson, Intercompany Technical Standardization in the Early American Automobile Industry, *Journal of Economic History* 24 (1954) 1–20.

[28] E. Wallerstein, Creating the LP Record (as told to Ward Botsford), *High Fidelity Magazine* (April 1976).

[29] M. Waterson, *Economic Theory of the Industry* (Cambridge University Press, Cambridge, 1984).

[30] O. E. Williamson, *The Economic Institutions of Capitalism* (The Free Press, New York, 1985).

[31] E. Winkler, MESA. Applied Feud Stirring over Pact, *Electronic News* (April 1990).

COMMENTARY
Richard N. Langlois and Paul L. Robertson

It has been roughly ten years since "Networks and Innovation in a Modular System" appeared in *Research Policy*. Significantly, those particular ten years were the Internet decade, a period during which many of the themes of our article emerged from obscurity – and perhaps even one or two of the article's predictions came true. And in the dog years of Internet time, a decade provides the kind of perspective that perhaps a century would grant in more conventional metric.[1] Such a perspective enables us to look back over the genesis of the paper and its contribution – and also to attempt the more difficult task of qualifying that contribution and of looking forward.

Genesis of the article

This article was part of a continuum of work in which we tried, both separately and together, to theorize about business institutions – be they firms, markets, or networks – in an explicitly dynamic or historical way (Langlois, 1988, 1992; Robertson and Alston, 1992). That work would eventually come together in a book called *Firms, Markets, and Economic Change: A Dynamic Theory of Business Institutions* (Langlois and Robertson, 1995), in which a version of this article appears as a chapter.

Rather than seeing business institutions as an equilibrium outcome of some kind of static (transaction) cost minimization, we argue that such institutions are forged often and importantly in the Schumpeterian crucible of innovation. The evolution of business institutions in this theory is thus influenced by two historically contingent factors. One is technological: the structure or form of the innovation driving change. The other is behavioral: the structure of relevant economic capabilities, including both the substantive content of those capabilities and the organizational structure under which they are deployed in the economy.[2]

One pattern typical in the history of business institutions emerges when a *systemic* innovation would yield significant gains to the owners of relevant assets. As a systemic innovation is one that requires simultaneous change in several stages of production,[3] such an innovation is likely to render obsolete some existing assets and, at the same time, to call for the use of capabilities not previously applied in the production of the product. If, in addition, the existing capabilities are under separate ownership – or, to put it loosely and somewhat inaccurately, the existing production system is coordinated through market mechanisms – then we arrive at one important rationale for the institution of the business firm. Under this scenario, the business firm arises because it can more cheaply redirect, coordinate, and where necessary create the capabilities necessary to make the innovation work. Because control of the necessary capabilities in the firm would be relatively more concentrated than in the existing organizational structure, such a firm could overcome not only the recalcitrance of asset-holders whose capital would have creatively to be destroyed but also the *dynamic transaction costs* of informing and persuading new input-holders with necessary capabilities.[4]

This scenario accurately describes the situation surrounding the creation and growth of many of the enterprises Alfred Chandler chronicled in *The Visible Hand* (1977). With the lowering of transportation and communications costs in the America of the nineteenth century, there arose profit opportunities for those who could create mass markets and take advantage of economies of scale in mass production. Examples range from steel and farm machinery to cigarettes and branded goods. Langlois and Robertson (1989) apply the theory to the case of Henry Ford and the moving assembly line. Because Ford and his engineers were reinventing the process of making automobile parts, it was far easier for them to own and to locate together the majority of the necessary assets and capabilities than it would have been to find, teach, persuade – and perhaps even create – outside suppliers. Mass production was a systemic innovation, one that took shape only slowly through trial and error.[5]

At the same time, however, we were well aware that the above scenario is by no means the only important one, let alone the only possible one. The superiority of the firm in that scenario rested on its ability cheaply to redeploy, coordinate, and create necessary capabilities in a situation in which (1) the entrepreneurial opportunity involved required systemic change, and (2) the necessary new capabilities were not cheaply available from an existing decentralized or market network. But when one or both of these conditions is missing, the benefits to the firm are attenuated, and its rationale slips away. In many circumstances, change – even sometimes rapid change – may proceed in autonomous fashion. Moreover, in highly developed economies, a wide variety of capabilities may be available for purchase on ordinary markets, in the form either of contract inputs or finished products. At the same time, it may also be the case that the existing network of capabilities that must be creatively destroyed (at least in part) by entrepreneurial change is not in the hands of decentralized input suppliers but is in fact concentrated in existing large firms.

What the article said and what it anticipated

It is here that "Networks and Innovation in a Modular System" fits into the picture: as an attempt to theorize about innovation and economic growth in a context of decentralized capabilities.

We presented a draft of the paper at the biennial meeting of the International Joseph A. Schumpeter Society at Airlie House in Virginia in the spring of 1990. We have to keep in mind that, unlike the 1990s, the 1980s had been the decade of the Japanese Success. American firms were routinely castigated for being too small and "fragmented" in comparison with the large Japanese Keiretsu, which seemed to some observers to be permanently capable of outcompeting the Americans.[6] The crises that were to afflict large firms on both continents lay in the future. The personal computer was a success story, but still something of a sideshow: what Bresnahan and Greenstein (1996) call the "competitive crash" in large-scale computing still lay in the future. The year 1990 had also seen the publication of Alfred Chandler's *Scale and Scope*, which traced and extolled the post-war success of the large multidivisional corporation.[7] Thus, to present a paper seeing virtue in fragmentation and decentralization was somewhat out of step with the times.

Academic economics in the 1980s had turned its attention to the phenomenon of network effects in a system of decentralized coordination, producing a number of important papers that influenced our thinking (David, 1985; Katz and Shapiro, 1985). But that literature was not particularly concerned with questions of organization, and it tended to see networks largely in terms of the demand-side costs and benefits of standardization.

Our paper's concern with modularity arose naturally from the project of articulating the effects on organization form of major autonomous innovation. As Robertson and Alston (1992) argue, the systemic or autonomous character of economic change depends on the way boundaries are drawn between tasks and how the process of production is conceived. And such boundary drawing is not often a matter of conscious design but is rather a process in which conscious intention interacts with historical accident, and in which considerations of organizational power and cognition play a role. But if, for whatever reason, boundaries are drawn and tasks are partitioned in a mostly decomposable way (Simon, in this volume), innovation will be channeled in an autonomous direction. This will lead to a pattern of innovation quite different from that driven by systemic change. But innovation will not therefore be any less rapid or radical. Quite possibly the reverse. And, since modular standards institutionalize the function of coordination (Kindleberger, 1983), the coordination benefits of common ownership and centralized control diminish, thus giving advantage to a network of decentralized producers.

In our account, as in that of the economics literature, network effects on the demand side matter. But we depart from most of the economics literature in seeing demand in Lancasterian terms, that is, as demand for abstract "attributes" that can be provided in a variety of ways. This allows us to unpack the black box a bit and attend to the details of alternative production possibilities. Our more important departure, however, is explicitly to integrate the supply side into our theory.

If, as we argue, the benefits of integration lie importantly in coordination, then pushing some of that coordination function into modular standards levels the playing field for decentralized producers. But our argument is even stronger. If coordination can take place through standardized "interfaces," then a decentralized network will have a clear advantage. This is because such a network can produce a more rapid rate of experimentation. Standardizing components lowers the barriers to entry for those who want to produce components, leading not merely to greater competition in the traditional sense but also to the trying out of a wider variety of alternative approaches. Such a "parallel paths" system leads to what Nelson and Winter (1977) call rapid trial-and-error learning. Baldwin and Clark (2000 and in this volume) have formalized our intuition in the language of finance theory. If we think of each player as offering an option on an experiment, then a network of players each conducting one experiment will outperform a single player conducting the same total number of experiments. This is because the value of a portfolio of options is greater than the value of an option on a portfolio.

There is even reason to think that the centrifugal force of modularity and decentralization is far more important a long-run tendency than is the centripetal force of internal vertical coordination. Langlois (2001) refers to this as the Vanishing Hand hypothesis. Driven by increases in population and income and by the reduction of technological and legal barriers to trade, the Smithian process of the division of labor always tends to lead to finer specialization of function and increased coordination through markets. But the components of that process – technology, organization, and institutions – change at different rates. The managerial revolution Chandler chronicled was the result of such an imbalance, in this case between the systemic coordination needs of high-throughput technologies and the abilities of contemporary markets and contemporary technologies of coordination to meet those needs. With further growth in the extent of the market and improvements in the technology of coordination – including increased standardization and modularity – the central management of vertically integrated production stages is likely increasingly to succumb to the forces of decentralization.

The limits to modularity

Modularity is unquestionably an important principle of design and an important characteristic of many artifacts. In many cases, design or development projects can benefit from carefully programmed procedures that allow the scope of individual activities to proceed within boundaries that correspond to the areas of expertise of design teams. As a number of articles in this collection suggest, it follows that modularity of product components is desirable to allow for the efficient use of modularity in the production of original designs and their subsequent updating. Nevertheless, we feel that the limits of modularity also need to be considered in detail. In particular, we argue that the use of modular systems must take into account not only technical but also human factors. Because they have broader ranges of characteristics than artifacts, people are often not susceptible to being treated as possessors of "interfaces" that can be standardized.[8] Moreover, these human characteristics may be subject to frequent and arbitrary autonomous changes. To the extent, therefore, that people are important parts of technological systems, they may substantially limit the usefulness of principles of modularity, or even render them counterproductive.

To appreciate this point, it is useful to review the evolution of thought on project organization techniques over the last 40 years. In the 1960s, the basic model for many projects was grounded in concepts of sequential interdependence (Thompson, 1967), in which downstream stages follow from those that precede them but there is no feedback or reciprocity. When this is the case, various stages such as planning, development, manufacturing, marketing, and use can all be designed without much reference to what might occur subsequently. From the mid 1980s, however, a number of authors (Stalk and Hout, 1990; Womack et al., 1990; Kodama, 1995; Fransman, 1995) have contended that sequential interdependence is too simple a model of project design and that other forms such as pooled or reciprocal interdependence (Thompson, 1967) provide a better way of organizing development processes. Thus the common practice of "throwing an object [or idea] over the wall" to the next stage of development became discredited. In response to the increased competition that American firms faced from Japanese counterparts, for example, Stalk and Hout (1990) have laid down rules for design teams that include mixed membership across functional areas, co-location of team members, and other ways of achieving quicker and tighter coordination. Smith and Reinertsen (1998) also support the use of cross-functional teams from the beginning of a project to generate cooperation from representatives of the marketing, development, and manufacturing departments, thereby enhancing the chances of generating new products that are both attractive to consumers and capable of being manufactured at a reasonable cost. This can be brought about by, among other things, increasing flows of tacit knowledge through direct interaction among representatives of different fields (von Krogh et al., 2000; Wong and Radcliffe, 2000).

More recently, important supporters of modularity (Baldwin and Clark, 2000; Sanchez, 2000), who are represented in the present volume, have argued that a separation of functions in design and development situations can deliver substantial benefits. They note that tightly-coupled teams may be less efficient than "silos," in which specialists can undertake their work without interference from people who are in other disciplines or concentrate on other stages in the sequence. Sanchez (2000: 118), for instance, has claimed that, "A loose coupling of component knowledge domains can lead to faster, more efficient learning processes by firms focused on developing new components within an industry." This is basically an argument in favor of the classical concept of the division of labor. It goes further than the use of sequential patterns of product development because each stage of a project can be treated as independent of activities at *earlier* as well as at later stages.

However, the use of silos relies on the presence of standardized interfaces so that each module can be developed and modified independently. As a result, it is constraining in contexts where no dominant design architecture has emerged and there can be no agreed interfaces. To counter this, some authors (Quinn et al., 1997; Smith and Reinertsen, 1998) have supported contingency models, in which different arrangements are appropriate depending on circumstances. Quinn et al., for example, contend that complexity is an important factor in the success of what they call "independent collaboration" in innovative situations. "In an increasing number of innovations . . . complexity is so high (as in advanced physics, aerospace, communications, or biotechnology projects) that teams, as they are ordinarily defined, cannot cope as well as collaboration among a large number of relatively independent units" (Quinn et al., 1997: 107). Hence, modularity and silos have vital roles within the larger project context because they provide foci for independent development.

Silos may exist for other reasons. Mindsets and "signature skills" are cited by Leonard-Barton (1995) as important influences on individual approaches to problem solving. As these often derive from professional training, they can be characteristic features of communities of practice (Wenger, 1998; Brown and Duguid, 2000), which help to differentiate the activities of one group from those of others. Another significant influence on the organization of design and development projects is the increased uncertainty of many development situations, especially when there is technological complexity. Woodward (1958, 1965) and Burns and Stalker (1994 [1961]), noted more than four decades ago that organizational arrangements may vary according to the degree of technological sophistication involved. Lawrence and Lorsch (1967) introduced similar insights into the area of research and development. They discovered that organizational structure diverges between research departments and those that engage in more routine activities. Thus, a high degree of differentiation is to be expected in development projects in which several functional areas or disciplines, each with its own mindset, signature skills, and knowledge realm, are expected to contribute to a collaborative venture. In respect to these and other issues, Miller et al. (1995) and Hobday (1998) have recently examined the structuring of complex development projects.

But, as Lawrence and Lorsch (1967), Chandler (1962) and Galbraith (1973) have all discussed, differentiation also requires integration in order to achieve coordination across subteams and subprojects, something that is widely recognized in the project management literature (Wheelwright and Clark, 1992; Clark and Fujimoto, 1991). Without suitable integrating mechanisms, "stickiness" may impede efficient knowledge flows, even within the same organization (Szulanski, 1996).

We believe that, at any given time, human participants play diverse roles and are influenced by a variety of factors, most of which are largely external to a design or development situation. The upshot is that it is often a severe challenge to integrate information within a project. This challenge can take many forms and, in addition to technical factors, involves organizational power, societal attitudes, and other attributes that may not lend themselves to the generation of unprobematical interfaces between aspects of a project. For this reason, we agree with Baldwin and Clark (2000: 2) that there are many influences that affect project development, some of which are subject to human control but others of which are not:

> What we see around us is not the result of some deus ex machina working outside of our influence or control. Human beings, working as individuals and in groups, create the new technologies, the new forms of organization, the new products and markets. To be sure, the consequences of their actions are not always intended or even anticipated. But the "things" themselves – the tangible objects, the devices, the software programs, the production processes, the contracts, the firms and markets – are the fruit of purposeful action. They are "designed."

In contrast to Baldwin and Clark, however, we wish to explore the aspects of development processes that are not subject to design in their sense. As artifacts are generally expected to be used, this implies that the interaction between people and artifacts should be a central consideration in the analysis of design and project development activities.[9] This is true not only of artifacts as a whole, but of individual modules. Therefore, the use of modular principles must allow for problems in achieving standardized interfaces between people and artifacts as well as grasping the advantages that may flow from standardization of interfaces between artifactual components. By looking at both sides – at the aspects of development that both are and are not amenable to design – we will be able to gain a better appreciation of the limits to modularity.

Part of our concern rests on considerations similar those in the Robertson and Alston article of 1992. In an unfairly neglected piece, Ames and Rosenberg (1965), have pointed out that the scope of usefulness of artifacts can vary. Some new technologies are integrative in comparison to earlier types of equipment because they are capable of undertaking work formerly done by several different machines, while other new technologies are differentiating because they apply to narrower ranges of activities than older equipment. Robertson and Alston (1992) have developed a schema based on modular principles to demonstrate that changes in the ranges of activities of equipment are likely to have different effects on industrial relations, depending on how closely they correspond to customary work patterns. They show that some types of technological change are more likely to be retarded or blocked because of worker resistance than are other types of technological change. In effect, Robertson and Alston show that standardized interfaces between equipment and the labor force can smooth change under certain conditions, as the proponents of modularity contend.

However, to leave the argument at this point begs the essential issues (1) of how standardized interfaces are to be created when people are involved in all of their changeability, and (2) of the practical implications for designers of dealing with people who are not informed or cooperative users of new equipment.

In their discussion of repair activities at Xerox, Brown and Duguid (2000) provide a good example of some of the limits to modularity. Xerox attempted to develop a system of diagnostic codes for its copying machines that would eliminate the need for repair persons to fossick around inside the machines to find the sources of problems. Essentially, repair problems were to be reduced to a suite of syllogisms in which the appearance of diagnostic code "x" would lead to repair activity "y." An additional "advantage" was that this would make each repair person independent of the others. As the code books would include everything that they needed to know, repair persons would never need to meet each other and there would be no need for common office space and other facilities. In the event, however, this independence was not achieved; the repair persons continued to meet on their own time, over breakfast and lunch, to discuss faults that were not treated adequately in the code books.

The Xerox case illustrates two points. The first, which we will not enlarge on, is the well-known problem of transmitting tacit knowledge. The second point – that design faults in the system could have been handled more effectively if the designers and users had worked together at various stages in the development process – is an excellent example of a major limitation of modularity in design activities.

Design projects may be thought of as collections of communities of practice.[10] According to Wenger (1998: 45):

> Over time, . . . collective learning results in practices that reflect both the pursuit of our enterprises and attendant social relations. Their practices are thus the property of a kind of community created over time by the sustained pursuit of a shared enterprise. It makes sense, therefore, to call these kinds of communities *communities of practice* [emphasis in original].

Each community of practice is centered on a given set of activities and its members are usually in direct contact with each other. In addition, Wenger discusses constellations of practice, which are larger groups who undertake similar activities but are not normally in direct contact. Heart surgeons in the same hospital or organic

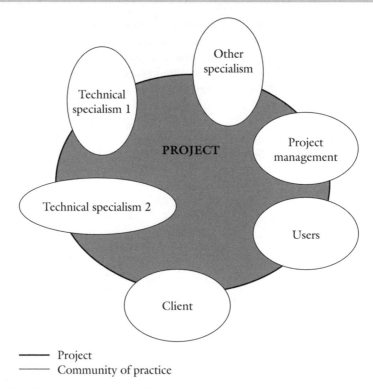

──── Project
──── Community of practice

Figure 3.6 Communities of practice in a development project.

chemists in the laboratory would belong to communities of practice, but heart surgeons or organic chemists in general would be part of constellations of practice.

Projects may therefore be conceived of as in figure 3.6, in which each group of specialists is in its own community of practice. This has clear advantages when specialized work is undertaken because it allows people with similar skills to concentrate their talents on particular problems. When work can be modularized in this way, transaction costs are reduced because communication is easier among members of a similar community of practice, who use similar terminology, than in multi-function teams. In addition, because the communities of practice extend in varying degrees beyond the boundaries of the project, they are able to import valuable knowledge from their wider networks.

However, the chances of a project succeeding may well be improved if the interested groups cooperate in both the initial planning stages and during implementation. Before proceeding very far, it is necessary to ask who is interested in the outcome(s) of the project, and what do they hope to achieve? How can their needs and preferences be met? Developers need answers to these questions before they begin to design prototypes. But involvement in the implementation phase is also needed, especially if goals shift during the course of a project. Furthermore, changes in goals may be accompanied by changes in the identities of the interested actors. New groups of users may need to be considered and incorporated in the development process.

Therefore, the final stages of the development and the early implementation phases are also times when close communication with potential users is likely pay off. This can be particularly important when the users are internal to the firm that has undertaken the development. As Leonard-Barton and Sinha (1993: 1134) argue:

> In the case of technology transfer inside a firm, the interaction of developers and users is not only possible, but may also be critical to success, since the technology is being developed for an internal, customized market. If internal developers fail to satisfy internal users, they do not usually have recourse to alternative markets for their products.

In the implementation phase, close communication between developers and users assists the transfer of two new types of knowledge that are generated *in the course of* the project. The first kind of learning flows from the efforts of the developers within their communities of practice, when they may not only investigate answers to the needs of their clients and potential users, but also encounter fresh insights on the nature of those needs. In addition, during the implementation phase, *users* can judge the suitability of the deliverable to *their* communities of practice, in the context of their existing work practices and artifacts. Therefore, a period of mutual adaptation is often required in order to fit the deliverable smoothly and efficiently into the environment of the users (Leonard-Barton, 1988; Tyre, 1991).

Timing can be vital at this phase as the "window of opportunity" (Tyre and Orlikowski, 1994) may be brief in the implementation phase. Both users and developers have a tendency to lose interest in refining the deliverable as implementation proceeds. Because users need to return quickly to their regular activities, they may find it easier to accept suboptimal performance from the deliverable than endure extended delays. Developers also become less willing to engage in adjustment as their attention turns to different assignments (Tyre and Orlikowski, 1994). Therefore, the need for learning and the communication of knowledge should be recognized, planned for and acted upon before it is no longer practical to implement the use of the deliverable efficiently and effectively.

Conclusions

The literature on modularity in design and development projects has made a highly important contribution to the project management literature, and acted as a corrective to excessive emphasis on development teams. But now that modularity has become widely accepted, more attention should be paid to exploring mixed modes of project organization. Further exploration is needed of the principles governing when communities of practice working in silos are superior to, or inferior to, development teams. An especially important contribution would flow from the explicit inclusion of human beings in the discussion, with recognition given to the effects of differential knowledge, political tactics, and many other essential human characteristics on the establishment and use of standardized interfaces.

NOTES

1 As one indication of the rapid passage of time, we might note that our trans-Pacific collaborations on the original paper were conducted in part over Bitnet, a now-forgotten precursor component of the Internet.
2 We use the term capabilities in the sense of Richardson (1972), and we see our work as broadly located within the modern capabilities literature.
3 This usage follows Teece (1986). The opposite of a systemic innovation is an *autonomous* one, in which change can proceed in one stage of production without requiring coordination with other stages.
4 Another way to put it is that dynamic transaction costs – or, more generally, dynamic *governance* costs – are the costs of not having the capabilities you need when you need them (Langlois, 1992).
5 It is significant that, once the contours of the mass-production process became clear, Ford found it desirable to (re)decentralize the production of parts, albeit within the context of the Ford organization (Ford and Crowther, 1923: 83–4). These capabilities also eventually diffused outside of Ford, both to competitors and to the network of independent suppliers who sprang up to serve the replacement-parts market.
6 For a perspective on the intellectual – as well as the actual – history of Japanese-American competition in the context of semiconductors, see Langlois and Steinmueller (1999).
7 On the other hand, 1990 also saw the publication of Michael E. Porter's *The Competitive Advantage of Nations*, which further focused attention on the relationship between firm-level and national capabilities. Porter's discussion of industrial districts corresponds to many of our own arguments. And, as we discuss at some length in Langlois and Robertson (1995), the "flexible specialization" literature of the 1980s (Piore and Sabel, 1984; Sabel and Zeitlin, 1985; Best, 1990) also provided some counterpoint to the Chandlerian current.
8 The professions are an example of modular production in which human interfaces are central. Langlois and Savage (2001) argue that, in professional production, standardization occurs importantly in professional training, which equips professionals with a more-or-less standardized "toolkit" from which they can choose routines. But professionals retain large amounts of discretion in order to be able to deal with non-routine events. Task boundaries as, for example, between physicians and nurses or between internists and surgeons are another aspect of modularity in the profession, but those boundaries are often permeable and changing at the margin.
9 In a number of places, Baldwin and Clark (2000) discuss the roles of users and other human beings in aspects of design and development processes. Our argument is not that they, and other contributors to the modularity literature, ignore this issue but that they severely understate its importance.
10 Much of this discussion draws on material in Garrety et al., (2001).

REFERENCES

Ames, Edward and Rosenberg, Nathan (1965). "The Progressive Division and Specialization of Industries," *Journal of Development Studies*, 1: 363–83.
Baldwin, Carliss Y. and Clark, Kim B. (2000). *Design Rules*, Vol. 1, *The Power of Modularity*, Cambridge, Ma.: MIT Press.
Best, Michael (1990). *The New Competition: Institutions of Industrial Restructuring*, Cambridge, Ma.: Harvard University Press.

Bresnahan, Timothy F., and Greenstein, Shane (1996). "The Competitive Crash in Large-Scale Commercial Computing," in Ralph Landau, Timothy Taylor, and Gavin Wright (eds.), *The Mosaic of Economic Growth*, Stanford: Stanford University Press.

Brown, John Seely and Duguid, Paul (2000). *The Social Life of Information*, Boston: Harvard Business School Press.

Burns, Tom and Stalker, G. M. (1994 [1961]). *The Management of Innovation*, Oxford: Oxford University Press.

Chandler, Alfred D. (1962). *Strategy and Structure: Chapters in the History of Industrial Enterprise*, Cambridge, Ma.: MIT Press.

Chandler, Alfred D. (1977). *The Visible Hand: the Managerial Revolution in American Business*, Cambridge, Ma.: The Belknap Press.

Chandler, Alfred D. (1990). *Scale and Scope: the Dynamics of Industrial Capitalism*, Cambridge, Ma.: The Belknap Press.

Clark, Kim B. and Takahiro, Fujimoto (1991). *Product Development Performance: Strategy, Organization, and Management in the World Auto Industry*, Boston: Harvard Business School Press.

David, Paul A. (1985). "Clio and the Economics of QWERTY," *American Economic Review*, 75(2): 332–7.

Ford, Henry, with Crowther, Samuel (1923). *My Life and Work*, Garden City: Doubleday.

Fransman, Martin (1995). *Japan's Computer and Communications Industry: The Evolution of Industrial Giants and Global Competitiveness*, Oxford: Oxford University Press.

Galbraith, Jay (1973). *Designing Complex Organizations*, Reading, Ma.: Addison-Wesley.

Garrety, Karin, Robertson, Paul L., and Badham, Richard (2001). "Communities of Practice, Actor Networks and Learning in Development Projects," paper presented to the ECIS Conference on The Future of Innovation Studies, Eindhoven, September 21–3.

Hobday, Mike (1998). "Product Complexity, Innovation and Industrial Organisation," *Research Policy*, 26: 689–710.

Katz, Michael, and Shapiro, Carl (1985). "Network Externalities, Competition, and Compatibility," *American Economic Review*, 75(3): 424–40.

Kindleberger, Charles P. (1983). "Standards as Public, Collective and Private Goods," *Kyklos*, 36(3): 377–96.

Kodama, Fumio (1995). *Emerging Patterns of Innovation: Sources of Japan's Technological Edge*, Boston: Harvard Business School Press.

Krogh, Georg von, Ichijo, Kazuo, and Nonaka, Ikujiro (2000). *Enabling Knowledge Creation: How to Unlock the Mystery of Tacit Knowledge and Release the Power of Innovation*, New York: Oxford University Press.

Langlois, Richard N. (1988). "Economic Change and the Boundaries of the Firm," *Journal of Institutional and Theoretical Economics*, 144(4): 635–57.

Langlois, Richard N. (1992). "Transaction-cost Economics in Real Time," *Industrial and Corporate Change*, 1(1): 99–127.

Langlois, Richard N. (2001). "The Vanishing Hand: the Changing Dynamics of Industrial capitalism," Working Paper 01–01, Center for Institutions, Organizations, and Markets, University of Connecticut. Available at: http://www.sp.uconn.edu/~langlois/Vanishing.html

Langlois, Richard N., and Robertson, P. L. (1989). "Explaining Vertical Integration: Lessons from the American Automobile Industry," *Journal of Economic History*, 49: 361–75.

Langlois, Richard N., and Robertson, P. L. (1995). *Firms, Markets, and Economic Change: A Dynamic Theory of Business Institutions*, London: Routledge, 1995.

Langlois, Richard N., and Savage, Deborah A. (2001). "Standards, Modularity, and Innovation: the Case of Medical Practice," in Raghu Garud and Peter Karnøe (eds.), *Path Dependence and Path Creation*, Hillsdale: Lawrence Erlbaum, 149–68.

Langlois, Richard N., and Steinmueller, W. Edward (1999). "The Evolution of Competitive Advantage in the Worldwide Semiconductor Industry, 1947–1996," in David C. Mowery and Richard R. Nelson (eds.), *The Sources of Industrial Leadership*, New York: Cambridge University Press, 19–78.

Lawrence, Paul R. and Lorsch, Jay W. (1967). *Organization and Environment: Managing Differentiation and Integration*, Boston: Division of Research, Graduate School of Business Administration, Harvard University.

Leonard-Barton, Dorothy (1988). "Implementation as Mutual Adaptation of Technology and Organization," *Research Policy*, 17: 251–67.

Leonard-Barton, Dorothy (1995). *Wellsprings of Knowledge: Building and Sustaining the Sources of Innovation*, Boston: Harvard Business School Press.

Leonard-Barton, Dorothy and Sinha, Deepak K. (1993). "Developer-User Interaction and User Satisfaction in Internal Technology Transfer," *Academy of Management Journal*, 36(5): 1125–39.

Miller, Roger, Hobday, Mike, Leroux-Demers, Thierry, and Olleros, Xavier (1995). "Innovation in Complex Systems Industries: The Case of Flight Simulation," *Industrial and Corporate Change*, 4(2): 363–400.

Nelson, Richard R. and Winter, Sidney G. (1977). "In Search of More Useful Theory of Innovation," *Research Policy*, 5: 36–76.

Piore, Michael J., and Sabel, Charles F. (1984). *The Second Industrial Divide*, New York: Basic Books.

Porter, Michael E. (1990). *The Competitive Advantage of Nations*, New York: The Free Press.

Quinn, James Brian, Baruch, Jordan J., and Zien, Karen Anne (1997). *Innovation Explosion: Using Intellect and Software to Revolutionize Growth Strategies*, New York: Free Press.

Richardson, G. B. (1972). "The Organisation of Industry," *Economic Journal*, 82: 883–96.

Robertson, Paul L. and Alston, Lee J. (1992). "Technological Choice and the Organization of Work in Capitalist Firms," *Economic History Review*, 45: 330–49.

Sabel, Charles F., and Zeitlin, Jonathan (1985). "Historical Alternatives to Mass Production: Politics, Markets, and Technology in Nineteenth-Century Industrialization," *Past and Present*, 108: 133–76.

Sanchez, Ron (2000). "Product and Process Architectures in the Management of Knowledge Resources," in Nicolai J. Foss and Paul L. Robertson (eds.), *Resources, Technology and Strategy: Explorations in the Resource-Based Perspective*, London: Routledge, 100–22.

Smith, Preston G. and Reinertsen, Donald G. (1998). *Developing Products in Half the Time: New Rules, New Tools*, New York: Van Nostrand Reinhold.

Stalk, George, Jr. and Hout, Thomas M. (1990). *Competing Against Time: How Time-Based Competition is Reshaping Global Markets*, New York: Free Press.

Szulanski, Gabriel (1996). "Exploring Internal Stickiness: Impediments to the Transfer of Best Practice within the Firm," *Strategic Management Journal*, 17, Special Issue: 27–43.

Teece, David J. (1986). "Profiting from Technological Innovation: Implications for Integration, Collaboration, Licensing, and Public Policy," *Research Policy*, 15: 285–305.

Thompson, James D. (1967). *Organizations in Action: Social Science Bases of Administrative Theory*, New York: McGraw-Hill.

Tyre, Marcie J. (1991). "Managing the Introduction of New Process Technology: International Differences in a Multi-Plant Network," *Research Policy*, 20: 57–76.

Tyre, Marcie J. and Orlikowski, Wanda J. (1994). "Windows of Opportunity: Temporal Patterns of Technological Adaptation in Organizations," *Organizational Science*, 5(1): 98–118.

Wenger, Etienne (1998). *Communities of Practice: Learning, Meaning, and Identity*, Cambridge: Cambridge University Press.

Wheelwright, Steven C. and Clark, Kim B. (1992). *Revolutionizing Product Development: Quantum Leaps in Speed, Efficiency, and Quality*, New York: The Free Press.

Womack, James P., Jones, Daniel T., and Roos, Daniel (1990). *The Machine that Changed the World*, New York: Rawson Associates.

Wong, W. L. P. and Radcliffe, D. F. (2000). "The Tacit Nature of Design Knowledge," *Technology Analysis and Strategic Management*, 13(4): 93–512.

Woodward, Joan (1958). *Management and Technology*, London: HMSO.

Woodward, Joan (1965). *Industrial Organization: Theory and Practice*, London: Oxford University Press.

PART TWO

MODULARITY AND ARCHITECTURES

CHAPTER FOUR

THE ROLE OF PRODUCT ARCHITECTURE IN THE MANUFACTURING FIRM

KARL ULRICH

1. INTRODUCTION

Product architecture is the scheme by which the function of a product is allocated to physical components. This paper argues that the architecture of the product can be a key driver of the performance of the manufacturing firm, that firms have substantial latitude in choosing a product architecture, and that the architecture of the product is therefore important in managerial decision making.

Product architecture is particularly relevant to the research and development (R & D) function of a company, because architectural decisions are made during the early phases of the innovation process where the R & D function often plays a lead role. While these architectural decisions are linked to the overall performance of the firm, they are also linked to specific R & D issues, including the ease of product change, the division between internal and external development resources, the ability to achieve certain types of technical product performance, and the way development is managed and organized.

In making these arguments, the paper builds on knowledge from several somewhat disparate research communities: design theory, software engineering, operations management and management of product development. My approach is to synthesize fragments of existing theory and knowledge into a new framework for understanding product architecture, and to use this framework to illuminate, with examples, how the architecture of the product relates to manufacturing firm performance. My intention is that industrial practitioners will benefit from the argument and develop a stronger conceptual foundation for decision making, and that researchers will benefit from the argument through an enhanced ability to formulate focused research questions around these issues.

The paper consists of eight remaining sections. Section 2 defines product architecture. Section 3 provides a typology of architectures. Sections 4 through 8 articulate the linkages among product architecture, product change, product variety, component standardization, product performance and the management of product development. Finally, Section 9 summarizes the key points, discusses how to establish a product architecture, and identifies three promising research directions.

2.   What is Product Architecture?

In informal terms, the architecture of the product is the scheme by which the function of the product is allocated to physical components. I define product architecture more precisely as: (1) the arrangement of *functional elements*; (2) the mapping from *functional elements to physical components*; (3) the specification of the *interfaces* among interacting physical components.

This section expands on this definition using the example of a *trailer* to illustrate the key points.

2.1   The arrangement of functional elements

The function of a product is what it does as opposed to what the physical characteristics of the product are. There have been several attempts in the design theory community to create formal languages for describing function [7], and there have been modest successes in narrow domains of application such as electro- and fluid-mechanical systems and digital circuits [33]. There have also been efforts to create informal functional languages to facilitate the practice of design [19, 11]. These languages are frequently used to create diagrams consisting of functional elements, expressed as linguistic terms like "convert energy", connected by links indicating the exchange of signals, materials, forces and energy. Some authors of informal functional languages provide a vocabulary of standard functional elements, while others rely on users to devise their own. Functional elements are sometimes called *functional requirements* [28] or *functives* [8], and the function diagram has been variously called a *function structure* [19, 11], a *functional description* and a *schematic description* [33]. Consistent with Pahl and Beitz, and Hubka and Eder, I call the arrangement of functional elements and their interconnections, a *function structure*. An example of a function structure for a trailer is shown in figure 4.1.

Function structures can be created at different levels of abstraction [8]. At the most general level, the function structure for a trailer might consist of a single functional element – "expand cargo capacity". At a more detailed level, the function structure could be specified as consisting of the collection of functional elements shown in figure 4.1, i.e. *connect to vehicle, protect cargo from weather, minimize air drag, support cargo loads, suspend trailer structure*, and *transfer loads to road*.

As they are expressed in more detail, function structures embody more assumptions about the physical working principles on which the product is based. For example, expand cargo capacity does not assume the trailer will be a device towed over the road (the trailer could be a lighter-than-air device), while the more detailed function structure shown in figure 4.1 does embody this assumption. For this reason,

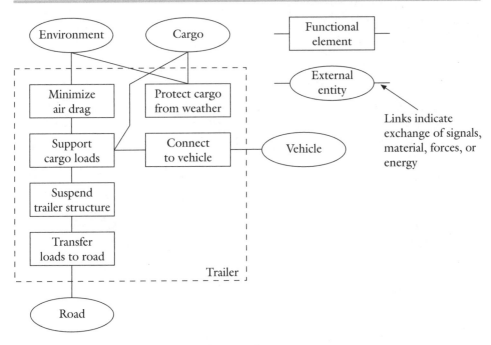

Figure 4.1   A function structure for a trailer.

two products that at the most general level do the same thing may have different function structures when described at a more detailed level.

While most functional elements involve the exchange of signals, materials, forces and energy, some elements do not interact with other functional elements. An example of such an element might be *harmonize aesthetically with vehicle.*

2.2   The mapping from functional elements to physical components

The second part of the product architecture is the mapping from functional elements to physical components. A discrete physical product consists of one or more components. For clarity, I define a component as a separable physical part of subassembly. However, for many of the arguments in the paper, a component can be thought of as any distinct region of the product, allowing the inclusion of a software subroutine in the definition of a component. Similarly, distinct regions of an integrated circuit, although not actually separate physical parts, could be thought of as components.

Physical components implement the functional elements of the product. The mapping between functional elements and components may be one-to-one, many-to-one, or one-to-many. Two different trailer designs and their associated mappings of functional elements to components are shown in figures 4.2 and 4.3.

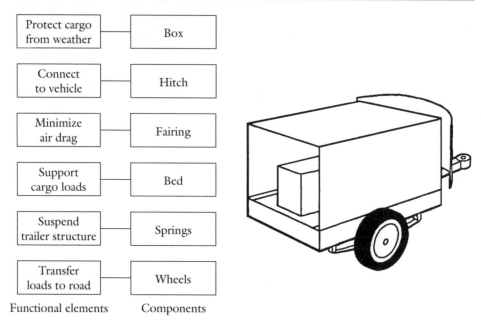

Figure 4.2 A modular trailer architecture exhibiting a one-to-one mapping from functional elements to physical components.

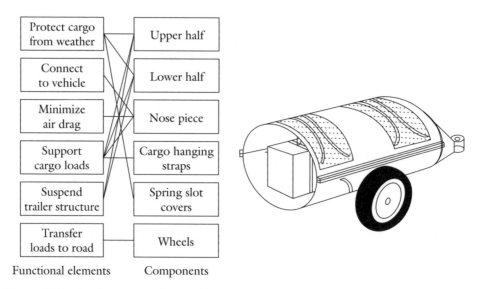

Figure 4.3 An integral trailer architecture exhibiting a complex mapping from functional elements to physical components.

The upper and lower halves of the trailer have slots cut in them. The strip of material remaining between two slots acts as a leaf spring. The cargo is hung by straps from the two springs in the upper half. The axle is attached to the spring in the lower half. Covers, shown shaded, are attached over the slots. The nose piece is the component containing the trailer hitch.

2.3   The specification of the interfaces between interacting physical components

By definition, interacting components are connected by some physical interface. Interfaces may involve geometric connections between two components, as with a gear on a shaft, or may involve non-contact interactions, as with the infrared communication link between a remote control and a television set. An interface specification defines the protocol for the primary interactions across the component interfaces, and the mating geometry in cases where there is a geometric connection.

For example, one of the interfaces for the trailer shown in figure 4.2 is between the box and the bed. The specification of the interface includes the dimensions of the contact surfaces between the two components, the positions and sizes of the bolt holes, and the maximum force the interface is expected to sustain.

Note that interfaces may be specified to adhere to a standard protocol. Examples of protocols that have been standardized across many different manufacturers' products are: SCSI (small computer systems interface), tyre/rim standards for automobiles, a stereo "phono" jack, a garden hose connection thread and a "ball-type" trailer hitch. Manufacturers sometimes choose to adopt a common protocol for interfaces used within their own product line, even though the interface may not adhere to an external standard.

3.   A TYPOLOGY OF PRODUCT ARCHITECTURES

A typology of architectures provides a vocabulary for discussing the implications of the choice of architecture on the performance of the manufacturing firm. The first distinction in the typology is between a *modular* architecture and an *integral* architecture. A modular architecture includes a one-to-one mapping from functional elements in the function structure to the physical components of the product, and specifies de-coupled interfaces between components. An integral architecture includes a complex (non one-to-one) mapping from functional elements to physical components and/or coupled interfaces between components.

3.1   Types of mappings from functional elements to physical components

The two trailers in figures 4.2 and 4.3 illustrate two extreme examples of mappings from functional elements to components. One trailer embodies a one-to-one mapping between functional elements and components. Assuming that the component interfaces are de-coupled (more on this later), this trailer has a modular architecture. In the field of software engineering, the notion of module *cohesion* or *strength* is similar to the one-to-one mapping of functional elements to components [25]. The other trailer embodies a mapping in which several functional elements are each implemented by more than one component, and in which several components each implement more than one functional element (a complex mapping). This trailer has an integral architecture. The phenomenon of a single component implementing several functional elements is called *function sharing* in the design theory community and is described in detail by Ulrich and Seering [34].

To some extent, whether or not functional elements map to more than one component depends on the level of detail at which the components and functional elements are considered. For example, if every washer, screw and filament of wire is considered a component, then each functional element will map to many components. In order to more precisely define what a one-to-one mapping between functional elements and components means, consider a product disassembled to the level of individual piece parts. (This level of disassembly has been called the *iota* level.[1]) In general, many possible subassemblies[2] could be created from these iota parts. If there is a partitioning of the set of iota parts into subassemblies such that there is a one-to-one mapping between these subassemblies and functional elements, then the product exhibits the one-to-one mapping characteristic of a modular architecture.

3.2 Interface coupling

In addition to one-to-one mappings, modular architectures include de-coupled component interfaces. Two components are coupled if a change made to one component requires a change to the other component in order for the overall product to work correctly. Two physical components connected by an interface are almost always coupled to some extent; there is almost always a change that can be made to one component that will require a change to the other component. (For example, arbitrarily increasing the operating temperature of one component by 1,000°C will require a change to nearly any imaginable neighbouring component.) However, in practical terms, coupling is relevant only to changes that modify the component in some useful way. (See [25] for a detailed discussion of the different types of coupling encountered in software.)

Figure 4.4 illustrates an example of an interface between two components, the bed and the box from the trailer in figure 4.2. The coupled interface embodies a dependency between the thickness of the bed and the vertical gap in the box

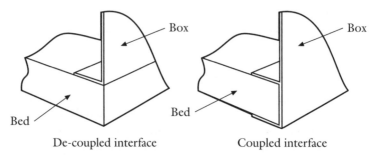

De-coupled interface   Coupled interface

Figure 4.4 Two example interfaces between the trailer box and trailer bed; one de-coupled, the other coupled.
The coupled interface requires that the box be changed whenever a change in the thickness of the bed is made to accommodate increased structural loading.

connection slot. The de-coupled interface involves no such dependency. For the coupled interface, when the thickness of the bed must be changed to accommodate a change in the cargo load rating, the box must change as well. Although the example in figure 4.4 is geometric, coupling may also be based on other physical phenomena, such as heat or magnetism.

3.3 Types of modular architectures

I divide modular architectures into three subtypes: *slot, bus* and *sectional*. Because each of the three subtypes is modular, each embodies a one-to-one mapping between functional elements and components, and the component interfaces are de-coupled; the differences among these subtypes lie in the way the component interactions are organized.

3.3.1 Slot

Each of the interfaces between components in a slot architecture is of a different type from the others, so that the various components in the product cannot be inter-changed. An automobile radio is an example of a component in a slot architecture. The radio implements exactly one function and is de-coupled from surrounding components, but its interface is different from any of the other components in the vehicle (e.g. radios and speedometers have different types of interfaces to the instrument panel).

3.3.2 Bus

In a bus architecture, there is a common bus to which the other physical components connect via the same type of interface. A common example of a component in a bus architecture would be an expansion card for a personal computer. Non-electronic products can also be built around a bus architecture. Track lighting, shelving systems with rails and adjustable roof racks for automobiles all embody a bus architecture. The bus is not necessarily linear; I also include components connected by a multi-dimensional network in the bus subtype.

3.3.3 Sectional

In a sectional architecture, all interfaces are of the same type and there is no single element to which all the other components attach. The assembly is built up by con-necting the components to each other via identical interfaces. Many piping systems adhere to a sectional architecture, as do sectional sofas, office partitions and some computer systems.

Figures 4.5 to 4.7 illustrate this typology for the trailer example, for a desk, and for a personal computer. I intend for the typology to provide a vocabulary for describing different product architectures. The types shown are idealized; most real

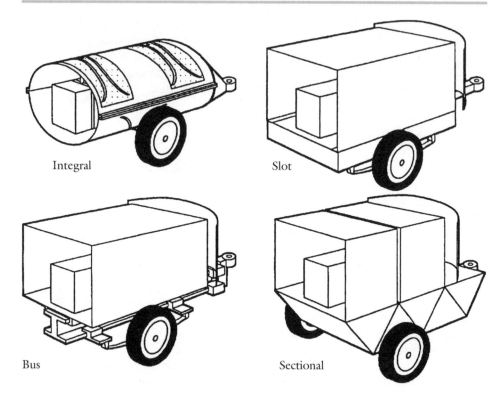

Integral   Slot

Bus   Sectional

Figure 4.5 Four trailer architectures.

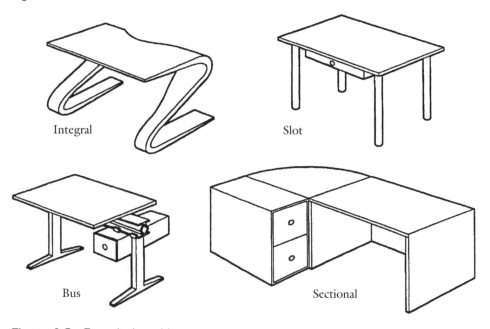

Integral   Slot

Bus   Sectional

Figure 4.6 Four desk architectures.

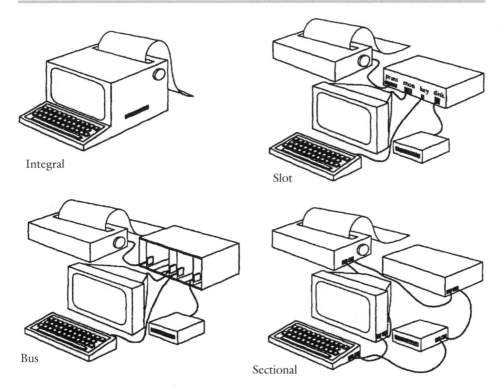

Figure 4.7 Four personal computer architectures.

products exhibit some combination of the characteristics of several types. Products may also exhibit characteristics of different types depending on whether one observes the product at the level of the overall final assembly or at the level of individual piece parts and subassemblies.

A firm can design and manufacture products without ever explicitly creating a product architecture or even a function structure. In the domains of software and electronic systems, the idea of a function structure (labelled as a *schematic, flow chart*, etc.) is prevalent in industrial practice [17, 25]. However, the notion of a function structure is just beginning to be disseminated in many mechanical domains. (See for example Ullman [30] for a recent mechanical design textbook adopting the idea.) If a product architecture is explicitly established during the product development process, this step usually occurs during the system-level design phase of the process after the basic technological working principles have been established, but before the design of components and subsystems has begun.

The examples in figures 4.5 to 4.7 suggest that firms possess substantial latitude in choosing a product architecture, although the architecture of many existing products may be less the result of deliberate choice and more the result of incremental evolution. Several scholars have prescribed a modular architecture as ideal. For example, Suh [28] argues that a modular architecture is an axiom of good design, and Alexander [1] presents an "optimal" design methodology, ensuring a lack of coupling between components. (Although neither author argues his point in my terminology.) I maintain that while product architecture is extremely important, no single architecture is optimal in all cases. The balance of the paper discusses the potential linkages between the architecture of the product and a set of issues of managerial importance. A recognition and understanding of these linkages is a prerequisite to the effective choice of an architecture for a particular product.

4. PRODUCT CHANGE

This section focuses on two types of product change: change to a particular artifact over its lifecycle (e.g. replacing a worn tyre) and change to a product line or model over successive generations (e.g. substituting the next generation suspension system in the whole product line). Section 5 and Section 6 treat two closely related concepts: product variety and component standardization.

4.1 Product architecture determines how the product can be changed

The minimum change that can be made to a product is a change to one component. The architecture of the product determines which functional elements of the product will be influenced by a change to a particular component, and which components must be changed to achieve a desired change to a functional element of the product. At one extreme, modular products allow each functional element of the product to be changed independently by changing only the corresponding component. At the other extreme, fully integral products require changes to every component to effect change in any single functional element. The architecture of a product is therefore closely linked to the ease with which a change to a product can be implemented. Here we consider how this linkage manifests itself in implementing change within the life of a particular artifact and in implementing change over several product generations.

4.2 Change within the life of a particular artifact

Products frequently undergo some change during their life. Some of the motives for this change are:

- Upgrade: As technological capabilities or user needs evolve, some products can accommodate this evolution through upgrades. Examples include changing the processor board in a computer printer or replacing a pump in a cooling system with a more powerful model. Some products, such as the Compaq Deskpro/M, have been promoted based on their ease of upgrade [26].
- Add-ons: Many products are sold by a manufacturer as a basic unit to which the user adds components, often produced by third parties, as needed. This type of change is common in the personal computer industry (e.g. the addition of

third-party mass storage devices to a basic computer). See Langlois and Robertson [14] for a thorough description of several such cases.

- Adaptation: Some long-lived products may be used in several different-use environments, requiring adaptation. For example, machine tools may have to be converted from 220V to 110V power. Engines may have to be converted from a gasoline to a propane fuel supply.
- Wear: Physical features of a product may deteriorate with use, necessitating replacement of the worn components to extend the useful life of the product. For example, many razors allow dull blades to be replaced, tyres on vehicles can usually be replaced, most rotational bearings can be replaced, and many appliance motors can be replaced.
- Consumption: Some products consume materials that are typically replaceable. For example, copiers and printers frequently contain toner cartridges, cameras contain film cartridges, glue guns contain glue sticks, torches contain gas cartridges, and watches contain batteries.
- Flexibility in use: Some products can be configured by the user to exhibit different capabilities. For example, many 35 mm cameras can be used with different lens and flash options, some boats can be used with several awning options, and some fishing rods accommodate several rod-reel configurations.

In each of these cases, changes to the product are most easily accommodated through modular architectures. The modular architecture allows the required changes that are typically associated with the product's function to be localized to the minimum possible number of components.

Although consumption and wear is frequently accommodated through a modular design with replaceable parts, another popular strategy is to dramatically lower the cost of the entire product, often through an integral architecture, such that the entire product can be discarded or recycled. For example, disposable razors, cameras and cigarette lighters have all been commercially successful products, and disposable pens dominate the marketplace. Section 7 explains how integral architectures can allow for a lower cost product under certain conditions.

4.3 Change across generations of the product

When a new model of an existing product is introduced to the marketplace, the product almost always embodies some functional change relative to the previous product. (In relatively rare cases, the firm changes only the name of the product.) The architecture of the product has profound implications for a firm's ability to implement this product change. For products with a modular architecture, desired changes to a functional element can be localized to one component. Products with integral architectures require changes to several components in order to implement changes to the product's function. This observation helps to explain industrial practice in the area of generational change.

For example, the Sony Walkman architecture allows the tape transport mechanism to be reused in many successive models, while the enclosure parts can be easily changed for each new model [24]. *Virtual design* is a term Sanderson [23] uses for this superposition of several product cycles involving changes to only a few components onto the longer life cycle of a technological platform. This virtual design is enabled by the modular product architecture exhibited by the Walkman at the level of major subassemblies.

Sanchez and Sudharshan [22] describe a development strategy they call *real-time market research*. Under this scheme, the firm introduces a product, gauges the market response, then develops and launches an incrementally-improved product extremely quickly. A modular architecture is essential to being able to quickly change the product in this way. The benefits of a modular architecture for exploring a market and fine-tuning a product are also described in Langlois and Robertson [14].

Cusumano and Nobeoka [4], in summarizing several previous studies of the world automobile industry, identify *project scope* – the percentage of unique components a manufacturer designs from scratch in-house – as a key variable relating to product development performance. The architecture of the product, and the degree of modularity in particular, dictate how much project scope will be required to achieve a particular level of functional change.

In software engineering, change is notoriously difficult; Korson and Vaishnavi [13] find strong empirical evidence that modular software architectures facilitate program change. Change to a product is not always confined to activities by a single manufacturer. In some markets, such as home entertainment, users create *virtual products* by assembling collections of products provided by diverse manufacturers. Modularity at the level of the entire system, when combined with standard interfaces, allows for the virtual product to evolve and change through independent actions by individual manufacturers [14].

5.   PRODUCT VARIETY

I define product variety as the diversity of products that a production system provides to the marketplace. Product variety has emerged as an important element of manufacturing competitiveness. Based on survey responses from 255 managers, Pine [20, 21] provides empirical evidence that both market turbulence and the need for product variety have increased substantially over the past decade and argues that variety will continue to increase in the future. Variety is also one of the elements of "lean production", which has been identified as a successful approach to automobile manufacturing [38].

High variety can be produced by any system at some cost. For example, an auto manufacturer could create different fender shapes for each individual vehicle by creating different sets of stamping dies, each of which would be used only once. Such a system is technically feasible, but prohibitively expensive. The challenge is to create the desired product variety economically.

The ability of a firm to economically produce variety is frequently credited to manufacturing *flexibility*. (See Suarez et al. [27] for a comprehensive review of the literature on flexibility.) When viewed at the level of the entire manufacturing system, this is a tautology – if a system is economically producing variety it is to some extent flexible. However, manufacturing flexibility is often equated with the flexibility of the process equipment in the plant (e.g. computer-numerical controlled milling machines), or with flexible assembly systems (e.g. programmable electronic chip insertion equipment). (See for example [12].) In this context, a flexible production process incurs small fixed costs for each output variant (e.g. low tooling costs) and small changeover costs between output variants (e.g. low set-up times). This notion of flexibility is consistent with Upton's definition [35]: ". . . the ability to change or adapt with little effort, time, or penalty". I argue that much of a manufacturing system's ability to create variety resides not with the flexibility of the equipment in the factory, but with the architecture of the product. This section shows how both the flexibility of the factory production process equipment and the product architecture interact to contribute to the ability to economically create product variety.

Variety is only meaningful to customers if the functionality of the product varies in some way.[3] This variation may be in terms of the set of functional elements implemented by the product (does the trailer protect the cargo from the environment at all?), or in terms of the specific performance characteristics of the product relative to a particular functional element (is the environmental protection *normal* or *heavy duty?*). Consider the trailer example. Assume customers' needs can be neatly divided in the following ways. Some customers want to minimize air drag, some do not. Two types of vehicle connection and three alternatives for the type of environmental protection are desired. Three alternatives are also desired for both the structural load rating and for the ride quality of the suspension system.[4] Under these assumptions, if variety incurred no cost, the firm would offer 108 distinct trailers to the marketplace ($2 \times 2 \times 3 \times 3 \times 3 = 108$).

If the firm uses the modular product architecture shown in figure 4.2, all of the 108 different trailers can be created from a total of only 12 different types of components: a single type of fairing (which is either included with the trailer or not), two types of hitches, three types of boxes, three types of beds, three types of spring assemblies and one type of wheel assembly. Because each functional element maps to exactly one physical component, and because the interfaces are de-coupled, the variety can be created by forming 108 combinations from a set of 12 component building blocks. I am not the first to observe that variety can be created by combinations of building blocks. In fact, this combinatorial approach to variety is part of a five-step technique called (somewhat confusingly) Variety Reduction Program [29]. Nevins and Whitney [18] also give several examples of such combinatorial assembly of product variants. The modularity of the product allows the variety to be created at final assembly, the last stage of the production process. Some firms are even delaying a portion of the final assembly until the product has moved through the distribution system and is ready to be shipped to a customer. This strategy has been called *postponement* [15].

If the firm wishes to offer all 108 variants and uses the integral product architecture shown in figure 4.3, 73 different types of components will be required: 27 types of upper halves, 27 types of lower halves, 12 types of nose pieces, three types of cargo hanging straps, three types of spring slot covers and one type of wheel assembly. Because in many instances each component implements several functional elements, there must be as many types of each component as there are desired combinations of the functional elements it implements. For example, to provide all of the different desired combinations of the two vehicle connection types, the two types of drag reduction, and the three load ratings, 12 distinct types of nose pieces will be required because the nose piece contributes to all three of the functional elements associated with the options.

5.1   Variety and flexibility

At first glance, producing 108 varieties of the integral design appears to be far less economical than for the modular design. In fact, the flexibility of the production process equipment is an additional factor in determining the basic economics of producing variety. If the trailer components can only be economically produced in large lot sizes because of the large set up times required for the process equipment, or if each type of component required large tooling investments, then in fact the integral design would be very expensive to produce with high variety. High variety under these conditions would require some combination of large inventory costs, large set-up costs, or large tooling costs.[5] However, if the integral trailer components could be produced economically in small lots (e.g. set-up costs are low) and without tooling investments, then variety could be offered economically for the integral design.

For example, consider the following production system for the integral trailer. The upper and lower halves are made by a computer controlled rolling machine followed by a computer controlled laser cutting machine. Plates of arbitrary thickness and material can be rolled to arbitrary diameters (within certain limits), and slots for the springs can be cut along arbitrary trajectories; all with small set-up times, no tooling investment, and rapid processing times. The nose piece is created by laser cutting, computer-controlled rolling and automated welding. The six components are then assembled manually. Because of the flexibility of the upper half, lower half and nose piece production processes, the required component types can be produced as they are needed in arbitrary combinations, and then assembled into the required trailer types. Such process flexibility allows economical high-variety production of a product with an integral architecture.

Flexible production process hardware can also have an impact on the production of the modular design. Using inflexible processes requiring expensive tooling and large lot sizes, the 12 different components required to assemble the 108 different product variants would be held in inventory ready for final assembly. Alternatively, the components for the modular design could be produced with flexible production equipment, eliminating the need for the inventories and tooling expense.

With a modular product architecture, product variety can be achieved with or without flexible component production equipment. In relative terms, in order to economically produce high variety with an integral architecture, the component production equipment must be flexible.

This argument assumes in all cases that the final assembly process itself is somewhat flexible, i.e. different combinations of components can be easily assembled to create the final product variety. This assumption is usually valid for products assembled manually, but some assembly systems, particularly high-volume automated assembly equipment, violate this assumption. For these systems, the flexibility of the final assembly process is also a key driver of the ability of the firm to offer product variety.

5.2   Infinite variety

Many flexible production processes can be programmed to produce an infinite variety of components. For example, a computer-controlled laser cutting system can cut along an arbitrarily specified trajectory. This flexibility allows systems incorporating these processes to create products that can be infinitely varied with respect to one or more properties. This ability to continuously vary the properties of components by a flexible process provides a subtle distinction between the variety that can be created by assembling products from a finite set of component alternatives, and the variety that can be created by flexible component production processes. Assembly from finite component choices is fundamentally a "set operation", in that it allows sets to be formed from discrete alternatives. Continuously variable process equipment can implement arbitrary mathematical relationships among component characteristics. For example, the laser cutting machine could be programmed to cut along a curve parameterized as a function of a set of other characteristics, such as expected climate of the use environment, the types of loads the trailer will carry, and the road quality in the customer's geographical region. Note that the ability to arbitrarily vary component characteristics can be achieved for both integral and modular architectures if components are fabricated with programmable processes.

A summary of the effect of product architecture and component process flexibility on the resulting performance characteristics of the production system is shown in figure 4.8.

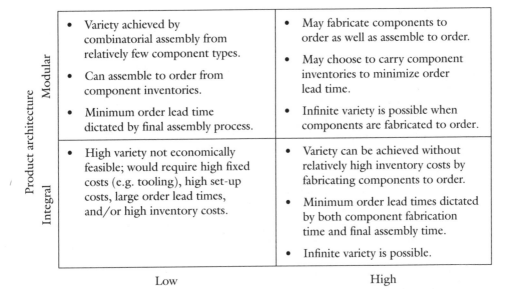

Figure 4.8 Product architecture *and* component process flexibility dictate the economics of producing variety.

6.   COMPONENT STANDARDIZATION

Component standardization is the use of the same component in multiple products and is closely linked to product variety. Common standardized components include tyres, batteries, bearings, motors, light bulbs, resistors and fasteners. Component standardization occurs both within a single firm (e.g. Quad-4 engines at General Motors) and across multiple firms (e.g. Timken roller bearings at Ford, General Motors, and Chrysler). I call the first case *internal* standardization, and the second case *external* standardization. For internal standardization, components may be designed and manufactured within the firm or provided by suppliers. For external standardization, components are typically designed and manufactured by suppliers.

6.1   A modular architecture makes standardization possible

Standardization can arise only when: (1) a component implements commonly useful functions; and (2) the interface to the component is identical across more than one different product. Otherwise, a component would either not be useful in more than one application or would not physically fit in more than one application.

A modular architecture increases the likelihood that a component will be commonly useful. When the mapping from functional elements to components is one-to-one, each component implements one and only one function. Such components are therefore useful in any other product applications where their associated functions occur. Components of a product exhibiting an integral architecture would only be potentially useful in other products containing the exact combination of functional elements, or parts of functional elements, implemented by the component.

A modular architecture also enables component interfaces to be identical across several products. Interfaces in modular architectures are decoupled, i.e. a particular component will not have to change when surrounding components are changed. Therefore, different sets of surrounding components, such as might occur in different applications, do not require different component interfaces. When interfaces are decoupled, an interface standard can be adopted and the same component can be used in a variety of settings.

6.2   What are the implications of standardization?

Component standardization, whether external or internal, has implications for the manufacturing firm in the areas of cost, product performance and product development.

Under most circumstances a standard component is less expensive than a component designed and built for use in only one product. This lower cost is possible primarily because the standard component will be produced in higher volume, allowing greater economies of scale and more learning. Higher component volume may also attract several competitors who exert price pressure on one another. When external standardization occurs, this cost advantage can be viewed in economic terms as a network externality [5, 6]. However, there are some circumstances under which the use of a standard component may incur higher unit costs than the use of a special component. Sometimes in an effort to standardize, firms will use a component with excess capability for a particular application. For example, a standard enclosure may be slightly larger than necessary in a particular application, or a standard power supply may provide slightly more power than is strictly necessary in a particular application. In these cases, firms may choose to adopt the standard components even if their unit cost is higher than that of a component more closely matched to the application. This standardization may be justifiable because of the economic savings from reduced complexity in, for example, purchasing, inventory management, quality control or field service.

Standard components, in general, exhibit higher performance (for a given cost) than unique designs. This performance advantage arises from the learning and experience the component supplier is able to accumulate. However, standardization may act as an inertial force preventing firms from adopting a better component technology because of compatibility issues in the installed base of products [5, 6].

The use of standard components can lower the complexity, cost and lead time of product development. An existing standard component represents a known entity and therefore can reduce the number of uncertain issues the development team must cope with. An existing standard component also requires no development resources and so can lower both the cost and, if the component development would have been on the project critical path, the lead time of a project.

7. PRODUCT PERFORMANCE

I define product performance as how well the product implements its functional elements. Typical product performance characteristics are speed, efficiency, life and noise. Product performance, as defined here, excludes *economic* performance, except to the extent that it arises from the product's technical performance, because economic performance is also highly dependent on the firm's production, service, sales and marketing activities.

Some performance characteristics arise only from the physical properties of a local region of the product. For example, the intensity of light from the tail of the trailer is a performance characteristic that arises only from the physical properties of those components implementing the aft illumination function. I call such characteristics *local performance characteristics.*

In contrast, many performance characteristics of a product arise inevitably from the physical properties of most, if not all, of the components of the product. These *global performance characteristics* are tied to the product's size, shape, mass and material properties. For example, vehicle fuel efficiency arises from, in addition to the trailer's aerodynamic profile, the trailer's mass. Mass is inevitably determined by every atom in the product. Other typical global performance characteristics include electromagnetic emissions, balance, aesthetics, power consumption, noise and vibration.

Local performance characteristics can be optimized through a modular architecture, but global performance characteristics can only be optimized through an integral architecture.

7.1   Local performance characteristics and modular architectures

Modular architectures allow for optimization of local performance characteristics for practical, more than for theoretical, reasons. First, as discussed in Section 6, a modular architecture may allow the use of a standard component. The use of a standard component allows the firm to exploit the performance refinements the supplier of this component has been able to make over the entire history of the component's use. Second, even when a standard component is not available and a component must be developed from scratch, a modular architecture allows the component to be designed, tested and refined in a focused way without disruptions and distractions arising from the need to address either interface coupling or other functional elements. All other things being equal, these benefits in design, testing and refinement lead to higher component performance. This explains why a trailer manufacturer trying to optimize light intensity or tyre life would likely adopt an architecture allowing the use of modular lamp and tyre components.

Note that what may be considered a component of one product is itself a product or system for the supplier of the component (whether the supplier is internal or external). As a result, the component itself may be designed with a highly integral architecture, but then may be used in a highly modular way as part of a larger product or system. For example, tyres exhibit a highly integral architecture, but may be used as a component in a trailer with a highly modular architecture.

7.2   Global performance characteristics and integral architectures

All physical products occupy space, exhibit some shape, and are composed of materials with mass and other physical properties. I illustrate the role architecture plays in global performance with the specific case of optimizing performance by minimizing the size and mass of a product; similar arguments can be made about other physical properties, such as natural frequency of vibration or electromagnetic radiation.

For most products, several key performance characteristics are closely related to the size and shape of the product or to its mass. For example, acceleration relates to mass, aerodynamic drag relates to size and shape, and, for our example, vehicle fuel efficiency relates to size and shape as well as to mass. In most cases, increasing global performance characteristics involves decreasing size and mass. (In relatively rare cases, increasing global performance involves increasing size and mass; improving the holding power of a boat anchor or increasing the passenger comfort of an automobile may be such cases.)

Two design strategies are frequently employed to minimize mass or size: *function sharing* and *geometric nesting*. Function sharing is a design strategy in which redundant physical properties of components are eliminated through the mapping of more than one functional element to a single component [34]. For example, a conventional motorcycle contains a steel tubular frame distinct from the engine and transmission. In contrast, several high-performance motorcycles contain no distinct frame. Rather, the cast aluminum transmission and motor casing acts as the structure for the motorcycle. (See, for example, the photograph of the BMW R1100RS in Ulrich and Eppinger [31]) The motorcycle designers adopted function sharing as a means of exploiting the fact that the transmission and motor case had incidental structural properties which were redundant to the structural properties of the conventional frame. Through function sharing the designers minimize the mass of the frame/motor/transmission system. In exploiting the secondary structural properties of the motor and transmission case, the designers mapped more than one functional element to a single component and therefore created an integral architecture.

Geometric nesting is a design strategy for efficient use of space and material and involves the interleaving and arrangement of components such that they occupy the minimum volume possible, or, in some cases, such that they occupy a volume with a particular desired shape. For example, the wheel, suspension, fender and brake system of a modern automobile are arranged in a way that barely allows clearance for wheel travel; they are tightly nested. An unfortunate consequence of nesting is the coupling of the interfaces between components, the other hallmark of an integral architecture. For example, in an automobile the brake system cooling is tightly coupled to the shape of the wheel well, the wheel covers and the fenders. A slight change to the shape of the wheel cover can require substantial changes to the brake disc design. Similarly, the road and wind noise from the wheels is coupled in a complex way to the shape of the wheel well and fender. Thus, a desire for increased global performance in the area of drag and aesthetics leads to a design strategy of geometric nesting. This design strategy causes components to be coupled, thereby sacrificing the modularity of the product architecture.

Minimizing size and mass is also part of a strategy for minimizing unit production costs for high-volume products, because as production volumes increase materials costs become more and more significant. This explains why integral architectures are sometimes employed to achieve very low unit costs, such as are required for disposable products like ball-point pens, razors and single-use cameras.

The examples in this section illustrate extreme conditions. Most products or systems will embody hybrid modular-integral architectures. For example, although the high-performance motorcycle may exhibit little modularity in the architecture of the engine, transmission and frame, the architecture of the ignition system may be quite modular (e.g. spark plug, wiring, coil, etc.). The designers of the motorcycle have avoided modularity only where the global performance penalties are most severe.

This view of how architecture relates to performance is another perspective on the notion of *product integrity* articulated by Clark and Fujimoto [3]. Product integrity can be viewed as the result of optimizing global performance characteristics. This optimization requires an integral architecture for some regions of the product, which in turn requires specific managerial approaches and techniques during new product development.

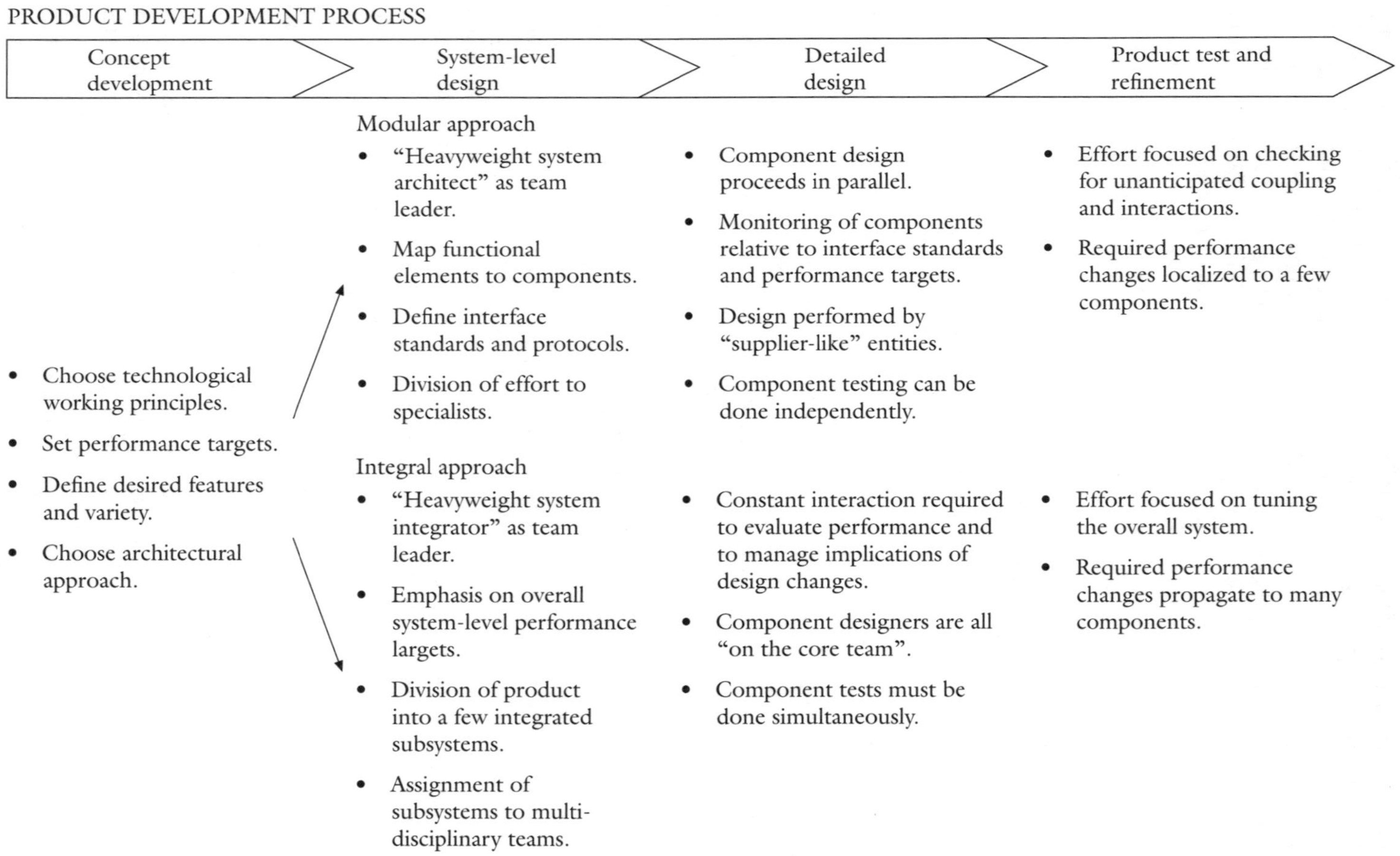

PRODUCT DEVELOPMENT PROCESS

Concept development	System-level design	Detailed design	Product test and refinement

Concept development
- Choose technological working principles.
- Set performance targets.
- Define desired features and variety.
- Choose architectural approach.

System-level design

Modular approach
- "Heavyweight system architect" as team leader.
- Map functional elements to components.
- Define interface standards and protocols.
- Division of effort to specialists.

Integral approach
- "Heavyweight system integrator" as team leader.
- Emphasis on overall system-level performance targets.
- Division of product into a few integrated subsystems.
- Assignment of subsystems to multi-disciplinary teams.

Detailed design

(Modular approach)
- Component design proceeds in parallel.
- Monitoring of components relative to interface standards and performance targets.
- Design performed by "supplier-like" entities.
- Component testing can be done independently.

(Integral approach)
- Constant interaction required to evaluate performance and to manage implications of design changes.
- Component designers are all "on the core team".
- Component tests must be done simultaneously.

Product test and refinement

(Modular approach)
- Effort focused on checking for unanticipated coupling and interactions.
- Required performance changes localized to a few components.

(Integral approach)
- Effort focused on tuning the overall system.
- Required performance changes propagate to many components.

Figure 4.9 Differences in product development management according to architectural approach.

8.   PRODUCT DEVELOPMENT MANAGEMENT

At a basic level the product development process can be viewed as consisting of four phases: concept development, system-level design, detailed design, and product testing and refinement. The activities of the concept development phase include: the selection of the technological working principles of a product; the choice of functional elements, features and performance targets in order to best meet customer needs; and a choice of architectural approach. The system-level design phase includes the development of the product architecture and the assignment of component development tasks to the extended product development team. The detailed design phase is primarily concerned with component design, testing and production process planning. The product testing and refinement phase involves assembling and testing prototypes and implementing any required changes to the component designs.

The architecture of the product has implications for the effectiveness of approaches to the three development phases following concept development. The following sections discuss these three phases and figure 4.9 summarizes the differences in effective approaches for modular and integral architectures.

8.1   System-level design

A modular architecture requires relatively more emphasis on this phase of development than does an integral architecture. For the modular architecture the focus of system-level design and planning is to carefully define component interfaces, specifying the associated standards and protocols. Performance targets and acceptance criteria are set for each component, corresponding to the particular functional element implemented by the component. Component design is frequently assigned to specialists, either internal or external to the firm. The development team leader can be viewed as a "heavyweight system architect".[6]

For the integral architecture, system-level design absorbs relatively less effort. The focus is on establishing clear targets for the performance of the overall system and on dividing the system into a relatively small number of integrated subsystems. These subsystems are frequently assigned to multi-disciplinary teams who will share the responsibility for designing the components that make up the subsystem. The leader of these teams can be viewed as a "heavyweight system integrator".

8.2   Detailed design

For the modular architecture, detailed design of each component can proceed almost independently and in parallel. Management of the detailed design process consists of monitoring the progress of each individual component design activity relative to the component performance targets and interface specifications. The component design teams are "supplier-like" in that interaction is structured and relatively infrequent. Testing of each component can be performed independently and clear objectives define completion of each component design activity.

For the integral architecture, component designers all form a "core team" and interact continually in order to analyze performance of the subsystem to which their component belongs and to manage changes required because of component interface coupling. Whether the components meet their performance targets depends on their interaction and not on whether they meet some pre-specified criteria. Testing of components cannot be completed in isolation; subsystems of components must be assembled and tested as a whole.

8.3   Product test and refinement

For the modular product, product testing and refinement is a checking activity. The tests are intended to detect unanticipated interactions among the components. These interactions are viewed as "bugs" and their resolution is usually localized to changes to one or two components.

For the integral product, product testing and infinement is a tuning activity. If the product performance must be altered in some way, changes are likely to be required to many components. Relatively more time will be spent in this phase than for the modular product.

8.4   Organizational implications

There are at least three organizational issues tied to a choice of architectural approach: skills and capabilities, management complexity, and the ability to innovate.

Highly modular designs allow firms to divide their development and production organizations into specialized groups with a narrow focus. This organizational structure may also extend to the supplier network of the firm. If the function of a component can be precisely specified and the interface between the component and the rest of the product is fully characterized, then the design and production of that component can be assigned to a separate entity. Such specialization may facilitate the development of deep expertise relative to a particular functional element and its associated component.

Required project management skills are different for different architectures. Modular architectures may require better systems engineering and planning skills, while integral architectures may require better coordination and integration skills. Firms with a long history of a particular architectural approach are likely to have developed the associated skills and capabilities.

A modular architecture enables a bureaucratic approach to organizing and managing development. This approach, for relatively well understood technologies, allows the complexity of the product development process to be dramatically reduced and may allow for better exploitation of supplier capabilities. Lovejoy articulates the highly non-linear theoretical reduction in complexity engendered by decomposing the design problem into de-coupled subproblems [16]. Von Hippel [36] argues that problem decomposition, and by implication product architecture, is important in managing development projects. Clark [2] provides evidence that automobile manufacturers with the shortest product development times adopt a "black box" approach to component development, in which the basic function of a component as well as its interfaces are specified, but the details of the design are not. For some domains the benefits of reduced complexity and enhanced supplier involvement may drive the choice of the architecture for at least parts of the product; software development is one such domain. In most cases the system-level performance penalties of a modular architecture are dwarfed by the benefits of a reduction in project management complexity.

A potential negative implication of a modular product architecture is the risk of creating organizational barriers to architectural innovation. These barriers appear to be unfortunate side effects of focus and specialization. This problem has been identified by Henderson and Clark [10] in the photolithography industry and may in fact be of concern in many other industries as well.

9.   CLOSING REMARKS

The overarching message of this paper is that manufacturing firm performance is linked to the architecture of the product. Product architecture consists of: (1) the arrangement of functional elements, or the function structure; (2) the mapping from functional elements to physical components; and (3) the specification of the interfaces between interacting components. Table 4.1 summarizes the key ideas in the paper. This closing section discusses how to establish a product architecture, identifies three research directions, and draws a few conclusions.

9.1   How to establish a product architecture

Dozens of issues are linked to the architecture of the product. The net effect is a complex set of relations among many areas of concern. While there are currently no deterministic approaches to choosing an optimal product architecture, the process can be guided. In most cases the choice will not be between a completely modular or completely integral architecture, but rather will be focused on which functional elements should be treated in a modular way and which should be treated in an integral way. Listed here are questions the product development team and firm management can ask in order to raise the important issues and to guide the development of an appropriate architecture. These questions are best posed during the concept development phase of the product development process. These questions also serve as a summary of the linkages between product architecture and the areas of managerial concern described in Sections 4 through 8.

9.1.1   Product change

- Which functional elements are likely to require upgrade?
- Are third-party add-ons desirable?
- Which functional elements may have to be adapted to new use environments over the life of the product?

Table 4.1 Summary of key ideas.

	Integral	Modular-slot	Modular-bus	Modular-sectional
Definition	• Complex mapping from functional elements to components. • And/or the component interfaces are coupled.	• One-to-one mapping between functional elements and components. • Interfaces between components are not coupled. • Component interfaces are all different.	• Component interfaces are all the same. • A single component (the bus) links the other components.	
Examples	• Automobile unit body. • Neon sign/lighting. • "Boom Box" (some internal components are modular-slot). • Cargo ship (hull in particular).	• Truck body and frame. • Table lamp with bulb and shade. • Consumer component stereo. • Tractor-trailer.	• Track lighting. • Shelves with brackets and rails. • Professional audio equipment in 19 inch rack.	• Stackable shelving units. • Freight train.
Product change	• Any change in functionality requires a change to several components	• Functional changes can be made to a product in the field. • Manufacturers can change the function of subsequent model generations by changing a single component.		
Product variety	• Variety not feasible without flexible component production processes.	• Products can be assembled in a combinatorial fashion from a relatively small set of component building blocks to create variety. • Variety possible even without flexible component production processes. • Variety confined to the choices of components within a pre-defined overall product structure.		• Variety in overall structure of the product possible (e.g. Lego blocks, piping).
Component standardization		• Components can be standardized across a product line.		

Table 4.1   (*cont'd*)

	Integral	Modular-slot	Modular-bus	Modular-sectional
		• Firms can use standard components provided by suppliers. • Interfaces may adhere to an industry standard.		
Product performance	• May exhibit higher performance for global performance characteristics like drag, noise, and aesthetics.	• May facilitate local performance. • De-coupling interfaces may require additional mass and space. • One-to-one mapping of functional elements to components prevents. *function sharing* – the simultaneous implementation of more than one functional element by a single component – potentially resulting in physical redundancy. • Standardized interfaces may result in additional redundancy and physical "overhead".		
Product development management	• Requires tight coordination of design tasks.	• Design tasks can be cleanly separated, thus allowing the tasks to be completed in parallel. • Specialization and division of labour possible. • Architectural innovation may be difficult. • Requires the top-down creation of a global product architecture.		

- Which functional elements will involve wear or consumption?
- Where will flexibility in configuration be useful to the user?
- Which functional elements can remain identical for future models of the product?
- Which functional elements must change rapidly to respond to market or techno-logical dynamics?

9.1.2   Product variety

- Which variants of the product are desirable to best match variation in customer preferences?
- What level of flexibility of component process is available or easily obtained?
- How much advantage does minimizing order lead time for custom products provide?

9.1.3   Component standardization

- Are existing components available internally or externally for any of the functional elements of the product?
- What are the cost implications of sharing a component with another product?
- Where can adopting a standard component reduce development time or complexity of project management?

9.1.4 Product performance

- Which local performance characteristics are of great value to customers and can therefore be optimized through a modular architecture?
- Which global performance characteristics are of great value to customers and can therefore be optimized through an integral architecture?

9.1.5 Product development management

- How much focus and specialization is present in the organization and in the supplier network?
- Is the product inherently large and complex?
- Is the development team geographically dispersed?
- Are barriers to architectural innovation developing in the organization because of specialization?
- Has the organization demonstrated an ability to change in structure and style?

9.2 Research directions

The research described in this paper is conceptual and foundational. My approach has been to synthesize fragments from several different disciplines, including software engineering, design theory, operations management and product development management. I have tried to create a coherent definition of product architecture and to use logical arguments and examples to illuminate the linkages between product architecture and important issues facing manufacturing firms. I hope to have motivated a set of problems and issues, but much analytical and empirical work remains. Three research directions seem particularly interesting and important.

First, the need to make decisions involving trade-offs motivates the development of decision support models. A single model of most of the trade-offs associated with the choice of a product architecture is unlikely, and even if it were developed would probably be too complex to be useful. However, focused problems can probably be usefully isolated, analyzed, and modelled. For example, a model integrating marketing science ideas (such as those in [9]) and production cost models could be used to evaluate the optimal variety that should be produced for each of two product architectures: integral and modular. The integral and modular architectures would each have their own cost structure and would likely lead to different levels of optimal product variety. Such a model could be used to coordinate systems engineering decisions involving product architecture, with market segment information and production cost information. Similar models could be built to support decisions involving component standardization, investments in production process flexibility and order lead time.

Second, I believe much insight would be gained by conducting an empirical study of the elements of difference in product architectures among the products manufactured by different firms. Such a study might lead to an identification of factors that dominate the choice of a product architecture. The results might also lead to an identification of multiple, equally effective, strategies involving different combinations of product architectures, organizational structures and production systems. I have used a methodology I call *product archaeology*, meaning the study of the physical artifact itself, to better understand design-for-manufacturing decision making [32]. This approach could also be applied to understanding the differences in product architectures among products from different manufacturers.

Finally, there is some evidence that the organization of the firm and the architecture of the product are interrelated. This linkage seems worthy of further research. Several specific questions could be addressed. Does the existence of a strong component supplier industry drive firms to organize in a particular way and to adopt a particular architecture? Do vertically integrated firms adopt more or less modular designs than firms working with outside suppliers? Does firm size or geographic location relate to the architecture of the product? Are firms able to change the architecture of their products without changing their organizational structure? If so, which organizational structures allow the most flexibility in product architecture.

9.3 Conclusions

While the concept of an explicit product architecture is prevalent in large electronic systems design and in software engineering, to my knowledge relatively few manufacturers of mechanical and electromechanical products explicitly consider the architecture of the product and its impact on the overall manufacturing system. Hopefully, the ideas in this paper will be useful, first, by raising the awareness of the far-reaching implications of the architecture of the product, and second, by creating a vocabulary for discussing and addressing the decisions and issues that are linked to product architecture.

In addition to providing a conceptual framework, I hope that by enumerating and discussing specific trade-offs the paper contributes directly to the decisions made during the concept development and systems engineering phases of product development. These decisions include: which variants of the product will be offered in the marketplace? How will the product be decomposed into components and subsystems? How will development tasks be allocated to internal teams and suppliers? What combination of process flexibility and modular product architecture will be used to achieve the desired product variety?

In the 1980s much attention was focused on the relationship between product design and manufacturing. While in many cases this attention led to improvements in production costs, it was focused on designing products to be easy to assemble and on reducing the cost of individual piece parts. The linkages between the product and the performance of the manufacturing firm are in fact much more extensive and include the relationship between the architecture of the product and the way the product will be changed, the variety offered in the marketplace, component standardization, the performance of the product and the management of product development.

ACKNOWLEDGMENTS

This research was supported by the National Science Foundation under contract number DDM-8914181 and by the MIT Leaders for Manufacturing Program, a partnership among MIT and 12 major corporations. Many of the ideas in the paper were developed during a collaborative research effort with the Square D Company. I am grateful to William Fonte, David Ellison, Steven Eppinger, George Favaloro, Frank Gillett, Stephen Graves, Rebecca Henderson, William Lovejoy, Wanda Orlikowski, B. Joseph Pine, Kamalini Ramdas-Jain, Henry Stoll, Bala Subramaniam, Mohan Tatikonda, Marcie Tyre and Daniel Whitney for their comments on earlier versions. The Research Policy reviewers also provided valuable recommendations for revision. Some of the ideas in this paper grew out of a previous paper with Karen Tung, Fundamentals of Product Modularity, Proceedings of the 1991 ASME Winter Annual Meeting Symposium on Issues in Design/Manufacturing Integration (ASME DE-Vol. 39).

NOTES

1 I have seen this term used at the General Motors Vehicle Assessment Center to describe the parts resulting from a complete disassembly of a vehicle, down to the last nut, bolt and washer.
2 A subassembly is a collection of components that: (1) can be assembled into a unit, and (2) can be subsequently treated as a single component during further assembly of the product.
3 Functionality, in this context, is used broadly to mean any attribute of the product from which the user derives a benefit, and so would include, for example, styling or colour changes.
4 Assume for the purpose of the example that the type of suspension and the load rating are independent choices. In practice, these two functional elements may in fact be related.
5 Inventory costs and set-up costs can be traded off against one another; inventory can be minimized by using small lot sizes, but this leads to high set-up costs.
6 This term is meant to complement the notion of a "heavyweight project manager" articulated by Wheelwright and Clark [37].

REFERENCES

[1] Christopher Alexander, *Notes on the Synthesis of Form* (Harvard University Press, Cambridge, 1964).
[2] Kim B. Clark, Project Scope and Project Performance: Effect of Parts Strategy and Supplier Involvement on Product Development, *Management Science* 35(10) (1989) 1247–63.
[3] Kim B. Clark and Takahiro Fujimoto, The Power of Product Integrity, *Harvard Business Review* 68(6) (1990).
[4] Michael A. Cusumano and Kentaro Nobeoka, Strategy, Structure and Performance in Product Development: Observations from the Auto Industry, *Research Policy* 21 (1992) 265–93.
[5] Joseph Farrell and Garth Saloner, Standardization, Compatibility, and Innovation, *Rand Journal of Economics* 16(1) (1985) 70–83.

[6]   Joseph Farrell and Garth Saloner, Installed Base and Compatibility: Innovation, Product Preannouncements, and Predation, *The American Economic Review* 76(5) (1986) 940–55.

[7]   Susan Finger and John R. Dixon, A Review of Research in Mechanical Engineering Design, *Research in Engineering Design* 1(1,2) (1989).

[8]   Theodore Fowler, *Value Analysis in Design* (Van Nostrand Reinhold, New York, 1990).

[9]   Paul E. Green and Abba M. Krieger, Models and Heuristics for Product Line Selection, *Marketing Science* 4(1) (1985).

[10] Rebecca M. Henderson and Kim B. Clark, Architectural Innovation: The Reconfiguration of Existing Product Technologies and the Failure of Established Firms, *Administrative Science Quarterly* 35 (1990) 9–30.

[11] Vladimir Hubka and W. Ernst Eder, *Theory of Technical Systems* (Springer-Verlag, New York, 1988).

[12] R. Jaikumar, Postindustrial Manufacturing, *Harvard Business Review* 64(6) (1986) 69–76.

[13] Timothy D. Korson and Vijay K. Vaishnavi, An Empirical Study of the Effects of Modularity on Program Modifiability, Technical Report CIS-86-001, Georgia State University, Department of Computer Information Systems, 1986.

[14] Richard N. Langlois and Paul L. Robertson, Networks and Innovation in a Modular System: Lessons from the Microcomputer and Stereo Components Industries, *Research Policy* 21 (1992).

[15] Hau Lee and Corey Billington, Designing Products and Processes for Postponement (paper presented at the Conference on Design Management, Anderson Graduate School of Management, UCLA, September 17–18, 1992).

[16] William S. Lovejoy, Rationalizing the Design Process (paper presented at the Conference on Design Management, Anderson Graduate School of Management, UCLA, September 17–18, 1992).

[17] Carver Mead and Lynn Conway, *Introduction to VLSI Systems* (Addison-Wesley, Reading, MA, 1980).

[18] James L. Nevins and Daniel E. Whitney, *Concurrent Design of Products and Processes* (McGraw-Hill, 1989).

[19] Gerhard Pahl and Wolfgang Beitz, in: Ken Wallace (Editor), *Engineering Design* (The Design Council, London, 1984).

[20] B. Joseph Pine II, Paradigm Shift: From Mass Production to Mass Customization, S.M. Thesis, MIT Sloan School of Management (1991).

[21] B. Joseph Pine II, *Mass Customization: The New Frontier in Business Competition* (Harvard Business School Press, 1992).

[22] Ron Sanchez and D. Sudharshan, Real-Time Market Research: Learning-by-Doing in the Development of New Products, *Proceedings of the International Conference on Product Development Management* Vol. II, Institute for Advanced Studies in Management, Brussels (1992).

[23] Susan Sanderson, Cost Models for Evaluating Virtual Design Strategies in Multicycle Product Families, *Journal of Engineering and Technology Management* 8 (1991) 339–58.

[24] Susan Sanderson and Mustafa Uzumeri, *Managing Product Families: The Case of the Sony Walkman*, Working Paper, Rensselaer Polytechnic Institute (1992).

[25] Stephen R. Schach, *Software Engineering* (Richard Irwin, Boston, 1990).

[26] Sean Silverthorne, Upgradable PCs Spreading, But Benefits are Debated, *Investor's Daily*, September 17 (1991).

[27] Fernando F. Suarez, Michael A. Customano and Charles H. Fine, Flexibility and Performance: A Literature Critique and Strategic Framework (Massachusetts Institute of Technology Sloan School of Management Working Paper 3298-91-BPS, 1991).

[28] Nam P. Suh, *The Principles of Design* (Oxford University Press, 1990).

[29] Toshio Suzue and Akira Kohdate, *Variety Reduction Program* (Productivity Press, Cambridge, MA, 1990).

[30] David G. Ullman, *The Mechanical Design Process* (McGraw-Hill, New York, 1992).

[31] Karl T. Ulrich and Steven D. Eppinger, *Product Design and Development*, McGraw-Hill, New York, 1995.

[32] Karl T. Ulrich and Scott Pearson, Does Product Design Really Determine 80% of Manufacturing Cost? (Massachusetts Institute of Technology Sloan School of Management working paper, 3601-93-MSA 1993).

[33] Karl T. Ulrich and Warren P. Seering, Synthesis of Schematic Descriptions in Mechanical Design, *Research in Engineering Design* 1 (1989) 3–18.

[34] Karl T. Ulrich and Warren P. Seering, Function Sharing in Mechanical Design, *Design Studies* 11 (1990) 223–34.

[35] David M. Upton, The Management of Manufacturing Flexibility: Work in Progress, Harvard Business School Working Paper 92-058, September 1991.

[36] Eric von Hippel, Task Partitioning: An Innovation Process Variable, *Research Policy* 19 (1990) 407–18.

[37] Steven C. Wheelwright and Kim B. Clark, *Revolutionizing Product Development: Quantum Leaps in Speed, Efficiency and Quality*, The Free Press, New York, 1992.

[38] J. P. Womack, D. T. Jones and D. Roos, *The Machine that Changed the World* (Rawson/Macmillan, New York, 1990).

COMMENTARY
Karl Ulrich

This commentary accompanies the reprinting in this volume of my 1995 *Research Policy* article "The Role of Product Architecture in the Manufacturing Firm" (Ulrich 1995). Here I provide some of the history and motivation behind the original article and comment on developments of the past decade.

Product architecture is the scheme by which the function of a product is allocated to its components. The "architecture paper" grew out of an applied research project in 1990 (with my former master's student Karen Tung) attempting to simplify one of the product lines of the Square D Company (since acquired by Schneider Electric). We discovered that the architecture of the product, in this case "lighting panel boards," was a critical determinant of the ability to create product variety. This fact surprised us because, through the early 1990s, most of the literature on product variety emphasized the role of production process flexibility, but did not discuss the architecture of the product. Perhaps most interestingly, we discovered that designers possess a great deal of latitude in selecting a product architecture and therefore architecture is an explicit or implicit choice of the firm and does not arise unavoidably from a core technology.

In investigating the literature on product architecture, we discovered fragments of theory in several different fields, but no comprehensive frameworks to help understand what product architecture is and how it relates to manufacturing performance.

Karen Tung and I wrote a preliminary paper in 1991 outlining some of our key findings (Ulrich and Tung, 1991). Over the next couple of years, I refined our early thinking and wrote the architecture paper reprinted here.

There are some very important antecedents to my work on architecture. An especially important influence for me was Simon's essay on architecture and complexity (Simon, 1981). I am pleased that the Simon article is reprinted in this volume. Clark's work on "design hierarchies" laid out influential ideas about how architecture can influence innovation (Clark, 1985). Another important antecedent is the software engineering literature (see, for example, Parnas et al., 1985.) Although the literature on software architecture at the time was largely heuristic and anecdotal, the software community had developed many promising ideas and design approaches.

The architecture paper is conceptual and is based in large measure on my observations of industrial practice. The paper does not contain quantitative analysis or mathematical modeling, yet has been quite influential on the direction of the product development research community. One of the important attributes of the architecture paper is that it brings together the perspectives of engineering design and management in a single integrated view. The engineering design literature had certainly discussed modularity before 1992. However, the commonly held view was that modularity was always desirable. In fact, an extreme version of this view was argued by Suh in the form of his "axiomatic design" theory (Suh, 1990). Suh held that a few intrinsic properties of a design, one of them essentially modularity, dictate design quality. In essence this view holds that design quality arises from its technical attributes independent of context. Having just spent several years struggling with applied research problems in design, I had come to believe that design decisions, including architectural choices, were strongly coupled to the economic context of the firm, which could vary substantially even for the same technical design problem. The architecture paper was an attempt to connect fundamental decisions in engineering design with the economic context of the product and firm.

Since I wrote the architecture paper, there has been a wealth of related work. Some of this work has focused on developing practical tools for making architectural choices. Steven Eppinger and I have distilled some of this practical knowledge in our textbook chapter on product architecture (Ulrich and Eppinger, 2000). David Robertson and I describe some of our work in applying many of the ideas in the architecture paper to the development of a major new platform for an automobile company (Robertson and Ulrich, 1998). A vibrant academic research community has also grown up around the problems of product architecture. See the review article by Vishwanathan Krishnan and me for some key references to this literature (Krishnan and Ulrich, 2001).

Several interesting issues remain to be explored and better understood. Let me provide one example of a problem motivated by recent developments in computer system design. The Linux operating system is a striking example of user-based design of a product. Linux is a freely available computer operating system that is substantially developed and maintained by its user community. Users have access to the source code and are free to attempt to make product improvements and enhancements. They may submit these designs to a committee for review, and the best designs are adopted as part of the canonical product. This system has resulted in one of the most reliable operating systems ever developed. Linux is a highly modular system comprised of a kernel and a bundle of features. What properties of this architecture enable user innovation? Could this scheme be extended beyond software? What would be the enabling architectural choices?

My work and that of others on product architecture is hardly complete. In my view, a primary contribution of the architecture paper was in identifying product architecture as one of the key decision variables of the firm. I believe that product architecture is as fundamental as, for example, supply chain configuration in determining firm performance. However, identifying the decision variables does not solve the decision problem. Therefore, further investments in understanding the implications of architectural choice for the enterprise are likely to provide significant returns in improved managerial decision making.

REFERENCES

Clark, K. B. (1985). "The Interaction of Design Hierarchies and Market Concepts in Technological Evolution," *Research Policy*, 14: 235–51.

Krishnan, V. and Ulrich, K. (2001). "Product Development Decisions: A Review of the Literature," *Management Science*, 47(1), January: 1–21.

Parnas, D. L, Clements, P. C. and Weiss, D. M. (1985). "The Modular Structure of Complex Systems," *IEEE Transactions on Software Engineering*, SE-11, March: 259–66.

Robertson, D. and Ulrich, K. (1998). "Planning for Product Platforms," *Sloan Management Review*, 39(4), Summer: 19–31.

Simon, H. A. (1981). "The Architecture of Complexity," *Proceedings of the American Philosophical Society*, 106: 467–82, reprinted in *The Sciences of the Artificial*, 2nd edn., Cambridge: MIT Press.

Suh, N. P. (1990). *The Principals of Design*, New York: Oxford University Press.

Ulrich, K. (1995). "The Role of Product Architecture in the Manufacturing Firm," *Research Policy*, 24: 419–40.

Ulrich, K. and Eppinger, S. (2000). *Product Design and Development*, 2nd edn., New York: McGraw-Hill.

Ulrich, K. and Tung, K. (1991). "Fundamentals of Product Modularity," *Proceedings of ASME Winter Annual Meeting Symposium on Design and Manufacturing Integration*, November, Atlanta: 73–9.

CHAPTER FIVE

MANAGING IN AN AGE OF MODULARITY

Carliss Y. Baldwin and Kim B. Clark

In the nineteenth century, railroads fundamentally altered the competitive landscape of business. By providing fast and cheap transportation, they forced previously protected regional companies into battles with distant rivals. The railroad companies also devised management practices to deal with their own complexity and high fixed costs that deeply influenced the second wave of industrialization at the turn of the century.

Today the computer industry is in a similar leading position. Not only have computer companies transformed a wide range of markets by introducing cheap and fast information processing, but they have also led the way toward a new industry structure that makes the best use of these processing abilities. At the heart of their remarkable advance is modularity – building a complex product or process from smaller subsystems that can be designed independently yet function together as a whole. Through the widespread adoption of modular designs, the computer industry has dramatically increased its rate of innovation. Indeed, it is modularity, more than speedy processing and communication or any other technology, that is responsible for the heightened pace of change that managers in the computer industry now face. And strategies based on modularity are the best way to deal with that change.

Many industries have long had a degree of modularity in their production processes. But a growing number of them are now poised to extend modularity to the design stage. Although they may have difficulty taking modularity as far as the computer industry has, managers in many industries stand to learn much about ways to employ this new approach from the experiences of their counterparts in computers.

A Solution to Growing Complexity

The popular and business presses have made much of the awesome power of computer technology. Storage capacities and processing speeds have sky-rocketed while costs have remained the same or have fallen. These improvements have depended on enormous growth in the complexity of the product. The modern computer is a bewildering array of elements working in concert, evolving rapidly in precise and elaborate ways.

Modularity has enabled companies to handle this increasingly complex technology. By breaking up a product into subsystems, or *modules*, designers, producers, and users have gained enormous flexibility. Different companies can take responsibility for separate modules and be confident that a reliable product will arise from their collective efforts.

The first modular computer, the System/360, which IBM announced in 1964, effectively illustrates this approach. The designs of previous models from IBM and other mainframe manufacturers were unique; each had its own operating system, processor, peripherals, and application software. Every time a manufacturer introduced a new computer system to take advantage of improved technology, it had to develop software and components specifically for that system while continuing to maintain those for the previous systems. When end users switched to new machines, they had to rewrite all their existing programs, and they ran the risk of losing critical data if software conversions were botched. As a result, many customers were reluctant to lease or purchase new equipment.

The developers of the System/360 attacked that problem head-on. They conceived of a family of computers that would include machines of different sizes suitable for different applications, all of which would use the same instruction set and could share peripherals. To achieve this compatibility, they applied the principle of *modularity in design*: that is, the System/360's designers divided the designs of the processors and peripherals into *visible* and *hidden* information. IBM set up a Central Processor Control Office, which established and enforced the visible overall design rules that determined how the different modules of the machine would work together. The dozens of design teams scattered around the world had to adhere absolutely to these rules. But each team had full control over the hidden elements of design in its module – those elements that had no effect on other modules. (See "A Guide to Modularity" below.)

When IBM employed this approach and also made the new systems compatible with existing software (by adding "emulator" modules), the result was a huge commercial and financial success for the company and its customers. Many of IBM's mainframe rivals were forced to abandon the market or seek niches focused on customers with highly specialized needs. But modularity also undermined IBM's dominance in the long run, as new companies produced their own so-called plug-compatible modules – printers, terminals, memory, software, and eventually even the central processing units themselves – that were compatible with, and could plug right into, the IBM machines. By following IBM's design rules but specializing in a particular area, an upstart company could often produce a module that was better than the ones IBM was making internally. Ultimately, the dynamic, innovative industry that has grown up around these modules developed entirely new kinds of computer systems that have taken away most of the mainframe's market share.

The fact that different companies (and different units of IBM) were working independently on modules enormously boosted the rate of innovation. By concentrating on a single module, each unit or company could push deeper into its workings. Having many companies focus on the design of a given module fostered

Table 5.1 A guide to modularity.

Modularity is a strategy for organizing complex products and processes efficiently.
A *modular* system is composed of units (or modules) that are designed independently
but still function as an integrated whole. Designers achieve modularity by partitioning
information into *visible design rules* and *hidden design parameters*. Modularity is beneficial
only if the partition is precise, unambiguous, and complete.

The visible design rules (also called *visible information*) are decisions that affect subsequent
design decisions. Ideally, the visible design rules are established early in a design process
and communicated broadly to those involved. Visible design rules fall into three categories:

- An *architecture*, which specifies what modules will be part of the system and what their
  functions will be.
- *Interfaces* that describe in detail how the modules will interact, including how they will
  fit together, connect, and communicate.
- *Standards* for testing a module's conformity to the design rules (can module X function
  in the system?) and for measuring one module's performance relative to another (how
  good is module X versus module Y?).

Practitioners sometimes lump all three elements of the visible information together and
call them all simply "the architecture," "the interfaces," or "the standards."

The hidden design parameters (also called *hidden information*) are decisions that do not
affect the design beyond the local module. Hidden elements can be chosen late and changed
often and do not have to be communicated to anyone beyond the module design team.

---

numerous, parallel experiments. The module designers were free to try out a wide
range of approaches as long as they obeyed the *design rules* ensuring that the
modules would fit together. For an industry like computers, in which technological
uncertainty is high and the best way to proceed is often unknown, the more experiments and the more flexibility each designer has to develop and test the experimental
modules, the faster the industry is able to arrive at improved versions.

This freedom to experiment with product design is what distinguishes modular
suppliers from ordinary subcontractors. For example, a team of disk drive designers
has to obey the overall requirements of a personal computer, such as data transmission protocols, specifications for the size and shape of hardware, and standards for
interfaces, to be sure that the module will function within the system as a whole. But
otherwise, team members can design the disk drive in the way they think works best.
The decisions they make need not be communicated to designers of other modules
or even to the system's architects, the creators of the visible design rules. Rival
disk-drive designers, by the same token, can experiment with completely different
engineering approaches for their versions of the module as long as they, too, obey
the visible design rules.[1]

MODULARITY OUTSIDE THE COMPUTER INDUSTRY

As a principle of production, modularity has a long history. Manufacturers have
been using it for a century or more because it has always been easier to make
complicated products by dividing the manufacturing process into modules or *cells*.

Carmakers, for example, routinely manufacture the components of an automobile at different sites and then bring them together for final assembly. They can do so because they have precisely and completely specified the design of each part. In this context, the engineering design of a part (its dimensions and tolerances) serves as the visible information in the manufacturing system, allowing a complicated process to be split up among many factories and even outsourced to other suppliers. Those suppliers may experiment with production processes or logistics, but, unlike in the computer industry, they have historically had little or no input into the design of the components.

Modularity is comparatively rare not only in the actual design of products but also in their use. *Modularity in use* allows consumers to mix and match elements to come up with a final product that suits their tastes and needs. For example, to make a bed, consumers often buy bed frames, mattresses, pillows, linens, and covers from different manufacturers and even different retailers. They all fit together because the different manufacturers put out these goods according to standard sizes. Modularity in use can spur innovation in design: the manufacturers can independently experiment with new products and concepts, such as futon mattresses or fabric blends, and find ready consumer acceptance as long as their modules fit the standard dimensions.

If modularity brings so many advantages, why aren't all products (and processes) fully modular? It turns out that modular systems are much more difficult to design than comparable interconnected systems. The designers of modular systems must know a great deal about the inner workings of the overall product or process in order to develop the visible design rules necessary to make the modules function as a whole. They have to specify those rules in advance. And while designs at the modular level are proceeding independently, it may seem that all is going well; problems with incomplete or imperfect modularization tend to appear only when the modules come together and work poorly as an integrated whole.

IBM discovered that problem with the System/360, which took far more resources to develop than expected. In fact, had the developers initially realized the difficulties of ensuring modular integration, they might never have pursued the approach at all because they also underestimated the System/360's market value. Customers wanted it so much that their willingness to pay amply justified IBM's increased costs.

We have now entered a period of great advances in modularity. Breakthroughs in materials science and other fields have made it easier to obtain the deep product knowledge necessary to specify the design rules. For example, engineers now understand how metal reacts under force well enough to ensure modular coherence in body design and metal-forming processes for cars and big appliances. And improvements in computing, of course, have dramatically decreased the cost of capturing, processing, and storing that knowledge, reducing the cost of designing and testing different modules as well. Concurrent improvements in financial markets and innovative contractual arrangements are helping small companies find resources and form alliances to try out experiments and market new products or modules. In some industries, such as telecommunications and electric utilities, deregulation is freeing companies to divide the market along modular lines.

In automobile manufacturing, the big assemblers have been moving away from the tightly centralized design system that they have relied on for much of this century. Under intense pressure to reduce costs, accelerate the pace of innovation, and improve quality, automotive designers and engineers are now looking for ways to parcel out the design of their complex electro-mechanical system.

The first step has been to redefine the cells in the production processes. When managers at Mercedes-Benz planned their new sport-utility assembly plant in Alabama, for example, they realized that the complexities of the vehicle would require the plant to control a network of hundreds of suppliers according to an intricate schedule and to keep substantial inventory as a buffer against unexpected developments. Instead of trying to manage the supply system directly as a whole, they structured it into a smaller set of large production modules. The entire driver's cockpit, for example – including air bags, heating and air-conditioning systems, the instrument cluster, the steering column, and the wiring harness – is a separate module produced at a nearby plant owned by Delphi Automotive Systems, a unit of General Motors Corporation. Delphi is wholly responsible for producing the cockpit module according to certain specifications and scheduling requirements, so it can form its own network of dozens of suppliers for this module. Mercedes' specifications and the scheduling information become the visible information that module suppliers use to coordinate and control the network of parts suppliers and to build the modules required for final production.

Volkswagen has taken this approach even further in its new truck factory in Resende, Brazil. The company provides the factory where all modules are built and the trucks are assembled, but the independent suppliers obtain their own materials and hire their own workforces to build the separate modules. Volkswagen does not "make" the car, in the sense of producing or assembling it. But it does establish the architecture of the production process and the interfaces between cells, it sets the standards for quality that each supplier must meet, and it tests the modules and the trucks as they proceed from stage to stage.

So far, this shift in supplier responsibilities differs little from the numerous changes in supply-chain management that many industries are going through. By delegating the manufacturing process to many separate suppliers, each one of which adds value, the assembler gains flexibility and cuts costs. That amounts to a refinement of the pattern of modularity already established in production. Eventually, though, strategists at Mercedes and other automakers expect the newly strengthened module makers to take on most of the design responsibility as well – and that is the point at which modularity will pay off the most. As modularity becomes an established way of doing business, competition among module suppliers will intensify. Assemblers will look for the best-performing or lowest cost modules, spurring these increasingly sophisticated and independent suppliers into a race for innovation similar to the one already happening with computer modules. Computer-assisted design will facilitate this new wave of experimentation.

Some automotive suppliers are already moving in that direction by consolidating their industry around particular modules. Lear Seating Corporation, Magna International, and Johnson Controls have been buying related suppliers, each attempting to become the worldwide leader in the production of entire car interiors. The big car manufacturers are indirectly encouraging this process by asking their suppliers to participate in the design of modules. Indeed, GM recently gave Magna total responsibility for overseeing development for the interior of the next-generation Cadillac Catera.

In addition to products, a wide range of services are also being modularized – most notably in the financial services industry, where the process is far along. Nothing is easier to modularize than stocks and other securities. Financial services are purely intangible, having no hard surfaces, no difficult shapes, no electrical pins or wires. Because the science of finance is sophisticated and highly developed, these services are relatively easy to define, analyze, and split apart. The design rules for financial transactions arise from centuries-old traditions of bookkeeping combined with modern legal and industry standards and the conventions of the securities exchanges.

As a result, providers need not take responsibility for all aspects of delivering their financial services. The tasks of managing a portfolio of securities, for example – selecting assets, conducting trades, keeping records, transferring ownership, reporting status and sending out statements, and performing custody services – can be readily broken apart and seamlessly performed by separate suppliers. Some major institutions have opted to specialize in one such area: Boston's State Street Bank in custody services, for example.

Other institutions, while modularizing their products, still seek to own and control those modules, as IBM tried to control the System/360. For example, Fidelity, the big, mass-market provider of money management services, has traditionally kept most aspects of its operations in-house. However, under pressure to reduce costs, it recently broke with that practice, announcing that Bankers Trust Company would manage $11 billion worth of stock index funds on its behalf. Index funds are a low-margin business whose performance is easily measured. Under the new arrangement, Bankers Trust's index-fund management services have become a hidden module in Fidelity's overall portfolio offerings, much as Volkswagen's suppliers operate as hidden modules in the Resende factory system.

The other result of the intrinsic modularity of financial instruments has been an enormous boost in innovation. By combining advanced scientific methods with high-speed computers, for example, designers can split up securities into smaller units that can then be reconfigured into derivative financial products. Such innovations have made global financial markets more fluid so that capital now flows easily even between countries with very different financial practices.

COMPETING IN A MODULAR ENVIRONMENT

Modularity does more than accelerate the pace of change or heighten competitive pressures. It also transforms relations among companies. Module designers rapidly move in and out of joint ventures, technology alliances, subcontracts, employment agreements, and financial arrangements as they compete in a relentless race to innovate. In such markets, revenue and profits are far more dispersed than they would be in traditional industries. Even such companies as Intel and Microsoft, which have substantial market power by virtue of their control over key subsets of visible information, account for less of the total market value of all computer companies than industry leaders typically do.

Being part of a shifting modular cluster of hundreds of companies in a constantly innovating industry is different from being one of a few dominant companies in a stable industry. No strategy or sequence of moves will always work; as in chess, a good move depends on the layout of the board, the pieces one controls, and the skill and resources of one's opponent. Nevertheless, the dual structure of a modular marketplace requires managers to choose carefully from two main strategies. A company can compete as an architect, creating the visible information, or design rules, for a product made up of modules. Or it can compete as a designer of modules that conform to the architecture, interfaces, and test protocols of others. Both strategies require companies to understand products at a deep level and be able to predict how modules will evolve, but they differ in a number of important ways.

For an architect, advantage comes from attracting module designers to its design rules by convincing them that this architecture will prevail in the marketplace. For the module maker, advantage comes from mastering the hidden information of the design and from superior execution in bringing its module to market. As opportunities emerge, the module maker must move quickly to fill a need and then move elsewhere or reach new levels of performance as the market becomes crowded.

Following the example of Intel and Microsoft, it is tempting to say that companies should aim to control the visible design rules by developing proprietary architectures and leave the mundane details of hidden modules to others. And it is true that the position of architect is powerful and can be very profitable. But a challenger can rely on modularity to mix and match its own capabilities with those of others and do an end-run around an architect.

That is what happened in the workstation market in the 1980s. Both of the leading companies, Apollo Computer and Sun Microsystems, relied heavily on other companies for the design and production of most of the modules that formed their workstations. But Apollo's founders, who emphasized high performance in their product, designed a proprietary architecture based on their own operating and network management systems. Although some modules, such as the microprocessor, were bought off the shelf, much of the hardware was designed in-house. The various parts of the design were highly interdependent, which Apollo's designers believed was necessary to achieve high levels of performance in the final product.

Sun's founders, by contrast, emphasized low costs and rapid time to market. They relied on a simplified, nonproprietary architecture built with off-the-shelf hardware and software, including the widely available UNIX operating system. Because its module makers did not have to design special modules to fit into its system, Sun was free of the investments in software and hardware design Apollo required and could bring products to market quickly while keeping capital costs low. To make up for the performance penalty incurred by using generic modules, Sun developed two proprietary, hidden hardware modules to link the microprocessor efficiently to the workstation's internal memory.

In terms of sheer performance, observers judged Apollo's workstation to be slightly better, but Sun had the cost advantage. Sun's reliance on other module makers proved superior in other respects as well. Many end users relied on the UNIX operating system in other networks or applications and preferred a workstation that ran UNIX rather than one that used a more proprietary operating system. Taking advantage of its edge in capital productivity, Sun opted for an aggressive strategy of rapid growth and product improvements.

Soon, Apollo found itself short of capital and its products' performance fell further and further behind Sun's. The flexibility and leanness Sun gained through its nonproprietary approach overcame the performance advantages Apollo had been enjoying through its proprietary strategy. Sun could offer customers an excellent product at an attractive price, earn superb margins, and employ much less capital in the process.

However, Sun's design gave it no enduring competitive edge. Because Sun controlled only the two hidden modules in the workstation, it could not lock its customers into its own proprietary operating system or network protocols. Sun did develop original ideas about how to combine existing modules into an effective system, but any competitor could do the same since the architecture – the visible information behind the workstation design – was easy to copy and could not be patented.

Indeed, minicomputer makers saw that workstations would threaten their business and engineering markets, and they soon offered rival products, while personal computer makers (whose designs were already extremely modular) saw an opportunity to move into a higher-margin niche. To protect itself, Sun shifted gears and sought greater control over the visible information in its own system. Sun hoped to use equity financing from AT&T, which controlled UNIX, to gain a favored role in designing future versions of the operating system. If Sun could control the evolution of UNIX, it could bring the next generation of workstations to market faster than its rivals could. But the minicomputer makers, which licensed UNIX for their existing systems, immediately saw the threat posed by the Sun-AT&T alliance, and they forced AT&T to back away from Sun. The workstation market remained wide open, and when Sun stumbled in bringing out a new generation of workstations, rivals gained ground with their own offerings. The race was on – and it continues.

NEEDED: KNOWLEDGEABLE LEADERS

Because modularity boosts the rate of innovation, it shrinks the time business leaders have to respond to competitors' moves. We may laugh about the concept of an "Internet year," but it's no joke. As more and more industries pursue modularity, their general managers, like those in the computer industry, will have to cope with higher rates of innovation and swifter change.

As a rule, managers will have to become much more attuned to all sorts of developments in the design of products, both inside and outside their own companies. It won't be enough to know what their direct competitors are doing – innovations in other modules and in the overall product architecture, as well as shifting alliances elsewhere in the industry, may spell trouble or present opportunities. Success in the marketplace will depend on mapping a much larger competitive terrain and linking one's own capabilities and options with those emerging elsewhere, possibly in companies very different from one's own.

Those capabilities and options involve not only product technologies but also financial resources and the skills of employees. Managers engaged with modular design efforts must be adept at forging new financial relationships and employment contracts, and they must enter into innovative technology ventures and alliances. Harvard Business School professor Howard Stevenson has described entrepreneurship as "the pursuit of opportunity beyond the resources currently controlled," and that's a good framework for thinking about modular leadership at even the biggest companies. (See "How Palm Computing Became an Architect" and "How Quantum Mines Hidden Knowledge" below.)

Table 5.2 How Palm Computing became an architect.

In 1992, Jeff Hawkins founded Palm Computing to develop and market a handheld computing device for the consumer market. Having already created the basic software for handwriting recognition, he intended to concentrate on refining that software and developing related applications for this new market. His plan was to rely on partners for the basic architecture, hardware, operating system software, and marketing. Venture capitalists funded Palm's own development. The handwriting recognition software became the key hidden module around which a consortium of companies formed to produce the complete product.

Sales of the first generation of products from both the consortium and its rivals, however, were poor, and Palm's partners had little interest in pursuing the next generation. Convinced that capitalizing on Palm's ability to connect the device directly to a PC would unlock the potential for sales, Hawkins and his chief executive, Donna Dubinsky, decided to shift course. If they couldn't get partners to develop the new concept, they would handle it themselves – at least the visible parts, which included the device's interface protocols and its operating system. Palm would have to become an architect, taking control of both the visible information and the hidden information in the handwriting recognition module. But to do so, Hawkins and Dubinsky needed a partner with deeper pockets than any venture capital firm would provide.

None of the companies in Palm's previous consortium was willing to help. Palm spread its net as far as US Robotics, the largest maker of modems. US Robotics was so taken with the concept for and development of Palm's product that it bought the company. With that backing, Palm was able to take the product into full production and get the marketing muscle it needed. The result was the Pilot, or what Palm calls a Personal Connected Organizer, which has been a tremendous success in the marketplace. Palm remains in control of the operating system and the handwriting recognition software in the Pilot but relies on other designers for hardware and for links to software that runs on PCs.

Palm's strategy with the Pilot worked as Hawkins and Dubinsky had intended. In order for its architecture to be accepted by customers and outside developers, Palm had to create a compelling concept that other module makers would accept, with attractive features and pricing, and bring the device to market quickly. Hawkins's initial strategy – to be a hidden-module producer while partners delivered the architecture – might have worked with a more familiar product, but the handheld-computer market was too unformed for it to work in that context. So, when the other members of the consortium balked in the second round of the design process, Palm had to take the lead role in developing both the proof of concept and a complete set of accessible design rules for the system as a whole.

We are grateful to Myra Hart for sharing with us her ongoing research on Palm. She describes the company in detail in her cases "Palm Computing, Inc. (A)," HBS case no. 396245, and "Palm Pilot 1995," HBS case, MO. 898090.

Table 5.3 How Quantum mines hidden knowledge.

Quantum Corporation began in 1980 as a maker of 8-inch disk storage drives for the minicomputer market. After the company fell behind as the industry shifted to 5.25-inch drives, a team led by Stephen M. Berkley and Dave Brown rescued it with an aggressive strategy, applying their storage expertise to developing a 3.5-inch add-on drive for the personal computer market. The product worked, but competing in this sector required higher volumes and tighter tolerances than Quantum was used to. Instead of trying to meet those demands internally, Berkley and Brown decided to keep the company focused on technology and to form an alliance with Matsushita-Kotobuki Electronics Industries (MKE), a division of the Matsushita Group, to handle the high-volume, high-precision manufacturing. With the new alliance in place, Quantum and MKE worked to develop tightly integrated design capabilities that spanned the two companies. The products resulting from those processes allowed Quantum to compete successfully in the market for drives installed as original equipment in personal computers.

Quantum has maintained a high rate of product innovation by exploiting modularity in the design of its own products and in its own organization. Separate, small teams work on the design and the production of each submodule, and the company's leaders have developed an unusually clear operating framework within which to coordinate the efforts of the teams while still freeing them to innovate effectively.

In addition to focusing on technology, the company has survived in the intensely competitive disk-drive industry by paying close attention to the companies that assemble personal computers. Quantum has become the preferred supplier for many of the assemblers because its careful attention to developments in the visible information for disk drives has enabled its drives to fit seamlessly into the assemblers' systems. Quantum's general managers have a deep reservoir of knowledge about both storage technology and the players in the sector, which helps them map the landscape, anticipating which segments of the computer market are set to go into decline and where emerging opportunities will arise. Early on, they saw the implications of the Internet and corporate intranets, and with help from a timely purchase of Digital Equipment Corporation's stagnating storage business, they had a head start in meeting the voracious demand for storage capacity that has been created by burgeoning networks. Despite what some observers might see as a weak position (because the company must depend on the visible information that other companies give out) Quantum has prospered, recently reporting strong profits and gains in stock price.

We are grateful to Steven Wheelwright and Clayton Christensen for sharing with us their ongoing research on Quantum. They describe the company in more detail in their case "Quantum Corp.: Business and Product Teams," HBS case no. 692023.

At the same time that modularity boosts the rate of innovation, it also heightens the degree of uncertainty in the design process. There is no way for managers to know which of many experimental approaches will win out in the marketplace. To prepare for sudden and dramatic changes in markets, therefore, managers need to be able to choose from an often complex array of technologies, skills, and financial options. Creating, watching, and nurturing a portfolio of such options will become more important than the pursuit of static efficiency *per se*.

To compete in a world of modularity, leaders must also redesign their internal organizations. In order to create superior modules, they need the flexibility to move quickly to market and make use of rapidly changing technologies, but they must also ensure that the modules conform to the architecture. The answer to this dilemma is modularity within the organization. Just as modularity in design boosts innovation in products by freeing designers to experiment, so managers can speed up development cycles for individual modules by splitting the work among independent teams, each pursuing a different submodule or different path to improvement.

Employing a modular approach to design complicates the task of managers who want to stabilize the manufacturing process or control inventories because it expands the range of possible product varieties. But the approach also allows engineers to create families of parts that share common characteristics and thus can all be made in the same way, using, for example, changes in machine settings that are well understood. Moreover, the growing power of information technology is giving managers more precise and timely information about sales and distribution channels, thus enhancing the efficiency of a modular production system.

For those organizational processes to succeed, however, the output of the various decentralized teams (including the designers at partner companies) must be tightly integrated. As with a product, the key to integration in the organization is the visible information. This is where leadership is critical. Despite what many observers of leadership are now saying, the heads of these companies must do more than provide a vision or goals for the decentralized development teams. They must also delineate and communicate a detailed operating framework within which each of the teams must work.

Such a framework begins by articulating the strategy and plans for the product line's evolution into which the work of the development teams needs to fit over time. But the framework also has to extend into the work of the teams themselves. It must, for example, establish principles for matching appropriate types of teams to each type of project. It must specify the size of the teams and make clear what roles senior management, the core design team, and support groups should play in carrying out the project's work. Finally, the framework must define processes by which progress will be measured and products released to the market. The framework may also address values that should guide the teams in their work (such as leading by example). Like the visible information in a modular product, this organizational framework establishes an overall structure within which teams can operate, provides ways for different teams and other groups to interact, and defines standards for testing the merit of the teams' work. Without careful direction, the teams would find it easy to pursue initiatives that may have individual merit but stray from the company's defining concepts.

Just like a modular product that lacks good interfaces between modules, an organization built around decentralized teams that fail to function according to a clear and effective framework will suffer from miscues and delays. Fast changing and dynamic markets – like those for computers – are unforgiving. The well-publicized problems of many computer companies have often been rooted in inadequate co-ordination of their development teams as they created new products. Less obvious, but equally important, are the problems that arise when teams fail to communicate the hidden information – the knowledge they develop about module technology – with the rest of the organization. That lack of communication, we have found, causes organizations to commit the same costly mistakes over and over again.

To take full advantage of modularity, companies need highly skilled, independent-minded employees eager to innovate. These designers and engineers do not respond to tight controls; many reject traditional forms of management and will seek employment elsewhere rather than submit to them. Such employees do, however, respond to informed leadership – to managers who can make reasoned arguments that will persuade employees to hold fast to the central operating framework. Managers must learn how to allow members of the organization the independence to probe and experiment while directing them to stay on the right overall course. The best analogy may be in biology, where complex organisms have been able to evolve into an astonishing variety of forms only by obeying immutable rules of development.

A century ago, the railroads showed managers how to control enormous organizations and masses of capital. In the world fashioned by computers, managers will control less and will need to know more. As modularity drives the evolution of much of the economy, general managers' greatest challenge will be to gain an intimate understanding of the knowledge behind their products. Technology can't be a black box to them because their ability to position the company, respond to market changes, and guide internal innovation depends on this knowledge. Leaders cannot manage knowledge at a distance merely by hiring knowledgeable people and giving them adequate resources. They need to be closely involved in shaping and directing the way knowledge is created and used. Details about the inner workings of products may seem to be merely technical engineering matters, but in the context of intense competition and fast changing technology, the success of whole strategies may hinge on such seemingly minor details.

NOTES

1 Practical knowledge of modularity has come largely from the computer industry. The term *architecture* was first used in connection with computers by the designers of the System/360: Gene M. Amdahl, Gerrit A. Blaauw, and Frederick P. Brooks, Jr., in "Architecture of the IBM System/360," *IBM Journal of Research and Development*, April 1964, p. 86. The scientific field of computer architecture was established by C. Gordon Bell and Allen Newell in *Computer Structures: Readings and Examples* (New York: McGraw-Hill, 1971). The principle of *information hiding* was first put forward in 1972 by David L. Parnas in "A Technique for Software Module Specification with Examples," *Communications of the ACM*, May 1972, p. 330. The term *design rules* was first used by Carver Mead and Lynn Conway in *Introduction to VLSI Systems* (Reading, Massachusetts: Addison-Wesley, 1980). Sun's architectural innovations, described in the text, were based on the work of John L. Hennessy and David A. Patterson, later summarized in their text *Computer Architecture: A Quantitative Approach* (San Mateo, California: Morgan Kaufman Publishers, 1990).

FURTHER READING

For more information on modular product design, see Steven D. Eppinger, Daniel E. Whitney, Robert P. Smith, and David Gebala, "A Model-Based Method for Organizing Tasks in Product Development," *Research in Engineering Design* 6, 1994. For more about modular processes, see James L. Nevins and Daniel E. Whitney, *Concurrent Design of Products and Processes* (New York: McGraw-Hill, 1989). For more information on the design of financial securities and the global financial system, see Robert C. Merton and Zvi Bodie, "A Conceptual

Framework for Analyzing the Financial Environment" and "Financial Infrastructure and Public Policy: A Functional Perspective," in *The Global Financial System: A Functional Perspective*, (Boston, Massachusetts: Harvard Business School Press, 1995).

For descriptions of how companies compete in industries using modular products, see Richard N. Langlois and Paul L. Robertson, "Networks and Innovation in a Modular System: Lessons from the Microcomputer and Stereo Component Industries," *Research Policy*, August 1992; Charles R. Morris and Charles H. Ferguson, "How Architecture Wins Technology Wars," HBR March–April 1993; Raghu Garud and Arun Kumaraswamy, "Changing Competitive Dynamics in Network Industries: An Exploration of Sun Micro-systems' Open Systems Strategy," *Strategic Management Journal*, July 1993, p. 351; and Clayton M. Christensen and Richard S. Rosenbloom, "Explaining the Attacker's Advantage: Technological Paradigms, Organizational Dynamics, and the Value Network," *Research Policy*, March 1995, p. 233.

COMMENTARY
Charles Y. Baldwin and Kim B. Clark

In "Managing in the Age of Modularity," which was written in June 1997, we proposed that a new technological phenomenon – the *modular design* of complex computer systems – caused the emergence of a large *modular cluster* of firms and markets in the computer industry. We went on to say that "managing" in this "modular environment" was different from managing a large, hierarchical corporation of the type that had emerged in the early 20th century.[1]

In 1997, there were about 1,000 publicly traded companies in the greater computer industry (the figure includes hardware, software and chip makers). Over the next three years (1997 to 2000), the "high tech" modular cluster grew rapidly both in number of firms and in total market capitalization, only to crash dramatically in 2000 and 2001. In the wake of these events, it is appropriate to reflect on what of actual value resides in modular designs and in the modular cluster as a form of economic organization.

The HBR article was part of a much larger project, which we embarked on 1987, and which continues. To date, we have finished the first of two planned volumes: *Design Rules: Volume 1, The Power of Modularity*. The article introduced several of the concepts found in the book:

- inspired by Herbert Simon (this volume) and Christopher Alexander (1964), it gave a definition of modularity, which others have found useful;[2]
- following David Parnas (1972a, b; et al., 1985), it described how to partition design information into visible design rules and hidden design parameters; and
- it distinguished modularity-in-design from modularity-in-production and modularity-in-use.

The article also made several sweeping statements to the effect that modularity was responsible for high rates of product innovation and economy-wide "evolution":

Through widespread adoption of modular designs, the computer industry has dramatically increased its rate of innovation. Indeed it is modularity, more than . . . any other technology, that is responsible for the heightened pace of change, that managers in [this] industry now face. . . . modularity drives the evolution of much of the economy

In the article, we did not back up these assertions. In particular, we did not describe the process of modular design evolution, which we were then attempting to explain in our other work. Thus, before proceeding here, we would like to describe briefly the theory on which we based our managerial recommendations. Our theory of modular design evolution can be summarized in two bullets:

- Modularity creates options.
- Modular designs evolve as the options are pursued and exercised.

Each of these points, however, needs some amplification.

1. Modularity creates options

When the design of an artifact is "modularized," the elements of the design are split up and assigned to modules according to a formal architecture or plan. Some of the modules are "hidden," meaning that design decisions in those modules do not affect decisions in other modules; some of the modules are "visible," meaning that they embody "design rules," which hidden module designers must obey if the modules are to work together. (See "A guide to modularity" in the article for further details.) In general, modularizations serve three purposes, any of which may justify expenditures to increase modularity:

- modularity makes complexity manageable;
- modularity enables parallel work; and
- modularity is tolerant of uncertainty.

In this context, "tolerant of uncertainty" means that particular elements of a modular design may be changed *after the fact* and *in unforeseen ways* as long as the design rules are obeyed.

Thus, modular designs offer alternatives that non-modular ("interdependent") designs do not provide. Specifically, in the hidden modules, designers may replace early, inferior solutions with superior solutions that are subsequently devised. We and several other authors in this volume have said that these alternatives can be modeled as "real options" within the formal theory of finance. Figure 5.1, taken from *Design Rules*, portrays how the option structure of a system changes as it goes from an interdependent to a modular design structure.[3]

The real options in a modular design are valuable. This is not a new or a controversial claim. Building on it, in *Design Rules* we sought to categorize the major options implicit in a modular design, and to explain how each type can be valued in accordance with modern finance theory. The key drivers of the "net option value" of a particular module, we discovered, were (1) the "technical potential" of a module (labeled σ, because it operates like volatility in financial option theory); (2) the

System before modularization   System after modularization

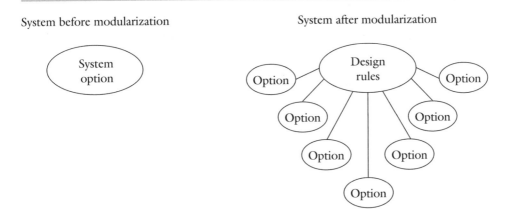

Figure 5.1 Modularity creates options.
Source: Baldwin and Clark, 2000, p. 237.

cost of mounting independent design experiments; and (3) the "visibility" of the module in question. The option value of a system made up of modules in turn can be approximated by adding up the net option values inherent in each module and subtracting the cost of creating the modular architecture. A positive value in this calculation justifies the investment of resources in a new modular architecture. But how will that value be realized? It will be realized over time via *modular design evolution*.

2. Modular designs evolve as the options are pursued and exercised

The promise implicit in a modular design is that parts of the system – the modules – can be modified after the fact at low cost. Foresighted actors seeking financial rewards will be motivated to pursue these options, and they will exercise the ones that are "in the money" at some future point in time (the actual date may be uncertain). Exercising an "in the money" option in this case means introducing a new, superior version of a particular module and reaping the economic rewards. The rewards take the form of positive cash flow from higher product revenue or lower process cost, or both.

The valuable options in a modular design thus motivate economic actors to pursue innovation, and the exercise of the options constitutes innovation. It follows that a modular design defines a set of evolutionary paths or trajectories in the sense originally defined by Nelson and Winter (1977), Sahal (1985), and Dosi (1988), and developed by many of the contributors to this volume.[4] There will be at least one trajectory per hidden module, and there may be more if the full potential of the actions we call "modular operators" is realized.[5]

As the history of a modular design unfolds, if the promise of the options is realized, we will "see" design evolution. The economically motivated actors in the system will pursue and then exercise design options on the basis of inherent economic value.

Their innovations will cause the individual hidden module designs to change over time in ways that create economic value. Architectures and interfaces will sometimes change, too, but less frequently.

This, we argue, is how innovation works in the microcosm of a modular system. Most changes will not be big sweeping disruptions of the whole, although those are not ruled out. Most changes instead will involve replacing one small modular element with another correspondingly small element that will do the same job in the system, only better. The overall picture is one of ordered, *but not wholly predictable*, progress towards higher economic value over time.

That is our theory in a nutshell. With it in mind, in the HBR article, we urged managers to embrace modularity and its option values, and to design their organizations and strategies with the demands of modular design evolution in mind:

> Being part of a shifting modular cluster of hundreds of companies in a constantly innovating industry is different from being one of a few dominant companies in a stable industry.

3.   The dot.com bubble and crash

But even as the article went to print, events in the economy at large were already beginning to run out of control. In June 1997, the NASDAQ market index was marching upward toward 1,500. Its climb continued for almost three years through the first part of 2000: for one brief moment, on March 10, 2000, the index reached the giddy height of 5,132. Then it gave back almost all its gains: in mid May 2002, it is hovering around 1,700, having closed as low as 1,423 on September 21, 2001.

The NASDAQ index is both symptomatic and symbolic of the so-called dot.com bubble and crash. Between 1997 and early 2000, thousands of computer software and hardware companies were formed. Several hundred went public. These fledgling companies did not have proven products, much less positive cash flow. Instead they were founded on the basis of product-ideas. According to their virtually universal business plan, if only the idea could be converted from a concept into a real product, the product was guaranteed to play an essential role in the vast new, modular system called the Internet. Revenue, profits, and cash would then flow to the firm that first made the product-idea real.

On this view, virtually all dot.com startups were formed to "pursue the option values inherent in a modular design." Today, most of those companies are running out of money, and very few are likely to survive. Large companies are announcing cutbacks and layoffs; smaller companies are going bankrupt or being acquired. For their part, investors have no reason to rejoice: from June 1997 to April 2001, much more value was destroyed than was created in the "modular sector" of the capital markets.

How do we square this bleak reality with the optimistic tone of our article? Can we hold to our theory of modularity as a source of options and and economic value in the aftermath of these events? In fact, the dot.com bubble and crash caused us to reflect critically on both our theory and our optimistic stance. In particular, we asked, in the real world (as opposed to the ideal world, which we modeled), do the benefits of modularity and the modular cluster form of organization justify the costs? If so, when and why?

In the glaring light of current events, we can see some large gaps in our theory. Two, which in hindsight seem especially important, are: (1) how can rational actors calibrate the "technical potential" of a module? and (2) how can rational investors as a group arrive at a sensible aggregate valuation of opportunities, when the opportunities themselves are dispersed in a large modular cluster of firms and markets? In the next sections of this commentary, we will explain why these questions are important, and what the answers may imply for the process of modular design evolution in the economy at large. We will then cycle back to the original focus of the article: how does managing in "the modular age" differ from previous ways of managing firms in a market economy?

4. What our theory does and does not predict

Many aspects of the dot.com phenomenon are wholly consistent with our theory of modular design evolution. Internet protocols, supplemented by the Hypertext Markup Language (HTML), and universal resource locators (URLs) constituted the design rules – the visible information – for a very large and economically potent modular system. Our theory predicts that when the architecture and interfaces of a new modular system become "good enough," hundreds, even thousands, of new design experiments in the hidden modules of the system will become valuable. The architectural transition that multiplies options and option values may arrive quite suddenly, and trigger a wave of investment. Furthermore, if the design rules are not privately owned (and the Internet and World Wide Web protocols are not), valuable options will be accessible to small new firms as well as to established older ones. Thus, in a modular system, it is not surprising to see an investment wave reflected in a wave of entry by small, new firms.[6]

After the initial "explosion" of options and investment, our theory predicts that candidate designs will compete with one another in a set of "tournaments."[7] In each module category, only one or two solutions will "win" and survive. Tournament competition, we said, would be especially fierce in those hidden modules with the lowest costs of experimentation and the highest technical potential. There, where most of the investment and entry take place, winners will be transient and subject to rapid turnover and substitution.

Hence the great wave of entry and the present "die-off" of Internet firms are fully consistent with our theory of modular design evolution in a large new system with non-proprietary design rules. What was not predicted, and indeed presents a problem for our theory, was the runup and subsequent crash of the NASDAQ index.

Our formal theory was an equilibrium theory in a stage-game, which we constrained by "rational expectations."[8] Within the framework imposed by rational expectations, *we assumed that the technical potential, σ, of each set of design experiments and the cost of each experiment were known to investors in advance of their investment.* We showed that these two factors together determined the number of profitable experiments that could be undertaken with respect to each specific module in the greater system. In other words, technical potential and experimental cost jointly determined a rational investment rule.

In a group of experiments aimed at a particular hidden module we envisioned the resolution of uncertainty taking place more or less as follows:

1   Initially, every design experiment in a given module category would "carry" value in proportion to its probability of "winning," (where winning meant emerging as the best design in that category). Thus, if each experiment initially had an equal probability of winning and equal cost to all the rest, then each would have the same economic value at the start of the process.
2   As the process unfolded, one design would emerge as best in each category, and the other experiments would be abandoned. Concomitantly, the sum of economic values in a given category, which was initially dispersed over all design-experiments in the category, would migrate to the winning design and to the firm that owned it.

Thus, we predicted, there would be great turbulence and risk across design-experiments within each category. There would be many starters, many losers, and only a few winners, especially in the low-cost categories with high technical potential. But, we thought much of this risk would disappear in the aggregate. The mathematics of real options and of extreme values pointed in this direction: as is well known, the standard deviation of the *highest* of a set of *independent* trials from a given distribution is much less than the standard deviation of the distribution itself.[9]

Under rational expectations, events in the system might unfold in many different ways, consistent with the underlying distributions, but the investors *ex ante* beliefs about the probabilistic structure would not be disconfirmed by what actually happened. Investors would see after the fact that this design-experiment turned out well, while that one turned out badly, but they would have no reason to change their beliefs about the basic probability distributions underlying the experiments. That being the case, investors would have no reason to want to revise their initial investment strategies with respect to module experiments!

Now, we submit, almost anyone who is aware of the dot.com phenomenon has had to change his or her beliefs about the probabilistic structure of the phenomenon. Even those whose expectations about *fundamental value* were essentially correct (that is, those who identified "the bubble" in 1997 or 1998) have had to revise their beliefs about other people's beliefs, and the effect of others' beliefs on actual market values in the short run and the long run. That means almost no one can honestly claim to have had "perfect rational expectations" about the dot.com phenomenon before the fact.

However, it is possible to move away from the rigid notion of a rational expectations equilibrium and still stay within the framework of a modular system and modular design evolution. If we do so, and assume that costs are generally better understood than probabilities, then two questions immediately arise. First, where do investors get their assessments of technical potential – the implicit σs – which condition their investment strategies? And second, how does knowledge about technical potential come to be "common knowledge" across a group of investors? These are reasonable questions to ask in the context of an evolutionary game, that is, a game played over multiple rounds, in which actors revise their view of the underlying probabilities and the value of strategies as new data come in.

Indeed, it seems unreasonable to believe that knowledge of the probabilistic reward structure of a new modular system would spring fully formed into the minds of investors at the very moment that the system itself came into being. And yet that is what a strict construction of rational expectations would have us assert. We think it is more reasonable (and interesting) to assume that investors must learn about the probabilistic reward structure of the system through their experiences with investment over time. In an evolutionary sense, investors may even influence the reward structure: it is well known that evolutionary games can develop along different trajectories, each of which provides different rewards for the players. Moreover, the players' interactions and experiences in an evolutionary game may or may not converge over time to an equilibrium set of consistent beliefs and stable strategies.

Thus, the dot.com phenomenon caused us to cut loose from the strict notion of "rational expectations equilibrium" that was inherent in our initial formulation of the theory. We have moved from it toward the more dynamic and provisional notion of equilibria in the setting of evolutionary games. This new framework is leading us to ask new questions: for example, which institutions in a modular system support the formation of consistent beliefs?; which beliefs need to be consistent?, and which can remain unreconciled?; how do different specifications of property rights (for example, the GNU public license) affect beliefs about reward structures?; and how do anticipated reward structures affect trajectories of innovation at different levels of a modular system?

5. Managing in a modular age

Where does the foregoing discussion take us in our recommendations to managers? We should start by saying that we still think that a modular cluster is a viable and useful form of economic organization in a market economy for industries that "play host" to modular design evolution. Those industries at present include: computers (hardware, software and chip design, though not chip fabrication); financial services; complex assembled goods like automobiles (the design evolution is in their parts, manufacturing processes, and supply chains); and Internet/Web services. In the wake of the dot.com bubble and crash, we fully expect to see a die-off of small firms and financial distress among some large firms in these sectors. But we do not expect to see any of these industries consolidate into a handful of large, vertically-integrated companies. This view of the future, which could be wrong, conditions our recommendations.

For managers in a modular cluster, it is essential (as we said in the article) to "know your product's place" in the design hierarchy of the modular system. Products that are hidden modules, especially small hidden modules with high technical potential, will be subject to very different competitive dynamics than products that embody visible design rules.

Table 5.4   Six modular operators.[10]

Operator	Definition
Splitting	Divides an interdependent system into modules
Substituting	Replaces one module with another
Augmenting	Adds a new module to the system
Excluding	Takes a module out of the system
Inverting	Creates new design rules and architectural modules
Porting	Makes a module compatible with two or more systems

We would now add: study the modular operators (see table 5.4) and the associated option values that are relevant to each of your products. Modular operators form a repertory of actions that can be performed in modular systems. Complex changes in a modular system can be represented as combinations of operators. The value of specific operator-moves can be modeled using real options methods from finance. In the operators and their option values reside both the opportunities and the threats to the products' revenue streams.

We would also say: do not be dogmatic about product and process boundaries. A process can be a module, and, if it is, the process can be a product. In fact, product definitions are endogenous in a modular system. The modular operators can be used to create new modules that can become new products, hence serve as the basis of new firms. As a result, products and firms will be ever-changing in the presence of modular design evolution. In addition, the greatest "turbulence," that is, the most rapid turnover of designs, will predictably arise in the small hidden modules with high technical potential: this is true whether the modules are specified as tangible objects or intangible processes.

In the article we emphasized that the internal organization of a firm – of any size – needed to reflect the modular structure of its products and processes, and to allow for decentralized, independent exercise of modular options. Unambiguous, binding design rules and simple, objective criteria of success and failure were desirable features for organizations competing in an evolving modular system. We would echo those recommendations today. Recent empirical work by Richard Bergin (2001) on the relative performance of Internet startups with a range of internal structures and organizational philosophies has increased our confidence in this claim. His results indicate that carefully designed "rules hierarchies" that match the modular structure of a firm's products and processes increase its likelihood of success in the tournament-type competitions that are characteristic of evolving modular designs. In effect, "guidance rules" and internal modularity of products and processes support efficient, repeated plays for valuable market positions. These plays can occur in rapid sequence or in parallel: a modular organizational structure supports them by holding down organizational complexity; by enabling parallel work; and by permitting adaptive responses to new market developments.

We would also say to managers that a cluster of firms and markets is by no means the only way to organize a modular system, nor is it necessarily the most efficient way to encourage modular design evolution. To our knowledge, at least two other, quite different, forms of organization have also succeeded in "hosting" modular design evolution. These are the Toyota Motor Corporation and the Open Source Software development community: their modular systems are, respectively, the Toyota Production System (TPS),[11] and a set of stable and evolving open-source code bases including Apache and Linux. Indeed, we think that Toyota and the Open Source developers have managed to drive the principles of modularity deeper into their design hierarchies than any cluster of firms and markets – given their implicit coordination problems – would be able to do.

Thus, taking full account of the events of the last four years, we would still end on an optimistic, albeit more cautious, note. We believe that "the modular age" can be and should be an age of opportunity. Modularity is a powerful design principle, and the modular operators as a group are demonstrably generators of opportunities and option value. In addition, the modular cluster form of organization is both viable and useful. It is here to stay, although (we now see) clusters need institutional mechanisms for coordinating beliefs, and these institutions themselves are still evolving. Finally, even in a cluster, there will be opportunities to create modular systems and reap the benefits of modular design evolution within individual firms. For managers and for the rest of us, the greater peril lies in ignoring the potential of modularity.

ACKNOWLEDGMENTS

Our thanks to Barbara Feinberg, who over many years and countless discussions has helped us to develop and refine our ideas. Thanks also go to Masahiko Aoki, Richard Bergin, Wayne Collier, Mark Gaynor, Karim Lakhani, Alan MacCormack, Jan Rivkin, John Rusnak, Sonali Shah, Steve Spear, Don Sull, Kevin Sullivan, Jonathan West, Jason Woodard, and members of the Negotiations, Organizations and Markets group at Harvard Business School for sharing key insights. We alone are responsible for errors, oversights and faulty reasoning.

NOTES

1 According to Alfred Chandler (1966; 1977), large, "modern" corporations arose as a means of coordinating large-volume, high-flow-through production and distribution systems. Oliver Williamson (1985: Chapter 11) has interpreted the structures of modern corporations as responses to hazards of market contracting. It is our position that the basic "task structures" and the economic incentives of modular design systems are different from the task structures and incentives of classic large-volume, high-flow-through production and distribution systems. Therefore the organizational forms that arise to coordinate modular design may not ressemble the classic structures of the modern corporation. In this respect, we echo Garud and Kumaraswamy, Langlois and Robertson, Sanchez and Mahoney, and Schilling, all in this volume.

2 See, for example, Gilmore and Pine (1999).

3 A "modular design structure" is a particular structure of interdependencies among design or process parameters or, equivalently, tasks. The actual structure of any design process or any set of tasks can be determined using the "Design Structure Matrix" mapping tools developed by Donald Steward (1981) and Steven Eppinger (1991). For numerous applications of this methodology, see http://web.mit.edu/dsm/publications_name.htm.

4   See David (1987), and Langlois and Robertson, Tushman and Murmann, and Wade, all in this volume.
5   Operators are "units of action" in a formal model of a complex adaptive system. The concept is due to John Holland (1992).
6   This thesis was first put forward by Langlois (1992) and Langlois and Robertson (this volume). A formal theory of "the Silicon Valley model" based on information encapsulation and tournament incentives has been constructed by Masahiko Aoki (1999; 2001). Aoki derives what we call a "modular cluster" as an equilibrium institutional form in a set of linked games of R&D and investment.
7   We adopt this term from Aoki (1999; 2001). Aoki derives tournament competition as an equilibrium incentive mechanism, whereas we see it as an optimal response to underlying real options. In this respect, our theories are complementary and mutually reinforcing.
8   In a rational expectations equilbrium of a stage-game, the probabilisitic structure of outcomes is known to all actors before play begins: standard deviations and correlations of the underlying distributions are "common knowledge" to investors in a game theoretic sense. On the constraints imposed by rational expectations in stage-games, see Samuelson (1997: Chapter 1).
9   We did ask ourselves, what if the trials were *not* independent? Then, the mathematics of real options says, each trial or experiment would be worth less. Holding costs fixed, rational investors should then invest in fewer trials, mount fewer experiments, start fewer firms. Thus, under rational expectations, our theory of modular design evolution with independent experiments can explain – rationally – why so many firms were started and then subsequently failed. But it cannot explain why those firms' aggregate market value rose and fell so dramatically. An alternate theory with correlated experimental outcomes can explain why the aggregate index rose and fell, but it begs the question of why so many *separate* firms were started to pursue essentially similar opportunities. Of course, there is a combination of anticipated independence and correlation that would make what actually happened "just right." That is an interesting calculation; but to assume that exactly those parameters were actually "expected" and "common knowledge" we think involves a heroic degree of retrofitting of the facts!
10 This list includes the operators we documented as occurring in modular computer designs, and whose financial valuations we modeled (Baldwin and Clark, 2000). It is by no means an exhaustive list of operators. Other candidate operators are: *replicating* a module; *combining* two or more modules; and *extending* a module. The identity and valuation of operators is an open line of research in the economics of modular designs.
11 For an analysis of the design rules and modular structure of TPS, see Spear (1999: especially Chapter 1 and 160–5).

REFERENCES

Alexander, Christopher (1964). *Notes on the Synthesis of Form*, Cambridge, MA: Harvard University Press.
Aoki, Masahiko (1999). "Information and Governance in the Silicon Valley Model," Stanford University, http://wwwecon.stanford.edu/faculty/workp/swp99028.html, viewed Jan 12, 2001.
Aoki, Masahiko (2001). *Towards a Comparative Institutional Analysis*, Cambridge, MA: MIT Press.
Baldwin, Carliss Y. and Clark, Kim B. (2000). *Design Rules, Volume 1, The Power of Modularity*, Cambridge, MA: MIT Press.

Bergin, Richard J. (2001). Venture Design, Scalability and Sustained Performance, unpublished DBA dissertation, Boston, MA: Harvard University, Graduate School of Business Administration.

Chandler, Alfred D. (1966). *Strategy and Structure*, Cambridge, MA: MIT Press.

Chandler, Alfred D. (1977). *The Visible Hand: The Managerial Revolution in American Business*, Cambridge, MA: Harvard University Press.

David, Paul A. (1987). "Some New Standards for the Economics of Standardization in the Information Age," in P. Dasgupta and P. Stoneman (eds.), *Economic Policy and Technological Performance*, Cambridge, UK: Cambridge University Press, 206–39.

Dosi, Giovanni (1988). "Sources, Procedures, and Microeconomic Effects of Innovation," *Journal of Economic Literature*, 26, September: 1120–71.

Eppinger, Steven D. (1991). "Model-based Approaches to Managing Concurrent Engineering," *Journal of Engineering Design*, 2: 283–90.

Gilmore, James H. and Pine, Joseph II (eds.), (1999). *Markets of One: Creating Customer-Unique Value Through Mass Customization*, Boston, MA: Harvard Business School Press.

Holland, John, H. (1992). *Adaptation in Natural and Adaptive Systems*, Cambridge, MA: MIT Press.

Langlois, Richard N. (1992). "External Economies and Economic Progress: The Case of the Microcomputer Industry," *Business History Review*, 66(1): 1–51.

Nelson, Richard R., and G. Winter, Sidney (1977). "In Search of a Useful Theory of Innovation," *Research Policy*, 6(1): 36–76.

Parnas, David L. (1972a). "A Technique for Software Module Specification with Examples," *Communications of the ACM*, 15, May: 330–6.

Parnas, David L. (1972b). "On the Criteria to Be Used in Decomposing Systems into Modules," *Communications of the ACM*, 15, December: 1053–8.

Parnas, David L., Clements, P. C., and Weiss, D. M. (1985). "The Modular Structure of Complex Systems," *IEEE Transactions on Software Engineering*, SE-11, March: 259–66.

Sahal, Devendra (1985). "Technical Guideposts and Innovation," *Research Policy*, 14: 61–82.

Samuelson, Larry (1997). *Evolutionary Games and Equilibrium Selection*, Cambridge, MA: MIT Press.

Spear, Steven J. (1999). The Toyota Production System: An Example of Managing Complex Social/Technical Systems, unpublished DBA dissertation, Boston, MA: Harvard University, Graduate School of Business Administration.

Steward, Donald V. (1981). "The Design Structure System: A Method for Managing the Design of Complex Systems," *IEEE Transactions on Engineering Management*, EM-28(3), August: 71–4.

Williamson, Oliver E. (1985). "The Economic Institutions of Capitalism," New York, NY: Free Press.

CHAPTER SIX

TOWARD A GENERAL MODULAR SYSTEMS THEORY AND ITS APPLICATION TO INTERFIRM PRODUCT MODULARITY

MELISSA A. SCHILLING

Modularity is a general systems concept: it is a continuum describing the degree to which a system's components can be separated and recombined, and it refers both to the tightness of coupling between components and the degree to which the "rules" of the system architecture enable (or prohibit) the mixing and matching of components. Since all systems are characterized by some degree of coupling (whether loose or tight) between components, and very few systems have components that are completely inseparable and cannot be recombined, almost all systems are, to some degree, modular.

Many systems migrate toward increasing modularity. Systems that were originally tightly integrated may be disaggregated into loosely coupled components that may be mixed and matched, allowing much greater flexibility in end configurations. For instance, personal computers originally were introduced as all-in-one packages (such as Intel's MCS-4, the Kenback-1, the Apple II, or the Commodore PET) but rapidly evolved into modular systems enabling the mixing and matching of components from different vendors. Publishers also have embraced modularity by utilizing recent information technology advances to enable instructors to assemble their own textbooks from book chapters, articles, cases, or their own materials. Even large home-appliance manufacturers now offer their products in modular configurations – for example, some stoves now offer customers the ability to remove the burners and plug in other cooking devices, such as barbecue grills and pancake griddles.

Increasing modularity is not, however, limited to products: scholars have noted increasing modularity in many different kinds of systems. For example, in recent research scholars have examined the disaggregation of many large, integrated, hierarchical organizations into loosely coupled production arrangements, such as contract manufacturing, alternative work arrangements, and strategic alliances (Ashkenas, Ulrich, Jick, and Kerr, 1995; Schilling and Steensma, 1999; Snow, Miles, and Coleman, 1992). Authors have even noted trends toward increasing modularity (particularly in the United States) in educational curricula, architecture, literature, and music (Blair, 1988).

Modularity exponentially increases the number of possible configurations achievable from a given set of inputs, greatly increasing the flexibility of a system. However, research also indicates that not all systems migrate toward increasing modularity; some appear to follow a path toward increasing integration. In product systems, for example, sets of components that once were easily mixed and matched may sometimes be bundled into a singe integrated package that does not allow (or that discourages) substitution of other components. Many commonly used software applications are now bundled into "software suites" that promote seamless integration. Although they do not prohibit using other vendor components, they discourage it by offering dramatically improved performance through the combination of the particular set of applications. Even bicycle componentry – once typically sold as individual components, such as brakes, gear sets, cranks, and derailleurs – now is sold predominantly in integrated component bundles that may not be mixed and matched.

In organizational systems, researchers have noted that whereas in many industries firms appear to be disaggregating, other industries (e.g., banking and health care) are characterized by increasing consolidation and integration. Presumably, if we were to undertake a detailed study of how the concepts of modularity and integration are used in the many disciplines that study systems, we would find many other examples of systems that had migrated toward or away from increasing modularity.

So what drives some systems toward increasing modularity and others toward increasing integration? Although the concept of modularity has been used by researchers in the fields of mathematics (Qi, 1988), knowledge structures and language development (Anderson, 1987; Baddeley, 1986; Crain and Thornton, 1998; Fodor, 1983, 1998; van der Lely, 1997), biological anatomy (Hall and Hughes, 1996; Wagner, 1995, 1996), and social systems (Cole, 1999), in none of their literature have these scholars revealed an explicit causal model of the adoption of increasingly modular forms. Researchers also have begun to look at the disaggregation of organizational systems (Achrol, 1997; Snow et al., 1992), but they have attributed the process largely to the increasing rate of technological change and globalization, developing a causal explanation little further.

The product modularity research is more extensive; researchers have looked at some of the advantages of the adoption of modular product designs, including its impact on the production configuration options available to firms and product configuration options available to customers (e.g., Baldwin and Clark, 1997; Garud and Kumaraswamy, 1995; Langlois, 1992; Sanchez, 1995; Sanchez and Mahoney, 1996). Researchers also have looked at the pricing effects and market segmentation opportunities of unbundling integrated product systems (e.g., Bryan and Clark, 1973; Grimes, 1994; Jacobides, 1997; Wilson, Weiss, and John, 1990), and they have considered how modularity might enable firms to reap some of the network externality advantages of a standards-based architecture while still producing unique, proprietary components (Garud and Kumaraswamy, 1995; Schilling, 1999). The study of modular product systems is still fairly new, however, and, to date, there are no explicit causal models that tie all of these constructs together to explain the adoption of increasingly modular product designs.

My purpose in this article is to develop an overarching causal model of the migration of systems toward or away from increasingly modular forms – a model that allows us to integrate existing constructs and to provide direction for future research. I first draw on the work of prominent systems theorists, such as Herbert Simon (whose work emphasizes economic systems) and Christopher Alexander (whose seminal work on architectural form lends powerful insight into systems in general), as well as the work of John Holland and Stuart Kauffman (who have done very significant work on complex adaptive systems). Once a common language and per-spective on systems is established, I then use this framework to develop a general theory of modularity. I do not claim, by any means, to provide a general modular systems theory in its final state. This research does, however, provide a very import-ant first step in this direction, and, as a more refined theory of modular systems evolves, it should prove to be a very powerful instrument for understanding the integration and disaggregation of many kinds of systems, including organizational, technological, social, and biological systems.

I then apply this general systems model to the more specific case of product modularity, integrating the existing constructs associated with product modularity (such as system integration and flexibility), while providing direction to other factors that might influence migration. Integrating these constructs within a more abstract model also provides insight into how the features of a system and its context interrelate and coevolve.

The interfirm product modularity model is valuable in its own right as a tool for scholars and managers of technological systems; however, it also provides valuable insight into how the general model might be applied to specific kinds of systems. In building the product modularity model, I draw from the burgeoning research on product and organizational modularity (e.g., Baldwin and Clark, 1997, 2000; Garud and Kumaraswamy, 1995; Langlois, 1992; Langlois and Robertson, 1992; Sanchez, 1995; Sanchez and Mahoney, 1996) and from the research on product bundling from the fields of consumer behavior and economics (e.g., Cready, 1991; Eppen, Hanson, and Martin, 1991; Grimes, 1994; Guiltinan, 1987; Hanson and Martin, 1990; Holt and Sherman, 1986; Lawless, 1991; Wilson et al., 1990).[1]

In the final section of the article, I discuss some of the implications of this work for practicing managers and future research. This section also highlights some of operational challenges for the empirical researcher.

Modular Systems

It is possible for us to view almost all entities – social, biological, technological, or otherwise – as hierarchically nested systems, meaning that at any unit of analysis, the entity is a system of components and each of those components is, in turn, a system of finer components, until we reach some point at which the components are "elementary particles" or until science constrains our decomposition (Simon, 1962).

Simon gives the very familiar example of a biological organism, "which is composed of organs, which are composed of cells, which contain organelles, which are composed of molecules, and so on" (Simon, 1995: 26). System hierarchies can also overlap, enabling components to serve multiple systems – for instance, an individual may simultaneously be a component of a family system, an organizational system (where the individual works), and several other community systems (e.g., the individual's church).

Furthermore, we can distinguish between a system and the context within which it exists; if the system is a solution to a problem, the context is what defines the problem and might include its physical environment, inputs that eventually become a part of the system, or even a point in time – anything that places demands upon the system (Alexander, 1964: 15). The identity of any unit as system or context is not fixed; this identity is determined by the level of analysis we choose. For example, an organization is a system within a context of an industry, but that industry is a system within the context of an economy. If we move in the other direction, we see that the organization is the context within which a particular production system (and many other systems) may operate, and so forth.

Fitness and adaptation

The fitness of the system is the degree to which the system and its context are "mutually acceptable" (Alexander, 1964: 19). The assumption here is that many complex systems adapt or evolve, shifting in response to changes in their context, or to changes in their underlying components in the pursuit of better fitness (Holland, 1994, 1995, 1999). A system may adapt purposefully, as when organizations alter themselves to better seek "value" (fitness in economic systems; Baldwin and Clark, 2000; Van de Ven, Poole, and Scott, 1995), and populations of systems can shift even when systems do not individually change, because the environment selects for particular attributes, thus causing the nature of systems characterizing a context to evolve.[2] Much more in-depth, systematic discussions of evolution versus adaptation exist elsewhere and, thus, are not undertaken here. The important point is that the context creates forces (sometimes conflicting ones) that draw a system toward a particular state.

A second important point is that a system often will not achieve an "optimal" fit with its context. First, inertia prevents a system from being perfectly responsive to shifts in its context: biological organisms might be incapable of purposeful change, and evolution through variation, selection, and retention requires many generations to achieve; organizations and other social systems tend to resist change even when the environment provides strong pressure; and before we can change technological systems, we often first must fumble around in search of better solutions. Thus, when the context shifts quickly, the system may demonstrate maladaptive features (Gell-Mann, 1995). Second, some systems might be incapable of attaining an optimal fit with their context, even given unlimited time: science may never render an ideal technological solution for a particular problem, and biological and social systems, particularly when they are complex, may entail a multitude of "conflicting compromises" that prevent the system from attaining an optimal configuration (Kauffman, 1993, 1995). Thus, although systems respond to fit their context, they may do so slowly and clumsily.

Finally, it is also important to recognize that as a system shifts in response to its context, it might also change its context in significant ways. For example, a new system state might create new potential inputs as a by-product of its adaptation, or it might alter the nature of demands upon the system by creating new competitive dynamics among systems: the system and its context coevolve (Gell-Mann, 1995). Such change in context may be the unintentional result of the system's response to its context or the deliberate result of purposeful behavior. Although in the article I often utilize a deterministic perspective, whereby the system responds to its environment (rather than acting voluntaristically upon it), because such a perspective is parsimonious and may be more accurate for many kinds of systems, this perspective is not a necessary assumption of the models. In the product modularity section of the article, I give several instances of how the system (or its producers) might intentionally change the context.

Coupling and recombination

I now turn specifically to modularity. As mentioned before, modularity is a general systems concept that has been applied to many kinds of systems, including technological, social, and biological (Baldwin and Clark, 1997, 2000; Garud and Kumaraswamy, 1995; Langlois, 1992; Robertson and Langlois, 1995; Sanchez, 1995; Worren, 1997). At its most abstract level, it refers simply to the degree to which a system's components can be separated and recombined. Also, as mentioned previously, since all systems are characterized by some degree of coupling between their components and since very few systems have components that are completely inseparable and nonrecombinable, almost all systems are, to some degree, modular.

The primary action of increasing modularity is to enable heterogeneous inputs to be recombined into a variety of heterogeneous configurations. Therefore, whether a system will respond to a shift in its context by becoming more modular is a function both of the degree to which the components of the system are separable ("what will be lost by separating the components?") and the pressure to be able to produce multiple configurations from diverse potential inputs ("will the ability to produce multiple configurations increase the system's fitness?"). I address both of these questions in turn in order to develop a causal model of modularity at the general systems level.

Separability

As mentioned before, the components of almost all systems are ultimately separable, although much may be lost in their separation. We can disassemble products, split apart social institutions, and even cut apart biological organisms. The more interesting question is whether the systems can be put back together again and then continue to function as before; still more interesting is whether we must put them back together in their original configuration. Some systems cease to function completely if they are decomposed. For example, many biological organisms will die if any of their components become separated from the whole. Other systems – for example, many product systems – will continue to function once a certain minimum configuration of components is recombined (although not necessarily in a way identical to how they functioned prior to disaggregation).

Systems are said to have a high degree of modularity when their components can be disaggregated and recombined into new configurations – possibly substituting various new components into the configuration – with little loss of functionality (Langlois, 1992; Sanchez, 1995). The components of such systems are relatively independent of one another; if they are compatible with the overall system architecture, they may be recombined easily with one another.

However, even in systems in which recombination is possible, there might be some combinations of particular components that work better together than others. Through optimization of the components working in a particular configuration, these combinations achieve a functionality unobtainable through combination of more independent components. The degree to which a system achieves greater functionality by its components being specific to one another can be termed its *synergistic specificity*; the combination of components achieves synergy through the specificity of individual components to a particular configuration. Systems with a high degree of synergistic specificity might be able to accomplish things that more modular systems cannot; they do so, however, by forfeiting a degree of recombinability.

Examples of this can be found in a wide range of systems. Some product systems achieve their functionality only through optimizing each of the components to work with each other. Each component becomes specific to the system; making these components nonspecific will entail loss of performance (Simon, 1962). Some organizational processes, such as the development of a new product by a team (the system), are greatly enhanced by collocating the team members (components of the system) and dedicating them full time to the project. The team members will develop skills and knowledge that are idiosyncratic to the particular project, making them less recombinable in other teams. However, they are able to achieve a greater understanding and commitment to the project by becoming specific to the project, and they may consequently achieve a superior outcome.

Such synergistic specificity is at the core of many complex systems. The components of the system may require such extensive interaction – and that interaction may be so directly influenced by the design or nature of each component – that any change in a component requires extensive compensating changes in other components of the system, or else functionality is lost (Sanchez and Mahoney, 1996).[3] High levels of synergistic specificity act as a strong force against the system's shifting to a more modular design.

Other systems, in contrast, achieve little synergistic specificity; their components are relatively independent and can be recombined in a variety of configurations, with little or no loss of functionality. For example, a stereo system might be composed of a variety of components that can be mixed and matched easily, with little or no loss of functional performance (for a detailed account of the modularization of stereo systems, see Langlois and Robertson, 1992). Similarly, temporary employees with very well-defined skills also can be redeployed fairly easily within a variety of organizations, with little loss of performance – if we leave the employee's social experience out of the picture!

Furthermore, the degree to which a system is characterized by synergistic specificity might change over time. For example, advances in science might enable components that achieve greater synergistic specificity or that are more independent. To illustrate, through the development of standards to govern interaction and exchange, the components of many technological and social systems are now more easily recombinable. Input-output specifications between computer components enable vendors to produce a seemingly endless array of components that will easily connect and function well together. Even the human body has become more modular; as our understanding of the rules regarding the systemic exchange within the body has increased, so too has our ability to replace defective organs (biological components) with those removed from another person or with those created synthetically. This last example illustrates vividly that modularity can be seen as a general property of systems and that scientific advancement might enable modularity where it was once unthinkable.

The degree, therefore, to which a system is separable is a continuum. Some systems are relatively inseparable (although very few are perfectly inseparable), whereas other systems may be decomposed easily, with no loss of performance. Separability – influenced primarily by the degree of synergistic specificity characterizing the system – will be one of the strongest factors conditioning whether a system will respond to pressures to become more modular.

I now turn to examining those factors in the system's context that will create such pressure to become more modular.

Heterogeneity of inputs and demands

As mentioned before, the primary action of modularity is to enable heterogeneous inputs to be recombined into a variety of heterogeneous configurations. Therefore, we must now ask, "when will the ability to produce multiple configurations increase the system's fitness?" The answer to this question is revealed already in the action of modularity: when there are heterogeneous inputs and heterogeneous demands placed upon the system. The more heterogeneous the inputs are that may be used to compose a system, the more possible configurations there are attainable through the recombinability enabled by modularity. Furthermore, the more heterogeneous the demands made of the system, the more valued such recombinability becomes.

The more potential configurations there are of a system, the more likely it is that configurations will be found that meet the heterogeneous demands made of the system. For a simple example, consider the following. Suppose a car can be assembled from a range of components. The wider the range of components that can be recombined into a car, the wider the range of possible car configurations achievable through modularity and the greater the potential opportunity cost of being "locked in" to a single configuration. Furthermore, the more heterogeneous the customers for cars are, the less likely they are to agree on a single configuration. By employing modularity, heterogeneous customers can choose a car configuration that more closely meets their preferences.

Close examination of this example reveals that each of these two factors reinforces the pressure created by the other. That is, if customers are heterogeneous, but the possible components of a system are perfectly homogeneous, modularity might enable flexibility in scale but might not significantly increase the range of possible functions of the product configuration. Conversely, even if there is a wide range of components, but customers all want the same thing, there is little to be gained through offering a modular system; it will be a simple matter to determine the best combination of components to meet customer demands and to integrate them into a nonmodular system (Langlois and Robertson, 1992). However, heterogeneity in the range of inputs, *combined with* heterogeneity in customers, creates powerful incentives to adopt a modular system.

Migration and equilibria

Systems can migrate toward increasing modularity, becoming decomposed at ever-finer levels, until they again find a balance between the pressure to become modular and the functionality gained through synergistic specificity. For example, consider a system composed of parts A, B, and C. If there are many other alternative components that these components could be combined with (say, D–Z), and if some of the demands placed upon this system would be better met by other configurations (e.g., A + F + G or C + B + M), there will be pressure to decompose the system. If, however, the tight coupling of A, B, and C yields something much greater than any of these components could yield if combined in another configuration (synergistic specificity), this performance advantage will act against the pressure to decompose the system. *The balance between the gains achievable through recombination and the gains achievable through specificity determines the pressure for or against the decomposition of the system.*

Should the gains from recombination win out, the system likely will be decomposed into a group of modular components. Furthermore, because systems are typically nested hierarchies (as mentioned previously), each of these components is likely a system of other components – a system that faces its own balance among the heterogeneity of demands, the heterogeneity of inputs, and its degree of separability. Should heterogeneity of inputs and demands again win out, it too might be decomposed into modular components. Such a trajectory might go on and on until we reach a level at which the system is relatively inseparable, is composed of relatively homogeneous inputs, or faces relatively homogeneous demands, or some combination of these.

Similarly, if a system should begin to incur more advantages from highly specific components (through, perhaps, scientific advance), or its inputs or demands become more homogeneous, the system may migrate toward less modularity. And if this system is, in turn, a component of a larger system, and if there are strong gains to be achieved through making this component specific to a particular combination, it might become more tightly integrated with another even larger system. Thus, the trajectory of systems (with regard to modularity) is bidirectional: as the environment changes (causing demands or inputs to become more or less heterogeneous) or the separability of the system changes, the system might migrate up or down a trajectory, toward or away from increasing modularity.

Overcoming inertia

There is one more element we must consider, even at this very general level of abstraction. As mentioned earlier, systems are characterized by inertia. They do not respond immediately and vigorously to every external influence. Therefore, it is altogether possible that a system will be relatively more or less modular than the balance of its separability, heterogeneity of inputs, and heterogeneity of demands would otherwise indicate. Whether and to what degree a system responds to changes in its context are influenced by forces in the context that create *urgency*. For example, competitive intensity or time constraints (such as the rapid obsolescence of products and processes caused by technological change) can catalyze the system's response to these balances. For instance, as discussed at greater length later in the article, despite heterogeneous inputs and customers, minicomputer companies did not begin to offer more modular minicomputers until the rise of workstations began to greatly increase competitive pressure in the minicomputer industry. Similarly, as mentioned earlier, several authors have argued that it has been the increasing pace of technological change and the competitive intensity of increasingly globalized industries that have caused whole organizational systems to begin to decompose and to use network configurations so that organizational components can be recombined quickly and fluidly to respond to environmental shifts (Achrol, 1997; Miles and Snow, 1986).

In sum, we can map the factors influencing whether a system migrates toward increasing modularity as in figure 6.1[4]: the heterogeneity of both inputs and demands increases pressure for the system to become more modular, and both reinforce

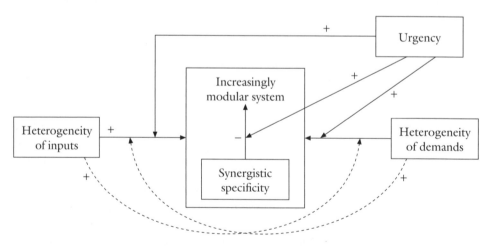

Figure 6.1 Modular systems[a]
[a] Solid lines represent direct effects; dashed lines represent indirect effects.

the effects of the other. The synergistic specificity of the system creates pressure against the system migrating toward modularity. Finally, factors creating urgency in the environment can catalyze the system's response to the balance of these forces.

I now apply this framework to a specific example: interfirm product modularity.

INTERFIRM PRODUCT MODULARITY

Products, like other kinds of systems, typically are bundles of components. A computer is a bundle of a CPU, a monitor, a keyboard, and a number of other components, many of which can be bought separately and assembled by the user, and some that typically are not. The monitor, in turn, is a bundle of many components (which are not typically sold separately to end users but may be exchanged among other intermediaries), such as LCDs, plastic housings, and so on.

Many product systems are modular; they can be decomposed into a number of components that can be mixed and matched in a variety of configurations (Garud and Kumaraswamy, 1995; Sanchez, 1995; Sanchez and Mahoney, 1996). The components are able to connect, interact, or exchange resources (such as energy or data) in some way, by adhering to a standardized interface. Unlike a tightly integrated product, whereby each component is designed to work specifically (and often exclusively) with other particular components in a tightly coupled system, modular products are systems of components that are "loosely coupled" (Orton and Weick, 1990; Sanchez and Mahoney, 1996; Weick, 1976).

Products can be made increasingly modular both by expanding the range of compatible components (increasing the range of possible product configurations) and by uncoupling integrated functions within components (making the product modular at a finer level). For example, a minicomputer manufacturer originally might offer a totally integrated, proprietary system in a single product configuration. However, greater market demand for flexibility might induce the manufacturer to begin to offer the system with a few different product configurations, each composed of the firm's own components. Should customers prefer to be able to combine the minicomputer with external components (such as off-the-shelf software or peripherals made by other vendors), the minicomputer manufacturer eventually might adopt a standard input-output protocol (a standardized interface) that makes the product compatible with other firms' components (employing interfirm product modularity). If pressure continues for even greater flexibility, the company might uncouple many of the functions of its core system and begin to sell them as modular components, which may then be combined in a greater number of product configurations with both the company's own components and other vendors' components. In each of these stages, the product has become increasingly modular.

The majority of products probably are modular at some level. The most obvious examples are products that employ interfirm modularity, enabling customers to assemble their own multivendor configuration. For example, many stereos, computers, shelving systems, and bicycles allow the customer to mix and match components from different vendors. There are a great many more products that are modular but that customers do not typically assemble themselves (although they may be able to choose the components). For instance, when a customer buys a car, he or she may be able to choose from a variety of product configurations available from the manufacturer (including engine size, upholstery options, automatic steering or transmission, and so on), and he or she may be able to choose components made by other vendors (such as a stereo system, tires, roof racks, security systems, and so on). Even aircraft are offered in this way: although Boeing and Airbus manufacture airframes, they do not manufacture engines. Engines are produced by such companies as GE, Pratt & Whitney, or Rolls-Royce. The engines generally are designed to be used in a few different aircraft models. Similarly, an aircraft is not committed to a single engine, although engineers might designate a "launch engine" as a preferred choice. The aircraft customer typically makes the final decision on which engine will be used in the aircraft.

Even more products are manufactured in a way that employs modularity within the firm but that does not extend the modularity to the customer level. For instance, firms might design their products so that particular components can be reused in a variety of product designs – employing Garud and Kumaraswamy's (1995) "economies of substitution." Different components might be included in multiple product configurations, but the end products themselves do not allow customer discretion over configuration.

Modularity within the firm not only enables economies in product design but may also greatly simplify coordination. If all components must be tightly integrated and optimized for each other, their production often requires that all individuals involved in such design and production also work in close contact. A modular product design, in contrast, can enable the production process to be decentralized. A firm that creates a well-defined standard interface can allow the individuals working on particular components to work in whatever departmental configuration they deem most desirable (even if that means that the departments are highly autonomous), and still be assured that the components will interact effectively.

There are a number of advantages and disadvantages of employing increasingly modular product designs, but the advantage most often cited is modularity's ability to greatly increase flexibility in the end product by allowing a variety of possible configurations to be assembled (Baldwin and Clark, 1997; Garud and Kumaraswamy, 1995; Sanchez, 1995). Modular technologies give users greater discretion over the function and scale of the end product, enabling users to create end products that perform functions more closely suited to their idiosyncratic needs. In the case of interfirm product modularity, it also enables customers to use components from a variety of different vendors, rather than being locked in to a single provider.

By applying the general modular systems framework developed earlier in the article to the specific case of modularity in products, we can simultaneously gain a deeper understanding of modularity as a general systems concept and explain why the dominant design of a product system should migrate toward or away from increasing modularity. I begin, as before, by considering those factors that will influence the separability of the system. I then look, in turn, at factors that increase the heterogeneity of inputs and the heterogeneity of demands placed upon the system. Next, I explore issues of urgency: those factors that will catalyze the system's response to pressure for increasing modularity and those factors that might prevent such catalysis (figure 6.2).

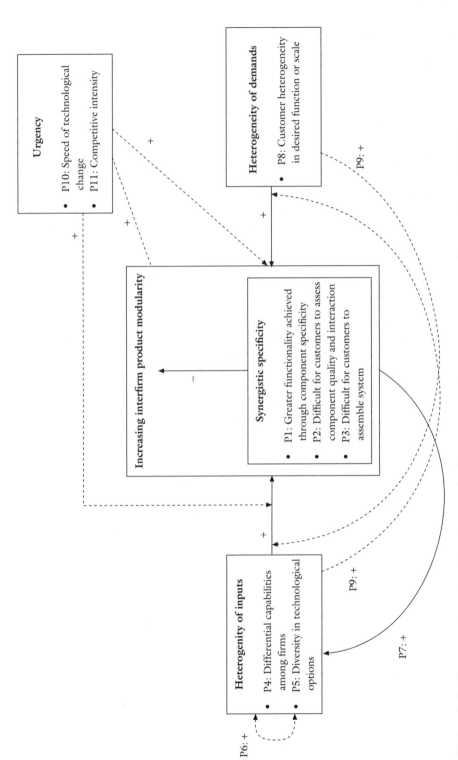

Figure 6.2 Factors influencing the migration toward (or away from) increasing interfirm product modularity.[α]

[α] Solid lines represent direct effects; dashed lines represent indirect effects.

Separability and synergistic specificity

Integrated product systems can achieve synergistic specificity both in the obvious way (through providing greater functionality by optimizing components to work together) and in a not-so-obvious way (through providing greater customer *confidence* that components will work well together, and through obviating the need for customer assembly).

Functionality achieved through specialized components

Even products that can be adapted easily to a standard interface may work *better* if they are optimized to be run with particular sets of other components. This is often argued to be the case for software suites, and it might explain the migration from many independent office software applications to integrated office software bundles.

After the first personal computer was introduced in the 1970s, there was rapid entry of competitors into the prepackaged software market. Early offerings included VisiCalc and Micropro Wordstar (both introduced in 1979), followed by WordPerfect, Lotus 1-2-3, and Microsoft's Multi-Tool Word for DOS. Although there were many other entrants during the 1980s, by the 1990s WordPerfect, Lotus, and Microsoft had risen to dominate the office software market. Initially, the companies competed via stand-alone software products, each differentiated from competitors in functionality and style. Personal computer users were likely to have a combination of products on their computers from multiple vendors.

However, after Microsoft's Windows 3.0 rose to become the dominant design in user interfaces (controlling roughly 90 percent of the market for IBM-compatible personal computers), software applications had to be Windows compatible in order to succeed. This eliminated some of the differentiation among the software offerings; each came to have a similar appearance and function. Furthermore, pressures for compatibility (between, for instance, a user's home computer and his or her office computer) forced software companies to enable a degree of integration between their products and competitors' products, further encouraging software products to become more homogeneous.

At the same time that the products became less differentiated, there was growing pressure to make different kinds of software programs work together better. Many users of office software programs wished to combine word processing, spreadsheets, databases, and presentation graphics in their files, and a product bundle that could integrate these functions seamlessly became much more valuable than were the components individually. Consequently, the early 1990s witnessed a move from stand-alone software products (such as WordPerfect or Microsoft Excel) to suites of integrated software products (such as Microsoft Office 97), designed to work better together than with other components. Through such integration and specificity, the product system yielded much greater functionality.[5]

Proposition 1: The degree to which functionality is achieved through component specificity$_{t0}$ will be negatively related to increasing interfirm product modularity$_{t1}$.

The degree to which functionality is achievable only through component specificity is related directly to the availability and effectiveness of standard interfaces (Baldwin and Clark, 1997; Garud and Kumaraswamy, 1995; Sanchez, 1995; Sanchez and Mahoney, 1996). The function of a standard interface is to make assets *nonspecific*, thereby facilitating the adoption of a modular structure. Without such an interface, firms might be able to provide components that could be mixed and matched with other vendors by developing *specialized* interfaces that coordinate the functions among a particular set of vendors' components, but the costs of developing such specialized interfaces would be very high, and the choice among configurations would be constrained to those configurations predetermined by the vendors that had produced the interfaces. (Some have argued that Microsoft's Windows is just such a constrained interface; this is discussed in greater length in the section on market power and architectural control.)

Customer ability and willingness to choose and assemble components

If it is difficult for a customer to choose appropriate components or to assemble those components into the product configuration, then a nonmodular product may offer the customer additional functionality by eliminating selection and assembly responsibilities. In order for a customer to choose components of a modular system, he or she must be able and willing to distinguish among the performance, quality, and value attributes of different components, which frequently means that the customer must have great understanding of how the components work both individually and together. For simple products, or those products where quality and performance are easily measured and the interaction among components well understood, the customer may have great confidence in his or her own ability to choose among components. However, where quality or performance are difficult to assess, the customer may be more likely to rely on a credible external source to choose components.

Even for a given product system, customers may vary in their degree of knowledge and motivation in choosing components. For example, although the average audio equipment customer usually buys a preassembled single-vendor stereo system (using brand name and limited technological information to assess overall system quality), more sophisticated audiophiles often purchase stereo components individually, from multiple vendors, in order to assemble a system that more closely matches their performance and price requirements.

Holt and Sherman (1986) suggest that where component quality is difficult to assess, customers may choose bundled or integrated products that are believed to provide an acceptable average quality across the components. Furthermore, where the nature of the *interaction* between components is uncertain, the customer may seek a product that has been assembled already to optimize its performance, thus making integrated solutions more attractive.

Proposition 2: The degree of difficulty customers face in assessing the quality and interaction of components$_{t0}$ will be negatively related to increasing interfirm product modularity$_{t1}$.

Furthermore, even when customers are willing and able to discriminate among components, they may be unwilling or unable to assemble the product configuration. Thus, an integrated product system may provide additional functionality in the form of preassembly[6] (Kinberg and Sudit, 1979; Porter, 1985).

> *Proposition 3: The degree of difficulty customers face in assembling components$_{t0}$ will be negatively related to increasing interfirm product modularity$_{t1}$.*

Heterogeneous inputs

The inputs into a product system include both the technological options available to achieve particular functions and the resources and capabilities of the firms involved in the production process. Heterogeneity in these inputs will increase the value to be obtained through modular product configurations.

Diversity of technological options available

When there are diverse technological options available to be incorporated into a product configuration, modular product designs will be more attractive to both customers and producers.

The diversity of available technological options might compel customers to seek more flexible solutions and make being tied to a single vendor less attractive. First, the number of available product configurations achievable through modularity is a direct function of the number of available components from which the customer may choose. A wider range of modular components quickly multiplies a customer's product configuration options, greatly increasing the flexibility gains to be reaped from modularity. Second, commitment to a single, integrated product system imposes an opportunity cost equivalent to the next best option available. When many different options are available, this opportunity cost is likely to be higher, because the next best solution is likely to be better than the next best solution when there are few options available. Third, when there is a great diversity in available technologies, the customer faces more ambiguity about which option is actually best. When there is little diversity in the technological options, customers sacrifice less by being committed to a single vendor, and they face less uncertainty about the optimality of their technology choice.

Diversity in the technological options available makes modularity more attractive to producers as well. It is usually difficult, and costly, for a firm to support multiple technologies (Garud and Kumaraswamy, 1995; Penrose, 1959; Teece, 1986). Very often, firms must choose one or two technology designs, gambling on those they believe to be the best match with (1) their capabilities and/or (2) consumer requirements. As with customers, a large number of diverse options can increase a firm's ambiguity about which technology to support. Furthermore, if the various technologies are incompatible (and products based on the technologies are, therefore, only offered as integrated systems), the firm might face a win-or-lose scenario: the firm either becomes a customer's sole supplier of an entire product system or it does no business with the customer at all.

Under conditions of modularity, the firm does not face such a win-or-lose scenario. Modularity enables compatibility between disparate technologies, lowering the risk to the firm of gambling on a particular technology. Multiple technologies can coexist more peacefully. The firm does not have to compete for a customer's business for an entire system; it can compete for a customer's business for a particular component, focusing on a technology in which it excels and allowing other vendors to supply other technologies.

> *Proposition 4: Greater diversity in the technological options available in the market$_{t0}$ will be positively related to increasing interfirm product modularity$_{t1}$.*

Differentiation in firm capabilities

Scholars of the resource-based view of the firm point out that firms have individual sets of core capabilities that distinguish them from competitors (Leonard-Barton, 1992). Because products often are made up of components that draw from different underlying production technologies, distribution and marketing requirements, or other required skill sets, a firm's core capabilities may put it at a performance or cost advantage in producing some components, while putting it at a disadvantage in producing others (Barney, 1991). A firm that specializes in those products in which it excels may earn higher returns than one that has its returns averaged across components in which it excels and those in which it does not. The greater the difference between the capabilities that firms possess, the greater the benefit they reap from specializing in different components. Thus, greater differentiation in firm capabilities can make modular solutions an attractive option for producers (Jacobides, 1997).

Great differentiation in firm capabilities can lead to increased pressure for modularity from customers as well. When differential capabilities among firms yield components with differential performance and value, the customer prefers to be able to choose from among various vendors in order to assemble the technology solution that provides the best fit with his or her needs. (Alternatively, when there is little difference between the capabilities that firms possess, their products may be more similar in terms of function, performance, or value, thus reducing the value of being able to mix and match components.)

> *Proposition 5: The degree to which firms in the market have different capabilities$_{t0}$ will be positively related to increasing interfirm product modularity$_{t1}$.*

Diversity in the technological options available and differentiation in firm capabilities will reinforce each other. The more differentiated firm capabilities are, the more likely firms will be to produce disparate technological options; likewise, the more technological options there are available to firms, the more likely they will be to choose to specialize in different things. Furthermore, when these two attributes are combined with the adoption of modular product designs, a circular dynamic may be engaged that propels a technology even further down a modularity trajectory: (1) the more different the sets of skills are among competitors, the more attractive modularity becomes, because it enables disparate technologies to be combined; (2) the use of modular product designs also enables firms to further specialize, encouraging them to pursue specialized learning curves and increasing their differentiation from competitors; and (3) the more firms travel down isomorphic learning paths, they more they develop disparate technologies (see figure 6.2). Such reinforcing effects can fuel a technology's motion along a trajectory, until it again hits a point at which inseparability of components grinds it to a halt at a new (potentially transient) equilibrium.

Proposition 6: The degree to which firms in the market have differentiated capabilities and the availability of diverse technological options will reinforce each other.

Proposition 7: The adoption of increasingly interfirm modular product designs$_{t1}$ may result in both the further differentiation of firm capabilities$_{t2}$ and the development of diverse technological options$_{t2}$.

Heterogeneous demands

Customer heterogeneity is an important factor that influences whether a technology will migrate toward increasing or decreasing modularity. When most customers desire roughly the same types of components and their requirements for each individual component are comparable, a firm is able to produce a bundle that is close to optimal for the majority of customers (Langlois and Robertson, 1992); through integrating the products, the firm may be able to create performance or cost advantages that outweigh the sacrifices customers make in not being able to choose their own components.

Alternatively, when customers for a particular technology solution have very different needs, it is more difficult for a single integrated solution to closely match their idiosyncratic requirements.[7] Consider the college textbook market. College course instructors have very heterogeneous preferences both for the type of material they wish to deliver and for the method of delivery. As inexpensive copying options proliferated (as did copyright clearinghouses, which facilitate the transfer of copyright privileges), many instructors moved away from the single, large, integrated textbook and began assembling their own course packets from articles, book chapters, cases, and their own course notes. Although the packets were somewhat ungainly (many had no consecutive page numbering system, and most lacked a table of contents and index), they offered the instructor greater flexibility in designing a course that met their needs. The instructor could not only determine the topic and sequence of the material but could also determine the depth to which a topic was explored. In response, publishing companies began designing their own customized textbook systems. One of the most widely used of these systems in the late 1990s was McGraw-Hill's Primis.

Primis allows instructors to assemble their own textbooks from a database of book chapters, articles, cases, and other materials (Venkatraman, 1997). The materials are not limited to McGraw-Hill's titles; Primis texts often include Harvard Business School cases, articles from journals, and book chapters from other publishers' texts, as long as copyright permissions are obtained. The materials are entered into a database and coded so that an instructor can choose materials and decide on their order, and a table of contents and indexing system are generated electronically. Books can be printed and shipped to bookstores within 5 to 10 days. McGraw-Hill's Electrobook Press also can print book runs of any quantity (McGraw-Hill frequently generates books for a single class) and does not require stopping for setups between titles. The ability to run small lots and to assemble and deliver books quickly allows instructors to update their texts from semester to semester.

Although McGraw-Hill uses a proprietary system for its database, the company still allows components from multiple vendors (in this case, publishers) to be combined, which creates great flexibility for the user. Should a standardized coding system be established for the industry, it is conceivable that the entire industry will migrate toward true interfirm modularity, whereby instructors will be able to download materials from multiple publishers, arrange payment for copying rights, and assemble and copy the text through any facility capable of printing and binding. (McGraw-Hill already is distributing Primis texts through university copy centers, who then collect payment for the texts. These centers would be a likely place for such printing and assembly.)[8]

> *Proposition 8: Customer heterogeneity in desired function or scale of product$_{t0}$ will be positively related to increasing interfirm product modularity$_{t1}$.*

The counter side of this proposition (that modular solutions are less likely when buyer needs are relatively homogeneous) is supported by an examination of the bicycle componentry industry. Until the last 10 years, the bicycle componentry industry was highly fragmented, composed of many small competitors providing differentiated products sold on an individual basis.

However, in the 1980s, Shimano radically altered the industry norms. In addition to spending considerably more on R&D and advertising than previous competitors, Shimano deployed its products very strategically. By 1984 it had invented the first click-shifting system – a breakthrough product that made bicycles more user friendly. It then combined these shifters into sets with derailleurs, crank sets, brakes, and other componentry that could not be mixed and matched. It also gave bike assemblers incentives to use a wholly Shimano system (causing it to be the target of an antitrust suit in 1989). Customers who wanted to have Shimano's click-shifting system on their bicycles were required to buy a bicycle that had the entire Shimano componentry set. (According to Shimano, the components were also optimized to work better with each other than if they were combined with other components – achieving synergistic specificity.)

The end result was a high-quality system of parts that had wide brand recognition. This, combined with the relative homogeneity of customer needs, enabled Shimano's componentry sets to become the dominant design in the bicycle componentry market. The vast majority of customers did not care enough (or were not well-informed enough) to compare the performance advantages of the various individual components. Although customers could have insisted on choosing among the various other components available to assemble a modular system, most were simply looking for a bicycle that had components of good quality and would function correctly. A well-known brand name and the endorsement of a salesperson often were enough to assure them that these needs were met. Since consumer needs were relatively homogeneous, Shimano was able to assemble an integrated component set that met the needs of the majority of bicycle customers.[9]

As of 1997, Shimano had gained a near monopoly position in the US bicycle component market, with an estimated market share of 86 to 98 percent. Other componentry manufacturers were forced to seek out market niches where Shimano's design had not become dominant – for example, bicyclists with more specialized needs. Racing cyclists, touring cyclists, or those who subject their bicycle to very grueling off-road adventures have different demands for individual components and are much more likely to assemble their own mix of components, thus avoiding a component package. These niche markets became the domain of componentry providers, such as Campagnola and Sachs.[10]

Furthermore, as the auto example provided in the general modular systems section illustrates, such heterogeneity of demands and the heterogeneity of inputs will have reinforcing effects upon each other.

> *Proposition 9: Heterogeneous inputs (diversity in technological options and differentiation in firm capabilities) and heterogeneous demands (customer heterogeneity) will each reinforce the effect of the other.*

Urgency

Some of the primary factors that create urgency in the contexts of product systems are speed of technological change and competitive intensity. Such factors increase the likelihood of the system responding to pressures to become more modular. Alternatively, when there is low urgency in the context or when a firm (or group of firms) is so powerful that it *experiences* less urgency, the product system might be pushed (or retained) at a point on a trajectory that seems a poor fit with the balance of the demands of its context and the synergistic specificity of the system. For example, firms might wish to prevent the adoption of modular product designs because modularity would decrease their market power or architectural control. Each of these situations is discussed below.

Speed of technological change

One of the major factors increasing the pressure to migrate toward modular techno-logy solutions is the speed of technological change. Where technology advances rapidly, both customers and producers desire flexibility in order to respond to the rapidly changing heterogeneity of inputs and demands. High-speed technological change can both increase the rate at which new and heterogeneous inputs proliferate and, by rapidly expanding the scope of possibilities for customers, nurture the rapid evolution of heterogeneous demands. Because the product design must be able to adapt quickly to fulfill heterogeneous demands (or to incorporate heterogeneous inputs), a modular solution becomes very attractive.[11]

For customers, modularity reduces switching costs and enables them to upgrade particular components as new technology becomes available, without replacing the entire system (Sanchez, 1995). Consider again the minicomputer industry. In the late 1970s companies such as Digital Equipment Corporation (DEC) and Data General began to challenge IBM's dominance in computing by offering minicom-puters. Smaller than a mainframe but considerably more powerful than personal computers or workstations of that era, minicomputers were rapidly adopted by small- to medium-size businesses. Minicomputers typically utilized a proprietary central processor, combined with a proprietary system bus and run with a propriet-ary operating system. This meant that a customer was locked into a single-vendor system that usually was not compatible with hardware or software from other vendors. Minicomputers generally were customized to individual customers to meet their particular needs, and if the customer wanted to develop a new project, they would have to hire consultants to do custom programming or would have to do their own programming in house (Streicher, 1991). This process was costly and slow, but at the time there were no other reasonable alternatives.

As microprocessor technology evolved, the processing power of PCs began to reach levels at which industrial control systems could be based entirely on a network of PCs. Customers began to move to networked PCs and workstations in droves. By adopting a workstation network based on standard interfaces, customers quickly could alter both the function and scale of their computing systems, upgrading individual components as new alternatives became available. They also could quickly adopt new software, enabling a given set of hardware to accomplish a much wider range of tasks.

DEC, Data General, and Hewlett-Packard all responded by moving toward increasingly modular, microprocessor-based products, configured in a client-server relationship, and were able to survive the minicomputer industry shakeout. DEC launched the VAX 4,000 Model 300 – a powerful local area network (LAN) server and a suite of network management software for multivendor LANs (Nesbitt, 1990).[12] Data General built a new line of RISC systems (the AViiON line of systems, servers, and workstations) embracing the UNIX operating system and various networking standards (*PR Newswire*, 1990). Hewlett-Packard also introduced a new line of RISC-based minicomputers based on open systems (the HP 3,000 and the HP 9,000 Series; Slofstra, 1990).

In contrast, Wang and Prime both stuck to their proprietary integrated systems and did not fare nearly as well. After suffering severe losses from 1986 through 1989, Wang announced that it would refocus its business on image processing technology. Prime saw its revenue bottom out in 1985 and chose to change its market domain, focusing instead on CAD/CAM products (Kiely, 1989). In 1992 Prime announced it would phase out its hardware operations.

In addition to increasing customer pressure for modularity, technological change may also make modularity more attractive to producers. Modularity enables a producer to incorporate new technologies into its products as they become available, while still being able to combine components within the existing product architecture (Henderson and Clark, 1990).[13] As long as new technology generations are compatible with the standard interface, components based on the new technology may still integrate with the installed base of components based on the previous technological generation. Modularity, therefore, increases the ease with which both customers and producers may upgrade their technology (Garud and Kumaraswamy, 1995), and it may slow the obsolescence of other parts of the product system.

> *Proposition 10: If there are pressures to increase or decrease the interfirm modularity of a product system, the speed of technological change$_{t0}$ will increase the likelihood of such a migration$_{t1}$.*

Competitive intensity

If a product market has heterogeneous inputs and heterogeneous demands, a high degree of competitive intensity will increase the likelihood of one or more competitors opting to offer a modular product in an effort to differentiate themselves competitively. Through offering modular products, firms may create product configurations that more closely fit customer needs, and thus enable them to penetrate more market niches. Furthermore, if those modular products meet the heterogeneous demands of customers better than tightly integrated products, many other competitors may be forced to follow suit. Modular products may erode a firm's market power and architectural control (as discussed later), but if competitive intensity is fierce, firms are more likely to bow to market pressure.

Competitive intensity also puts great pressure on firms to lower costs. Modularity may impact the end cost to customers through its influence on both switching and product costs. When customers choose a nonmodular solution, they are making a commitment to a single source and forfeiting the many other options that would be achievable through reconfiguring heterogeneous inputs. Once a solution is chosen, the customer bears significant switching costs to change vendors. However, modularity enables purchasing from multiple sources, thus decreasing switching costs (Jacobides,

1997; Sanchez, 1995). If a customer decides to change to a product from another vendor, that customer need only change components – not the entire system.[14]

Modularity also can impact the price customers pay for products by influencing both firm costs and margins. In a market characterized by product design modularity, component vendors might benefit by increased specialization (Langlois, 2000). Consider first the alternative case. A firm that produces all of the components of a system faces greater fixed and variable costs: it must have the equipment required to produce a variety of components, not all of which will be based on the same manufacturing technologies; it might have to employ more people in order to ensure a wider range of available skills; it likely will have higher inventory costs because it must hold both the raw materials for a wider range of products and the range of end products themselves; and it might face greater setup costs to vary production, although flexible and lean manufacturing systems may attenuate some of these costs (Lei, Hitt, and Goldhar, 1996). In contrast, a firm that specializes in producing only one or a few components can avoid these costs and can focus on those components that best leverage its core capabilities and maximize its performance/value ratio.

Furthermore, modularity can increase the degree of competition among component providers both because it lowers customer switching costs and lowers entry barriers by enabling competitors who only produce one or a few components (but not the entire system) to enter the market. This can result in greater pressure on firm profit margins and may translate into lower costs for consumers.

We can see all three of these price/cost effects in the minicomputer case discussed earlier: customers found modular minicomputers (or networked workstations, which are also a modular alternative) more attractive than conventional minicomputers because they enabled changes to be made to the system without changing the whole system or relying on a single vendor (lowered switching costs), and because increased competition between minicomputer and microcomputer providers resulted in lower prices (lowered margins). Furthermore, both the microcomputers and the modular minicomputer components were less expensive to produce than highly customized minicomputer solutions (lowered production costs).

> *Proposition 11: If there are pressures to increase or decrease the interfirm modularity of a product system, competitive intensity$_{t0}$ will increase the likelihood of such a migration$_{t1}$.*

A particularly interesting competitive dynamic arises when industries are characterized by strong network externality effects. Under conditions of network externalities, a consumer's benefit from using a good is related directly to the number of other users of the same good (Katz and Shapiro, 1986). Network externalities are likely to be particularly important when the products interact in a physical network (e.g., telecommunications, computer networks) or when complementary goods (e.g., software for computers, videotaped movies for videoplayers) play a key role in the function of the product. In such systems the fitness (or value) of the system, thus, is closely linked to the size of its installed base and the availability of complementary goods. Furthermore, product designs with an initial advantage in installed base or complementary goods availability can reap self-reinforcing feedback effects: customers are more likely to choose the product design (increasing the installed base), and complementary goods producers are more likely to support the product design (increasing the availability of complementary goods). Through this cycle of increasing returns, the product rises rapidly to a position of dominant design (Arthur, 1989).

In such markets, rapidly gaining a large installed base (and encouraging the proliferation of complementary goods) is of extreme importance. This creates a dilemma for the firm about whether to protect or diffuse its technology: although a firm might wish to protect its proprietary technologies (through patents, secrecy, and so on) in order to appropriate rents, product systems based on open standards might more rapidly accumulate an installed base and be compatible with a wider range of complementary goods. Proprietary systems, therefore, might be at more risk of being locked out of the market by a competing standards-based design (Schilling, 1999).

Modular systems offer an attractive compromise. By encapsulating proprietary technology within a component that conforms to an open standards-based architecture, firms can reap the advantages of compatibility with a wide range of complementary goods while still retaining the rent-generating potential of their proprietary component. Network externalities, therefore, can increase the pressure for modular systems. However, a firm that already has a firmly entrenched position as the dominant design also can use network externalities to its favor, resisting modularity in an effort to gain market power and architectural control.

Market power and architectural control

Thus far, I have focused on arguments in which firms bow to market pressure and offer products that best fit the balance of the pressures created by heterogeneous inputs and demands, as well as the synergistic specificity of the product system. However, even when other variables indicate that a firm should experience strong pressure to offer increasingly modular products, the firm might continue to focus on integrated systems if its strategy is to increase market power or architectural control. If the firm possesses some unique asset or position in the market that enables it to resist the pressure created by heterogeneous inputs and demands, it might be able to push the market to an otherwise unlikely equilibrium.

For example, Prybeck, Alvarez, and Gifford (1991) have pointed out that a firm possessing proprietary control over an important component in a system can restrict market access by offering that component only as part of a total product system. If potential entrants to the industry must be able to provide an entire system (rather than individual components), integrated systems can act as a significant barrier to entry (lowering competitive intensity) – particularly if one proprietary component of the integrated system is highly desired by customers and can be protected from compatibility with other providers' components.

Consider again Microsoft's Windows. Windows reaped tremendous network externality benefits early in its history by being tied to DOS (which had reaped network externality benefits of its own through its initial bundling with IBM personal computers). Its huge installed base and complementary goods advantages gave Microsoft great control over the evolution of the personal computer operating system standard. Microsoft was able to make Windows an increasingly large and integrated product, despite consumer and competitive pressure for increased flexibility and "leaner" programs. By incorporating ever more utility programs into the core program, Microsoft has expanded Windows to take over the roles of many other software components. Whereas a user once purchased an operating system, uninstaller programs, disk compression programs, and memory management programs separately, Windows 95 and 98 integrate all of these products, and more, into the operating system. Many have argued that doing so has decreased consumer choice and made the operating system a "bloated, unwieldy product only experts can use without confusion, crashes and endless compatibility problems" (Elgan, 1998: 17). This "feature creep" has had a major impact on competition in the industry: many utility producers, such as Qualitas, Stac Electronics, Microhelp, Quarterdeck, and others, have abandoned their once-profitable products.

Similarly, a firm with a unique and powerful asset or position in the market may avoid modular product designs because it wishes to retain architectural control of the product. For example, many industry observers have argued that Microsoft provides incomplete information to third-party applications developers regarding the "hooks" that allow software to be compatible with Windows. By strategically excluding some vendors from access to the full details of the interface, Microsoft retains more control over what products can be made compatible. This enables Microsoft to protect its market power in product categories that might otherwise have been overrun with competitors, and it gives the company great control over the evolution of the architecture of personal computer software.[15]

Strategy, then, may defy pressures for increasing modularity if a firm possesses a unique and powerful advantage. However, it does so at a risk: if the benefits of a modular product design are very strong, the firm's integrated system eventually might be rejected by the market in favor of modular alternatives, even if that means giving up some unique, desirable feature. The firm that has concentrated on protecting its integrated product position then might be at a disadvantage in competing in modular component markets. The methods by which and reasons why firms choose to resist (or promote) modularity in an environment encouraging a different solution are as varied as firms themselves – thus, I offer no propositions for this topic. I develop these two examples merely to illustrate how firm strategy sometimes might be at odds with the migration path suggested by the nature of the technology and its context.

IMPLICATIONS, LIMITATIONS, AND SUGGESTIONS FOR FUTURE RESEARCH

The model of interfirm product modularity has immediate implications for management and public policy, which are discussed below. The research implications of both the general model and its application to product modularity are even farther reaching. If the model holds up to theoretical and empirical scrutiny, it opens up a wide range of future research possibilities. These possibilities, and the challenges they pose, are discussed in the section on implications for future research.

Implications for management and public policy

The ability to understand, predict, and explain a product system's migration toward increasing or decreasing modularity should prove very valuable both to incumbents and new entrants in an industry. For incumbent firms, understanding the pressures that drive a market toward or away from product modularity will help them both to predict competitive shifts in their market and to influence the path their market will take. For instance, if there are strong pressures for a market to become more modular (e.g., technology is changing very rapidly and customers want the flexibility to be able to put together their own set of components), a firm that produces only integrated product systems may be at risk of losing its market share to competitors (either other incumbents or new entrants) who provide modular alternatives.

An incumbent that recognizes there are strong pressures for increasing modularity can resist such a shift by actively opposing the development (or adoption) of a standardized interface. Alternatively, it might choose to usher in the era itself, possibly securing first mover advantages. This might have been McGraw-Hill's strategy in providing modular textbooks. The growing popularity of reading packets that were being provided by copy centers demonstrated the value users ascribed to being able to assemble their own texts. It also demonstrated that this method of "publishing" was open to nontraditional competitors – any company capable of securing copyright permissions and offering duplication and binding could put together a packet. McGraw-Hill's strategy was to leverage its own resources to provide a product that had advantages over those provided by a copy center. Specifically, McGraw-Hill could provide better copy quality since it could work with electronically produced originals, as well as generate a table of contents and indexing system. Also, by drawing largely on its own titles, it could avoid much of the difficulty and expense of obtaining copyright permissions.

Although McGraw-Hill's move may precipitate an industry-wide shift toward modularity that induces other incumbents to offer similar products (as well as open the door for new competitors), McGraw-Hill may secure some first mover advantages by building the Primis brand name and by securing relationships with authors and instructors. McGraw-Hill is aware that Primis will cannibalize some of its traditional textbook sales, but the company prefers to cannibalize its own sales than to give share away to competitors.

For potential new entrants, identifying the forces that either encourage or discourage increasing modularity can alert them to a new market opportunity and shape their tactics for entry. If a market has pressures for modularity, yet there are no modular providers, new entrants might be able to capture a portion of the market quickly (and radically alter the industry dynamics) by offering a modular alternative. Such firms would have a strong interest in developing and promoting a standardized interface.

Conversely, when there are strong pressures for integration, an entrant might benefit by forging alliances with incumbent firms. For instance, if the entrant is able to offer a component that provides desirable technological features that could be integrated with an existing product system, the entrant might be able to enter a market successfully by engaging in a bundling relationship with an established product system provider. The bundling relationship can help the new entrant to overcome entry barriers, rapidly reach an established customer base, and might give the firm access to the incumbent firm's capital to fund fast growth or technological development.

Being able to identify the forces driving an industry either toward or away from modularity also could be very useful for public policy makers. One major implication of the model is that some industries will benefit (both on customer and producer sides) from increasing integration, whereas some will not. The model helps to clarify, among other things, when integration is desirable from the customer's point of view and when it actually constitutes an injurious tie-in (Grimes, 1994). It also has important implications for what degree of concentration we should expect to see in an industry. If the industry has strong customer, technological, and firm pressures to deliver an integrated product, we would expect to see greater industry concentration and larger firms, since only such firms may be able to deliver a wholly integrated product system. Alternatively, if the industry has strong pressures for modularity, we would expect the industry to become more fragmented; therefore, an oligopolistic industry structure might be an indicator that consumer welfare is being expropriated and deserves closer scrutiny.

Implications for future research

The general modular systems theory developed here ultimately might prove useful for understanding the integration and disaggregation of many kinds of systems. By using the theory to derive a more specific model of interfirm product modularity, I have demonstrated the applicability of the theory to one particular kind of system. However, the general model hopefully can be used to derive specific causal and explanatory models for many kinds of modular systems, including (but not limited to) organizational systems (e.g., "why do firms form integrated hierarchies or disaggregate into loosely coupled systems of contracts?"), biological systems (e.g., "when does it benefit protein strands to integrate into large, tightly integrated organisms?"), and social systems (e.g., "does the logic of modularity explain why populations of people should shift from large urban centers to networks of much smaller, more dispersed neighborhoods?").

Even within each of these areas there are multitudes of different kinds of systems to which this model may apply. The challenges then, are to derive the more specific applications of the model to these many systems and see to what degree it remains effective and robust, and to identify what kinds of systems, if any, the model may not apply to and why this would be the case.

The model also yields some operationalization challenges because of the circularity of the relationships. A factor might increase the likelihood of modularity, which, in turn, would increase the intensity of the factor (which is why many of the propositions in the interfirm product modularity model include time anchors). These circular relationships, and the fact that all systems may be modular at some level, mean that any empirical test of the model must attempt to measure *change* in the degree of modularity and should be designed to capture temporal effects.

There is much left to be done before we can have great faith in the reliability and validity of the model's ability to explain the integration and disaggregation of different kinds of systems. However, if future research refines and validates the model, we will have a powerful new tool for understanding systems. Even if the model fails under future scrutiny – but in the process spurs the development of better models that can achieve such a task – it will have served a useful purpose.

NOTES

I gratefully acknowledge the advice and assistance of Carliss Baldwin, Richard Langlois, N. Venkatraman, Shawn Berman, Peter Arnold, Henry Chesbrough, Andy Hoffman, Jonathan Hibbard, Dorothy Paun, P. R. Balasubramanian, and John Henderson, and I acknowledge especially the comments of several anonymous reviewers for their generous help and support.

1   Despite the fact that the product bundling research does not deal explicitly with modularity, this research proves very informative about modular product systems. First, it lends insight into when customers will seek to buy a predetermined bundle of products, versus assembling their own heterogeneous bundle configurations. Second, it addresses the issue of whether (and when) firms will prefer to offer bundled packages versus components.

2   In technological systems, we can think of the nature of systems characterizing a context as the "dominant design." A dominant design is a system architecture that establishes dominance in a class of products (Abernathy, 1978; Anderson and Tushman, 1990; Sahal, 1981).

3   We see an excellent example of this in software systems. In many software systems there are thousands of interdependent programs because of redundancies in the code or because of shared data. Any design change results in a "cascade" of required changes in other programs, known as a *ripple effect* (Fichman and Kemmerer, 1993). Because of this, many stakeholders in this industry are advocating the adoption of object-oriented programming, despite the major investment in new skills and new systems this will require for many firms. With object-oriented programming, software modules are designed to be *encapsulated* so that they do not require the sharing of data, and the range of their interdependencies with other modules is limited to those intended by the interface. Encapsulation allows information within the module to be hidden; modules can interact without requiring full knowledge of the contents of each module.

4   For simplicity, the model depicts only the case of increasing modularity. However, it is a straightforward matter to convert the model to show causal factors for decreasing modularity by reversing the signs on the main effects of heterogeneity of inputs, heterogeneity of demands, and synergistic specificity.

5   A similar argument can be found in the marketing strategy literature on product bundling. Firms often combine components together into a bundle because the combination of particular components improves their performance relative to their performance as

components (Eppen et al., 1991; Guiltinan, 1987; Hanson, 1987; Hanson and Martin, 1990; Porter, 1985; Wilson et al., 1990).

6   In markets in which the customer is able to choose among components but unable (or unwilling) to assemble them, a market for third-party assemblers may arise or one of the component producers may take over assembly of the end-product configuration. For instance, airlines choose the airframe they will purchase and usually the engine (components that are produced by different manufacturers); however, airlines are not involved in the assembly of these components.

7   Consumer behavior researchers have made a very similar argument regarding bundling, pointing out that when buyers are heterogeneous, it becomes very difficult to offer a bundled product system that meets all of their needs (Bryan and Clark, 1973; Cready, 1991; Eppen et al., 1991; Jeuland, 1984; Kinberg and Sudit, 1979; Porter, 1985). Unbundled solutions, therefore, become much more attractive.

8   There has been some concern that the modularization of texts could result in gaps or inconsistencies in materials. Chapters chosen from different books may not share the same terminology and may have been intended for people with different knowledge backgrounds – in essence, they may not fit as well together as chapters from a book that was planned as an integrated product (Venkatraman, 1997). That is, they forfeit synergistic specificity. To resolve this, there has been some discussion of authors writing chapters that stand alone better. Most book chapters currently are not designed to be modular components; however, if the publishing industry were to move increasingly toward modularity in assembling texts, one would expect authors increasingly to plan for modularity in writing them.

9   This example also demonstrates how a producer can leverage on highly desirable proprietary component into control over a whole product system – a topic discussed at greater length in the section on market power and architectural control.

10   Although modularity may be the dominant form in industries characterized by heterogeneous customer needs, and integrated systems may be dominant where customer needs are similar, there may still be niche providers who will provide the alternative form for those customers not falling into the majority group.

11   It is also possible that the migration to more modular technology designs will foster more rapid technological change. The decomposition of a system into simpler components might enable each component to be improved more rapidly – as implied by the earlier arguments about specialization's improving a firm's ability to travel down a particular learning curve. Alexander (1964), Holland (1995), and Kauffman (1995) have made parallel arguments. However, in technological systems there is likely to be a complex web of interactions between the design (i.e., the interfaces and overall architecture) and contextual factors that will condition whether this relationship holds. This possibility warrants a much more in-depth examination than can be included here – I suggest it only as a potential area of future inquiry.

12   A local area network server enables a more distributed computing environment, whereby workstations are linked in a network and interact with a central server. A multivendor LAN allows components from different vendors to be linked in a network – a much more modular solution than minicomputers.

13   Alexander made a similar argument when he pointed out that a complex adaptive system will be able to move from a state of misfit with its context to "perfect fit" much faster if it is composed of subsystems that are relatively independent of each other (1964: 40–1).

14   This is very consistent with the marketing and economics literature on bundling, where authors posit that consumer price sensitivity will decrease the likelihood of bundling (Nagle, 1987).

15 Note that architectural control also could be maintained by a consortium of loosely coupled organizations, if consortium members were able to maintain a cooperative agreement. However, in the computer industry such consortiums (e.g., the Open Software Foundation) have proven to be very difficult to sustain.

REFERENCES

Abernathy, W. J. (1978). *The productivity dilemma*. Baltimore: Johns Hopkins University Press.

Achrol, R. S. (1997). Changes in the theory of interorganizational relations in marketing: Toward a network paradigm. *Academy of Marketing Science*, 25: 56–71.

Alexander, C. (1964). *Notes on the synthesis of form*. Cambridge, MA: Harvard University Press.

Anderson, J. R. (1987). Methodologies for studying human knowledge. *Behavioral and Brain Sciences*, 10: 467–505.

Anderson, P., and Tushman, M. (1990). Technological discontinuities and dominant designs: A cyclical model of technological change. *Administrative Science Quarterly*, 35: 604–34.

Arthur, W. B. (1989). Competing technologies, increasing returns, and lock-in by historical events. *Economic Journal*, 99: 116–31.

Ashkenas, R., Ulrich, D., Jick, T., and Kerr, S. (1995). *The boundaryless organization: Breaking the chains of organizational structure*. San Francisco: Jossey-Bass.

Baddeley, A. (1986). Modularity, mass-action and memory. *Quarterly Journal of Experimental Psychology: Human Experimental Psychology*, 38: 527–33.

Baldwin, C. Y., and Clark, K. B. (1997). Managing in an age of modularity. *Harvard Business Review*, 75(5): 84–93.

Baldwin, C. Y., and Clark, K. B. (2000). *Design rules. Volume 1: The power of modularity*. Cambridge, MA: MIT Press.

Barney, J. B. (1991). Firm resources and sustained competitive advantage. *Journal of Management*, 17: 99–120.

Blair, J. G. (1998). *Modular America: Cross-cultural perspectives on the emergence of an American way*. Westport, CT: Greenwood.

Bryan, L., and Clark, S. (1973). *Unbundling full-service banking*. Cambridge, MA: Harcomm Associates.

Cole, M. (1999). Context, modularity, and the cultural constitution of development. In P. Lloyd and C. Fernyhough (Eds.), *Lev Vygotsky: Critical assessments: Future directions*, vol. IV: 74–100. New York: Routledge.

Crain, S., and Thornton, R. (1998). *Investigations in universal grammar: A guide to experiments on the acquisition of syntax and semantics*. Cambridge, MA: MIT Press.

Cready, W. (1991). Premium bundling. *Economic Inquiry*, 29: 173–9.

Elgan, M. (1998). An open letter to Bill Gates. *Windows Magazine*, 9(5): 17.

Eppen, G., Hanson, W., and Martin, K. (1991). Bundling – new products, new markets, low risk. *Sloan Management Review*, 32(4): 7–14.

Fichman, R., and Kemmerer, C. (1993). Adoption of software engineering process innovations: The case of object orientation. *Sloan Management Review*, 34(2): 7–22.

Fodor, J. (1983). *The modularity of mind*. Cambridge, MA: MIT Press.

Fodor, J. (1998). *In critical condition: Polemical essays on cognitive science and the philosophy of mind*. Cambridge, MA: MIT Press.

Garud, R., and Kumaraswamy, A. (1995). Technological and organizational designs for realizing economies of substitution. *Strategic Management Journal*, 16: 93–109.

Gell-Mann, M. (1995). Complex adaptive systems. In H. Morowitz and J. Singer (Eds.), *The mind, the brain and complex adaptive systems. SFI studies in the sciences of complexity*, vol. XXII: 11–23. Reading, MA: Addison-Wesley.

Grimes, W. (1994). Antitrust tie-in analysis after Kodak: Understanding the role of market imperfections. *Antitrust Law Journal*, 62: 263–325.

Guiltinan, J. (1987). The price bundling of services: A normative framework. *Journal of Marketing*, 51: 74–85.

Hall, V. R., and Hughes, T. P. (1996). Reproductive strategies of modular organisms: Comparative studies of reef-building corals. *Ecology*, 77: 950–63.

Hanson, W. (1987). *The strategic role of bundling.* Technical Report and Reprint Series, Working paper No. 44. Chicago: University of Chicago Press.

Hanson, W., and Martin, K. (1990). Optimal bundle pricing. *Management Science*, 36: 155–74.

Henderson, R., and Clark, K. B. (1990). Architectural innovation: The reconfiguration of existing product technologies and the failure of established firms. *Administrative Science Quarterly*, 35: 9–30.

Holland, J. (1994). *Adaptation in natural and artificial systems: An introductory analysis with applications to biology, control, and artificial intelligence.* Cambridge, MA: MIT Press.

Holland, J. (1995). *Hidden order: How adaptation builds complexity.* Cambridge, MA: Perseus.

Holland, J. (1999). *Emergence: From chaos to order.* Cambridge, MA: Perseus.

Holt, C., and Sherman, R. (1986). Quality uncertainty and bundling. In P. M. Ippolito and D. T. Scheffman (Eds.), *Empirical approaches to consumer protection economics*: 221–50. Washington, DC: U.S. Government Printing Office.

Jacobides, M. (1997). Unbundling, standardization and competitive dynamics. Paper presented at the 1997 Strategic Management Society Conference, Barcelona, Spain.

Jeuland, A. (1984). Comments on "Gaussian Demand and Commodity Bundling." *Journal of Business*, 57: S231–S234.

Katz, M., and Shapiro, C. (1986). Technology adoption in the presence of network externalities. *Journal of Political Economy*, 94: 822–41.

Kauffman, S. A. (1993). *The origins of order.* New York: Oxford University Press.

Kauffman, S. A. (1995). *At home in the universe.* New York: Oxford University Press.

Kiely, T. (1989). No mean feat for mini makers. *New England Business*, 11(7): 16–25.

Kinberg, Y., and Sudit, E. (1979). Country/service bundling in international tourism: Criteria for the selection of an efficient bundle mix and allocation of joint revenues. *Journal of International Business Studies*, 10(2): 51–63.

Langlois, R. (1992). External economies and economic progress: The case of the microcomputer industry. *Business History Review*, 66: 1–50.

Langlois, R. (2000). Capabilities and vertical disintegration in process technology: The case of semiconductor fabrication equipment. In N. J. Foss, and P. L. Robertson (Eds.), *Resources, technology, and strategy*: 199–206. London: Routledge.

Langlois, R., and Robertson, P. (1992). Networks and innovation in a modular system: Lessons from the microcomputer and stereo component industries. *Research Policy*, 21: 297–13.

Lawless, M. (1991). Commodity bundling for competitive advantage: Strategic implications. *Journal of Management Studies*, 28: 267–80.

Lei, D., Hitt, M. A., and Goldhar, J. D. (1996). Advanced manufacturing technology: Organizational design and strategic flexibility. *Organization Studies*, 17: 501–23.

Leonard-Barton, D. (1992). Core capabilities and core rigidities: A paradox in managing new product development. *Strategic Management Journal*, 13: 111–25.

Miles, R. E., and Snow, C. C. (1986). Organizations: New concepts for new forms. *California Management Review*, 28(3): 62–73.

Nagle, T. (1987). *The strategy and tactics of pricing.* Englewood Cliffs, NJ: Prentice-Hall.

Nesbitt, P. (1990). Long arm of the LAN; Local are network; DEC introduces networking as part of new strategy. *PC User*, 138: 24–8.

Orton, J., and Weick, K. (1990). Loosely coupled systems: A reconceptualization. *Academy of Management Review*, 15: 203–23.

Penrose, E. (1959). *The theory of the growth of the firm*. Oxford: Basil Blackwell.

Porter, M. (1985). *Competitive advantage: Creating and sustaining superior performance*. New York: Free Press.

PR Newswire. (1990). Two founders to leave Data General. December 12.

Prybeck, F., Alvarez, F., and Gifford, S. (1991). How to price for successful product bundling (Part II). *Journal of Pricing Management*, 2: 16–20.

Qi, L. (1988). Odd submodular functions, Dilworth functions and discrete convex functions. *Mathematics of Operations Research*, 13: 435–47.

Robertson, P., and Langlois, D. (1995). Innovation, networks, and vertical integration. *Research Policy*, 24: 543–62.

Sahal, D. (1981). *Patterns of technological innovation*. Reading, MA: Addison-Wesley.

Sanchez, R. (1995). Strategic flexibility in product competition. *Strategic Management Journal*, 16: 135–59.

Sanchez, R., and Mahoney, J. (1996). Modularity, flexibility, and knowledge management in product and organizational design. *Strategic Management Journal*, 17: 63–6.

Schilling, M. (1999). Technology success and failure in winner-take-all markets: Testing a model of technological lock-out. Unpublished doctoral dissertation, University of Washington, Seattle.

Schilling, M., and Steensma, K. (1999). Technological change, globalization, and the adoption of modular organizational forms. Working paper, Boston University.

Simon, H. (1962). The architecture of complexity. *Proceedings of the American Philosophical Society*, vol. 106: 467–82.

Simon, H. (1995). Near decomposability and complexity: How a mind resides in a brain. In H. Morowitz and J. Singer (Eds.), *The mind, the brain and complex adaptive systems. SFI studies in the sciences of complexity*, vol. XXII: 25–43. Reading, MA: Addison-Wesley.

Slofstra, M. (1990). HP makes major midrange move. *Computing Canada*, 16(3): 1–3.

Snow, C., Miles, R., and Coleman, H. J. (1992). Managing 21st century network organizations. *Organizational Dynamics*, 20(3): 5–20.

Streicher, T. (1991). Minicomputer technology: Where it's been, where it's headed. *Instrumentation and Control Systems*, 64(12): 31–41.

Teece, K. J. (1986). Profiting from technological innovation: Implications for integration, collaboration, licensing, and public policy. *Research Policy*, 15: 285–305.

Van de Ven, A., Poole, A., and Scott, M. (1995). Explaining development and change in organizations. *Academy of Management Review*, 20: 510–41.

van der Lely, H. K. (1997). Narrative discourse in grammatical specific language impaired children: A modular language deficit? *Journal of Child Language*, 24: 221–56.

Venkatraman, N. (1997). *The college textbook marketplace in the 1990s: McGraw-Hill's launch of Primis*. Teaching case, Boston University.

Wagner, G. P. (1995). Adaptation and the modular design of organisms. *Advances in Artificial Life*, 929: 317–28.

Wagner, G. P. (1996). Homologues, natural kinds and the evolution of modularity. *American Zoologist*, 36: 36–43.

Weick, K. E. (1976). Educational organizations as loosely coupled systems. *Administrative Science Quarterly*, 21: 1–19.

Wilson, L., Weiss, A., and John, G. (1990). Unbundling of industrial systems. *Journal of Marketing Research*, 27: 123–38.

Worren, N. (1997). Creating dynamic capabilities: The role of individual vs. organizational learning. Dissertation proposal, Oxford University, Oxford, UK.

COMMENTARY
Melissa A. Schilling

In the article, Toward a General Modular Systems Theory and its Application to Inter-firm Product Modularity, I argued that since modularity was a general systems concept, we might be able to develop a general systems theory of modularity. Such a theory, if articulated abstractly enough, could be used to derive more specific models for a wide range of systems. In the paper, I developed a simple causal model for modularity (what factors may drive a system to adopt increasingly or decreasingly modular forms) and then demonstrated its application to inter-firm product modularity.

Since publishing the general systems model, a colleague and I have applied a variation of it to the adoption of modular organizational forms at the industry level (Schilling and Steensma, 2001). However, we are still at only the beginning steps of having a general systems theory of modularity. First, while a causal model is useful and interesting, there are many other models that remain to be built. For instance, a model of the outcomes of the adoption of increasingly modular forms would be valuable, as would be more development of the different ways that a system can manifest modularity. Secondly, before a unified theory can be readily applied to multiple disciplines, it would be helpful if we had a greater understanding of the way that different disciplines use the concept of modularity. By comparing and contrasting the way that modularity is defined and used in other disciplines, we are both more likely to develop a more complete theory, and more likely to employ a language that is readily understood by multiple disciplines.

Towards furthering this objective, I offer here a brief review of how modularity is used in four different disciplines: psychology, biology, American studies, and mathematics. Admittedly, these reviews are greatly constrained by my lack of experience in these disciplines. Perhaps, however, they will provide a useful launching pad for others who are better equipped to bridge multiple disciplines, and who are interested in further developing a general systems theory of modularity. A review of the use of modularity in technology and organizations seems superfluous here, therefore I will focus on the use of modularity in the other disciplines, and relate them back to modularity in technology and organizations in the final section.

Modularity in multiple disciplines

Modularity in psychology

Probably the most noted work on modularity in psychology is Jerry Fodor's book, *The Modularity of Mind* (1996). In the book, he proposes a "modified" modularity theory of cognitive processes. His theory builds on the premise of faculty psychology that there are certain faculties innate in the mind, and mental "organs" that are biologically predisposed to perform certain types of computational processes.[1] Fodor does not argue that the entire mind is modular; rather he proposes that the central cognitive system responsible for complex cognitive activities (such as analogical reasoning) is not modular, but that input systems (which interpret the neural signals from physical stimuli, and are responsible for basic cognitive activities such as language and vision) are likely to be modular (Coltheart, 1999).

Input systems, or "domain specific computational mechanisms" (such as the ability to perceive spoken language) are termed vertical faculties, and according to Fodor they are modular in that they possess a number of characteristics Fodor argues constitute modularity. Fodor's list of features characterizing modules includes the following:

1   Domain specific (modules only respond to inputs of a specific class, and thus a "species of vertical faculty" (Fodor, 1996: 37).
2   Innately specified (the structure is inherent and is not formed by a learning process).
3   Not assembled (modules are not put together from a stock of more elementary subprocesses but rather their virtual architecture maps directly onto their neural implementation).
4   Neurologically hardwired (modules are associated with specific, localized, and elaborately structured neural systems rather than fungible neural mechanisms).
5   Autonomous (modules are independent of other modules).

Fodor does not argue that this is formal definition or an all inclusive list of features necessary for modularity. He argues only that cognitive systems characterized by some of the features above are likely to be characterized by them all, and that such systems can be considered modular. He also notes that the characteristics are not an all-or-nothing proposition, but rather each of the characteristics may be manifest in some degree, and that modularity itself is also not a dichotomous construct – something may be more or less modular: "One would thus expect – what anyhow seems to be desirable – that the notion of modularity ought to admit of degrees" (Fodor, 1996: 37).

For Fodor, one of the most important features of modularity (though not explicitly on his list) is information encapsulation. Information encapsulation implies that all (or most) of the necessary information or processing needed to perform a computation is within the module. The module does not have to interact with other information within the individual. Information encapsulation enables input systems to do their jobs quickly, by not accessing or using all of the information conceivably available. Fodor notes, "The informational encapsulation of the input systems is, or so I shall argue, the essence of their modularity. It's also the essence of the analogy between the input systems and reflexes; reflexes are informationally encapsulated with bells on" (Fodor, 1996: 71).

Notably, Fodor's "not assembled" feature contrasts sharply with the use of modularity in other fields in which modular systems are seen to be hierarchically nested (that is, modules are themselves composed of modules, which in turn are composed of modules, and so on) However, Coltheart (1999) notes that Fodor's commitment to the non-assembled feature appears weak, and other scholars (for example, Block, 1995) have proposed that Fodor's modules could be decomposed into finer modules. For instance, while Fodor distinguishes between separate modules for spoken and written language, Block might further decompose the spoken language module into modules for phonetic analysis and lexical forms (Coltheart, 1999): "Decomposition stops when all the components are primitive processors – because the operation of a primitive processor cannot be further decomposed into sub-operations" (Block, 1995).

Though Fodor's work on modularity may be considered the most extensive, there is other work in psychology on modularity worth noting for its symmetry with modularity in other disciplines. For instance, while Fodor focused on cognitive input systems as modules, Coltheart (1999) proposes that there may be many different kinds of cognitive modules, and distinguishes between, for example, knowledge modules and processing modules. The former is a body of knowledge that is independent of other bodies of knowledge, while the latter is a mental information-processing system independent from other such systems.

With respect to the evolution from integrated systems to modular systems, Hulme and Snowling note, "interaction between systems in probably the norm in development, and it may only be after a very extensive period of development that the relative modularity or autonomy of different systems in the adult is achieved" (1992: 906). Their point is that in the child, cognitive processes likely entail extensive interaction and integration, and autonomy of modules is only achieved after the individual's cognitive processes are well developed and the mind has a relatively complete cognitive map of which processes and knowledge are most closely related. This is highly analogous to arguments made by Christensen, Verlinden and Westerman (2001) and Baldwin and Clark (1997) that new technological innovations tend to be introduced in integrated form. It may take extensive effort and experience before the architecture of the technological system is understood well enough to enable definition of design rules that facilitate the modularization of the system.

Also analogous to arguments made about modularity in technological systems, psychologists have emphasized the role of modularity in breaking up complex systems into smaller, more specialized parts: "any large computation should be split up into a collection of small, nearly independent, specialized subprocesses" (Marr, 1982: 325). From my limited perusal of the topic, it would seem that modularity in cognitive systems relates very directly to modularity in biological systems (in particular the evolution of homologous parts), but I found no evidence of any direct connection between studies of modularity in psychology and biology. If such connections are truly lacking, then there are likely to be important synergies ripe for discovery between the two groups of scholars.

Modularity in biology

As in some of the other disciplines, the term modularity may be used in multiple ways in biology. For example, it may be used to refer to organisms that have an indeterminate structure wherein modules of various complexity (for example, leaves, twigs) may be assembled without strict limits on their number or placement. Many plants and sessile benthic invertebrates demonstrate this type of modularity (by contrast, many other organisms have a determinate structure that is predefined in embryogenesis) (Andrews, 1998). The term has also been used in a broader sense in biology to refer to the reuse of homologous structures across individuals and species. Even within this latter category, there may be differences in how a module is perceived. For instance, evolutionary biologists may focus on the module as a morphological component (subunit) of a whole organism, while developmental biologists may use the term module to refer to some combination of lower-level components (for example, genes) that are able to act in a unified way to perform a function (Bolker, 2000). In the former, the module is perceived a basic component, while in the latter the emphasis is on the module as a collective. As Bolker (2000) states:

> Formulating a definition of modularity that is both comprehensive and practical is a non-trivial task. It is surprisingly hard to define something we easily recognize in the biological world, namely its organization into individualized yet interconnected units across a range of physical and functional scales. Part of the difficulty may be precisely that it is often easy to recognize modularity, and to develop practical, working definitions that are never made explicit. For example, evolutionary biologists and morphologists readily identify the tetrapod forelimb as a discrete structure that is homologous across different taxa, despite its structural, functional and adaptive diversity. Developmental biologists recognize the limb bud as an embryonic region with unique intrinsic patterning and developmental integration that can be physically displaced or induced ectopically, yet retains its fundamental structure and identity . . . Such local definitions of modularity are restricted to a single context, or at most a single level of the biological hierarchy, precisely because they are based on particular functions or mechanisms within that context. They have great power within a level, but limited ability to bridge different levels.

Instead of providing definitions, some biology scholars have provided a list of features that should characterize a module (much as Fodor did in *The Modularity of Mind*). For instance, Raff (1996) provides the following list of characteristics that developmental modules should possess:

1   discrete genetic specification;
2   hierarchical organization;
3   interactions with other modules;
4   a particular physical location within a developing organism;
5   the ability to undergo transformations on both developmental and evolutionary time scales.

To Raff's mind, developmental modules are "dynamic entities representing localized processes (as in morphogenetic fields) rather than simply incipient structures . . . (. . . such as organ rudiments)" (Raff, 1996: 326). Bolker, however, attempts to construct a definitional list of characteristics that is more abstract, and thus more suited to multiple levels of study in biology. She argues that:

1   A module is a biological entity (a structure, a process, or a pathway) characterized by more internal than external integration.
2   Modules are biological individuals (Hull, 1980; Roth, 1991) that can be delineated from their surroundings or context, and whose behavior or function reflects the integration of their parts, not simply the arithmetical sum. That is, as a

whole, the module can perform tasks that its constituent parts could not perform if dissociated.

3   In addition to their internal integration, modules have external connectivity, yet they can also be delineated from the other entities with which they interact in some way.

Another stream of research on modularity in biology that should be of particular interest to scholars in other disciplines is that of Gunter Wagner. Wagner's work (for example, Wagner and Altenburg, 1996; Wagner, 1996) explores how natural selection may have resulted in modular organisms, and the roles modularity plays in evolution. Wagner's work suggests that modularity is both the result of evolution, and facilitates evolution – an idea that shares a marked resemblance to work on modularity in technological and organizational domains.

Modularity in American studies

Although I have frequently suspected that it may be fruitful to conceive of social systems as modular systems (for example, the disintegration of the urban center into more loosely coupled neighborhoods), I found very little use of the modularity construct among studies of population or culture. Fortunately, the one very notable exception, Blair's *Modular America* (1988), is so rich and extensive that it provides ample fuel for our discussion here. Blair's central premise is that as Americans began to replace social structures inherited from Europe (predominantly England and France), they evolved a uniquely American tendency towards modularity, in fields as diverse as education, music, and architecture.

Blair observes that when the word module first emerged in the sixteenth and seventeenth centuries, it meant something very close to model. It implied a small-scale representation or example. By the eighteenth and nineteenth centuries, the word had come to imply a standard measure of fixed ratios and proportions. For example, in architecture, the proportions of a column could be stated in modules (that is, "a height of fourteen modules equaled seven times the diameter measured at the base" (1988: 2)) and thus multiplied to any size while still retaining the desired proportions.

However, in America the meaning and usage of the word shifted considerably:

> Starting with architectural terminology in the 1930s, the new emphasis was on any entity or system designed in terms of modules as subcomponents. As applications broadened after World War II to furniture, hi-fi equipment, computer programs and beyond, modular construction came to refer to any whole made up of self-contained units designed to be equivalent parts of a system, hence, we might say, "systemically equivalent." Modular parts are implicitly interchangeable and/or recombinable in one or another of several senses (Blair, 1988: 3).

Blair defines a modular system as "one that gives more importance to parts than to wholes. Parts are conceived as equivalent and hence, in one or more senses, interchangeable and/or cumulative and/or recombinable" (p. 125). Blair describes the emergence of modular structures in education, industry, architecture, music, literature, sports, law, and religion. The first four will be briefly overviewed here for illustrative purposes:

The college curriculum.   Blair notes that in the late 1800s, American universities began to replace the European fixed curriculum with the more modular elective system, partially in response to declining enrollments. In the new curricula, a "course" no longer referred to a course of study as it did in England, but rather to a class, and classes were interchangeable. Credits emerged as a standard unit and gave students the freedom to piece together their own educational path. The college curriculum had been broken into a set of systemically equivalent parts, allowing for substitutability and a rationalization of assembly processes. A nearly identical process was taking place in manufacturing, and the symmetry of these processes is captured in a quote from Laurence Veysey (1965: 312): "Assembly-line methods of registration arrived at Harvard in the autumn of 1891, and efficient orange perforated registration cards were introduced in 1896. At most universities, courses were now rationalized into a numerical system of units for credit; the catalogue began to resemble the inventory of a well-stocked and neatly labeled general store."

Industrial assembly by the "American System of Manufactures."   The move to a manufacturing system in which standardized parts could be substituted into an assembled product was prompted in large part by a demand for guns that outstripped supply. Early production of muskets in both Europe and America was performed by craftsmen, who laboriously produced an entire gun from start to finish. If the gun was damaged, a gunsmith would have to fit another unique component to the gun. Production was slow, and difficult to expand due to a lack of gunsmiths in America. Around the turn of the nineteenth century, a new approach was developed (termed the "uniformity system" by Eli Whitney, one of its proponents) which would come to be known as the American System of Manufactures. The approach would employ specialized machines (rather than specialized craftsmen) so that unskilled laborers could produce uniform components that could be assembled into a functional weapon. Originally, it was much more expensive and difficult to produce parts which were so precisely manufactured as to be interchangeable. Without military loyalty to interchangeability and government backing of the development costs, the system might have died out quickly. Throughout the nineteenth century the production method spread from guns, to a wide range of assembled products including farm machinery, bicycles, and automobiles.

Skyscraper architecture.   Traditional European conceptions of architecture demanded that buildings be conceived of as wholes, with due attention paid to the building's proportions and stylistic coherence. All aspects of the building's size and style had to be carefully coordinated. In America, however, the combination of the advent of structural steel and the liberation from European norms enabled the rise of a new type of building: the skyscraper. By European standards, the American skyscraper was a vulgar and aesthetically distasteful piece of work. Its proportions were determined by practicality rather than beauty. Skyscrapers were modular constructions in that once the basic building blocks (floors) were established, they could be piled up to almost any height. Blair terms this *additive open-endedness*, and demonstrates its close relationship to modularity in literature and music.

Blues and jazz. As described by Blair, blues music is composed of stanzas that may flow in any order, and are held together only by their emotional congruity. The traditional blues singer may interchange, add, or delete stanzas to suit the mood. Jazz music is similar, though because it is typically played by an ensemble, it requires somewhat more architecture in order to ensure that even when playing emergent improvisational sets, the individual musicians are able to follow each other appropriately. To accomplish this, jazz music has basic structural units that provide underlying rules:

> Every jazz improvisation is based on a theme. Usually it is . . . a standard song in 32-bar form – the "AABA" form of our popular tunes, in which the 8-bar main theme (A) is first presented, then repeated, then followed by a new 8-bar idea – the so-called bridge (B) – and in conclusion the first 8 bars are sounded once more (Berendt, 1983: 148).

By utilizing these standardized structural units, jazz musicians can abandon the overarching hierarchical form of traditional European music while still retaining a sense of where they are in relation to each other. As noted by Blair:

> All members of a jazz group know that the composition will take place in 32-bar segments, though they may not be aware in advance of how many such units will be played or what embellishments of timbre and chordal elaboration may emerge as the sequence moves on. These modular building blocks of musical time are . . . essential to the very existence of jazz (p. 76).

In his concluding chapter, Blair does not commit to a firm view of what causes Americans to pursue more modular structures in the diverse domains in which it has appeared, but he does suggest that it may in some way be related to the American ideology of liberal individualism, and a preference for anti-hierarchical organization.

Modularity in math

The use of the term "modular" in mathematics is thought to have originated with the theory of congruent numbers by Carl Friedrich Gauss (1777–1855). His congruence theory was published in 1801 in his *Disquisitiones Arithmeticae*, and a translation may be found in Smith's (1959) *A Source Book in Mathematics*. In the first section, "Concerning congruence of numbers in general," Gauss begins:

> If a number *a* divides the difference of the numbers *b* and *c*, *b* and *c* are said to be *congruent with respect to a*; but if not, *incongruent*. We call *a* the *modulus* (Smith, 1959: 107).

What this means is that if from any starting number, say 3, one can get to another number, say 21, by the addition of a series of a third number (the modulus), say 6, then the first number and the second number are said to be congruent with respect to the modulus. In this example, 3 and 21 are congruent modulus 6 (3 + 6 + 6 + 6 = 21). To the non-mathematician this seems a strange observation, but it enables several interesting techniques. One of the simpler techniques, termed "casting-out-nines," was once employed by children as a game and is now often taught in grade schools as a method of checking arithmetic.

Casting-out-nines can be used for addition, subtraction, multiplication and division (Loy, 1999). It enables the reduction of numbers into their much simpler casting-out-nines equivalents. To obtain the casting-out-nines equivalents, the digits of the number are added up, omitting the nines, or any pair of digits that add to nine. If the resulting number has more than one digit, the process is repeated until a single-digit number is reached. The function is then performed on these much smaller numbers, and the casting-out-nines equivalent answer should be the same as the casting-out-nines equivalent of the original answer. This technique is much easier to explain with an example:

Casting-out-nines equivalent

1,645   7 (1 + 6 = 7, the 4 and 5 can be omitted because they add to 9)
+ 2,378   2 (2 and 7 are omitted, 3 + 8 = 11, 1 + 1 = 2)
4,023   9 (4 + 2 + 3 = 9)

Much of modern number theory arose from Gauss's original work on congruent numbers. Gauss's use of the *modulus* can be related to Blair's additive open-endedness; for any given starting number and any given modulus (which may be considered a standardized module), there is an infinite quantity of congruent numbers that may be obtained. The casting-out-nines example also demonstrates that the modulus nine may be used to break complex problems down into simpler problems, much as modularity may be used to break complex technological systems into simpler components. The analogies are a bit rough here, and the use of number theory and the term "modular" have evolved into areas in which it becomes even more difficult to identify symmetries with the way modularity is used in other fields. However, a more experienced mathematician might be able to identify more relationships between modularity in math and modularity in other disciplines than I have done.[2]

Pervasive themes

Comparing the use of modularity by discipline reveals several themes that extend across two or more disciplines (see table 6.1). One theme that showed up in psychology and biology but nowhere else in the current study is *innately specified*. Innately specified (as used here) implies that the purpose or structure of the module is predetermined by some biological mandate. It may be possible to construe a type of innate specification for modules in other types of systems, but as I did not stumble upon it in my review, I leave that to the reader.

Table 6.1 The use of modularity by discipline.

Concept	Psychology	Biology	American studies	Mathematics	Technology and organizations
Domain specific	X	X			X
Innately specified	X	X			
Hierarchically nested	X	X	X	X	X
More internal integration than external integration (localized processes and autonomy)	X	X	X	?	X
Informationally encapsulated	X		?		X
Near-decomposability (segmentability, delineation between modules, or breaking down complexity)	X	X	X	X	X
Substitutability	X	?	X	?	X
Recombinability		X	X		X
Expandability		X	X	X	X
Module as homologue		X	X	X	X
Modules may be different in kind	X	X	X		X
Evolution from greater integration to greater modularity	X				X

Domain specificity, that modules respond only to inputs of a specific class (or perform functions only of a specific class) is a theme that clearly spans psychology and biology, and it can be argued that it also spans technological and organizational systems. Domain specificity would be seen in the latter disciplines as specialization of function.

Hierarchically nested is a theme that recurs in every discipline. Though originally disavowed by Fodor, other psychologists have embraced it, and it is readily apparent in the use of modularity in biology (for example, each module of an organism can be decomposed into finer modules), social processes and artifacts (for example, we can think of a skyscraper in terms of blocks of floors, a single floor, elements of a floor, and so on), mathematics (for example, the modulus 6 may be further divided into the moduli 1, 2 and 3), and technological and organizational systems (for example, an organization may be composed of divisions, which are composed of teams, which are composed of individuals).

Greater internal than external integration is a theme that showed up in every discipline but mathematics. Often referred to as autonomy, this theme acknowledged that there may be interaction or integration between modules, but the greater interaction and integration occurs within the module. This theme is very closely related to *information encapsulation*, which shows up explicitly in both the psychology and technology research.

Near decomposability (as termed by Simon, 1962) shows up in all of the disciplines, but is manifest in a matter of degrees. For instance, in psychology and biology it may refer merely to the ability to delineate one module from another (recognizing the boundaries of the module). In several of the social artifacts, mathematics, and technological or organizational systems, however, it refers to the ability to actually separate components from one another. In several of the disciplines this decomposability also enables the complexity of a system (or process) to be reduced. This is aptly captured in the quote from Marr (1982: 325) about psychological processes where he notes that, "any large computation should be split up into a collection of small, nearly independent, specialized subprocesses" (Marr, 1982: 325). Reducing complexity is also the express purpose of casting-out-nines in mathematics.

Substitutability and *recombinability* are closely related constructs. The former refers to the ability to substitute one component for another as in Blair's "systemic equivalence" while the latter may refer both to the indeterminate form of the system and the indeterminate use of the component. In college curricula, for example, each course is designed with a credit system that ensures a uniform number of contact hours, and approximately uniform educational content, yielding substitability. By virtue of their substitutability, each student may create their own curricula (recombinability of the curriculum as a system) and each course may be said to be recombinable with a variety of students' curricula (recombinability of the component within multiple systems). Both substitutability and recombinability are immediately recognizable in Blair's social processes and artifacts, and are also well captured in Garud and Kumaraswamy's (1995) discussion of economies of substitution in technological systems.

Blair's systemic equivalence also demonstrates the relationship between substitutability and the *module as a homologue*. Blair's systemic equivalence refers to the ability for multiple modules to perform approximately the same function within a system, while in biology a module as a homologue refers to different modules sharing approximately the same form or function in different organisms. The extreme of the module as homologue is found in mathematics, where (in the simplest case) the modules refer to the reuse of a particular number and thus each module is exactly alike.

In all but mathematics, there was an emphasis that *modules may be different in kind*. In Fodor's discussion of modular cognitive system, each module performs a unique task. In biology, even modules that are considered homologous may be somewhat different in form and function (for example, a whale's fin versus a human's hand). In Blair's book, he points out that while jazz music may be composed of structural units that conform to the same underlying rules, those components vary significantly. Similarly in studies of technology and organization, modular systems may be composed of modules that are very similar (as in shelving units that may be piled one on top of the other) or very different (as in a stereo system where each component performs unique functions) or any combination in between.

The last theme is not a characteristic given for modules or modular systems, but rather is a proposition about how a system's modularity may change over time. In both psychology research and in technology research it has been argued that *a system may migrate from greater integration to greater modularity*, and intriguingly, approximately the same reasoning is given in both disciplines. In psychology, Hulme and Snowling (1992) argue that only after the cognitive architecture of an individual is well developed and experienced with the variety of computations it will perform can the cognitive process become more modular. In essence, once the brain understands the computational processes well, it is able to parse them out and dedicate particular modules to them. A very similar argument has been made in technological research where it is often argued that technological innovations are often introduced in integrated form, and only after the system is very well understood can the architecture of that system be designed so as to make the system modular.[3]

I have not included every feature of modularity, or argument about modularity, made in each of the disciplines in this section; I have only tried to tease out those themes that recur in at least two distinct disciplines. I have also not attempted to cover every discipline in which modularity may play a role, nor can I claim to have done full justice to the use of the term in the disciplines covered here. However, given those limitations, the preceding discussion still offers us the following conclusion: while there are some marked differences between the ways that modularity is defined or used by the different disciplines, there are also many significant similarities. Exploring both the similarities and differences should enable us to further develop a more complete understanding of modularity.

NOTES

1   One rather dire implication of this is that there may also be endogenous limits on what the mind can process. This is not the same as Simon's bounded rationality; rather it is an implication that the mind is epistemically bounded such that there may be concepts or theories the mind is incapable of entertaining (Fodor, 1996: 120).

2   I am deeply indebted to Barry Mazur and Paul Garret for this explanation of modularity in math, however all mistakes remain my own.

3   In a related vein, Blair noted that it was initially much more expensive to develop machinery and manufacturing processes that would enable modular production of guns.

REFERENCES

Andrews, J. (1998). "Bacteria as modular organisms," *Annual Review of Microbiology*, 52: 105–26.

Baldwin, C. Y. and Clark, K. B. (1997). "Managing in an age of modularity," *Harvard Business Review*, September–October: 84–93.

Berendt, J. (1983). *The jazz book: From New Orleans to jazz rock and beyond*, trans. H. and B. Bredigkeit with Dan Morgenstern, London: Granada.

Blair, J. G. (1988). *Modular America: Cross-cultural perspectives on the emergence of an American way*, New York: Greenwood Press.

Block, N. (1995). "The mind as the software of the brain," in E. Smith and D. Osherson (eds.) *Thinking: An invitation to cognitive science*. Cambridge, MA: MIT Press.

Bolker, J. A. (2000). "Modularity in development and why it matters to Evo-Devo," *American Zoologist*, 40: 770–6.

Christensen, C., Verlinden, M., and Westerman, G. (2001). "Disruption, dis-integration, and the dissipation of differentiability," Harvard Business School Working Paper 00–074.

Coltheart, M. (1999). "Modularity and cognition," *Trends in cognitive sciences*, 3(3): 115–20.

Fodor, J. (1996). *The modularity of mind*, Cambridge, MA: MIT Press, original edition 1983.

Garud, R. and Kumaraswamy, A. (1995). "Technological and organizational designs to achieve economies of substitution," *Strategic Management Journal*, 16: 93–110.

Hull, D. L. (1980). "Individuality and selection," *Annual Review of Ecological Systems*, 11: 311–32

Hulme, C. and Snowling, M. (1992). "Deficits in output phonology: An explanation of reading failure?" *Cognitive Neuropsychology*, 9: 47–72

Loy, J. (1999). Casting out nines, http://www.jimloy.com/number/nines.htm

Marr, D. (1982). *Vision*, Oxford, UK: W. H. Freeman Publishers.

Raff, R. A. (1996). *The shape of life*, Chicago: Chicago University Press.

Roth, V. L. (1991). "Homology and hierarchies: Problems solved and unresolved," *Journal of Evolutionary Biology*, 4: 167–94.

Schilling, M. A. and Steensma, H. K. (2001). "The use of modular organizational forms: An industry-level analysis," *Academy of Management Journal*, 44: 1149–68.

Simon, H. A. (1962). "The architecture of complexity," *Proceedings of the American Philosophical Society*, 106: 467–82.

Smith, D. E. (1959). *A source book in mathematics*, New York: Dover Publications, original edition 1929.

Veysey, L. (1965). *The emergence of the American university*, Chicago: University of Chicago Press.

Wagner, G. (1996). "Homologues, natural kinds and the evolution of modularity," *American Zoologist*, 36: 36–43.

Wagner, G. and Altenberg, L. (1996). "Perspective: complex adaptations and the evolution of evolvability," *Evolution*, 50: 967–76.

PART THREE

NETWORKS AND STANDARDS

CHAPTER SEVEN

THE ECONOMICS OF NETWORKS

NICHOLAS ECONOMIDES

1. INTRODUCTION

Network industries play a crucial role in modern life.[1] The modern economy would be very much diminished without the transportation, communications, information, and railroad networks. This essay will analyze the major economic features of networks. In the course of the analysis it will become clear that many important non-network industries share many essential economic features with network industries. These non-network industries are characterized by strong complementary relations. Thus, the lessons of networks can be applied to industries where vertical relations play a crucial role; conversely, the economic and legal learning developed in the analysis of vertically related industries can be applied to network industries.

2. CLASSIFICATION OF NETWORKS

Formally, networks are composed of links that connect nodes. It is inherent in the structure of a network that many components of a network are required for the provision of a typical service. Thus, network components are complementary to each other. Figure 7.1 represents the emerging *information superhighway* network. Clearly, services demanded by consumers are composed of many complementary components. For example, interactive ordering while browsing in a "department store" as it appears in successive video frames requires a number of components: a database engine at the service provider, transmission of signals, decoding through an interface, display on a TV or computer monitor, etc. Clearly, there are close substitutes for each of these components; for example, transmission can be done through a cable TV line, a fixed telephone line, a wireless satellite, PCN, etc.; the in-home interface may be a TV-top box or an add-on to a PC, etc. It is likely that the combinations of various components will not result in identical services. Thus, the information superhighway will provide substitutes made of complements; this is a typical feature of networks.

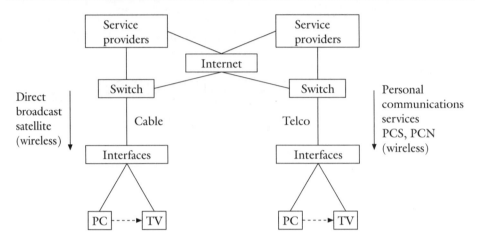

Figure 7.1 An information superhighway.

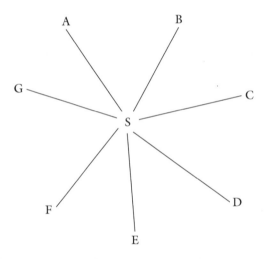

Figure 7.2 A simple star network.

Figure 7.2 shows this feature in a simple star telephone network. A phone call from *A* to *B* is composed of *AS* (access to the switch of customer *A*), *BS* (access to the switch of customer *B*), and switching services at *S*. Despite the fact that goods *AS* and *BS* look very similar and have the same industrial classification, they are *complements* and not substitutes.[2]

Networks where services *AB* and *BA* are distinct are named "two-way" networks in Economides and White (1994). Two-way networks include railroad, road, and many telecommunications networks. When one of *AB* or *BA* is unfeasible, or does not make economic sense, or when there is no sense of direction in the network so that *AB* and *BA* are identical, then the network is called a one-way network. In a typical one-way network, there are two types of components, and composite goods

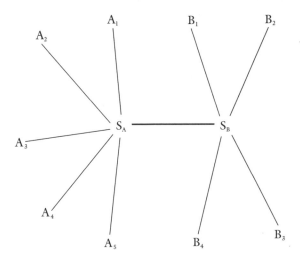

Figure 7.3 A simple local and long distance network.

are formed only by combining a component of each type, and customers are often not identified with components but instead demand composite goods. For example, broadcasting and paging are one-way networks.[3]

The classification in network type (one-way or two-way) is not a function of the topological structure of the network. Rather, it depends on the interpretation of the structure to represent a specific service. For example, the network of figure 7.3 can be interpreted as a two-way telephone network where SA represents a local switch in city A, A_i represents a customer in city A, and similarly for SB and B_j.[4] In this network, there are two types of local phone calls $A_iS_AA_k$ and $B_jS_BB_l$ as well as long distance phone call $A_iS_AS_BB_j$. We can also interpret the network of figure 7.3 as an automatic teller machine network (ATM). Then a transaction (say a withdrawal) from bank B_j from ATM A_i is $A_iS_AS_BB_j$. Connections $A_iS_AA_k$ and $B_jS_BB_l$ may be feasible but there is no demand for them.

We have pointed out earlier that the crucial relationship in both one-way and two-way networks is the complementarity between the pieces of the network. This crucial economic relationship is also often observed between different classes of goods in non-network industries. In fact, Economides and White (1994) point out that a pair of vertically related industries is formally equivalent to a one-way network. Figure 7.4 can represent two industries of complementary goods A and B, where consumers demand combinations A_iB_j. Notice that this formulation is formally identical to our long-distance network of figure 7.3 in the ATM interpretation.

The discussion so far was carried under the assumption of *compatibility*, i.e. that various links and nodes on the network are costlessly combinable to produce demanded goods. We have pointed out that links on a network are potentially complementary, but it is *compatibility that makes complementarity actual*. Some network goods and some vertically related goods are immediately combinable because of their inherent properties. However, for many complex products, actual complementarity can be achieved only through the adherence to specific technical compatibility

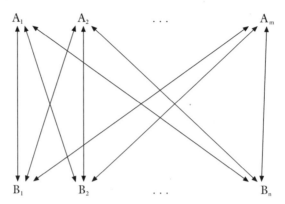

Figure 7.4 A pair of vertically related markets.

standards. Thus, many providers of network or vertically related goods have the option of making their products partially or fully incompatible with components produced by other firms. This can be done through the creation of proprietary designs or the outright exclusion or refusal to interconnect with some firms.

Traditionally, networks were analyzed under the assumption that each network was owned by a single firm. Thus, economic research focused on the efficient use of the network structure as well as on the appropriate allocation of costs.[5] In the 70s, partly prompted by the antitrust suit against AT&T, there was a considerable amount of research on economies of scope, i.e. on the efficiency gains from joint operation of complementary components of networks.[6]

Once one of the most important networks (the AT&T telecommunications network in the US) was broken to pieces, economic research focused in the 80s and 90s on issues of interconnection and compatibility. Similar research on issues of compatibility was prompted by the reduced role of IBM in the 80s and 90s in the setting of technical standards in computer hardware and software. Significant reductions in costs also contributed and will contribute to the transformation toward fragmented ownership in the telecommunications sector in both the United States and abroad. Costs of transmission have fallen dramatically with the introduction of fiberoptic lines. Switching costs have followed the fast cost decreases of microchips and integrated circuits. These cost reductions have transformed the telecommunications industry from a natural monopoly to an oligopoly. The same cost reductions have made many new services, such as interactive video and interactive games, feasible at low cost. Technological change now allows for joint transmission of digital signals of various communications services. Thus, the monopoly of the last link closest to home is in the process of being eliminated,[7] since both telephone lines and cable lines (and in some cases PCS and terrestrial satellites) will provide similar services.[8,9]

In a network where complementary as well as substitute links are owned by different firms, the questions of interconnection, compatibility, interoperability, and coordination of quality of services become of paramount importance. We will examine these issues in detail in the next few sections. We first focus on a fundamental property of networks, i.e. the fact that they exhibit *network externalities*.

3. NETWORK EXTERNALITIES

Networks exhibit positive consumption and production externalities. A positive consumption externality (or network externality) signifies the fact that the value of a unit of the good increases with the number of units sold. To economists, this fact seems quite counterintuitive, since they all know that, except for potatoes in Irish famines, market demand slopes downwards. Thus, the earlier statement, "the value of a unit of a good increases with the number of units sold," should be interpreted as "the value of a unit of the good increases with the *expected* number of units to be sold." Thus, the demand slopes downward but shifts upward with increases in the number of units expected to be sold.

3.1 Sources of network externalities

The key reason for the appearance of network externalities is the complementarity between the components of a network. Depending on the network, the externality may be direct or indirect. When customers are identified with components, the externality is direct. Consider for example a typical two-way network, such as the local telephone network of figure 7.2. In this n-component network, there are $n(n-1)$ potential goods. An additional $(n+1\text{th})$ customer provides direct externalities to all other customers in the network by adding $2n$ potential new goods through the provision of a complementary link (say ES) to the existing links.[10]

In typical one-way networks, the externality is only indirect. When there are m varieties of component A and n varieties of component B as in figure 7.4 (and all A-type goods are compatible with all B-type), there are mn potential composite goods. An extra customer yields indirect externalities to other customers, by increasing the demand for components of types A and B and thereby (because of the presence of economies of scale) potentially increasing the number of varieties of each component that are available in the market.

Financial exchange networks also exhibit indirect network externalities. There are two ways in which these externalities arise. First, externalities arise in the act of exchanging assets or goods. Second, externalities may arise in the array of vertically related services that compose a financial transaction. These include the services of a broker, of bringing the offer to the floor, matching the offer, etc. The second type of externalities are similar to other vertically related markets. The first way in which externalities arise in financial markets is more important.

The act of exchanging goods or assets brings together a trader who is willing to sell with a trader who is willing to buy. The exchange brings together the two complementary goods, "willingness to sell at price p" (the "offer") and "willingness to buy at price p" (the "counteroffer") and creates a composite good, the "exchange transaction." The two original goods were complementary and each had no value without the other one. Clearly, the availability of the counteroffer is critical for the exchange to occur. Put in terms commonly used in finance, minimal liquidity is necessary for the transaction to occur.

Financial markets also exhibit positive size externalities in the sense that the increasing size (or thickness) of an exchange market increases the expected utility of all participants. Higher participation of traders on both sides of the market (drawn from the same distribution) decreases the variance of the expected market price and increases the expected utility of risk-averse traders. *Ceteris paribus*, higher liquidity increase traders' utility. Thus, financial exchange markets also exhibit network externalities.[11,12]

3.2 The "macro" approach

There are two approaches and two strands of literature in the analysis of network externalities. The first approach assumes that network externalities exist, and attempts to model their consequences. I call this the "macro" approach. Conceptually this approach is easier, and it has produced strong results. It was the predominant approach during the 80s. The second approach attempts to find the root cause of the network externalities. I call this the "micro" approach. In industrial organization, it started with the analysis of mix-and-match models and has evolved to the analysis of various structures of vertically related markets. In finance, it started with the analysis of price dispersion models. The "micro" approach is harder, and in many ways more constrained, as it has to rely on the underlying microstructure. However, the "micro" approach has a very significant benefit in defining the market structure. We discuss the "macro" approach first.

3.2.1 Perfect competition

As we have noted earlier, network externalities arise out of the complementarity of different network pieces. Thus, they arise naturally in both one- and two-way networks, as well as in vertically related markets. The value of good X increases as more of the complementary good Y is sold, and vice versa. Thus, more of Y is sold as more X is sold. It follows that the value of X increases as more of it is sold. This positive feedback loop seems explosive, and indeed it would be, except for the inherent downward slope of the demand curve. To understand this better, consider a fulfilled expectations formulation of network externalities as in Katz and Shapiro (1985), Economides (1993b), Economides (1996a), and Economides and Himmelberg (1995). Let the willingness to pay for the nth unit of the good when n^e units are expected to be sold be $p(n; n^e)$.[13] This is a decreasing function of its first argument because the demand slopes downward. $p(n; n^e)$ increases in n^e; this captures the network externalities effect. At a market equilibrium of the simple single-period world, expectations are fulfilled, $n = n^e$, thus defining the fulfilled expectations demand $p(n, n)$. Figure 7.5 shows the construction of a typical fulfilled expectations demand. Each curve D_i, $i = 1, \ldots, 4$, shows the willingness to pay for a varying quantity n, given an expectation of sales $n^e = n_i$. At $n = n_i$, expectations are fulfilled and the point belongs to $p(n, n)$ as $p(n_i, n_i)$. Thus $p(n, n)$ is constructed as a collection of points $p(n_i, n_i)$.

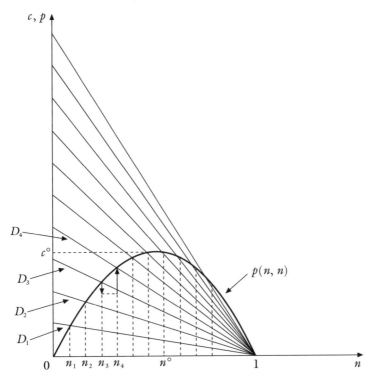

Figure 7.5 Construction of the fulfilled expectations demand.

To avoid explosions and infinite sales, it is reasonable to impose $\lim_{n \to \infty} P(n, n) = 0$; it then follows that $p(n, n)$ is decreasing for large n. Economides and Himmelberg (1995) show that the fulfilled expectations demand is increasing for small n if either one of three conditions hold: (i) *the utility of every consumer in a network of zero size is zero*, or (ii) *there are immediate and large external benefits to network expansion for very small networks*, or (iii) *there is a significant density of high-willingness-to-pay consumers who are just indifferent on joining a network of approximately zero size*. The first condition is straightforward and applies directly to all two-way networks. The other two conditions are a bit more subtle, but commonly observed in networks and vertically related industries.

When the fulfilled expectations demand increases for small n, we say that *the network exhibits a positive critical mass under perfect competition*. This means that, if we imagine a constant marginal cost c decreasing parametrically, the network will start at a positive and significant size n° (corresponding to marginal cost c°). For each smaller marginal cost, $c < c^\circ$, there are three network sizes consistent with marginal cost pricing: a zero size network; an unstable network size at the first intersection of the horizontal through c with $p(n, n)$; and the Pareto optimal stable network size at the largest intersection of the horizontal with $p(n, n)$. The multiplicity of equilibria is a direct result of the coordination problem that arises naturally in the typical network externalities model. In such a setting, it is natural to assume that the Pareto optimal network size will result.[14]

In the presence of network externalities, it is evident that perfect competition is inefficient: the marginal social benefit of network expansion is larger than the benefit that accrues to a particular firm under perfect competition. Thus, perfect competition will provide a smaller network than is socially optimal, and for some relatively high marginal costs perfect competition will not provide the good while it is socially optimal to provide it.

One interesting question that remains virtually unanswered is how to decentralize the welfare maximizing solution in the presence of network externalities. Clearly, the welfare maximizing solution can be implemented through perfect price discrimination, but typically such discrimination is unfeasible. It remains to be seen to what extent mechanisms that allow for non-linear pricing and self-selection by consumers will come close to the first best.

3.2.2 Monopoly

Economides and Himmelberg (1995) show that a monopolist who is unable to price-discriminate will support a smaller network and charge higher prices than perfectly competitive firms. This is despite the fact that the monopolist has influence over the expectations of the consumers, and he recognizes this influence, while no perfectly competitive firm has such influence.[15] Influence over expectations drives the monopolist to higher production, but the monopolist's profit-maximizing tendency towards restricted production is stronger and leads it to lower production levels than perfect competition. Thus, consumers and total surplus will be lower in monopoly than in perfect competition. Therefore the existence of network externalities does not reverse the standard welfare comparison between monopoly and competition; it follows that *the existence of network externalities cannot be claimed as a reason in favor of a monopoly market structure.*

3.2.3 Oligopoly and monopolistic competition under compatibility

Cournot oligopolists producing compatible components also have some influence over expectations. A natural way to model the influence of oligopolists on output expectations is to assume that every oligopolist takes the output of all others as given and sets the expectation of consumers of his own output. In this setting, M compatible Cournot oligopolists support a network of a size between monopoly ($M = 1$) and perfect competition ($M = \infty$). The analysis can easily be extended to monopolistic competition among compatible oligopolists if firms face downward-sloping average cost curves as shown in figure 7.6. Firms produce on the downward-sloping part of the firm-scaled fulfilled expectations demand. At a symmetric equilibrium, firm j's output is determined at the intersection of marginal cost c and marginal revenue MR_j. Price is read off the fulfilled expectations firm-scaled inverse demand $p(Mq, Mq)$. At a monopolistically competitive equilibrium, the AC curve is tangent to the fulfilled expectations demand at q_j.

Monopolistic competition with network
externalities and M compatible goods

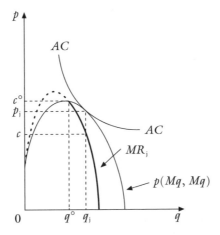

Figure 7.6 Monopolistic competition with network externalities and M compatible goods.

3.2.4 Oligopoly under incompatibility

One of the most interesting issues in the economics of networks is the interaction of oligopolists producing incompatible goods. A full analysis of such a market, in conjunction with the analysis of compatible oligopolists, will allow us to determine the incentives of individual firms to choose technologies that are compatible or incompatible with others.

Given any set of firms $S = \{1, \ldots, N\}$, we can identify a subset of S that adheres to the same technical "standard" as a coalition. Then the partition of S into subsets defines a coalition structure $C_S = \{C_1, \ldots, C_k\}$. Compatibility by all firms means that there is a single coalition that includes all firms. Total incompatibility, where every firm adheres to its own unique standard, means that $k = N$.

A number of criteria can be used to define the equilibrium coalition structure. A purely non-cooperative concept without side payments requires that, after a firm joins a coalition, it is better off at the resulting market equilibirum, just from revenues from its own sales.[16] At a non-cooperative equilibirum with side payments, firms divide the profits of a coalition arbitrarily to induce firms to join a coalition. Yet firms do not cooperate in output decisions. Katz and Shapiro (1985) show that the level of industry output is greater under compatibility than at any equilibrium with some incompatible firm(s). This is not sufficient to characterize the incentives of firms to opt for compatibility.

Intuitively, a firm benefits from a move to compatibility if (i) the marginal externality is strong; (ii) it joins a large coalition; and (iii) it does not thereby increase competition to a significant degree by its action. On the other hand, the coalition benefits from a firm joining its "standard" if (i) the marginal externality is strong;

(ii) the firm that joins the coalition is large; (iii) competition does not increase significantly as a result of the firm joining the coalition. Clearly, in both cases, the second and the third criteria may create incentives that are in conflict; this will help define the equilibrium coalition structure.[17]

Katz and Shapiro (1985) show that if the costs of achieving compatibility are lower for all firms than the increase in profits because of compatibility, then the industry move toward compatibility is socially beneficial. However, it may be true that the (fixed) cost of achieving compatibility is larger than the increase in profits for some firms, while these costs are lower than the increase in total surplus from compatibility. Then profit maximizing firms will not achieve industry-wide compatibility while this regime is socially optimal. Further, if a change leads to less than industry-wide compatibility, the private incentives to standardize may be excessive or inadequate. This is because of the output changes that a change of regime has on all firms. Similarly, the incentive of a firm to produce a one-way adapter, that allows it to achieve compatibility without affecting the compatibility of other firms, may be deficient or excessive because the firm ignores the change it creates on other firms' profits and on consumers surplus.

3.2.5 Coordination to technical standards with asymmetric technologies

So far it was assumed that the cost of standardization was fixed and the same for both firms. If standardization costs are different, firms play a standards coordination game. A 2×2 version of this game is presented in figure 7.7. Entries represent profits. In this game, we will assume that firm i has higher profits when "its" standard i get adopted, $a > g$, $b < h$. Profits, in case of disagreement, will depend on the particulars of the industry. One standard assumption that captures many industries is that in case of disagreement profits will be lower than those of either standard, e, $c < g$; $d, f < b$. Under these circumstances, the setting of either standard will constitute a non-cooperative equilibrium.[18] There is no guarantee that the highest joint profit standard will be adopted. Since consumers surplus does not appear in the matrix, there is no guarantee of maximization of social welfare at equilibrium. For an analysis with continuous choice of standard specification see Berg (1988).

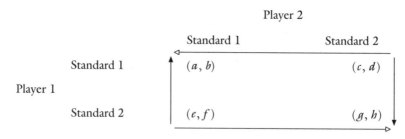

Figure 7.7

3.3 The "micro" approach

The micro approach starts with an analysis of the specific micro-structure of a network. After identifying the physical aspects of a network, such as nodes and links, we identify the goods and services that are demanded on the network. We distinguish between the case where only end-to-end services are demanded and the case when there is also demand for some services that do not reach from end to end. The case when only end-to-end services exist is easier and has been dealt with in much more detail in the literature. However, many important networks, such as the railroad and telephone networks, provide both end-to-end and partial coverage service. We examine this case later.

We start with a simple case where only end-to-end services are demanded. Suppose that there are two complementary types of goods, A and B. Suppose that each type of good has a number of brands available, A_i, $i = 1, \ldots, m$, B_j, $j = 1, \ldots, n$, as in figure 7.4. Let consumers demand 1:1 combinations $A_k B_j$. We call each of the complementary goods A_i or B_j *components*, while the combined good $A_i B_j$ is called a *composite good* or *system*. Potentially all combinations $A_i B_j$, $i = 1, \ldots, m$; $j = 1, \ldots, n$, are possible. Thus complementarity exists in potential. Complementarity is actualized when the components A_i and B_j are combinable and function together without extra cost, i.e. when the components are *compatible*. Often it is an explicit decision of the producers of individual components to make their products compatible with those of other producers. Thus, compatibility is a *strategic* decision and should be analyzed as such.

Modern industrial organization provides a rich collection of environments for the analysis of strategic decisions; because of shortage of time and space, this survey will discuss the decision on compatibility only in few environments.

3.3.1 Mix-and-match: compatibility versus incompatibility

The *mix-and-match* literature does not assume a priori network externalities; however, it is clear that demand in mix-and-match models *exhibits* network externalities. The mix-and-match approach was originated by Matutes and Regibeau (1988), and followed by Economides (1988), Economides (1989), Economides (1991a), Economides (1991b), Economides (1993c), Economides and Salop (1992), Economides and Lehr (1995), Matutes and Regibeau (1989), Matutes and Regibeau (1992), and others. To fix ideas, consider the case of figure 7.4 with $m = 2$, $n = 2$, technologies are known, coordination is costless, price discrimination is not allowed, and there are no cost asymmetries created by any particular compatibility standard. Figure 7.8 shows the case of compatibility. The incentive for compatibility of a vertically integrated firm (producing A_1 and B_1) depends on the relative sizes of each combination of complementary components. Reciprocal compatibility, (i.e. simultaneous compatibility between A_1 and B_2, as well as between A_2 and B_1) increases demand (by allowing for the sale of $A_1 B_2$ and $A_2 B_1$) but also increases competition for the individual components. Therefore, when the hybrid demand is large compared with the own-product demand (including the case where the two demands are

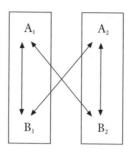

Figure 7.8 Mix-and-match compatibility.

equal at equal prices), a firm has an incentive to want compatibility.[19] When the demand for hybrids is small, a firm does not want compatibility. Thus, it is possible, with two vertically integrated firms, that one firm wants compatibility (because it has small own-product demand compared with the hybrids demand) while the other one prefers incompatibility (because its own-product demand is large compared with the hybrids demand). Thus, there can be conflict across firms in their incentives for compatibility, even when the technology is well known. The presumption is that opponents will not be able to counteract and correct all incompatibilities introduced by an opponent, and, therefore, in situations of conflict we expect that incompatibility wins.

These results hold both for zero-one decisions (i.e. compatibility vs. incompatibility) and for decisions of partial (or variable) incompatibility. The intuition of the pro-compatibility result for the zero-one decision in the equal hybrid- and own-demand is simple. Starting from the same level of prices and demand in both the compatibility and incompatibility regimes, consider a price increase in one component that produces the same decrease in demand in both regimes. Under incompatibility, the loss of profits is higher since *systems* sales are lost rather than sales of *one component*. Therefore, profits are more responsive to price under incompatibility; it follows that the residual demand facing firms is more elastic under incompatibility, and therefore firms will choose lower prices in that regime.[20] This is reminiscent of Cournot's (1838) celebrated result (see Cournot, 1927) that a vertically integrated monopolist faces a more elastic demand and will choose a lower price than the sum of the prices of two vertically disintegrated monopolists.[21]

So far we have assumed that compatibility is reciprocal – i.e. that the same adapter is required to make both $A_1 B_2$ and $A_2 B_1$ functional. If compatibility is not reciprocal (i.e. if different adapters are required for $A_1 B_2$ and $A_2 B_1$) the incentive of firms to achieve compatibility depends on the cross substitution between own-products and hybrids. Roughly, if the substitutability among A-type components is equal to the substitutability among B-type components, the earlier results of the reciprocal setup still hold.[22] Nevertheless, if the degree of substitutability among the As is different than among the Bs, one firm may create an advantage for itself by introducing some incompatibilities. However, it is *never* to the advantage of *both* vertically integrated firms to create incompatibilities.

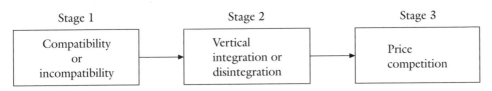

Figure 7.9 Compatibility decisions are less flexible than vertical integration decisions.

The issue of compatibility and coordination is much more complicated if there are more than two firms. A number of coalitions can each be formed around a specific technical standard, and standards may allow for partial compatibility, or may be mutually incompatible. Not enough research has been done on this issue. Research in this area is made particularly difficult by the lack of established models of coalition formation in non-cooperative settings. The analysis based on coalition structures is more complicated in the "micro" approach because of the specifics of the ownership structure.

The studies we referred to this far take the ownership structure as given (i.e. as parallel vertical integration), and proceed to discuss the choice of the degree of compatibility. In many cases, vertical integration is a decision that is more flexible (and less irreversible) than a decision on compatibility. Thus, it makes sense to think of a game structure where the choice of technology (which implies the degree of compatibility) *precedes* the choice of the degree of vertical integration. Economides (1996b) analyzes the choice of asset ownership as a consequence of the choice of technology (and of the implied degree of compatibility). It posits a three-stage game of compatibility choice in the first stage, vertical integration in the second stage, and price choice in the third stage. Incentives for vertical mergers in industries with varying degrees of compatibility are compared. In analyzing the stage of compatibility choice, the influence of the anticipation of decisions on (vertical) industry structure on compatibility decisions is evaluated (see figure 7.9).

3.3.2 Changes in the number of varieties as a result of compatibility decisions

Economides (1991b) considers the interplay of compatibility and the number of varieties of complementary goods. There are two types of goods, A and B, consumed in 1:1 ratio. There are two brands of good A, A_1 and A_2, each produced by an independent firm. The number of B-type brands, each also produced by an independent firm, is determined by a free-entry condition, so that industry B is in monopolistic competition. In a regime of compatibility, each B-type component is immediately compatible with either A_1 or A_2. In a regime of incompatibility, each brand B_1 produces two versions, one compatible with A_1 and one compatible with A_2. The two cases are shown in figure 7.10 and figure 7.11.

Under incompatibility, each B-type firm incurs higher fixed costs; it follows that *ceteris paribus* the number of B-type brands will be smaller under incompatibility.

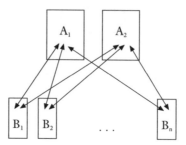

Figure 7.10 Compatibility.

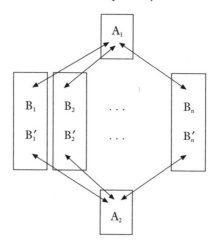

Figure 7.11 Incompatibility.

An A-type firm prefers incompatibility or compatibility according to the equilibrium profits it realizes in each regime. These profits, and the decision on compatibility, depends on the specifics of the utility function of consumers, and in particular on the impact of an increase of the number of varieties on utility. In industry demand is not sensitive to increases in the number of varieties of composite goods n (and does not increase much as n increases), then equilibirum profits of an A-type firm decrease in the number of firms; therefore profits of an A-type firm are higher at the smaller number of firms implied by incompatibility, and an A-type firm prefers incompatibility. Conversely, when consumers have a strong preference for variety and demand for composite goods increases significantly in n, equilibrium profits of an A-type firm increase in the number of firms; therefore its profits are higher at the larger number of firms implied by compatibility, and an A-type firm prefers compatibility.

Church and Gandal (1992b), Chou and Shy (1990a), Chou and Shy (1990b), and Chou and Shy (1990c) also examine the impact of the number of varieties of complementary (B-type) goods on the decisions of consumers to buy one of the A-type goods under conditions of incompatibility.

3.3.3 Quality coordination in mix-and-match

The framework of mix and match models applies to both variety and quality features that are combinable additively in the utility function. That is, in the standard mix-and-match model, the utility accruing to a consumer from component A_i is added to the utility from component B_j. However, in some networks, including telecommunications,[23] the utility of the composite good A_iB_j is not the sum of the respective qualities. In particular, the quality of voice in a long distance call is the minimum of the qualities of the component parts of the network, i.e. the local and the long distance transmission. Thus, significant quality coordination problems arise in a network with fragmented ownership. Economides (1994b) and Economides and Lehr (1995) examine this coordination problem.

Let A and B be components that are combinable in a 1:1 ratio. Suppose that the quality levels of the components are q_A and q_B, while the quality level of the composite good is $q_{AB} = \min(q_A, q_B)$. Consumers have varying willingness to pay for quality improvements as in Gabszewicz and Thisse (1979) and Shaked and Sutton (1982), and firms play a two-stage game of quality choice in the first stage, followed by price choice in the second stage. As mentioned earlier, Cournot (1927) has shown that an integrated monopolist producing both A and B will charge less than two vertically related monopolists, each producing one component only. This is because of the elimination of double marginalization by the integrated monopolist. Economides (1994b) and Economides and Lehr (1995) show that an integrated monopolist also provides a higher quality than the two independent monopolists. In bilateral monopoly, marginal increases in quality have a bigger impact on price. Being able to sell the same quality at a higher price than under integrated monopoly, the bilateral monopolists choose lower quality levels, which are less costly. Despite that, because of double marginalization, prices are higher than in integrated monopoly, a lower portion of the market is served, and firms realize lower profits.[24] Thus, *lack of vertical integration leads to a reduction in quality*. Note that this is not because of lack of coordination between the bilateral monopolists in the choice of quality, since they both choose the same quality level.[25]

In this setting, Economides and Lehr (1995) examine various ownership structures where, for at least one of the types of components there is more than one quality level available. Clearly, a situation where all components have the same quality is not viable, since competition would then drive prices to marginal cost. Further, for a "high" quality composite good to be available, both an A- and a B-type goods must be of "high" quality. They find that a third (and fourth) "low" quality goods have a hard time surviving if they are produced by independent firms. In contrast, in parallel vertical integration (with firm i, $i = 1, 2$, producing A_i and B_i), firms prefer not to interconnect – i.e. to produce components that are incompatible with those of the opponent.

4.   NETWORK EXTERNALITIES AND INDUSTRY STRUCTURE

4.1   Invitations to enter

In the presence of strong network externalities, a monopolist exclusive holder of a technology may have an incentive to invite competitors and even subsidize them. The realization of network externalities requires high output. A monopolist may be unable credibly to commit to a high output as long as he is operating by himself. However, if he licenses the technology to a number of firms and invites them to enter and compete with him, market output will be higher; and since the level of market output depends mainly upon other firms, the commitment to high output is credible.

   The invitation to enter and the consequent increase in market output has two effects; a *competitive effect* and a *network effect*. The competitive effect is an expected increase in competition because of the increase of the number of firms. The network effect tends to increase the willingness to pay and the market price because of the high expected sales. Economides (1993b) and Economides (1996a) show that, if the network externality is strong enough, the network effect is larger than the competitive effect, and therefore an innovator-monopolist invites competitors and even subsidizes them on the margin to induce them to increase production.

4.2   Interconnection or foreclosure by a local monopolist?

Many telecommunications, airline networks and railroad networks have the structure of figure 7.12. In a railroad network, there may be direct consumer demand for links *AB*, *BC*, as well as *AC*. This figure can also represent a telephone network with demand for local telephone services (*AB*) and for long distance services (*ABC*); in that case, there is no direct demand for *BC*, but only the indirect demand arising from long distance calls *ABC*. In many cases, one firm has a monopoly of a link that is necessary for a number of services (here *AB*), and this link is a natural monopoly. This bottleneck link is often called an essential facility. The monopolist can foreclose any firm by denying access to the bottleneck facility. What are his incentives do so?

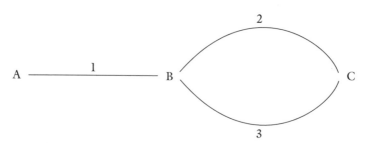

Figure 7.12   *AB* is a bottleneck facility.

Network in extensive and collapsed form

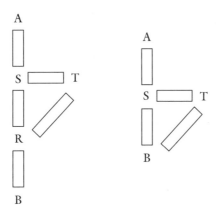

Figure 7.13   Intermodal competition.

Economides and Woroch (1992) examine intermodal competition in the context of a simple network pictured in figure 7.13. S and R are local switches; AS and BR is local service (in different cities); SR and STR are alternative long distance services. The diagram is simplified by eliminating R without any essential loss. Suppose that an integrated firm offers end-to-end service (ASB), while a second firm offers service of partial coverage only (STB). They find that, although the integrated firm has the opportunity to foreclose the opponent, it prefers not to. In fact, *the integrated firm is better off by implementing a vertical price squeeze on the opponent*, and charging a significantly higher price to the opponent for the use of the monopolized link than it "charges" itself.[26] Thus, foreclosure, although feasible, it not optimal for the integrated firm.[27]

Economides and Woroch (1992) also find that vertical disintegration is not desirable for the firm that offers end-to-end service. Once disintegrated, its constituent parts realize lower total profits. This is because, besides appropriating monopoly rents for its AS monopoly, the integrated firm (ASB) was creating a significant restriction of competition in SB–STB market by its *de facto* price discriminating strategy. After disintegration, the SB–STB market becomes much more competitive, even if AS price discriminates between SB and STB. Thus, even if network ASB were to receive the full rent earned by the new owner of SB, its after-divestiture profits would be lower than before divestiture.[28]

Even in simple networks, there may be relations among firms that are neither purely vertical nor purely horizontal. Thus, the conventional wisdom about vertical and horizontal integration fails. Economides and Salop (1992) discuss pricing in various ownership structures in the model of figure 7.8. They call the ownership structure of this figure, where each firm produces a component of each type, *parallel vertical integration*. They also consider the *independent ownership* structure, where each of the four components is owned by a different firm. In both of these structures, no firm is purely vertically or purely horizontally related to another firm. Thus, starting from independent ownership, or starting from parallel vertical integration, a merger to *joint ownership*, where all components are produced by the same firm, can either increase or decrease prices. Thus, simple prescriptions against mergers may easily fail.

In the model of figure 7.13, Economides and Woroch (1992) consider the case where link *ST* is owned by a firm that owns a vertically related link (either *AS* or *BT*), or is owned by an independent firm. Clearly, the strategic structure of the game remains unaffected when link *ST* changes hands between two firms that also own a link that is vertically related to *ST*. Therefore, if *ST* has a fixed cost, it is a liability to such a firm; each firm would like the opponent to own it. However, if the link is owned by a third party, it has a positive value because of its monopoly position in the chain. Thus, each original owner has an incentive to sell *ST* to a third party. The direct implication is that the value of links depends on what other links a firm owns. Thus, general prescriptions on the desirability of unbundling of ownership are suspect.

Often parts of the network are regulated, while other parts are not. This is the typical arrangement in telephony in the US, where only local telephone companies are tightly regulated, since their market is traditionally considered a natural monopoly.[29] Baumol and Sidak (1994a) and Baumol and Sidak (1994b) propose that, to attract efficient entrants in the long distance market and to discourage inefficient entrants, a local telephone company should charge them an *interconnection (or access) fee* equal to the marginal cost of provision of service plus any opportunity cost that the local telephone company incurs.[30] This is correct under a set of strict assumptions: first that the end-to-end good is sold originally at the competitive price; second that the entrant produces the same complementary good (long distance service) as the incumbent;[31] third, that there are no economies of scale in either one of the complements. Economides and White (1995) and Economides and White (1996) discuss how the relaxation of these assumptions leads to different interconnection charges. For example, if competition between an entrant and the incumbent reduces the market power of the incumbent, entry may increase social welfare even when the entrant produces at higher cost than the incumbent.

5. Sequential Games

In network markets, and more generally in markets with network externalities, when firms and consumers interact in more than period, *history matters*. Both consumers and firms make production and consumption decisions based on sizes of installed base and on expectations of its increases over time. The same underlying technology and consumers' preferences and distribution can lead to different industrial structures depending on the way things start. Thus, strategic advantages, such as first mover advantages, can have long run effects.[32]

Network externalities and historical events are particularly important in the speed of adoption of an innovation that creates services on a network. Cabral (1990) discusses the adoption of innovations under perfect competition in the presence of network externalities. His main conclusion is that, when network externalities are strong, the equilibrium adoption path may be discontinuous. This is another way

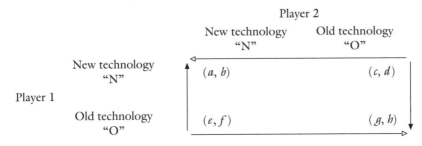

Figure 7.14

of saying that there are two network sizes supported as equilibria at the same time instant. This may occur at the start of the network, and then it is called positive critical mass by Economides and Himmelberg (1995). It may also occur at other points in the network evolution. In practice, discontinuities in the size of the network over time do not occur since that would imply an infinite size of sales at some points in time. Continuity and smoothness of the network path is restored if instantaneous marginal production costs are increasing. Under this assumption, Economides and Himmelberg (1995) find that the adoption path is much steeper in the presence of externalities. Further, driven by the externality, in early stages the network can expand so quickly as to exhibit increasing retail prices even when marginal costs are falling over time. Their analysis is applied to the fax market in the US and Japan.

The analysis is more complex when we depart from the assumption of perfect competition. Accordingly, this analysis tends to be in the form of simple two-period models. We analyze it with reference to the standard simultaneous choice coordination game of section 3.2.5, where we now interpret the first strategy as sticking to the old technology, and the second as the adoption of a new one (figure 7.14). Network externalities for both technologies mean that $a > c$, e; $b > d$, f, $g > c$, e; $h > d$, f. If both firms are worse off when they are not coordinated, both the "new technology" (i.e. (N, N)) and the "old technology" (i.e. (O, O)) will arise as equilibria. Clearly, one of the equilibria can be inefficient. If the (O, O) equilibrium is inefficient and is adopted, Farrell and Saloner (1985) call the situation *excess inertia*.[33] Similarly, if the (N, N) equilibrium is inefficient and it is adopted, the situation is called *excess momentum*.

Farrell and Saloner (1985) discuss a two-period model where consumers have varying willingness to pay for the change of the technology, measured by θ. Users can switch in Period 1 or 2, and switching is irreversible. Users fall in four categories according to the strategy they pick: (i) they never switch, whatever the behavior of others in the first period; (ii) they switch in Period 2 if other users have switched in Period 1 – jumping on the bandwagon; (iii) they switch in Period 1; (iv) switch in Period 2 even if others have not switched in Period 1. The last strategy is dominated by strategy (iii). Consumers of low θ use strategy (i), consumers of intermediate θ use strategy (ii), and consumers of high θ use strategy (iii). Consumers would like to coordinate themselves and switch in the first period (thereby getting the bandwagon rolling) but are unable to do so, thus creating excess inertia. This inertia can be reduced through communication among the consumers, through contracts, through coordination in committees or through new product sponsorship and special intro-ductory pricing.[34]

In a sequential setting, preannouncement (i.e. announcement of a new product before its introduction) may induce some users to delay their purchase. Also pene-tration pricing can be important. Katz and Shapiro (1986a) examine the effects of sponsorship (allowing firms to price differently than at marginal cost). Katz and Shapiro (1986b) examine the effects of uncertainty in product adoption and introduction.

Nevertheless, there is much more work to be done on multiperiod and on con-tinuous time dynamic games with network externalities. The issues of foreclosure and predation have not been sufficiently discussed in the context of network externalities. More generally, much more work is required on multiperiod dynamic games in this context, especially for durable goods.

6. MARKETS FOR ADAPTERS AND ADD-ONS

Not enough research has been done on the economics of adapters and interfaces. One strand of the mix-and-match literature assumes that compatibilities introduced by one firm cannot be corrected by the other, so that adapters are unfeasible. Eco-nomides (1991a) assumes that adapters are provided by a competitive industry at cost, but decisions of the firms determine the extent of incompatibility, and there-fore the cost of the adapters. Farrell and Saloner (1992) assume that converters make the technologies only partially compatible, in the sense that hybrid goods that utilize incompatible components as well as an adapter give lower utility than a system composed of fully compatible components. In this framework, the availability of converters can reduce social welfare, since, in the presence of converters, some consumers would buy the converter and the "inferior" technology rather than the "best" technology, although the "best" technology gives more externalities.

7. CONCLUDING REMARKS

In this paper, we have noted some of the interesting issues that arise in networks and vertically related industries, especially in the presence of a fragmented ownership structure. As is evident, many open questions remain. One of the most important issues that remains largely unresolved is the joint determination of an equilibrium market structure (including the degree of vertical integration) together with the degree of compatibility across firms. The extent of standardization in markets with more than two participants and the structure of "standards" coalitions also remain open questions. Markets for adapters and add-ons have not been sufficiently analyzed. An analysis of market structure in multiperiod dynamic games with network extern-alities is also unavailable. Further, issues of predation and foreclosure in networks have not been fully analyzed yet. On a more fundamental level, there is no good prediction yet of the "break points" that define the complementary components in a modular design structure. Even if these break points are known, little analysis has been done of competition in a multilayered structure of vertically related components.

Nevertheless, it is exactly this kind of modelling that is needed for an analysis and evaluation of the potential structures of the "information superhighway."

NOTES

Plenary session address, E.A.R.I.E. conference, Chania, Greece, September 1994. I thank Larry White for helpful comments.

1   The literature on networks is so extensive that it is futile to attempt to cover it. This paper discusses only some issues that arise in networks and attempts to point out areas in which further research is necessary.
2   *AS* and *BS* can also be components of *substitute* phone calls *ASC* and *BSC*.
3   The 1994 spectrum auction will allow for a large two-way paging network.
4   In this network, we may identify end-nodes, such as A_i and B_j, end-links, such as A_iS_A and S_BB_j, the interface or gateway S_AS_B, and switches S_A and S_B.
5   See Sharkey (1995) for an excellent survey.
6   See Baumol et al. (1982).
7   It is already eliminated in some parts of the United Kingdom, where cable TV operators offer telephone service at significantly lower prices than British Telecom.
8   These significant changes in costs and the convergence of communications services open an number of policy questions on pricing, unbundling, deregulation, and possibly mandated segmentation in this sector. It is possible that ownership breakup of local and long distance lines is no longer necessary to improve competition. For example, European Union policy mandates open competition by 1998 in any part of the telecommunications network, but does not advocate vertical fragmentation of the existing integrated national monopolies; see European Commission (1994). The reduction in costs and the elimination of natural monopoly in many services may make it possible for this policy to lead the industry to competition.
9   Another important network, the airline network, faces significant change in Europe. Airlines have not benefited from significant cost reductions and technological change; the present reform is just the abolition by the European Union of the antiquated regime of national airline monopolies, and its replacement by a more competitive environment.
10 This property of two-way networks was pointed out in telecommunications networks by Rohlfs (1974) in a very early paper on network externalities. See also Oren and Smith (1981).
11 For a more detailed discussion of networks in finance see Economides (1993a). Economides and Schwartz (1995a) discuss how to set up *electronic call markets* that bunch transactions and execute them all at once. Call markets have inherently higher liquidity because they take advantage of network externalities in exchange. Thus, transaction costs are lower in call markets. Economides (1994a) and Economides and Heisler (1994) discuss how to increase liquidity in call markets. The survey of institutional investors reported by Economides and Schwartz (1995b) find that many traders who work in the present continuous market environment would be willing to wait a number of hours for execution of their orders if they can save in transaction costs, including bid-ask spreads. Thus, the time is right for the establishment of call markets in parallel operation with the continuous market.
12 The increase of utility in expectation due to market thickness was pointed out by Economides and Siow (1988), and earlier and in less formal terms by Garbade and Silber (1976a), Garbade and Silber (1976b), and Garbade and Silber (1979). The effects are similar to those of search models as in Diamond (1982) and Diamond (1984).

13 In this formulation n and n^e are normalized so that they represent market shares rather than absolute quantities.

14 It is possible to have other shapes of the fulfilled expectations demand. In general $p(n, n)$ is quasiconcave under weak conditions on the distribution of preferences and the network externality function. Then, if none of the three causes mentioned above are not present, the fulfilled expectations demand is downward sloping.

15 A monopolist unable to influence expectations will clearly produce less than a monopolist able to influence expectations.

16 See Economides (1984), Yi and Shin (1992a), and Yi and Shin (1992b).

17 Economides and Flyer (1995) examine the incentives for coalition formation around compatibility standards.

18 Standard 1 is an equilibrium if $a > e$, $b > d$. Similarly, Standard 2 is an equilibrium if $g > c$, $h > f$.

19 Matutes and Regibeau (1988) and Economides (1989) find that compatibility is always the firms' choice because they assume a locational setting with uniform distribution of consumers in space that results in equal own-product and hybrid demands at equal prices. The exposition here follows the more general framework of Economides (1988) and Economides (1991a).

20 These results also hold when firms can price discriminate between buyers who buy the pure combination A_iB_i and buyers who buy only one component from firm i. Thus, firms practice mixed bundling. See Matutes and Regibeau (1992) and Economides (1993c).

21 See Economides (1988) for a discussion of Cournot's result, and Economides and Salop (1992) for an extension of the result to (parallel) vertical integration among two pairs of vertically related firms.

22 Economides (1991a, p. 52).

23 See also Encaoua et al. (1992) for a discussion of the coordination of the timing of different legs of airport transportation.

24 Consumers also receive lower surplus in comparison to vertically integrated monopoly.

25 The *reliability* of the network, measured by the percentage of time that the network is in operation, or by the probability of a successful connection, is measured by the product of the respective reliabilities of the components (another non-linear function).

26 This result is dependent on the linear structure of the demand system, and may not hold for any demand structure.

27 Church and Gandal (1992a) find that sometimes firms prefer foreclosure, but their model does not allow for a vertical price squeeze.

28 This result is in contrast to Bonanno and Vickers (1988) because of the absence of two-part contracts in Economides and Woroch (1992).

29 This is changing for some customers through the existence of competitive access providers, who directly compete with the local telephone company for large customers, and the potential for competition by cable companies.

30 Kahn and Taylor (1994) have very similar views.

31 Armstrong and Doyle (1994) relax this assumption.

32 See Arthur (1988), Arthur (1989), David (1985). David argues that the QWERTY keyboard was abopted mainly because it appeared first while the DVORAK keyboard was superior. This is disputed by Liebowitz and Margolis (1990).

33 See Katz and Shapiro (1992) for a different view arguing for excess momentum (which they call *insufficient friction*).

34 See also Farrell and Saloner (1988) for mechanisms to achieve coordination, and Farrell and Saloner (1985) for a discussion of network product sponsorship.

REFERENCES

Armstrong, M. and C. Doyle, 1994, *Interconnection and the Effects of Entry*, mimeo.

Arthur, W. B., 1988, Self-reinforcing mechanisms in economics, in: P. W. Anderson, K. J. Arrow and D. Pines, eds., *The Economy as an Evolving Complex System* (Addison Wesley).

Arthur, W. B., 1989, Competing technologies, increasing returns, and lock-in by historical events, *The Economic Journal* 99, 116–31.

Baumol, W. J. and J. G. Sidak, 1994a, The pricing of inputs sold to competitors, *Yale Journal of Regulation* 11(1), 171–202.

Baumol, W. J. and J. G. Sidak, 1994b, *Toward Competition in Local Telephony* (The MIT Press and The American Enterprise Institute, Washington, DC).

Baumol, W. J., J. Panzar and R. Willig, 1982, *Contestable Markets and the Theory of Inustry Structure* (Harcourt Brace Jovanovich, New York).

Berg, S.V., 1988, Duopoly compatibility standards with partial cooperation and standards leadership, *Information Economics and Policy* 3, 35–53.

Bonanno, G. and J. Vickers, 1988, Vertical separation, *Journal of Industrial Economics* 36(3), 257–65.

Cabral, L., 1990, On the adoption of innovations with 'network' externalities, *Mathematical Social Sciences* 19, 229–308.

Chou, C. and O. Shy, 1990a, *Do Consumers Always Gain When More People Buy the Same Brand?* mimeo.

Chou, C. and O. Shy, 1990b, *Supporting Services and the Choice of Compatibility*, mimeo.

Chou, C. and O. Shy, 1990c, *Partially Compatible Brands and Consumer Welfare*, mimeo.

Church, J. and N. Gandal, 1992a, Integration, complementary products, and variety, *Journal of Economics and Management Strategy* 1(4), 653–75.

Church, J. and N. Gandal, 1992b, Network effects, software provision and standardization, *Journal of Industrial Economics* 40(1), 85–104.

Cournot, A., 1927, *Researches into the Mathematical Principles of the Theory of Wealth* (Macmillan, New York).

David, P. A., 1985, Clio and the economics of QWERTY, *American Economic Review* 75(2), 332–7.

Diamond, P., 1982, Aggregate demand management in search equilibrium, *Journal of Political Economy* 90, 881–94.

Diamond, P., 1984, *A Search-Equilibrium Approach to the Micro Foundations of Macroeconomics* (MIT Press, Cambridge, MA).

Economides, N., 1984, *Equilibrium coalition structures*, Discussion Paper No. 273, Department of Economics, Columbia University.

Economides, N., 1988, *Variable compatibility without network externalities*, Discussion Paper No. 145, Studies in Industry Economics, Stanford University.

Economides, N., 1989, Desirability of compatibility in the absence of network externalities, *American Economic Review* 78(1), 108–21.

Economides, N., 1991a, Compatibility and the creation of shared networks, in: M. Guerin-Calvert and S. Wildman, eds., *Electronic Services Networks: A Business and Public Policy Challenge* (Praeger Publishing Inc., New York).

Economides, N., 1991b, *Compatibility and market structure*, Discussion Paper EC-91-16, Stern School of Business, NYU.

Economides, N., 1993a, Network economics with application to finance, *Financial Markets, Institutions and Instruments* 2(5), 89–97.

Economides, N., 1993b, A monopolist's incentive to invite competitors to enter in tele-communications services, in: G. Pogorel, ed., *Global Telecommunications Services and Technological Changes* (Elsevier, Amsterdam).

Economides, N., 1993c, *Mixed bundling in duopoly*, Discussion Paper EC-93-29, Stern School of Business, NYU.

Economides, N., 1994a, How to enhance market liquidity, in: R.A. Schwartz, ed., *Global Equity Markets* (Irwin Professional, New York).

Economides, N., 1994b, *Quality choice and vertical integration*, Discussion Paper EC-94-22, Stern School of Business, NYU.

Economides, N., 1996a, Network externalities, complementarities, and invitations to enter, *European Journal of Political Economy*, 12, 211–32.

Economides, N., 1996b, *Vertical integration and compatibility of complementary components*, mimeo.

Economides, N. and F. Flyer, 1995, *Technical standards coalitions for network goods*, Discussion Paper EC-95-12, Stern School of Business, NYU.

Economides, N. and J. Heisler, 1994, *Equilibrium fee structure in a monopolist call market*, Discussion Paper EC-94-15, Stern School of Business, NYU.

Economides, N. and C. Himmelberg, 1995, *Critical mass and network size with application to the US fax market*, Discussion Paper EC-95-11, Stern School of Business, NYU.

Economides, N. and W. Lehr, 1995, The quality of complex systems and industry structure, in: W. Lehz (Editor), *Quality and Reliability of Telecommunications Infrastructure*. (Lawrence Erlbaum, Hillsdale, NJ).

Economides, N. and S. C. Salop, 1992, Competition and integration among complements, and network market structure, *Journal of Industrial Economics* 40(1), 105–23.

Economides, N. and R. A. Schwartz, 1995a, Electronic call market trading, *Journal of Portfolio Management* 21(3), 10–18.

Economides, N. and R. A. Schwartz, 1995b, Equity trading practices and market structure: assessing asset managers' demand for immediacy, *Financial Markets, Institutions and Instruments* 4(4): 1–46.

Economides, N. and A. Siow, 1988, The division of markets is limited by the extent of liquidity: spatial competition with externalities, *American Economic Review* 78(1), 108–21.

Economides, N. and L. J. White, 1994, Networks and compatibility: implications for antitrust, *European Economic Review* 38, 651–62.

Economides, N. and L. J. White, 1995, Access and interconnection pricing: how efficient is the "efficient component pricing rule"? *Antitrust Bulletin* XL(3), 557–79.

Economides, N. and White, L. J., 1996, The inefficiency of ECPR yet again: a reply to Larson, *The Antitrust Bulletin*, XLIII(2), 429–44.

Economides, N. and G. A. Woroch, 1992, *Benefits and pitfalls of network interconnection*, Discussion Paper EC-92-31, Stern School of Business, NYU.

Encaoua, D., M. Moreaux and A. Perrot, 1992, *Demand Side Network Effect in Airline Markets*, mimeo.

European Commission, 1994, *Europe and the Global Information Society – Bangemann Report*.

Farrell, J. and G. Saloner, 1985, Standardization, compatibility, and innovation, *Rand Journal of Economics* 16, 70–83.

Farrell, J. and G. Saloner, 1988, Coordination through committees and markets, *Rand Journal of Economics* 19(2), 235–52.

Farrell, J. and G. Saloner, 1992, Converters, compatibility, and the control of interfaces, *Journal of Industrial Economics* 40(1), 9–36.

Gabszewicz, J. and J.-F. Thisse, 1979, Price competition, quality, and income disparities, *Journal of Economic Theory* 20, 340–59.

Garbade, K. and W. Silber, 1976a, Price dispersion in the government securities market, *Journal of Political Economy* 84.

Garbade, K. and W. Silber, 1976b, Technology, communication and the performance of financial markets, 1840–1975, *Journal of Finance* 33.

Garbade, K. and W. Silber, 1979, Structural organization of secondary markets: clearing frequency, dealer activity and liquidity risk, *Journal of Finance* 34, 577–93.

Kahn, A. and Taylor, W., 1994, The pricing of inputs sold to competitors: comment, Yale *Journal of Regulation* 11(1), 225–40.

Katz, M. and C. Shapiro, 1985, Network externalities, competition and compatibility, *American Economic Review* 75(3), 424–40.

Katz, M. and C. Shapiro, 1986a, Technology adoption in the presence of network externalities, *Journal of Political Economy* 94, 822–41.

Katz, M. and C. Shapiro, 1986b, Product compatibility choice in a market with technological progress, *Oxford Economic Papers* 38, 146–65.

Katz, M. and C. Shapiro, 1992, Product introduction with network externalities, *Journal of Industrial Economics* 40(1), 55–84.

Liebowitz, S.J. and S.E. Margolis, 1990, The fable of keys, *Journal of Law and Economics* 33(1), 1–26.

Matutes, C. and P. Regibeau, 1988, Mix and match: product compatibility without network externalities, *Rand Journal of Economics* 19(2), 219–34.

Matutes, C. and P. Regibeau, 1989, Standardization across markets and entry, *Journal of Industrial Economics* 37, 359–71.

Matutes, C. and P. Regibeau, 1992, Compatibility and bundling of complementary goods in a duopoly, *Journal of Industrial Economics* 40(1), 37–54.

Oren, S. and S. Smith, 1981, Critical mass and tariff structure in electronic communications markets, *Bell Journal of Economics* 12(2), 467–87.

Rohlfs, J., 1974, A theory of interdependent demand for a communications service, *Bell Journal of Economics* 5(1), 16–37.

Shaked, A. and J. Sutton, 1982, Relaxing price competition through product differentiation, *Review of Economic Studies* 49, 3–14.

Sharkey, W. W., 1995, Network Models in Economics. In: M. O. Ball et al. (Editors), *Handbook in OR and MS*, 8: 713–65.

Yi, S.-S. and H. Shin, 1992a, *Endogenous Formation of Coalitions Part I: Theory*, mimeo.

Yi, S.-S. and H. Shin, 1992b, *Endogenous Formation of Coalitions Part II: Applications to Cooperative Research and Development*, mimeo.

COMMENTARY
Nicholas Economides

Introduction

Since the publication of the *Economics of Networks* survey in 1996 there has been significant progress in the analysis of network industries both from the theoretical and the empirical points of view. But there are still many fundamental issues in network economics where there is no full understanding of the way in which markets work in network industries. Despite the lack of full understanding of these industries by economists, network economics has been applied in the last few years in a number of antitrust cases, the most prominent of which is the Microsoft antitrust case. Before turning to a very brief analysis of the Microsoft case from a network economics point of view, we define the features of network markets that have key antitrust implications.

Features of network markets with key antitrust implications

To help set a foundation for the application of antitrust in network markets, it is important to understand the implication of network effects on competition. Network effects define crucial features of market structure that have to be taken into consideration in understanding competition and potentially anti-competitive actions in these markets.

As discussed in detail in the *Economics of Networks* survey, a market exhibits network effects (or network externalities)[1] when the value to a buyer of an extra unit is higher when more units are sold, everything else being equal. In a traditional network, network externalities arise because a typical subscriber can reach more subscribers in a larger network.[2] In a virtual network,[3] network externalities arise because larger sales of component A induce larger availability of complementary components $B_1, \ldots,$ B_n, thereby increasing the value of component A. The increased value of component A results in further positive feedback.[4] For example, the existence of an abundance of Windows-compatible applications increases the value of Windows.

There are a number of crucial features of markets with network effects that distinguish them from other markets. First, markets with strong network effects where firms can choose their own technical standards are "winner-takes-most" markets. That is, in these markets, there is extreme market share and profits inequality.[5] The market share of the largest firm can easily be a multiple of the market share of the second largest, the second largest firm's market share can be a multiple of the market share of the third, and so on. This geometric sequence of market shares implies that, even for small n, the nth firm's market share is tiny.

For example, abundance of applications written for Windows increases the value of Windows and induces more consumers to buy Windows. This increases the incentive for independent applications writers to write applications for Windows, and this further increases sales and market share for Windows. Moreover, consumers are willing to pay more for the brand with the highest market share (since it has more associated applications), and therefore profits associated with this brand can be a large multiple of profits of other platforms. This implies a very large market share for Windows, a small market share for the Mac, a very small market share for the third competitor, and almost negligible shares for the fourth and other competitors.

Second, due to the natural extreme inequality in market shares and profits in such markets at any point in time, there should be no presumption that there were anti-competitive actions that were responsible for the creation of the market share inequality or the very high profitability of a top firm. Great inequality in sales and profits is the natural equilibrium in markets with network externalities and incompatible technical standards. No anti-competitive acts are *necessary* to create this inequality.[6]

Third, because winner-takes-most is the natural equilibrium in these markets, attempting to superimpose a different market structure, (say one of all firms having approximately equal market shares), is futile and counterproductive. If a different market structure is imposed by a singular structural act (say a breakup of a dominant firm), the market would naturally deviate from it and instead converge to the natural inequality equilibrium. If forced equality is imposed as a permanent condition, it would create significant social inefficiency, as discussed below.

Fourth, under incompatibility once few firms are in operation, the addition of new competitors, say under conditions of free entry, does not change the market structure in any significant way. The addition of a fourth competitor to a triopoly hardly changes the market shares, prices, and profits of the three top competitors.[7] This is true under conditions of free entry. Therefore, although eliminating barriers to entry can encourage competition, the resulting competition does not significantly affect market structure. In markets with strong network effects, antitrust authorities cannot significantly affect equilibrium market *structure* by eliminating barriers to entry.

Fifth, the fact that the natural equilibrium in network industries is *winner-takes-most* with very significant market inequality does not imply that competition is weak. Competition on which firm will create the top platform and reap most of the benefits is, in fact, very intense.

Sixth, there is a more fundamental concern about the application of antitrust in network industries.[8] In industries with significant network externalities, under conditions of incompatibility between competing platforms, monopoly may maximize social surplus. When strong network effects are present, a very large market share of one platform creates significant network benefits for this platform which contribute to large consumers' and producers' surpluses. It is possible to have situations where a breakup of a monopoly into two competing firms of incompatible standards *reduces* rather than increases social surplus because network externalities benefits are reduced. This is another way of saying that *de facto* standardization is valuable, even if done by a monopolist.[9]

Seventh, in network industries, the costs of entry may be higher but the rewards of success may also be higher compared to non-network industries. Thus, it is unclear if there is going to be less entry in network industries compared to traditional industries. If a requirement for entry is innovation, one can read the previous statement as saying that it is unclear if innovation would be more or less intense in network industries. The dynamics of the innovation process in the winner-takes-most environment of network industries are not sufficiently understood by academic economists so that they could give credible advice on this issue to antitrust authorities. However, in the last two decades we have observed very intense competition in innovative activities in network industries financed by capital markets.

Eighth, the existence of an installed base of consumers favors an incumbent. However, competitors with significant product advantages or a better pricing strategy can overcome the advantage of an installed base.[10] Network effects intensify competition, and an entrant with a significantly better product can unseat the incumbent. In network industries, we often observe Schumpeterian races for market dominance. This is a consequence of the winner-takes-most natural equilibrium combined with the high intensity of competition that network externalities imply.

Implications for the Microsoft antitrust case

The Microsoft case has certainly been the most important antitrust case of the "new economy" this far. Unfortunately, its legal battle was fought to a very large extent without the use of the economics tools that are at the foundation of the new economy and were key to the business success of Microsoft. There are a number of reasons for this. First, often, legal cases are created and filed before an economist is found who will create the appropriate economic model to support the case. Second, the economic theory of networks is so inadequate and unsettled that there is no commonly accepted body of knowledge on market structure with network externalities, based on which one could evaluate deviations toward anticompetitive behavior. Third, the legal system has tremendous inertia to new ideas and models. Fourth, the legal system rewards the use of well-treaded principles and traditions. Fifth, the legal system is ill-equipped to deal with complex technical matters. When it got down to the technical details of software, courts have had a very hard time understanding the way things work and how it could be changed. Sixth, given all these facts, lawyers on both sides find it easier to fight the issues on well-trodden ground even if the problems are really of a different nature. It is as if there is a dispute among two parties in the middle of a heavily forested area, but the lawyers of both parties fight it as if the dispute happened on the open plains, because they know the way disputes on the plains are resolved, while the law of dispute resolution in forests has yet to be established.

In the Microsoft case, generally, the plaintiffs used network economics more extensively and more effectively than the defendants. The plaintiffs convinced the courts (both the district court and the court of appeals) that the existence of an installed base of applications for the Windows operating system created a barrier to entry in the market for operating systems for personal computers, which they called "the applications barrier to entry." And this, despite the fact it was well understood that the fixed cost in the market for operating systems, although considerable in absolute terms, was small in terms of the size of the market. The existence of barriers to entry was significant in the argument that Microsoft had market power.

Microsoft stressed the importance of innovation in the computing industry and its role in that process. But Microsoft did not stress the importance of the *de facto* *compatibility* that Microsoft has imposed in the PC industry. Compatibility has very important benefits for all industry participants and for consumers. Microsoft failed to compare the present state of the PC industry with an industry with fragmented technical standards and show the benefits of compatibility, even if compatibility is imposed by a monopolist. Microsoft further failed to convincingly show the benefits that compatibility brings to innovation.

Even more fundamentally, Microsoft failed to convincingly discuss market structure in network industries *in the absence of anticompetitive actions.* A perfectly competitive industry with many equal participants, near marginal cost pricing, and small profits was presumed to be *the* alternative to the actual situation-in which Microsoft's alleged anticompetitive actions were judged. The fact that, in network industries, market structure has very significant inequalities in quantities, prices, and profits, was almost completely lost to the court. High market shares and high profits were presumed to be arising entirely out of Microsoft's anticompetitive actions.

Instead Microsoft stressed the view that the software market was experiencing Schumpeterian competition, in which the high speed of innovation and new successful entry present a huge threat to incumbents. That view is consistent with the relatively low prices that Microsoft charged for Windows 95 and 98.[11] It is also consistent with network economics, which stresses races for reaching the leading position as well as the possibility of replacement of the leader by new entrants. While Microsoft made the general Schumpeterian argument, it did not adequately connect it to the network economics theory.

Overall, the Microsoft case failed to use network economics sufficiently. Thus, the Microsoft case failed to create the appropriate case law standards on which new network economics cases can be adjudicated. One hopes that in the next new economy antitrust cases, there will be deeper understanding of the economics of networks and of the way the law should apply to network industries.

NOTES

1   The word externality means that a good's value is not intermediated in a market. For the purposes of this paper, we will use the words "network effects" and "network externalities" interchangeably.
2   See Economides (1996).
3   A virtual network is a collection of compatible goods (that share a common technical platform). For example, all VHS video players make up a virtual network. Similarly, all computers running Windows 98 can be thought of as a virtual network.
4   Despite the cycle of positive feedbacks, it is typically expected that the value of component A does not explode to infinity because the additional positive feedback is expected to decrease with increases in the size of the network.
5   See Economides and Flyer (1998).
6   For example, Litan et al. (2000) err in reasoning that Microsoft's very high profitability is a clear indication of monopolization in the antitrust sense. High profitability for the top platform is natural in this winner-take-most market.
7   See Economides and Flyer (1998). Table 7.1 below, taken from this paper, shows market coverage and prices as the number of firms with incompatible platforms increases. Maximum potential sales were normalized to 1.

Table 7.1   Quantities, market coverage, and prices among incompatible platforms.

Number of firms I	Sales of largest firm q_1	Sales of second firm q_2	Sales of third firm q_3	Market coverage $\sum_{j=i}^{I} q_j$	Price of largest firm P_1	Price of second firm P_2	Price of third firm P_3	Price of smallest firm P_1
1	0.6666			0.6666	0.222222			2.222e-1
2	0.6357	0.2428		0.8785	0.172604	0.0294		2.948e-2
3	0.6340	0.2326	0.0888	0.9555	0.170007	0.0231	0.0035	3.508e-3
4	0.6339	0.2320	0.0851	0.9837	0.169881	0.0227	0.0030	4.533e-4
5	0.6339	0.2320	0.0849	0.9940	0.169873	0.0227	0.0030	7.086e-5
6	0.6339	0.2320	0.0849	0.9999	0.169873	0.0227	0.0030	9.88e-11
7	0.6339	0.2320	0.0849	0.9999	0.169873	0.0227	0.0030	0

Note that the addition of the fourth firm onward makes practically no difference in the sales and prices of the top three firms.

8 In the Microsoft case, both sides had the chance to address this issue, but failed to do so.
9 Economides and Flyer (1998), show that, in market conditions similar to the ones in the OS software market, social welfare (total social surplus) can be higher in monopoly. Table 7.2 below, taken from this paper, shows profits, consumers' and total surplus in a market where firms produce incompatible products, as the number of competitors I increases.

Table 7.2 Profits, consumers' and total surplus among incompatible platforms.

Total number of firms I	Profits of largest firm Π_1	Profits of second firm Π_2	Profits of third firm Π_3	Total industry profits $\sum_{j=1}^{I} \Pi_j$	Consumers' surplus CS	Total surplus TS
1	0.1481			0.1481	0.148197	0.29629651
2	0.1097	7.159e-3		0.1168	0.173219	0.29001881
3	0.1077	5.377e-3	3.508e-4	0.1135	0.175288	0.28878819

10 A clear example of this is the win of VHS over Beta in the United States consumer video recorders market. Beta was first to market and had a significant installed base in the five years of the coexistence of the two competing standards. However, because VHS (1) introduced earlier a recording tape of longer duration; (2) used wide and inexpensive licensing of its technology; and (3) its licensees had a much wider distribution system, VHS emerged as the winner, and Sony stopped selling Beta recorders to the US consumer market.
11 See a very extensive discussion of this issue by Economides (2001).

REFERENCES

Economides, Nicholas (1996). "The Economics of Networks," *International Journal of Industrial Organization*, 14(2), 675–99, http://www.stern.nyu.edu/networks/top.html.

Economides, Nicholas, and Fredrick Flyer (1998). "Compatibility and Market Structure for Network Goods," Discussion Paper EC-98-02, Stern School of Business, New York University, http://www.stern.nyu.edu/networks/98-02.pdf.

Economides, Nicholas (2001). "The Microsoft Antitrust Case," *Journal of Industry, Competition and Trade: From Theory to Policy*, 1(1), 7–39.

Litan, Robert E., Roger G. Noll, William D. Nordhaus, and Frederic Scherer (2000). "Remedies Brief Of Amici Curiae In Civil Action No. 98-1232 (TPJ)."

CHAPTER EIGHT

THE ART OF STANDARDS WARS

CARL SHAPIRO AND HAL R. VARIAN

Standards wars – battles for market dominance between incompatible technologies – are a fixture of the information age. Based on our study of historical standards wars, we have identified several generic strategies, along with a number of winning tactics, to help companies fighting today's – and tomorrow's – battles.

There is no doubt about the significance of standards battles in today's economy. Public attention is currently focused on the Browser War between Microsoft and Netscape (oops, America OnLine). Even as Judge Jackson evaluates the legality of Microsoft's tactics in the Browser War, the Audio and Video Streaming Battle is heating up between Microsoft and RealNetworks over software to deliver audio and video over the Internet. The 56k Modem War of 1997 pitted 3Com against Rockwell and Lucent-Microsoft's Word and Excel have vanquished WordPerfect and Lotus 1-2-3 respectively. Most everyone remembers the Video-Cassette Recorder Duel of the 1980s, in which Matsushita's VHS format triumphed over Sony's Betamax format. However, few recall how Philips's digital compact cassette and Sony's minidisk format both flopped in the early 1990s. This year, it's DVD versus Divx in the battle to replace both VCRs and CDs.

Virtually every high-tech company has some role to play in these battles, perhaps as a primary combatant, more likely as a member of a coalition or alliance supporting one side, and certainly as a customer seeking to pick a winner when adopting new technology. The outcome of a standards war can determine the very survival of the companies involved. How do you win one?

HISTORICAL EXAMPLES

Happily, companies heading off to fight a standards war do not have to reinvent the wheel. The fact is, standards wars are *not* unique to the information age. Unlike technology, the economics underlying such battles changes little, if at all, over time. We begin with three instructive standards battles of old. From these and many more historical episodes we have distilled the battle manual for standards wars that follows.

North versus South in railroad gauges[1]

As railroads began to be built in the early 19th century, tracks of varying widths (gauges) were employed in the United States. By 1860, seven different gauges were in use in America. Just over half of the total mileage was of the 4'8½" standard. The next most popular was the 5' gauge concentrated in the South. Despite clear benefits, railroad gauge standardization faced three major obstacles: it was costly to change the width of existing tracks; each group wanted the others to make the move; and workers whose livelihoods depended upon the incompatibilities resisted the proposed changes, in fact to the point of rioting. Nonetheless, standardization was gradually achieved between 1860 and 1890. How?

The Westward expansion provided part of the answer. The big eastern railroads wanted to move western grain to the East, and pushed for new lines to the West to be at standard gauge. Since the majority of the Eastbound traffic terminated on their lines, they got their way. The Civil War played a role, too. The Union military had pressing needs for efficient East-West transportation, giving further impetus for new western lines to be built at standard gauge. In 1862, when Congress specified the standard gauge for the transcontinental railroads, the Southern states had seceded, leaving no one to push for the 5' gauge. After the war, the Southern railroads found themselves increasingly in the minority. For the next twenty years, they relied upon various imperfect interconnections with the North and West: cars with a sliding wheel base, hoists to lift cars from one wheel base to another, and, most commonly, building a third rail.

Southern railroad interests finally threw in the towel and adopted the standard gauge in 1886. On two days during the Spring of 1886, the gauges were changed, converting 5' gauge into the now-standard 4'8½" gauge on more than 11,000 miles of track in the South to match the Northern standard – a belated victory for the North.

Many of the lessons from this experience are very relevant today:

- Incompatibilities can arise almost by accident, yet persist for many years.
- Network markets tend to tip towards the leading player, unless the other players coordinate to act quickly and decisively.
- Seceding from the standard-setting process can leave you in a weak market position in the future.
- A large buyer (in this case the US government) can have more influence than suppliers in tipping the balance.
- Those left with the less popular technology will find a way to cut their losses, either by employing adapters or by writing off existing assets and joining the bandwagon.

Edison versus Westinghouse in electric power: the battle of the systems[2]

Another classic 19th century standards battle concerned the distribution of electricity. Thomas Edison promoted a direct current (DC) system of electrical power generation and distribution. Edison was the pioneer in building power systems, beginning in New York City in 1882. Edison's direct current system was challenged by the alternating current (AC) technology developed and deployed in the US by George Westinghouse.

Thus was joined the "Battle of the Systems." Each technology had pros and cons. Direct current had, for practical purposes relating to voltage drop, a one-mile limit between the generating station and the user, but was more efficient at generating power. Direct current had also had two significant commercial advantages: a head start and Edison's imprimatur.

Unlike railroads, however, standardization was less of an imperative in electricity. Indeed, the two technologies initially did not compete directly, but were deployed in regions suited to their relative strengths. DC was most attractive in densely populated urban areas, while AC made inroads in small towns. Nonetheless, a battle royal ensued in the 1887–1892 period, a struggle that was by no means confined to competition in the marketplace, but rather extended to the courtroom, the political arena, public relations, and academia. We can learn much today from the tactics followed by the rival camps.

The Edison group moved first with infringement actions against the Westinghouse forces, which forced Westinghouse to invent around Edison patents, including patents involving the Edison lamp. Edison also went to great lengths to convince the public that the AC system was unsafe, going so far as to patent the electric chair. Edison first demonstrated the electric chair using alternating current to electrocute a large dog, and then persuaded the State of New York to execute condemned criminals "by administration of an alternating current." The Edison group even used the term "to Westinghouse" to refer to electrocution by alternating current.

Ultimately, three factors ended the Battle of the Systems. First and foremost, advances in polyphase AC made it increasingly clear that AC was the superior alternative. Second, the rotary converter introduced in 1892 allowed existing DC stations to be integrated into AC systems, facilitating a graceful retreat for DC. Third, by 1890 Edison had sold his interests, leading to the formation of the General Electric Company in 1892, which was no longer a DC-only manufacturing entity.[3] By 1893, both General Electric and Westinghouse were offering AC systems and the battle was over.

The battle between Edison and Westinghouse illustrates several key aspects of strategy in standards wars:

- Edison fought hard to convince consumers that DC was safer, in no small part because consumer expectations can easily become self-fulfilling in standards battles.
- Technologies can seek well-suited niches if the forces towards standardization are not overwhelming.
- Ongoing innovation (here, polyphase AC) can lead to victory in a standards war.
- A first-mover advantage (of DC) can be overcome by a superior technology (of AC), if the performance advantage is sufficient and users are not overly entrenched.
- Adapters can be the salvation of the losing technology and can help to ultimately defuse a standards war.

RCA versus CBS in color television[4]

Our third historical example is considerably more recent: the adoption of color television in the United States fifty years ago. Television is perhaps the biggest bandwagon of them all. Some 99% of American homes have at least one television, making TV sets more ubiquitous than telephones or flush toilets.

We begin our story with the inauguration of commercial black and white television transmission in the United States on July 1, 1941. At that time, RCA – the owner of NBC and a leading manufacturer of black and white sets – was a powerful force in the radio and television world. However, the future of television was clearly to be color, which had first been demonstrated in America by Bell Labs in 1929.

Throughout the 1940s, CBS, the leading television network, was pushing for the adoption of the mechanical color television system it was developing. During this time RCA was busy selling black and white sets, improving its technology, and, under the legendary leadership of David Sarnoff, working on its own all-electronic color television system. As the CBS system took the lead in performance, RCA urged the FCC to wait for an electronic system. A major obstacle for the CBS system was that it was not backward-compatible: color sets of the CBS-type would not be able to receive existing black and white broadcasts without a special attachment.

Despite this drawback, the FCC adopted the CBS system in October 1950, after a test between the two color systems. The RCA system was just not ready. As David Sarnoff himself said, "The monkeys were green, the bananas were blue, and everyone had a good laugh." This was a political triumph of major proportions for CBS.

The market outcome was another story. RCA and Sarnoff refused to throw in the towel. To the contrary, they re-doubled their efforts, on three fronts. First, RCA continued to criticize the CBS system in an attempt to slow its adoption. Second, RCA intensified its efforts to place black and white sets and thus build up an installed base of users whose equipment would be incompatible with the CBS technology. "Every set we get out there makes it that much tougher on CBS," said Sarnoff at the time. Third, Sarnoff intensified RCA's research and development on its color television system, with around-the-clock teams working in the lab.

CBS was poorly placed to take advantage of its political victory. To begin with, CBS had no manufacturing capability at the time, and had not readied a manufacturing ally to move promptly into production. As a result, the official premier of CBS color broadcasting, on June 25, 1951, featuring Ed Sullivan among others, was largely invisible, only seen at special studio parties. There were about 12 million TV sets in America at the time, but only a few dozen could receive CBS color. Luck, of a sort, entered into the picture, too. With the onset of the Korean War, the US government said that the materials needed for production of color sets were critical instead for the war effort and ordered a suspension of the manufacture of color sets.

By the time the ban was modified in June 1952, the RCA system was ready for prime time. A consensus in support of the RCA system had formed at the National Television Systems Committee (NTSC). This became known as the NTSC system, despite the fact that RCA owned most of the hundreds of patents controlling it. This re-labeling was a face-saving device for the FCC, which could be seen to be following the industry consortium rather than RCA. In March 1953, Frank Stanton, the President of CBS, raised the white flag, noting that with 23 million black and white sets in place in American homes, compatibility was rather important. In December 1953, the FCC officially reversed its 1950 decision.

However, yet again, political victory did not lead so easily to success in the market. In 1954, Sarnoff predicted that that RCA would sell 75,000 sets. In fact, only 5,000 sets were purchased, perhaps because few customers were willing to pay $1,000 for the $12\frac{1}{2}''$ color set rather than $300 for a 21" black-and-white set. With hindsight, this does not seem surprising, especially since color sets would offer little added value until broadcasters invested in color capability and color programming became widespread. All this takes time. The chicken-and-egg problem had to be settled before the NBC peacock could prevail.

As it turned out, NBC and CBS affiliates invested in color transmission equipment quite quickly: 106 of 158 stations in the top 40 cities had the ability to transmit color programs by 1957. This was of little import to viewers, since the networks were far slower in offering color programming. By 1965, NBC offered 4,000 hours of color, but CBS still showed only 800 color hours, and ABC 600. The upshot: by 1963, only about 3% of TV households had color sets, which remained three to five times as expensive as black and white sets.

As brilliant as Sarnoff and RCA had been in getting their technology established as the standard, they, like CBS, were unable to put into place all the necessary components of the system to obtain profitability during the 1950s. As a result, by 1959, RCA had spent $130 million to develop color TV with no profit to show for it. The missing pieces were the creation and distribution of the programming itself: content. Then, as now, a "killer app" was needed to get households to invest in color television sets. The killer app of 1960 was "Walt Disney's Wonderful World of Color," which Sarnoff obtained from ABC in 1960. RCA's first operating profit from color television sales came in 1960, and RCA started selling picture tubes to Zenith and others. The rest is history: color sets got better and cheaper, and the NBC peacock became famous.

We can all learn a great deal from this episode, ancient though it is by Internet time.

- Adoption of a new technology can be painfully slow if the price/performance ratio is unattractive and if it requires adoption by a number of different players.[5]
- First-mover advantages need not be decisive, even in markets strongly subject to tipping.
- Victory in a standards war often requires building an alliance.
- A dominant position in one generation of technology (such as RCA enjoyed in the sale of black-and-white sets) does not necessarily translate into dominance in the next generation of technology.

WAR OR PEACE?

Standards wars are especially bitter – and especially crucial to business success – in markets with strong *network effects* that cause consumers to play high value on compatibility.[6] We do not consider it a coincidence that there is a single worldwide standard for fax machines and for modems (for which compatibility is crucial), while multiple formats persist for cellular telephones and digital television (for which compatibility across regions is far less important).

We do not mean to suggest that every new information technology must endure a standards war. Take the compact disk (CD) technology, for instance. Sony and Philips pooled together and openly licensed their CD patents as a means to establish their new CD technology. While CDs were completely incompatible with the existing audio technologies of phonographs, cassette players, and reel-to-reel tapes, Sony and Philips were not in a battle with another new technology. They "merely" had to convince consumers to take a leap and invest in a CD player and compact disks.

What is distinct about standards wars is that there are *two* firms, or more commonly alliances, vying for dominance. In some cases, one of the combatants may be an incumbent that controls a significant base of customers who use an older technology, as when Nintendo battled Sony in the video game market in the mid-1990s. Nintendo had a large installed base from the previous generation when both companies introduced 64-bit systems. In other instances, both sides may be starting from scratch, as in the battle between Sony and Matsushita in videotape machines as well as in the browser war between Netscape and Microsoft.

Standards wars can end in: a *truce*, as happened in 56k modems and color television where a common standard was ultimately adopted; a *duopoly*, as we see in video games today with Nintendo and Sony battling toe-to-toe; or a *fight to the death*, as with railroad gauges, AC versus DC electric power, and videotape players. True fight-to-the-death standards wars are unique to markets with powerful positive feedback based on strong network effects. Thus, traditional principles of strategy, while helpful, need to be supplemented to account for the peculiar economics of networks.

Before entering into a standards battle, would-be combatants are well-advised to consider a peaceful solution.[7] Unlike many other aspects of competition, where coordination among rivals would be branded as illegal collusion, declaring an early truce in a standards war can benefit *consumers* as well as vendors, and thus pass antitrust muster.[8]

Even bitter enemies such as Microsoft and Netscape have repeatedly been able to cooperate to establish standards when compatibility is crucial for market growth. First, when it appeared that a battle might ensue over standards for protecting privacy on the Internet, Microsoft announced its support for Netscape's *Open Profiling Standard*, which subsequently became part of the *Platform for Privacy Preferences* being developed by the Word Wide Web Consortium. Second, Microsoft and Netscape were able to reach agreement on standards for viewing 3-D images over the Internet. In August 1997, they decided to support compatible versions of *Virtual Reality Modeling Language*, a 3-D viewing technology, in their browsers. Again, Microsoft was pragmatic rather than proud, adopting a language invented at Silicon Graphics. Third, Microsoft and Netscape teamed up (along with Visa and MasterCard as well as IBM) to support the *Secure Electronic Transactions* standard for protecting the security of electronic payments by encrypting credit card numbers sent to online merchants. Cooperative standard-setting often takes place through the auspices of formal standard-setting organizations such as the American National Standards Institute or the International Telecommunications Union.[9]

We must note, however, the clear analogy between technology battles and military battles: the more costly a battle is to both sides, the greater are the pressures to negotiate a truce; and one's strength in battle is an overriding consideration when meeting to conduct truce talks. Whether you are planning to negotiate a product standard or fight to the death, you will benefit from understanding the art (read: economics and strategy) of standards wars.

CLASSIFICATION OF STANDARDS WARS

Not all standards wars are alike. Standards battles come in three distinct flavors. The starting point for strategy in a standards battle is to understand which type of war you are fighting. The critical distinguishing feature of the battle is the magnitude of the switching costs, or more generally the adoption costs, for each rival technology. We classify standards wars depending on how compatible each player's proposed new technology is with the current technology.

When a company or alliance introduces new technology that is *compatible* with the old, we say that they have adopted an "Evolution" strategy. Evolutionary strategies are based on offering superior performance with minimal consumer switching or adoption costs. The NTSC color television system selected by the FCC in 1953 was evolutionary: NTSC signals could be received by black-and-white sets, and the new color sets could receive black-and-white signals, making adoption of color far easier for both television stations and households. In contrast, the CBS system that the FCC had first endorsed in 1950 was not backward compatible.

When a company or alliance introduces new technology that is *incompatible* with the old, we say that they have adopted a "Revolution" strategy. Revolutionary strategies are based on offering such compelling performance that consumers are willing to incur significant switching or adoption costs.

If both your technology and your rival's technology are compatible with the older, established technology, but incompatible with each other we say the battle is one of "Rival Evolutions." Competition between DVD and Divx (both of which will play CDs), the 56k modem battle (both types communicate with slower modems), and competition between various flavors of Unix (which can run programs written for older versions of plain vanilla Unix) all fit this pattern.

If your technology offers backward compatibility and your rival's does not, we have "Evolution versus Revolution." The "Evolution versus Revolution" war is a contest between the backward compatibility of Evolution and the superior performance of Revolution. Evolution versus Revolution includes the important case of an upstart fighting against an established technology that is offering compatible upgrades. The struggle in the late 1980s between Ashton Tate's dBase IV and Paradox in the market for desktop database software fit this pattern. (The mirror image of this occurs if your rival offers backward compatibility but you do not: "Revolution versus Evolution.")

Finally, if neither technology is backward compatible we have "Rival Revolutions." The contest between Nintendo 64 and the Sony Playstation, and the historical example of AC versus DC in electrical systems, follow this pattern.

These four types of standards battles are described in figure 8.1.

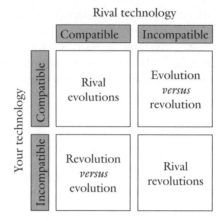

Figure 8.1 Types of standards wars.

KEY ASSETS IN NETWORK MARKETS

In our view, successful strategy generally must harness a firm's resources in a manner that harmonizes with the underlying competitive environment. In a standards battle, the competitive environment is usefully characterized by locating the battle in figure 8.1. What about the firms' resources?

Your ability to successfully wage a standards war depends on your ownership of seven key assets:

- control over an installed base of users;
- intellectual property rights;
- ability to innovate;
- first-mover advantages;
- manufacturing capabilities;
- strength in complements; and
- brand name and reputation.

What these assets have in common is that they place you in a potentially unique position to contribute to the adoption of a new technology. If you own these assets, your value-added to other players is high. Some assets, however, such as the ability to innovate or manufacturing capabilities, may even be more valuable in peace than in war.

No one asset is decisive. For example, control over an older generation of technology does not necessarily confer the ability to pick the next generation. Sony and Philips controlled CDs but could not move unilaterally into DVDs. Atari had a huge installed base of first-generation video games in 1983, but Nintendo's superior technology and hot new games caught Atari flat-footed. The early leader in modems, Hayes, tried to buck the crowd when modems operating at 9,600 kbps were introduced, and ended up in Chapter 11.

Don't forget that *customers* as well as technology suppliers can control key assets, too. A big customer is automatically in "control" of at least part of the installed base. America Online recognized this in the recent 56k modem standards battle. Content providers played a key role in the DVD standards battle. IBM was pivotal in moving the industry from $5\frac{1}{4}''$ diskettes to $3\frac{1}{2}''$ disks. Most recently, TCI has not been shy about flexing its muscle in the battle over the technology used in TV set-top boxes.

Control over an installed base of customers

An incumbent firm, like Microsoft, that has a large base of loyal or locked-in customers is uniquely placed to pursue an Evolution strategy offering backward compatibility. Control over an installed base can be used to block cooperative standard setting and force a standards war. Control can also be used to block rivals from offering compatible products, thus forcing them to play the more risky Revolution strategy.

Intellectual property rights

Firms with patents and copyrights controlling valuable new technology or interfaces are clearly in a strong position. Qualcomm's primary asset in the digital wireless telephone battle was its patent portfolio. The core assets of Sony and Philips in the CD and DVD areas were their respective patents. Usually, patents are stronger than copyrights, but computer software copyrights that can be used to block compatibility can be highly valuable. This is why Lotus fought Borland all the way to the Supreme Court to try to block Borland's use of the Lotus command structure (see below), and why Microsoft watched the trial intently to protect Excel's ability to read macros originally written for Lotus 1-2-3.

Ability to innovate

Beyond your existing intellectual property, the ability to make proprietary extensions in the future puts you in a strong position today. In the color TV battle, NBC's R&D capabilities were crucial after the FCC initially adopted the CBS color system. NBC's engineers quickly developed a color system that was compatible with the existing black-and-white sets, a system which the FCC then accepted. Hewlett-Packard's engineering skills are legendary in Silicon Valley; it is often in their interest to compromise on standards since they can out-engineer their competition once the standard has been defined, even if they have to play some initial catch up.

First-mover advantages

If you already have done a lot of product development work and are farther down the learning curve than the competition, you are in a strong position. Netscape obtained stunning market capitalization based on a their ability to bring new technology to market quickly. RealNetworks currently has as big lead on Microsoft in audio and video streaming.

Manufacturing capabilities

If you are a low-cost producer, due to either scale economies or manufacturing competence, you are in a strong position. Cost advantages can help you survive a standards war, or capture share competing to sell a standardized product. Compaq and Dell both have pushed hard on driving down their manufacturing costs, which gives them a strong competitive advantage in the PC market. Rockwell has lower costs than its competitors in making chipsets for modems. HP has long been a team player in Silicon Valley, welcoming standards because of their engineering and manufacturing skills. These companies benefit from open standards, which emphasize the importance of efficient production.

Strength in complements

It you produce a product that is a significant complement for the market in question, you will be strongly motivated to get the bandwagon rolling. This, too, puts you in a natural leadership position, since acceptance of the new technology will stimulate sales of the other products you produce. This force is stronger, the larger are your gross margins on your established products. Intel's thirst to sell more CPUs has been a key driver in their efforts to promote new standards for other PC components, including interfaces between motherboards and CPUs, busses, chipsets, and graphics controllers.

Reputation and brand name

A brand-name premium in any large market is highly valuable. But reputation and brand name are especially valuable in network markets, where expectations are pivotal. It's not enough to have the best product; you have to convince consumers that you will win. Previous victories and a recognized name count for a lot in this battle. Microsoft, HP, Intel, Sony, and Sun each have powerful reputations in their respective domains, giving them instant credibility.[10]

PREEMPTION

Preemption is one of two crucial marketplace tactics that arise over and over again in standards battles. The logic of preemption is straightforward: build an early lead, so positive feedback works for you and against your rival. The same principle applies in markets with strong learning-by-doing: the first firm to gain significant experience will have lower costs and can pull even further ahead. Either way, the trick is to exploit positive feedback. With learning-by-doing, the positive feedback is through lower costs. With network externalities, the positive feedback comes on the demand side; the leader offers a more valuable product or service.

One way to preempt is simply to be first to market. Product development and design skills can be critical to gaining a first-mover advantage. But watch out: early introduction also can entail compromises in quality and a greater risk of bugs, either of which can doom your product. This was the fate of the color television system promoted by CBS and of Japan's HDTV system. The race belongs to the swift, but speed must come from superior product design, not by marketing an inferior system.

In addition to launching your product early, you need to be aggressive early on to build an installed base of customers. Find the "pioneers" (a.k.a. gadget freaks) who are most keen to try new technology and sign them up swiftly. Pricing below cost (i.e., *penetration pricing*) is a common tactic to build an installed base. Discounting to attract large, visible, or influential customers is virtually unavoidable in a standards war.

In some cases, especially for software with a zero marginal cost, you can go beyond free samples and actually *pay* people to take your product. As we see it, there is nothing special about zero as a price, as long as you have multiple revenue streams to recover costs. Some cable television programmers pay cable operators to distribute their programming, knowing that a larger audience will augment their advertising revenues. In the same fashion. Netscape is prepared to give away its browser for free, or even pay OEMs (original equipment manufacturers) to load it on new machines, in order to increase the usage of Navigator and thus direct more traffic to the Netscape Web site.

The big danger with negative prices is that someone will accept payment for "using" your product and then not really use it. This problem is easily solved in the cable television context, because programmers simply insist that cable operators actually carry their programming once they are paid to do so. Likewise, Netscape can check that an OEM loads Navigator (in a specified way) on new machines, and can conduct surveys to see just how the OEM configuration affects usage of Navigator.[11]

Before you go overboard giving your product away, or paying customers to take it, you need to ask three questions. First, if you pay someone to take your product, will they really use it and generate network externalities for other, paying customers? Second, how much is it really worth to you to build up your installed base? Where is the offsetting revenue stream, and when will it arrive? Third, are you fooling yourself? Beware the well-known "Winner's Curse": the tendency of the most optimistic participant to win in a bidding war, only to find that they were overly optimistic and other bidders were more realistic.

Penetration pricing may be difficult to implement if you are building a coalition around an "open" standard. The sponsor of a proprietary standard can hope to recoup the losses incurred during penetration pricing once it controls an established technology. Without a sponsor, no single supplier will be willing to make the necessary investments to preempt using penetration pricing. For precisely this reason, penetration pricing can be particularly effective when used by a company with a proprietary system against a rival touting its openness.

Another implication is that the player in a standards battle with the largest profit streams from related products stands to win the war. We have seen this with smart cards in Europe. They were introduced with a single application – public telephone service – but soon were expanded to other transactions involving small purchases. Eventually, many more applications such as identification and authentication will be introduced. Visa, MasterCard, and American Express are already jockeying for position in the smart card wars. Whichever player can figure out the most effective way to generate multiple revenue streams from an installed base of smart card holders will be able to bid most aggressively, but still profitably, to build up the largest base of customers.

EXPECTATIONS MANAGEMENT

The second key tactic in standards wars is the management of expectations. Expectations are a major factor in consumer decisions about whether or not to purchase a new technology, so make sure that you do your best to manage those expectations. Just as incumbents will try to knock down the viability of new technologies that emerge, so will those very entrants strive to establish credibility.

Vaporware is a classic tactic aimed at influencing expectations: announce an upcoming product so as to freeze your rival's sales. In the 1994 antitrust case brought by the Justice Department against Microsoft, Judge Sporkin cited vaporware as one reason why he found the proposed consent decree insufficient. In an earlier era, IBM was accused of the same tactic. Of course, drawing the line between "predatory product pre-announcements" and simply being late bringing a product to market is not so easy to draw, especially in the delay-prone software market. Look at what happened to Lotus in spreadsheets and Ashton-Tate and database software. After both of these companies repeatedly missed launch dates, industry wags said they should be merged and use the stock ticker symbol "LATE." We must note with some irony that Microsoft's stock took a 5.3% nosedive in late 1997 after Microsoft announced a delay in the launch of Windows 98 from the first to the second quarter of 1998.

The most direct way to manage expectations is by assembling allies and by making grand claims about your product's current or future popularity. Sun has been highly visible in gathering allies in support of Java, including taking out full-page advertisements listing the companies in the Java coalition. Indicative of how important expectations management is in markets with strong network externalities, WordPerfect even filed a court complaint against Microsoft to block Microsoft from claiming that its word processing software was the most popular in the world. Barnes & Noble did the same thing to Amazon, arguing that their claim to being the "world's largest bookstore" was misleading.

ONCE YOU'VE WON

Moving on from war to the spoils of victory, let's consider how best to proceed once you have actually *won* a standards war. Probably you made some concessions to achieve victory, such as promises of openness or deals with various allies. Of course, you have to live with those, but there is still a great deal of room for strategy. In today's high-tech world, the battle never really ends. So, take a deep breath and be ready to keep moving.

Staying on your guard

Technology marches forward. You have to keep looking out for the next generation of technology, which can come from unexpected directions. Microsoft, with all its foresight and savvy, has had to scurry to deal with the Internet phenomenon and try to defuse any threat to their core business.

You may be especially vulnerable if you were victorious in one generation of technology through a preemption strategy. Going early usually means making technical compromises, which gives that much more room for others to execute an incompatible Revolution strategy against you. Apple pioneered the market for personal digital assistants, but U.S. Robotics perfected the idea with their Palm Pilot. If your rivals attract the power users, your market position and the value of your network may begin to erode.

The hazards of moving early and then lacking flexibility can be seen in the case of the French Minitel system. Back in the 1980s, the French were world leaders in on-line transactions with the extensive Minitel computer network, which was sponsored and controlled by France Telecom. Before the Internet was widely known, much less used, million of French subscribers used the Minitel system to obtain information and conduct secure on-line transactions. Today, Minitel boasts more than 35 million French subscribers and 25,000 vendors. One reason Minitel has attracted so many suppliers is that users pay a fee to France Telecom each time they visit a commercial site, and a portion of these fees are passed along to vendors. Needless to say, this is quite a different business model than we see on the Web.

Now, however, the Minitel systems is seen as inflexible, and France is lagging behind in moving onto the Internet. Just as companies that invested in dedicated word processing systems in the 1970s were slow to move to more generalized personal computers in the 1980s, the French have been slow to invest in equipment that can access the Internet. Only about 3% of the French population uses the Internet, far short of the estimated 20% in the US and 9% is the UK and Germany. Roughly 15% of French companies have a Web site, versus nearly 35% of US businesses. Only in August 1997 did the French government admit that the Internet, not Minitel, was the way of the future rather than an instrument of American cultural imperialism. France Telecom is now in the planning stages to introduce next-generation Minitel terminals that will access the Internet as well as Minitel.

What is the lesson here? The French sluggishness to move to the Internet stems from two causes that are present in many other settings. First, France Telecom and the vendors had an incentive to preserve the revenue streams they were earning from Minitel. This is understandable, but it should be recognized as a choice to harvest an installed base, with adverse implications for the future. Milking the installed base is sometimes the right thing to do, but make this a calculated choice, not a default decision. Second, moving to the Internet presents substantial collective switching costs – and less incremental value – to French consumers in contrast with, say, American consumers. Precisely because Minitel was a success, it reduced the attractiveness of the Internet.

The strategic implication is that you need a migration path or roadmap for your technology. If you cannot improve your technology with time, while offering substantial compatibility with older versions, you will be overtaken sooner or later. Rigidity is death, unless you build a really big installed base, and even this will fade eventually without improvements.

Offer customers a migration path

To fend off challenges from upstarts, you need to make it hard for rivals to execute a revolution strategy. The key is to anticipate the next generation of technology and co-opt it. Look in all directions for the next threat and take advantage of the fact that consumers will not switch to a new incompatibility technology unless it offers a marked improvement in performance. Microsoft has been the master of this strategy with its "Embrace and Extend" philosophy of anticipating or imitating improvements and incorporating them into its flagship products.[12] Avoid being frozen in place by your own success. If you cater too closely to your installed base by emphasizing backward compatibility, you open the door to a Revolution strategy by an upstart. This is precisely what happened to Ashton-Tate in databases, allowing Borland and later Microsoft to offer far superior performance with their Paradox and FoxPro products. Your product road map has to offer your customers a smooth migration path to ever-improving technology, and it must stay close to, if not on, the cutting edge.

One way to avoid being dragged down by the need to retain compatibility is to give older members of your installed base free or inexpensive upgrades to a recent but not current version of your product. This is worth doing for many reasons: users of much older versions have revealed that they do not need the latest bells and whistles and thus are less likely to actually buy the latest version; the free "partial" upgrade can restore some lost customer loyalty; you can save on support costs by avoiding "version-creep"; and you can avoid being hamstrung in designing your latest products by a customer-relations need to maintain compatibility with older and older versions. To compromise the performance of your latest version in the name of compatibility with ancient versions presents an opening for a rival to build an installed base among more demanding users. Happily, this "lagged upgrade" approach is easier and easier with distribution so cheap over the Internet.

Microsoft did a good job with this problem with migration to Windows 95. Politely put, Windows 95 is a kludge, with all sorts of special workarounds to allow DOS programs to execute in the Windows environment, thereby maintaining compatibility with customers' earlier programs. Microsoft's plan with Windows 98 is to move the consumer version of Windows closer to the professional version, Windows NT, eventually ending up with only one product, or at least only one interface.

Commoditize complementary products

Once you've won, you want to keep your network alive and healthy. This means that you've got to attend not only to your own products, but to the products produced by your complementors as well. Your goal should be to retain your franchise as the market leader, but have a vibrant and competitive marker for complements to your product.

This can be tricky. Apple has flipped back and forth on its developer relations over the years. First they wanted to just be in the computer business, and let others develop applications. Then they established a subsidiary, Claris, to do applications development. When this soured relations with other developers they spun Claris off. And so it went – a back-and-forth dance.

Microsoft faced the same problem, but with a somewhat different strategy. If an applications developer became successful, Microsoft just bought them (or tried to – Microsoft's intended purchase of Intuit was blocked by the Department of Justice). Nowadays a lot of new business plans in the software industry have the same structure: "Produce product, capture emerging market, be bought by Microsoft."

Our view is that you should try to maintain a competitive market in complementary products and avoid the temptation to meddle. Enter into these markets only if integration of your core product with adjacent products adds value to consumers, or if you can inject significant additional competition to keep prices low. If you are truly successful, like Intel, you will need to spur innovation in complementary products to continue to grow, both by capturing revenues from new complementary products and by stimulating demand for your core product.

Competing against your own installed base

You may need to improve performance just to compete against your installed base, even without an external threat. How can you continue to grow when your information product or technology starts to reach market saturation? One answer is to drive innovation ever faster. Intel is pushing to improve hardware performance of complementary products (such as graphics chips and chipsets) and helping develop applications that crave processing power so as to drive the hardware upgrade cycle. Competition with one's own installed base is not a new problem for companies selling durable goods. The stiffest competition faced by Steinway in selling pianos is from used Steinways.

One way to grow even after you have a large installed base is to start discounting as a means of attracting the remaining customers who have demonstrated (by waiting) that they have a relatively low willingness-to-pay for your product. This is a good instinct, but be careful. First, discounting established products is at odds with a penetration pricing strategy to win a standards war. Second, if you regularly discount products once they are well established, consumers may learn to wait for the discounts. The key question: can you expand the market and not spoil your margins for traditional customers?

Economists have long recognized this as the "durable-goods monopoly" problem. Ronald Coase, recent winner of the Nobel Prize in Economics, wrote 35 years ago about the temptation of a company selling a durable product to offer lower and lower prices to expand the market once many consumers already purchased the durable good. He conjectured that consumers would come to anticipate these price reductions and hold off buying until prices fall. Since then, economists have studied a variety of strategies designed to prevent the resulting erosion of profits. The problem raised by Coase is especially severe for highly durable products such as information and software.

One of the prescriptions for solving the durable-goods monopoly problem is to *rent* your product rather than sell it. This will not work for a microprocessor or a printer, but rapid technological change can achieve the same end. If a product becomes obsolete in two or three years, used versions won't pose much of a threat to new sales down the line. This is a great spur for companies like Intel to rush ahead as fast as possible increasing the speed of their microprocessors. The same is true on the software side, where even vendors who are dominant in their category (such as Autodesk in computer-aided design) are forced to improve their programs to generate a steady stream of revenues.

Protecting your position

A variety of defensive tactics can help secure your position. This is where antitrust limits come in most sharply, however, since it is illegal to "maintain a monopoly" by anticompetitive means.

One tactic is to offer ongoing attractive terms to important complementors. For example, Nintendo worked aggressively to attract developers of hit games and used its popularity to gain very strong distribution. This tactic can, however, cross the legal line if you insist that your suppliers, or distributors, deal with you to the exclusion of your rivals. For example, FTD, the floral network, under pressure from the Justice Department, had to cancel its program giving discounts to florists who used FTD exclusively. Since FTD had the lion's share of the floral delivery network business, this quasi-exclusivity provision was seen as protecting FTD's near-monopoly position. Ticketmaster was subjected to an extensive investigation for adopting exclusivity provisions in its contracts with stadiums, concert halls, and other venues. The Justice Department in 1994 attacked Microsoft's contracts with OEMs for having an effect similar to that of exclusive licenses.

A less controversial way to protect your position is to take steps to avoid being held up by others who claim that your product infringes their patents or copyrights. Obviously, there is no risk-free way to do this. However, it makes a great deal of sense to ask those seeking access to your network to agree not to bring the whole network down in an infringement action. Microsoft took steps along these lines when it launched Windows 95, including a provision in the Windows 95 license for OEMs that prevented Microsoft licensees from attempting to use certain software patents to block Microsoft from shipping Windows 95. Intel regularly asks companies taking licenses to its open specifications to agree to offer royalty-free licenses to other participants for any patents that would block the specified technology. This "two-sided openness" strategy prevents *ex post* hold-up problems and helps safely launch a new specification.

Leveraging your installed base

Once you have a strong installed base, basic principles of competitive strategy dictate that you seek to leverage into adjacent product spaces, exploiting the key assets that give you a unique ability to create value for consumers in those spaces. In some cases, control over an interface can be used to extend leadership from one side of the interface to the other.

But don't get carried away. You may be better off encouraging healthy competition in complementary products, which stimulates demand for your core product, rather than trying to dominate adjacent spaces. Acquisitions of companies selling neighboring products should be driven by true synergies of bringing both products into the same company, not simply by a desire to expand your empire. Again, legal limits on both 'leveraging" and on vertical acquisitions can come into play. For example, the FTC forced Time Warner to agree to carry a rival news channel on its cable systems when Time Warner acquired CNN in its merger with Turner.

Geographic expansion is yet another way to leverage your installed base. This is true for traditional goods and services, but with a new twist for network products: when expanding the geographic scope of your network, make sure your installed base in one region becomes a competitive advantage in another region. But careful: don't build a two-way bridge to another region where you face an even stronger rival; in that case, more troops will come across the bridge attacking you than you can send to gain new territory.

Geographic effects were powerful in the FCC auctions of spectrum space for PCS services, the successor to the older cellular telephone technology. If you provide Personal Digital Assistance (PDA) wireless services in Minneapolis, you have a big advantage if you also provide such services in St. Paul. The market leader in one town would therefore be willing to outbid rivals in neighboring locations. In the PCS auctions, bidders allegedly "signaled" their most-preferred territories by encoding them into their bids as an attempt to avoid a mutually unprofitable bidding war. The Department of Justice is investigating these complaints. Our point is not to offer bidding strategy, but to remind you that geographic expansion of a network can be highly profitable. Network growth generates new customers and offers more value to existing customers at the same time.

Staying a leader

How can you secure a competitive advantage for yourself short of maintaining direct control over the technology, e.g., through patent or copyright protection? Even without direct control over the installed base or ownership of key patents, you may be able to make the other factors work for you, while garnering enough external support to set the standards you want.

If you have a good development team, you can build a bandwagon using an "openness" approach of ceding current control over the technology (e.g., through licenses at low or nominal royalties) while keeping tight control over improvements and extensions. If you know better than others how the technology is likely to evolve, you can use this informational advantage to preserve important future rights without losing the support of your allies. IBM chose to open up the PC, but then they lost control because they did not see what the key assets would be in the future. Besides the now-obvious ones (the design of the operating system and manufacturing of the underlying microprocessor), consider the example of interface standards between the PC and the monitor. During the 1980s, IBM set the first four standards: the Monochrome Graphics Adapters (MGA), the Color Graphics Adapter (CGA), the Enhanced Graphics Adapter (EGA), and the Video Graphics Adapter (VGA), the last in 1987. But by the time of the VGA, IBM was losing control, and the standard started to splinter with the Super VGA around 1988. Soon, with the arrival of the VESA interface, standard-setting passed out of IBM's hands altogether. By anticipating advances in the resolution of monitors, IBM could have done more to preserve its power to set these interface standards, without jeopardizing the initial launch of the PC.

Developing proprietary extensions is a valuable tactic to recapture at least partial control over your own technology. You may not be able to exert strong control at the outset, but you may gain some control later if you launch a technology that takes off and you can be first to market with valuable improvements and extensions.

One difficulty with such an approach is that your new technology may be *too* successful. If the demand for your product grows too fast, many of your resources may end up being devoted to meeting current demand rather than investing in R&D for the future. This happened to Cisco. All of their energies were devoted to the next generation of networking gear, leaving them little time for long-run research. If you are lucky enough to be in Cisco's position, do what they did: use all the profits you are making to identify and purchase firms that are producing the next-generation products. As Cisco's CEO, John Chambers, puts it: "We don't do research – we buy research!"

Allow complementors, and even rivals, to participate in developing standards, but under *your* terms. Clones are fine, so long as you set the terms under which they can operate. Don't flip-flop in your policies, as Apple did with its clone manufacturers: stay open, but make sure that you charge enough for access to your network (e.g., in the form of licensing fees) that your bottom line does not suffer when rivals displace your own sales. Build the opportunity costs of lost sales into your access prices or licensing fees.

REAR-GUARD ACTIONS

What happens if you fall behind? Can you ever recover?

That depends upon what you mean by "recover." Usually it is not possible to wrest leadership from another technology that is equally good and more established, unless your rival slips up badly. However, if the network externalities are not crushing, you may be able to protect a niche in the market. And you can always position yourself to make a run at leadership in the next generation of technology.

Atari, Nintendo, Sega, and Sony present a good example. Atari was dominant in 8-bit systems, Nintendo in 16-bit systems, Sega made inroads by being first-to-market with 32-bit systems, and Sony is giving Nintendo a run for their money in 64-bit systems. Losing one round does not mean you should give up, especially if backward compatibility is not paramount.

This leaves a set of tricky issues of how to manage your customers if you have done poorly in one round of the competition. Stranding even a small installed base of customers can have lasting reputational effects. IBM was concerned about this when they dropped the PC Jr. in the mid-1980s. Apart from consumer goodwill, retaining a presence in the market can be vital to keeping up customer relations and brand identity, even if you have little prospect of making major sales until you introduce a new generation of products. Apple faces this problem with their new operating system, Rhapsody. How do they maintain compatibility with their loyal followers while still building a path to what they hope will be a dramatic improvement in the operating environment?

Adapters and interconnection

A tried and true tactic when falling behind is to add an adapter, or to somehow interconnect with the larger network. This can be a sign of weakness, but one worth bearing if the enhanced network externalities of plugging into a far larger network are substantial. We touched on this in our discussion of how to negotiate a truce; if you are negotiating from weakness, you may simply seek the right to interconnect with the larger network.

The first question to ask is whether you even have the right to build an adapter. Sometimes the large network can keep you out. Atari lacked the intellectual property rights to include an adapter in their machines to play Nintendo cartridges, because of Nintendo's lock-out chip. In other cases, you may be able to break down the door, or at least try. The dominant ATM network in Canada, Interac, was compelled to let non-member banks interconnect. In the telephone area, the FCC is implementing elaborate rules that will allow competitive local exchange carriers to interconnect with the incumbent monopoly telephone networks.

The most famous legal case of a less-popular network product maneuvering to achieve compatibility is the battle between Borland and Lotus in spreadsheets. To promote its QuattroPro spreadsheet as an alternative to the dominant spreadsheet of the day, Lotus 1-2-3, Borland not only made sure than QuattroPro could import Lotus files, but copied part of the menu structure used by Lotus. Lotus sued Borland for copyright infringement. The case went all the way to the Supreme Court; the vote was deadlocked so Borland prevailed based on its victory in the First Circuit Court of Appeals. This case highlights the presence of legal uncertainty over what degree of imitation is permissible; the courts are still working out the limits on how patents and copyrights can be used in network industries.

There are many diverse examples of "adapters." Conversion of data from another program is a type of adapter. Translators and emulators can serve the same function when more complex code is involved. Converters can be one-way or two-way, with very different strategic implications. Think about WordPerfect and Microsoft Word today. WordPerfect is small and unlikely to gain much share, so they benefit from two-way compatibility. Consumers will be more willing to buy or upgrade WordPerfect if they can import files in Word format and export files in a format that is readable by users of Word. So far, Word will import files in WordPerfect format, but if Microsoft ever eliminates this feature of Word, WordPerfect should attempt to offer an export capability that preserves as much information as possible.

The biggest problem with adapters, when they are technically and legally possible, is performance degradation. Early hopes that improved processing power would make emulation easy have proven false. Tasks become more complex.

Digital's efforts with its Alpha microprocessor illustrate some of the ways in which less popular technologies seek compatibility. The Alpha chip has been consistently faster than the fastest Intel chips on the market. Digital sells systems with Alpha chips into the server market, a far smaller market than the desktop and workstation markets. And Digital's systems are far more expensive than systems using Intel chips. As a result, despite its technical superiority, the Alpha sold only 300,000 chips in 1996 compared to 65 million sold by Intel. This leaves Digital in the frustrating position of having a superior product but suffering from a small network. Recognizing that Alpha is in a precarious position, Digital has been looking for ways to interconnect with the Intel (virtual) network. Digital offers an emulator to let its Alpha chip run like an Intel architecture chip, but most of the performance advantages that Alpha offers are neutralized by the emulator. Hoping to improve the performance of systems using the Alpha chip, Digital and Microsoft announced in January 1998 an enhanced Alliance for Enterprise Computing, under which Windows NT server-based products will be released concurrently for Alpha- and Intel-based systems. Digital also has secured a commitment from Microsoft that Microsoft will cooperate to provide source-code compatibility between Alpha- and Intel-based systems for Windows NT application developers, making it far easier for them to develop applications to run on Alpha-based systems in native mode.

Adapters and converters among software programs are also highly imperfect. Converting files from WordStar to WordPerfect, and now from WordPerfect to Word, is notoriously buggy. Whatever the example, consumers are rightly wary of translators and emulators, in part because of raw performance concerns and in part because of lurking concerns over just how compatible the conversion really is: consider the problems that users have faced with Intel to Motorola architectures, or dBase to Paradox databases.

Apple offers a good example of a company that responded to eroding market share by adding adapters. Apple put in disk drivers that could read floppy disks formatted on DOS and Windows machines in the mid-eighties. In 1993, Apple introduced a machine that included an Intel 486 chip and could run DOS and Windows software along with Macintosh software. But Apple's case also exposes the deep tension underlying an adapter strategy: the adapter adds (some) value, but undermines confidence in the smaller network itself.

Finally, be careful about the large network changing interface specifications to avoid compatibility. IBM was accused of this in mainframe computers. Indeed, we suggested this very tactic in the section above on strategies for winners, so long as the new specifications are truly superior, not merely an attempt to exclude competitors.

Survival pricing

The marginal cost of producing information goods is close to zero. This means that you can cut your price very low and still cover (incremental) costs. Hence, when you find yourself falling behind in a network industry, it is tempting to cut price in order to spur sales, a tactic we call *survival pricing*.

However, the temptation should be resisted. Survival pricing is unlikely to work. It shows weakness, and it is hard to find examples where it made much difference. Computer Associates gave away "Simply Money" (for a $6.95 shipping and handling fee), but this didn't matter. Simply money still did not take off in its battle against Quicken and Money. On the other hand, Computer Associates got the name and vital statistics of each buyer, which was worth something in the mail list market, so it wasn't a total loss. IBM offered OS/2 for as little as $50, but look where it got them. Borland priced QuattroPro very aggressively when squeezed between Lotus 1-2-3 and Microsoft Excel back in 1993.

The problem is that the purchase price of software is minor in comparison with the costs of deployment, training, and support. Corporate purchasers, and even individual consumers, were much more worried about picking the winner of the spreadsheet wars than they were in whether their spreadsheet cost $49.95 or $99.95. At the time of the cut-throat pricing, Borland was a distant third in the spreadsheet market. Lotus and Microsoft both said they would not respond to the low price. Frank Ingari, Lotus's vice president for marketing, dismissed Borland as a "fringe player" and said the $49 price was a "last gasp move."

Survival pricing – cutting your price after the tide has moved against you – should be distinguished from penetration pricing, which is offering a low price to invade another market. Borland used penetration pricing very cleverly in the early 1980s with its Turbo Pascal product. Microsoft, along with other compiler companies, ignored Turbo Pascal, much to their dismay later on.

Legal approaches

If all else fails, sue. No, really. If the dominant firm has promised to be open and has reneged on that promise, you should attack its bait-and-switch approach. The Supreme Court in the landmark *Kodak* case opened the door to antitrust attacks along these lines, and many companies have taken up the invitation. The key is that a company may be found to be a "monopolist" over its own installed base of users, even if it faces strong competition to attract such users in the first place. Although the economics behind the *Kodak* case are murky and muddled, it can offer a valuable lever to gain compatibility or interconnection with a dominant firm.

CONCLUSIONS AND LESSONS

Before you can craft standards strategy, you first need to understand what type of standards war you are waging. The single most important factor to track is the compatibility between the dueling new technologies and established products. Standards wars come in three types: Rival Evolutions, Rival Revolutions, and Revolution versus Evolution.

Strength in the standards game is determined by ownership of seven critical assets:

- control of an installed base;
- intellectual property rights;
- ability to innovate;
- first-mover advantages;
- manufacturing abilities;
- presence in complementary products; and
- brand name and reputation.

Our main lessons for strategy and tactics, drawn from dozens of standards wars over the past century and more, are these:

- *Before you go to war, assemble allies.* You'll need the support of consumers, suppliers of complements, and even your competitors. Not even the strongest companies can afford to go it alone in a standards war.
- *Preemption is a critical tactic during a standards war.* Rapid design cycles, early deals with pivotal customers, and penetration pricing are the building blocks of a preemption strategy.
- *Managing consumer expectations is crucial in network markets.* Your goal is to convince customers – and your complementors – that you will emerge as the victor. Such expectations can easily become a self-fulfilling prophecy when network effects are strong. To manage expectations you should engage in aggressive marketing, make early announcements of new products, assemble allies, and make visible commitments to your technology.
- *When you've won your war, don't rest easy.* Cater to your own installed base and avoid complacency. Don't let the desire for backward compatibility hobble your ability to improve your product; doing so will leave you open to an entrant offering less compatibility but superior performance. Commoditize complementary products to make your systems more attractive for consumers.
- *If you fall behind, avoid survival pricing; it just signals weakness.* A better tactic is to establish a compelling performance advantage, or to interconnect with the prevailing standard using converters and adapters.

ACKNOWLEDGEMENTS

This material is adapted from our book, *Information Rules: A Strategic Guide to the Network Economy* (Harvard Business School Press, Boston, MA, 1998). We are indebted to our colleagues Joseph Farrell and Michael L. Katz who have greatly contributed over the past 15 years to our understanding of these Issues.

NOTES

1   For a lengthy discussion of railroad gauge standardization, see Amy Friedlander, *Emerging Infrastructure: The Growth of Railroads* (Reston, VA: Corporation for National Research Initiatives, 1995).

2   For further details on the Battle of the Systems, see Julie Ann Bunn and Paul David, "The Economics of Gateway Technologies and Network Evolution: Lessons from Electricity Supply History," *Information Economics and Policy*, 3/2(1988).

3   In this context, Edison's efforts can be seen as an attempt to prevent or delay tipping towards AC, perhaps to obtain the most money in selling his DC interests.

4   A very nice recounting of the color television story can be found in David Fisher and Marshall Fisher, "The Color War," *Invention & Technology*, 3/3 (1997). See, also, Joseph Farrell and Carl Shapiro, "Standard Setting in High-Definition Television," *Brookings Papers on Economic Activity: Microeconomics* (1992).

5   For color TV to truly offer value to viewers, it was not enough to get set manufacturers and networks to agree on a standard; they had to produce sets that performed well at reasonable cost, they had to create compelling content, and they had to induce broadcasters to invest in transmission gear. The technology was just not ready for the mass market in 1953, much less 1950. Interestingly, the Europeans, by waiting another decade before the adoption of PAL and SECAM, ended up with a better system. The same leapfrogging is now taking place in reverse: the digital HDTV system being adopted in the US is superior to the system selected years before by the Japanese.

6   For a fuller discussion of positive feedback, network effects, and network externalities, see Chapter 7 of Carl Shapiro and Hal R. Varian, *Information Rules: A Strategic Guide to the Network Economy* (Boston, MA: Harvard Business School Press, 1998). See, also, Michael Katz and Carl Shapiro, "Systems Competition and Network Effects," *Journal of Economic Perspectives*, 8/2 (1994); Brian Arthur, *Increasing Returns and Path Dependence in the Economy* (Ann Arbor, MI: University of Michigan Press, 1994).

7   We recognize, indeed emphasize, that building an alliance of customers, suppliers, and complementors to support one technology over another in a standards battle can be the single most important tactic in such a struggle. We explore alliances and cooperative strategies to achieve compatibility separately in Chapter 8 of *Information Rules* [Shapiro and Varian, op. cit.]. See, also, David B. Yoffie, "Competing in the Age of Digital Convergence," *California Management Review*, 38/4 (1996).

8   For a discussion of the antitrust treatment of standards, see the Federal Trade Commission Staff Report, *Competition Policy in the New High-Tech, Global Marketplace*, Chapter 9, "Networks and Standards"; Joel Klein, "Cross-Licensing and Antitrust Law," 1997, available at www.usdoj.gov/atr/public/speeches/1123.htm; Carl Shapiro, "Antitrust in Network Industries," 1996, available at www.usdoj.gov/atr/public/speeches/shapir.mar; Carl Shapiro, "Setting Compatibility Standards: Cooperation or Collusion?" Working Paper, University of California, Berkeley, 1998.

9   We cannot explore cooperation and compatibility tactics in any depth here. We discuss tactics for participation in formal standard setting in Chapter 8 of *Information Rules* [Shapiro and Varian, op. cit.].

10 Even these companies have had losers, too, such as Microsoft's Bob, Intel's original
    Celeron chip, and Sun's 386 platform. Credibility and brand name recognition without
    allies and a sound product are not enough.
11 Manufacturers do the same thing when they pay "slotting allowances" to supermarkets
    for shelf space by checking that their products are actually displayed where they are
    supposed to be displayed.
12 Indeed, the strategy has been so successful that some have amended the name to
    "Embrace, Extend and Eliminate."

COMMENTARY
Carl Shapiro and Hal R. Varian

In the course of research for *The Art of Standards Wars* we investigated several
historical examples of such wars, including railroad gauges, AC versus DC power,
and telephone networks. Our reading of these episodes confirmed our belief that
"technology changes, economic laws do not." The same forces that were at work
in the telephone battles of 1910 show up in Internet backbones in 2000, albeit in
somewhat different forms.

One striking fact that emerges from the historical record is that standardization
is difficult. The first attempts to standardize parts for arms manufacture occurred
in the 1770s in France. Thomas Jefferson was quick to recognize the potential of
interchangeable parts and pushed for this technology in the US.

The Springfield Armory, Eli Whitney, Samuel Colt, and other legendary nineteenth century inventors tried their hand at making interchangeable parts, but progress
was slow. In fact, it really wasn't until Henry Ford and the advent of mass production that interchangeable parts became commonplace. Much of the difficulty in
realizing the dream of interchangeable parts was technological: the relatively primitive measurement and manufacturing technology required that parts be laboriously
hand fitted in order to mesh together smoothly. When Henry Ford announced in
1926 that "there is no fitting in mass production" he was signalling the end of more
than a century of effort.

But, in a way, the conquest of the technological dimension of interchangeable
parts led directly to the socio-economic problem of making parts that were interchangeable not only *within* a particular product, but even *across* manufacturers. It is
these forces that are the most interest to us as economists.

Between 1904 and 1908, more than 240 companies entered the fledgling automotive business. In 1910 there was a mini-recession, and many of these entrants
went out of business. Parts suppliers realized that it would be much less risky to
produce parts that they could sell to more than one manufacturer. Simultaneously,
the smaller automobile manufacturers realized that they could enjoy some of the
cost savings from economies of scale and competition if they also used standardized
parts that were provided by a number of suppliers.

Guess which companies were *not* interested in parts standardization? The two largest
companies in the industry: Ford Motor Company and General Motors. Why? Because
they were well able to achieve strong economies of scale in their own operations,
and had no interest in "interconnecting" with anyone else: standardization would

(partially) level the playing field regarding economies of scale at the component level. As usual, then and now, standardization benefits entrants, complementors, and consumers, but may hold little interest for dominant incumbents.

The Society of Automotive Engineers worked tirelessly to standardize part design. Eventually, Ford and GM did sign on to this effort, initially for products that they did not manufacture (oil, gasoline) but eventually for most generic parts. Recently, several auto firms have found it attractive to spin off their part suppliers, presumably to achieve procurement cost savings via competition and perhaps even greater returns to scale. As the design of the automobile has stabilized, some of the need for differentiation via unique parts has been eliminated.

The more we look at the history of technological change, the more we have become aware of what we like to call "combinatorial innovation," a concept closely related to what Martin Weitzman calls "recombinant growth." The idea is that every now and then a set of standardized parts or components comes along, triggering a wave of experimentation by innovators who tinker with the many *combinations* of these components. The result: a wealth of new products build on the newly available components. Weitzman's example is the Wright brothers: they took kite technology, bicycle technology, and the gasoline engine and combined them to create a totally new invention: the flying machine.

Moving to more modern times, the personal computer was essentially an accident. Intel's 4004 chip and its successor, the 8080, could only do basic computations; they were designed for use in calculators, cash registers, automatic teller machines, and other industrial products. However, some engineers at a small company named MITS recognized that the 8080 was powerful enough to be used in a general purpose programmable device and in 1974 they released the Altair, the world's first personal computer.

Intel never envisioned the 8080 being used for this purpose. In fact, when the Altair was released, Gordon Moore himself thought personal computers had no future. This is a telling illustration of the startling and unexpected fruits that can be harvested from a set of components capable of being re-purposed for uses entirely different from those envisioned by their original designers.[1]

We believe that the same forces that drove the Wright brothers and the personal computer have been at work in the last five years. And now, at the turn of a new century, we have seen component parts like TCP/IP, HTTP, HTML, CGI, and so on being combined and recombined to create new inventions: web pages, chat rooms, online auctions, exchanges, search engines, and so on. The difference between *this* burst of recombinant activity and the earlier episodes is that now the components are all *ideas*, many of which are no more tangible than a string of computer code.[2]

Combinatorial innovation can take place extraordinarily rapidly in the information age, precisely because the components are virtual, not physical. Today's raw material for tomorrow's new products are protocols, software, and collections of bits, all of which can be zapped around the world in fractions of a second, at virtually no incremental cost. Manufacturing lags and parts shortages are just not a problem: there are no capacity and production constraints for bits. All of this implies that the recombination of *ideas* today can occur at a much faster pace than the recombination of *physical parts* we saw in previous episodes of innovation. The result: everything moves on Internet time, and we see an incredibly rapid pace of innovation, similar in form to what we have seen in historical episodes, but moving much more rapidly.

The benefits from having a robust set of component parts can hardly be overestimated, as they provide the basic infrastructure for innovation. But, as we said earlier, standardization is hard, both from the engineering viewpoint of design, and from the economic point of aligning incentives. Standardization involves the age-old problem of seeking consensus from very different individuals and organizations who may have sharply different interests. Today's technology, built on ideas, is poised to rocket ahead, but there is no reason to think that the economic and political obstacles to standardization can be solved more rapidly in the twenty-first century than in the nineteenth century. The implication: the economics of standardization may serve as the limiting or gating factor determining the pace of adoption and diffusion of new information technologies over the decades ahead.

In our article, we provide a framework for understanding and managing the economic forces at work in standardization, especially in situations where market conditions are critical to the bargaining positions of different players in the standardization process. For the reasons just given, we see standardization as one of the key factors determining the pace and direction of adoption of information technologies in the next decade. We hope we have contributed something to the understanding of this critical phenomenon.

NOTES

1 http://www.thetech.org/exhibits_events/online/revolution/moore/i_c.html
2 Of course, modern technological miracles are hardly confined to software and the Internet. We see parallel combinatorial innovation taking place in a number of industries today, ranging from photonics to biotechnology to magnetic data storage technology.

PART FOUR

FIELD-LEVEL AND ORGANIZATIONAL DYNAMICS

DYNAMICS OF ORGANIZATIONAL COMMUNITIES AND TECHNOLOGICAL BANDWAGONS: AN EMPIRICAL INVESTIGATION OF COMMUNITY EVOLUTION IN THE MICROPROCESSOR MARKET

JAMES WADE

The *market success* of a technology or design arises not simply because of its efficiency or technological superiority, but from the level of organizational support that the technology attracts. Here, organizational support refers to all organizations that have a stake in a given design or technology. For instance, Garud and Kumaraswamy (1993) suggest that Sun Microsystem's success is largely due to its open systems strategy. By providing rivals easy access to its technology, Sun has been able to create a broad network of organizational support for its products, including microprocessor manufacturers, software producers, and producers of Sun clones. Organizational support increases customer confidence that the technology will survive, thus making customers more likely to adopt. In turn, as more customers adopt the technology, it becomes increasingly viable for other firms to copy the product and produce associated products, making potential customers even more likely to adopt the system (Katz and Shapiro, 1985). Increasing returns can lead to nonobvious outcomes in which newer and technologically superior designs are not adopted because of the support that the older system has garnered (David, 1985).

Most observers agree, for instance, that the Beta video cassette standard (sponsored by Sony) was superior to the VHS standard (sponsored by Matsushita) in both compactness and quality. A key difference in strategy between the two firms was that Matsushita freely licensed out its technology to vendors, while Sony kept its system proprietary. Possibly because of VHS system's increased organizational support, VHS systems flooded the market and overwhelmed the Beta standard. Thus, at some level of support, irreversible technological bandwagons may develop. Despite the strategic importance of this issue, little empirical research has addressed how organizational support for a design or technology evolves.

Past Research

Most empirical work that examines the spread of technological innovations has investigated the diffusion of a single innovation. Various factors such as social contagion are theorized to speed up or slow down this diffusion rate. Fischer and Carroll (1988), for instance, investigated the diffusion of the telephone and the automobile. One characteristic of these models is that there is only a single innovation vying for acceptance in the market. In many markets, however, many designs compete for dominance.

This fact is implicit in the economic literature on competing, incompatible standards (see David and Greenstein, 1990, for a review). One strength of this literature is its identification of the problems associated with increasing returns. Increasing returns associated with network externalities occur when the utility that a user derives from a good increases with the number of other adopters (Katz and Shapiro, 1985). With telephones, for instance, it is obvious that a telephone's value increases as the total number of telephones increases; the user can speak to more people through the telephone. Similarly, Swann (1987) has suggested and provided empirical evidence that the degree to which a microprocessor product can attract organizational support serves as an information externality indicating the status of the product as a potential industry standard. Thus, a large number of firms supporting a design may encourage customers to buy the design which, in turn, leads to more firms joining the community. At some point these processes may feed upon each other and start irreversible technological bandwagons rolling.

Factors which increase the rate at which a system gains organizational support are also of strategic importance because they are likely to increase entry barriers to potential competitors with competing systems (Porter, 1985). For instance, Gallini (1984) has suggested that licensing out technology may deter the entry of new potential standards. A large number of suppliers providing compatible products increases the costs of entry to potential competitors because of the large installed base that would have to be overcome. To enter viably once an existing system has garnered extensive organizational support, a competitor not only has to provide the base product but also a wide variety of supporting products – a cost that may be prohibitive. Further, customers of the existing systems will be reluctant to switch because their sunk investments in the old system would be lost (Hannan and Freeman, 1989; Lieberman and Montogomery, 1988) and because of supplier-specific learning by customers

(Wernerfelt, 1984). Consequently, understanding how technologies garner organizational support is quite important because it may shed light onto the factors that start technological bandwagons rolling or, correspondingly, bring them to a halt.

Economic theorists use mathematical models to show that the presence of increasing returns may lead to nonoptimal outcomes such as inferior technologies being adopted (Farrell and Saloner, 1985). In particular, Arthur (1989) has suggested that early events can have disproportionate effects on the outcome of technological adoption, regardless of the relative merit of the competing technologies. In effect, once a given technology receives a certain level of support, a technological bandwagon develops and that design becomes dominant. The drawbacks in these models are two-fold. First, almost all the models are mathematically derived and have not been tested empirically. Second, the process by which a given design gains supporters is not specified, just its consequences.

In the organizations literature, Tushman and Rosenkopf (1992) have taken a more sociological approach and described the battle to become the dominant design as a competition between multiple technologies. Each technology can be thought of as being supported by a community of organizations that have a stake in the technology or design.[1] The degree to which a community attracts these stakeholders can prove crucial to the fate of the community. In fact, the emergence of a dominant design is closely tied to the notion of key stakeholders converging upon and supporting a single design. And, the emergence of a dominant design can have profound effects on interorganizational dynamics, particularly in industries where increasing returns are present (Baum, Korn, and Kotha, 1995). Thus far, however, just as in the literature on the economics of standards, this theory yields little insight into the underlying processes by which competing designs garner support.

One commonality between the organizations and economic literatures is their recognition that it is often mistaken to view firms in a market atomistically. In the economic literature, the competition is not simply between firms, but between standards. Further, each standard could be supported by a multitude of firms. Similarly, the dominant design theory implies that communities of organizations support rival technological approaches and that interorganizational dynamics determine the emergence of a dominant design. Again, the important boundaries to be considered are not simply those between firms, but between rival technological communities. What, then, does determine the process by which these technological communities gain organizational support? In order to understand the issues involved in this question, the concept of technological communities is explored in greater detail below. Then hypotheses are developed and tested using data from the microprocessor market. Finally, implications for strategy are drawn and I speculate on the broader implications of this study for future technology research.

TECHNOLOGICAL COMMUNITIES

Technical change and interorganizational interdependence will be modeled here from the perspective of organizational communities. In ecological theory, a community is defined as a set of interdependent populations (Hawley, 1950). At the community level, population ecology can be closely tied to a network perspective. A community is defined as a set of interdependent populations (Hawley, 1950). Members of a given population in a community are structurally equivalent because they have equivalent ties to other populations in the community and similar patterns of resource flows (Dimaggio, 1986).

Because I am arguing that interdependencies within and among competing technological communities play a major role in the technological evolution of this industry, a key theoretical issue that needs to be addressed concerns how these communities should be defined. Below I explore two possible alternative possibilities. The first bases community membership on compatibility, while the second bases it on sponsorship. In the economic literature, a sponsor is a firm that creates a design and has a proprietary interest in it (David and Greenstein, 1990).

Communities based on designs

One way that organizational communities could be formed is by grouping products that have some degree of hardware and/or software compatibility. Essentially, the basic design embodies a technological paradigm (Dosi, 1982), defining a technological trajectory that will be followed by subsequent products in that design family. *A community based on a technological paradigm or design, then, includes the sponsor of the design, and all organizations that have a stake in and support the design.* Forms of organizational support might include firms copying the designs, firms producing associated products (e.g., software for a computer design), and even user groups. The Apple Macintosh, for example, has a variety of customer user groups associated with it, as does the IBM personal computer. Thus, the IBM personal computer community is made up of a population of clonemakers, a population of software manufacturers, as well as many others (see figure 9.1).[2] This definition of a community is closely tied to the economic literature on technical standardization (David and Greenstein, 1990). Because products within a community are compatible, each community and its associated design represent a potential technical standard for the industry.

Communities based on sponsors

Alternatively, community membership can be based solely on sponsorship. Using this approach, *a community consists of a sponsor and all those organizations who have a stake in and support any of its designs.* Rather than focusing purely on technical compatibility, ties between a sponsor and other firms form the community, regardless of the number of distinct designs that the sponsor has produced.

At first glance, defining a community by sponsorship rather than by compatibility appears to make the economic literature on standards less relevant. However, this is not necessarily the case. As discussed earlier, most of the theory in the literature on standards is based on the notion of increasing returns. In this market, for instance, as a design gains increased support from customers and producers, the system

IBM personal computer community

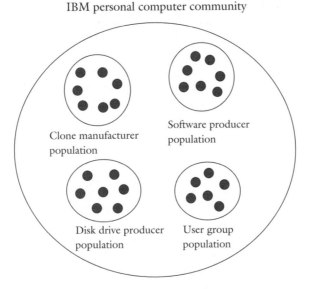

Clone manufacturer
population

Software producer
population

Disk drive producer
population

User group
population

Apple Macintosh community

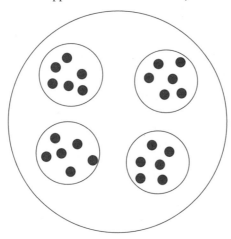

Figure 9.1 Design communities in the personal computer market.

becomes more valuable to users. Increasing returns may also apply at the level of the sponsor, regardless of the number of designs that the sponsor supports because of reference or minimum quality standards. Reference or minimum quality standards signal that a given product conforms to the content and level of certain defined characteristics (David and Greenstein, 1990). In the same way, the level of organizational support that a community has and the identity of the sponsor may send a signal to customers regarding the reliability and level of support that all the sponsor's designs enjoy. In effect, the state of a sponsor's overall network may be a proxy for its reputation and be the source of positive feedbacks.

From a sociological perspective, a community defined at the level of the sponsor is the most relevant level of analysis. Customers, employees, and firms producing associated products are likely to develop general relationships and interdependencies with the sponsor that transcend issues of product compatibility. Moreover, the fates of designs developed by the same sponsor and the attractiveness of those designs to potential community members are unlikely to be independent of each other. In short, social ties between people and organizations are likely to be embedded in economic activity (Granovetter, 1985).

Summary

In summary, one definition of an organizational community is based purely on compatibility and is consistent with the economic literature on technical standards. The alternative definition of community is more sociological in nature. In this case the ties and interdependencies administered by the dominant sponsoring firm are considered paramount to compatibility. Since both definitions of community have merit and will have similar predictions, I will test the hypotheses using both definitions. This strategy should help determine which conceptualization of a community offers more explanatory power.

CONTEXT OF THE STUDY

I explore these issues using quarterly data on all merchant producers of microprocessors from 1971 to 1989. General microprocessors perform both the primary execution and control functions in a system. They resemble and are often the central processing unit in a computer. Before the advent of the microprocessor, integrated circuit chips were designed for specific tasks. For instance, each new function on a calculator was performed by a logic chip specially designed for that task. Because of the level of specialization, it was difficult for firms to find mass market applications for their chips and reap economies of scale. Microprocessors can be programmed to perform any function desired and thus overcame this limitation. With the introduction of the first four-bit microprocessor in 1971, Intel started an industry whose sales have grown to over 600 million in the third quarter of 1989.[3]

Firms producing microprocessors generally pursue one of two strategies. First, a firm can design and produce an original microprocessor. This firm can be conceptualized as a sponsor because it holds a proprietary interest in the design (David and Greenstein, 1990). A prominent sponsor in this industry is Intel, best known for designing the microprocessor family used in the IBM personal computer.

A second strategy is to copy an existing product. Essentially, these firms are imitators and are commonly referred to as second sources. While this strategy of imitation or followership is common in many markets, no precise theoretical term has been consistently used to describe it. For the sake of simplicity, firms following this strategy will be referred to hereafter as second sources.

Here, I investigate one particular type of organizational support, the *rate at which communities attract second sources*. Of course, second sourcing is only one type of organizational support in this market. Other firms provide support in terms of providing compatible software and peripheral devices such as memory and input–output devices. I suggest, however, that the processes governing the rates of entry of other types of organizational support are likely to be similar. I expect, for instance, that firms entering a microprocessor community with input–output devices will follow the same pattern as second sources. These groups can be thought of as inter-dependent populations which form the organizational community. Thus, while I am examining one type of organizational support here, I expect the results to be generalizable to other types of support. Undoubtedly, there are cross-effects between different types of organizational support. Because of the exploratory nature of this study, however, these cross-effects are not empirically considered here.

In this study, I do not control for differing strategies by sponsors, with regard to their licensing and patent protection strategies. Specification problems could arise if sponsors could easily prevent second sources from copying their designs. It is unlikely, however, that this is a significant problem because patent protection in this industry has been traditionally weak and customers in the semiconductor market generally support second sourcing because of the volatility of the industry (Webbink, 1977). Thus, the noninclusion of these factors is not likely to be a serious limitation to the study.

The results of this study have strategic implications for both sponsors and those firms considering supporting an organizational community. From the perspective of new sponsors, for instance, garnering increased organizational support can be critical to their survival. By understanding the factors that drive this process, sponsors may be able to manipulate these bandwagon effects to their advantage and increase their chances of survival.

Second sources (and other forms of organizational support) also face critical uncertainties. If a second source joins an established community with extensive organizational support, the firm has increased confidence that the community will survive, but will probably face intense competition from other second sources. In contrast, if the firm joins a new community, the second source may benefit from first mover effects, but only if the community survives and is able to attract additional organizational support. By understanding how technological bandwagons develop, however, second sources and other potential stakeholders may be able to identity communities, early on, that have greater chances of surviving and prospering.

THEORY AND HYPOTHESES

Arthur (1989) has portrayed the eventual failure or success of competing products or technologies with competing technologies as a path-dependent process in which chance events near the beginning of the process can disproportionately affect the outcome. Carroll and Harrison (1994) have demonstrated in a simulation that such outcomes may be compatible with Hannan's (1986) density-dependent model of organizational evolution. Hannan's theory postulates that at the beginning of an industry increases in the numbers of firms legitimate the population and founding rates increase, while mortality rates fall. Essentially, increased numbers of an organizational form lead to increased legitimacy as customers and the capital market increasingly take the form for granted. While Hannan (1986) is the first theorist to directly link legitimation or "taken-for-grantedness" with numbers of an organizational form, the idea of taken-for-grantedness has its roots in institutional theory which suggests that legitimacy is directly and positively related to organizational survival (Meyer and Rowan, 1977; Meyer, 1983). At some point, however, the population becomes "taken for granted" and further increases in numbers only exacerbate competition, leading to an increase in the failure rate and a decrease in the founding rate.[4]

In their simulation, Carroll and Harrison (1994) set up two competing populations, each of which had a competitive effect on the other that was proportional to the number of firms in a given population. The simulation was set up, however, so that one population's competitive effect on the other was much weaker. If, for instance, the two populations both had an equivalent number of firms, stronger competitive effects would be generated in the less fit population (higher failure rates and lower founding rates). Theorizing that each population grew according to Hannan's (1986) density-dependent theory of legitimation and competition, they found that chance played a major role in determining which population survived. In fact, the competitively superior population only won the contest 66 percent of the time. Whether the inferior population could win depended on how many organizations were in the inferior population when the competitively dominant population began.

While boundaries around populations have traditionally corresponded to industry boundaries, perhaps different technologies, designs, or sponsorship might also create boundaries between sets of firms. Thus, Carroll and Harrison's (1994) two simulated populations could be reconceptualized as two communities in the same industry utilizing different designs or technologies. If so, one of the key processes governing the outcome would be the rate at which each community attracts organizational support, which in turn may be governed by Hannan's (1986) density-dependent theory of organizational evolution.

Hannan's (1986) density-dependent model proposes that at the beginning of an industry increased density (number of firms) is mutualistic and increases the founding rate. At the level of a technological community, this proposition is consistent with Porter's argument (1985) that licensing serves to speed up the process by which a product becomes the industry standard or "dominant design." The existence of many producers of compatible products yields information about the status of a community's products as a possible industry standard (Swann, 1987). It instils confidence in customers that the product will persist in the market and that a steady supply of parts and a variety of peripheral components will continue to be available. Thus, in effect, with increasing density, the community becomes institutionalized and achieves a "taken-for-granted" character (Meyer, 1983; Meyer and Rowan, 1977).

However, these mutualistic effects are likely to have limits. At some point customers should see a given community as established and reliable, and the addition of another community member will not significantly increase the system's value to customers.

Thus, further increases in density within the community will simply exacerbate competition. The following hypothesis is suggested:

Hypothesis 1: The rate at which communities gain second source support will at first increase with the number of second sources in that community. However, as density continues to increase further, the rate of entry will fall as competitive effects dominate.

The rate at which firms enter a community may also be affected by the number of communities in operation. Entering a community inevitably entails some risks. If these communities compete to have their products become the "dominant" design, only one winner, or at most a few, is likely (Anderson and Tushman, 1990).[5] A firm which bets on a losing community's products is likely to follow that community into oblivion, particularly if the firm has only limited diversification into other markets. Obviously, it might be more difficult to pick the "winner" in an environment with many communities. In fact, *Business Week* (1991a) asserted that because there are so many competing personal computer designs, customers are buying less than they ordinarily would because they are afraid of being stuck on a losing standard. Similarly, it might be that the greater the number of communities in the market, the slower will be the rate at which communities gain support because of this increased uncertainty. The following hypothesis is proposed:

Hypothesis 2a: The greater the number of other communities in the market, the lower will be the rate of second source entry into a focal community.

Hannan's density dependence theory of organizational evolution, however, suggests a different pattern. In earlier research on the microprocessor industry, Wade (1993) found that the entry of new sponsors followed the pattern predicted by the density-dependent model of legitimation and competition. That is, as the number of communities first increased, the entry rate of sponsors rose, because of legitimation. As density continued to rise, however, competition dominated and the entry rate fell. Similar to the approach taken here, Wade (1993) defined communities at the level of the sponsor and at the level of the design and found these effects using either definition of community.

Just as an increased number of communities in an industry is proposed to increase the entry rates of sponsors due to legitimation, an initial increase in the number of technological communities supporting designs may have the same legitimating effect at a lower level of a analysis, that is, on second source entry into technological communities. Potential entrants may be loath to enter the market if there are very few communities. At this point, the future of the microprocessor technology is unknown and the risks are likely to be quite high.

This legitimation process may be particularly important for systemic technologies like microprocessors that require compatible associated components (in this case memory and input–output devices) to function. In this case, if the technology perishes, customers lose not only their investments in the primary product, the microprocessor, but also in a wide range of other associated products. Moreover, this uncertainty is likely to be quite severe in the case of technologies that are radical technological discontinuities such as microprcessors. In fact, while Intel sold the first microprocessor in the second quarter of 1971, the marketing department made no press announcement until December of that year because they had significant doubts on whether the microprocessor was a viable and cost-effective product (Rogers and Larsen, 1984). With more communities in the market, however, this uncertainty about the microprocessor technology declines as it becomes "taken for granted" and becomes the accepted way to accomplish a particular task. In addition, under conditions of ambiguity (as would exist in this market's early history), organizations are quite vulnerable to social bandwagon pressures (Abrahamson and Rosenkopf, 1993; Dimaggio and Powell, 1983; Meyer and Rowan, 1977). Thus, as the number of communities in the market initially increases, entry into them should rise.

At some point, however, further increases in density should make it more difficult to enter. This decline might be purely because of competitive effects, or it could be that with many communities in the market potential entrants are less certain about the likely "winner" (as suggested in Hypothesis 2a) and are less likely to enter. Similarly, as Barnett (1990) finds in the telephone industry, a large number of incompatible products may fragment the industry, since any two products are less likely to work together. Further, as the number of communities rises and fragmentation increases, existing customers are locked into an increasing number of communities with incompatible products. Thus, as the number of communities rises (holding the market size constant), the potential market for any given design is likely to be reduced and, in turn, discourages entry by potential second sources. The following hypothesis is proposed:

> *Hypothesis 2b: As the number of other communities in the market initially increases, second source entry into a focal community will increase. At some point, however, a further increase in the number of communities will cause entry into the community to decline.*

The rate at which firms enter a particular community is likely also to be affected by the number of firms that are supporting other communities. These firms may be creating a base of support for existing communities that acts as an entry barrier for prospective entrants with new designs (Gallini, 1984). Indeed, Wade (1993) finds support for this contention in an earlier study on the microprocessor industry. He found that as the number of second sources in the market increased, the entry rate of sponsors of new designs declined. Possibly, the same process occurs at a lower level of analysis, that is, for entry into a focal community. The presence of extensive organizational support implies that there is likely to be a large number of supporting products, and many customers who may be effectively "locked in" to existing standards, creating scarce resources and poor opportunities for potential entrants. Customers will be reluctant to switch to a new incompatible system because their existing investments will be lost. The following hypothesis is suggested:

> *Hypothesis 3: At the level of a given community, the greater the number of second sources supporting other communities, the lower will be the entry rate of second sources into that community.*

In considering which community to join, second sources are also likely to be influenced by differences in technology between communities. An important distinction between communities may be the extent to which their technology is based upon an architectural innovation. Architectural innovation has been described as the reconfiguration of an established system to link together existing components in a new way (Henderson and Clark, 1990). Unlike radical innovations, which give rise to new markets and often rely on new scientific principles (Dess and Beard, 1984; Dewar and Dutton, 1986), in an architectural innovation, the basic scientific knowledge underlying the technology has not changed. Architectural innovation is often triggered by a change in a component which creates new interactions and linkages with other components in the system. For instance, the development of the jet engine altered the relationships between the structural components of an airplane because of the different stresses that it placed on the airframe.

Existing firms copying a new architecture face a difficult problem. Because the components of the systems are similar these firms may apply their knowledge of the old architecture to the new one. Since the interrelationships between the components of the system have changed, however, this knowledge is of dubious value. In fact, the firms' knowledge of the old architecture, embedded in their existing organizational routines, may cause them to misunderstand the new one. New entrants, however, will have no such constraints, and architectural innovations may allow them to make inroads into the industry. Such was the case in Henderson and Clark's (1990) compelling case study which analyzed several architectural changes that have occurred in the semiconductor photolithographic alignment industry. After each architectural change, new entrants replaced the older, more established firms.

Essentially, while architectural change may not appear to be a large change at the component level, it is a competence-destroying change at the system-wide level from the perspective of incumbent firms whose existing routines do not enable them to cope with the change. Thus, architectural change or innovation may lower entry barriers for new communities and allow their supporters to proliferate. Potential second sources may be attracted to communities based on architectural innovations because the performance enhancements that the design offers will be attractive to customers and effective competition from other communities may be minimized.

In microprocessors, the dominant architecture is called Complex Instruction Set Code (CISC). This architecture focuses on building complex instructions into the hardware of a microprocessor. A new architecture introduced in the last decade is called Reduced Instruction Set Code (RISC). Although the underlying design philosophy of a RISC processor is different, it uses the same basic technology as a CISC processor. Proponents of the RICS architecture contend that by leaving out seldom-used instructions designers can make chips smaller and faster. Because RISC processors only have simple instructions burned into the hardware, the emphasis shifts to the software side in comparison to CISC, for which the emphasis remains largely on the hardware side. RISC is an architectural innovation in the sense that the linkages between the software and hardware components of the processor have changed. The following hypothesis is proposed:

> *Hypothesis 4: Communities based on RISC technology will have higher rates of second source entry than other communities.*

Another determinant of the rate at which a community attracts organizational support might be its dominance in the market, particularly if positive network externalities are present. In the economics of standards literature (Katz and Shapiro, 1985; Farrell and Saloner, 1985; David and Greenstein, 1990), theorists have generally equated dominance with the number of products sold that are compatible with a given standard. A larger network size will make the communities' products more valuable to customers because of the wider variety of supporting products available, and more attractive to potential supporters because of the larger customer base. In the microprocessor market, for example, network externalities are particularly relevant because of all the peripheral devices and software that are sold along with microprocessors. Further, a dominant community in this type of industry is also likely to have a large base of customers effectively locked into its network; because of the switching costs involved, these customers will likely remain loyal to the original community. The following hypothesis is suggested:

> *Hypothesis 5: The greater a community's dominance, the greater the entry rate of second sources into that community.*

While I have suggested that innovativeness will not necessarily be the primary factor in the ability of a community to attract organizational support, it should certainly have an impact. Here, I investigate the rate at which a community introduces products that are technologically superior to its previous products. The rate at which a community improves its own products is important because it is often less ambiguous than technological differences between the processors manufactured by two different communities. Because microprocessors have multiple performance dimensions and vary widely in their architecture across communities, comparing their technical characteristics across communities is difficult. Thus, while an Intel microprocessor may be superior in one dimension, its Motorola counterpart may be superior in another. Within a community a comparison is much easier because it is natural for the sponsor and the analysts in the industry to compare products that are common to a sponsor.

Because of the ambiguity involved in evaluating processors across communities, the rate at which a community improves its products should send a signal to prospective supporters and customers that the community is viable because the sponsor is continuing to invest in the technology. These signals which build reputation are particularly important when there are information asymmetries between players (Weigelt and Camerer, 1988). In this industry, it is almost certain that sponsors have a greater knowledge and understanding of their designs than a potential second source because significant economies of scale are achieved through learning by doing (Webbink, 1977). The following hypothesis is proposed:

> *Hypothesis 6: The shorter the time since a community has last innovated, the greater the rate at which it will attract second source support.*

METHOD

The data include all firms that produced microprocessors between the beginning of the market in 1971 and 1989. Data on firms' quarterly dates of participation in the industry as sponsors or second sources were gathered from a leading data research firm in the industry and from *IC Master*, a directory that engineers use to select microprocessors.

The research firm collects data on microprocessors and sells this information to firms in the industry.[6] The data are collected through a survey using multiple sources and its accuracy and coverage are aided by the fact that the firm has offices throughout the world, including Europe and Japan. Estimated yearly shipment data by product were reported by the research firm in 1975 and quarterly data thereafter. Entries were defined as being in the quarter when a firm first put a microprocessor into full production and exits were recorded when shipping ceased.

This information was supplemented by data from *IC Master*, an annual directory (published since 1976) used by engineers to select integrated circuits that meet their performance requirements. Before 1983 *IC Master* also listed the quarter in which the product was first shipped. This information made it possible to extend the data on entries and exits back to the beginning of the industry in 1971.[7] After 1982, yearly dates could be inferred from a product's inclusion in the yearly volume. When only yearly dates were available, sponsors were assumed to enter during the year before their first listing and to exit during the year of their last listing. *IC Master* was published each January or February, so this strategy is reasonable.

By combining these two primary sources, it was possible to construct a fairly exhaustive list and history of the products in the industry. When there were inconsistencies between the two primary sources, they were resolved by consulting numerous secondary sources, including, *Predicast's F&S Indexes* (various years), *Electronics* (various years), *Microprocessors and Microsystems*, Swann (1986), *EDN's* annual Microprocessor Survey (1974–89), as well as various historical accounts of the industry.

Using multiple sources in determining entry dates is essential in this market because firms close to producing a product have an incentive to have their product publicized so that it will be considered for purchase. In addition, while having a license is a very strong indicator that a second source is producing a product, it is not a guarantee. In rare cases, this could lead to a listing in *IC Master* and other sources before the firm is actually shipping the product. Because the research firm uses multiple sources, it is more immune to this type of strategic behavior. Triangulating on the date of entry and exit using multiple sources made it unlikely that an incorrect date would be used. Secondary sources and the judgement of the author were relied upon to adjudicate any conflicting dates between the two primary sources.

The primary heuristic used to group products into communities defined at the level of the design was hardware and software compatibility. Because of technological progress, new products by a sponsor would sometimes lose some compatibility with earlier products, but if any degree of compatibility remained it would be assigned to that design community. For example, while the 8086 is not hardware compatible with many of the earlier 8085's peripheral devices, it does share a high degree of software compatibility. Thus, since this product is assumed to build on the architecture of the earlier product, it is considered to be in the same design group. Both *EDN's* Annual Survey of Microprocessors and Money's *Microprocessor Data Book* contained information on compatibility between designs. Using the sources, it was possible to judge the compatibility of a sponsor's products. Sponsor communities were then formed by grouping together products that were developed by the same sponsor.

In some cases, a firm designs and markets a product that shares some compatibility with an existing sponsor's design, but has a unique mix of features and an architecture that cannot be directly tied to any product in the original design community. For example, while Zilog's Z80 was similar to Intel's 8080 in that the 8080's instruction set was a subset of the Z80's, it had over 50 more instructions, and its bus structure was unique. It is argued here that the technological trajectories of the two products (designs) which are only partially compatible and have different capabilities or features are likely to diverge over time if they have two independent sponsors. Thus, in this situation, the two products were grouped into separate communities and Zilog and Intel were considered to be two separate sponsors. Thirty communities were formed at the level of the sponsor, while there were 38 communities defined at the level of the design, indicating that introducing more than one design is relatively rare.

Entry and exit dates assigned were quarterly. In the few cases where only a yearly entry or exit date was available, the event was randomly assigned to a quarter during the year. For the 53 second sources in communities defined at the level of the sponsor, four ending dates and six starting dates were randomly assigned to quarters within the year. All independent variables were lagged by one quarter.

Data

Population density measures

Community density was simply defined as the number of technological communities in the market other than the focal community. For one set of analyses, communities were defined at the level of the sponsor, while in the other the design was the unit of analysis. The number of community members was the number of firms belonging to a community, including both the sponsor and the second sources. The number of second sources outside the community was computed by summing second source density across all communities at each point in time and subtracting the number of second sources in the focal community.

Communities based on architectural innovations. Any community whose primary design was based on RISC technology was given a value of one for this dummy variable.

Community dominance. Economic theorists have implicitly equated dominance in an industry with increasing return with the standard's installed base, that is, the total number of units sold conforming to a given standard (David and Greenstein, 1990). One problem with simply using the number of units sold is that it assumes that products are homogeneous. That is, the role of technological change within a standard (a community in may case) is never addressed. Thus, while telephones are roughly equal, this is not the case with microprocessors. Simply counting up the number of microprocessors sold by a community would be misleading because there is significant heterogeneity in the value of these processors both within and across communities. In order to address this issue, I compute each community's installed sales base which is equal to the total value of all products ever sold by the community.

One problem that this operationalization shares with many of the mathematical models in the economics literature is that it does not take into account retirements.[8] Thus, I also use another measure of dominance, the community's sales in the previous quarter. The installed sales base reflects the cumulative history of the community, while sales in the previous quarter reflect the community's recent performance.

Quarterly sales for each community were constructed from 1975 to 1989 by using quarterly product shipment data supplied by the data research firm and multiplying it by pricing information obtained from *EDN*'s Annual Survey of Microprocessors. Annual price data were converted to quarterly measures by interpolating between years. Because the survey was published in November, the prices given were assumed to be for the fourth quarter.

One problem that arose was that the shipment data provided by the data research firm covered only 20 of the 30 communities. However, the remaining communities appeared to be quite small. To obtain an estimate for these missing values, I consulted the data research firm's estimates for microcomponent sales which included microprocessors, microcontrollers and microperipherals. In their data, the firm estimated the amount of sales in the market not included in their firm-level data. Over the period, this figure averaged 1.25 percent of total sales. Because microprocessors are the most visible component of this market, it is likely that this figure represents an upper bound for the percentage of sales encompassed by the communities' missing sales values. Consequently, 1.25 percent of the total sales calculated was equally allocated to the communities' missing sales values. Because the actual sales of the missing communities are very low relative to overall market sales, more complicated variations are not likely to affect the results. Before 1975 no unit shipment information was available. Consequently, Hypothesis 5, suggesting that more dominant communities would attract second sources at a higher rate, was only tested over the restricted time period.

Microprocessor sales. Overall quarterly microprocessor sales were used as a control in the models run over the entire time period. From 1975 onward, quarterly market sales were obtained by summing sales across all communities. Here, I use the growth rate in microcomponents published in *Electronics* to interpolate sales back to 1971. Because sales in 1975 are so small compared with later years, changes in the interpolation assumptions will not affect the results. This overall sales measure had a 0.99 correlation with total annual sales for the market that were estimated by the research firm between 1979 and 1989.

Innovation. Innovation occurred at the level of the community and was defined in two ways. An innovation of *Type I* occurred when a community member (usually the sponsor) shipped a product that was technological superior to anything previously produced by the community. A list of these types of innovations and their dates of occurrence were constructed for both communities defined at the level of the design and those defined at the level of the sponsor.

When the community was defined at the level of the sponsor, an additional definition of innovation was also used. Innovation *Type II* was defined as the introduction of a new design or an improvement in an existing design. Communities defined at the level of the sponsor may produce several designs. Sometimes, the first new product of a new design is not always the community's most advanced product. However, the introduction of a new design obviously involves creation, which is a key part of the innovative process. Thus, Innovation *Type II* counted a new design by an existing sponsor as an innovation, even if the sponsor had a product in another design group that was technologically superior.

The technological ranking of a product was determined by consulting Money's *Microprocessor Data Book* (1981, 1990) and descriptions of products given in *EDN*'s Annual Survey of Microprocessors. I classified a new product as being more technologically advanced than previous products if the firm made a significant architectural improvement that increased processor performance. Common types of improvement included increases in the internal or external databus size or an increase in the size or number of internal registers. Because the size of the databus determines how much information can be transmitted at one time, an increase from an 8- to a 16-bit bus size yields a significant performance improvement. Ranking the products was aided by the fact that both sources naturally compared the performance of new products by a sponsor to its previous products.

One community sponsored by Matsushita was excluded from this analysis because insufficient information was available on the technical characteristics of its products.[9] Using the dates of the innovations, a clock was constructed for each community which was reset to zero each time there was an innovation. Because a community entered the market, by definition, when it introduced its first product, this clock was collinear with age until a community introduced its second innovative product.[10] When the community was defined at the level of the sponsor, 43 innovations of *Type I* were recorded. Seven of these could only be determined to the nearest year and were randomly assigned to a quarter within that year.

Procedure

Entry rates of second sources into technological communities were estimated using the Poisson event count model. This model has commonly been used by organizational ecologists in estimating the founding rates over time within organizational populations (Carroll and Hannan, 1989; Hannan and Freeman, 1989). In analyzing this entry rate, the unit of analysis will be each community. Thus, each community will have an observation for each quarter that it is in existence. Two analyses will be performed: one with the sponsor forming the center of the community and one with the design forming the community center.

Social event counts often display overdispersion in that the variance of the dependent variable exceeds the mean. Overdispersion can be a serious problem when using the Poisson distribution because it can lead to erroneously small standard errors (Cameron and Trevedi, 1986). The accepted procedure in this case is to rerun these analyses using the negative binomial model and see if it significantly improves over the Poisson. Because the negative binomial model never significantly improved over the Poisson, use of the Poisson model is appropriate for these data.[11] Thus, the analyses reported here were undertaken using the Poisson model as described in the *LIMDEP User's Manual* (Greene, 1991).

RESULTS

Table 9.1 shows the results for second source entry into communities defined at the level of the sponsor. Model 1 uses a linear effect of community density, while Model 2 adds the squared effect. As expected from Hypothesis 1, the linear effect is positive, while the squared effect is negative and significant. Further, the inflection point at which the effect of density switches from increasing to decreasing entry rates occurs within the observed range of the data. Since each community behaves the way an organizational population does, this finding suggests that each community should be seen as a distinct organizational microenvironment.

Hypothesis 2a contended that the total number of communities in the population should deter second source entry, reasoning that a larger number would lessen potential entrants' ability to pick the likely "winner," thus reducing entry. On the other hand, Hypothesis 2b proposed the counter argument, namely, that the number of communities would influence second source entry in the manner predicted by Hannan's (1986) density-dependent theory of organizational evolution. As shown in Models 1 and 2, no support is found for Hypothesis 2a; the linear community density term has no significant effect. Model 3 adds the squared community density

Table 9.1 Poisson regression models of second source entry into communities (by quarter, community defined at the level of the sponsor).

Independent variables[a]	Models												
	1	2	3	4	5	6	7	8	9	10	11	12	13
Number of community members	0.267**	0.782**	0.716**	0.741**	0.693**	0.613**	0.566**	0.800**	0.969**	1.06**	1.01**	0.909**	0.851**
	(0.0710)	(0.194)	(0.194)	(0.203)	(0.204)	(0.206)	(0.207)	(0.201)	(0.216)	(0.229)	(0.229)	(0.236)	(0.237)
Number of community members²		-0.0532**	-0.0488**	-0.0621**	-0.0589**	-0.0599**	-0.0592**	-0.0645**	-0.0862**	-0.0974**	-0.0930**	-0.0879**	-0.0860**
		(0.0193)	(0.0192)	(0.0210)	(0.0208)	(0.0206)	(0.0206)	(0.0210)	(0.0238)	(0.0256)	(0.0255)	(0.0253)	(0.0251)
Second source support for other communities	-0.0513*	-0.0552**	-0.0678**	-0.107**	-0.108**	-0.110**	-0.104**	-0.0833**	-0.0757**	-0.0751**	-0.0752**	-0.0759**	-0.0702**
	(0.0254)	(0.0257)	(0.0267)	(0.0311)	(0.0310)	(0.0322)	(0.0311)	(0.0300)	(0.0307)	(0.0305)	(0.0304)	(0.0311)	(0.0303)
Number of other communities	0.0340	0.0141	0.373*	0.453*	0.476**	0.541**	0.575**	-0.189*	-0.191*	-0.195*	-0.198*	-0.175	-0.164
	(0.0641)	(0.0665)	(0.224)	(0.233)	(0.233)	(0.242)	(0.247)	(0.107)	(0.108)	(0.106)	(0.106)	(0.106)	(0.106)
Number of other communities²			-0.0187*	-0.0223**	-0.0231**	-0.0252**	-0.0266**						
			(0.0102)	(0.0104)	(0.0105)	(0.0107)	(0.0108)						
Community age	-0.118**	-0.0894	0.0790	0.115	0.119	0.192*	0.205**	0.102	0.0935	0.0817	0.0824	0.132	0.145
	(0.0554)	(0.0556)	(0.0563)	(0.0950)	(0.0946)	(0.0990)	(0.0959)	(0.0929)	(0.0951)	(0.0956)	(0.0952)	(0.0985)	(0.0955)
Microprocessor sales index	0.113	0.167	0.537**	0.285	0.293	0.249	0.259	0.129					
	(0.131)	(0.133)	(0.221)	(0.231)	(0.231)	(0.231)	(0.232)	(0.194)					
Community established by architectural innovation				2.94**	2.88**	2.92**	2.79**	2.83**	3.17**	3.31**	3.21**	3.07**	2.89**
				(1.07)	(1.06)	(1.05)	(1.02)	(1.05)	(1.07)	(1.06)	(1.05)	(1.04)	(1.01)
Community sales									0.960**				
									(0.430)				
Outside community sales									-0.0117	-0.0479	-0.0343	-0.0678	-0.0871
									(0.213)	(0.214)	(0.214)	(0.217)	(0.219)
Community installed base										0.110**	0.105**	0.0853**	0.0820**
										(0.0300)	(0.0375)	(0.0394)	(0.0392)
Time since innovation (Type I)						-0.221**						-0.166*	
						(0.0960)						(0.0983)	
Time since innovation (Type II)							-0.352**						-0.299**
							(0.121)						(0.122)
Constant	-2.71**	-3.26**	-4.52**	-4.99**	-4.99**	-5.08**	-5.14	-0.886	-1.09*	-1.11	-0.931	-0.861	-0.842
	(0.631)	(0.684)	(1.20)	(1.27)	(1.27)	(1.33)	(1.37)	(1.14)	(1.17)	(1.20)	(1.15)	(1.14)	(1.13)
-2 × log likelihood	372.0	362.9	359.3	351.5	355.07	348.9	344.0	341.5	337.8	335.3	339.0	335.8	331.5
Number or events	52	52	52	52	52	52	52	51	51	51	51	51	51
N	948	948	948	948	889	889	889	913	913	913	854	854	854

** $p < 0.05$; * $p < 0.10$
[a] Standard errors are in parentheses.

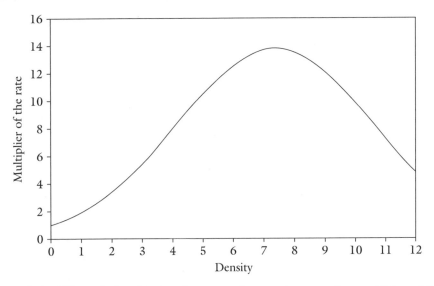

Figure 9.2 Effect of the density of community members on the multiplier of the rate of second source entry.

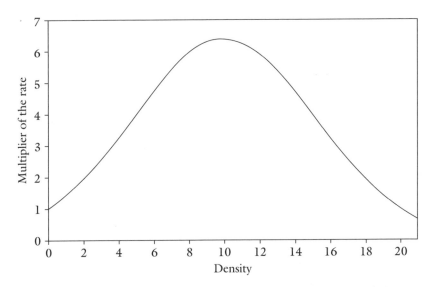

Figure 9.3 Effect of the density of communities on the multiplier of the rate of second source entry.

term to the equation. Consistent with Hypothesis 2b, the linear term becomes positive and significant, while the squared term becomes negative and significant. Apparently, density dependence operates at two levels. Importantly, the inflection points at which further increases in density lead to a decrease in the entry rate fall within the observed range of the data for both community density and second source density (see figures 9.2 and 9.3).

Hypothesis 3 predicted that the more second source support other communities had, the lower would be the entry rate into the focal community. As expected, this variable is negative and significant (see Model 3). Testing Hypothesis 4, Model 4 adds a variable indicating whether a community was established by the introduction of an architectural innovation. As can be seen, this type of community attracts second sources at a higher rate than others. Hypothesis 6 predicted that communities that had innovated more recently would attract organizational support at a higher rate. Because one community was excluded for lack of innovation data, Model 5 reestimates Model 4 using the slightly smaller data set. Importantly, the results do not change, indicating that the exclusion did not affect the results. Models 6 and 7 support Hypothesis 6, showing that firms that have innovated more recently attract second sources at a higher rate. Moreover, the results are consistent across both types of innovation discussed in the Methods section.

Hypothesis 5 predicted that dominant communities would have higher rates of second source entry than smaller, less dominant communities. Dominance was measured by the estimated total sales by the network the previous quarter, and by the community's installed sales base (the value of all processors ever sold by the community). Since this information was available only from 1975 onward, Model 8 reestimates Model 4 over this period only to see if the results reported previously are sensitive to the dropping of the earlier observations. The number of other communities squared is no longer significant and was not included in the model, while the linear term is negative and significant. The fact that the number of communities do not have their expected curvilinear effect should not necessarily be taken as a refutation of Hypothesis 2b because this analysis was not done over the entire period. In fact, this finding is not surprising since the linear effect signifies the legitimation process and would be expected to have the greatest impact early in the population's history. The fact that the linear effect becomes negative lends support to this interpretation and suggests that the microprocessor market had become "taken-for-granted" (legitimated) by 1975. Moreover, Hannan and Carroll (1992) have suggested that it is important to test density dependence over the entire history of the population and note that studies that do not support the theory often have truncated observation windows.[12] Still, however, this result should only be taken as suggestive since the two primary data sources only extended back to 1975. Recall that the data were extended back to 1971 using the first shipment dates given in *IC Master*.

Models 9 and 10 separately add each community's sales and its installed sales base. These measures are significant in the expected positive direction (Hypothesis 5). Model 11 reestimates Model 10 using the restricted sample containing the innovation data and the results do not change. Models 12 and 13 add the time since innovation to the analyses. As expected from Hypothesis 5, these variables are significant in the expected negative direction.[13] With the exception of the number of other communities in the market (which while still negative drops from significance), the earlier results do not change.

Table 9.2 reanalyzes entry rates, but defines the community at the level of the design. Overall, the results are very similar to those in table 9.1. However, as seen in Models 1–3, the number of other communities (in this case, designs) has no effect on entry rates of second sources. Recall that in table 9.1 the effects of this variable

Table 9.2 Poisson regression models of second source entry into communities (by quarter, community defined at the design level).

Independent variables[a]	Models										
	1	2	3	4	5	6	7	8	9	10	11
Number of community members	0.315** (0.0726)	0.725** (0.185)	0.712** (0.184)	0.731** (0.181)	0.694** (0.188)	0.653** (0.194)	0.733** (0.185)	0.890** (0.203)	0.960** (0.210)	0.918** (0.211)	0.880** (0.221)
Number of community members^2		-0.0409** (0.0173)	-0.0398** (0.0173)	-0.0446** (0.0180)	-0.0424** (0.0180)	-0.0471** (0.0181)	-0.0436** (0.0179)	-0.0629** (0.0210)	-0.0708** (0.0220)	-0.0678** (0.0220)	-0.0704** (0.0222)
Second source support for other communities	-0.0530** (0.0256)	-0.0524** (0.0258)	-0.0517** (0.0258)	-0.0615** (0.0274)	-0.0635** (0.0272)	-0.0629** (0.0272)	-0.0486* (0.0284)	-0.0386 (0.0290)	-0.0377 (0.0287)	-0.0391 (0.0285)	-0.0394 (0.0285)
Number of other communities	0.0808 (0.0627)	0.0598 (0.0641)	0.215 (0.193)	0.0657 (0.0649)	-0.0707 (0.0645)	-0.0882 (0.0654)	-0.0655 (0.0973)	-0.0750 (0.0986)	-0.0730 (0.0968)	-0.0768 (0.0970)	-0.0490 (0.0972)
Number of other communities^2			-0.00710 (0.00798)								
Community age	-0.173** (0.0571)	-0.158** (0.0566)	-0.157** (0.0567)	-0.102 (0.0763)	-0.0946 (0.0759)	-0.0147 (0.0831)	-0.101 (0.0767)	-0.121 (0.0798)	-0.141* (0.0820)	-0.135* (0.0816)	-0.0713 (0.0879)
Mircroprocessor sales	0.0790 (0.123)	0.126 (0.124)	0.295 (0.223)	0.0197 (0.158)	0.0102 (0.158)	-0.0766 (0.160)	0.171 (0.177)				
Community established by architectural innovation				0.941 (0.828)	0.936 (0.821)	1.00 (0.799)	0.925 (0.830)	1.14 (0.849)	1.21 (0.853)	1.18 (0.844)	1.15 (0.818)
Community sales								0.959** (0.423)			
Outside community sales								0.0670 (0.193)	0.0383 (0.196)	0.0455 (0.195)	-0.0276 (0.197)
Community installed base									0.106** (0.0368)	0.104** (0.0369)	0.0896** (0.0388)
Time since innovation						-0.232** (0.0973)					-0.202** (0.0994)
Constant	-3.38** (0.717)	-3.73** (0.743)	-4.42** (1.18)	-3.83** (0.753)	-3.78** (0.747)	-3.72** (0.759)	-2.02* (1.22)	-2.14* (1.24)	-2.20* (1.23)	-2.03 (1.24)	-2.15* (1.23)
-2 × log likelihood	419.4	413.3	412.5	412.0	409.56	403.08	399.8	396.4	394.0	391.4	386.8
	57	57	57	57	57	57	56	56	56	56	56
N	1125	1125	1125	1125	1066	1066	1078	1078	1078	1019	1019

** $p < 0.05$; * $p < 0.10$

[a] Standard errors are in parentheses.

conformed to density dependence. Apparently, it is the presence of a sponsor, not simply a design, which leads to the legitimation and competition effects of the density-based theory. In retrospect, this result is not too surprising since in evaluating the likely survival of a new technology early on, when there are, for instance, two designs in the market, a new sponsor rather than a sponsor producing a second design is likely to have a greater legitimating effect. In the first case, the technology will not perish if one of the sponsors fails, while in the second it will.

Another difference in results using this level of analysis is that the architectural innovation dummy no longer has a positive and significant effect. This finding should not be too surprising since two of the design communities based on architectural innovations were introduced by former sponsors, Intel and Motorola. Because Henderson and Clark (1990) predict that older firms will experience great difficulty in adjusting to architectural innovations, including these communities in that category understandably weakens the effects of the architectural innovation dummy. Apparently, existing sponsors that create a second design that is an architectural innovation are handicapped by their existing routines that were ingrained in their development of the first design. The only other anomaly from the analyses at this level is that second source support for other communities is no longer significant once community sales is added to the analysis. Other effects in table 9.2 parallel those of table 9.1.

Overall, the results for second source entry are more consistent for the analyses in which communities are defined at the level of the sponsor. All six hypotheses are supported when communities are defined at the level of the sponsor, while I only find support for three hypotheses when the community is defined at the level of the design. In retrospect, as discussed above, part of this difference may be due to the fact that each way of defining a community may have slightly different theoretical implications. The greater support found for communities defined at the level of the sponsor, as well as the effects of organizational level variables, does suggest that a sociological approach is valuable and that researchers investigating the evolution of standards, particularly those taking an economics approach, need to take into account organization level variables. Further, this pattern supports Hawley (1950), who suggested that the center of the community is the dominant player that integrates and administers its interdependencies – in this case, the sponsor.

DISCUSSION AND CONCLUSIONS

This paper has identified factors which influence the rate at which firms join technological communities. In so doing, I have identified processes influencing the development of technological bandwagons. Below, I first discuss why organizational support is a valuable resource in industries characterized by network externalities and how the present study supports that view. After this, I discuss how technological bandwagons develop and explore the strategic implications of the findings. I conclude by suggesting that the community level of analysis can be a powerful conceptual and empirical tool in increasing our understanding of cycles of technological change.

Organizational support as a resource

The present study suggests that organizational support is a valuable resource for firms in a community. Consistent with the economic literature on standards (Gallini, 1984), I find second source entry into a focal community is reduced when there are a large number of second sources supporting other communities. Moreover, in a complementary study, Wade (1993) finds that increased second source support also reduces the entry rate of new sponsors into the market. Effectively, this means that sponsors who are able to gain increased organizational support can both discourage competition from other potential sponsors, as well as reduce the rate at which existing communities can garner organizational support.

Banbury and Mitchell (1995) also offer some evidence that having many followers introduce similar products enhances the market share of those first to market. Moreover, they find that increased market share reduces failure rates. Because sponsors are in a sense first movers and second sources are followers that by definition produce identical products, these findings may suggest that organizational support might also have a positive impact on a sponsor's market share and indirectly increase its survival chances. More research is needed to determine the conditions under which increased organizational support produces increased performance.

Undoubtedly, extensive organizational support should have other significant effects on community members and on the evolution of markets which have not yet been addressed. For instance, the product life cycle literature has been the subject of much criticism because there is no clear specification of the forces which drive the product through its life cycle and little consideration of the different competitive positions of firms in the market (Boyd and Walker, 1990; Lambkin and Day, 1989). In particular, it has been difficult for analysts to explain variations from the expected bell-type curve. The present study may be able to address why some products and product classes never progress past the introductory stage, but simply perish as sales never take off. Possibly, in markets with increasing returns, one factor which may determine if the product class (or at a lower level of analysis, the product form) enters the growth stage may be the level of organizational support that it is able to attract. In addition, research is needed to determine how these benefits are distributed across community members. Are they evenly distributed or do sponsors derive the lion's share of these benefits?

Technological bandwagons and strategy

This study has also shed light on how technological bandwagons may develop. The findings suggest that small differences in network size may have disproportionate effects on the ultimate outcome (Arthur, 1989; Katz and Shapiro, 1985; Farrell and Saloner, 1985; Swann, 1987). In particular, the finding here that the total processor sales by a community throughout its history increases entry by second sources suggests that small differences in sales initially may be important. Communities with higher sales early on attract second sources which, in turn, increases the production capacity of the community. Possibly, the existence of more organizational support also makes the community more attractive to customers and generates increased sales. Empirical research is needed to investigate these linkages to performance.

The finding that, early on, the addition of each new community member accelerates the rate at which second sources join a community indicates that early success by a sponsor in attracting second sources may be critical. It suggests that, initially, the addition of one community member may produce a bandwagon effect, increasing the probability of gaining further organizational support and of having the community become legitimated and "taken-for-granted" (Meyer, 1983; Meyer and Rowan, 1977). Because legitimation is a source of increasing returns, it suggests that, consistent with Arthur (1989) and Chakravarthy (1994), differences in entry patterns between communities, early on, can have a critical impact on success. Apple, for instance, is now attempting to reverse its strategy of discouraging vendors from cloning its personal computer. Most analysts feel, however, that Apple's window of opportunity has passed and that they will be unsuccessful in attracting organizational support (*Wall Street Journal*, 1994).

Because small differences can generate these bandwagon effects, it is not inconceivable that chance could play a large role. Thus, one community may gain substantial organizational support, while another does not simply because two firms decided to join it for idiosyncratic reasons. In turn, other entrants use the fact that the previous two firms joined as a signal that the community is viable and also enter, creating a bandwagon effect. Of course, those two firms that started the bandwagon rolling may have joined after a calculated decision process. Possibly, that community offered technical assistances or had a liberal licencing policy. One possible strategy for a sponsor, then, might be to make joining particularly attractive, early on, by offering extensive technical support to the first few second sources. In turn, their entry may generate bandwagon effects which induce others to join, regardless of whether they are offered the same technical assistance.

Of course, the ability of a sponsor to attract second sources may be a double-edged sword. Early on, organizational support may legitimize a community's designs and increase its viability. However, second sources also represent competition and may be undesirable (Swann, 1987). For example, while the IBM personal computer (PC) clearly dominates the market, IBM's position in this market has eroded greatly over time. While IBM had captured 75 percent of the market in the early 1980s, its market share dropped to just under 12 percent by 1991 (*Business Week*, 1991b) because of competition from clone manufacturers. If, however, the processes investigated here apply to all forms of organizational support, it suggests a possible strategy for sponsors in industries that have proprietary control over their technology and designs.

Barnett (1990) suggests that differentiated populations that are complementary will be mutualistic, while those that are not differentiated will compete. Thus, increasing organizational support for complementary products should yield the benefits of having increased organizational support without the competition. For instance, an increased number of firms manufacturing associated hardware and software should increase the value of the community to customers, and raise entry barriers for potential competitors without the possible detrimental effect of increased competition to the sponsor. Thus, a viable strategy for a sponsor with proprietary control over its technology may be to restrict access to the components that it manufactures, but allow access and, in fact, use the strategies outlined above, to encourage entry by firms into associated products. This strategy is consistent with that of Morris and Ferguson (1993), who suggested that defining and maintaining ownership of a system's critical architecture can be a source of competitive advantage.

Often, however, retaining strict control of a system's critical architecture may not be a viable option if sponsors have only limited proprietary control over their products, as in this industry. Moreover, new sponsors may need to share their primary technology with rivals or direct competitors (an open systems strategy) in order to attract manufacturers of associated components since these vendors are more likely to be attracted to a community which already has a large installed base (Garud and Kumaraswamy, 1995). Garud and Kumaraswamy (1993) note, however, that sponsors adopting an open systems strategy have several advantages. Being the sponsor of an open system allows the sponsor to retain a competitive advantage because of the time lag between its implementation of the technology and its diffusion to others (Garud and Kumaraswamy, 1993). Thus, if the sponsor has core competencies that allow upgradability of components and skills, the sponsor will enjoy transient monopoly positions as it brings upgrades of its technology to market faster than rivals can imitate (Garud and Kumaraswamy, 1993, 1995; MacMillan, McCaffery, and Wijk, 1985).

The finding that sponsor communities based on architectural innovations gain increased organizational support also has compelling strategic implications. The architectural innovation introduced here – RISC technology – did not appear until relatively late in the industry's development. During this period there were a high number of technological communities with a wide range of organizational support already on the market. Moreover, the market was extremely concentrated, as Intel-based processors had captured over 50 percent of the market. Apparently, despite this competitive pressure architectural innovations are able to garner higher than expected organizational support. Perhaps this occurs because, as Henderson and Clark (1990) suggest, existing sponsors find it difficult to copy the new technology successfully. This competitive disadvantage lowers entry barriers for sponsors of architectural innovations and their supporters.

This finding suggests that a viable strategy for potential sponsors in crowded markets may be to concentrate their efforts on developing products that are architectural innovations rather than on products that are simply incremental extensions of the existing technology. Indeed, in an earlier study of this market, Wade (1993) found that higher concentration led to the increased entry of specialist sponsors, primarily those specializing in RISC technology. He speculated, consistent with resource partitioning (Carroll, 1985), that in periods of high concentration existing generalist communities primarily serve the center of the market where economies of scale can be most easily achieved. This crowding of the center of the market may open up pockets of resources (or new niches) at the periphery of the market where specialists can thrive, particularly those specialists whose technology is based on an architectural innovation. Initially, incumbents will be unlikely to see the new niche as attractive because economies of scale will not be present. Moreover, because the technology is an architectural innovation, incumbents will have great difficulty in copying the new products. Thus, when these communities based on architectural innovations first emerge, they may represent opportunities for potential second sources and producers of associated products. Because communities based on architectural innovations attract increased organizational support, potential entrants can join such a community, early in its history, and enjoy first mover advantages, while at the same time minimizing the risk of joining the "wrong" community – one that will be unable to attract additional organizational support and subsequently be unsuccessful in the market.

Conclusions

This study illustrates that in industries with increasing returns firms cannot be considered atomistically. Competing technologies and standards can usefully be envisioned as separate organizational communities, each supported by a set of interdependent populations. This study, however, has barely scratched the surface. In fact, the interorganizational relationships examined here represent only a small part of the relevant linkages. Here, technological communities were centered around designs or sponsors, with second sources as members. As Tushman and Rosenkopf (1992) point out, relationships with suppliers, professional associations, universities, customers, and suppliers of complementary products will surely have an impact on the evolution of technologies. Examining a broader set of community linkages is a promising avenue for future research.

Similarly, a broad number of outcomes could be considered using this approach at multiple levels of analysis. For example, while Wade (1993) has examined the entry rate of communities into the market, no research thus far has investigated the factors leading to the success or failure of individual communities. Similarly, the performance of an individual firm is likely to be a reflection of its position in a community, and its strategy, as well as its community's role in the broader macrocommunity. In this market, for example, second sources throughout the market could be viewed as a strategic group because they follow a similar strategy of imitation. Future research could compare and investigate the relative effects of strategy and community-level variables on firm performance.

At a broader level, a community level of analysis can enhance our understanding of the evolution of standards and dominant designs. Anderson and Tushman (1990: 605) note that multiple disciplines suggest that "technological change can fruitfully be characterized as a sociocultural process of variation, selection and retention," Similarly, Abernathy and Utterback (1982) have described technological change in an industry as periods of intense variation in products when the industry first emerges followed by incremental process innovations as the industry matures. The period of incremental innovation is often triggered by the emergence (or selection) of a dominant design or standard. Similar models have been put forward by Sahal (1981) and Tushman and Anderson (1986), and applied to a wide variety of settings, including products as diverse as the typewriter (David, 1985) and the automobile (Abernathy, 1978).

By examining processes within and between communities researchers may be able to model these technology cycles directly. Variation or the emergence of new designs and alternative standards can be directly modeled as the emergence of new communities. Similarly, processes that increase the failure rate of entire communities can be tied to the emergence of a dominant design or standard. In short, by using a community-level framework, researchers have a conceptual and empirical tool that may enable them to get further inside the black box of technological change (Rosenberg, 1982).

ACKNOWLEDGEMENTS

I am grateful for the comments that I received on this research from David Barron, Glenn Carroll, Charles O'Reilly, Michael Hout, Joseph Porac, three anonymous *Strategic Management Journal* reviewers and participants in the *Strategic Management Journal* special issue conference on Technological Change and the New Competitive Landscape. Thanks are also due to Jack Brittain, Jon Green, David Howell, William D. Mensch and Paul Magin, who provided data and insight into the industry.

NOTES

Key words: organizational ecology; technology; standards; networks

1   Tushman and Rosenkopf (1992) and Rosenkopf and Tushman (1994) argue that the product class, which may contain multiple technologies or standards, defines the boundary of the organizational community. I argue in this paper, however, that each technology or standard can be viewed as forming a separate organizational community.

2   The community construct is related to but conceptually distinct from the term strategic group. A community defined at the level of the design consists of a set of interdependent populations bound to a particular design. In the IBM personal computer's case, one such population is those firms that produce software for the IBM personal computer. A strategic group, on the other hand, consists of firms following similar strategies (Porter, 1980). In this instance, it could be argued that all firms producing software for any type of personal computer (Apple or IBM) and those producing software for the more scientifically oriented workstation market form two strategic groups. Of course, there may be important differences in the strategies followed (or in their access to resources) by these software producers that would argue for more fine grained strategic groups. In any case, however, the strategic group concept cuts across community boundaries.

3   Microcontrollers is a market that is related to the microprocessor market. Here, however, I investigate only microprocessors since industry insiders that I interviewed viewed the two products as being in separate markets. For more details on the differences between the two markets, see Wade (1993).

4   Zucker (1989) has suggested that density and density squared are simply *indicators* of two unobservable variables, competition and legitimation (Zucker, 1989). The view taken here, however, corresponds with that of Hannan and Carroll (1992), who argue that "growth in density controls these processes – it does not reflect them, as the language of *indicators* connotes. Increasing density combines with other social processes in conveying institutional standing as taken-for-grantedness. Growth in density relative to the abundance of resources that sustains a population intensifies competition." It should also be noted that the idea of legitimation as taken-for-grantedness is different and distinct from coercive isomorphism (Dimaggio and Powell, 1983) or conformity to institutional rules.

5   Anderson and Tushman (1990) speculate that dominant designs may not emerge if demand is low or if technological competition is cut short. They further suggest that a dominant design may also not emerge in product classes with limited demand or where there is a demand for custom-made products. None of these conditions exist in the microprocessor market.

6   The data were obtained on the condition that the research firm's identity be kept confidential.

7   Secondary sources as well as extensive industry histories were examined to determine if any products introduced in the early period had disappeared prior to *IC Master*'s first publication in 1976 and no conclusive evidence was found. Although great care was taken in examining the early history of the industry, the absence of any definitive source made it possible that some error could be present. For instance, it recently came to my attention (from a supplementary source) that Texas Instruments may have manufactured a clone of Intel's 8008 for a brief period, prior to 1975.

8   On the one hand, calculating the installed sales base as the total value of all processors sold by a community introduces some error since it does not take into account micro-processor retirements by customers. On the other hand, however, a customer's likeli-hood of purchasing subsequent processors from the community may increase with each processor purchased because of learning by doing (Arrow, 1962). That is, the firm's prior experience is likely to be devalued if it switches to another community's processors. Similarly, continued experience with a community may strengthen social ties (Granovetter, 1985) between customers and the community, making defection less likely.

9   It was difficult to evaluate SPARC community products because Sun requires only software compatibility from its members. *EDN*, a journal that evaluates all the micro-processors each year, did not note any major differences in the technological capabilities of the SPARC processors. Thus it was assumed that these processors were at the same approximate technological level. Only one SPARC member, Fujitsu, introduced more than one compatible SPARC processor during the period studied. It was not clear if this processor was superior to its previous one or simply a variation. Some evidence in *EDN* suggested it was simply a stripped down version of the previous processor and thus no innovations were counted for this community. Supplementary analyses were run, however, to test the sensitivity of the results to this assumption and the results did not change.

10 A reviewer made the point that the introduction of a new design was a more radical change than an improvement in an existing design and suggested that these two types of innovation be separated. Because only a small number of designs were introduced by incumbent sponsors (eight out of 38), however, this variable would be collinear with age.

11 Because the negative binomial simply adds an estimate for overdispersion, the Poisson and the negative binomial are nested models. Moreover, because -2 times the likelihood ratio is chi squared distributed, it is possible to compare the models' goodness of fit by taking the difference between the likelihood ratios of the two models using one degree of freedom. In no case did this difference ever approach the critical value of 3.84 ($p < 0.05$). Thus, the use of the Poisson model is appropriate. An additional model which has recently been developed for these types of data is the quasi-likelihood model which corrects for autocorrelation (Barron, 1992). However, because this model uses the overdispersion term to correct for autocorrelation, it is not appropriate for these data since this term is insignificant and effectively zero (Barron, personal communication).

12 While I suggest that the reason that the nonmonotonic effect of the number of commun-ities disappears is because of the truncated observation period, it could be argued that

the models' run over the entire period are not fully specified. That is, the effects of the number of communities might disappear if I controlled for the dominance of the communities. While I do not have sales data for individual communities prior to 1975, it is possible to perform some sensitivity analyses. In one case, I assumed that the installed sales base for each community prior to 1975 remained at its 1975 level. In another analysis, I make the extreme assumption that the installed sales base for each community is zero prior to 1975. In both cases, the number of communities has the nonmonotonic effect predicted by Hypothesis 2b. Thus (while still possible), it appears unlikely that the confirmation of Hypothesis 2b in models covering the entire time period simply occurs because the model is not fully specified.

13 An anonymous reviewer suggested that higher average rates of innovation could actually decrease entry by second sources. Higher rates could produce higher uncertainty about successful entry on the part of second sources due to the emergence of improved designs from the sponsor before entry costs are recovered. To rule out this possibility, I included in supplementary models the total number of innovations introduced by a community up to the time of measurement. After age is controlled for, a high value for this variable reflects a high average rate of innovation. However, this variable was never negative and significant as the above argument would suggest.

REFERENCES

Abernathy, W. J. (1978). *The Productivity Dilemma*. Johns Hopkins University Press, Baltimore, MD.

Abernathy, W. J. and J. M. Utterback (1982). "Patterns of industrial innovation." In M. L. Tushman and W. Moore (eds.), *Readings in the Management of Innovation*. Pitman Publishing, Marshfield, MA, pp. 97–108.

Abrahamson, E. and L. Rosenkopf (1993). "Institutional and competitive bandwagons: Using mathematical modeling as a tool to explore innovation diffusion," *Academy of Management Review*, 18, pp. 487–517.

Anderson, P. and M. L. Tushman (1990). "Technological discontinuities and dominant designs: A cyclical model of technological change," *Administrative Science Quarterly*, 35, pp. 604–33.

Arrow, K. J. (1962). "The economic implications of learning by doing," *Review of Economic Studies*, 29, pp. 155–73.

Arthur, W. B. (1989). "Competing technologies, increasing returns, and lock-in by historical events," *Economic Journal*, 99, pp. 116–31.

Banbury, C. M. and W. Mitchell (1995). "The effect of introducing important incremental innovations on market share and business survival," *Strategic Management Journal*, Summer Special Issue, 16, pp. 161–82.

Barnett, W. P. (1990). "The organizational ecology of a technological system," *Administrative Science Quarterly*, 35, pp. 31–60.

Barron, D. N. (1992). "The analysis of count data: Overdispersion and autocorrelation." In P. V. Marsden (ed.), *Sociological Methodology*, Vol. 22. Blackwell, Cambridge, MA, pp. 179–220.

Baum, J. A. C. and H. Korn, and S. Kotha (1995). "Dominant designs and population dynamics in telecommunications services: Founding and failure of facsimile transmission service organizations, 1965–1992," *Social Science Research*, 24, 97–135.

Boyd, H. W. and O. C. Walker (1990). *Marketing Management: A Strategic Approach*. Irwin, Homewood, IL.

Business Week (10 June 1991a). "Computer confusion: A jumble of competing, conflicting standards is chilling the market," pp. 72–8.

Business Week (17 June 1991b). "IBM: As markets and technology change can Big Blue remake its culture?," p. 29.

Cameron, A. and P. Trevedi (1986). "Econometric models based on count data: Comparisons and applications of some estimators and tests," *Journal of Applied Econometrics*, 1, pp. 29–53.

Carroll, G. R. (1985). "Concentration and specialization: Dynamics of niche width in populations of organizations," *American Journal of Sociology*, 90, pp. 1262–83.

Carroll, G. R. and J. R. Harrison (1994). "On the historical efficiency of competition between organizational populations," *American Journal of Sociology*, 100, pp. 720–49.

Carroll, G. R. and M. T. Hannan (1989). "Density dependence in the evolution of populations of newspaper organizations," *American Sociological Review*, 54, pp. 524–41.

Chakravarthy, B. (1994). "Competing in turbulent industries: In search of a framework," paper presented at the *Strategic Management Journal*'s Special Issue Conference on Technological Change and the New Competitive Landscape, University of North Carolina, Chapel Hill, NC.

David, P. (1985). "Clio and the economics of QWERTY," *Economic History*, 75, pp. 332–7.

David, P. and S. Greenstein (1990). "The economics of compatibility standards: An introduction to recent research," *Economics of Innovation and New Technology*, 1, pp. 3–42.

Dess, G. G. and D. Beard (1984). "Dimensions of organizational task environments," *Administrative Science Quarterly*, 29, pp. 52–73.

Dewar, R. D. and J. E. Dutton (1986). "The adoption of radical and incremental innovations: An empirical analysis," *Management Science*, 32, pp. 1422–33.

Dimaggio, P. J. (1986). "Structural analysis of organizational fields: A blockmodel approach." In B. M. Staw and L. L. Cummings (eds.), *Research in Organizational Behavior*, Vol. 8. JAI Press, CT, pp. 335–70.

Dimaggio, P. J. and W. W. Powell (1983). "The iron cage revisited: Institutional isomorphism and collective rationality in organizational fields," *American Sociological Review*, 48, pp. 147–60.

Dosi, G. (1982). "Technological paradigms and technological trajectories: A suggested interpretation of the determinants and directions of technological change," *Research Policy*, 11, pp. 147–62.

EDN (various years). Cahner's Publishing Company, Boston, MA.

Electronics (various years). Penton Publishing, San Jose, CA.

Farrell, J. and G. Saloner (1985). "Standardization, compatibility, and innovation," *Rand Journal of Economics*, 16, pp. 71–83.

Fischer, C. S. and G. R. Carroll (1988). "Telephone and automobile diffusion in the United States, 1902–1937," *American Journal of Sociology*, 93, pp. 1153–78.

Gallini, N. T. (1984). "Strategic deterrence by market sharing: Licensing in research and development markets," *American Economic Review*, 74, pp. 93–141.

Garud, R. and A. Kumaraswamy (1993). "Changing competitive dynamics in network industries: An exploration of Sun Microsystems' open systems strategy," *Strategic Management Journal*, 14(5), pp. 351–69.

Garud, R. and A. Kumaraswamy (1995). "Technological and organizational designs for realizing economies of substitution," *Strategic Management Journal*, Summer Special Issue, 16, pp. 93–109.

Granovetter, M. (1985). "Economic action and social structure: The problem of embeddedness," *American Journal of Sociology*, 91, pp. 481–510.

Greene, W. H. (1991). *LIMDEP, Version 6.0: Users Manual.* Econometric Software, New York.

Hannan, M. (1986). "A model of competitive and institutional processes in organizational ecology," Technical Report 86–13. Department of Sociology, Cornell University, Ithaca, NY.

Hannan, M. T. and J. Freeman (1989). *Organizational Ecology.* Harvard University Press, Cambridge, MA.

Hannan, M. T. and G. R. Carroll (1992). *Dynamics of Organizational Populations.* Oxford University Press, New York.

Hawley, A. (1950). *Human Ecology.* Ronald Press, New York.

Henderson, R. M. and K. B. Clark (1990). "Architectural innovation: The reconfiguration of existing firms," *Administrative Science Quarterly*, 35, pp. 9–30.

IC Master (various years). United Technical Publications, Garden City, New York.

Katz, M. and C. Shapiro (1985). "Network externalities, competition, and compatibility," *American Economic Review*, 75, pp. 424–40.

Lambkin, M. and G. S. Day (1989). "Evolutionary processes in competitive markets: Beyond the product life cycle," *Journal of Marketing*, 53, pp. 4–20.

Lieberman, M. B. and D. B. Montgomery (1988). "First-mover advantages," *Strategic Management Journal*, Summer Special Issue, 9, pp. 41–58.

MacMillan, I., M. L. McCaffery and G. V. Wijk (1985). "Competitor responses to easily imitated products," *Strategic Management Journal*, 6(1), pp. 75–86.

Meyer, J. W. (1983). "Institutionalization and the rationality of formal organizational structure." In J. W. Meyer and W. R. Scott (eds.), *Organizational Environments: Ritual and Rationality.* Sage, Beverly Hills, CA, pp. 261–82.

Meyer, J. W. and B. Rowan (1977). "Institutionalized organizations: Formal structure as myth and ceremony," *American Journal of Sociology*, 83, pp. 340–63.

Microprocessors and Microsystems (various years). Butterworth Heinemann, Oxford, UK.

Money, S. A. (1981). *Microprocessor Data Book.* McGraw-Hill, New York.

Money, S. A. (1990). *Microprocessor Data Book* (2nd ed.). Academic Press, San Diego, CA.

Morris, C. R. and C. H. Ferguson (1993). "How architecture wins technology wars," *Harvard Business Review*, pp. 86–96.

Porter, M. E. (1980). *Competitive Strategy: Techniques for Analyzing Industries and Competitors.* Free Press, New York.

Porter, M. E. (1985). *Competitive Advantage: Creating and Sustaining Superior Advantage.* Free Press, New York.

Predicast's F&S Indexes (various years). Predicast, Cleveland, OH.

Rogers, E. M. and J. K. Larsen (1984). *Silicon Valley Fever: Growth of High Technology Culture.* Basic Books, New York.

Rosenberg, N. (1982). *Inside the Black Box: Technology and Economics.* Cambridge University Press, New York.

Rosenkopf, L. and M. L. Tushman (1994). "Community organization and technological evolution: Inter-organizational cooperation over the technology cycle," working paper, Wharton School, University of Pennsylvania.

Sahal, D. (1981). *Patterns of Technological Innovation.* Addison-Wesley, Reading, MA.

Swann, G. M. P. (1986). *Quality Innovation: An Economic Analysis of Rapid Improvements in Microelectronic Components.* Frances Pinter Publishers, London.

Swann, G. M. P. (1987). "Industry standard microprocessors and the strategy of second source production." In H. Landis Gabel (ed.), *Product Standardization and Competitive Strategy.* Elsevier, Amsterdam, pp. 239–62.

Tushman, M. L. and P. Anderson (1986). "Technological discontinuities and organization environments," *Administrative Science Quarterly*, 31, pp. 439–65.

Tushman, M. L. and L. Rosenkopf (1992). "On the organizational determinants of technological change: Towards a sociology of technological evolution." In B. Staw and L. Cummings
(eds.), *Research in Organizational Behavior*, Vol. 14. JAI Press, Greenwich, CT., pp. 311–
47.

Wade, J. (1993). "Organizational sources of technological designs in the microprocessor
market," University of Illinois Faculty Working Paper 93–0151.

Wall Street Journal (17 October 1994). "Playing catchup, Apple finally gives in and attempts
cloning, but it's awfully late," p. A1.

Webbink, D. W. (1997). *The Semiconductor Industry: A Survey of Structure, Conduct, and
Performance*. Staff Report to the Federal Trade Commission. US Government Printing
Office, Washington, DC.

Weigelt, K. and C. Camerer (1988). "Reputation and corporate strategy: A review of recent
theory and applications," *Strategic Management Journal*, 9(5), pp. 443–54.

Wernerfelt, B. (1984). "A Resource-based view of the firm." *Strategic Management Journal*,
5(2), pp. 171–80.

Zucker, L. (1989). "No legitimacy, no history (Comment on Carroll and Hannan)," *American Sociological Review*, 54, pp. 542–45.

COMMENTARY
James Wade

Introduction

At the time that I wrote this paper, I was attempting to fill what I felt were some
important gaps in the literature. One of these gaps was primarily empirical. While
theorists had suggested that one of the factors driving a technology's success was the
level of organizational support that it received, little research had empirically investigated the process by which a given technology gained such support. Because prior
work suggested that whether or not a technology gains organizational support
can determine its future viability, I felt that understanding the process by which this
occurs is of key importance to both firms sponsoring new technologies and technology researchers.

On a broader level, while much work in this area implied that rival technologies
are supported by multiple populations and that a community level perspective was
called for, relatively little research had used this approach. Tushman and Rosenkopf
(1992) were an exception in that they conceived of communities as being defined by
different groups involved in a battle for technological dominance within a product
class (see also Garud and Rappa, 1994). In their view, each community contains
multiple populations supporting different standards.

Because I felt that standards create boundaries between actors within the same
product class, I took a slightly different approach in defining communities. I defined
each standard as being a community, each of which was supported by multiple
populations. What I feel is beneficial about this approach is that it allows us to
examine competitive and mutualistic interactions at multiple levels of analysis. We
can examine not only interactions between populations supporting different technological standards, but also interactions between populations supporting the same
standard. In this commentary I will first address what I feel are some of the most

interesting issues raised by the study and discuss areas in which future research might prove fruitful. In so doing, I will attempt to tease out connections between my original arguments and other relevant research in the area. Finally, I will address how some of these ideas are of growing importance in the evolving internet economy.

Technological variation and standard setting

I felt that one of the most interesting findings in the paper was that technological standards based on architectural innovations attracted high levels of organizational support. Such communities are likely to have an advantage because competitors using older technologies may tend to misunderstand the new technology because interrelationships between key components have changed. Essentially, incumbents are hampered by their old architectural knowledge which is of dubious value, while new entrants have no such constraints (Henderson and Clark, 1990). As I discussed in the paper, the important architectural innovation that emerged in the micro-processor market were RISC (Reduced Instruction Set Code) based microprocessors. This technology was an architectural innovation because it shifted the emphasis from the hardware built into a microprocessor to the software.

Although I did not really address it in the paper, RISC microprocessors emerged quite late in the industry's evolution. Inmos, for instance, shipped its first RISC based processor in mid 1985 while the first shipment of the SPARC standard RISC pro-cessors developed by Sun were shipped in approximately 1988. Both of these ship-ments occurred well after Intel based processors held over half of the market. This rather late entry is striking since it occurred after a dominant design had already emerged. More specifically, by the third quarter of 1984 Intel-based processors had captured over 50 per cent of the market and its share had increased to over 75 per cent by 1988. The emergence of many new RISC based microprocessors this late is surprising since Intel would seem to have an insurmountable advantage due to its large installed base and extensive organizational support. Indeed, according to the dominant design theory, new entrants were unlikely to successfully enter the market unless there was a competence destroying technological discontinuity that rendered the existing capabilities of incumbents obsolete (Tushman and Anderson, 1986).

Other work by others and myself suggests a possible explanation for this phenom-enon. In a follow-up paper, I proposed that concentrated markets may paradoxically provide opportunities for new entrants with new technological approaches (Wade, 1996). This may occur because of what Carroll (1985) has called resource partitioning. Carroll suggested that when a market first emerges, firms tend to become generalists and vie for the widest possible resource space. Later, however, when a market becomes concentrated and scale economies become important, the surviving generalists cater to the center of the market. Thus, because of economies of scale, incumbents only develop products that will appeal to the average consumer. As a result, specialized niches are neglected by the incumbents after a dominant design emerges. Because of the economies of scale that the remaining few incumbents enjoy, producing specialized products for these specialized niches would be costly for them. As a result, opportun-ities for new entrants whose designs cater to specialist applications are created.

This raises the possibility that in highly concentrated environments entry barriers for specialists, especially those pursuing new technological approaches are small. Such a circumstance is important since it means that even when markets are dominated by a few large firms that are tied to existing technological trajectories, new technological trajectories may emerge. Similar results have been documented in non-technological settings. Mezias and Mezias (2000), for instance, found that increased concentration among generalists in the movie industry increased the founding rates of small specialist producers and distributors. Moreover, they showed that these new specialists were more innovative in that they were more likely to create new film genres.

These findings may have implications for theories of technological change such as the dominant design theory. The dominant design theory proposes that technological change occurs through a variation, selection and retention process (Tushman and Anderson, 1986; Utterback and Abernathy, 1975). Variation is provided by technological breakthroughs that occur randomly and stochastically. These breakthroughs are followed by a period of ferment in which many designs compete in the market. Eventually, one design dominates and future technological change proceeds incrementally until the next discontinuity.

If new technological approaches are more likely to emerge in concentrated markets, it raises the possibility that the timing of technological breakthroughs may not be entirely random. Indeed, it may be that the emergence of a dominant design may bring with it the seeds of its own destruction (Wade, 1996). Swaminathan (1995) made a similar argument suggesting that increasing concentration may set the stage for discontinuities that ultimately lead to the emergence of new organizational forms.

I want to stress, of course, that I do not believe that new technological approaches that emerge in highly concentrated environment will always supersede the existing dominant design. In the microprocessor market, RISC processors occupy a small niche at the high end of the market. In addition, some of the larger firms such as Intel have incorporated some RISC technology into their own microprocessors. I am simply making an evolutionary argument that concentrated environments may lead to greater technological variation and, in turn, greater strategic opportunities for firms advocating new and novel approaches. Such approaches, however, may or may not end up being successful.

Such a model does, however, suggest a cyclical process in which dominance by a single technological approach paradoxically leads to increased variation. Future research needs to investigate whether specialists advocating new approaches have higher life chances in environments that are highly concentrated and how the level of organizational support that they attract affects this process. Although it is not a technology-based industry, the recent history of the coffee industry suggests that specialists can under some circumstances actually replace incumbents. In this industry, specialty coffee makers that emerged in the early 1980s eventually came to dominate the industry and claim the lion's share of the market (see Rindova and Fombrun, 1999). The barriers to success, however, are likely to be higher in technology based industries in which incumbents have substantial advantages due to network externalities. Older technologies are likely to be supported by large number of organizational populations that produce supporting products. Again, a key factor will be whether new entrants can attract organizational support for their new products.

In the paper, I argued that architectural innovations may allow new entrants to garner such support. It may also be that the timing of when an architectural innovation is introduced is quite important. More specifically, architectural innovations may be most likely to succeed and gain organizational support when industry concentration is high. Other factors may also interact with industry concentration and increase the probability of a new technology's acceptance. For example, perhaps radical competence destroying innovations are most likely to emerge and gain organizational support in highly concentrated markets. In general, existing technological standards may be vulnerable when industry concentration is high. Clearly, of course, it is not a given that in these environments, standards based on new technologies will supplant older ones. As many researchers have noted, technological superiority does not always lead to dominance. Jointly investigating the characteristics of new standards and the industry conditions under which they are most likely to thrive would be a fruitful avenue for future research.

Collective action and standard setting

In my paper, I identified several industry level factors that might affect the level of organizational support that a given standard would attract. What was neglected in the paper is how social interactions between and within standard communities affect technological evolution. More specifically, standard supporters often undertake collective strategies that closely resemble the tactics used by social movements. For instance, when cochlear implant technology emerged, a debate developed between whether the standards should be based on single or multi-channel technologies. Proponents of each side attempted to mobilize organizations and governmental bodies to support them (Garud and Rappa, 1994). Supporters of cochlear implant technology sought to increase the technology's acceptance by encouraging interactions between potential supporters from academia and industry (Garud and Rappa, 1994). These collective strategies are often employed by standard supporters in an effort to gain support from other populations that can speed up a standard's acceptance. Such tactics are often critical in competitions between technologically complex technologies, because the criteria for determining which technology is superior is often ambiguous and socially constructed.

Collective strategies will be particularly crucial when new technologies emerge that threaten older established technologies. Their situation is akin to new organizational forms which must employ collective strategies to create ties to external supporters and gain legitimacy (Aldrich and Fiol, 1994; Aldrich, 1999; Swaminathan and Wade, 2001). Once an older technology has garnered extensive organizational and consumer support, advocates of a new approach not only have to provide the base technology – but a host of supporting technologies. Recruiting organizations to join their new community will be critical if the new technology is to survive. Because of network externalities and the organizational support that older technologies enjoy, new technological approaches may not be pursued even if they are clearly technologically superior.

According to social movement theorists, a key task that must be accomplished by activists advocating change is the development of a collective action frame. According to Klandermans (1997), collective action frames are systems of shared beliefs that justify the existence of social movements and mobilize action. Resonant collective action frames identify the problem that needs to be corrected, target opponents, provide a plan that will correct the situation and provide compelling reasons why collective action should be undertaken. Powerful collective action frames can link together multiple populations and make successful mobilization more likely.

Dowell, Swaminathan, and Wade (forthcoming) suggest that framing processes played an important role in the attempt to develop a standard for high definition television (HDTV) and I use their analysis as an illustrative example. When HDTV was first demonstrated in the US by the Japanese company NHK, the majority of broadcasters showed little interest in the new technology (Brinkley, 1997). Their ambivalence was not surprising, given the large investments in equipment such as transmitting equipment and cameras that would be required. In the mid eighties, however, the FCC was planning to take away some of the broadcaster's unused spectrum and give it to two-way radio users such as police and ambulance services. Spectrum is simply the channels allocated to a particular use and broadcasters only used about half of their allocated channels.

The broadcaster's solution was to argue that they should keep the unused spectrum so that it could be used for HDTV which required much greater bandwidth. Dowell et al. (forthcoming), argue that their efforts to elicit the support of government officials, the FCC and other populations such as television equipment manufacturers was largely unsuccessful because they did not have a resonant collective action frame. The broadcaster's position that the public deserved clear pictures was simply not as compelling as two-way radio users' framing that they needed the spectrum to improve public safety.

The broadcasters' situation markedly changed, however, when they modified their frame so that it tied US involvement in HDTV as being essential to US competitiveness in the world economy. This frame was quite compelling because Japan had essentially come to dominate the entire consumer electronics market. Indeed, Zenith was the only American television manufacturer left in the market. By identifying a specific antagonist, namely Japan, that resonated with multiple populations, the broadcasters were able to mobilize support from key government officials and various populations of equipment manufacturers (Dowell et al., forthcoming). Indeed, successfully identifying a salient antagonist may be a critical part of the framing process (Swaminathan and Wade, 2001).[1] Overall, then, framing may be a critical strategic tool that supporters of a new technology can use to attract organizational support from multiple populations and have important effects on technological evolution.

Interestingly, although the broadcasters were allowed to keep their spectrum, HDTV has still not substantially penetrated the market. Part of the reason for its lack of success is that after the broadcasters were allowed to keep their spectrum they did not actively support HDTV because of the huge costs that they would incur if they actually had to broadcast it on a large scale. Thus, while the equipment manufacturers actively tried to come up with a standard, the broadcasters turned their attention to other possible uses of the spectrum such as interactive digital TV. This example illustrates that even within a given standard or technology, it is not advisable to treat technology supporters as unitary actors with common goals. Indeed, in this instance, the broadcasters were simply supporting the technology to achieve other goals. One advantage of conceptualizing competing standards as communities is that it makes it possible to disentangle and analyze the political tactics and collective strategies employed by different populations both within and across communities.

Organizational support and modularity

One important topic that I did not address in my earlier paper was how modularity might influence the organizational support that a community can attract. Because many products are becoming increasingly complex systems composed of multiple subsystems, a products degree of modularity is becoming increasingly strategically important (Baldwin and Clark, 1997; Langlois and Robertson, 1992; Schilling, 2000; Garud and Kumaraswamy, 1995, Sanchez, 1995; Tushman and Murmann, 1998). According to Schilling (2000), modularity refers to how tightly coupled the components in a system are and whether it is possible to mix and match components. Modularity can be advantageous because it allows firms to produce systems that can appeal to consumers with heterogeneous needs and preferences (Schilling, 2000; Garud and Kumaraswamy, 1995; Sanchez, 1995). Moreover, in modular systems, technological breakthroughs in one component can often be integrated into the system without replacing all of the components (Schilling, 2000; Sanchez, 1995).

From my perspective, designing a modular product is an interesting option because it increases the potential number of populations that a firm producing a core component can gain support from. And, when network externalities are present a firm using a modular strategy might gain organizational support from multiple populations and start a technological bandwagon rolling that leads to its design becoming dominant (Schilling, 2000). As I argued in my paper, the existence of many populations supporting a technological community or standard legitimate the community's products and allow them to achieve a taken for granted character (Meyer, 1983). For these reasons, a modular strategy may be particularly advantageous when a new technology first emerges.

Schilling (2000) suggests that new entrants should carefully analyze whether there are pressures for modularity within an industry. If there are such pressures, but no modular systems are in the market, it presents an opportunity for new entrants to introduce such a system and capture a large share of the market. Such drivers toward modularity include the competitive intensity in the market, the speed of technological change, and heterogeneous demand (Schilling, 2000). Essentially, new entrants should look for mismatches between the extent of modular strategies that are present in an industry and the extent of modularity that should be present.

Carroll's theory of resource partitioning that I discussed earlier may suggest when one such mismatch will be likely to occur. Recall that Carroll's theory suggests that as an industry becomes more concentrated the surviving generalists target the center of the market. In so doing, these generalists are likely to pursue integrated strategies (Schilling, 2000) and neglect specialized niches. I found in my earlier work that resource partitioning lowered entry barriers for technological communities based on architectural innovations and allowed such communities to gain organizational support more quickly (Wade, 1995, 1996).

It may also be that such industry conditions are ripe for exploitation by new technological communities using modular strategies. Firms along with their network partners who pursue modular strategies can offer a wide variety of specialized products to serve niches that are neglected by the large generalists. Because of the economies of scale that the large generalists have in constructing a standardized product that appeals to a large number of consumers, they may not immediately attempt to compete with the new modular entrants. In addition, because the organizational routines, skills, and structures required for implementing a modular strategy are very different than those used in a integrated product strategy, incumbents may find it quite disruptive to change their strategy. Essentially, changing their strategy would be a core change that would disrupt organizational activities and would be unlikely to be successful (Hannan and Freeman, 1977, 1984). Thus, in general, we might expect that modular communities might paradoxically have enhanced life chances in markets dominated by a few large firms who are pursuing integrated product strategies. At the same time, however, some caution is warranted. Firms undertaking a modular strategy, must ensure that enough degrees of freedom are built into key components of the system that allow for significant improvement's in the product's capabilities (Garud and Kumaraswamy, 1995). Failure to accomplish this could actually result in a loss of organizational support.

Conclusions

In this commentary, I have attempted to further develop and extend some of the ideas that I raised in my earlier paper. One topic that I did not yet explore, however, is the tension between individual and collective outcomes. As I noted in the paper, gaining organizational support can be viewed as a double-edged sword. While gaining such support may enhance a new technology's viability and increase the probability that it will become the standard, it also can generate unwanted competition. For instance, while the IBM personal computer is the standard, IBM's market share dropped from 75 per cent in the early eighties to under 12 per cent by 1991.

Many of the papers in this volume provide some answers to this dilemma. For instance, Garud and Kumaraswamy (1995) illustrate how firms can construct networks of firms and still maintain some control over their core products using economies of substitution. Shapiro and Varian (1999) stress how firms must keep their networks alive and healthy by encouraging competition between producers of complementary products but maintain dominance in their core area. In my view, building networks and alliances can only become more important in the evolving Internet economy. Because of the rapid flow of information along the internet, networks and alliances can be built much more quickly and their effects can rapidly diffuse. This rapid diffusion will be particularly crucial when new technologies emerge since small differences in initial market penetration can make the difference between success and failure (Arthur, 1989).

I have suggested, contrary to the popular view, that concentrated environments may create opportunities for sponsors of new technologies. Capitalizing on such opportunities, however, will require great strategic acumen. As I noted earlier, modularizing some components of a product in this type of environment may enable sponsors to recruit other populations into their community and either overcome a incumbent technology or, at least create a viable specialized niche. At the same time, however, sponsors must take care that the overall network that is created both ensures the overall viability of the new technology standard and, at the same time, enables them to exercise some control over the standard so that they can extract profits for themselves.

In general, firms hoping to create and sustain a competitive advantage for their technologies must essentially become skilled network architects and employ collective strategies that attract the "right" kind of organizational support. Who to include and exclude from their networks becomes of critical importance. For instance, Burt's (1992) structural holes theory may offer some guidance. Perhaps, firms who manage to build non-redundant networks that are rich in structural holes will be more likely to have their standard adopted and reap the highest returns. Maintaining such networks over time represents an additional challenge. For instance, if firms in a network feel that a small set of firms (perhaps the sponsor) is appropriating all the rents at their expense they are likely to leave the network or sabotage its standard setting efforts. Garud et al. (2002), for instance describe the difficulties Sun faced in maintaining organizational support for its JAVA language. Theories of networks may shed some light on this problem. In any event, exploring these issues is an exciting and important task for researchers in this area.

NOTES

1   Garud, Jain, and Kumaraswamy (2002) chronicled a similar process in Sun's efforts to mobilize support for its Java programming language. They note how Sun framed its opposition to Microsoft's competing technology using a Star Wars metaphor. Sun's CEO suggested that, "there are two camps, those in Richmond (Microsoft) that live on the Deathstar, and the rest of us, the rebel forces." (Quoted in Surowiecki, 1997.)

REFERENCES

Aldrich, H. (1999). *Organizations Evolving*, Thousand Oaks, CA: Sage.

Aldrich, H. and M. C. Fiol (1994). "When Fools Rush In? The Institutional Context of Industry Creation," *Academy of Management Review*, 19: 645–70.

Arthur, W. B. (1989). "Competing Technologies, Increasing Returns and Lock-in by Historical Events," *Economic Journal*, 99: 116–31.

Baldwin, Carliss Y. and Clark, Kim B. (1997). "Managing in an Age of Modularity," *Harvard Business Review*, September–October: 84–93.

Brinkley, J. (1997). Defining Vision: The Battle for the Future of Television, New York: Harcourt Brace and Company.

Burt, R. S. (1992). *Structural Holes: The Social Structure of Competition*. Cambridge, MA: Harvard University Press.

Carroll, G. R. (1985). "Concentration and Specialization: Dynamics of Niche Width in Populations of Newspaper Organizations," *American Journal of Sociology*, 90: 1262–83.

Dowell, G., Swaminathan, A. and Wade, J. B. (forthcoming). "Pretty Pictures and Ugly Scenes: Political and Technological Maneuvers in High Definition Television," in P. Ingram and B. Silverman (eds.), "The New Institutionalism in Strategic Management," in J. Baum (ed.), *Advances in Strategic Management*, 19, New York, NY: Elsevier Science.

Garud, R., Jain, S., and Kumaraswamy, A. (2002). "Institutional Entrepreneurship in the Sponsor of Common Technological Systems: The Case of Sun Microsystems and JAVA," *Academy of Management Journal*, 45(1): 196–214.

Garud, R. and Kumaraswamy, A. (1995). "Technological and Organizational Designs for Realizing Economies of Substitution," *Strategic Management Journal*, Summer Special Issue, 16: 93–109.

Garud, R. and M. A. Rappa (1994). "A Socio-cognitive Model of Technology Evolution: The Case of Cochlear Implants," *Organization Science*, 5: 344–62.

Hannan, M. T. and Freeman, J. H. (1977). "The Population Ecology of Organizations," *American Journal of Sociology*, 82: 929–64.

Hannan, M. T. and Freeman, J. H. (1984). "Structural Inertia and Organizational Change," *American Sociological Review*, 49: 149–64.

Henderson, R. M. and Clark, K. B. (1990). "Architectural Innovation: The Reconfiguration of Existing Product Technologies and the Failure of Established Firms," *Administrative Science Quarterly*, 35: 9–30.

Klandermans, B. (1997). *The Social Psychology of Protest*. Cambridge, MA: Blackwell Publishers.

Langlois, R. N. and Robertson, P. L. (1992). "Networks and Innovation in a Modular System: Lessons from the microcomputer and Stereo Component Industries," *Research Policy*, 21: 297–313.

Meyer, J. W. (1983). "Institutionalization and the Rationality of Formal Organization Structure," in J. W. Meyer and W. R. Scott (eds.), *Organizational Environments: Ritual and Rationality*, Beverley Hills, CA: Sage.

Mezias, J. M. and Mezias, S. J. (2000). "Resource Partitioning, the Founding of Specialist Firms, and Innovation: The American Feature Film Industry, 1912–1929," *Organization Science*, 11: 306–22.

Rindova, V. P. and Fombrun, C. (1999). "Constructing Competitive Advantage: The Role of Firm-Constituent Interactions," *Strategic Management Journal*, 20: 691–710.

Sanchez, R. (1995). "Strategic Flexibility in Product Competition," *Strategic Management Journal*, Summer Special Issue, 16: 135–59.

Schilling, Melissa A. (2000). "Toward a General Modular Systems Theory and its Application to Inter-firm Product Modularity," *Academy of Management Review*, 25: 312–34.

Shapiro, C. and Varian, H. R. (1999). "The Art of Standards Wars," *California Management Review*, 41: 8–32.

Surowiecki, J. (1997). "Culture wars: Behind the Java hype is a struggle for computer-world hegemony," *Slate*, (http://slate.msn.com/?id-2621), September 27.

Swaminathan, A. (1995). "The Proliferation of Specialist Organizations in the American Wine Industry: 1941–1990," *Administrative Science Quarterly*, 40: 653–80.

Swaminathan, A. and Wade, James B. (2001). "Social Movement Theory and the Evolution of New Organizational Forms," in C. B. Schoonhoven and E. Romanelli (eds.), *The Entrepreneurship Dynamic in Population Evolution*, Stanford, CA: Stanford University Press, 286–313.

Tushman, M. L. and Anderson, P. (1986). "Technological Discontinuities and Organizational Environments," *Administrative Science Quarterly*, 31: 439–65.

Tushman, M. L and Murmann, J. P. (1998). "Dominant Designs, Innovation Types and Organizational Outcomes", in B. M. Staw and L. L. Cummings (eds.), *Research in Organizational Behavior*, 20: 231–66. Greenwich, CT: JAI Press.

Tushman, M. L., and Rosenkopf, L. (1992). "On the Organizational determinants of Technological Change: Towards a Sociology of Technological Evolution," In B. M. Staw and L. L. Cummings (eds.), *Research in Organizational Behavior*, 14: 311–47, Greenwich, CT: JAI Press.

Utterback, J. and Abernathy, W. (1975). "A Dynamic Model of Process and Product Innovation," *Omega*, 33: 639–56.

Wade, J. (1995). "Dynamics of Organizational Communities and Technological Bandwagons: An Empirical Investigation of community Evolution in the Microprocessor Market," *Strategic Management Journal*, Summer Special Issue, 16: 111–33.

Wade, J. (1996). "A Community-Level Analysis of Sources and Rates of Technological Variation in the Microprocessor Market," *Academy of Management Journal*, 39: 1218–44.

CHAPTER TEN

DOMINANT DESIGNS, TECHNOLOGY CYCLES, AND ORGANIZATIONAL OUTCOMES

MICHAEL L. TUSHMAN AND JOHANN PETER MURMANN

Organization theorists, strategy scholars, economists, and historians of technology have all highlighted the powerful role of technology in shaping organizational outcomes. It is by now a well-established observation that technological change is one of the prime movers of industrial, strategic, and organizational change (e.g., Henderson and Clark, 1990; Barley, 1990; Tripsas, 1997; Tushman and Anderson, 1986). Mastering the "black box of technology" represents a crucial organizational capability for succeeding in competitive markets (e.g., Rosenberg, 1976; Rosenbloom and Christensen, 1994; Tushman and O'Reilly, 1997). Yet with all the interest in technology and organizational outcomes, confusion abounds in basic concepts and fundamental ideas; there is little clarity on a mid-range theory of technology and technological change, or their impacts on organizational outcomes (e.g., Podolny and Stuart, 1995; Teece, 1996; Nelson, 1995). Confusion on dominant designs and technology cycles contributes to this condition.

Dominant designs and their effects on industry and organizational evolution have been at the core of several distinct research streams over the past 20 years. Dominant designs appear to be a crucial linchpin in both technological as well as organizational evolution. For example, the emergence of quartz movements in watches (dominating tuning fork and escapements) and Windows operating systems (dominating OS/2 and Mac) in PCs, both triggered profound changes in technological as well as organizational evolution in their respective product classes. Dominant designs and subsequent technological discontinuities together define technology cycles (Anderson and Tushman, 1990; Van de Ven and Garud, 1994).

Dominant designs end eras of ferment and initiate eras of incremental technological change. The emergence of dominant designs have been linked by economists to shifting industry structures (Abernathy and Clark, 1985; Klepper, 1996; Langlois and Robertson, 1992), by strategy scholars to product class and firm performance (e.g., Henderson, 1995; Teece and Pisano, 1994; McGrath, MacMillan and Tushman, 1992; Prahalad and Hamel, 1994), by organizational theorists to entry/exit rates and organizational fate (e.g., Hunt and Aldrich, 1998; Wade, 1996; Podolny and Stuart, 1995; Baum, Korn, and Kotha, 1995; Rosenkopf and Tushman, 1998), by technology management scholars to shifts in innovation types, firm performance, and industry structure (e.g., Iansiti and Clark, 1994; Lee, O'Neal, Pruett, and Thomas, 1995; Utterback, 1994; Suarez and Utterback, 1995; Christensen and Bower, 1996), and by historians of technology to industrial and organizational evolution (e.g., Landes, 1983; Hughes, 1983; Hounshell, 1995). Shaping a technology cycle via actions on a dominant design, or innovating across technology cycles (e.g., substituting Windows for DOS in operating systems) may be at the core of dynamic organizational capabilities (Teece and Pisano, 1994).

The emergence of dominant designs is an important juncture in both technology cycles and organizational evolution. Yet with all the interest in dominant designs, it remains a concept whose fundamental definition, unit of analysis, causal mechanisms, boundary conditions, and linkages to organizational outcomes remain confused and ambiguous (Ehrnberg, 1995). To clarify this strategically important concept, our paper proceeds in four sections. We start with an extended example to ground the phenomena of dominant designs and organizational outcomes. We then move to review what both historians of technology and evolutionary economists have observed about technological change and its organizational impacts. The third section reviews three contrasting approaches to the concept of dominant designs and confronts these approaches with the empirical literature on dominant designs. We induce a set of observations and hypotheses about dominant designs at the subsystem and linking levels of analysis, about nested hierarchies of dominant designs, and about dominant designs over time. Our final section develops a set of hypotheses linking dominant designs and technology cycles to environmental conditions and organization evolution.

AN ILLUSTRATION OF THE PHENOMENON: DOMINANT DESIGNS, TECHNOLOGY CYCLES, AND ORGANIZATIONAL OUTCOMES

To appreciate the phenomenon of dominant designs, technology cycles, and organizational outcomes, consider an abbreviated history of the passenger airplane and its associated industry. An airplane is the integration of a number of essential subsystems: propulsion, lifting, landing, control systems, passenger compartment, systems architecture, and linking mechanisms (Vincenti, 1990, 1994). During the infancy of airplanes, designers experimented with configuring these major components of the plane in different ways. The purpose of changing the subsystems and their integration was to permit stable and controllable flight.

The first successful airplane of the Wright brothers had two wings and was powered by a 12-horsepower, 4-cylinder internal combustion fuel engine driving two propellers. With the exception of the engine, the airplane was made out of wood and fabric. The evolution that has transformed this early design into the contemporary jet airliner proceeded through cycles of variation, selection, and retention for each subsystem and its linkage mechanisms. We have selected several subsystems that reveal the emergence of dominant designs at the system, subsystem, and basic component levels of analysis.

Propulsion

The propulsion system of the Wright brothers' airplane consisted of an internal combustion engine and two wooden propellers. Metal replaced wood as the dominant material for propeller blades by the 1930s. Trying to scale up propulsive power, engineers examined the effects of mounting up to eight engines on the airplane. Around 1926–1927, the three-engine approach as embodied in the Ford Tri-Motor became the dominant design for commercial airplanes until the emergence of the DC-3 in 1936 ushered in the subsequent period of two-motor designs. The two-motor, internal combustion propulsion period was broken, in turn, by jet engines in 1959 by De Havilland and Boeing.

During the period of internal combustion engines, several crucial innovations occurred within the engine subsystem. For example, after testing a number of different materials, engineers converged on sodium-cooled exhaust valves as the dominant design in motor cylinders in the early 1930s. Further, a dramatic increase in engine performance was achieved by adding lead to the engine fuel. The outcome of much experimentation with different lead levels was a 90-octane standard that remained the standard until 1945 when it was replaced with a 100-octane standard (Hanieski, 1973).

When theoretical work in aeronautics in the 1920s predicted that it was possible to travel at least twice as fast as previously assumed, designers looked for a propulsion technology that would not have the speed limitations of propellers. The German design community experimented with a number of different propulsion concepts: rockets, controlled bomb explosion, pure jets, and turbine jets (Constant, 1980; Jewkes, Sawers, and Stillerman, 1961). From these variations, the turbine jet (turbojet) engine emerged as the most viable option. Initially turbojets had many fewer parts than traditional piston engines, but over the course of 50 years jet designers have added so many parts that jet engines have again become very complex. Within turbojet technology a large number of alternative architectures were tried until the ducted fan type axial flow turbojet became the dominant design, largely because of its fuel efficiency (Constant, 1980).

For the turbojet to become a viable technology, material scientists had to mix hundreds of different alloys to find a material that could withstand the enormous heat of a jet engine. Engineers found the Nimonic 80 alloy to be the most effective heat resistant material for constructing a gas turbine, and it became the dominant material. A similar process of search, development, and experimentation with a large variety of alloys led to the selection of alloy G. 18B for the rotor and rim of the turbine (Hanieski, 1973). Without solving these "material" bottlenecks, the turbojet would not have replaced the piston engine. To successfully incorporate jet engines into airplane technology, it was necessary to make a number of complementary changes in other subsystems. For example, airframes had to be made much stronger in order to withstand the higher levels of stress created by jet engines. The introduction of jet engines could not be accomplished in a modular way by simply mounting them in the space allocated for the traditional piston engines. Before jet engines could become the dominant design for commercial airplanes, systemic innovation in many components both in the airplane and its larger technological context (e.g., runways) had to be achieved.

Landing function

The pioneer airplanes (for example, the 1910 Nieuport model) typically were equipped with a four-wheel fixed gear, resembling a little cart. Efforts to make landing gear more robust led to the tripoid design where two big wheels were mounted below the fuselage and a very small wheel at the bottom of the tail, giving the entire fuselage a downward slope toward the rear. The tripoid configuration became the dominant design for commercial airplanes until the tri-cycle undercarriage was introduced in 1938 by Douglas's model 4E (Miller and Sawers, 1968). By introducing a third leg of equal length, an airplane would be less inclined to flip onto its face (i.e., the front end of the fuselage) during landing. Landing gears that put the commercial airplane in a fully horizontal position became the dominant design up to the present day.

In the 1930s engineers started to explore a number of different design ideas for making the landing gear more aerodynamic. These attempts can be classified into two broad design approaches, the enclosing of wheels and the construction of retractable landing gear (Vincenti, 1994). Trying out a number of different methods of enclosure, designers put airplanes into service that either had their wheels enclosed (a design called wheel pants or spats) or had the entire landing gear enclosed (a design called trouser pants). Similarly, a number of different retraction mechanisms were devised. Retractable landing gear promised to deliver the greatest aerodynamic gains, but these devices were much more complicated than wheel and trouser pants, leading designers initially to focus on enclosing the landing gear. The period from 1928–1935 marked the era of greatest variation: unstreamlined fixed gears, wheel pants, trousers gear, and retractable landing gears showed up in commercial airplanes and competed with one another (see figure 10.1). In the end, however, it was the laterally retracting landing gear that became the dominant design for all commercial airplanes, winning the design competition not only against wheel and trouser pants but also against mechanisms where wheels would retract backwards or into the sides of the fuselage. Only very small and slow private airplanes currently do not use retractable landing gears. As Vincenti (1994, p. 19) observes, "Airplanes today exhibit different kinds of landing gear in an ordered way, and the topic no longer arouses any discussion. Fixed gear, either unstreamlined or with wheel pants, predominate at low speeds and retractable gear at high, with the changeover occurring around 200–250 mph."

Fixed landing gear

Wheel pants landing gear

Trouser landing gear

Retractable landing gear

Figure 10.1 Variations in landing gear, 1928–1935.
Source: Vincenti, 1994.

Early systems architecture

Aeronautical engineers experimented with a great many design alternatives in the overall airplane body before a particular configuration emerged as the dominant design. Trying to make airplanes more controllable (so that pilots could fly curves and travel over longer distances), the Wright brothers and other designers experimented with changing the size of the various main components and placing them in different relations to one another. During this process, designers not only built monoplanes with either low- or high-mounted wings but also created double- and triple-wing airplanes. In some designs the propeller was placed in front of the wings facing forward, in others it was placed behind the wings facing backwards. To achieve more stability and greater distance some designers built airplanes with two propellers powered by independent engines; others tried to perfect the airplane configuration with single-engine motor power.

After experimenting and learning about the advantages and disadvantages of various configurations, the engine-forward, tail-aft biplane by World War I had become the dominant design, which designers typically took as the starting point in their efforts to create better airplane designs (Vincenti, 1990). As engines became more powerful, designers switched from the biplane to the single wing configuration. After the emergence of the engine-forward, tail-aft monoplane as the dominant design for the overall configuration, engineers focused on experimenting with small variations of this design to find the most aerodynamic airplane shape as well as on improving the individual subsystems. This architecture remained the standard until jet engines triggered a fundamental shift in airplane architecture.

Dominant designs, technology cycles, and industry dynamics

In addition to the dramatic fluctuations in demand during the two world wars and the Great Depression, innovation at the subsystem and integration levels had profound effects on organization and industry dynamics (Rae, 1968). During the airframe revolution between 1925 and 1935 the introduction of the all metal, low-wing monoplane, the controllable-pitch propeller, the retractable landing gear, and wing flaps, led to significant entry of new firms, exit of incumbents, mergers, and dramatic reconfigurations of market shares. Former leaders like Curtiss-Wright were overtaken by firms like Boeing, Douglas, Lockheed, and Martin.

When in 1936 Douglas integrated this set of innovations into its DC-3, the firm achieved so economical an airplane that it very quickly became the largest manufacturer of commercial airplanes in the world until the jet era in the 1950s. As other firms tried to imitate Douglas's design formula, the all-metal, low-wing monoplane, the controllable-pitch propeller, the retractable landing gear, and wing flaps became standard design subsystems for the next 20 years. By 1941 almost eight out of 10 commercial airplanes were DC-3 configurations (Klein, 1977).

When jet engines became commercially viable in the mid-1950s, Boeing was quicker to respond to this propulsion substitution than others. Indeed, Boeing tested a prototype of its 707 a full year before Douglas began developing its DC-8 jet airliner. Boeing captured a leading position in the beginning of the jet era and has succeeded in remaining the largest producer of commercial airplanes until today. Douglas was reduced to the status of a very small player in the market and Lockheed abandoned the commercial jet market altogether.

Radical innovations in individual subsystems have also led to a large amount of entry and exit in the populations of firms associated with the production of individual components and subsystems (Rae, 1968). For instance, the leading manufacturers of water-cooled aircraft engines in the early 1920s – Curtiss Aeroplane and Motor Corporation, the Wright Aeronautical Corporation, and the Packard Motor Car Company – were challenged by dynamic competitors like Lawrence and Pratt & Whitney who entered the industry to pioneer the development of air-cooled engines. While Wright was able to make the transition to air-cooled engines and remain a major producer in the 1930s, the other leading firms were overtaken by Pratt & Whitney, and many exited the industry (Klein, 1977).

This highly abbreviated discussion of the commercial airplane's evolution anchors several ideas we will discuss. To understand the airplane's technical evolution requires an understanding of its multiple subsystems and their linkages, or integration, into a working system (see also Clark, 1985). For each subsystem and linking mechanism, patterns of experimentation, trial and error, or variation led to the emergence (or selection) of a dominant design which led to incremental change in the standardized design which led, in turn, to the subsequent discontinuous technological change. Dominant designs at the subsystem level change over time as eras of incremental technological advance are broken by subsequent technological discontinuities. For example, in landing gears the initial competition between four-wheel-fixed versus the tripod design led to the emergence of the tripod as the industry standard. This standard was, in turn, broken by the tri-cycle undercarriage and, in turn, retractable landing gears. During the period when each subsystem was in a period of incremental change, the DC-3, as a bundle of standard subsystems, was the dominant design at the system level of analysis.

In the airplane's evolution, dominant designs emerged from a battle between alternatives. Even in simple subsystems, the closing on a dominant design was a result of social, political, and economic forces of compromise and accommodation. For example, the standard 100-degree angle mandatory for flush riveting in commercial airplanes emerged from protracted negotiation between rival parties that was finally settled by an aeronautical board. Further, dominant designs apply at both the system (e.g., DC-3) and subsystem (e.g., landing gear, engine) levels of analysis. In airplanes not all subsystems were equally important. Some more core subsystems (e.g., propulsion) directed the nature and pace of other more peripheral subsystems (e.g., the entertainment system). Finally, dominant design and technology cycles affect firm performance and industry structure. In airplanes transitions involving core subsystems had more sweeping effects than those of more peripheral subsystems.

A Context for Dominant Designs and Technology Cycles: History of Technology and Evolutionary Economics

As historians of technology and evolutionary economists have intensively studied technological change and its organizational impacts, they offer both empirical evidence and conceptual tools for understanding the phenomena of dominant designs and technology cycles.

History of technology

Historians of technology have uncovered much evidence that variation and selection processes shape the evolution of technological change (e.g., Hounshell, 1995; Bijker, Hughes, and Pinch, 1987). Gilfillan (1935) pioneered the study of technological change with a systematic examination of the history of ships. He showed that in the late eighteenth century, screw propulsion emerged as the standard design for ships from an array of competing propulsion variants including water jets, setting poles, duck's feet, and reciprocating paddles, among others. Once the screw propeller emerged as the standard, technical change was driven by the technological issues inherent in screw propulsion.

Basalla's (1988) research on nuclear reactors, cotton gins, barbed wire, and railway propulsion systems, Noble's (1984) research on automatically controlled machine tools, Hughes's (1983) history of electric power systems, Aitken's (1985) research on radio systems, Pinch and Bijker's (1987) discussion of bicycles, and Constant's (1980) research on turbojet propulsion each describe a process driven by variation (or diversity), a selection process leading to continuity and, eventually, the period of continuity broken by subsequent diversity. These histories of technology describe the selection process leading to a dominant design as a social/political process shaped by economic and technical conditions. "Superior" technologies often do not survive these selection processes as social, political, and random forces shape selection processes. For example, Noble (1984) argues that the victory of numerical control (NC) machine tools over record-playback (RP) was driven not by technical merits so much as a powerful political coalition between MIT and the Air Force (see also Davies's (1997) discussion of telecommunication systems, and Hunt and Aldrich's (1998) discussion of the World Wide Web).

David Landes's (1983) work on the evolution of watches describes how both subsystem and linking technologies advanced incrementally for over 100 years until quartz and tuning fork technologies challenged escapements for dominance in the oscillation subsystem. After a period of variation, where tuning fork, quartz, and escapement oscillation modes competed with each other, the quartz movement became the dominant design. By the mid-1980s, while it was still possible to buy a tuning fork or mechanical watch, more than 80 percent of all watches were of quartz design. Landes (1983) also observed that the emergence of the quartz movement had cascading effects on all other watch subsystems as well as manufacturing processes. These cascading changes in core and linking subsystems and their associated manufacturing processes destroyed the Swiss firms' highly evolved and interrelated competencies. The escapement-to-quartz transition led to the demise of the Swiss (through the early 1990s) and fueled the rise of Japanese competitors (see also Glassmeier, 1991).

Similarly, Jenkins's (1975) thorough analysis of the photography industry through 1925 describes five fundamental transitions in the technology of image capturing (e.g., wet to dry gelatin on glass, to dry gelatin on film). He describes technology variation within technological regimes as well as between regimes. In each case a dominant design emerged which, in turn, triggered profound changes in manufacturing, marketing, and organization controls. Further, for each technological transition, new firms replaced incumbents.

Much like Vincenti's (1990, 1994) discussion of airplanes, other historians of technology observe that products are technological systems made up of subsystems and linking mechanisms (e.g., Hughes, 1983, p. 55). Processes of variation, selection, and retention occur at the subsystem and linkage levels of analysis. Thus, Aitken (1985) focused on the spark/wave generators, Constant (1980) focused on the propulsion system, while Landes (1983) focused on the energy and oscillation subsystems. Further, not all subsystems are of equal importance. Some subsystems are central or core to the product, while others are more peripheral. These critical subsystems, or critical problems, shift over time (Hughes, 1983). For example, only after batteries replaced springs did the oscillation subsystem emerge as a critical technology battleground in watches (Landes, 1983).

Research on the history of technological change provides much insight to the notions of technology cycles and dominant designs. Technological progress seems to be both socially driven as well as driven by forces inherent in the technology itself. Prior to the emergence of a dominant design, the battle between variants is driven by social and political forces; by different communities of practitioners each pushing its own variant (see Noble's [1984] discussion of the machine tool industry and Yates's [1993] discussion of the insurance firms' attempts to shape the early card-punch/tabulation industry). In contrast, after the standard emerges (e.g., 110 cycle AC power or quartz movements), further technological progress is driven by inherent technological and economic forces, and by a more consolidated community of practitioners (Hounshell, 1995). This period of autonomous technical progress is, in turn, broken by the subsequent technological discontinuity and the subsequent period of variation, selection, and retention at the subsystem level (e.g., piston to turbojets, dry gelatin on glass to film). Finally, transitions to dominant designs and the subsequent technological discontinuity are associated with sweeping organizational and industrial changes as seen in the airplane, radio, photography, power, machine tool, and watch industries.

Evolutionary economics and the economics of standards

Scholars in economics interested in technological change have developed a set of concepts that mesh well with ideas from historians of technology (see Rosenberg, 1976, 1994). Nelson and Winter (1982) employ the phrase "natural trajectories" to describe the phenomenon that technologies typically evolve by exploiting latent economies of scale and the potential for increased mechanization of operations that were previously done by hand. Nelson and Winter maintain that designers of a technology have at every given point in time beliefs about what is technically feasible or worth trying. Thus, the development of a technology is very much constrained and directed by the cognitive framework that engineers bring to the development situation. This idea of natural trajectories is associated with incremental elaboration of a standard design. Natural trajectories and periods of incremental innovations of a standard design occur because it is economically efficient to elaborate a design approach into which substantial resources have been invested and which is already well understood. Only when further performance improvements either are blocked or yield diminishing returns do engineers look for fundamentally different design approaches (Dosi, 1982).

Dosi (1984) elaborates the ideas of Nelson and Winter and describes in more detail how natural trajectories are unseated by new ones. In his study of devices that amplify, rectify, and modulate electrical signals. Dosi examined the dynamics of how thermoionic valve technology (vacuum tubes or electronic tubes) was replaced by a new trajectory based on semiconductor technology. Borrowing ideas about the evolution of scientific disciplines, he developed the ideas of technological paradigms and technological trajectories.[1] Dosi's definition of technological paradigm is a multidimensional construct as he uses the concept to refer to a generic technological task, the material technology selected to achieve the task, the physical/chemical properties exploited, and the technological and economic dimensions and tradeoffs focused on (1982, p. 153).

Dosi identifies two origins for new technological paradigms. Either designers cannot improve a technology on the existing paradigm and therefore engage in extraordinary problem solving to find a radically new solution for the generic technological task (here he follows Nelson and Winter), or scientific breakthroughs may open up new possibilities for achieving the technological task. In the second case, innovative designers seize the opportunity and create a technological alternative to existing designs. Once designers adopt a new paradigm, they focus on incrementally improving the technology along key dimensions identified by the paradigm. Dosi argues that technological paradigms have a powerful exclusion effect: they focus the technological imagination and the efforts of engineers as well as the organizations they work for in rather precise directions while they make them "blind" with respect to other technological possibilities (1984, p. 15). This exclusionary effect stabilizes the paradigm even further and explains why technological evolution is so highly directional and only under special circumstances shifts to a very different path.

Since there are always a number of different pathways that are technically possible in a given technological paradigm, what determines the selection of a particular trajectory? Dosi maintains that economic forces together with institutional and social factors operate as a *selective device*. For him, the most important economic forces are the pressures on firms to achieve adequate returns on their investments. Because of these pressures, managers and designers pursue pathways that promise to bring about marketable applications.

The Nelson and Winter, and Dosi theorizing has stimulated substantial research. Langlois and Robertson (1992) explored the microcomputer and stereo industries. They found that in these industries technological evolution was modular, that distinct standards evolved at the subsystems level of analysis, and that product competition shifted from integrated stereo systems to dis-integrated modular systems. Other research finds that periods of uncertainty are indeed resolved by the emergence (or lock-in) of standards and, in turn, increasing returns to scale of the selected standard (e.g., David and Greenstein, 1990; Arthur, 1988, 1989; David, 1985). These selected technologies (e.g., the QWERTY keyboard or the internal combustion engine) are selected not because they are the optimal technologies, but rather because of a complex array of political, social, and institutional factors as well as simple luck (see Nelson, 1995). For example, Saloner (1990) investigated the battle between different operating systems for UNIX-based computers. He documented in great detail how rivals formed two coalitions to push their preferred UNIX version to the industry standard.

Industry standards have important effects on industry structure and organizational fates. Prior to the emergence of standard, many smaller firms compete based on product innovation. After the standard, however, process innovation and associated production investments raise barriers to entry, drive cost-based competition, and the shake-out of an industry now dominated by larger firms (e.g., Gort and Klepper, 1982; Klepper and Grady, 1990; Malerba and Orsenigo, 1996, 1997). These industry dynamics occur at both the component as well as the system levels of analysis (Langlois and Robertson, 1992). Further, Teece and Pisano (1994) and Bercovitz, de Figueiredo, and Teece (1997) have described how path dependencies and the development of co-specialized assets hold firms hostage to existing standards and their associated technological trajectories. This work illustrates the difficulties yet importance of building dynamic organizational capabilities in the face of changing technological trajectories.

Literature on Dominant Designs and Technology Cycles

The work on dominant designs and the linkage between dominant designs and organizational evolution was initiated by Abernathy (1978) and Abernathy and Utterback (1978). Over the past 20 years the concept has been used by a range of authors in a variety of ways. Confusion over the concept, its underlying causal mechanisms, and its level of analysis renders research in the field confusing and hinders our understanding of the phenomenon and its effects on environmental conditions and organizational dynamics. Building on evolutionary economics and history of technology literatures, we focus on several unresolved issues: (1) what are dominant designs, (2) what is the appropriate level of analysis to understand dominant designs, (3) and how do they evolve?

Contrasting approaches to dominant designs

Important differences exist in the ways scholars have defined the concept of a dominant design. These differences are illustrated in the work of Abernathy and Utterback (1978), Anderson and Tushman (1990), and Henderson and Clark (1990). We first review these contrasting points of view and then move to the larger empirical literature.

Since Abernathy (1978) and Abernathy and Utterback (1978) pioneered the concept of dominant designs, we begin with their initial concepts. Exploring the relation between product and process innovation, Abernathy and Utterback (1978) see dominant designs as turning points that lead an industry to move from a custom-made to a standardized-product manufacturing system. This transition from flexible to specialized production processes is marked by a series of steps. The first step is the development of a model that has broad appeal. This design satisfies the needs of a broad class of users; it is not a radical innovation but rather a creative synthesis of innovations that were introduced in earlier products. This dominant product design, for example, Ford's Model T and Douglas' DC-3, attracts significant market share and forces other competitors to imitate this dominant configuration (Abernathy, 1978, pp. 61–2). After the dominant design is in place, subsequent innovations focus on incrementally changing the product; innovations become more cumulative and competition moves from product differentiation to price.

From its first formulations, dominant designs were defined as a set of subsystems at the product level of analysis (e.g., the automobile or airplane) and emerged in a deterministic fashion as the "weight of many innovations that tilted the economic balance in favor of one approach" (Christensen, Suarez, and Utterback, 1996, quoting Abernathy (1978)). While this design may not be the best along all performance dimensions, Abernathy and Utterback regard it as the best compromise that then forced all other participants to imitate the design.

This notion of dominant designs at the product level of analysis and as the best synthesis of existing innovations has been continued by Utterback and his colleagues as well as by a range of other researchers. Suarez and Utterback (1995), for example, suggest that there were single dominant designs in the typewriter, automobile, calculator, TV, TV tube, and transistor product classes. They observe that dominant designs (e.g., the Underwood Model 5 or the all steel, closed body automobile) are singular events which were synthesized from fragments of extant innovations. Suarez and Utterback (1995) observe that economies of scale are not a mechanism that drives convergence. Rather, the emergence of the best compromise makes it possible to sell the product to many different users; economies of scale are relevant after a dominant design is in place (p. 418). Similarly, Christensen, Suarez, and Utterback (1996) explore the disk-drive industry over 30 years. Through a careful analysis of a set of disk-drive subsystems, Christensen, Suarez, and Utterback observe that a single dominant design emerged in 1983 as a synthesis of five interrelated subsystems.

Single dominant designs, the product as the primary level of analysis, and the dominant design as the best synthesis of extant innovation, all symbolized in the image of the Model-T or the DC-3, pervade the literature on dominant designs. For example, Kodama (1995), Tushman and Anderson (1986), Christensen and Bower (1996), Teece (1986), Abernathy and Clark (1985), and Leonard-Barton (1995) all use similar imagery – a single package of innovations that dominate all others.

In sharp contrast to these ideas is the work of Anderson and Tushman (1990). These authors introduce the notion of technology cycles – periods of variation (eras of ferment) initiated by technological discontinuities that are closed by the selection out of a dominant design. Dominant designs usher in eras of incremental change that are, in turn, broken by subsequent technological discontinuities, and the next cycle of variation, selection, and retention (Anderson and Tushman, 1990). Dominant designs are, then, a key transition point between eras of ferment (e.g., the period between 1928–1935 of four competing landing gears) and eras of incremental change (e.g., sustained improvements in retractable landing gears after 1935). Once a dominant design emerges, uncertainty associated with design approaches vanishes and subsequent technical progress elaborates the selected variant.

Building on the history of technology literature, rather than seeing a dominant design as that single best bundle of subsystems that establishes dominance, Anderson and Tushman (1990) observe that dominant designs emerge out of an evolutionary process characterized by variations, selection of a dominant design leading, in turn, to a retention period. From this evolutionary perspective, dominant designs are not driven by technical or economic superiority, but by sociopolitical/institutional processes of compromise and accommodation between communities of interest moderated by economic and technical constraints. The more complex the product, the more accentuated these institutional forces intrude in the emergence of a dominant design (Rosenkopf and Tushman, 1994, 1998). Where social, political, and institutional forces shape technological progress prior to the dominant design, technology drives subsequent technical evolution after the dominant design. These cycles get reinitiated at the next technological discontinuity (see figure 10.2).

Anderson and Tushman (1990) in their work on the glass, cement and minicomputer product classes observe that while dominant designs occur at the product level, they do not embody the best, most superior combination of components; rather, dominant designs lie behind the technological frontier. Similarly, Rosenkopf and Tushman's (1998) analysis of the flight simulator industry found that successive dominant designs (full-flight simulators and, in turn, modular simulators) were

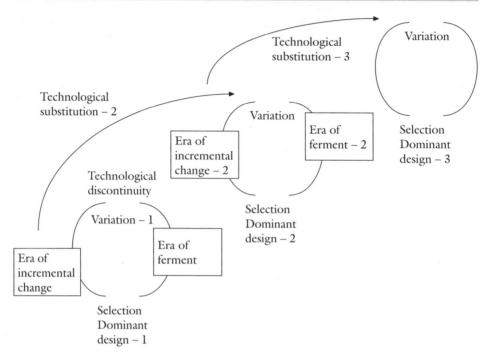

Figure 10.2 Technology cycles over time.

driven not by a logic of technological superiority, but through compromise and accommodation between powerful sets of alliances made up of suppliers, users, and governmental agencies.

This evolutionary perspective on dominant designs focuses on rivalry among alternatives and associated product class uncertainty. Eras of ferment are fundamentally more uncertain than eras of incremental change (Anderson and Tushman, 1990). Except for simple, non-assembled products (e.g., cement), this uncertainty can not be adjudicated by technology alone; rather, dominant designs emerge out of a social, political, economic process of compromise and accommodation played out in the community (Rosenkopf and Tushman, 1994). Reflecting this evolutionary approach, Anderson and Tushman (1990) observe that dominant designs can only be known in retrospect (i.e., there is no optimal design) and that they are defined when a single variant accounts for over 50 percent of new product sales or installations. Further, as technological discontinuities trigger subsequent technology cycles, dominant designs shift over time (e.g., tripod landing gears replaced by retractable landing gears in airplanes). Since variation is crucial to the evolution of a dominant design, if variation is constrained either by governmental regulation (e.g., railway track regulations in Europe) or by limited demand (e.g., space shuttles), no dominant design will emerge.

While the work of Abernathy and Utterback (1978) and Anderson and Tushman (1990) differ on the underlying causal mechanisms driving dominant designs, these approaches both take the product as the unit of analysis. In contrast, Clark (1985) and Henderson and Clark (1990) focus attention on product subsystems and associated linking mechanisms. Such a focus on subsystems leads Henderson and Clark (1990) to induce several innovation types: incremental, architectural, modular, and radical, at the system level of analysis. These innovation types differ in terms of changes in subsystems and linking mechanisms. Further, building on Alexander (1964), Clark (1985) observes that not all subsystems are of equal importance; that products have their own hierarchical order such that change in higher subsystems (e.g., the engine in an automobile) will have more cascading effects than lower-order subsystems. Dominant designs appear at the subsystem level of analysis and change over time (Clark, 1985). While Clark (1985) and more recently Baldwin and Clark (1997) adopt an evolutionary approach to dominant design, this approach shifts to design hierarchies; products as made up of differentially more or less central subsystems.

Henderson and Clark (1990) put special attention on linking mechanisms as vital subsystems. Building on evolutionary logic, these authors observe that dominant designs emerge out of variation and selection processes on core subsystems (i.e., components) and their linking mechanisms. While this research does not explore the consequences of dominant designs, it does explore the devastating effects of architectural (i.e., linking) innovations on incumbent firms in the photolithography industry. Such seemingly minor linking innovations in alignment equipment led to drastic shifts in industry leadership. Incumbents lost their leadership position over four successive architectural (i.e., linking) innovations. Henderson (1993, 1995) retains her focus on subsystems and linking mechanisms in her analysis of the unexpectedly old age of photolithography. Optical photolithography extended its dominance through fundamental changes in core subsystems (i.e., optics) and linking mechanisms (see also Abernathy, Clark, and Kantrow, 1983; Leonard-Barton, 1995; Rosenkopf and Tushman, 1994; and Meyer and Lehnerd, 1997 for work on design hierarchies and subsystem levels of analysis).

Toward a refined model of dominant designs: nested hierarchies of technology cycles

Differences in points of view regarding underlying causal mechanisms and units of analysis reflected in the work of Abernathy and Utterback (1978), Anderson and Tushman (1990), and Henderson and Clark (1990) can be reconciled with reference to the history of technology and evolutionary economics literatures as well as the emerging empirical literature on dominant designs.

Dominant designs do indeed exist. While levels of analysis differ and are often confused, dominant designs have been found in typewriters, TVs, electronic calculators (Suarez and Utterback, 1995), automobiles (Abernathy, 1978), VCRs (Cusumano, Mylonadis, and Rosenbloom, 1992), flight simulators (Rosenkopf and Tushman, in press; Miller et al., 1995), cochlear implants (Van de Ven and Garud, 1994), fax transmission services (Baum, Kom, and Kotha, 1995), mainframe computers (Iansiti and Khanna, 1995), photolithography (Henderson, 1995), personal mobile stereos

(Sanderson and Uzumeri, 1995), microprocessors (Wade, 1995, 1996), disk drives (Christensen, Suarez, and Utterback, 1996), in the glass, cement, and minicomputer product classes (Anderson and Tushman, 1990), and in cardiac pacemakers (Hidefjall, 1997). In a broad range of industries, periods of product variation are closed with the emergence of a dominant design (e.g., laterally retractable landing gears). After a dominant design emerges, subsequent product variation clusters around the accepted archetype (e.g., continual improvement of retractable landing gears). This dominant design literature when coupled with the history of technology literature indicates that dominant designs are a robust phenomenon.

While support for the existence of dominant designs has been strong, the impact of this literature has been diminished because of confusion in levels of analysis (Freeman, 1978). Where dominant designs have been most often described at the product level, the demonstration of the phenomenon is centered at the subsystem level of analysis. For example, where Abernathy (1978) describes the Model-T as an early dominant design in automobiles, his empirical referent is the internal combustion engine dominating battery and steam powered engines. Similarly, Anderson and Tushman (1990) refer to dominant designs in minicomputers but only provide data on the CPU. Finally, Christensen and colleagues (1998) describe a single dominant design in disk drives, but suggest that only two subsystems drive their standard–intelligent interfaces and the Winchester architecture. It seems that the appropriate unit of analysis in understanding dominant designs is at the subsystem level and that core subsystems (e.g., the engine in automobiles) drive subsequent, interrelated changes in lower-level subsystems.

There are several important exceptions to this unit of analysis confusion. These studies support the notion that core subsystems drive system-level innovation. Henderson (1993, 1995) found that optical photolithography was able to remain dominant over time due to shifts in component (i.e., lens), linking, and complementary technologies. Iansiti and Khanna (1995) demonstrate that IBM was able to control the evolving dominant design in mainframe computers over a 20-year period through sustained attention to innovation in multiple subsystems (e.g., boards, cables, and solid-state logic). Similarly, Sanderson and Uzumeri's (1995) research on Sony's dominance in personal portable stereos and Tripsas's (1997) work on Mergenthaler's dominance for over 100 years in typesetting are both anchored on constant changes in subsystems and linking innovations.

Consistent with Henderson and Clark's (1990) and Baldwin and Clark's (1997) work, the empirical work suggests that products are composed of a nested hierarchy of subsystems and linking mechanisms (see figure 10.3). Further, consistent with Anderson and Tushman (1990) and Tushman and Rosenkopf (1992), the evolutionary processes of variation, selection, and retention operate at the subsystem and linking levels of analysis.

Observation 1. *Products can be decomposed into subsystems and linking mechanisms. Subsystems can, in turn, also be decomposed into their own subsystems and linking mechanisms.*

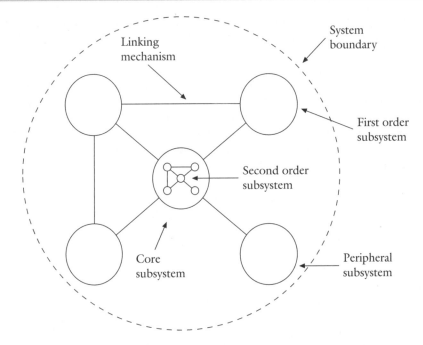

Figure 10.3 System composed of subsystems and linking mechanisms.
Source: Tushman and Rosenkopf (1992).

Not all subsystems are equivalent. Rather, products are composed of hierarchically ordered subsystems that are coupled together by linking mechanisms that are as crucial to the product's performance as are the subsystems themselves (see figure 10.3). Those more core subsystems are either tightly connected to other subsystems or represent a strategic performance bottleneck (e.g., Hughes, 1983; Clark, 1985). In contrast, a peripheral subsystem is one that is only weakly connected to other subsystems.

Shifts in core subsystems have cascading effects on other more peripheral subsystems. Technological evolution in peripheral subsystems is paced by core subsystems in order to maintain the system's overall performance (Ulrich and Eppinger, 1995). In contrast, changes in peripheral subsystems have only minor effects on other subsystems. For example, in airplane engines. Constant (1980) demonstrated how the success of jet engines (engines with no pistons, cylinders, or propellers) drove complementary changes in all other engine subsystems.

Observation 2. *Subsystems differ in their degree of centrality. Core subsystems are those that are tightly coupled to other subsystems. In contrast, peripheral subsystems are only weakly coupled to other subsystems.*

Hypothesis 1. *Changes in core subsystems will have greater system-wide effects than changes in peripheral subsystems.*

Products range from non-assembled (e.g., cement, chemicals) to simple assembled (e.g., skis, tennis racquets), to complex assembled (e.g., flight simulators, airplanes), to open systems (e.g., radio or TV systems) (Tushman and Rosenkopf, 1992). The greater the product's complexity, the greater the number of interfaces and linkage demands. For example, where in skis the linkage between subsystems is accomplished physically, in flight simulators the linkage between the motion systems, flight instrumentation, and computer hardware is accomplished through a complex set of software-based linking mechanisms (Rosenkopf and Tushman, 1998). Systems integration in complex products is strategically crucial to product performance (see Iansiti, 1998).

> **Observation 3.** *The more complex the product, the greater the centrality of linking mechanisms.*

Any single product might have several core subsystems and core subsystems shift over time. Once a particular core subsystem closes on a dominant design, the product's strategic action moves to another core subsystem or another key dimension of merit. For example, in watches, after quartz movements became the dominant design in oscillation, SMH (via the Swatch watch) changed the basis of competition in the low-cost watch sector by treating the case, once a peripheral subsystem, as a core subsystem. Swatch's injection-molded plastic cases required system-wide shifts in other components and linking mechanisms. Similarly, in power systems, Hughes (1983) describes core subsystems changing over time as network system bottlenecks shifted as subsystem problems (e.g., generator efficiency, energy transfer, or motor loads) were sequentially solved.

> **Hypothesis 2.** *For complex products, core subsystems will shift over time.*

Products as hierarchically ordered systems composed of subsystems and linking mechanisms is consistent with the empirical literature on dominant designs. Abernathy (1978) focused his attention on one of the automobile's core subsystems – the engine. Similarly, while Tushman and Anderson (1986) and Cusumano, Mylonadis, and Rosenbloom (1992) discussed minicomputers and VCRs respectively, they actually only gathered data on the minicomputer's and VCR's core subsystems, the CPU and the scanner of a VCR, respectively. More recently, Baldwin and Clark (1997) explicitly model mainframes as a set of interlinked modules. Singh (1997) models hospital software systems as composed of components and linkages, while Meyer and Lehnerd (1997) model product platforms as sets of subsystems and associated interfaces. Similarly, Baum, Korn, and Kotha (1995) and Sanderson and Uzumeri (1995) describe fax machines and Sony's Walkman as composed of core subsystems and linking mechanisms. Finally, Iansiti and Clark (1994) and Iansiti and Khanna (1995) focus on subsystems and linking mechanisms in mainframes. They observe that the discreteness of technological evolution is hidden in technological transitions at the component level.

If products are made up of nested hierarchies, the phenomenon of dominant designs applies most fundamentally at the subsystem and linking levels of analysis. Except for simple, non-assembled products where the best technology most likely dominates, in more complex products, innovation patterns for each subsystem and linking mechanism are shaped not by optimizing processes, but by evolutionary processes of variation, selection, and retention. Where deterministic, technology-driven processes do characterize eras of incremental change after dominant designs emerge, sociopolitical/institutional processes characterize eras of ferment prior to the emergence of a dominant design (see figure 10.2). Dominant designs are pivot points between alternative modes of technological change (Tushman and Rosenkopf, 1992; Miner and Haunschild, 1995).

The process of adjudication between alternative variants (e.g., tuning forks, escapement, or quartz movements in watches or OS/2, Mac, or Windows operating systems for PCs) is not driven by optimizing processes (Nelson, 1995). Rather, the empirical work in ships (Gilfillan, 1935), machine tools (Noble, 1984), cochlear implants (Van de Ven and Garud, 1994), microprocessors (Garud and Kumaraswamy, 1993; Wade, 1995), fax transmission (Baum, Korn, and Kotha, 1995), and the World Wide Web (Hunt and Aldrich, 1998) indicates that technological uncertainty during eras of ferment is adjudicated through a process of population-level compromise and accommodation played out in political, institutional, and economic domains. This population-level learning is driven by social-, political-, and institutional-level action that is accentuated for open systems (e.g., standards in cell phones) but minimized in simple, non-assembled products (Miner and Haunschild, 1995). If, however, governments become involved (as in cellular telephony) or in low-volume markets (e.g., satellites), then variation and selection processes are dampened such that either no dominant design emerges or dominant designs emerge that are locally idiosyncratic (e.g., railway track gauges in Europe).

Observation 4.   *Dominant designs apply at the subsystem and linking levels of analysis.*

Hypothesis 3.   *For simple, non-assembled products, dominant designs emerge out of a technological/optimizing logic.*

Hypothesis 4.   *For complex products, subsystem and linking dominant designs emerge out of social/political processes between communities of interest.*

Hypothesis 5.   *Dominant designs will either not emerge in regulated or low-volume markets or will be locally idiosyncratic.*

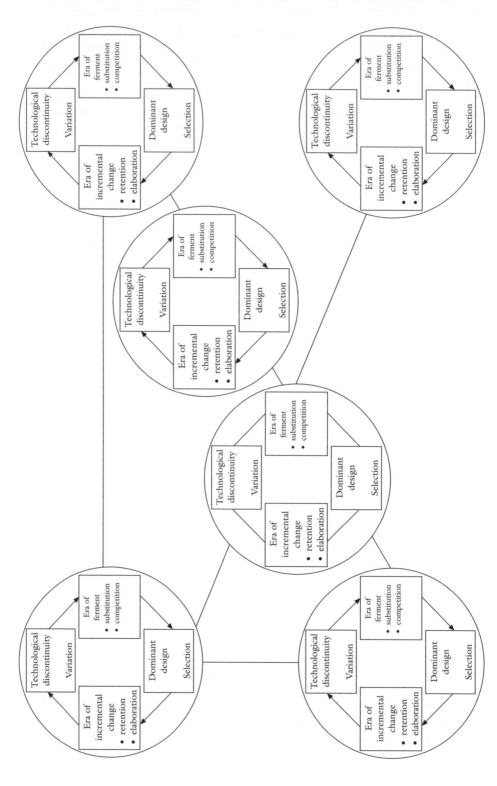

Figure 10.4 Subsystems, linking mechanisms, and technology cycles.

Once an era of ferment is closed with the emergence of a dominant design, subsequent technological progress is driven by forces internal to the selected variant (e.g., the Windows operating system or quartz movements). Eras of incremental change are eventually broken by subsequent technological discontinuities (e.g., automatic kinetic energy replacing batteries in watches). These discontinuities, in turn, initiate a subsequent technology cycle. Thus, Anderson and Tushman's (1990) work on technology cycles applies not at the product level of analysis, but rather at the subsystem and linking levels of analysis (Rosenkopf and Tushman, 1994). However, when all core subsystems are in eras of incremental change (i.e., have stable dominant designs), then the concept of dominant design applies at the product level. For example, the DC-3, the Fordson tractor, and full-flight simulators are each dominant designs at the product level that were made up of a bundle of core subsystems each in eras of incremental change (Utterback, 1994; Rosenkopf and Tushman, 1998).

> *Observation 5.* Dominant designs at the product level of analysis are found when all core subsystems are in eras of incremental change.

Technological change at the product level is driven by a hierarchy of technology cycles at the subsystem and linkage levels of analysis. The action in product evolution is driven by shifts in its core subsystems. For example, in cell phones in the late 1990s, the battle between transmission subsystems (GSM in Europe vs. CDMA and TDMA in the United States) is more strategically important than human interface subsystems. For core subsystems, an era of ferment begins with a technological discontinuity and ends with the selection of a dominant design. The era of incremental change is eventually broken by the next discontinuity; dominant designs, then, evolve over time. Once a core subsystem closes on a dominant design, the basis of technological competition shifts to other core subsystems or to more peripheral subsystems (e.g., Hughes, 1983; Vincenti, 1994). Second-order or component technology cycles (e.g., octane fuel or engine valves) are nested in subsystem technology cycles (e.g., airplane engines) (see Rosenbloom and Christensen's (1994) discussion of nested hierarchies and value networks) (see figures 10.3 and 10.4).

> *Hypothesis 6.* Dominant designs at the subsystem and linkage levels of analysis will evolve over time as technological discontinuities initiate subsequent technology cycles.
>
> *Hypothesis 7.* Dominant designs in core subsystems will have greater impact on the product than dominant designs in peripheral subsystems.
>
> *Hypothesis 8.* Once a dominant design emerges in a core subsystem, the basis of competition shifts to other core or more peripheral subsystems.

DOMINANT DESIGNS, TECHNOLOGY CYCLES, AND ORGANIZATIONAL OUTCOMES

What are the effects of dominant designs and evolving technology cycles on environmental conditions and organizational outcomes? While the units of analysis are often mixed, the empirical literature on the effects of dominant designs are unequivocal. Dominant designs have important effects on competitive environments and organizational outcomes. Shaping dominant designs and, in turn, technology cycles are fundamental to creating dynamic organizational capabilities (Tushman and O'Reilly, 1997; Bercovitz, deFigueiredo, and Teece, 1997).

Dominant designs are at the juncture between uncertain eras of ferment and more certain eras of incremental change (Anderson and Tushman, 1990) (see figure 10.3). Anderson and Tushman (1997) found that uncertainty during eras of ferment was hazardous to firms; both demand and technological uncertainty during eras of ferment were more hazardous to firms than the technological discontinuities themselves or macroeconomic conditions. Van de Ven and Garud (1994) and Rosenkopf and Tushman (1998) found that community networks during eras of ferment were more dispersed than during eras of incremental change, and that these community networks became more stable and consolidated as dominant designs shifted in the cochlear implant and flight simulator industries, respectively.

> *Hypothesis 9.   Eras of ferment are more uncertain than eras of incremental change.*

The emergence of a dominant design has powerful effects on bases of competition in a product class. Rivalry shifts from product to process innovation when dominant designs emerge (Abernathy and Utterback, 1978; Utterback 1994). Requisite organizational forms differ between eras of ferment and eras of incremental change. Hunt and Aldrich (1998) found that in the Web community, r-specialist forms play a dominant role in eras of ferment, while k-strategists thrive during eras of incremental change.

Shifting bases of competition differentially affect incumbents versus new entrants. Suarez and Utterback (1995) and Utterback and Suarez (1993) found that the closing on a dominant design was associated with a sharp drop in the number of firms in a product class and that the probability of success of new entrants drops after a dominant design. Similarly, Baum, Korn, and Kotha (1995) found that failure rates of incumbents decreased after a dominant design, while failure rates of new entrants were less before than after a dominant design. Wade's (1996) study of the microprocessor market between 1971 and 1989 found that new entrants were the primary sources of new technological designs, that entry patterns followed traditional density-dependent patterns, that new entrants initiated alternative designs during eras of incremental change that, in turn, triggered subsequent eras of ferment. Finally, Christensen and colleagues (1996) found a window of opportunity around a dominant design in the disk-drive industry; just prior to the dominant design new entrants had significantly less probability of failure than just after the dominant design.

> *Hypothesis 10.* Bases of competition will be different in eras of ferment than during eras of incremental change. During the former competition hinges on major product innovation, while during the latter competition shifts to process innovation and incremental technological change.
>
> *Hypothesis 11.* Once a dominant design emerges, product class entry rates will decrease and exit rates will increase.
>
> *Hypothesis 11A.* Entry rates of new firms will decrease and incumbents will have greater survival rates after the dominant design.
>
> *Hypothesis 12.* Dominant designs in core subsystems will have greater effects on entry and exit rates than dominant designs in peripheral subsystems.

Shaping the emergence and subsequent destruction of dominant designs is strategically crucial to firms. Christensen et al. (1996), Teece (1987), Cusumano and Selby (1995), Sanderson and Uzumeri (1995) and Iansiti and Khanna (1995) found that those firms that captured the dominant design outperformed others. In contrast, as seen so clearly in Cusumano, Mylonadis, and Rosenbloom's (1992) discussion of VCRs, Sanderson and Uzumeri's (1995) discussion of personal mobile stereos, and Teece's (1987) discussion of medical electronics, losing the battle between product variants is devastating. Similarly, as seen in the photolithography (Henderson, 1995), disk drive (Christensen and Bower, 1996; Rosenbloom and Christensen, 1994), tire (Sull, Tedlow, and Rosenbloom, 1997), typesetting (Tripsas, 1997), and automobile industries (Abernathy, 1978), losing control of an evolving dominant design is catastrophic. In sharp contrast, controlling an evolving dominant design, as IBM did in mainframes (Iansiti and Khanna, 1995), as Mergenthaler did in typesetting (Tripsas, 1997), as Microsoft has done in operating systems (Cusumano and Selby, 1995), and Sony did with its Walkman (Sanderson and Uzumeri, 1995), is associated with sustained market power (see also Morone, 1993).

> *Hypothesis 13.* Sustained competitive advantage is gained by shaping dominant designs in core subsystems over time.
>
> *Hypothesis 13A.* Firms that gain control of core subsystems will be systematically more successful than those that control peripheral subsystems.
>
> *Hypothesis 14.* Firms that lose the dominant design in a core subsystem will face severe performance decline.

What are the organizational determinants of surviving through technology cycles – of both shaping dominant designs, managing during periods of incremental change and, in turn, initiating a subsequent technological discontinuity to reinitiate the technology cycle? There is substantial literature on dynamic organizational capabilities. Perhaps most clearly, during eras of incremental change, small changes in existing subsystems and linking mechanisms is the forte of incumbents. Highly inertial veterans are designed to take advantage of scale economies and to execute incremental change (Tushman and Romanelli, 1985; Nelson and Winter, 1982). During eras of incremental change, such minor organizational changes are associated with predictability, efficiency, and incremental innovation (Myers and Marquis, 1969; Dougherty and Hardy, 1996; Tushman and O'Reilly, 1997).

> *Hypothesis 15. Eras of incremental change will be dominated by veteran firms.*

While veteran firms thrive during eras of incremental change, inertial forces hold these firms hostage to their pasts – core competencies become core rigidities (Leonard-Barton, 1992). For example, in the Swiss watch industry during the 1980s, incremental improvements in escapements hindered these dominant firms from taking advantage of the subsequent technological discontinuity (i.e., the quartz movement) that the Swiss themselves invented (Glassmeier, 1991).

Technological discontinuities, and in turn, subsequent technology cycles, are strongly resisted by organizational inertia and the history of the current era of incremental change. Organizational inertia affects both subsystem and linking technology transitions. Henderson and Clark (1990) and Henderson (1993) found that over a series of subsystem and linking technology transitions, incumbent firms in the photolithography industry were either unable to innovate or were incompetent in doing so. Similarly, Christensen and Bower (1996) and Christensen and Rosenbloom (1995) found that in the disk-drive industry, in wave after wave of shifts in linking mechanisms, veteran firms were dominated by new entrants. Christensen and his colleagues suggest that while veteran firms can initiate substantial subsystem changes to existing customers, when evolving technologies open up potentially new customer bases, existing customers and extant resource allocation practices hold veteran firms hostage to their pasts.[2]

Discontinuous shifts in subsystem technologies (for example, the quartz versus escapement transition for Swiss producers) are inconsistent with inertial force as well as with interrelated organizational capabilities rooted in different operating principles and complementary assets (Tripsas, 1997; Barnett, 1997). Discontinuous subsystem innovations are usually initiated by new firms or by innovative users (e.g., Von Hippel, 1988; Cooper and Smith, 1992; Tripsas, 1997; Foster, 1986). Veteran firms either ignore these technological discontinuities or react incompetently. For example, where veteran firms were well aware of fundamentally new microprocessor, reprographic, and oscillation technologies, it was new firms that initiated RISC and reprographic technologies and the quartz movement (Wade, 1995; Von Hippel, 1988; Glassmeier, 1991). Similarly, Sull, Tedlow, and Rosenbloom (1997) found that competence-destroying technological change (i.e., radial tires) in the tire industry triggered slow and incompetent moves by incumbents. In the United States, every veteran tire firm but one was dominated by new players. Finally, Methé, Swaminathan, and Mitchell (1996) found that in the telecommunications industry, veteran firms initiated competence-enhancing technological discontinuities, while new firms initiated competence-destroying technological discontinuities.

Hypothesis 16. For both subsystem and linking technologies, technological discontinuities and subsequent eras of ferment are more frequently initiated by new firms than by veterans.

Where most incumbent firms are anchored to incremental subsystem and linkage change by strong inertial forces, some are not (Morone, 1993; Hurst, 1995; Tushman and O'Reilly, 1997). Strong organizational linking capabilities seem to be important in shaping dominant designs over time (McGrath, MacMillan, and Tushman, 1992; Tripsas, 1997). Organizational linking mechanisms must be able to attend to a product's linking requirements. As a product's subsystems and linking mechanisms shift over time, so too must the organization's architecture (Ulrich and Eppinger, 1995). For example, Sanderson and Uzumeri (1995) described how Sony was able to generate seven generations of Walkman over a 10-year period by fundamental shifts in the product's subsystem and linking mechanisms. To prosper over several technology cycles, Sony invested in complex organizational linking mechanisms including: multiple, distinct platform teams, and multiple project managers yet integrated by a single senior team. Similar intra-organizational heterogeneity with strong senior team integration was also found to drive multiple technology cycles at Honda (Nonaka, 1988) and at NEC, Canon, and Epson (Imai, Nonaka, and Takeuchi, 1985).

Because a product's linkage mechanisms are so crucial in all but the most simple products, a firm's integrative capability reflected in its diversity of organizational linkage mechanisms and competencies is an important determinant of shaping evolving dominant designs for linking technologies (Iansiti, 1998; Henderson and Clark, 1990). Further, as dominant designs in all but the most simple products are an institutional phenomenon, those firms most effective at shaping evolving dominant designs will have diverse external linkages and capabilities (Tripsas, 1997, Podolny and Stuart, 1995; Wade, 1995; Powell and Brantley, 1991). These external capabilities help shape evolving coalitions in favor of the focal firm (Rosenkopf and Tushman, 1998).

Hypothesis 17. For complex products, those firms that shape dominant designs in linking mechanisms will have stronger organizational linking capabilities than those less successful firms.

Hypothesis 18. For complex products, those most successful firms in shaping dominant designs will have denser and more diverse external networks than those less successful firms.

Those rare firms that do make the transition across technology cycles do so through complex organizational forms, dense external linkages, and revolutionary organizational changes. Those disk-drive firms that made it through several technology cycles did so through a combination of intra-organizational experimentation, option creation, and discontinuous organizational changes (Bowman and Hurry, 1993; Burgelman, 1994; Christensen and Bower, 1996). Cusumano and Selby (1995) describe how Microsoft was able to cannibalize its DOS product and move rapidly into Windows through product diversity coupled with discontinuous organizational changes. Tripsas (1997) describes how only the Mergenthaler firm was able to survive through four technological discontinuities in the typesetter industry. She finds that dynamic capabilities come from building integrative capabilities during eras of incremental change, hosting complex organizational forms, as well as the ability to initiate major organizational changes. Similarly, Tushman and O'Reilly (1997) describe how CibaVision was able to build its conventional lens business even as it worked to destroy the product with either extended wear or disposable lenses. Such dynamic capabilities in the face of discontinuous technological change come from building into the firm internally inconsistent organizational architectures – architectures that simultaneously drive both incremental as well as revolutionary technological change – as well as the ability to initiate discontinuous organizational changes (Bradach, 1997; Levinthal, 1997a, 1997b; Brown and Eisenhardt, 1997).

Hypothesis 19.   Those firms that shape dominant designs over time do so by simultaneously generating both incremental and discontinuous technological change.

Hypothesis 20.   Dynamic capabilities, the ability of veterans to move through successive technology cycles, is rooted in internally inconsistent organizational architectures and in the ability to execute discontinuous organizational changes.

Given the power of organizational inertia, shifts between eras of ferment and eras of incremental change seem to require discontinuous organizational changes (Tushman and Romanelli, 1985; Levinthal, 1997b; Sastry, 1997). It may be important to distinguish levels of analysis in initiating discontinuous organizational change. Anderson and Tushman (1990) found that in the cement, glass, and minicomputer industries, both competence-enhancing and -destroying process technological changes were initiated by incumbents; only competence destroying product changes were initiated by new players. It may be that discontinuous technological changes that are isolated to peripheral subsystems and/or single functions (e.g., process innovation within operations) can be initiated by revolutionary subunit change. Such localized technological discontinuities may not disrupt other subsystems and/or complementary assets. Tripsas (1997) found, for example, that those typesetting discontinuities that did not affect other complementary assets were initiated by incumbents (see also Mitchell, 1989).

In contrast, discontinuous technological change in a core subsystem will be initiated by system-wide organizational change (or more likely, by new entrants) (Romanelli and Tushman, 1994). Further, as shifts in linking technologies run counter to organization-wide embedded competencies, shifts in these technologies will also be associated with discontinuous, system-wide organizational changes (e.g., Henderson and Clark, 1990). Thus, as level of analysis is important in categorizing technological change, it may also be important in categorizing organizational changes associated with evolving technology cycles (e.g., Tushman and O'Reilly, 1997; Brown and Eisenhardt, 1997).

> *Hypothesis 21. The locus of discontinuous organizational changes will shift for core versus peripheral subsystem technological discontinuities. Discontinuous shifts in core subsystems will be associated with organization-wide discontinuous change. In contrast, discontinuous shifts in peripheral subsystems will only be associated with subunit organizational changes.*
>
> *Hypothesis 21A. Discontinuous shifts in linking technologies will be associated with organization-wide discontinuous changes.*

CONCLUSION

Our review of the history of technology, economics, and technology management literatures indicates that dominant designs and technology cycles are important phenomena for scholars of organizations; one must understand the development and evolution of dominant designs to understand how firms and their product classes evolve. We have found it useful to clarify appropriate levels of analysis. We have explored the causal mechanisms of dominant designs at the subsystem and linkage levels of analysis and, under limited conditions, at the product level. We have also explored how dominant designs and technology cycles affect environmental conditions and organizational outcomes.

Dominant designs are most fundamentally found at the subsystem and linkage levels of analysis. They do not arise through the invisible hand of the market. Rather, dominant designs are an outcome of institutional forces moderated by economics constraints and technological possibilities. Dominant designs emerge through the more visible interactions of compromise and accommodation among interest groups. Because of the sociopolitical nature of dominant design evolution, they can only be known in retrospect, and they are amenable to managerial action. The more complex the product, the greater the intensity of these sociopolitical dynamics and the greater the potential to shape dominant designs and technology cycles through strategic action both within and outside the firm. Strategic technological action takes place, then, at the subsystem and linkage levels. Dominant designs appear at the product level only when subsystems and linking mechanisms are in eras of incremental change.

A focus on subsystems permits the identification of core versus peripheral subsystems – of design hierarchies. Not all subsystems are equally important. Core subsystems pace innovations in more peripheral subsystems and are, as such, more strategically important to both firm and product class evolution. Further, dominant designs are a transition point in larger technology cycles. Dominant designs end an era of ferment and initiate the subsequent era of incremental change. As technological discontinuities disrupt eras of incremental change, dominant designs evolve over time. Eras of incremental change are dominated by incumbents, while eras of ferment are dominated by new entrants. Yet those rare firms that do move across technology cycles, that do exhibit dynamic capabilities, do so through complex organizational architectures, creating strategic options, and through discontinuous organizational change. We argued that the locus of discontinuous organizational change would be contingent on the type and locus of subsystem change.

Dominant designs and technology cycles are classic phenomenon-driven meso concepts (Pfeffer, 1997); they cross levels of analysis as well as literature streams. Dominant designs and technology cycles are concepts that can help integrate and bridge strategy, organizational and economic literatures with respect to organization evolution. Not only are dominant designs and technological discontinuities crucial to understanding the phenomenon of organizational evolution, they also may provide leverage for managerial action in shaping technological evolution and, in turn, organizational fates. Through taking action on core subsystems and shaping eras of ferment, managers can actually shape the nature of technological change to their advantage. Similarly, initiating a new technology cycle is a way of moving from today's dominant design tomorrow's era of ferment and, in turn, next dominant design. Linking technology cycles and dominant designs to organizational architectures and competencies is a way to get more deeply to the roots of dynamic organizational capabilities.

The phenomena of technology cycles and dominant designs lie at the intersection of both strategy and organization theory as well as at the intersection of theory and practice. Given their centrality to such crucial organizational phenomena, and given the number of unresolved issues, much exciting theoretical and empirical work remains in coupling dominant designs and technology cycles to environmental conditions and organizational evolution.

ACKNOWLEDGMENTS

We thank Howard Aldrich, Philip Anderson, Andy Henderson, Rita McGrath, Charles O'Reilly, Richard Nelson, Simon Rodan, Lori Rosenkopf, and Barry Staw for their helpful comments. We also thank Walter Vincenti for pointing us to valuable sources on the history of airplanes and landing gears.

NOTES

1 From a study of the evolution of farm tractors, locomotives, aircrafts, tank ships, electric power generation systems, computers, and passenger ships, Sahal (1981) develops very similar concepts which he calls "technological guideposts" and "innovation avenues." He also finds that certain design approaches serve as the starting point for incremental innovations over long periods until they are overthrown by other radical design approaches.

2   Christensen and Bower (1996) categorize technological changes not in terms of techno-
    logical trajectories, but as technologically sustaining or disruptive. Sustaining technological
    changes enhance existing customer's dimensions of merit (e.g., capacity in disk drives),
    while disruptive technologies shift a product's key dimensions of merit (e.g., weight or
    size). Where Christensen and Bower's (1996) sustaining/disruptive dimensions focus on
    customers or markets (independent of subsystems), Anderson and Tushman's (1990)
    notion of competence enhancing/destroying technological change applies for subsystems
    (independent of customer). Chritensen and Bower (1996) observe that sustaining techno-
    logical changes are relatively easy for incumbents, while shifting value chains and initiating
    disruptive technological changes is very difficult for incumbents.

REFERENCES

Abernathy, W. (1978). *The productivity dilemma*. Baltimore: Johns Hopkins University Press.

Abernathy, W., and Clark, K. (1985). Innovation: Mapping the winds of creative destruction. *Research Policy*, 14, 3–22.

Abernathy, W., Clark, K., and Kantrow, A. (1983). *Industrial renaissance*. New York: Basic Books.

Abernathy, W., and Utterback, J. (1978). Patterns of industrial innovation. *Technology Review*, *80*, 40–7.

Aitken, H. (1985). *The continuous wave*. Princeton: Princeton University Press.

Alexander, C. (1964). *Notes on the synthesis of form*. Cambridge, MA: Harvard University Press.

Anderson, P., and Tushman, M. (1997). Organizational environments and industry exit: Effects of uncertainty, munificence and complexity. Working paper, Dartmouth, Tuck School.

Anderson, P., and Tushman. M. (1990). Technological discontinuities and dominant designs: A cyclical model of technological change. *Administrative Science Quarterly*, 35, 604–33.

Arthur, W. B. (1988). Competing technologies: An overview. In G. Dosi, C. Freeman, R. Nelson, G. Silverberg, and L. Soete (Eds.), *Technical change and economic theory*. London: Pinter.

Arthur, B. (1989). Competing technologies. Increasing returns, and lock-in by historically small events. *The Economic Journal*, *99*(394), 116–31.

Baldwin, C., and Clark, K. (1997). Design rules: The power of modularity. Working paper, Harvard Business School.

Barley, S. (1990). The alignment of technology and structure through roles and networks. *Administrative Science Quarterly*, *35*(1), 61–103.

Barnett, W. (1997). The dynamics of competitive intensity. *Administrative Science Quarterly*, 42, 128–60.

Basalla, G. (1988). *The evolution of technology*. New York: Cambridge University Press.

Baum, J. A. C., Korn, H. J., and Kotha, S. (1995). Dominant designs and population dynamics in telecommunications services: Founding and failure of facsimile transmission service organizations, 1965–1992. *Social Science Research*, 24, 97–135.

Bercovitz, J., de Figueiredo, J., and Teece, D. (1997). Firm capabilities and managerial decision making. In R. Garud, P. Nayyar, and Z. Shapira (Eds.), *Technological innovation: Oversights and foresights*. Cambridge: Cambridge University Press.

Bijker, W., Hughes, T., and Pinch, T. (1987). *The social construction of technological systems*. Cambridge, MA: MIT Press.

Bowman, N., and Hurry, D. (1993). Strategy through the options lens: An integrated view of resource investments and incremental choice processes. *Academy of Management Review*, *18*(4), 760–82.

Bradach, J. (1997). Using the plural form in the management of restaurant chains. *Administrative Science Quarterly, 42*(2), 276–303.

Brown, S., and Eisenhardt, K. (1997). The art of continuous change: Linking complexity theory and time paced evolution. *Administrative Science Quarterly, 42,* 1–34.

Burgelman, R. (1994). Fading memories: A process theory of strategic business exit. *Administrative Science Quarterly, 39,* 24–36.

Christensen, C., and Bower, J. (1996). Customer power, strategic investment, and the failure of leading firms. *Strategic Management Journal, 17,* 197–218.

Christensen, C., and Rosenbloom, R. (1995). Explaining the attacker's advantage: Technological paradigms, organizational dynamics, and the value network. *Research Policy, 24,* 233–57.

Christensen, C., Suarez, F., and Utterback, J. (1998). Strategies for survival in fast-changing industries. *Management Science, 44*(12), Part 2 of 2, S207–S220.

Clark, K. B. (1985). The interaction of design hierarchies and market concepts in technological evolution. *Research Policy, 14,* 235–51.

Constant, E. W. (1980). *The origins of the turbojet revolution* (Vol. 5). Baltimore: The Johns Hopkins University Press.

Cooper, A., and Smith, C. (1992). How established firms respond to threatening technologies. *Academy of Management Executive, 6*(2), 55–70.

Cusumano, M., Mylonadis, Y., and Rosenbloom, R. (1992). Strategic maneuvering and mass market dynamics: The triumph of VHS over Beta. *Business History Review,* 51–93.

Cusumano, M., and Selby, R. (1995). *Microsoft secrets.* New York: Free Press.

David, P. (1985). Clio and the economics of qwerty. *Economic History,* 30–49.

David, P. A., and Greenstein, S. (1990). The economics of compatibility standards: An introduction to recent research. *Economics of Innovations and New Technology, 1,* 3–41.

Davies, A. (1997). Innovation in large technical systems: Case of telecommunications. *Industrial and Corporate Change, 5,* 1143–80.

Dosi, G. (1982). Technological paradigms and technological trajectories. *Research Policy, 11,* 147–62.

Dosi, G. (1984). *Technical change and industrial transformation.* New York: St. Martin's Press.

Dougherty, D., and Hardy, C. (1996). Sustained product innovation in large, mature organizations. *Academy of Management Journal, 39,* 1120–53.

Ehrnberg, E. (1995). On the definition and measurement of technological discontinuities. *Technomation, 5,* 437–52.

Foster, R. (1986). *Innovation: The attacker's advantage.* New York: Summit Books.

Freeman, J. (1978). The unit of analysis in organizational research. In M. Meyer (Ed.), *Environments and organizations.* San Francisco: Jossey Bass.

Garud, R., and Kumaraswamy, A. (1993). Changing competitive dynamics in network industries: An exploration of Sun Microsystem's open system strategy. *Strategic Management Journal, 14,* 351–69.

Gilfillan, S. C. (1935). *Inventing the ship.* Chicago: Follet Publishing Company.

Glassmeier, A. (1991). Technological discontinuities and flexible production networks: The case of Switzerland and the world watch industry. *Research Policy, 20,* 469–85.

Gort, M., and Klepper, S. (1982). Time paths in the diffusion of product innovations. *Economic Journal, 92,* 630–53.

Hanieski, J. F. (1973). The airplane as an economic variable: Aspects of technological change in aeronautics, 1903–1955. *Technology and Culture, 14*(4), 535–52.

Henderson, R. (1995). Of life cycles real and imaginary: The unexpectedly long old age of optical lithography. *Research Polity, 24,* 631–43.

Henderson, R. (1993). Underinvestment and incompetence as responses to radical innovation. *Rand Journal of Economics, 24*, 248–69.

Henderson, R., and Clark, K. (1990). Architectural innovation: The reconfiguration of existing product technologies and the failure of existing firms. *Administrative Science Quarterly, 35*, 9–30.

Hidefjall, P. (1997). *The pace of innovation: Patterns of innovation in the cardiac pacemaker industry.* Linkoping University.

Hounshell, D. (1995). Hughesian history of technology and Chandlerian business history. *History and Technology, 12*, 205–24.

Hughes, T. (1983). *Networks of power.* Johns Hopkins Press.

Hunt, C., and Aldrich, H. (1998). The second ecology: The creation and evolution of organizational communities in the world wide web. In B. Staw and L. Cummings (Eds.), *Research in Organizational Behavior, 20*, Greenwich, CT: JAI Press, 267–301.

Hurst, D. (1995). *Crisis and renewal.* Boston: Harvard Business School Press.

Iansiti, M. (1998). *Technology integration.* Boston, MA: Harvard Business School Press.

Iansiti, M., and Clark, K. (1994). Integration and dynamic capability. *Industry and Corporation Change, 3*, 557–606.

Iansiti, M., and Khanna, T. (1995). Technological evolution, system architecture and the obsolescence of firm capabilities. *Industrial and Corporate Change, 4*(2), 333–61.

Imai, K., Nonaka, I., and Takeuchi, H. (1985). Managing the new product development process: How Japanese firms learn and unlearn. In K. Clark et al. (Eds.), *The uneasy alliance.* Harvard Business School Press.

Jenkins, R. (1975). *Images and enterprise.* Baltimore: Johns Hopkins Press.

Jewkes, J., Sawers, D., and Stillerman, R. (1961). *The sources of invention.* New York: Norton.

Klein, B. (1977). *Dynamic economics.* Cambridge, MA: Harvard University Press.

Klepper, S. (1996). Entry, exit, growth, and innovation over the product cycle. *American Economic Review, 86*(3), 562–83.

Klepper, S., and Grady, E. (1990). The evolution of new industries and the determinants of market structure. *Rand Journal of Economics, 27*–44.

Kodama, F. (1995). *Emerging patterns of innovation.* Boston: Harvard Business School Press.

Landes, D. (1983). *Revolution in time.* Cambridge, MA: Harvard University Press.

Langlois, R. N., and Robertson, P. L. (1992). Networks and innovation in a modular system: Lessons from the microcomputer and stereo component industries. *Research Policy, 21*, 297–313.

Lee, J.-R., O'Neal, D. E., Pruett, M. W., and Thomas, H. (1995). Planning for dominance: A strategic perspective on the emergence of dominant design. *R & D Management, 25*(1), 3–15.

Leonard-Barton, D. (1992). Core capabilities and core rigidities: A paradox in managing new product development. *Strategic Management Journal, 13*, 111–25.

Leonard-Barton, D. (1995). *Wellsprings of knowledge.* Boston, MA: Harvard Business School Press.

Levinthal, D. (1997a). Three faces of organizational learning: Wisdom, inertia and discovery. In R. Garud, P. Nayyar, and Z. Shapira (Eds.), *Technological innovation: Oversights and foresights.* Cambridge: Cambridge University Press.

Levinthal, D. (1997b). Adaptation on rugged landscapes. *Management Science, 43*(7), 934–50.

Malerba, F., and Orsenigo, L. (1996). The dynamics and evolution of industries. *Industrial and Corporate Change, 5*(1), 51–88.

Malerba, F., and Orsenigo, L. (1997). Technological regimes and sectoral patterns of innovative activity. *Industrial and Corporate Change, 6*(1), 83–118.

McGrath, R., MacMillan, I., and Tushman, M. (1992). The role of executive team actions in shaping dominant designs: Towards shaping technological progress. *Strategic Management Journal, 13,* 137–61.

Methé, D., Swaminathan, A., and Mitchell, W. (1996). The underemphasized role of established firms as sources of major innovations. *Industrial and Corporate Change, 5,* 1181–204.

Meyer, M., and Lehnerd, A. (1997). *The power of product platforms.* New York: Free Press.

Miller, R., Hobday, M., Leroux-Demers, T., and Olleros, X. (1995). Innovation in complex system industries: The case of flight simulation. *Industrial and Corporate Change, 4*(2), 363–400.

Miner, A., and Haunschild, P. (1995). Population level learning. In B. Staw and L. Cummings (Eds.), *Research in organizational behavior* (Vol. 17, pp. 115–66). Greenwich, CT: JAI Press.

Mitchell, W. (1989). Whether and when? Probability and timing of incumbents' entry into emerging industrial subfields. *Administrative Science Quarterly, 34,* 208–34.

Morone, J. (1993). *Winning in high tech markets.* Boston, MA: Harvard Business School Press.

Myers, S., and Marquis, D. (1969). *Successful industrial innovation.* Washington, DC: NSF.

Nelson, R. (1995). Recent evolutionary theorizing about economic change. *Journal of Economic Literature, 33,* 48–90.

Nelson, R., and Winter, S. (1982). *An evolutionary theory of economic change.* Cambridge, MA: Harvard University Press.

Noble, D. (1984). *Forces of production.* New York: Knopf.

Nonaka, I. (1988). Creating order out of chaos: Self renewal in Japanese firms. *California Management Review, 30*(3), 57–73.

Pinch, T., and Bijker, W. (1987). The social construction of facts and artifacts. In W. Bijker, T. Hughes, and T. Pinch, *The social construction of technological systems.* Cambridge, MA: MIT Press.

Podolny, J., and Stuart, T. (1995). A role-based ecology of technological change. *American Journal of Sociology, 100,* 1224–60.

Powell, W., and Brantley, P. (1991). Competitive cooperation in biotechnology: Learning through networks. In N. Nohria and R. Eccles (Eds.), *Networks and organizations.* Cambridge, MA: Harvard Business School Press.

Prahalad, C., and Hamel, G. (1994). *Competing for the future.* Boston. MA: Harvard Business School Press.

Rae, J. B. (1968). *Climb to greatness: The American aircraft industry* 1920–1960. Cambridge, MA: The MIT Press.

Romanelli, E., and Tushman, M. (1994). Organization transformation as punctuated equilibrium: An empirical test. *Academy of Management Journal, 34,* 1141–66.

Rosenberg, N. (1994). *Exploring the Black box: Technology, economics and history.* Cambridge: Cambridge University Press.

Rosenberg, N. (1976). *Perspectives on technology.* Cambridge: Cambridge University Press.

Rosenbloom, R. S., and Christensen, C. (1994). Technological discontinuities, organization capabilities, and strategic commitments. *Industry and Corporate Change, 3,* 655–86.

Rosenkopf, L., and Tushman, M. (1994). The coevolution of technology and organization. In J. Baum and J. Singh (Eds.), *Evolutionary dynamics of organizations.* Oxford University Press.

Rosenkopf, L., and Tushman, M. (1998). The coevolution of community networks and technology: Lessons from the flight simulator industry. *Industrial and Corporate Change, 7,* 311–46.

Sahal, D. (1981). *Patterns of technological innovation*. Reading, MA: Addison-Wesley.

Saloner, G. (1990). The economics of computer interface standardization: The case of UNIX. *Economics of Innovation and New Technology*, 1, 135–56.

Sanderson, S., and Uzumeri, M. (1995). Product platforms' and dominant designs: The case of Sony's Walkman. *Research Policy*, 24, 583–607.

Sastry, A. (1997). Problems and paradoxes in a model of punctuated organizational change. *Administrative Science Quarterly*, 42(2), 237–75.

Singh, K. (1997). The impact of technological complexity and interfirm cooperation on business survival. *Academy of Management Journal*, 40, 339–67.

Suarez, F. F., and Utterback, J. M. (1995). Dominant designs and the survival of firms. *Strategic Management Journal*, 16, 415–30.

Sull, D., Tedlow, R., and Rosenbloom, R. (1997). Managerial commitments and technological change in the U.S. tire industry. *Industrial and Corporate Change*, 6, 461–500.

Teece, D. (1996). Firm organization, industrial structure and technological innovation. *Journal of Economic Behavior and Organizations*, 31, 193–224.

Teece, D. (1987). Profiting from technological innovation. In D. Teece (Ed.), *The competitive challenge*. New York: Harper & Row.

Teece, D. (1986). Profiting from technological innovation. *Research Policy*, 15, 285–306.

Teece, D., and Pisano, G. (1994). Dynamic capabilities of firms. *Industry and Corporate Change*, 3, 537–56.

Tripsas, M. (1997). Unraveling the process of creative destruction: Complementary assets and incumbent survival in the typesetter industry. *Strategic Management Journal*, Summer Special Issue, 18, 119–42.

Tushman, M., and Anderson, P. (1986). Technological discontinuities and organization environments. *Administrative Science Quarterly*, 31, 439–65.

Tushman, M., Anderson, P., and O'Reilly, C. (1997). Technology cycles, innovation streams and ambidextrous organizations. In M. Tushman and P. Anderson (Eds.), *Managing strategic innovation*. New York: Oxford University Press.

Tushman, M., and O'Reilly, C. (1997). *Winning through innovation: A practical guide to leading organizational change and renewal*. Boston, MA: Harvard Business School Press.

Tushman, M., and Romanelli, E. (1985). Organizational evolution: A metamorphosis model of convergence and reorientation. In L. Cummings & B. Staw (Eds.), *Research in organizational behavior* (Vol. 7). Greenwich, CT.: JAI Press.

Tushman, M., and Rosenkopf, L. (1992). On the organizational determinants of technological change: Towards a sociology of technological evolution. In B. Staw and L. Cummings (Eds.), *Research in organization behavior* (Vol. 14). Greenwich, CT: JAI Press.

Ulrich, K., and Eppinger, S. (1995). *Product design and development*. New York: McGraw-Hill.

Utterback, J. (1994). *Mastering the dynamics of innovation*. Boston: Harvard Business School Press.

Utterback, J., and Suarez, F. F. (1993). Innovation, competition, and industry structure. *Research Policy*, 22(1), 1–21.

Van de Ven, A., and Garud, R. (1994). The coevolution of technical and institutional events in the development of an innovation. In J. Baum and J. Singh (Eds.), *Evolutionary dynamics of organizations*. Oxford University Press.

Vincenti, W. (1990). *What do engineers know and how do they know it?* Baltimore: Johns Hopkins Press.

Vincenti, W. (1994). The retractable landing gear and the northrup "Anomaly": Variation-selection and the shaping of technology. *Technology and Culture*, 35(1), 1–33.

Von Hipple, E. (1988). *Sources of innovation*. New York: Oxford University Press.

Wade, J. (1996). A community-level analysis of sources and rates of technological variation in the microprocessor market. *Academy of Management Journal*, *39* (5), 1218–44.

Wade, J. (1995). Dynamics of organizational communities and technological bandwagons. *Strategic Management Journal*, *16*, 111–33.

Yates, J. (1993). Co-evolution of information-processing technology and use. *Business History Review*, *67*, 1–51.

COMMENTARY
George Westerman and Michael L. Tushman

Modularity, markets and service innovation

In the few years since Tushman and Murmann (1998), much has been written about technology cycles, dominant designs, and organizational evolution. We briefly review this ongoing work with particular reference to product modularity, technology/market strategy, and moderators of technology cycles. Much of what we know about the management of innovation has been derived through studies of product-based innovation. Lessons from studying transitions in product technologies have been generalized to other industries and technologies. Cumulatively, the past 15 to 20 years of research has extended and focused the constructs and theory, leading to an ever-greater understanding of technology cycles and organizational evolution strategy. While building dynamic capabilities is strategically important, it is clearly difficult for incumbents to execute (Lehrer, 2000; Rosenbloom, 2000; Sorensen and Stuart, 2000; Foster and Kaplan, 2001).

But even as research on product innovation accelerates, the percentage of the economy in the service sector is rapidly increasing. In 1999, over 80 percent of all employment in the United States was in service industries, up from 67 percent in 1980 (United Nations, 1999) Unfortunately, most of the studies of innovation retain their product-orientation. While many of the concepts, including modularity, nested hierarchies, core and peripheral components, and organizational architectures may apply to services, the application of all of the concepts is far from clear.

This commentary has two sections. The first takes the frameworks synthesized by Tushman and Murmann (1998) and extends them with key ideas from recent technology, strategy, innovation, and organizational research. The second examines these product-anchored ideas in the light of the service economy. While page limits prevent a full elaboration of ideas, we hope that our commentary will bring additional clarity to innovation in products, and spur debate on innovation in services.

Innovation streams, modularity, and technology cycles

Tushman and Murmann (1998) synthesized the literature on innovation and organizational outcomes, with a focus on dominant designs and technology cycles. They adopted the view of a product as a nested hierarchy of core and peripheral components, each of which has its own technology cycles. Competence-destroying change in core components is associated with negative outcomes for industry leaders, while discontinuities in peripheral components are less problematic. By developing a theoretical framework underlying technology cycles, Tushman and Murmann (1998) added clarity to the research that has focused on technological change, innovation and organizational outcomes. In this section, we describe important extensions to the Tushman and Murmann framework that have arisen over the past few years.

Before getting to our review, let's consider a simple example. An optical scanner is a complex assembled product, consisting of a number of components including optics and image capture, a location/position mechanism, sensors, interface logic, power supply, software drivers, and character recognition software, among others. Each component requires specific competencies to develop, improve, and manufacture. The components must, in turn, be coupled appropriately to provide high system performance and quality. Further, some of these components are core to the product, while others are more peripheral. For example, the power supply is peripheral as there are only a few very simple rules that govern its interactions with the rest of the system. Other components, such as the image capture and positioning subsystems, have much more complex interdependencies with other components and their performance mechanisms actually drive the other subsystems. During the late 1990s, competence destroying change in one of the core subsystems (location/positioning) challenged industry incumbents. Scanning firms rooted in flat-bed technology had to simultaneously compete in cost focused rivalry with existing customers even as they innovated in the emerging "knitting" technology which promised portable scanners to the consumer market (see Radov and Tushman, 2000).

With this example to ground our understanding of Tushman and Murmann's main concepts, we can look at recent extensions to the framework. The extensions can be grouped into three areas

- product structure and competence;
- technology cycles, innovation streams, and senior teams; and
- moderators of product and industry transitions.

Product structure and competence

Gatignon et al. (2000) developed empirically-based measures for key innovation concepts such as competence enhancing and destruction, architectural innovation, and radical innovation. While validating their measures, they discovered that the concepts of competence enhancing and destruction consisted of two distinct dimensions: new competence acquisition and competence enhancing/destroying. Of the two, new competence acquisition in a core component was a more important determinant of organizational outcomes than competence destruction.

In our scanner example, a discontinuity in a core subsystem, such as the location/positioning subsystem, has multiple independent effects. First, new competence is required to develop the positioning system and this is difficult to acquire. Second, destruction of existing competencies makes the adoption more difficult. Finally, if the location/positioning subsystem is a core component, then non-standard linkages to other components cause the discontinuity to have cascading effects throughout the product.

Further Gatignon et al. (2000) found that once the effects of innovation type and characteristics were controlled, architectural innovations had no impact on organizational outcomes. Thus there is clearly a need to push research on the nature of innovation and on innovation characteristics and their differential impacts on organizational outcomes.

Research on another key characteristic of product structure, namely modularity, can be considered an important extension to Tushman and Murmann's ideas of nested hierarchy, dominant designs, and the nature of component linkages. After the closing on a dominant design in a core subsystem, standard interfaces between components provide real options, which allow rapid customization and evolution of product designs (Baldwin and Clark, 2000; Schilling, 2000; McGrath, 2001). Modularity may also provide options that allow manufacturers to explore multiple trajectories at once (Garud and Kumaraswamy, 1995; Garud and Kotha, 1994).

After standards emerge, modularity also allows easy variation in feature sets across and between product generations (Sanderson and Uzumeri, 1995). At its limit, modularity leads to simple build-to-order customization for the mass market (Pine, 1992).

Shifting to a more or less modular product form can require changes in organizational structure to maintain competitive advantage. Here, it is not the modularity of a product, but rather the dynamics of modularity in core components that drive industry transitions (Christensen, et al., 2002). When modular design rules become industry standards, those standards become mechanisms for coordinating designs across the boundaries of firms (Baldwin and Clark, 2000; Sanchez and Mahoney, 1996). Then, economies of scale and specialization drive product class performance. At these junctures, when integrated products become disintegrated bundles of standardized components with standard interfaces, incumbents often get selected out of the product class (for example, Langlois and Robertson, 1992; Sull, 1999; Rosenbloom, 2000). Then, virtual firms, which assemble subsystems produced by outside suppliers, tend to dominate more vertically integrated firms.

In contrast, discontinuous innovation in a modular component can change the level of modularity in the product. If the component dominates product performance (that is, is a core subsystem), and if markets demand more performance than current products deliver, then this discontinuous innovation can cause a shift back to interdependent product forms. Highly interdependent components require a high degree of coordination that is very difficult to achieve across organizational boundaries. Thus, the shift from modular to integrated products drives competitive advantage to more vertically integrated organizational forms over their non-integrated competitors (Christensen, et al., 2002; Chesbrough and Kusunoki, 2001; Tushman and Smith, 2001). Accordingly, in the late 1990s, incumbent scanner manufacturers, facing both modular and interdependent product forms, either had to spin out the emerging knitting/consumer business from the flat-bed business, or find a way to simultaneously host integrated and disintegrated organizational forms.

Technology cycles, innovation streams, and senior teams

Tushman and Murmann (1998) describe technology cycles as driven by technological discontinuities leading to an era of ferment that is closed by the emergence of a dominant design. Once a dominant design emerges, in particular for core subsystems, an era of incremental change ensues as the standards get further elaborated. For complex products, these emerge through socio-political and economic mechanisms. These technology cycles are reinitiated at subsequent technological discontinuities.

Tushman and Murmann pay little attention to the role of market segments or new markets in the dynamics of technology cycles. Different tiers of a market can demand very different types (as opposed to degrees) of performance. Christensen (1997) finds that moving to a new, previously unimportant, dimension of merit can be disruptive to an incumbent, especially when products in these new markets are inferior on traditional performance dimensions. For example, the move to portable scanners, which may have lower performance and lower margins than desktop scanners, could be disruptive to incumbent scanner manufacturers. Christensen and Rosenbloom (1995) also show that market segments interact, as technologies from one market segment can evolve to displace technologies in existing segments. Product movement down-market and up-market adds a vital new dimension to the literature on technology cycles. It may be that dynamic capabilities are rooted in driving streams of innovation – innovations that differ along technical and market dimensions, or both (Abernathy and Clark, 1985; Tushman and Smith, 2001).

But dynamic capabilities are rooted in a firm's ability to compete simultaneously in different competitive regimes (Rosenkopf and Nerkar, 2001; Lehrer, 2000). Tushman and Murmann (1998) suggest that ambidextrous organizational forms permit firms to both explore and exploit simultaneously. An ambidextrous firm or business unit hosts multiple inconsistent organizational architectures within the same business unit (Tushman and O'Reilly, 1997). By simultaneously pursuing multiple experiments at different locations in technology and market space, the ambidextrous manager and the senior team build a portfolio of options from which to make strategic choices (McGrath, 2001). If an option has value, it can be exercised rapidly. If not, the experiment can be closed down. By creating technology cycles and instigating discontinuities inside the firm, the senior team has options from which to make strategic product or market bets. Leonard-Barton's (1995) work on falling forward, Brown and Eisenhardt's (1997) on time paced innovation, experiments and probes, and Burgelman's (1994) work on internal selection environments are consistent with these ideas of creating multiple selection environments within business units. In our scanner example, the general manager of a scanner business unit would be wise to pursue multiple experiments. At the same time as she incrementally improves existing flat-bed products, she might sponsor projects to investigate new optical or sensor technologies targeted to new customer sets.

If a business unit must develop capabilities to explore and exploit simultaneously, where do these inconsistent activities occur? Where does integration occur? Christensen (1997) suggests that because inertial processes are so strong, disruptive technologies cannot be commercialized within the same company as incumbent technologies.

Products for less demanding markets must be commercialized by units spun out from the incumbent unit. In contrast, Tushman and O'Reilly (1997) and Tushman and Smith (2001) argue that a single senior team must own the innovation stream, and this team must build an ambidextrous organizational form. Ambidextrous organizations use highly differentiated subunits, weak tactical integration, and strong senior team integration. Resolving the innovation stream and organizational form question is an empirical question, but some form of organizational differentiation to pursue discontinuous innovation appears to be required.

Ambidextrous organizational forms require senior teams that have the capability of hosting and managing multiple inconsistent architectures. The characteristics of the senior team and its processes are important determinants of their ability to handle the organizational contradictions of exploitation and exploration. Recent work by Rotemberg and Saloner (2000), Tripsas and Gavetti (2000), Gavetti and Levinthal (2000), Edmondson (1999), Pelled et al. (1999), and Dunbar et al. (1996) indicate that dynamic capabilities are at least partly rooted in a senior team's ability to develop and take advantage of multiple cognitive schemes and time frames anchored by a common vision.

Moderators of product and industry transitions

Tushman and Murmann (1998) suggest two major factors that can prevent technology cycles from following their regular pattern. Small market size or strong regulatory influence can either prevent the emergence of a discontinuity or influence the selection processes leading to a dominant design. These constraints on technology cycles entrench the power of incumbents. In the scanner example, small markets such as satellite reconnaissance or highly regulated markets such as medical imaging experience truncated technology cycles. In small markets, there are too few customers and manufacturers to trigger a period of ferment. In the medical field, incumbents may be able to influence regulatory selection environment, and, even if not, regulatory delays enable incumbents to be forewarned about new technologies (for example, Lehrer, 2000).

Recent work suggests that other moderators can affect the impact of technology cycles on firms and industry structure. First, the presence of complementary assets (Teece, 1986; Tripsas, 1997) can raise switching costs for customers, thus reducing effects of technology cycles on incumbents. For example, if customers had transaction-specific investments related to knowledge of an incumbent's particular image manipulation software, they might be unwilling to shift to an entrant that uses different software, even if its scanner is much better.

Another moderator of technology cycles is the set of institutional structures that can entrench incumbents. For example, Japan's leading disk drive manufacturers did not experience the negative effects of disruptive innovation that Christensen (1997) observed in American firms. Chesbrough (1999) suggests that Japan's immobile labor markets, long-term supplier relationships, and restricted capital markets can prevent the emergence and/or success of startups. If no entrants can arise, then incumbents have less to fear from technological change. Incumbents can adopt innovations at a slower pace, thus avoiding some of the negative consequences of market/technology uncertainty in new products. The same institutional forces can affect other aspects of incumbent innovation processes as well. For example, West (2000) found that the limited mobility of the Japanese labor force enabled Japanese semiconductor manufacturers to use more decentralized organizational structures for new product/process development than their American counterparts.

Modularity and open standards, which were described earlier, should be mentioned again as a moderator of technology cycles. Information encapsulated in open standards and modular component interfaces can substitute for the intense coordination required in more interdependent designs (Sanchez and Mahoney, 1996). In so doing, modularity and open standards create external economies of scope (Langlois, 1992) and economies of substitution (Garud and Kumaraswamy, 1993), allowing very rapid evolution of product designs (Baldwin and Clark, 2000). Modularity and open standards can be an important moderator of technology cycles by increasing the pace of variation, but it is unclear whether it works only for certain types of products or in certain parts of the technology cycle. For example, some innovations may actually de-modularize a dominant product design (Christensen, et al., 2002). Additionally, high levels of uncertainty during a period of ferment may make it difficult to specify standard modular interfaces.

Technology cycles, innovation streams and services

Much of the learning about product-based innovation may apply to services. However, there are important distinctions between products and services that may require changes to product-based theory. In this section, we examine the three dimensions of technology cycles mentioned above, examining how product-based theory may or may not apply in the world of services. We conclude that, because of four major distinctions between products and services, incumbent service providers may be more able to adopt innovations and adapt to technology cycles than might be expected from the product-based innovation literature. To the extent that a service is more like a product along these four dimensions, we would expect service providers to be more like product manufacturers in adaptability. Similarly, if a manufacturer's products are more like services along these dimensions, we would expect that firm to be more adaptable than firms producing less "service-like" products.

In order to ground the services discussion, another example is needed. One service that many of us use every week is the corner drugstore. In a drugstore, the major "product" is the process of selling health-related products. Here, the customer conducts many parts of the process in a self-service mode. She selects merchandise, pays at a checkout counter, and carries the product home. Other parts of the process, including stocking the shelves, identifying what products to sell at what prices (merchandising), and filling prescriptions, are performed by the retailer.

The service can be provided in other ways. For example, many retailers and health insurers sell prescriptions through mail order. Here, the components of the process are arranged in a different architecture, and most of the process steps are performed by the retailer. The customer places an order, provides payment, and waits for the prescription to arrive in the mail. Prices are much lower than in traditional retail, but the direct contact which pharmacists and customer value is removed. Recently, another innovation has arisen: online retailing. New competence is required in internet selling and (for some firms) order fulfillment and customer service, but customers may be the same and some processes, such as store-based prescription-filling, may still be useful.

The three forms of drug retailing can be considered analogous to discontinuities and technology cycles. Each version serves somewhat different markets, with different pricing and service levels. Each new form of selling threatened and took market share from existing forms. Yet, some major incumbents were able to adopt and be successful with all three versions.

Major distinctions between products and services

While products and services are similar in many ways, there are also important distinctions that may affect the nature of technological change and its effects on incumbent firms. These include (Regan, 1963; Zeithaml et al., 1985):

1 *Production/consumption simultaneity.* In most services, unlike most manufacturing, production and consumption occur simultaneously. The product is the process, and is executed at or near the place of consumption, with high involvement from the customer. In most instances, each time the user uses a service, the "manufacturing" process must be executed again.
2 *Intangibility.* Services are not tangible artifacts. Performance and quality are difficult to conceptualize, and even more difficult to assess. It can be very difficult to compare service quality across multiple suppliers. Even price comparisons can be difficult in many services because services can be highly heterogeneous and tailored to the customer.
3 *The human element (output heterogeneity):* Many service processes are delivered by people, not by manufacturing machinery. Even highly automated service processes, such as in financial services, often have an important human component for interfacing with the consumer or handling exceptions. Because of this, service quality can vary widely from execution to execution and from location to location. On the other hand, the human element also allows for a level of personalization that is not possible with many products.
4 *Perishability.* Services cannot be produced and then stored for a later date. Similarly, consumers cannot stockpile services and use them later. This implies that service providers can be severely hurt by demand fluctuations, but also that they have frequent contact with their customers.

In the remainder of this commentary, we treat the implications of these distinctions in more detail. We do this by examining the effects of each of these distinctions on the three major components of the Tushman and Murmann (1998) model.

"Product" structure and competence in services

Like products, service delivery processes can be thought of as nested hierarchies of components and linkages. Service components are subprocesses (or activities) that often have a significant human element. Humans introduce a level of flexibility that may make intangible service processes more malleable and reconfigurable than products, and thus more able to absorb technological change.

First, when individuals act as interfaces between process steps, non-modular interfaces between process steps can be made more modular. That is, a person's ability to interpret a set of inputs may enable her to quickly adjust to changing conditions or requests. In essence, individuals can make a core component somewhat less core, and thus make evolution in components less harmful to incumbents. For example, some drug chains were very quick in allowing customers to order a prescription through the internet and pick it up in a local store. The chains initially implemented this by automatically generating special faxes in the local pharmacy. Pharmacists receiving these special faxes knew that they did not need to call physicians or verify insurance coverage because those steps had already been performed by pharmacists in the online group. Later, a more optimal automatic connection was made between store-based pharmacy systems and online systems. In essence, they used the human element to make competence acquisition and architectural innovation more incremental.

Second, simultaneity and perishability can bring the service provider much closer to the customer. The provider has the opportunity to learn, with each service instance, the precise needs of the consumer, and act on those specific needs (Middleton, 1983). This allows a level of mass customization (Pine, 1992) that is not often possible in products. Additionally, innovations and process upgrades can be introduced as needed, and the consumer will always experience the most up-to-date version. So, a service provider can pilot new or modified services on a small subset of customers and obtain rapid feedback.

Technology cycles in services

It is clear that discontinuities do occur in services. The supermarket, the discount broker, ATM machines, containerized transport, and mail order pharmacy all represented order-of-magnitude improvements in price/performance for certain customer or business segments. What is less clear is whether service discontinuities follow the same types of technology cycles as with products.

Other major product-based concepts from technology cycles also occur in services. For example, the technological cycle of variation, selection, and retention occurred in retail electronic commerce. Radical variation in websites gave way to a dominant bricks-and-clicks feature set (common site layout, shopping cart, shared brands, pricing closer to offline prices, allowing returns at stores), after which retailers began to concentrate on service quality and profitability. Modularity and market discontinuities also occur. For example, standard rating tools for mortgages created modularity which led to the disintegration of the mortgage industry. Market discontinuities created by Internet brokerage caused great difficulty for leading brokerage firms for several years. Finally, innovation streams occur in services, as evidenced by the senior managers of some leading drugstore chains, who were able to maintain growth and profitability in their retail stores while adopting mail service pharmacy in the early 1990s, and then electronic commerce in the early 2000s.

Yet, we suggest that the distinctions between services and products have strong implications for the nature of technology cycles in services. For example, simultaneity and the human element may allow services firms to approach a discontinuity in a much more incremental way. During a discontinuity, service providers can use rapid feedback from customers (Middleton, 1983) and interim processes linked by humans (similar to the idea of transitional product designs in Garud and Kumaraswamy, 1996) to engage in rapid variation and learning. Using humans to link new and existing services, they can leverage complementary assets in ways that startups cannot. In fact, Barras (1986, 1990) suggests that services innovations have a reverse product cycle effect, moving from improving efficiency of existing processes to improving service quality to creating new services.

Services may also call for a different process of managing innovation streams. Instead of investigating whole new product forms, innovation streams in services may involve adding or changing particular subprocesses, and then plugging them into the service as needed. Once these process steps are found to be useful, more radical changes may be possible (for example, Barras' reverse product cycle). Organizationally, innovations in services tend to be more integrated than innovations in processes (Easingwood, 1986; Sundbo, 1997). This implies that the organizational structures used to pursue innovation streams in services may be much more tightly integrated with incumbent subunits than would be possible in products.

Finally, the nature of some services may affect technology cycles and innovation streams. For example, consulting firms tend to develop ad hoc informational solutions that are highly customized to a particular client's needs. Yet, over time, in a quest for efficiency and higher service levels, they may begin to formalize the innovation. Other drivers of trajectories in services include the extent to which the service involves physical versus information goods, and the extent of scale-intensity and supplier-domination in the service (see Gallouj and Gallouj, 2001 for a review).

Moderators of industry transitions in services

Earlier, we mentioned that regulation and complementary assets are important moderators of technology cycles in the product world. Intangibility of services adds another moderator, namely the difficulty of comparing performance across service providers. When customers are unable to make simple price/performance comparisons across providers, they cannot make informed, rational decisions as to which providers have superior services (Zeithaml, 1981; Edgett and Parkinson, 1993). This may slow consumer adoption of new processes (Zeithaml, 1981; Zeithaml et al., 1985). It may also increase the importance of measures which customers can assess more readily. Thus, convenience and risk reduction may be more important in services (Heskett, 1986). These in turn are driven by the scale and quality of complementary assets such as brand/image (risk reduction), locations (convenience) and control over the customer's assets or transaction history (convenience). By slowing the diffusion of innovations, and emphasizing the value of the augmented offering (Storey and Easingwood, 1998), intangibility may make customers less willing to switch providers, thus entrenching incumbent service providers.

For example, in drug retailing, it can be difficult to identify significant differences in quality and pricing between different drugstore chains. Convenience (good location, maintaining a patient's insurance information on file), image (friendly staff, clean stores) or perceived risk reduction (trusted brand, drug-interaction screening) may drive the purchase decision. More traditional measures become important only when a provider falls significantly below expectations.

Negative implications of service–product distinctions

The distinctions between services and products have negative as well as positive implications. While recognizing these, we have until now chosen to emphasize the value of the four service-product distinctions in improving an incumbent's adaptability to technological change.

However, the negative implications of the service-product distinctions cannot be ignored. They relate primarily to new service development and marketing (see Cooper and Edgett (1999: 19) for a list, and Edgett and Parkinson (1993) for a review). For example, since service consumers interact frequently with the provider for each use of the service, the entire customer base can be affected by a problem in a service process. Modifying a service component to attract new customers may cause disruptions that affect all customers, not just new ones. This inconsistency across processes can have negative implications for perceived performance (Heskett et al., 1997; Frei et al., 1999).

Additionally, the elements that may promote rapid variation in services can also have negative consequences. For example, intangibility, simultaneity, and perishability can make incremental variation easier by promoting easier variation and more learning opportunities, but can also lead to proliferation of services that confuses customers and provider personnel (Easingwood, 1986). In addition to potential confusion, there can be long-term costs to service proliferation, since it can be very difficult to shut down existing services once some customers have begun to use them. Perishability, while providing more opportunities for customer contact, can also lead to troubles when expensive infrastructure is not utilized to capacity (Sasser, 1976).

Another negative implication arises when the human element becomes a source of inertia rather than flexibility. While some humans can shield consumers from process issues, others may introduce process issues. Even in steady state, service delivery processes conducted by humans may have much higher variability in quality than machine-conducted processes(Zeithaml et al., 1985; Levitt, 1972, 1981). Launching a new service to be delivered by thousands of people who may be low skilled and/or geographically dispersed can place great demands on the information and training infrastructure (Edgett and Jones, 1991). Thus, we would expect that, to the extent that processes are highly human-intensive, and the company's labor pool has diversity in skill and motivation levels, the benefit of humans' ability to flexibly reconfigure processes may be outweighed by the costs of humans' inconsistency. That is, beyond a certain critical point, human intensity may become a source of inertia rather than adaptability.

Conclusions

In this commentary, we attempted to extend the Tushmann and Murmann framework to include important recent research in the product domain. Most notably, we linked the framework to research on modularity, market discontinuities, senior teams, and additional moderators of technological transitions. Further, we speculated on how concepts rooted in products may apply to services (see table 10.1). While

Table 10.1 Key concepts, extensions, and their applicability to services.

	Tushman and Murmann (1998)	Extensions	Services
Product structure	Components and linkages Core and peripheral Competence destruction	Modularity and Standards New competence acquisition vs. competence destruction	Service components may be more malleable and re-configurable than product components. High human intensity in the process or high variation in labor skill and motivation may be associated with reduced service quality or adaptability.
Technology cycles, innovation streams, and senior teams	Discontinuity Dominant design Variation-selection-retention Ambidextrous organizations	New markets/ multiple market tiers Innovation streams Modularity and interdependence Experimentation in technology and market axes	Technology cycles occur, but they may not follow the same process of emergence or selection. Innovation streams may use much more integrated organizational structures than in products. Opportunity to approach discontinuous innovations incrementally. Incumbents may be more able to survive transitions.
Moderators of product and industry transitions	Small markets Regulation	Complementary assets Institutional effects Modularity and open systems	Difficulty in comparing performance across service providers may aid incumbents during transitions.

intangibility, simultaneity, heterogeneity, and perishability have well-documented negative consequences for new service development, we suggest that they may also make incumbent service providers more adaptable and able to weather technological discontinuities. We hope that the extensions and conjectures in this commentary help to stimulate additional research in these areas.

REFERENCES

Abernathy, W. J. and Clark, K. B. (1985). "Innovation: Mapping the Winds of Creative Destruction," *Research Policy*, 14 (February): 3–22.

Baldwin, C. Y. and Clark, K. B. (2000). *Design Rules: The Power of Modularity*, Cambridge, MA: MIT Press.

Barras, R. (1986). "Towards a Theory of Innovation in Services," *Research Policy*, 15(4): 161–73.

Barras, R. (1990). "Interactive Innovation in Financial Services: The Vanguard of the Service Revolution," *Research Policy*, 19(3): 215–37.

Brown, S. L. and Eisenhardt, K. M. (1997). "The Art of Continuous Change: Linking Complexity Theory and Time-Paced Evolution in Relentlessly Shifting Organizations," *Administrative Sciences Quarterly*, 42: 1–34.

Burgelman, R. A. (1994). "Fading Memories: A Process Theory of Strategic Business Exit in Dynamic Environments," *Administrative Science Quarterly*, (March): 25–55.

Chesbrough, Henry (1999). "The Differing Organizational Impact of Technological Change: A Comparative Theory of National Institutional Factors," *Industrial and Corporate Change*, 8(3): 447–86.

Chesbrough, Henry W., and Kusunoki, Ken (2001). "The Modularity Trap: Innovation, Technology Phase-Shifts and the Resulting Limits of Virtual Organizations," in I. Nonaka and David Teece (eds.), *Managing Industrial Knowledge: Creation, Transfer and Utilization*, Thousand Oaks, CA: Sage Publications.

Christensen, C. M. (1997). *The Innovator's Dilemma*, Boston: HBS Press.

Christensen, C. M. and Rosenbloom, R. S. (1995). "Explaining the Attacker's Advantage: Technological Paradigms, Organizational Dynamics and the Value Network," *Reserach Policy*, 24: 233–57.

Christensen, C. M., Verlinden, M., and Westerman, G. (2002). "Disruption, Dis-integration, and the Dissipation of Differentiability," forthcoming, *Industrial and Corporate Change*.

Cooper, R. and Edgett, S. (1999). *Product Development for the Service Sector*, Cambridge, MA: Perseus Books.

Dunbar, R. L. M., Garud, R., and Raghuram, S. (1996). "Run rabbit, run! But can you survive?" *Journal of Management Inquiry*, 5(2): 168–75.

Easingwood, C. (1986). "New Product Development for Service Companies," *Journal of Product Innovation Management*, 4: 264–75.

Edgett, S. and Jones, S. (1991). "New Product Development in the Financial Services Industry: A Case Study," *Journal of Marketing Management*, 7(3).

Edgett, S. and Parkinson, S. (1993). "Marketing for Service Industries – A Review," *The Service Industries Journal*, 13(3): 19–39.

Edmondson, A. (1999). "Psychological Safety and Learning Behavior in Work Teams," *Administrative Science Quarterly*, 44: 350–83.

Foster, R., and Kaplan, S. (2001). *Creative destruction: why companies that are built to last underperform the market – and how to successfully transform them*, New York: Currency.

Frei, F., Kalakota, R., Leone, A., and Marx, L. (1999). "Process Variation as a Determinant of Bank Performance: Evidence from the Retail Banking Study," *Management Science*, 45(9): 1210–20.

Gallouj, C. and Gallouj, F. (2001). "Neo-Schumpeterian Perspectives on Innovation in Services," in M. Boden and I. Miles (eds.), *Services and the Knowledge-Based Economy*, London: Continuum.

Garud, R. and Kotha, S. (1994). "Using the Brain as a Metaphor to Model Flexible Productive Units," *Academy of Management Review*, 19(4): 671–98.

Garud, R. and Kumaraswamy, A. (1993). "Changing competitive Dynamics in Network Industries: An Exploration of Sun Microsystems' Open Systems Strategy," *Strategic Management Journal*, 14: 351–69.

Garud, R. and Kumaraswamy, A. (1995). "Technological and Organizational Designs to Achieve Economies of Substitution," *Strategic Management Journal*, 16: 93–110.

Garud, R. and Kumarawamy, A. (1996). "Technological Designs for Retention and reuse," *International Journal of Technology Management*, 11(7, 8): 883–91.

Gatignon, H., Tushman, M. L. Anderson, P., and Smith, W. (2000). "A Structural Approach to Assessing Innovation: Construct Development of Innovation Types and Characteristics and Their Organizational Effects," Harvard Business School Working Paper, presented at Academy of Management, Washington DC, August 2001.

Gavetti, G. and Levinthal, D. (2000). "Looking Forward and Looking Backward: Cognitive and Experimental Search," *Administrative Science Quarterly*, 45(1): 113–37.

Heskett, J. (1986). *Managing in the Service Economy*, Boston, MA: HBS Press.

Heskett, J., Sasser, E., and Schlesinger, L. (1997). *The Service Profit Chain*, Boston, MA: Harvard Business School Press.

Langlois, R. N. (1992). "External Economies and Economic Progress: The case of the Microcomputer Industry," *Business History Review* (Spring 1992).

Langlois, R. N. and Robertson, P. L. (1992). "Networks and Innovation in a Modular Systems; Lessons from the Microcomputer and Stereo Component Industries," *Research Policy*, 21: 297–313.

Lehrer, M. (2000). "The Organizational Choice Between Evolutionary and Revolutionary Capability Regimes," *Industrial and Corporate Change*, 9: 489–520.

Leonard-Barton, D. (1995). *Wellsprings of Knowledge*, Boston, MA: Harvard Business School Press.

Levitt, T. (1972). "Production-line approach to services," Harvard Business Review, 50(4): 41.

Levitt, T. (1981). "Marketing Intangible Products and Product Intangibles," *Harvard Business Review*, 53(3) (May/June 1981): 94–102.

McGrath, R. (2001). "Exploratory learning, innovative capacity, and managerial oversight," *Academy of Magement Journal*, 44(1): 118–31

Middleton, V. (1983). "Product Marketing – Goods and Services Compared, *The Quarterly Review of Marketing*, 8(4): 1–10.

Pelled, L., Eisenhardt, K., and Xin, K. (1999). "Exploring the Black Box: An Analysis of Work Group Diversity, Conflict and Performance," *Admistrative Science Quarterly*, 44(1): 1–28.

Pine, B. J. (1992). *Mass Customization: The New Frontier in Business Competition*, Boston, MA: HBS Press.

Radov, D. and Tushman, M. (2000). "Greeley Hard Copy: Portable Scanner Initiative (A), (B), & (C)," HBS Cases # 9–401–003, (004) and (005), Boston: HBS Press.

Regan, W. (1963). "The Service Revolution," *Journal of Marketing*, 27(3).

Rosenbloom, R. (2000). "Leadership, Capabilities, and Technological Change: The Transformation of NCR in the Electronic Era," *Strategic Management Journal*, 21: 1083–103.

Rosenkopf, L. and Nerkar, A. (2001). "Beyond Local Search: Boundary-spanning, Exploration, and Impact in the Optical Disc Industry," *Strategic Management Journal*, 22: 287–306.

Rotemberg, J. and Saloner, G. (2000). "Visionaries, Managers, and Strategic Direction," *Rand Journal of Economics*, 31(4): 693–716.

Sanchez, R. and Mahoney, T. (1996). "Modularity, Flexibility, and Knowledge Management," *Strategic Management Journal*, 17: 63–76.

Sanderson, S. and Uzumeri, M. (1995). "Managing product families: The case of the Sony Walkman," *Research Policy*, 24(5): 761.

Sasser, E. (1976). "Match Supply and Demand in Service Industries," *Harvard Business Review*, 54(6): 133.

Schilling, M. (2000). "Toward a General Modular Systems Theory and its Application to Interfirm Product Modularity," *Academy of Management Review*, 25(2): 312–34.

Sorensen, J. B. and Stuart, T. E. (2000). "Aging, Obsolescence, and Organizational Innovation," *Administrative Science Quarterly*, 45: 81–112.

Storey, C. and Easingwood, C. (1998). "The Augmented Service Offering: A Conceptualization and Study of its Impact on New Service Success," *Journal of Product Innovation Management*, 15(4): 335–51.

Sull, D. N. (1999). "The Dynamics of Standing Still: Firestone Tire & Rubber and the Radial Revolution," *Business History Review*, 73 (Autumn 1999): 430–64.

Sundbo, J. (1997). "Management of Innovation in Services," *The Service Industries Journal*, 17(3): 432–55

Teece, D. J. (1986). "Profiting from Technological Innovation: Implications for Integration, Collaboration, Licensing and Public Policy," *Research Policy*, 15: 285–305.

Tripsas, M. (1997). "Unraveling the Process of Creative Destruction," *Strategic Management Journal*, 18 (1997) (Summer Special Issue): 119–42.

Tripsas, M. and Gavetti, G. (2000). "Capabilities, Cognition, and Inertia: Evidence from Digital Imaging", *Strategic Management Journal*, 21: 1147–61.

Tushman, M. L. and Murmann, J. P. (1998). "Dominant Designs, Technology Cycles, and Organizational Outcomes," *Research in Organizational Behavior*, 20: 231–66.

Tushman, M. L. and O'Reilly, C. A. (1997). *Winning Through Innovation*, Boston: HBS Press.

Tushman, M. and Smith, W. (2001). "Technological Change, Ambidextrous Organizations, and Organizational Evolution," in J. A. C. Baum (ed.), *Companion to Organizations*, Oxford, UK: Blackwell Publishers.

United Nations (1999). *1999 Statistical Yearbook*, Department of International Economic and Social Affairs Statistical Office, United Nations, New York, as cited in Fitzsimmons and Fitzsimmons (2001), *Service Management*, Third Edition, New York: McGraw-Hill.

West, J. (2000). "Institutions, Information Processing, and Organization Structure in Research and Development: Evidence from the Semiconductor Industry," *Research Policy*, 29(3): 349–73.

Zeithaml, V. (1981). "How Consumer Evaluation Processes Differ Between Goods and Services," in J. Donnelly and W. George (eds.), *Marketing of Services*, Chicago: American Marketing Association, 39–47.

Zeithaml, V., Parasuraman, A., and Berry, L. L. (1985). "Problems and strategies in services marketing," *Journal of Marketing*, 49(2): 33–46.

CHAPTER ELEVEN

MODULARITY, FLEXIBILITY, AND KNOWLEDGE MANAGEMENT IN PRODUCT AND ORGANIZATION DESIGN

Rᴏɴ Sᴀɴᴄʜᴇᴢ ᴀɴᴅ Jᴏsᴇᴘʜ T. Mᴀʜᴏɴᴇʏ

Iɴᴛʀᴏᴅᴜᴄᴛɪᴏɴ

Daft and Lewin identify the "modular organization" as a new paradigm that has as its premise "the need for flexible, learning organizations that continuously change and solve problems through interconnected coordinated self-organizing processes" (1993: i). This paper investigates approaches to *managing knowledge* in a firm's product-creation processes that facilitate specific forms of "coordinated self-organizing processes" capable of improving a firm's *strategic flexibility* to respond advantageously to a changing environment (Sanchez, 1993, 1994b, 1995). To do so, we investigate concepts of *modularity* in both product designs and organization designs.

We explain how advanced technological knowledge about component interactions can be used to fully specify and standardize the component interfaces that make up a modular product architecture, creating a nearly independent system (Simon, 1962) of "loosely coupled" components. We then suggest that just as some work may be coordinated by specifying standard operating procedures (Cyert and March, 1963) that govern *processes* directly, much work in product development may be coordinated by specifying standardized component interfaces that govern the *outputs* of component development processes. In essence, the standardized component interfaces in a modular product architecture provide a form of *embedded coordination* that greatly reduces the need for overt exercise of managerial authority to achieve coordination of development processes, thereby making possible the concurrent and autonomous development of components by *loosely coupled organization structures* (Orton and Weick, 1990). Thus, using technological knowledge to create *modularity in product designs* becomes an important strategy for achieving *modularity in organization designs*.

This paper is organized in the following way. The next section builds on Simon's (1962) notion of "nearly decomposable" systems by proposing that product designs and organization designs follow the fundamental principles of decomposition.

We then investigate modularity in product and organization designs. We suggest that although organizations ostensibly design products, it can also be argued that *products design organizations*, because the coordination tasks implicit in specific product designs largely determine the feasible organization designs for developing and producing those products.[1]

The following section considers how learning processes create *information structures* in product development processes, and it evaluates the characteristic information structures and resulting learning efficiencies of three models for organizing product development processes: sequential development, overlapping problem solving, and modular product design.

We conclude by suggesting that the emerging prominence of modular product designs is being accompanied by new knowledge management strategies (Grant, 1993; Sanchez, 1996c) that allow product creation to be carried out more effectively through flexible, "modular" organization structures.

NEARLY DECOMPOSABLE SYSTEMS

A complex system – whether product design or organization structure – consists of parts that interact and are interdependent to some degree. Simon (1962) argues that *hierarchy* is an organizing principle of complex systems, which are essentially composed of interrelated subsystems that in turn have their own subsystems, and so on.

This paper applies Simon's (1962) *structural* conception of hierarchy in complex systems to the analysis of product designs and of organizational processes for developing new products. In so doing, we use a more general conception of "hierarchy" than that usually invoked in organizational economics and strategic management (e.g., Mahoney, 1992b, 1992c; Williamson, 1975), where hierarchy typically denotes subordination to an *authority* relationship. Our interest here, however, is in understanding hierarchical systems for creating new products in which there is *little or no overt exercise of managerial authority*.[2]

In this discussion, "hierarchy" refers to a decomposition of a complex system into a structured ordering of successive sets of subsystems, in the manner suggested by Simon (1962) – i.e., a partitioning into relationships that collectively define the parts of any whole. We suggest that hierarchy, in this structural sense, may be a feature of both designs for products and designs for organizations that create products (Sanchez, 1995, 1996b).

Simon (1962) further defines a *nearly decomposable system* as one in which interactions among subsystems are weak (but not necessarily negligible). The interactions between the divisions of a multidivisional organization are representative of a nearly decomposable system (Mahoney, 1992a; Williamson, 1975). The tasks within a multidivisional firm are intentionally designed to require low levels of coordination so that they can be carried out by an organizational structure of quasi-independent divisions functioning as *loosely coupled subsystems* (Weick, 1976).

An important property of this structural hierarchical decomposition is that the impacts of environmental disturbances may be localized within specific subsystems, increasing the survivability and adaptability of the overall system in a turbulent environment (Orton and Weick, 1990). Extending these insights to product designs and organizations that create new products, we suggest that new approaches to decomposing and structuring product designs have enabled the adoption of more structurally decomposed – and thus more adaptable – organization designs for creating products.

MODULARITY IN PRODUCT AND ORGANIZATION DESIGNS

Product designs differ fundamentally in the degree to which a design has been decomposed into "loosely coupled" vs. "tightly coupled" components. The degree to which components are loosely coupled or tightly coupled in a product *design* depends on the extent to which a change in the design of one component requires compensating design changes in other components. *Modularity* is a special form of design which intentionally creates a high degree of independence or "loose coupling" between component designs by standardizing component interface specifications. This section explains how modular design achieves the loose coupling of component designs and in the process creates an *information structure* that can provide *embedded co-ordination* of loosely coupled component development processes (Sanchez, 1995).

Modular product designs

A component in a product design performs a function within a system of interrelated components whose collective functioning make up the product. Relationships between components are defined by the specifications of inputs and outputs linking components in a design,[3] and a complete set of component interface specifications constitutes a *product architecture* (Abernathy and Clark, 1985; Clark, 1985).

Traditional engineering design follows a methodology of constrained optimization, which tries to obtain the highest level of product performance within some cost constraint or the lowest cost for a product meeting a minimum performance constraint. This design methodology typically leads to product designs composed of highly integrated, tightly coupled component designs. Specifications of input and output interfaces between components must therefore reflect the idiosyncratic characteristics of each tightly coupled component design. As a consequence, *processes* for developing tightly coupled component designs require intensive managerial coordination, since a change in the design of one component is likely to require extensive compensating changes in the designs of many interrelated components. Thus, product designs composed of tightly coupled components will generally require development processes carried out in a *tightly coupled organization structure* coordinated by a managerial *authority hierarchy*, an organization design typically achieved within a single firm.

Some firms, however, are now using an alternative design methodology that intentionally creates loosely coupled component designs by specifying *standardized component interfaces* that define functional, spatial, and other relationships between components that, once specified, are not permitted to change during an intended period in a product development process. The "intended period" during which standardized component interfaces are not permitted to change may range from key stages in the development of a new product architecture (Cusumano and Selby, 1995) to the entire commercial lifetime of a product family (Sanchez, 1995). Standardizing component interface specifications during a period of time allows processes for developing component designs to become loosely coupled, because they can be effectively coordinated simply by requiring that all developed components conform to the standardized component interface specifications.[4] Thus, controlling the required *output* of component development processes by standardizing component interfaces permits effective coordination of development processes without the continual exercise of managerial authority. The specification for standardized component interfaces provides, in effect, an *information structure* (Radner, 1992) that coordinates the loosely coupled activities of component developers.

A *modular product architecture* (Sanchez, 1994a; Ulrich and Eppinger, 1995) is a special form of product design that uses standardized interfaces between components to create a *flexible* product architecture. In modular product design, the standardized interfaces between components are specified to allow for *a range of variations* in components to be substituted into a product architecture. *Modular components* are components whose interface characteristics are within the range of variations allowed by a modular product architecture. The modular architecture is *flexible* (Sanchez, 1995) because product variations can be leveraged by substituting (Garud and Kumaraswamy, 1993) different modular components into the product architecture without having to redesign other components. This loose coupling of component designs within a modular product architecture allows the "mixing and matching" of modular components to give a potentially large number of product variations distinctive functionalities, features, and/or performance levels (Sanderson and Uzumeri, 1990; Sanchez, 1994a; Ward et al., 1995).

Modular product architectures can be an important source of *strategic flexibility* (Sanchez, 1995) when they enable a firm to respond more readily to changing markets and technologies by rapidly creating product variations based on new combinations of new or existing modular components. The standardized component interfaces of a modular product architecture also enable the coordination of a loosely coupled organization structure linking geographically dispersed component developers. Thus, a firm may be able to use a modular product architecture to coordinate a global network (Kogut and Bowman, 1995; Kogut and Kulatilaka, 1994) or "constellation" (Normann and Ramirez, 1993) of component developers and suppliers to source a broad range of component variations, thereby further enhancing the ability of the firm to leverage new product variations. In this way, "loose coupling [within a product architecture] facilitates continuous change" (Spender and Grinyer, 1995) by improving the ability of a firm to generate new product variations. As table 11.1 indicates, modular product architectures that allow mixing and matching[5] of modular components are now appearing in diverse product markets (Sanderson and Uzumeri, 1990; Sanchez, 1991).

Table 11.1 Examples of products with modular designs.

Products	Form of modular product design	References
Aircraft	Common wing, nose, and tail components allow several models to be leveraged by using different numbers of fuselage modules to create aircraft of different lengths and passenger/freight capacities (used by Boeing, McDonnell-Douglas, and Airbus Industries).	Woolsey (1994)
Automobiles	Automakers have long used many basic modular components specified by the Society of Automotive Engineers.	Nevins and Whitney (1989)
	Some automakers use common (modular) components in many different models. Also, the Taurus platform design is leveraged to provide a basis for the Taurus and Mercury Sable sedans and wagons and for the Ford Taurus Windstar minivan.	*Automobile* (1994)
	Ford is converting its auto and struck engines to modular engine designs with high levels of common (modular) parts. The 4.6 L V-8 introduced in 1992 was Ford's first modular engine.	*Ford Engineering World* (1990)
	Chrysler's LH car designs are modular. Several models have been leveraged from common power train and engine components. The interior of each model is composed of four easy-to-install units that arrive ready-built from separate suppliers. The Chrysler Neon uses numerous modular assemblies.	Tully (1993)
Consumer electronics	Over 160 variations of the Sony Walkman were leveraged by "mixing and matching" modular components in a few basic modular product designs.	Sanderson and Uzumeri (1990)
	Several upgraded models of Sony HandyCam video cameras were leveraged from an initial system design by successively introducing improved modular components.	Sanchez (1994a)
Household appliances	General Electric leverages several models of dishwashers by installing different modular doors and controls on common assemblies of enclosures, motors, and wiring harnesses.	Sanchez and Sudharshan (1993)
Personal computers	Personal computers often consist largely of modular components like hard disk drives, flat screen displays, and memory chips, coupled with some distinctive components like a microprocessor chip and enclosure.	Langlois and Robertson (1992)
Software	Software designs are creating modules of routines which can be combined to create customized applications programs.	Cusumano (1991)
	Software designers attain modularity through loose coupling. The objective is often to minimize coupling – i.e., to make modules as independent as possible. Loose coupling between modules signifies a well-designed system. Modular programming (1) allows one module to be written without knowledge of the code in another module (a decomposition using an "information hiding"	Parnas, Clements and Weiss (1985)

Table 11.1 (*cont'd*)

Products	Form of modular product design	References
	regime), and (2) allows modules to be reassembled and replaced without design of the whole system. Separating *action* (what the module does) and *logic* (how the module accomplishes the action) is a "composite" approach to software engineering that has been deployed by NASA and GTE, among others.	
	Software for designing application-specific integrated circuits (ASICs) provides modular circuit elements which can then be linked together to provide the specific functionalities needed to customize an ASIC for a specific product application.	von Hippel (1994)
Test instruments	Philips created a flexible chassis for receiving modular components which permit the configuration of large numbers of specialized oscilloscopes for testing various kinds of electronic products.	*Electronics* (1986)
Power tools	Black and Decker designed its entire line of power tools in the 1980s to incorporate a high degree of common modular components.	Utterback (1994)

Modular organization designs

Specifying the required *outputs* of component development processes permits those processes to be partitioned into tasks (von Hippel, 1990) that can be performed *autonomously and concurrently* by a loosely coupled structure of development organizations. In effect, the *information structure* provided by the standardized component interface specifications of a modular product architecture provides a means to embed coordination of loosely coupled component development processes. The information structure of a modular product architecture thus provides the "glue" of embedded coordination that allows a loosely coupled development organization to achieve syntheses (Spender and Grinyer, 1995) in the form of developed products.[6]

A loosely coupled product creation organization in which each participating component development unit can function autonomously and concurrently under the embedded coordination of a modular product architecture appears to correspond closely to Daft and Lewin's notion of *modular organizations* "that continuously change and solve problems through interconnected coordinated self-organizing processes" (1993: i). A firm using a modular product architecture to coordinate development processes has a means to quickly link together the resources and capabilities of many organizations to form product development "resource chains" that can respond flexibly – i.e., broadly, quickly, and at low cost (Sanchez, 1995, 1996b) – to environmental change.

MODELS FOR MANAGING KNOWLEDGE AND LEARNING IN PRODUCT CREATION

Product development projects can be thought of as "programmed" innovation in which firms create new products by applying existing knowledge and creating new knowledge about components and their interactions. To create the information structure of fully specified and standardized component interfaces in a modular product architecture requires a high level of architectural knowledge (Sanchez, 1996c; Wright, 1994) about how components function and interact in a product. To the extent that a firm has inadequate knowledge of components and their interactions, creating a new product architecture requires learning by experimenting (Baldwin and Clark, 1994) with new component designs and alternative arrangements of components.

Innovation during product development may therefore involve (i) creating new information about the functions components can perform, which implies learning about components *per se*, or (ii) creating new information about the ways components interact and can be configured, which implies learning about product architectures (Henderson and Clark, 1990). Extending the notion of learning at component and architectural levels, figure 11.1 identifies four modes of learning – radical, architectural, modular, and incremental – that can occur in product innovation process (see Henderson and Clark, 1990).

Learning about component functions and designs

	Moderate	Significant
Moderate	**Incremental learning at the component level** Incremental learning through component development leads to limited functional improvements and design variations in components used within an existing product architecture.	**Modular learning at the component level** Learning about new kinds of component technologies leads to significant changes in feasible component functions and designs that can be accommodated within an existing product architecture.
Significant	**Architectural learning** Learning about new product market opportunities leads to new product architectures based on changes in the ways existing kinds of components are combined and configured in product designs.	**Radical learning at architectural and component levels** Learning about new market opportunities and new product and component technologies leads to major changes in both kinds of components used and ways components are configured to form a product architecture.

Learning about component interactions and configurations

Figure 11.1 Modes of learning in product creation processes.

Research in strategy has often emphasized the challenges to organizations of "radical" learning (Dewar and Dutton, 1986). More recently, attention has also been paid to the importance of "architectural" learning (Morris and Ferguson, 1993; Henderson and Clark, 1990). Significant benefits may also be realized, however, by effectively leveraging new products based on "modular" or "incremental" forms of learning that can take place within an existing product architecture (Sanchez, 1995, 1996b). All these forms of learning are vital to organizational renewal and development, but not all processes for learning during product development are equally efficient. This section considers ways in which processes for architectural, modular, and incremental learning during product development may be managed to improve the efficiency of both component and architectural levels of learning.

Much recent research into improving the effectiveness and efficiency of product development has focused on processes for knowledge creation and information transfer in product creation projects (e.g., Clark and Fujimoto, 1991; Wheelwright and Clark, 1992). The product creation process generally consists of product concept development, feasibility testing, product design, component development processes, pilot production, and final production (Takeuchi and Nonaka, 1986). We now analyze more closely three alternative approaches to creating knowledge and transferring information in product design and component development processes: "traditional" sequential development, overlapping problem solving, and modular product development.

"Traditional" sequential development processes

The "traditional" model of product design and development follows a sequential staging of design and development tasks (Takeuchi and Nonaka, 1986), as suggested in figure 11.2(a). In this model, after defining the product concept, design and development tasks are sequenced so that technology and component development tasks with the greatest need for new knowledge and with the greatest impact on other component design and development tasks are undertaken first. As the firm develops new technical knowledge about components and their interactions at each stage, it makes component design decisions and communicates new information about component interface specifications that allow the next stage of component design and development tasks to proceed. This process is repeated at each stage of development until all components and their interfaces are fully specified. Thus, a critical feature of the sequential development process is that the information structure of component interface specifications – i.e., the new product architecture – is the *output* of the design and development process.

Recent research has made evident the likelihood of breakdowns, losses, and delays in information flows when product development processes are organized as a sequence of development tasks (e.g., Clark and Wheelwright, 1993). A sequential ordering of design and development tasks, for example, typically results in recursive information flows that often slow the development process, as suggested by the information feedback flows in figure 11.2(a). A sequential process is also likely to "lose information" as development proceeds from one stage to the next, because

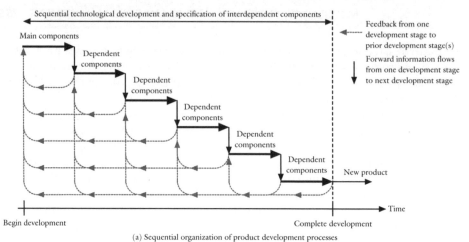

(a) Sequential organization of product development processes

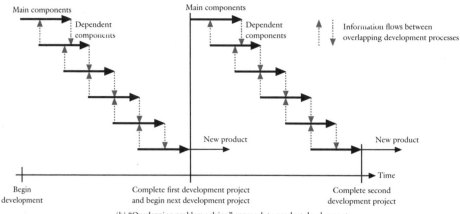

(b) "Overlapping problem solving" approach to product development

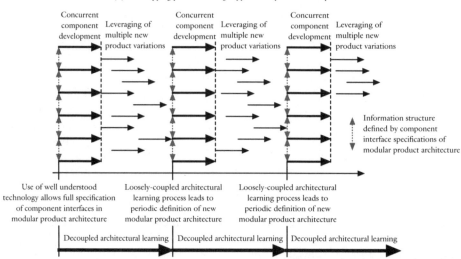

(c) Modular organization of product development processes

Figure 11.2 (a) "Traditional" sequential organization of product development processes (b) "Overlapping problem solving" approach to product development (c) "Modular" organization of product development processes.

the information and assumptions underlying upstream design decisions may not be transferred intact to downstream stages of development. Technical incompatibilities between interdependent components may then actually be "designed into" down-stream components.

We suggest here that in addition to these well-known effects, the incomplete information structure of an *evolving* product architecture also has profound implications for feasible approaches to organizing this kind of development process. Because the information structure of an evolving product architecture is incomplete and indefinite until all stages of component development are completed, the desired outputs of specific component development tasks cannot be fully specified before beginning development. Coordinating incompletely specified but interdependent development tasks will require managerial adjudication of many technical and financial issues likely to arise between component development groups. The authority hierarchy needed to manage a sequential development process requires, in effect, the *tightly coupled organization structure* of a single firm or a firm with strong ties to a "quasi-integrated" group of dependent component suppliers (Nishiguchi, 1994; Sanchez, 1995).[7]

Overlapping problem solving

An alternative model for managing product development organizes the sequential development processes of figure 11.2(a) into staggered but overlapping stages, as shown in figure 11.2(b). Overlapping development stages make possible greater sharing of current information through processes of *overlapping problem solving* (Clark and Fujimoto, 1991; Clark and Wheelwright, 1993) that link closely inter-related component design and development tasks. Overlapping problem solving, which is often carried out in a team-based organizational structure (Takeuchi and Nonaka, 1986), improves information flows between overlapping development tasks, as suggested by the information feedbacks in figure 11.2(b), allowing some inter-related component development to proceed more quickly and reducing information losses between stages.

Although it offers improvements over a sequential development process, an overlapping problem solving process also has an evolving information structure (i.e., product architecture) and thus also requires intensive managerial coordination of incompletely specified development tasks within the boundaries of a single firm or within a small group of quasi-integrated component developers. Clark and Fujimoto (1991), for example, have observed that development projects using overlapping problem solving are more successful when they are managed by a "heavyweight project manager" who has the *authority* to make design and specification decisions and adjudicate disputes between development groups.

Modular product design

Modular product design follows a new model for managing learning and knowledge in product creation processes. In contrast to the evolving information structures characteristic of the sequential and overlapping problem solving models, a modular product design process creates a complete information structure – i.e., the fully specified component interfaces of a modular product architecture – that defines required outputs of component development processes *before* beginning development of components. To fully specify component interfaces in a modular product architecture, a firm must have, or have access to, advanced *architectural* knowledge about relevant components and their interactions.

When a firm can use advanced architectural knowledge to specify a new modular architecture within which development of modular components can take place, learning at the modular or incremental levels through developing new and improved components may be improved by being *intentionally separated* from and made only *loosely coupled* to processes for creating new architectural knowledge. Moreover, processes for learning at both levels may become more efficient.

Improved component-level learning

When learning through the development of individual components can take place within the stable information structure of a fully specified product architecture, learning inefficiencies due to breakdowns, losses, and delays in information flows between component development activities can be avoided. In effect, adopting a modular design process allows learning at the component level to be "insulated" from disruptions by unexpected changes in product architecture during development projects.

Because fully specified component interfaces allow component-level learning processes to be carried out *concurrently and autonomously* by geographically dispersed, loosely coupled development groups, as suggested in figure 11.2(c), a firm may be able to combine its capabilities more readily with those of an extensive network of component developers, thereby increasing the absorptive capacity of the firm (Cohen and Levinthal, 1990) and its potential for realizing the full *combinative capabilities* (Bartlett, 1993; Kogut and Zander, 1992) of the firm's current architectural knowledge. Decoupling architectural and component levels of learning may therefore allow a firm to be more effective in exploiting its current stock of architectural knowledge (March, 1991). After the initial round of concurrent component development suggested in figure 11.2(c), a developing firm may use the stability of a modular product architecture to accelerate network-based development of new kinds of "mix and match" modular components for leveraging product variations.

A modular product design process may therefore enable a firm to accelerate its *learning about markets* by enabling the firm to leverage many different variations of a product more quickly and at reduced cost. In effect, allowing more focused component-level learning within a current product architecture may facilitate an evolutionary process of real-time market research (Sanchez and Sudharshan, 1993) that supports accelerated creation of market knowledge in an enterprise (Baldwin and Clark, 1994). The decoupling of architectural and component learning processes may also create a more efficient environment for involving suppliers and customers in "localized learning" in developing specific components. Boeing's use of a modular design process in developing the 777 aircraft (Woolsey, 1994), for example, created a decoupled component-level learning environment that facilitated the involvement of Boeing's lead customers in developing improved designs for key components which directly affect customers' use of the 777. Use of modular product architectures to achieve a managed separation of architectural and component learning may therefore provide a framework that supports expanded involvement of lead users (von Hippel, 1988) in product development.

Improved architectural-level learning

The loose coupling of learning at the component and architectural levels may also improve architectural learning processes. Henderson and Clark (1990) suggest that organizations tend to lose their abilities to innovate at the architectural level, because over time organizations develop organizational structures and information channels that are focused on component-level activities. Compartmentalization of organizations and information around components creates "filters" that block flows of information that would suggest opportunities for architectural innovation. A further set of concerns about architectural learning arises from the "project" nature of most product development processes. The time-sensitive, high-pressure environment which often characterizes new product development projects is likely to impose severe constraints on the time and resources which can be devoted to learning at the "architectural" level. Using specific product development projects as the *context* for creating new technical knowledge may therefore lead to an excessive focus on incremental (and perhaps modular) learning which can be applied immediately to current development needs. Learning at the architectural level, when intentionally decoupled from learning at the component level, may become more open to technological and market change, less dominated by the near-term demands of component-level learning during development projects, and thus less suceptible to falling into patterns of myopic learning (Levinthal and March, 1993).

Using modular product architectures as mechanisms for coordinating organizational learning

The process of periodically revising or creating a new modular product architecture provides an important coordinating mechanism for periodically linking loosely coupled processes for learning at architectural and component levels. Learning at the architectural level may suggest advantageous changes in components compatible with a current product architecture (i.e., opportunities for modular learning), as well as possibilities for significant changes in both components and product architectures (opportunities for radical innovations). Periodic redefinitions of modular product architectures may therefore provide a "programmed" opportunity for reconnecting and coordinating architectural and component-level learning.

The shifting focus of knowledge management in modular product development

Modularity in product designs and organization designs for developing products may lead to a fundamental shift in the nature and focus of strategic learning activities in firms. Firms that create new products through modular product development are likely to place increasing emphasis on learning at the architectural level, while focusing and intensifying component-level learning in one or a few key components of subsystems that are critical to overall product performance and in which a firm possesses superior development capabilities.

Examples of this new pattern of "modular learning" can be found in a growing number of industries, from high-tech to industrial. As an example of the latter, we cite Venkatesan's (1992) analysis of product competition in the earth-moving equipment industry. Venkatesan (1992) discusses the product architecture of a backhoe/loader – a complex mechanical system composed of a number of subsystems of components such as hydraulics, drive train, chassis, ground-engaging tools, vehicle electronics, operator cab, and engine. Venkatesan (1992: 101–103) describes the process of deciding which components and subsystems will become the focus of a firm's own learning efforts and which the firm will manage by using its architectural knowledge to define modular component interface specifications:

> The first thing to decide is what subsystems will be indispensable to the company's competitive position over subsequent product generations. This choice will vary from company to company and ultimately drive product differentiation. . . . [W]hen capable subsystem suppliers exist, it is not so important to be able to design and manufacture the sub-system in-house as it is to have *the ability to specify and control the performance characteristics of the subsystem.* [italics added for emphasis]

Venkatesan's (1992) observations suggest that much strategic learning is now directed at improving a firm's architectural knowledge needed to control the specifications of subsystems and components in a modular product architecture. This kind of architectural learning is becoming a strategically important means for assessing and coordinating an extended network of component development capabilities in other organizations (Sanchez, 1996d; Sanchez and Heene, 1996). As more firms begin to use modularity not just to create greater product variety, but also as a new framework for aggressive strategic learning and more effective knowledge management, new innovation dynamics are being created whose implications for technology-driven competition invite further investigation.

Conclusions

A useful tool for management and organization science is to make use of the world's redundancy to describe the complexity of our world as simply as possible (Simon, 1981: 222). The principle of the decomposability of systems deepens our understanding of the architecture of complexity, whether the system in question is physical, biological, social, or economic. Our effort to understand more fully the potential for *intentionally decomposing* complex products and organizational phenomena into loosely coupled subsystems suggests an approach to gaining new insights into the structure and dynamics of changing product markets and evolving organizational forms.

Extending the principle of decomposition, this paper has suggested that the creation of modular product architectures not only creates flexible product designs, but also enables the design of loosely coupled, flexible, "modular" organization structures. Embedding coordination in fully specified and standardized component interfaces can reduce the need for much overt exercise of managerial authority across the interfaces of organizational units developing components, thereby reducing the intensity and complexity of a firm's managerial task in product development and giving it greater flexibility to take on a larger number and/or greater variety of product creation projects.

Adam Smith (1776) showed early insight into the importance of managing knowledge by suggesting that a firm organized around processes based on the specialized *content* of knowledge may gain efficiencies in producing physical products. Here we make an analogous argument about knowledge-intensive work: organizing a firm around specialized *processes for creating and applying* knowledge can lead to important dynamic efficiencies in the production of *intellectual* products in the form of new product and component designs and technologies.

We expect that the knowledge management processes of product-creating firms pursuing greater dynamic efficiencies will become increasingly focused on the codification of architectural knowledge about component interactions needed to specify modular product architectures and on using that architectural knowledge to coordinate loosely coupled modular organization structures for component and product development. In general, while firms may develop specialized knowledge about some strategically important modular components, we expect firms to undertake internal development of fewer components, as more product-creating firms learn how to use modular architectures to source more components through loosely coupled networks of component suppliers. Growing strategic use of modularity as a framework for more effective strategic learning and knowledge management may result in increasingly dynamic product markets. These are likely to be characterized by expanding interactions among modular development organizations through "quick-connect" global electronic networks (Sanchez, 1996a). The consequences of this new modular creation environment will be previously unattained levels of product variety and change.

Discontinuities in product technology (Tushman and Anderson, 1986) lead to changes in the *content* of product markets – i.e., to new kinds of products made by new organizations. This paper, however, has described the rise of modular product design as a recent discontinuity in *coordination technology* (Sanchez, 1996b) that is leading to changes in the *processes and structures* of product markets – i.e., to new kinds of product development processes carried out by new forms of product development organizations. Thus, the possibilities for adapting new coordinating technologies and knowledge management processes based on modularity concepts are making it possible as never before for *organizational form* to become a variable to be managed strategically.

Finally, this paper concludes that the increased flexibilities that can result from the embedded coordination of standardized interfaces in modular architectures may not be limited to product development processes. The flexibilities to be derived from the standardized interfaces of modular architectures also appear to be attainable in the design of marketing, distribution, and other processes. Thus, we suggest that standardizing interfaces in modular system architectures of many types may be a new dominant design for achieving increased flexibility and interorganizational connectivity among broadly de-integrating organizations.[8]

ACKNOWLEDGEMENTS

The comments of Kathy Alexander, Stephen Bowden, Charles Galunic, Philip Gorman, Rob Grant, Jim Hagen, Kathryn Rudie Harrigan, Doug Johnson, Dong-Jae Kim, Bruce Kogut, Georgine Kryda, Arie Lewin, James Mahoney, Mark Pruett, Tom Roehl, Anju Seth, J.-C. Spender, Devanathan Sudharshan, Greg Winter, and especially Carliss Baldwin on earlier drafts are gratefully acknowledged. All remaining errors are the authors' responsibility.

NOTES

Key words: coordination; knowledge management; modularity; strategic flexibility.

1 Product design should be recognized as a strategic activity with important economic implications. A 1986 study at Rolls-Royce suggested that design determines 80 per cent of the final production costs of 2000 components, and General Motors executives maintain that 70 percent of the total cost of manufacturing truck transmissions is determined in the design stage (Whitney, 1988).

2 In fact, Radner (1992: 1392) poses the question "Would a hierarchical design of the processes of production [necessarily] lead to hierarchical management?" In effect, what we are suggesting in this paper is that specific forms of hierarchical designs of processes *need not* be accompanied by hierarchical management.

3 Note that tight or loose coupling of components in a product *design* is different from tight or loose coupling in an actual (usually physical) product. A personal computer design, for example, may have loosely coupled components in that different microprocessors or hard disk drives may be substituted into the computer design without requiring a redesign of the other components. Nevertheless, the components in the physical computer will be tightly coupled in the sense that all components must function properly for the computer to function as a system.

4 Specifying standardized interfaces to create loosely coupled components allows each component within a product design to be treated as a "black box" (Wheelwright and Clark, 1992) by the product developing firm. In developing new car models, many car makers now provide their suppliers with only a "black box" specification of the (standardized) functional, spatial, and other interfaces of the required component, leaving the actual design and development of the component to the supplier (Clark and Fujimoto, 1991). This design principle is also evident in software development, where object-oriented programming methods require that each component of a program be written by software developers who have no knowledge of the code used by other developers in writing their program components. Decomposition of program design allows a regime of "information hiding" among program component developers (Parnas, 1972) analogous to "black box" component development in the automobile industry. (For further discussion of standards and interfaces, see David and Greenstein, 1990.)

5 Shirley (1990) investigates the potential for product designs using modular components to provide a large number of product variations while reducing overall manufacturing costs. We suggest that modularity in product design creates many options for product

variations in the form of feasible combinations of modular components, some of which may be drawn from a "design library" of existing components. In this regard, leveraging product variations from modular designs is a specific expression of Kogut and Zander's (1992) "combinative capabilities" in the context of creating new products.

6   In a more general sense, embedded coordination is the coordination of organizational processes achieved by any means other than the continuous exercise of managerial authority and may include, for example, clan coordination through tradition (Ouchi, 1980). We thank the editors for bringing this point to our attention.

7   A further argument for the necessity of carrying out sequential development processes within a single firm is the difficulty of contracting for component development services when the *performance* of a contractor would be difficult to assess, given the high degree of dependence of each development group's work on the effort of other development groups (Alchian and Demsetz, 1972; Ouchi, 1980).

8   We observe, for example, that modularity in product designs can facilitate modularity in manufacturing processes as well as in development processes. In industries whose product designs are typically most modularized (e.g., personal computers), production, assembly, and servicing of components are commonly carried out by globally dispersed, loosely coupled organizations.

REFERENCES

Abernathy, W. J. and K. B. Clark (1985). "Innovation: Mapping the winds of creative destruction," *Research Policy*, 14, pp. 3–22.

Alchian, A. A. and H. Demsetz (1972). "Production, information costs, and economic organization," *American Economic Review*, 62, pp. 777–95.

Automobile (August 1994). "1995 SAAB 900SE turbo coupe," pp. 97–8.

Baldwin, C. and K. B. Clark (1994). "Modularity-in-design: An analysis based on the theory of real options," working paper, Harvard Business School, Cambridge, MA.

Bartlett, C. A. (1993). "Commentary: Strategic flexibility, firm organization, and managerial work in dynamic markets." In P. Shrivastava, A. S. Huff and J. Dutton (eds.), *Advances in Strategic Management*, Vol. 9. JAI Press, Greenwich, CT, pp. 292–98.

Clark, K. B. (1985). "The interaction of design hierarchies and market concepts in technological evolution," *Research Policy*, 14(5), pp. 235–51.

Clark, K. B. and T. Fujimoto (1991). *Product Development Performance: Strategy, Organization, and Management in the World Auto Industry*. Harvard University Press, Boston, MA.

Clark, K. B. and S. C. Wheelwright (1993). *Managing New Product and Process Development*. Free Press, New York.

Cohen, W. M. and D. A. Levinthal (1990). "Absorptive capacity: A new perspective on learning and innovation," *Administrative Science Quarterly*, 35, pp. 128–52.

Cusumano, M. A. (1991). *Japan's Software Factories: A Challenge to U.S. Management*. Oxford University Press, New York.

Cusumano, M. A. and R. W. Selby (1995). *Microsoft Secrets: How the World's Most Powerful Software Company Creates Technology, Shapes Markets, and Manages People*. Free Press, New York.

Cyert, R. M. and J. G. March (1963). *A Behavioral Theory of the Firm*. Prentice-Hall, Englewood Cliffs, NJ.

Daft, R. L. and A. Y. Lewin (1993). "Where are the theories of the 'new' organizational forms? An editorial essay," *Organization Science*, 4(4), pp. i–vi.

David, P. A. and S. Greenstein (1990). "The economics of compatibility standards: An introduction to recent research," *Economic Innovation and New Technology*, 1(1), pp. 3–41.

Dewar, R. D. and J. E. Dutton (1986). "The adoption of radical and incremental innovations: An empirical analysis," *Management Science*, 32(11), pp. 1422–33.

Electronics (7 April 1986). "How Philips sweated the cost out of its new scopes", pp. 39–41.

Ford Engineering World (1990). "4.6 L V-8 is Ford's first modular engine," 15(3), pp. 1–4.

Garud, R. and A. Kumaraswamy (1993). "Changing competitive dynamics in network industries: An exploration of Sun Microsystems' open systems strategy," *Strategic Management Journal*, 14(5), pp. 351–69.

Grant, R. (1993). "Organizational capability within a knowledge-based view of the firm," School of Business Administration Working Paper Series, STRAT2277-03-1293, Georgetown University.

Henderson, R. M. and K. B. Clark (1990). "Architectural innovation: The reconfiguration of existing product technologies and the failure of established firms," *Administrative Science Quarterly*, 35, pp. 9–30.

Kogut, B. and E. H. Bowman (1995). "Modularity and permeability as principles of design." In E. H. Bowman and B. Kogut (eds.), *Redesigning the Firm*. Oxford University Press, New York, pp. 243–60.

Kogut, B. and N. Kulatilaka (1994). "Operating flexibility, global manufacturing, and the option value of a multinational network," *Management Science*, 40(1), pp. 123–39.

Kogut, B. and U. Zander (1992). "Knowledge of the firm, combinative capabilities, and the replication of technology," *Organization Science*, 3(3), pp. 383–97.

Langlois, R. N. and P. L. Robertson (1992). "Networks and innovation in a modular system: Lessons from the microcomputer and stereo component industries," *Research Policy*, 21(4), pp. 297–313.

Levinthal, D. A. and J. G. March (1993). "The myopia of learning," *Strategic Management Journal*, Winter Special Issue, 14, pp. 95–112.

Mahoney, J. T. (1992a). "The adoption of the multidivisional form of organization: A contingency model," *Journal of Management Studies*, 29(1), pp. 49–72.

Mahoney, J. T. (1992b). "Organizational economics within the conversation of strategic management." In P. Shrivastava, A. S. Huff and J. Dutton (eds.), *Advances in Strategic Management*, Vol. 8. JAI Press, Greenwich, CT, pp. 103–55.

Mahoney, J. T. (1992c). "The choice of organizational form: Vertical financial ownership versus other methods of vertical integration," *Strategic Management Journal*, 13(8), pp. 559–84.

March, J. G. (1991). "Exploration and exploitation in organizational learning," *Organization Science*, 2(1), pp. 71–87.

Morris, C. R. and C. H. Ferguson (1993). "How architecture wins technology wars," *Harvard Business Review*, 71(2), pp. 86–96.

Nevins, J. L. and D. E. Whitney (eds.) (1989). *Concurrent Design of Products and Processes: A Strategy for the Next Generation in Manufacturing*. McGraw-Hill, New York.

Nishiguchi, T. (1994). *Strategic Industrial Outsourcing: The Japanese Advantage*. Oxford University Press, Oxford.

Normann, R. and R. Ramirez (1993). "From value chain to value constellation: Designing interactive strategy," *Harvard Business Review*, 71(4), pp. 65–77.

Orton, J. D. and K. E. Weick (1990). "Loosely coupled systems: A reconceptualization," *Academy of Management Review*, 15(2), pp, 203–23.

Ouchi, W. G. (1980). "Markets, bureaucracies, and clans," *Administrative Science Quarterly*, 25, pp. 120–142.

Parnas, D. L. (1972). "On the criteria to be used in decomposing systems into modules," *Communications of the ACM*, 15, pp. 1053–58.

Parnas, D. L., P. C. Clements and D. M. Weiss (1985). "The modular structure of complex systems," *IEEE Transactions on Software Engineering*, 11, pp. 259–266.

Radner, R. (1992). "Hierarchy: The economics of managing," *Journal of Economic Literature*, 30, pp. 1382–415.

Sanchez, R. (1991). "Strategic flexibility, real options, and product-based strategy," Ph.D. dissertation, Massachusetts Institute of Technology, Cambridge, MA.

Sanchez, R. (1993). "Strategic flexibility, firm organization, and managerial work in dynamic markets: A strategic options perspective." In P. Shrivastava, A. S. Huff and J. Dutton (eds.), *Advances in Strategic Management*, Vol. 9. JAI Press, Greenwich, CT, pp. 251–91.

Sanchez, R. (1994a). "Towards a science of strategic product design," paper presented at the Second International Product Development Management Conference on New Approaches to Development and Engineering, 30–1 May, 1994, Gothenburg, Sweden.

Sanchez, R. (1994b). "Higher order organization and commitment in strategic options theory: A reply to Christopher Bartlett." In P. Shrivastava, A. S. Huff and J. Dutton (eds.), *Advances in Strategic Management*, Vol. 10B. JAI Press, Greenwich, CT, pp. 251–91.

Sanchez, R. (1995). "Strategic flexibility in product competition," *Strategic Management Journal*, Summer Special Issue, 16, pp. 135–59.

Sanchez, R. (1996a). "Quick-connect technologies for product creation: Implications for comeptence-based competition." In R. Sanchez, A. Heene and H. Thomas (eds.), *Dynamics of Competence-based Competition: Theory and Practice in the New Strategic Management*. Elsevier, Oxford.

Sanchez, R. (1996b). "Strategic product creation: Managing new interactions of technologies, markets, and organizations," *European Management Journal*, 14(2), pp. 121–38.

Sanchez, R. (1996c). "Managing articulated knowledge in competence-based competition." In R. Sanchez and A. Heene (eds.), *Strategic Learning and Knowledge Management*. Wiley, Chichester.

Sanchez, R. (1996d). "Integrating technology strategy and marketing strategy." In D. O'Neal and H. Thomas (eds.), *Integrating Strategy*. Wiley, Chichester.

Sanchez, R. and A. Heene (eds.) (1996). *Strategic Learning and Knowledge Management*. Wiley, Chichester.

Sanchez, R. and D. Sudharshan (1993). "Real-time market research: Learning-by-doing in the development of new products," *Marketing Intelligence and Planning*, 11(7), pp. 29–38.

Sanderson, S. W. and V. Uzumeri (1990). "Strategies for new product development and renewal: Designbased incrementalism," working paper, Center for Science and Technology Policy, Rensselaer Polytechnic Institute, Troy, NY.

Shirley, G. V. (1990). "Models for managing the redesign and manufacture of product sets", *Journal of Manufacturing and Operations Management*, 3(2), pp. 85–104.

Simon, H. A. (1962). "The architecture of complexity," *Proceedings of the American Philosophical Society*, 106, pp. 467–82.

Simon, H. A. (1981). *The Sciences of the Artificial*. MIT Press, Cambridge, MA.

Smith, A. (1776). *An Inquiry into the Nature and Causes of the Wealth of Nations*. The Modern Library, New York.

Spender, J.-C. and Grinyer, P. H. (1995). "Organizational renewal: Top management's role in a loosely coupled system," *Human Relations*, 48(8), pp. 909–26.

Takeuchi, H. and I. Nonaka (1986). "The new new product development game," *Harvard Business Review*, 64(1), pp. 137–46.

Tully, S. (8 February 1993). "The modular corporation," *Fortune*, pp. 106–14.

Tushman, M. L. and P. Anderson (1986). "Technological discontinuities and organizational environments," *Administrative Science Quarterly*, 31, pp. 439–65.

Ulrich, K. T. and S. Eppinger (1995). *Product Design and Development*. McGraw-Hill, New York.

Utterback, J. M. (1994). *Mastering the Dynamics of Innovation: How Companies Can Seize Opportunities in the Face of Technological Change*. Harvard Business Press, Boston, MA.

Venkatesan, R. (1992). "Strategic souring: To make or not to make," *Harvard Business Review*, 70(6), pp. 98–107.

von Hippel, E. (1998). *The Sources of Information*. Oxford University Press, New York.

von Hippel, E. (1990). "Task partitioning: An innovation process variable," *Research Policy*, 19(5), pp. 407–18.

von Hippel, E. (1994). "Sticky information and the locus of problem solving," *Management Science*, 40(4), pp. 429–39.

Ward, A., J. V. Liker, J. J. Cristiano and D. K. Sobek (1995). "The second Toyota paradox: Delaying decisions can make better cars faster," *Sloan Management Review*, Spring, pp. 43–61.

Weick, K. E. (1976). "Educational organizations as loosely coupled systems," *Administrative Science Quarterly*, 21, pp. 1–19.

Wheelwright, S. C. and K. B. Clark (1992). *Revolutionizing Product Development: Quantum Leaps in Speed, Efficiency, and Quality*. Free Press, New York.

Whitney, D. E. (1998). "Manufacturing by design," *Harvard Business Review*, 66(4), pp. 83–91.

Williamson, O. E. (1975). *Markets and Hierarchies*. Free Press, New York.

Woolsey, J. P. (April 1994). "777," *Air Transport World*, pp. 22–31.

Wright, R. W. (1994). "The effects of tacitness and tangibility on the diffusion of knowledge-based resources," *Academy of Management Best Papers Proceedings*, pp. 52–6.,

COMMENTARY
Ron Sanchez

Introduction

The 1996 *Strategic Management Journal* paper co-authored with Joe Mahoney and reprinted in this volume undertook to lay out a broad yet fundamental view of how modular product architectures can impact product creation processes, market strategies, organization designs, competitive dynamics, and industry structures. The paper also suggested some ways in which modular architectures could provide a new framework for learning and knowledge management processes within firms and industries. Some of the modularity concepts presented in the paper were greeted with considerable skepticism or incomprehension at the time.[1] I am happy to be able to say now that modularity concepts are becoming better understood and increasingly accepted in both management practice and academia.

In this retrospective appraisal of the paper, I summarize what I believe are the main ideas contributed by the paper, discuss Herbert Simon's important influence on those ideas, and identify what I believe are some of the more interesting and significant extensions of modularity ideas developed since 1996. In this discussion, I suggest some connections of modularity concepts to standards, networks, complexity, co-evolution of technological and social systems, and other concepts developed in some of the papers reprinted in this volume. I conclude with comments on the enabling role of modular architectures in eBusiness.

The main ideas about modularity

In essence, the *Strategic Management Journal* paper makes the following arguments:

- Modular architectures are product designs that are strategically conceived as "platforms" for substituting (Garud and Kumaraswamy, 1993) a range of component variations in order to configure a range of product variations. The key to "designing in" substitutability of components is the specification and standardization (David, 1987) of interfaces between components to allow the "mixing and matching" (Sanderson and Uzumeri, 1990) of component variations in the modular architecture. The range of component variations which the interfaces in an architecture can accommodate determines the *flexibility* of the architecture to configure new product variations, which in turn greatly affects the *strategic flexibility*[2] of a firm to respond to changing market demands in the near term (Sanchez, 1995).
- The standardization of interfaces that support substitutability of component variations enables component development processes to become loosely coupled (Weick, 1976). Loose coupling of development processes results because the standardization of interfaces creates, in effect, a stable technical infrastructure for the product type. A stable technical infrastructure provides a well-defined information structure that specifies how the component parts of the product as a system function together. As long as all component development groups develop components that conform to the standardized interfaces, the decisions made by one development group do not affect other groups' development processes. Product development processes can then be coordinated through the information structure of standardized interface specifications, avoiding the need for authority-based hierarchical coordination (Mahoney, 1992). Thus, standardized interfaces may make it possible for a firm to adopt a "modular" development process that draws on the resources of networks of component developers around the globe (Langlois and Robertson, 1992). Using the standardized interfaces of a modular architecture to coordinate a modular development organization is one instance of the general proposition made in the paper that *products design organizations*. In essence, the way a firm decomposes and interrelates the components in its product designs will greatly affect the organization designs a firm can adopt for developing, producing, and supporting its products.
- To specify component interfaces that allow substitutability of component variations, a firm must have high levels of architectural knowledge – that is, knowledge about how components interact in a product as a system. Architectural knowledge used to specify interfaces between components can be distinguished from component-level knowledge that enables a firm to design a given type of component.[3] In conventional development processes (see figure 11.2(a) in the 1996 paper), the component designs and interfaces in a product design are co-evolving and complexly interdependent, and architectural and component forms of knowledge are thus tightly coupled. In modular development processes, however, interfaces are specified and standardized before beginning component development processes, and component designs are constrained to conform to

the standardized interface specifications (see figure 11.2(c) in the paper). The standardizing of component interfaces based on the firm's current architectural knowledge largely decouples architectural knowledge-based processes from the component-level knowledge used to develop specific component designs during product development. This decoupling of architectural and component-level knowledge during product development greatly reduces the complexity of the learning environment during development and can therefore increase the efficiency with which current architectural and component-level knowledge can be applied and new knowledge of both types generated.

Herbert Simon's influence

The initial impetus for the 1996 paper was my research into using modular product architectures as platforms that give firms strategic options to leverage a range of new product variations quickly and inexpensively (Sanchez, 1991, 1993, 1995). As Joe Mahoney and I discussed modularity concepts, however, it became clear to us that an architecture essentially referred to a well decomposed and specified system, and in particular that modular architectures had many of the properties that Herbert Simon (1962) had attributed to "nearly decomposable systems." Simon's paper *The Architecture of Complexity* suggested a fundamental connection between our ideas about modular architectures and Simon's ideas about nearly decomposable systems.

The key connection was the shared concept of *decomposability*. Simon proposed that hierarchy is an organizing principle of nature, which he clearly saw as consisting of systems that cover the spectrum from the subatomic to the galactic, from the elegantly simple to the enormously complex. In Simon's structural conception of hierarchy, decomposition represents a partitioning of a system into interacting subsystems, of subsystems into sub-subsystems, and so on, down to the most elemental building blocks of a system. A "nearly decomposable system" is the term Simon used to refer to a system in which the interactions among subsystems are relatively weak compared to the interactions between the parts within subsystems.

Because the first step in creating an architecture is the decomposition of a product or process design into interacting functional components, an architecture represents a hierarchical ordering of parts through decomposition, as described by Simon. Moreover, a modular architecture is a *design* that intentionally creates weak interactions between component designs in order to allow the substitution of component design variations into the architecture. Thus, a modular architecture has the essential distinguishing property of Simon's nearly decomposable systems.

Simon observed that nearly decomposable systems often demonstrate high levels of adaptability. Because of the weak interactions between subsystems in a nearly decomposable design, it may be possible for one part of a nearly decomposable system to change without having to make changes in other parts of the system – thereby increasing the adaptive capability or evolvability of the system. Analogously, improved adaptability of product designs through substitution of new component design variations is also an important benefit sought through modular architectures.

Although these basic similarities are important, there is also a noteworthy differ-ence between Simon's concept of nearly decomposable systems and the concept of modular architectures. These differences no doubt arise from the different perspectives from which Simon on the one hand and Joe Mahoney and I on the other approached the study of systems. Simon's perspective was essentially that of the natural scientist interested in describing and explaining nature as he saw it, and the outcome of such a process is descriptive, positive scientific theory. Joe Mahoney and I approached the study of modularity primarily as management researchers interested in devising better strategies for managing human systems, and the outcome of our investigation was intended to be new prescriptive (normative) management theory. Thus, an essential differentiator between the two perspectives is that Simon's concept of near decomposability may describe all kinds of natural systems, while the concept of modular architectures applies to product or process system designs that are motivated by a *strategic intention* to create more adaptable products and processes and thereby improve the strategic flexibility of an organization. In the hierarchical ordering of concepts, therefore, modular architectures are a subset of nearly decomposable systems – but a subset of central importance to management theory and strategy.

Important extensions of modularity concepts

My research to date has largely confirmed the key propositions about modularity made in the 1996 *Strategic Management Journal* paper. For example, the paper suggests that specifying and standardizing interfaces in modular product develop-ment allows parallel, concurrent development of components, and that concurrent development of components should greatly reduce both time and resource require-ments for developing new products compared to conventional development processes (compare figure 11.2(c) to 11.2(a) in the 1996 paper). Evidence gathered from a growing number of companies suggests that this modular process for developing products can in fact reduce development costs, resource requirements, and time to market by 50–80 percent compared to conventional development processes (Sanchez, forthcoming). Moreover, the reduced complexity that results from the decoupling of architectural and component-level knowledge in modular development processes can indeed significantly improve both the efficiency and effectiveness of organiza-tional learning and knowledge leveraging (Sanchez and Collins, forthcoming).

Further, my research has progressively led to the view that modularity concepts are not just relevant for product and process designs, but rather suggest fundament-ally important new conceptions of organization and management (Sanchez, 1997 and forthcoming; Schilling, 2000). Today I propose that modularity should be seen as a fundamental approach to organizing and managing, not just as a strategy for designing products. The logic behind this more extensive view took a while to come into clear focus, but now seems quite evident: modularity is essentially a way of designing systems to be more adaptable, and both organizations as systems and management processes as systems can therefore be made more adaptable by adopt-ing modular system designs. In addition, my research has also suggested strongly that achieving the full benefits of modularity in product strategies requires extending modularity practices to many interrelated activities in an organization. Following are three of the key aspects of this subsequent, more extensive view of modularity.

Modularity in the marketing processes

Modular product architectures can enable firms to offer more product variations more frequently and at lower costs. As noted in the 1996 paper, this flexibility of modular architectures makes it possible to learn about markets through *real-time market research* – a process of introducing a changing array of new product variations to discover which combinations of functions, features, and performance levels the market will prefer at various price points (Sanchez and Sudharshan, 1993). However, the flexibility of modular architectures also makes it possible to probe markets more widely and more finely. Both new capabilities have significant implications for the marketing process (Sanchez, 1999).

Traditional marketing is essentially concerned with discovering convergence (means) in the distributions of demand for different products in order to identify the attributes of products for which demand is most likely to be significant. The time-consuming and often costly methods of traditional marketing research may become quite problematic to use when market preferences are diverse and evolving rapidly. When many product variations can be leveraged from a modular architecture, however, an alternative mission for marketing research is discovering the evolving divergence (variance) in demand that might be served through a highly configurable modular architecture. In essence, much of the risk inherent in defining new products to serve diverse and evolving consumer preferences may be managed more satisfactorily through the flexibility of well-conceived modular product architectures than through traditional marketing research methods.

Modularity also challenges the central concept of market segmentation in marketing theory and practice. Market segmentation has been a foundational concept in marketing theory and practice for so long that the reasons behind the concept of segmentation are often overlooked. In essence, consumers have been grouped into market segments because the cost of creating products for individual consumers has been assumed to be prohibitive. Modular architectures, however, make it possible to segment markets much more finely than ever before – even to the level of mass-customized or personalized products for individual consumers. When a firm develops a modularity-based mass-customization capability, the usual marketing assumption about the prohibitive cost of serving individual customer preferences no longer holds. Once a product market starts to "go modular," the marketing process becomes much more concerned with defining menus of component variations to offer to individual customers than with grouping of customers into traditional market segments to be served by specific differentiated products.

Modularity in knowledge management

Modular architectures can greatly improve an organization's ability to identify and leverage its current knowledge and to identify opportunities for strategically important organizational learning (Sanchez and Collins, forthcoming). A firm's knowledge becomes embodied in specific components of its products and processes and in the firm's processes for coordinating those components in its products and processes as systems. Firms that develop products in the modular way usually develop "design libraries" of available modular component designs that can be used in their existing architectures. The component designs that a firm has in its design library represent an inventory of the readily available intellectual assets (component designs) that can be used immediately to configure new product variations. A firm that creates a design library of available product and process components can begin to see more clearly its current capabilities to configure new products in the short run – in effect, it begins to "know what it knows how to do" better than firms that do not systematically define and catalog available component designs. When new product opportunities come along that would require new component designs, the lack of suitable component designs in the design library helps a firm to understand its current capability limitations – in effect, to "know what it does *not* know how to do" in the short run. A firm may then focus its organizational learning on developing appropriate new component designs to meet new product opportunities. In this way, modular architectures provide a framework that helps a firm discover and focus on opportunities for strategically important organizational learning and capability development.

The adoption of standardized component interfaces within a firm or an industry also creates a stable technical infrastructure (for some period of time) for a given type of product architecture (for example, the "Wintel" personal computer architecture). A stable technical infrastructure gives rise to a socio-technical system that is populated by people who develop architectural or component level knowledge about the product architecture – in effect, forming a "community of practice" based on the architecture (Wade, 1995). Firms may then define their own modular architectures to be consistent (either partially or entirely) with the prevailing industry interface standards. Adopting industry standard interfaces makes it possible for a firm to invite the participation of external component developers and producers in its own product creation and realization processes, because those developers already have expertise in the technical system requirements of such components. Thus, adopting modular architectures that incorporate industry standard interface specifications is a critical step in strategies for accessing a world of external expertise that can improve a firm's own product creation and realization capabilities (Sanchez, 2000a, 2000b).

Modularity in competence-based strategic management

The competence-based perspective on strategic management is concerned with devising new management theory and practice that incorporates essential dynamic, systemic, cognitive, and holistic dimensions of the management task (Heene and Sanchez, 1997; Mahoney and Sanchez, 1997; Sanchez, 2001). Modularity brings important new possibilities to the advancement of competence-based management in several of these dimensions.

The dynamic challenge in managing arises from the ongoing changes in both market preferences for products and the technological means for creating new products. The configurability of modular architectures can make it possible for a firm to rapidly change or upgrade its products by substituting new, higher performing component variations into its product architectures – thereby improving the ability of the firm to respond to market and technology dynamics.

The systemic dimension involves managing change in an organization as a system. When organizations are composed of units that interact in inflexible, idiosyncratic ways, change processes become very complex, and managers can have great difficulty in realigning organizations with changing market and technology conditions. The concept of modular architectures, however, can be applied to process designs as well as product designs to create more configurable, evolvable organization designs. An organization's processes becomes modular when they are decomposed into intentionally loosely-coupled activities that interact in standardized ways – that is, through standardized process interfaces. When various internal and external organization units understand the standardized process interfaces of the organization (and have adequate incentives to work within that structure), those units may be substituted into the organization's process architecture to configure variations in the organization's chain of resources that can help the organization respond to changing environmental conditions. In this respect, standardizing an organization's activity interfaces is as essential to outsourcing manufacturing, distribution, and support activities as standardizing product component interfaces is to outsourcing component development (Sanchez, 2000b).

The modularity perspective also provides both conceptual arguments and empirical evidence against the proposition that the resource endowments of firms alone can adequately explain the differential performances of firms – a central tenet of the resource-based view in strategy theory (Barney, 1986, 1991). Modularity is a new way of *coordinating* resources in the creation and realization of products. The same development resources coordinated through conventional or modular development processes can have very different levels of productivity and market impacts. Thus, any strategy theory that aspires to explain differential performance in product creation, for example, must look not just to the development resources within a firm, but to the ability of the firm to coordinate its development resources in the most effective way.

The cognitive challenge in managing derives from the increasing complexity of modern organizations and their environments. Managers need frameworks that can help them to adequately conceptualize essential processes and capabilities in their organizations and the changes that both must undergo for an organization to remain competitive. Many firms today, for example, do both market and technology forecasting in an effort to conceptualize future market conditions and technology possibilities. Interpreting such forecasts to define specific objectives for the future is likely to remain problematic, however, without a framework for integrating technology and market trends to define a plan of action. As platforms for using available technologies to serve emerging market needs, modular architectures offer a useful and perhaps essential framework for defining the new kinds of products that will be both possible and desirable in the future, for defining the new kinds of components that will be needed in those products, and the new architectural and component-level capabilities a firm will need to create and realize its future generation product architectures. In some firms today, the definition of future generation modular architectures and the capabilities that will be needed to create and realize those architectures has become the driver of long-term product strategies and strategic capability development processes (Sanchez, 2000a, forthcoming; Sanchez and Collins, forthcoming).

Modularity in eBusiness

The 1996 paper suggested that increasing adoption of modular architectures would result in more dynamic product markets "characterized by expanding interactions among modular development organizations through 'quick-connect' global electronic networks." The rise of internet-mediated eBusiness has brought the era of "quick-connect" global eBusiness relationships into existence, and modular architectures are the foundation for both the *process* and the *content* of eBusiness.

The Internet itself is a modular communication architecture with well defined and standardized interfaces for "quick-connecting" computer systems around the world. The flexible, "platform-independent" interfaces of the internet make it possible for any company with a computer equipped with a browser to "plug and play" in the global internet communication architecture. Of course, connected buyers must still find the right connected suppliers, and vice versa. On the B2B (business to business) side, a large number of both general and industry-specific electronic marketplaces are now emerging to provide meeting places for buyers and suppliers. Within the industry marketplaces, modularity concepts are prominent in the standardized processes through which buyers and suppliers interact in eBusiness platforms. The automobile industry eBusiness marketplaces, for example, require that interested suppliers submit offers to provide components through standardized process interfaces – that is, standard document formats that allow consistent electronic data integration (EDI) and dissemination to interested buyers throughout the industry. Thus, the B2B eBusiness platforms being put in place today are effectively creating modular process architectures for managing the information content and coordination of buyer-supplier interactions globally. On the content dimension, B2B platforms are also encouraging greater standardization of component interfaces and even component designs. Because a firm cannot readily contract for a component development or production services if the technical specifications of the component are not fully determined, companies now have significant new incentives to fully specify and standardize their component interfaces in order to use eBusiness marketplaces to invite offers to supply components from the global pool of connected component suppliers.

On the B2C (business to consumer) side, modular architectures play an even more visible role. The mass-customization and personalization[4] of products for individual customers virtually requires the use of flexible modular product architectures to configure individual product variations for individual customers. Moreover, as more consumers around the world choose their preferred combinations of components for mass-customized or personalized products, firms offering such products must expand the resources they can access to provide both new product component variations and new process component variations (assembly, shipping, and support services). Thus, behind the growing use of modular architectures to configure product variations for individual customers is the increasing creation of modular supply chains to provide new modular component variations and to assemble, ship, and service specific product variations (Sanchez, forthcoming).

As eBusiness becomes more widely adopted as a standard business process on both the B2B and B2C sides, considerable new incentives are being created for firms to adopt standardized components for both their product and process architectures. As more firms adopt modular architectures to serve demand for mass-customized and personalized products and to standardize product and process components and interfaces to coordinate global supply chains, more eBusiness processes are beginning to grow and to become important new marketplaces for firms that are "modular capable." Thus, today a powerful new "virtuous circle" driven by the benefits of increasing modularity and connectivity is taking shape in the global business environment. The dynamic of this virtuous circle is setting the stage for the next chapter in the evolution of modularity concepts.

NOTES

1 A version of the 1996 paper was rejected by the journal *Organization Science* in 1995. In her rejection letter, the area editor characterized the paper as presenting "a naive view of product development."
2 The strategic flexibility of a firm can be represented as the sum of the *strategic options* available to a firm to introduce new product variations. Strategic flexibility increases with the number of (positive net present value) strategic options a firm has, and decreases with the time and cost required to exercise each strategic option (Sanchez, 1993, 1995).
3 Of course, for a component supplier, the component is its product, and the component maker must have architectural knowledge about how its component functions as a system. Architectural knowledge at the component level can then be distinguished from knowledge about how the individual subassemblies or parts within the component must be designed. Thus, in a fundamental sense, *architectural knowledge is knowledge about how the parts of a system function together*, whether the system be at the level of a component, a product, or the macro-system that defines the context of use of a product.
4 Mass-customization configures individual product variations from a menu of standard component variations. Product personalization configures individual products that include at least one component that is made specifically to suit an individual customer's requirements (Sanchez, 1999). Products like personal computers are commonly mass-customized, while articles of clothing and footwear typically are increasingly available offered as personalized products that conform exactly to a an individual's body measurements.

REFERENCES

Barney, J. (1986). "Strategic factor markets: Expectations, luck, and business strategy," *Management Science*, 32, 1231–41.

Barney, J. (1991). "Firm resources and sustained competitive advantage," *Journal of Management*, 17, 99–120.

David, P. A. (1987). "Some new standards for the economics of standardization in the information age," in P. Dasgupta and P. Stoneman (eds.), *Economic Policy and Technological Performance*, Cambridge: Cambridge University Press.

Garud, R. and Kumaraswamy, A. (1993). "Changing competitive dynamics in network industries: An exploration of Sun Microsystems' open systems strategy," *Strategic Management Journal*, 14(5), 351–69.

Heene, A. and Sanchez, R. (eds.) (1997). *Competence-Based Strategic Management*, Chichester: John Wiley & Sons.

Langlois, R. and Robertson, P. (1992). "Networks and innovation in a modular system: Lessons from microcomputer and stereo components industries," *Research Policy*, 21(4), 297–313.

Mahoney, J. T. (1992). "Organizational economics with in the conversation of strategic management," in P. Shrivastava, A. S. Huff, and J. Dutton (eds.), *Advances in Strategic Management*, vol. 8, Greenwich, CT: JAI Press.

Mahoney, J. T. and Sanchez, R. (1997). "Competence theory building: Reconnecting management research and management practice," in A. Heene and R. Sanchez (eds.), *Competence-Based Strategic Management*, Chichester: John Wiley & Sons.

Sanchez, R. (1991). "Strategic flexibility, real options, and product-based strategy," Ph.D. dissertation, Cambridge, MA: Massachusetts Institute of Technology.

Sanchez, R. (1993). "Strategic flexibility, firm organization, and managerial work in dynamic markets: A strategic options perspective," in P. Shrivastava, A. S. Huff, and J. Dutton (eds.), *Advances in Strategic Management*, vol. 9, Greenwich, CT: JAI Press.

Sanchez, R. (1995). "Strategic flexibility in product competition," *Strategic Management Journal*, 16 (Summer Special Issue), 135–59.

Sanchez, R. (1997). "Strategic management at the point of inflection: Systems, complexity, and competence theory," *Long Range Planning*, 30(6), 939–46.

Sanchez, R. (1999). "Modular architectures in the marketing process," *Journal of Marketing*, 63 (Special Issue), 92–111.

Sanchez, R. (2000a). "Product and process architectures in the management of knowledge resources," in N. J. Foss and P. L. Robertson (eds.), *Resources, Technology and Strategy*, London: Routledge.

Sanchez, R. (2000b). "Modular architectures, knowledge assets, and organizational learning: New management processes for product creation," *International Journal of Technology Management*, 19(6), 610–29.

Sanchez, R., (ed.) (2001). *Knowledge Management and Organizational Competence*, Oxford: Oxford University Press.

Sanchez, R. (forthcoming). *Modularity, Strategic Flexibility, and Knowledge Management*, Oxford: Oxford University Press.

Sanchez, R. and Collins, R. P. (forthcoming). "Competing – and learning – in modular markets," *Long Range Planning*.

Sanchez, R. and Sudharshan, D. (1993). "Real-time market research: Learning-by-doing in the development of new products," *Marketing Intelligence and Planning*, 11(7), 29–38.

Sanderson, S. W. and Uzumeri, V. (1990). "Strategies for new product development and renewal: Design-based incrementalism," working paper, Center for Science and Technology Policy, Troy, NY: Rensselaer Polytechnic Institute.

Schilling, M. A. (2000). "Towards a general modular systems theory and its application to interfirm product modularity," *Academy of Management Review*, 25, 312–34.

Simon, H. A. (1962). "The architecture of complexity," *Proceedings of the American Philosophical Society*, 106 (December), 467–82.

Wade, J. (1995). "Dynamics of organizational communities and technological bandwagons: An empirical investigation of community evolution in the microprocessor market," *Strategic Management Journal*, 16, 111–33.

Weick, K. E. (1976). "Educational organizations as loosely coupled systems," *Administrative Science Quarterly*, 21, 1–19.

INDEX

Note: page numbers in italics refer to figures; page numbers in bold refer to tables.

Gallini, N. T., 276
games machines, standards wars, 252, 253, 254, 262, 265
Gandal, N., 231
Garrard, 99
Garud, R., 51, 52, 275, 299, 313, 336
  economies of substitution, 182, 212, 312
  path creation theories, 5
gases
  atomic bonding, 27
  hierarchic structure, 17, 18
  molecular interactions, 23–4
  perfect, 24
gateway technologies, 49, 62
Gatignon, H., 349–50
Gauss, Carl Friedrich (1777–1855), *Disquisitiones Arithmeticae*, 209–10
General Electric (GE), 182, 249
general modular systems theory, development, 172–214
General Motors Corporation, 96, 132, 153–4, 270, 271, 376
  Vehicle Assessment Center, 144
general systems theory, 15
general-purpose technology (GPT), 9
genetic programs, 33–4, 38
geometric nesting, 134, 135
Gifford, S., 194
Gilfillan, S. C., 322
GNU (operating system), public license, 167
Goodwin, Richard, 38
GPT (general-purpose technology), 9
Graham, I., 52
gravitational forces, 27
Greenstein, Shane, 102
GTE, **367**
gunsmiths, 208

Hamel, G., 51, 52
handwriting recognition, **157**
Hannan, M. T., 281–2, 283, 291, 294
hardware–software networks, 4
Harrison, J. R., 281
Hawkins, Jeff, **157**
Hawley, A., 296
Hayes, 254
HDTV *see* high-definition television (HDTV)

heat exchange, nearly decomposable systems, 24–5, 39
Heifetz, Jascha, 88
Henderson, Rebecca M.
  architectural innovations, 70, 139, 285, 296, 299
  dominant design theories, 326, 329, 330, 338
  organizational theories, 373
Hewlett-Packard, 55, 93, 191, 255
  reputation, 256
  RISC systems, 192
  standards, 256
hidden design parameters, 3–4
hierarchic span, 18, 23, 27–8
hierarchic systems, 16–18
  and product design, 363
  redundancy in, 30–1
hierarchy
  in complex systems, 363
  evolutionary explanation, 23
  structural concept of, 363
  use of term, 16–17
high-definition television (HDTV), 97, 269
  standards, 257, 310
high-fidelity systems
  attributes, 80
  compatibility issues, 86, 96–7
  development, 84–9: early, 85, 98–9
  frequency response, 85
  hardware networks, 87–8
  international standards, 86
  and microcomputers compared, 96–7
  modular vs. appliances, 86, 89, 97, 185
  modularity, 97
  post-war developments, 85–6
  software networks, 87–8
  see also FM receivers; records (high-fidelity)
Hill, C., 52
Himmelberg, C., 222–3, 224, 235
history, and complex systems, 23
Hitt, M., 52
Hobday, Mike, 106
Holland, John, 174
Holt, C., 185
home-entertainment systems, 97
homeostasis, 15
Honda, 55, 63, 339
  Accord, 50